X4290 West, Troy, CA. July 1950. A.C. Phelps photo.

Pacific Fruit Express

Pacific Fruit Express

Second Edition

Anthony W. Thompson

Robert J. Church

Bruce H. Jones

SIGNATURE PRESS

Berkeley and Wilton, California

Pacific Fruit Express
Second Edition

Published by Signature Press
11508 Green Road
Wilton, CA 95693

Publisher's Cataloging-in-Publication
(Provided by Quality Books, Inc.)
Thompson, Anthony W. (Anthony Wayne), 1940–
    Pacific Fruit Express / Anthony W. Thompson,
Robert J. Church, Bruce H. Jones. –2nd ed.
        p. cm.
        Includes bibliographic references and index
        ISBN: 1-930013-03-5

        1. Pacific Fruit Express Company. 2. Railroads
—California—Freight-cars. 3. Refrigerator cars
—California. I. Church, Robert J., 1939–
II. Jones, Bruce H. III. Title

HE2791.P33T56 2000   385.065'09794
            QBI00-500066

Library of Congress Catalog Card No. 00-191352

Acknowledgements for Art
Dust jacket and Page 1. The Laramie ice deck and a passing train are depicted by artist Jan Rons in watercolor.
Frontispiece. This oil painting by artist and author John R. Signor shows a "transition era" refrigerator block in the Salinas Valley.
Dedication page. A pencil sketch by retired CSRM Curator Jim Neider illustrates the familiar scene of icing refrigerator cars.

Book design and typography by Anthony W. Thompson.

Second edition, second printing, May, 2003

Printed in the United States of America

Preface and Acknowledgements

It is evident in reading standard railroad histories that Pacific Fruit Express is typically regarded as a sidelight, a detail, in the greater scope of railroad affairs, and many historians have evidently summarized or paraphrased their predecessor's remarks without additional research. Thus this book is hardly the last word on the subject; indeed, as Vivian Mercier put it, it is closer to being the first. Our task has accordingly been extensive, and given that railroad slang has for decades referred to refrigerator cars as "reefers," we have resisted only with difficulty the temptation to subtitle this book, "Reefer Madness."

As listed below and in the Bibliography, we have interviewed persons knowledgeable about PFE, and have researched the railroad trade press, and professional journals for both railroad and refrigeration engineering subjects, to supplement PFE records in assembling this history. It is our hope that it will extend and enrich understanding of the Pacific Fruit Express Company.

We have been helped in this project by numerous individuals and institutions. Without their assistance, this history could not have been written. We wish to thank them by acknowledgement here, hopefully without significant omissions. If we have left anyone out, our apologies in advance for the oversight.

Researching the extensive published record on PFE and on refrigerated transportation would not have been possible without assistance from several libraries and institutions. Foremost among these was the Library of the California State Railroad Museum (referred to throughout this book as CSRM) in Sacramento, which now has the majority of archival materials saved from PFE's last headquarters in Brisbane, Calif. Particular thanks go to CSRM Director Walter P. Gray III and Senior Curator Steven E. Drew for facilitating our access to these materials, and to Librarian Ellen Halteman and Archivist Blaine Lamb. We had additional help at CSRM from the Railway & Locomotive Historical Society's archivist, Jackie Pryor.

Also very important to our work was the Union Pacific Railroad Museum in Omaha, where many PFE documents were found. Museum Director Don Snoddy provided outstanding help on numerous occasions, as did Ken Longe, Wm. W. Kratville and George Cockle.

Other libraries which were of assistance included the A.C. Kalmbach Memorial Library of the National Model Railroad Association (NMRA), and its director Bruce Metcalf; the Sherman Library in Corona del Mar, Calif., with William Hendricks and William Thompson; the Carnegie Library of Pittsburgh; the Library of Congress; the California State Library in Sacramento; the Libraries of Carnegie Mellon University in Pittsburgh, of Stanford University, and of the University of California at Santa Barbara; the Denver Public Library and its Western History Department; the Smithsonian Institution's superb Pullman collection; the Bancroft Library of the University of California; the Huntington Library; and the DeGolyer Library of Southern Methodist University.

Additional bibliographic help was provided by Doug Gurin, Richard Hendrickson, Keith Jordan, and John Ryczkowski. Kyle Wyatt of the Nevada State Railroad Museum was of particular help with the pre-1906 era.

Many photographers and holders of photographic collections have generously shared information as well as providing photos. These include Richard Steinheimer, Stan Kistler, Richard Kindig, Don Sims, Guy Dunscomb, Wil Whittaker, Donald Duke, and Al Phelps, Western railroad photographers extraordinaire. Others who made available both knowledge and photographs were Howard Ameling, D.G. Biernacki, Phil DaCosta, V.W. Davis, Dean Dickerhoof, Frank Ellington, Dick Flock, Richard Hendrickson, Don Hofsommer, John Illman, Dick Kuelbs, Jim Lekas, Bob Lorenz, Bob Malinoski, Arnold Menke, Terry Metcalfe, Gordon Mills, Jeff Moreau, Jim Morley, William Myers, Dan Nelson, Clint Nestell, Jim Orem, Frank Peacock, Steve Peery, Doug Peterson, Jim Providenza, Byron Rose, John Shaw, John Signor, Milton Sorensen, Al Westerfield, Jeff Winslow, and Charles Winters. These photographers and collectors, who provided photos of subjects not covered in official photography, or who have helped preserve original builder's or railroad photos, deserve our gratitude.

We greatly appreciate the generosity of Simmons-Boardman Publishers, who gave permission to use several drawings from the *Car Builders' Cyclopedias*, and of Carstens Publications (*Railroad Model Craftsman* and *Railfan and Railroad*), Kalmbach Publishing Co. (*Trains* and *Model Railroader*), and Hundman Publishing (*Mainline Mod-*

eler), both for permission to use HO scale drawings of PFE cars and for the loan of photographs from their collections.

We were fortunate to be able to interview a number of persons associated with PFE (specifics are listed in the Bibliography), to gain valuable insight into the company's history, operations, and idiosyncrasies. These individuals gave us numerous hours of their time for taped interviews and in reviewing text drafts. Several also provided photographs from their personal collections. Earl Hopkins, retired General Mechanical & Engineering Officer, was extraordinarily valuable on refrigerator cars, particularly on mechanical refrigerators, the development of which at PFE was overseen by him. The late Pete Holst's incomparable memory, dating back to his start with PFE in 1917, together with his knowledge of car service and refrigeration issues, was essential. Ed Chiasson, the last VP & GM of the UP-SP ownership period, was similarly helpful on corporate issues and trailer service. The above interviewees, and a number of other persons knowledgeable about PFE, among those listed below, have also read, commented on and suggested corrections to drafts of parts of this book, although of course any errors which remain are the sole responsibility of the authors.

Before and since PFE ceased to be a car line in 1985, a number of people have been generous to all three authors with their time, assistance, and knowledge. The following PFE personnel were particularly helpful by participating in informal interviews, allowing access to documents prior to closure of the Brisbane office, clarifying points of detail, or other assistance: Tom Ellen, VP & GM; Don Schumacher, Auditor; Tim Walsh, Industrial Relations; Marvin Dike, Plant Manager; Mike Coz, District Agent; Bob Torassa, District Superintendent; Edna Clark, Customer Service and Public Relations; Jim Segurson, Asst. to VP & GM; Layton Batson, Fleet Management; the late Duane Autrey, Controller; J. Neil Cline, Purchasing Agent; and Rick Fend, Market Development. Those interviewed with non-PFE backgrounds include G.M. "Buck" Haynie and Allen M. Shelley, SP engineers; Al Phelps, SP clerk; Bill Fisher, SP signal maintainer; Bob Fletcher, Federal-State Agricultural Shipping Point Inspector; David S. Alltucker, George Chorn, and Jim Seagrave, who iced PFE cars while in college; and John A. Church, who farmed in Idaho.

Other individuals were also of assistance. The magazine articles that were the nucleus for the project were encouraged by Bob Mohowski and especially by Bill Schaumburg. Additional drawings were specially commissioned from Chuck Yungkurth and Eric Neubauer. John Signor's magnificent map of PFE's territory was a welcome addition to the book, as were the artworks created by Signor, Jan Rons, and Jim Nider. Stan Kistler provided outstanding darkroom work for some of the photos. Valuable feedback on earlier work and on chapter drafts was provided by John H. White, Jr., C.J. Riley, Larry Kline, Campbell Thompson, Kyle Wyatt, Jim Eager, Dan Church, David Church, and Don Smith. And we are grateful for support from all the freight car experts and enthusiasts who continually reminded us that there was an audience for this work. We thank you all.

Finally, to our wives, Mary, Jeanne, and Joy, who provided understanding, as well as encouragement when the job seemed never-ending, our deepest appreciation. Our own enthusiasm for Pacific Fruit Express and its history has survived undimmed.

Tony Thompson, Bob Church, Bruce Jones

Preface to the Revised Edition

We have been fortunate to have the opportunity to include additional material in this new edition of the book (some of which no doubt should have been in the first edition), as well as to correct a number of minor errors and omissions. A few photographs have also been replaced with better ones which subsequently came to light, and others have been improved with modern computer technologies.

We have largely maintained our historical cutoff in the early 1990's (except for acknowledging the merger of Union Pacific and Southern Pacific in 1996), rather than try to bring the entire text up to today's date. The history of UPFE deserves to be researched and written, but we have decided it should not be part of this book.

Our thanks to a number of people who have contributed new material, or have identified errors, including Richard Hendrickson, Robert B. Rogers, Jim Seagrave, John Carlson, and Dick Harley. Greg Henschen and Dick Harley also contributed some of the tabular matter in the added portion of the Appendix.

Tony Thompson

Colton, 1948

Table of Contents

Dedicated to the Men and Women of Pacific Fruit Express.

Without their pride, loyalty, morale, and conscientious
dedication to the task, PFE could not have been what it was.

I

THE COMPANY

HISTORY AND ORGANIZATION

BY
BRUCE H. JONES

Part of the office staff at 85 Second Street, San Francisco, in 1942, poses with a Blue Star service flag, presented for employees in military service (574 at this time), with a single, small Gold Star emblematic of a death in service. Present were, from left to right, kneeling, Kathryn Martin, Gloria Grolla, Marnell Wilson, Jean Schranlin, Jeanne Weber, Kathryn Sharkey, Laverne Burnett and Frances Tucker. Standing, Eunice Patterson, Margaret Curran, Ira Flinn, Carol Olsen, Annette Havel, R.G. Herda (AGM San Francisco), Bessie Bering, A.J. Mello (Purchasing Agent), Mary Moran, Carmel Leffmann, Mildred Simons, G.P. Torburn (Car Dept.), Fred Garrigues (Personnel), George Culver, Mary Shea, Helen Leffmann, and Mary Griffin. PFE photo, courtesy T.D. Walsh.

1

COMPANY HISTORY

The Flood Building, 870 Market St. in San Francisco, famed as one of the very few downtown buildings to survive the 1906 earthquake and fire. PFE had western offices in this building from 1907-13, then moved its headquarters here in 1913. PFE moved to the SP Building at 65 Market St. in 1923. The narrower street is Powell. San Francisco Public Library, Neg. 4507.

The Pacific Fruit Express Company was, by almost any measure, the greatest refrigerator car line in America for virtually its entire life; but it was also more. It became a pivotal part of the phenomenal growth of western agriculture in the first three decades of the twentieth century. It played no small part in the transformation of, for example, the orange, from a rare and treasured object to a commodity which could be enjoyed for breakfast every day of the year. Its eventual decline took place as perishable transportation became the province of the highway truck instead of the railroad. The story of PFE is thus the story of the development of Western agricultural industry and mar-

kets, just as much as it is a railroad car line story.

Settlement of the Western states continued steadily after the Gold Rush of 1848, and a farming industry grew up to feed the local population. As more and more acreage came under cultivation, the production capacity of the land soon exceeded the local demand. The farmers' concern over this matter was expressed in the *Pacific Rural Press* of September 25, 1875:

"It has become painfully apparent that the utmost capacity for the consumption of fresh fruit by the people who buy in the markets of California has been more than reached by the supply this year when the volume of the product has been much less than it would have been but for late frosts last spring, and that, if next year's product be as large as there is reason to expect, the supply will be considerably in excess of the demand. Hence it results that we must either diminish the amount of fresh fruit which would be thrown upon the market in the ordinary course of business, or make serious losses, or find a foreign market."

Since overseas export of fresh fruits and vegetables would not begin until 1892 a "foreign market" was anything beyond the area of local consumption.

By the time farmers were looking toward broader markets for their products, the railroad had reached them; the Pacific Railroad was completed on May 10, 1869. By the end of the 19th century, this and other new railroads provided routes for farmers to ship their products to distant markets. The railroads moved to meet that demand and aid agricultural development in the West, by means of advertising campaigns extolling the virtues of western agriculture to eastern farmers, development of agricultural and irrigation techniques, and land sales.

In the 1870's, though, this interrelation between farmers and the railroads had not emerged. Indeed, long distance shipment of agricultural products was in its infancy. As described in more detail in Chapter 3, the idea of the refrigerated freight car first emerged in the 1840's and was proving viable for produce shipment by the 1860's. As late as 1885, however, produce was predominantly shipped in ventilated box cars, not in refrigerator cars. During the same period, privately owned refrigerator car lines began to enter the business of produce shipment, including the movement of California produce to the east.

Most railroads did not initially wish to own and main-

tain refrigerator cars which they saw as relatively expensive and specialized equipment, nor did they want to diverge from their "common carrier" identity in order to build and maintain the ancillary facilities required by a refrigerator car operation, such as ice houses and car icing platforms. This left the field to private ownership of car fleets.

The Chicago meat packers already owned large fleets of private refrigerator cars, in which they shipped dressed meat to market. Their knowledge of car operations, along with their investments in car repair shops and in icing facilities along major railroad lines, positioned them well to enter the produce trade. Although it was not possible to use the existing fleet of meat cars to ship produce, new cars could be added to their car fleets for shipping produce.

By 1895, Armour Car Lines, owned by the meat packing company of the same name, had become a giant among the private car operators, absorbing about twenty smaller car lines as it expanded. Toward the end of the 19th century, through its near monopoly in the fruit and vegetable trade of not only California but also the Southeast and much of the Midwest and Northeast, Armour inflicted abuses upon shippers and railroads alike in its routing of cars and in icing charges.

Although freight rates for shipments were required to follow uniform, published schedules, Armour, as it became the largest private car line, was able to extract favorable car use contracts from railroads. Armour would not allow its cars to be supplied to shippers along a particular railroad unless that railroad contracted to obtain all its refrigerator cars from Armour. This was called an "exclusive contract." Part of Armour's persuasion in obtaining these contracts was to agree to route its meat traffic preferentially over roads with which it had exclusive contracts. The shipper was thus obliged to use Armour cars exclusively, and also to pay Armour's icing charges, whether or not he furnished

In this scene at Vacaville, Calif., on July 30, 1887, wagons of produce are being loaded into Southern Pacific and Central Pacific box cars. The SP "California Fast Freight Line" car is worthy of note (see Chapter 3 for discussion). Williamson collection, neg. 12448, CSRM.

In a vivid image from the steam age, an SP cab-forward hauls PFE reefers through Altamont Pass. Charles Smiley collection.

his own ice. Armour could then charge amounts for icing which bore little relation to costs, and in fact were typically much larger than the true cost.

The car line in whose cars a load was handled also decided the route the car was to take to its destination. Armour and other private car lines, by their own admission, received rebates from certain railroads in exchange for favorable routing over the roads offering the rebates. This resulted in circuitous routes and delays to shippers as car owners sought to maximize profits through the rebating practice. Some car lines also occasionally moved empty cars from city to city, since they were paid on a mileage basis for car movements. These practices brought complaints from railroads who used Armour's and others' cars for their perishable traffic, and from shippers who had to bear the costs of the icing and poor routing.

Although the complaints did somewhat reduce rebating after 1898, shippers turned to the U.S. Government to seek relief from these abuses. They found a favorable climate in Washington. Regulation of the railroads had been of interest to Congress since the inception of the railroad industry.

THE CALIFORNIA FRUIT CASE AND THE HEPBURN ACT

Almost with the inception of the Pacific Railroad and the flurry of railroad building in the following years there came a rising volume of complaints by farmers and other users of the railroads of abuses in rates and service. Political reformers, aided by the Granger Movement, were able in 1887 to pass the Interstate Commerce Act into law. At first welcomed by many railroads, since the Act was expected to bring an end to ruinous rate wars, the Interstate Commerce Commission (ICC) soon began to make decisions which

were unwelcome to the railroads. However, the ICC's original powers were quite limited, and adverse decisions were circumvented by railroad lawyers. In several cases, the U.S. Supreme Court upheld a limited scope for the ICC, rendering it ineffective as a regulatory entity.

After the reform-minded Progressive era began at the turn of the century, additional regulatory and enforcement powers were given to the ICC by the Elkins Act of 1903, followed by the Hepburn (1906) and Mann-Elkins (1910) Acts. The Hepburn Act is particularly important here, as it was one of the pivotal reasons for the creation of the Pacific Fruit Express Company.

As agriculture gained momentum in the West, farmers formed cooperative organizations to pool resources and effort. These cooperatives were not only packing, shipping and marketing organizations but political ones as well. Through the co-ops farmers could speak collectively to the regulatory agencies about abuses, both real and perceived. One complaint in particular, brought before the Interstate Commerce Commission in 1900, became known as the California Fruit Case. Originally brought by the Consolidated Forwarding Company and the Southern California Fruit Company, the case would eventually be heard by the Supreme Court. The details of this complaint, its litigation and its effects provide insight into the increasingly effective regulation of the railroad industry by the ICC.

In order to break up the rebating practices of private car lines, chiefly Armour, the Southern Pacific and Santa Fe railroads each decided to take the problem of routing perishable shipments into their own hands. They gave a notice in their tariff for citrus fruits to the effect that "in guaranteeing through rates, the absolute and unqualified right of the routing beyond its own terminals is reserved to the initial carrier giving the guarantee." Connecting lines that wished to be included in the tariff were required to consent to those terms. In simple terms, if SP or Santa Fe originated the shipment, they then decided upon the route it took to its destination. This stopped rebating but was challenged by shippers in the California Fruit Case.

The complaint stated that the railroads could not lawfully have the exclusive right to decide upon routing of perishable shipments, denying the shipper a choice of routes. The complaint further stated that this established a "tonnage pool" of traffic between connecting carriers, thus violating the Fifth Section (anti-pooling clause) of the Interstate Commerce Act. On April 19, 1902, after two years of hearings the ICC ruled against the railroads. At this time, however, the ICC had no direct power to enforce its rulings. If a railroad refused to obey a ruling, the ICC had to seek enforcement by the courts.

SP and Santa Fe did ignore this ruling and the matter was taken by the ICC to the U.S. Circuit Court at Los Angeles. On September 6, 1904 Judge O.M. Wellborn held that the route-controlling practice by the railroads was indeed "pooling," a violation of the Interstate Commerce Act and destructive to competition. An injunction was granted to prevent the railroads from continuing their control of routing.

This injunction was immediately appealed by SP and Santa Fe to the U.S. Supreme Court which, on February 26, 1906, reversed the lower court decision, declaring "there is nothing in the provisions of the Interstate Commerce Act which forbade the adoption of a regulation that served to break up rebating by connecting lines and, in its practical operation, the actual routing is generally conceded to the shipper, and his requests to divert shipments en route are usually allowed; nor is the pooling of freights of competing railroads accomplished by the adoption of such a rule." By upholding the railroads' position, the Supreme Court also established the important precedent that the courts could interpret or modify orders of the Interstate Commerce Commission, thus involving themselves in the regulatory process.

There was a separate series of shipper complaints on icing charges. The ICC declared in a 1905 decision regarding shipping rates that "the owner of a commodity transported can no more provide the refrigeration than he can provide the transportation itself" and that "furnishing of refrigeration is a part of the transportation itself and that the railway is obliged to publish and maintain these charges for icing." The railroads insisted that "the providing of refrigeration is a local service, not part of transportation, which is not and cannot be put under supervision of any government tribunal (the ICC); that the service is furnished by private persons and not subject to the jurisdiction of the Commission." This reiterated the railroads' reluctance to get into the business of a complete refrigera-

tor car operation, preferring instead to transport cars owned, loaded and iced by others. However, the ICC responded by declaring, "In view of the great importance of these charges to the shipper, we suggest that the Congress make that service, by express provisions in the law, a part of transportation, and recommend that these refrigeration and icing charges should be put on the same basis as all other freight ratings." The ICC further stated, "We do not at this time recommend that carriers should be prohibited from using private cars or from employing the owners of such cars to perform the icing services if they find that course to their advantage, but we do recommend that these charges should also be published and maintained the same as the transportation charge and be subject to the same supervision and control."

Congress, responding to the ICC and to its own reform agenda, passed the above-mentioned Hepburn Act early in 1906. Although best known for empowering the ICC to set maximum freight rates, and in requiring the railroads, not the ICC, to seek court relief in disagreements on rulings, it also made railroad companies responsible for the reasonableness of icing charges over their lines. The provisions of the Interstate Commerce Act were amended to require the railroads to provide refrigerator cars (whether their own cars or leased private cars), show charges for protective services (icing, heating and ventilation) in their tariffs and include such charges in their freight bills. This Act thus eliminated the worst feature of "exclusive contracts," the abuse of icing charges, and made the railroads responsible for fair access by shippers to the supply of refrigerator cars.

As railroads could no longer benefit from traffic agreements in "exclusive contracts," nor could the private car lines reap the profits associated with earlier practices, particularly icing, the pre-1906 relationship between railroads and the private car lines obviously could not continue. Many railroads were motivated by the Hepburn Act to terminate their private car agreements and establish their own refrigerated freight services, car fleets, and facilities. A number of railroads, however, continued to lease or contract for their supply of refrigerator cars from private owners, although these arrangements were far less lucrative than formerly.

THE HARRIMAN PERIOD

While the Hepburn Act made its way toward passage in 1906, one railroad executive in particular watched with great interest. That interest was to lead to the incorporation of the Pacific Fruit Express Company, or PFE. The beginning of PFE, though it arose from a complex series of events involving economic, regulatory and legal questions, was

Edward Henry Harriman, Chairman of the Union Pacific from 1898 to 1909, was also the founder of Pacific Fruit Express. Here he sits before the roll-top desk in his New York office, in 1907 or 1908. His overcoat and top hat are atop the desk. UP Railroad Museum, photo H-139.

ultimately attributable to one man, Edward Henry Harriman.

Born February 25, 1848, Harriman left school at 14, found success as a stock broker before he was 20 years old, and soon became established on Wall Street as a financier. He entered railroading on a small scale in 1881, and soon acquired considerable railroad experience and knowledge through his association with Stuyvesant Fish and the Illinois Central. Elected a Director of the IC in 1883, he became Vice President in 1887. He also assisted in one of the financial reorganizations of the Erie. A few years later, he began to invest in the Union Pacific Railroad which, though laboring under a mountain of debt arising from the Credit Mobilier affair, and having lost its Pacific Coast outlet at Portland when the Oregon Short Line (OSL) and Oregon Railroad and Navigation Co. (OR&N) were severed in the bankruptcy of 1893, was struggling to reorganize.

Harriman became a director of the Union Pacific on December 6, 1897 and became Chairman of the Board in

May, 1898. Using $25 million in capital raised through his financial connections in the East, he embarked upon a remarkable rehabilitation program for the UP, bringing it into first-class physical and financial shape by the turn of the century. He also re-acquired the OSL and the OR&N to complete UP's lines in the Pacific Northwest. These huge expenditures, on a road many considered marginal, were a surprise to the railroad business. Harriman was unfazed. "The way to save money," he said, "is to spend it wisely and productively."

Harriman began very early to consider ways of securing UP's western traffic. Though a strong bridge route, the UP was peculiarly vulnerable to its neighbors. The growing strength of James J. Hill's railroads to the north, and, to the south, the Gould roads, the Santa Fe, and particularly Southern Pacific's connections to New Orleans and Chicago, made the connection to the Central Pacific at Ogden a lifeline for the UP. SP was obliged by federal statute to exchange most of its traffic at Ogden with the UP, but should the SP turn unfriendly, it could route traffic elsewhere than Ogden. Harriman explored ways to acquire or control the CP's line from Ogden to San Francisco.

But as long as Collis P. Huntington, last of the Big Four, remained in control of that road and its lessee, the Southern Pacific Company, Harriman made no headway. The situation was much changed upon the death of Huntington on August 13, 1900. During the year following Huntington's death the UP went into the market to purchase all the SP stock it could. Harriman was able to raise the necessary cash for stock purchases by selling UP bonds, and by early 1901 nearly $100 million worth of four percent bonds had been sold. When Edwin Hawley, a close associate of Huntington's, pledged his personal SP holdings to the UP, the tide turned in Harriman's favor. By March 31, 1901, UP held a 38% share of Southern Pacific; later, additional shares of SP were purchased, bringing UP ownership of SP to more than 45%. Harriman, for all intents and purposes, now held control of the Southern Pacific. He well understood he had acquired more than just the Central Pacific. As he told his associates, "We have bought not only a railroad, but an empire."

Harriman promptly set about making capital improvements on the Southern Pacific as he had on the Union Pacific, infusing vast amounts of money into the physical plant of the SP. Many of these projects to improve existing lines had been conceived in Huntington's day, but Harriman provided the capital and the decisiveness to carry them out. His bold confidence, and the accuracy and rapidity of his decision-making, never ceased to surprise and impress the men he worked with. When the board authorized $18 million for SP improvements, and Julius Kruttschnitt, who would supervise the spending, inquired as to the pace he should set (expecting, he said, to be told to spend so large a sum carefully), Harriman replied, "Spend it in a week if you can."

Under Harriman's Presidency, Southern Pacific and Union Pacific each had nominally separate boards of directors, though in fact many directors sat on both boards. The operating organizations were likewise separate on a local basis, but a combined management team at the top, many chosen from the SP, directed the entire system. In a remarkable tribute to Harriman's organizational and leadership skills, this unified operation of an 18,000-mile system worked well. The Director of Operations for both railroads was Kruttschnitt, who had been Vice President of the SP under Huntington. He and Harriman instituted a method of financial control which has persisted on both UP and SP: the Authorization for Expenditure (AFE). An AFE had to be issued for a major purchase to be made, or work to be done. Since AFE's were issued at headquarters, central cognizance of all expenditures was assured. Each AFE expired annually, requiring re-issuance if a project

could not be carried out when planned. The AFE's for each part of the organization constituted its project budget.

PACIFIC FRUIT EXPRESS IS FOUNDED

Both SP and UP had been in the business of eastward shipment of perishables in the pre-Harriman years, having small fleets of non-refrigerated "ventilator" cars in service. By 1900, the UP had 1162 cars in perishable service, and the SP had 992 cars, a combined total of 2054 cars, while competitor Atchison, Topeka and Santa Fe Railway, through its subsidiary, Santa Fe Refrigerator Despatch (SFRD), had 1570 produce cars on its roster. Many of each railroad's cars of this type were ventilated cars. These pre-Harriman cars are described in Chapter 3.

In the years after 1900, shipments of California produce increased prodigiously. By 1905, there were roughly 30,000 carloadings a year and the Harriman lines were only getting about 40 percent of that traffic. Much of the remaining 60 percent was carried by SFRD. The UP, SP and SFRD all had "exclusive car contracts" with Armour to supply part of their car needs at this time, so that Armour Lines was carrying the lion's share of California traffic. Private car lines in the trade had ordered 11,000 new cars in the two years since January 1, 1904. There was clearly an opportunity for Harriman to move into this growing business.

In addition to the growth of the California produce traffic, there was another motivation for Harriman. UP and SP relied on Armour Car Lines to supply both cars and protective service (icing, ventilation or heating) for the combined railroads. Not only had Armour been involved in the routing and rebating abuses which had brought about the California Fruit Case, but also its service to its customers, shippers and railroads alike, was the source of chronic complaints.

Finally, and perhaps most important, the geography of the SP and UP provided a way in which a car fleet could receive good utilization. Many railroads served only one or a few produce districts, and the harvest season was often short. This was why so few railroads were willing to invest in expensive refrigerator cars: their annual usage might be only a few weeks' time. But UP and SP in combination served a vast and varied territory, with harvest seasons ranging from spring fruit in the Southwest, to fall potatoes in the Northwest, to winter citrus in California. Thus a car fleet serving the two railroads could literally be used year-round. As PFE's publicists liked to say in later years, the PFE car fleet "followed the sun." These factors, along with the additional impetus given by the requirements of the Hepburn Act, gave Harriman ample reason to establish his own refrigerated car line.

Harriman's style was decisiveness backed up with capital. Therefore, he determined that the Southern Pacific should join the Union Pacific in the incorporation of a subsidiary company to furnish them and their allied lines with refrigerated cars and service (both shops and protective services). The Pacific Fruit Express Company was incorporated under the laws of the state of Utah in the city of Salt Lake on December 7th, 1906.

At the December 13th, 1906, meeting of the Executive Committee of the Union Pacific Railroad Company, Harriman had a few things to say about the establishment of PFE, as stated in the following extract from the Committee minutes for that date.

"The chairman [Harriman] stated that the contract between [the UP] and Armour Car Lines with reference to the transportation of fruit and other perishable freight, contained a provision authorizing the termination thereof upon six months' notice from either party, and that the latter had given notice of its intention to terminate such contract; that he [Harriman] was advised that under the Interstate Commerce Act, as amended, railroad companies are required to provide refrigerator cars and to show the charges for such cars and for the service of refrigeration, ventilation, etc., in their tariffs, and to include such charges in their freight bills; that under the circumstances it seemed advisable for this Company and the Southern Pacific Company to provide for the incorporation of a company whose stock should be taken by them, to acquire and furnish them and their allied lines refrigerator cars required by them and to take over and carry on the business of furnishing cars for traffic origination upon their lines which require refrigeration and ventilation of such cars; and that, pursuant to this plan he had heretofore caused a

corporation known as 'Pacific Fruit Express Company' to be organized with an authorized capital stock of $12,000,000. He further stated that, under the laws of the State of Utah, it was necessary that 10 per cent of the authorized capital stock should be paid in cash at the time of the organization of the company, and that he had directed the treasurer of the Union Pacific Railroad Company to pay that amount, one-half of it to be repaid to said company by the Southern Pacific Company."

The original paid-in cash stock of $1.2 million (the 10% amount) was divided into shares with a par value of $100 per share. The initial subscribers were all residents of Salt Lake City, Utah. The UP and SP, of course, were the origin of the capital funds, and the subscribers were individuals chosen to hold this stock. Their names and amount held were as follows. W.H. Bancroft was assigned 11,996 shares, and P.L. Williams, D.E. Burley, J.A. Reeves, and F.H. Knickerbocker were assigned 1 share each.

At the same meeting Harriman further stated that "in furtherance of this plan, he had some time ago authorized the purchase for account of said Pacific Fruit Express Company of 6000 refrigerator cars [raised to 6600 cars shortly thereafter] at a cost of $1700 each." It was pure E. H. Harriman style to "cause" an organization such as PFE to simply come into existence and begin serving his purposes, with $12 million of authorized capital (most of it used for the car purchase), and tell his board about it afterwards.

Until the first general election of officers of PFE could take place, W.H. Bancroft was appointed President of the company. The first two employees, hired in January, 1907, were C.M. Secrist, listed as "General Manager," and L.A. Resseguie, Clerk. Secrist, who had 15 years' background

This is PFE car no. 1, the first of 6600 cars of its class, delivered in 1906-07, and the progenitor of the largest fleet of refrigerator cars in the world. This photo was taken in the early 1920's, and shows that era's paint scheme. PFE photo, CSRM.

with traffic departments of the Harriman roads, soon was elected as the first chief executive officer of the new subsidiary, and was then listed as "President and General Manager" of PFE. By July, 1907, there were 10 employees, six of them clerks.

In 1908, the capital stock of each railroad was increased to $5.4 million, and later in 1923, the stock was increased to $12 million for each railroad, representing 240,000 shares of stock. The latter total amount of stock remained in force for the remainder of PFE's life.

The original offices of PFE were located at 135 Adams Street in Chicago. There was also a PFE office in San Francisco's Flood Building, which had survived the 1906 earthquake. Starting in July, 1907, PFE's General Agent was J.W. McClymonds and A. Faget was listed as the Consulting Engineer (at a salary equal to that of Secrist).

PFE was in business, then, right from its incorporation, although its primary business at first was managing the car fleet operations. Not until October 1, 1907, were the Armour and UP icing facilities, and Armour's western car shops, turned over to PFE under a purchase agreement. At that point, PFE became what it was to be throughout the rest of its life, a complete perishable transportation organization.

PFE BEGINS OPERATION

Managing and directing the operation of a fleet of 6600 refrigerator cars was an immense task, but PFE did not quite start from scratch. A number of existing shops and icing facilities were acquired in 1907. PFE took over the Armour Car Line California repair shops at Sacramento, Los Angeles, Riverside and Colton. These shops had been built around 1899 when Armour was running about 5000 cars in the California fruit trade and had only a light repair capability, since Armour, being an eastern concern, had its heavy shops in the Midwest and sent cars "home" for heavy repairs. This served PFE well in its early operations, however, since all their cars were purchased new and only light running repairs were needed for the first few years.

As the old Armour shops became inadequate for PFE's needs, they were enlarged and in some cases replaced. In 1909, the Riverside shop was closed and operations moved to Colton; the Sacramento facility was moved to Roseville upon completion of the new Southern Pacific yard there. In the 1920's, additional shop facilities would be built.

PFE was contractually responsible for handling all car icing on the lines of the SP and UP and in 1908 it built the first of its major ice manufacturing plants at Roseville. The Roseville plant was enlarged and improved over the years, eventually becoming the largest ice manufacturing plant in the world. Other new plants were built and older ones

C.M. Secrist, VP & GM, 1907-1923.

upgraded, until in its peak years PFE owned and operated nineteen ice manufacturing plants. In 1907, PFE had purchased 80% of the ice it used from commercial firms, most of it natural ice, but by 1921, over two-thirds of PFE's ice requirements were met from its own plant production, and the great majority of that ice was manufactured, not natural ice. Of 1.6 million tons of ice used by PFE in 1921, only 100,000 tons were natural.

When PFE could not justify the cost of a company-owned plant, it contracted for ice from local ice companies, or supplied ice in PFE cars from PFE plants. In such situations, either PFE or the ice company might build the car icing platforms (ice decks). This flexible strategy permitted operations in all growing and packing regions regardless of their level of traffic. These developments are described in much more detail in Chapter 13.

The function of PFE was to supply refrigerator cars and protective services (icing, ventilation or heating) to railroads with which it had contracts. Its two major "customers" under the Car Hire Contract were its parents, SP and UP and their subsidiaries, but PFE also provided services to several other railroads. Usually these services were provided through an "agreement" which only committed PFE to supply cars as available, but cars were leased from

Harvesting natural ice at Laramie. Men called "spudders" are completing separation of the ice raft into 22-inch square blocks, which then go into the ice storage house. This plant was built by UP in 1906 and purchased by PFE shortly after. UP Railroad Museum.

the Western Pacific, as described below and in Chapter 5.

PFE earned its revenue through mileage charges for equipment. The mileage rate, initially 1¢ per mile, applied whether the car was loaded or empty and was charged to the railroads. PFE did not bill shippers directly. The railroads collected freight charges from the shippers according to tariff rules, then paid the per-mile car rental and protective services fees to PFE, keeping their share of the charges for hauling the car over their lines. In PFE's early days, its contract provided that SP and UP did not pay the standard 1¢ per mile, but paid only ¾¢ per mile for loaded cars, and paid no charge for empty cars.

THE UN-MERGER CASE CHANGES
PFE'S PARENTS

On February 1, 1908, the U.S. government initiated an action against the Harriman Lines (UP, SP, CP) under the Sherman Anti-Trust Act of 1890. As legal maneuvering continued, Harriman died on September 9, 1909 and would not see the dismantling of his empire. Although a lower court dismissed the case, called the Pacific Railroad Case, on June 11, 1911, the government appealed the decision to the U.S. Supreme Court, and on December 2, 1912, the Court ordered the separation or "un-merger" of

the Union Pacific and the Southern Pacific Railroads.

Procedures for this un-merger began to take place almost immediately; joint traffic offices were closed, solicitation agreements canceled and the pooled SP and UP freight car fleets divided between the two railroads. As PFE was already owned by the two railroads as separate stockholders, it was not directly affected by the changes, and its cars remained its property. In 1913, PFE's headquarters was moved from Chicago to San Francisco, and consolidated with existing PFE offices in the Flood Building.

The Wilson administration was not satisfied with the 1913 outcome of the Pacific Railroad Case, and on February 11, 1914, filed another Sherman Act suit against the SP, this time to separate the Central Pacific from the SP. Although the district court denied the government's petition on March 10, 1917, the government appealed to the Supreme Court. Proceedings were interrupted by the period of government control of American railroads during World War I, through the United States Railroad Administration (USRA) during the 26 months prior to March, 1920. Early in 1921, the case was resumed, and on May 29, 1922, the Supreme Court held that the SP's 1899 acquisition of the CP was an "unlawful restraint of trade." SP applied for a rehearing of the case, which was denied on October 9, 1922.

11

Part of the 1923 Western Pacific car purchase was car 50187. Built by AC&F, the car was to remain in WP ownership all its life, although always maintained and distributed to shippers by PFE. AC&F photo, courtesy ACF Industries, Al Westerfield collection.

Meanwhile, SP was pursuing another solution to the problem. Congress had enacted the Transportation Act of 1920 to encourage consolidation, not competition, of railroads, and the SP now applied to the ICC, under the ICC's 1920 Transportation Act powers, to acquire the CP as a legal railroad consolidation. In December, 1922, as the ICC hearings began to trend in the SP's favor, the SP and UP met privately to negotiate an agreement for the SP to keep the CP, subject to certain arrangements with the UP. That draft agreement was submitted to the ICC in January, and officially accepted on February 6, 1923.

This agreement had two important effects on PFE. One was a condition of the ICC settlement, requiring that SP solicit traffic for preferential routing via UP originating or terminating on the following parts of the SP lines: north of Santa Margarita on the Coast line, north of Caliente (in the Tehachapis) on the Valley line, south of Kirk on the Cascade line. Off-line, the requirement extended to territory north of the Oklahoma-Texas border to the Ohio River and on to Buffalo, New York. PFE was primarily affected in California, and for many years all originating traffic in the Salinas Valley, for example, went via Ogden, while that originating in Southern California went via El Paso, without regard for its final destination. (This situation was essentially voided by the ICC in 1966, in response to a series of cases filed by the D&RGW.)

The second important effect had to do with the Western Pacific. Although the ICC had imposed no conditions in its settlement regarding the WP, the SP negotiated an agreement privately to forestall any ICC conditions. That WP agreement is discussed in the following section.

WESTERN PACIFIC

In the spring of 1923, refrigerator cars began to appear in PFE's fleet bearing the emblem of the Western Pacific. This was an outcome of the "un-merger" process just described, and was a major change from the earlier relationship of the Southern Pacific and the PFE with the

Western Pacific. The SP had naturally regarded the WP as an interloper, right from WP's completion in 1909, though WP traffic was a minute percentage of what SP was carrying over the Sierra. Hostile rather than merely competitive relations prevailed. When the USRA took control of the railroads at the end of 1917, an SP Vice President, William R. Scott, was appointed manager of the WP, and among the changes he instituted was a paired-track arrangement between Alazon and Weso in northern Nevada. Though WP terminated this arrangement at the end of the USRA period, it had been recognized by both railroads as a useful feature from the operational standpoint, and was reinstituted later.

On PFE's part, ice was supplied by contract to the WP for its facilities, for example at Portola, where there was no ice manufacturing capability. At first PFE owned some of the WP ice decks, but between 1915 and 1924 all were sold to WP. PFE operated (managed) the icing stations, at least as early as 1914. Carlin in eastern Nevada was a "joint" facility, with WP and PFE ice houses initially on opposite sides of the same ice pond (see Chapter 12 for details).

In the earliest days of the Western Pacific, most freight equipment had been leased from the Denver and Rio Grande. Among the exceptions were 100 truss-rod underframe refrigerator cars, 36 ft. long, purchased from Armour in 1910. When the WP emerged from receivership and Rio Grande control in 1916, it began to buy its own freight car fleet, and at least as early as 1916, WP made an agreement with PFE to supplement their refrigerator car supply. The arrangement was that PFE would furnish ventilated refrigerator cars, as needed by the WP (subject to car availability), at standard rates. PFE also had such an agreement (not a contract) at that time with the Denver and Salt Lake Railroad.

In mid-1922, the WP announced plans to purchase new refrigerator cars of its own. It is not clear whether this was a genuine intent to operate a separate car line, or was a negotiating tactic with PFE or SP. There exists correspondence from the SP to the PFE, dated in mid-1922,

Western Pacific 2-8-2 No. 302 races eastward across Nevada with a perishable block. Every recognizable car is a PFE reefer. Otto C. Perry photo OP-20019, Western History Dept., Denver Public Library.

directing PFE to undertake "discussions to obtain a car hire contract." Discussions did take place in the fall of 1922. Meanwhile, WP had not supplied car specifications to any prospective builder, as late as December, 1922. They did, however, set up a new, subsidiary organization, the Western Refrigerator Line, on Jan. 1, 1923, to operate WP's new cars.

Meanwhile, SP was embroiled with the ICC, as described above, in the effort to retain ownership of the Central Pacific. Although the ICC imposed no conditions on the SP regarding relations with the WP, it is clear from surviving correspondence that the SP perceived an obligation to provide reasonable conditions for its small rival. As early as January 16, 1923, SP and WP had initialed a memorandum of agreement to negotiate arrangements on several topics. The joint trackage operations in Nevada were one such topic. Another was refrigerator cars.

Paul Shoup, the SP Vice President who had negotiated the agreement with UP which the ICC accepted, was also SP's negotiator with WP for the lease by PFE of the WP refrigerator cars, which had not yet been built. He communicated memoranda of all his meetings to William Sproule, SP President, to C.M. Secrist, PFE's VP & GM and to C.R. Gray, the UP President. The UP soon indicated that it was content to let the SP reach what agreement it wished, on behalf of PFE, with the WP. During March, 1923, Secrist raised the point that PFE would want the WP cars to be "painted and branded the same as PFE equipment." A draft contract was then made up by SP, including a clause that the cars "should carry the words 'Pacific Fruit Express'

in standard letters of the latter," but that the "trade mark of the WRL may be carried if desired by that line."

Secrist replied on April 3, 1923, that he felt "if the Western Pacific desires any marking of their own on the leased cars, it should be the medallion of the railroad and not the marking of the Western Refrigerator Line," though he would "prefer no marking of this kind." As a basis, he stated that "I would be adverse to establishing the W.R.L. by carrying their advertising on our cars. [The] WP Railroad is already established." A revised contract was then drawn up by April 17, with the provision that "these cars will be lettered 'Pacific Fruit Express' and numbered in our series, but...will carry the medallion of the Western Pacific." The contract went into effect on May 1, 1923.

An interesting detail is that the cars were already under construction by American Car and Foundry by this time, and the first few cars were moved to Sacramento, for acceptance by PFE, with WRL lettering. As described in Chapter 5, this was then changed to PFE lettering at Roseville. Thus the cars never operated in revenue service under the Western Refrigerator Line name.

The Western Pacific built these cars as part of a car hire agreement with PFE, and for the express purpose of having them operated as part of the PFE fleet. In this way, WP arranged to have a dependable source of cars for its shippers, while also obtaining a guaranteed payment toward the carrying charges on the borrowed cost of the cars. Very likely this was a more certain source of income from the cars than would have been the case with WP or WRL operation. It has been asserted by some authors that WP

During the 1920's, PFE acquired just over 22,000 refrigerator cars. Here a string of completed but unpainted cars for PFE has been pulled out of the plant at General American in 1922. GATC photo, courtesy Jim Lekas.

did operate these cars at various periods, but this was never the case. PFE not only was responsible for making the cars available to shippers, and was the agent collecting (and keeping) the mileage payments, but PFE maintained and later rebuilt the cars in its own shops. Capital improvements to the cars were at WP's expense.

The rental fee paid on the WP cars is worth detailing. There was an initial request by WP that PFE pay a rental equivalent to 6% of the cars' cost, which was equal to the interest and charges WP was obligated to pay on its equipment trust. (Financially solid PFE usually enjoyed 4% trusts.) Since the cars cost about $3200, 6% would have been $192 per car annually. In response, PFE wished to pay a flat fee, a fee which was rather less than the mileage payments which the cars would earn under PFE management (though more than the cars could earn with only WP's lighter traffic). Thus PFE was able to earn a modest net income on the cars, without the capital cost of constructing them. The flat fee was $136 per year, while PFE's average car earned about $175 per year in mileage charges in the 1920's. When the contract was renewed in 1938 and extended in 1942, the same $136 fee was continued until 1950.

This WP-PFE contract placed the PFE in a delicate position. PFE was required to distribute cars for loading on both SP and WP in a fair and equitable fashion, which could become quite difficult during equipment shortages (endemic during the 1920's). Yet A.E. Chiasson, PFE's last VP & GM before the 1978 split-up, recalls that "both SP and WP had confidence in the integrity of PFE to carry out properly its obligations under the contract. I do not recall a single instance where PFE's judgement was questioned by either railroad."

The contract renewal in 1951 raised the annual car rental fee to $204. More contentious at that time was the issue of modernization of WP's cars. Most by this time

were in very poor condition, and a substantial number had been scrapped. The 1951 contract provided that WP would provide the sum of $3 million to recondition 900 of its best cars. The concern of PFE was that American Refrigerator Transit (ART) might bid for the WP's business without asking any such capital outlay, since it was known that ART had actively sought the contract. The WP, however, continued its contract with PFE.

After the ice cars' life expired and all were scrapped in the early 1960's, the WP contract was modified to provide that PFE would supply ice cars, mechanical cars, or both, as needed by WP shippers, subject as always to car availability. As the decade wore on, however, consistent shortages of mechanical cars were encountered. The WP did not feel able to finance a contribution of mechanical cars to PFE, and eventually sought other arrangements. The Western Pacific found that Fruit Growers Express (FGE) would supply cars if WP purchased a certain stock ownership in FGE. WP finally elected to terminate the PFE contract on June 30, 1967. This ended a car leasing contract of more than 40 years duration.

THE TWENTIES

At the time of the 1913 "un-merger," PFE's management structure underwent a change. The Presidency of PFE was arranged to alternate annually between representatives of the UP and SP. This was to maintain a political balance between the two parent companies. At first each railroad usually chose a senior executive, such as a Vice-President, to act as PFE President, but in later years one of the railroad's directors was usually chosen. In the years before 1920, for example, Julius Kruttschnitt served for the SP, while F.W. Charske served for UP many times between 1920 and 1940.

Since UP and SP maintained New York offices in

separate buildings, a fascinating little drama occurred each October, in which SP's PFE President (in even-numbered years) would ship, from 165 Broadway, the actual filing cabinets containing all PFE documents to the incoming UP President, at 120 Broadway. The next October they were solemnly shipped back up the street. The President was required, under PFE's incorporation papers, to be a share-holder, so each year one share of stock was enrolled in the name of the new President.

The rotating President in New York was, of course, only titular head of PFE. Direct management of PFE was accomplished by the Vice President and General Manager or VP & GM in San Francisco, a title created in 1913 and immediately bestowed upon C.M. Secrist, who had served as operating head of PFE since 1907.

During 1919, there were contacts among UP, SP and AT&SF executives regarding the possibility of pooling or commonly owning the PFE and SFRD refrigerator cars. But discussions died out over concerns about division of territory and traffic; SP in particular felt unwilling to open its own rich territories to joint traffic solicitation.

In December, 1923, C.M Secrist died while on a duck-hunting trip in the Hanford, California, area. Upon his death there was considerable discussion as to who would succeed him, with both UP and SP anxious to have one of "their" people running PFE. After several months' delay, Horace Giddings was appointed. Born in 1872, Giddings had come from Armour Car Lines to the PFE at its inception in 1907. Beginning as an agent, he rose through the operational ranks of the Car Service Department, taking office as VP & GM in January, 1924. By this time, PFE's offices were located in the Southern Pacific Building at 65 Market Street, San Francisco, where they would remain until 1930.

Giddings was known as a hard worker and was a self-educated and well-read man, common in the days of practical rather than formal education. He kept a tight rein on payrolls and worked toward the centralization of services such as diversion and passing. He remained as VP & GM until his retirement on September 30, 1942, bringing the PFE through years of great growth in the 1920's, then the Depression, and the first years of World War II.

On Aug. 31, 1920, the ICC authorized an increase in the refrigerator car mileage rate, from 1¢ per mile to 2¢. At this time, the preferential ¾¢ rate enjoyed by SP and UP (and also by AT&SF) was discontinued.

By 1927, it was clear that PFE was performing extremely well financially. It may be of interest to list the dividends paid to the owning railroads in the first 21 years of PFE's existence, as well as the per cent return on investment, based on the capital stock in existence for each year. In 1907 and 1918-1920, no dividends were paid. In

1908 and 1911, a 5% dividend, or $270,000, was paid to each railroad; in 1909, 1910, 1912, 1913, 1915-1917, and 1921, $540,000, or 10%, was paid to each; in 1914, $810,000, or 15% was paid. In 1922, $1.08 million, or 20%, was paid. During these years the capital stock had been $5.4 million per railroad. In 1923, the stock was increased to $12 million per railroad. In that year, a $4.2 million dividend, or 35%, was paid to each railroad, and in 1924-26, a $2.4 million dividend, or 20%, was paid to each, while in 1927 a 30% dividend, $3.6 million was paid. For these 21 years, then, dividends to each railroad averaged 11.9% per year, including the non-dividend years, not a bad investment at all. Another way to summarize it is that each railroad had received $21.75 million on an investment of $12 million.

In 1928, Southern Pacific culminated several years of complaining about its share of PFE revenues by insisting on a revised Car Hire Contract with UP. The SP's contention was that it originated and handled a significantly greater share of PFE traffic than did UP, and consequently incurred greater expenses than did UP. The percentage of PFE loadings originating on SP lines had in fact varied between 68 and 73 per cent during the 1920's (see Appendix). As a result, the revised Contract of 1928 continued

Horace Giddings, VP & GM, 1924-1942.

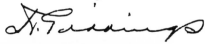

An SP perishable block, running as the third section of train 842, rolls eastward near Wellton, Ariz., on July 26, 1935. Consolidation 2529 is doing its utmost to maintain 45 MPH. Otto C. Perry photo OP-15827, Western History Dept., Denver Public Library.

the practice of PFE dividends being equally split between the two equal stockholders, but added the feature that each railroad would be entitled to "special compensation" over and above its dividend. This compensation was intended to reflect the actual share of traffic for each year, and SP received substantially more than did UP. At this time, PFE dividends were regarded by the IRS as internal matters for UP and SP, and were not directly subject to income taxes.

PFE contracted in 1926 with the Denver and Salt Lake Railroad to supply it with reefers, and this was renewed in 1930 despite a desire by the Denver and Rio Grande Western to join the D&SL in an agreement with American Refrigerator Transit. Carl Gray, UP's President, quietly arranged to extend PFE's contract, and telegraphed UP's Board Chairman, R.S. Lovett, that "When the D&RGW wake up to this there will be some stir." The D&SL contract was renewed periodically until the D&SL was consolidated with D&RGW; in February, 1953, the contract was terminated.

As shown above, PFE was a profitable enterprise from the beginning. Throughout the 1920's, car loadings, mileage and profits continued to rise. In the larger growing regions such as the Imperial and San Joaquin Valleys of California it was not unheard of to load 500 to 1000 cars per day or 20,000 per season. As PFE's carloadings soared, many thousands of new cars were needed. From 1918, when PFE already had the largest refrigerator car fleet in North America, until 1926, over 23,000 more cars were purchased (not counting the 2775 WP cars), as detailed in Chapter 5. By 1926, PFE owned more than a third of all

refrigerator cars in U. S. service, and had more than twice as many cars as its nearest rival, Santa Fe's Refrigeration Department (SFRD), although SFRD was also growing. By the end of the 1920's, PFE reached a fleet size of 40,000 cars, a size it was to maintain into the 1950's.

From the first, and especially in the 1920's, PFE's managers understood SFRD to be the competition in California, and information about SFRD's activities, real or rumored, was often used to justify PFE's own plans. SFRD appears to have done the same regarding PFE.

An interesting detail of PFE's car purchases, in the 1920's and for years thereafter, was the specification that most wood parts were to be Oregon fir. Moreover, it was required that the fir be shipped to the builder's plant via UP or SP. Car specifications even contained a helpful list of mills located on SP and UP lines which would be suitable sources of the wood. Thus the two owning railroads not only generated traffic for themselves, but also directed business to their on-line industries.

As the PFE car fleet grew, additional shops were needed. In 1926 a complete shop was built at Nampa, Idaho and a light repair facility was built at Pocatello, Ida. These shops served the growing traffic originating out of the areas in the Pacific Northwest served by lines of the Union Pacific. During 1926 and 1927, in order to gain more room, the Roseville shop was relocated a few miles west to Antelope, on the western end of the SP yard. The light repair shop at Tucson, Ariz., was built in 1928 to handle cars originating and returning to the farming areas of the Imperial Valley and Arizona. The dry climate of Tucson was ideal for

PFE ice crews often included athletes building up both bank accounts and muscles during the summer. This Imperial Valley crew in the 1920's is University of Southern California football players. E.L. DeGolyer photo collection, DeGolyer Library.

refinishing cars and after 1966 all PFE cars would be directed to Tucson for painting.

PFE now had five shops at Los Angeles, Colton, and Roseville, Calif.; Tucson, Ariz.; and Nampa, Ida. as well as a number of light repair facilities. Empty cars were expedited back from their destinations for cleaning and reloading without much thought given to westbound traffic. This was because of the rate structure, based on mileage, loaded or empty, and a critical need for cars in the western growing regions at harvest time. Shippers were intolerant of car shortages, making their complaints well known to both PFE and the ICC. But shipper attitudes on car quality were another matter. PFE maintained its cars very well, and shippers often objected if a "foreign" car was spotted on their siding instead of a PFE car. Use of foreign cars was a necessity in the August-October peak rush, when 15,000 to 25,000 foreign cars would be loaded out of a total of 100 to 125,000 carloads in those three months.

PFE's annual net income in the early 1920's was mostly paid to the parent railroads in the form of dividends, as listed above. The rest became an "earned surplus" which was typically used for capital projects. The accumulated surplus in 1920 was $3.3 million, but by 1930 it had risen to more than $10 million. This surplus was mostly held in the form of investments, particularly as offsets for car investment trusts, and as capital property such as ice plants. In effect, each owning railroad had a 50% equity in this earned surplus, as well as receiving annual dividends.

PROHIBITION AND THE PFE

PFE was affected by the fluctuations of the larger national economy around it but certain events had a greater effect than had others. The Eighteenth Amendment to the U.S. Constitution (Volstead Act) brought Prohibition of the manufacture and sale of alcoholic beverages throughout the United States. Becoming effective on January 16, 1920, Prohibition seemed only to fire the ingenuity of those determined to keep up the supply of alcohol, Prohibition or no Prohibition.

Among those were people of European descent who had settled along the east coast and who were accustomed to regular use of wine. The Volstead Act permitted up to 250 gallons of wine to be made annually for personal use, and soon there were literally thousands of basement wineries kept going by grapes from California. Many California grape growers had posted signs in their vineyards stating "Prohibition will ruin this vineyard," but soon grape sales for transport east replaced at least part of former sales to commercial wineries. Grape prices rose, from $5 per ton to $110 per ton, delivered, and so did the demand for freight refrigerators to ship them. The grape shipments were an important part of PFE's traffic throughout the Prohibition period of the 1920's, but declined sharply when Prohibition was repealed by the ratification of the Twenty-First Amendment on December 5, 1933.

Icing crews were often made up of immigrant labor, particularly near the border with Mexico. In addition to the Mexican laborers, many a college student put himself through school icing cars in the 110-degree heat of an Imperial Valley or Central Valley summer. College athletes, often with the help of their coaches, were able to obtain jobs on the decks to keep them in shape in the off-seasons, and many times a friendly scrimmage between hastily-organized teams would take place between trains.

PFE shops had well-organized athletic teams in sports such as baseball, basketball and boxing, and in some instances shop Superintendents would recruit potential employees based upon athletic ability as well as shop skills. Of course in the days of manual labor in car repair or icing, a strong back was the rule rather than the exception.

Like much of industry during the period of a burgeoning economy of the early and mid-1920's, PFE management was paternalistic toward its employees, establishing employee welfare programs such as hospitalization and life insurance. This policy followed the pattern of the parent railroads. Both of PFE's parents, SP and UP, had systems of hospitals staffed by company-employed doctors and nurses which served any and all employees

THE GREAT DEPRESSION

The Stock Market Crash of October, 1929, and the subsequent economic depression lasting nearly until the beginning of World War II had less effect on PFE than on many railroads. People still had to eat, albeit perhaps less fresh produce, and foodstuffs still needed to be shipped to points of consumption. The agricultural areas of California and the Pacific Northwest provided year-round traffic for the PFE car fleet and, in fact, the fleet reached its greatest strength on September 30, 1930, with 41,261 cars on the roster. In January, 1930, PFE moved into its first separate office facility in San Francisco, at 64 Pine Street. By 1935, PFE moved its offices again, this time to the Wells Fargo Building at 85 Second Street, San Francisco.

The PFE labor forces became unionized during the Depression, culminating changes in labor relations stemming from the USRA period. Since PFE was not a common carrier itself, the establishment of the USRA in 1917 had had only two significant impacts on PFE: restrictions on car purchases, as mentioned in Chapter 5, and the effect on wages. The USRA indirectly affected wages on PFE and the railroad industry in general through the establishment of labor rules and wage guidelines.

The USRA granted substantial wage increases to railroad workers, which were then the springboard for further wage demands after World War I. The work rules, issued in a USRA Circular, would later form some of the framework for formal agreements between organized labor and the railroad industry, PFE included. Although unions had been active in organizing railroad employees since before the turn of the century, they did not succeed in representing any PFE employees until the 1930's.

In September 12th, 1933, a meeting was held in the Eagles' Hall at Roseville for the purpose of organizing the icing platform men and other workers on the PFE and the SP. The carmen, by far the largest labor force on the PFE, had "recently organized" according to an article carried in the Sept. 13, 1933, *Sacramento Bee* reporting the meeting. Other crafts gradually gained union representation on the PFE during the balance of the 1930's and in the 1940's.

Turning to financial issues, many PFE employees believed that the subsidiary was a "cash cow" for the parent railroads, helping keep them afloat during the Depression. That this was at least partly true is suggested by a plan, never implemented, to lease PFE's cars to the parent railroads in 1933. Under this scheme, PFE would no longer pay taxes on its income. Instead, UP and SP would have the tax obligation, but since neither were paying any taxes in those hard times, the usual PFE tax bill could be avoided. Complexities in state and local taxes, as well as concerns about the practice in more normal times, combined to scuttle the idea.

PFE's profitability played a more direct role in a transaction SP had with the Reconstruction Finance Corporation (RFC), one of the "alphabet soup" government agencies created in the early 1930's as part of the Roosevelt administration's efforts to combat the Depression.

The RFC was in the business of loaning money to bail out companies in trouble. In March, 1933 SP applied to the RFC for a loan, which was partly secured by PFE stock. The SP pledged its $12 million of PFE stock to the RFC, along with $16 million in stock of other subsidiaries such as the Arizona Eastern, as collateral for the $22 million loan. Ten-year railroad bonds were then issued, and the proceeds of bond sales used to pay off the loan by 1936. Although there was nothing in the articles of incorporation of the PFE that prevented SP from pledging its half of the PFE stock for whatever purpose it saw fit, it would seem that had SP defaulted on the loan, the history of the PFE might have taken a considerably different direction.

Even PFE cars hosted their share of unauthorized passengers in the Depression. Photo courtesy Doug Peterson.

When depression conditions reappeared after a brief respite, SP returned to the RFC in 1938 and 1939 for an additional $20 million, although PFE stock was not again pledged as security. As economic circumstances improved, SP repaid all its RFC loans by June, 1942. Lest these loans seem a criticism of SP's finances, it should be pointed out that SP is among the very few American railroads never to have fallen into bankruptcy.

During the depression, PFE's revenue had continued to generate substantial income for its parents. In the period 1929-1939, PFE never paid less than $1.5 million annually to each railroad (12.5% annual return on investment) in dividends alone, and similar amounts were also paid as compensation. Total payments, to UP and SP combined, were $51.1 million in dividends and $53.2 million in compensation for the 1929-39 period, inclusive. To give a single illustration of the impact of these monies, in 1937 Southern Pacific netted less than $2 million, about $0.52 per share of stock, and paid no dividend (it had paid no dividends since 1931). Its receipts from PFE in that year were nearly $3.5 million.

But money was still scarce, causing PFE to undertake a new approach to its car fleet. As described in Chapter 7, cars needing work were simply renewed in kind, or "reconditioned," instead of being thoroughly rebuilt. During 1937-41, nearly 11,000 cars were reworked in this way in PFE shops.

WORLD WAR II

From 1940 until the declaration of war in December, 1941, pressure on U.S. industry, including the transportation sector, steadily increased. Mindful of the Federalization of the railroads during World War I, railroad management went out of its way to cooperate with both private and government demand for service as the United States moved toward a state of war on two fronts, across both the Atlantic and Pacific Oceans. However, few of the arrangements made to meet this demand, such as certain equipment pooling agreements, survived beyond the wartime period.

The initial panic on the West Coast following the attack on Pearl Harbor on Dec. 7, 1941 was not lost on the managers and executives of PFE. Immediately after the attack there was a flurry of communication from PFE executives to officers of its owning roads regarding protection from sabotage and bombings. The SP wrote back that it was busy with its own problems, while the UP was a bit more helpful, quoting National Fire Protection Association guidelines for protection against incendiary bombs. The guidelines suggested a supply of sand and shovels to extinguish magnesium bombs which, NFPA determined, would penetrate roofs and explode on the floors of facili-

Kenneth V. Plummer, VP & GM, 1942-1958.

ties. By Dec. 30, 1941, Giddings had written back that the shovels and sand had been ordered to protect the facilities.

Horace Giddings was succeeded by Kenneth V. Plummer in October, 1942, upon Giddings' retirement from service. Born February 26, 1893, Plummer began his railroad career on October 16, 1912, with the Southern Pacific as a car record agent. He went to the Western Pacific Railroad on February 1, 1918, as an agent and then went on loan to the USRA from October 1, 1918 until the USRA ended, March 1, 1920. He returned from USRA to a position in the President's office of the Southern Pacific Company, beginning his tenure with the PFE on April 18, 1922, as a clerk to the VP & GM and AGM (Assistant General Manager) offices. He went "up through the ranks" at PFE, reaching the District Agent's position at Sacramento and making Superintendent on May 1, 1938.

Plummer became an AGM in 1939, and was elevated to VP & GM on October 1, 1942, at a salary of $30,000. His previous employment with Southern Pacific made him acceptable to that company and in the opinion of some, may have accelerated his ascent to the VP & GM's office over other candidates. There was always some conjecture around PFE that the Southern Pacific exercised greater influence on the PFE partly because of the physical proximity of the offices of SP and PFE and perhaps also because SP originated the majority of PFE's total perishable traffic until about 1976 or so, as is tabulated in the Appendix.

Plummer was considered the last of the informally educated men to hold the position of VP & GM and was outstanding in his abilities to deal with shippers and the public. He traveled extensively in this capacity, working closely in PFE operations with his Assistant General Manager, Charles Ahern. These men, working side by side, Ahern "inside" the PFE and Plummer "outside," presided over the most successful days of the PFE.

Plummer also took over at a time when PFE, like all parts of the railroad industry, had come under tremendous pressure to perform. Although there was no counterpart of the USRA in World War II, the ICC and the ODT (Office of Defense Transportation) cooperated in policies designed to best utilize the total capacity of U. S. railroads. An important issue was efficient use of refrigerator cars.

Prior to the War, both reefers and box cars moved eastward from the Pacific coast with far greater traffic than was available for the westward return. But west coast war industries, and export traffic through Pacific ports, reversed the movement of loaded box cars, creating a situation in which empty box cars returning from California passed empty reefers returning from the East. The solution to this wasteful cross-haul of empties was to create pooling arrangements in which refrigerator cars were loaded when box cars were not available for Pacific coast destinations. The ICC, at the ODT's request, issued Service Order No. 104 in January, 1943, ordering this pooling, which initially applied only to cars of PFE and SFRD, but in September was extended to all refrigerator cars.

In prewar years the PFE had directed its cars "home" to one of its own shops or light repair points for repairs and cleaning; foreign owners did the same. During the War, however, PFE was obligated to repair, "OK," and load foreign reefers if they were available, and foreign roads were obligated to do the same for PFE's cars. In 1940 the number of PFE cars loaded in foreign line service was 5990; by 1945 this had jumped to 171,917. PFE lost some of the quality control it had over its fleet but the pooling arrangement brought about greater cooperation among owners and carried over to a degree in the post-war years.

Another effect of the War was upon westbound loadings. In prewar years PFE largely ignored westbound traffic because of the critical need to turn cars around quickly for eastbound loading and because PFE was paid by the car-mile, whether cars were loaded or empty.

In 1940 only 19.6 per cent of westbound miles in PFE cars were with loads, but in 1944 this percentage jumped to a high of 45.3 per cent. By 1946 the percentage of loaded westbound miles had dropped to 25.8 per cent, indicating that PFE was regaining control of its fleet and returning to business as usual.

During World War II, American domestic industry was anxious to convey to the public that its able-bodied employees were essential to the war. This UP poster does so for ice deck workers. UP Railroad Museum.

In retrospect it might appear that PFE and its parents perhaps let go of a golden opportunity to continue development of the westbound traffic secured during the war. A vigorous pursuit of that traffic may have better prepared PFE to weather future changes in the transportation of perishable commodities and in the railroad industry itself. There were, however, three circumstances peculiar to the refrigerated car industry which contradict this idea.

First, PFE's primary responsibility was to its shippers of perishables. There was usually a critical need for empty cars at the loading points, particularly during the August-October rush in California. The right number of empty cars had to be supplied to each harvesting area, and these had to be assembled just as each perishable movement began. It is understandable that priority was given to getting the cars back west, loaded or not.

Second, the cars had to be maintained in a first-class condition for the handling of foodstuffs and this limited what could be loaded in them for a westbound trip. Many kinds of "rough" freight would not be suitable. Moreover, the cubic capacity of a refrigerator car of the same outside length as a boxcar was less because of the ice bunkers, floor racks, and lower roof height. Some PFE reefer classes were fitted with collapsible bunkers to offset this disadvantage, but an ice refrigerator car was still a smaller car.

A third factor is that the cars, once unloaded, were sometimes damp inside and unsuitable for loading of dry commodities. Thus even the lading shipped in reefers without icing, to take advantage of their insulation, such as canned goods, pharmaceuticals, dry packaged goods like crackers and cereal, wine and other bottled beverages, and paper and printed articles such as magazines, could not always be placed in an available reefer. Although as late as 1946 nearly 22 per cent of all loading in refrigerator cars nationwide was of this type of "dry traffic," the introduction of insulated boxcars after 1950 essentially captured that lading from refrigerator cars.

On paper, PFE was strictly an operating organization. While there was much communication and good relations between shippers and PFE people, it was officially up to the railroads which contracted for PFE's service to solicit perishable traffic over their lines. But even if PFE was not supposed to solicit any of its traffic, perishable or otherwise, it certainly cooperated closely with SP and UP in contacts with shippers, and often acted to facilitate its traffic.

Yet PFE's owning roads had plenty of their own box cars to load, and for box cars, no mileage rate needed to be paid to a subsidiary. Thus if either parent road could load one of its box cars westbound it did not, in essence, have to share the revenue with the other parent through mileage charges. There was a small amount of westbound traffic in perishables, mainly in meat and fish, but these commodities had to ride in reefers dedicated to that service and did not usually come west in PFE cars.

In later years PFE's eastern General Agencies worked to develop westbound traffic in PFE equipment, particularly trailers, as well as secure favorable eastbound routes from receivers, as described below. However, the "dry" westbound loadings were often better suited for insulated boxcars, which PFE did not own, and for non-refrigerated trailers. Thus PFE was competing for this traffic with many other sources of transportation services.

THE FIFTIES – END OF THE GOLDEN AGE

The post-war 1940's and Fifties were the "salad days" of PFE. The physical plant was at full strength (see map, page 432). There were 19 ice manufacturing plants in 1950. One had been sold by this time, and the last natural ice plant at Laramie was to be converted to an ice manufacturing plant in 1951. There were five major shops, numerous light repair facilities and many icing platforms at loading

points which either contracted locally for ice or used ice which was shipped in. The total number of PFE employees had surpassed 5500 in the 1950's, near the all-time peak. On July 1, 1946, the car mileage rate had been raised from 2¢ to 2.5¢, and July 1, 1949, increased again to 3¢. In 1948, PFE moved its headquarters yet again, to 116 New Montgomery Street, San Francisco, where it would remain for over thirty years, the longest at a single address.

Among the many features of the Hepburn Act of 1906 was the mandating of uniform accounting methods, later called "ICC accounting," for all railroads. Since it was not a common carrier, PFE was not bound by this requirement, and it used its own accounting procedures. The differences that arose in accounting descriptions between PFE and the SP and UP were vexing, and finally in 1948, the parent railroads directed that PFE should adopt ICC accounting, to be consistent with their own.

The PFE shops had possessed the capability to build cars from scratch since 1917, and continued to build many of the newer classes of ice and mechanical cars during the 1950's (see details in Chapters 8, 9 and 11). Testing and innovation continued to be the hallmark of PFE car design and development, as described in more detail in Chapters 6 through 9. Car were also rebuilt in PFE shops for many years (Chapters 6 and 7), because the cost of doing so was, for tax purposes, a maintenance expense, and thus was deductible from income, while new equipment had to be capitalized and was not deductible.

But in 1949 the IRS decided that rebuilding cars "like new," as was PFE's practice, was not merely maintenance. The rebuilt cars had a life expectancy of 15 years, not much different, the IRS concluded, from a new car. By 1950, the IRS notified PFE, after detailed examination of tax records, that back taxes and interest for 7 years, to and including 1944, were due. The total bill was nearly $12 million. PFE paid $10.95 million in 1951 and $0.98 million in 1952. Remarkably, PFE paid these bills out of cash reserves and

PFE was cost conscious even in its prosperous 1950's. CSRM.

MATERIAL CONSERVATION PROGRAM DO YOU KNOW	
I LINING BOARD	COSTS $ .62
I PLYWOOD SHEET 9/16"X 48"X 105"	COSTS $8.62
I MASONITE SHEET 5/16"X 48"X 105"	COSTS $4.89
I SIDING BOARD	COSTS $ .62
I B.H. PAD BOARD	COSTS $ 1.01
I FLOOR RACK SLAT	COSTS $ .46
I B.H. POST 4"X 5 3/4"	COSTS $3.23
I SIDE FASCIA	COSTS $ 1.68

WASTE IS EXPENSIVE - HELP SAVE ALL MATERIAL POSSIBLE

1951-52 earnings, although it was necessary to forego a dividend to the parent railroads in those two years. After PFE learned in 1949 that the IRS was disallowing rebuilding expenses, all such work in the shops was discontinued. Similar discontinuances took place on most other U.S. railroads which had been rebuilding cars. Programmed heavy repairs to many PFE classes did continue.

PFE continued to operate the largest fleet of refrigerator cars in North America. In 1950, about 38,500 cars, over one-third of all reefers, bore PFE's name, while runners-up Santa Fe (SFRD) and Fruit Growers Express owned about 14,500 and 12,000 cars, respectively. The PFE fleet continued to be, as it had been since the 1920's, one of the most modern and progressive in the country. Chapters 5 through 8 give more details on features of these cars.

In the immediate post-war period, PFE ordered a single class of 5000 steel ice cars, class R-40-23, which was the largest single order ever placed for steel reefers. At that time, PFE management was continuing to press the view, as they had since the end of the 1920's, that PFE's "natural" fleet size was about 40,000 cars. Whenever the roster fell much below that size, PFE was sure to approach SP and UP about purchase of more cars. But within a few years,

carloadings would begin a precipitous decline (see graph), and the PFE fleet would shrink to reflect that decrease in demand.

Throughout its life, PFE obtained remarkable utilization of its car fleet. Before 1940, when American reefers averaged barely three revenue trips per year, PFE was averaging ten trips. The accompanying graph shows this clearly since the carloading scale is ten times the car number scale. Even in the 1950's, when the U.S. average climbed to nearly four revenue trips, PFE continued to obtain ten. This was one source of PFE's financial success.

In the first half of the 1950's, PFE was earning a net income of $20 million or more each year. After payment of $4 to 6 million in dividends and $10 to $13 million in "special compensation" to the two owning railroads, there was still a surplus each year of $2 to 4 million. Each year's surplus was added to the "undistributed earnings" account, also called "accumulated surplus," which by the end of 1956 had reached more than $44 million. A calculation in 1957 of the value of PFE to the Southern Pacific concluded that over the 29-year period from the start of the revised PFE contract in 1928, until 1957, SP had received $82.7 million in dividends and $127 million in special

A study in wheel sets and hand tools provides a foreground for PFE 93612, an R-30-9 class car which has just received a steel superstructure frame (see Chapter 7). In the background are the ice plant office and pre-cooling shed. Richard Steinheimer photo at PFE's Los Angeles Shop, December, 1950, DeGolyer Library.

compensation, totalling more than $209 million. This was more than $7.2 million average income per year; based on the investment by SP of $12 million in capital stock, this was an annual return of fully 60 per cent! To say that PFE was a profitable contribution to the finances of SP and UP in the '50's would be quite safe. Moody's *Manual of Investments*, in corroboration, regularly cited the PFE dividend during the 1950's as important to net income of both Southern Pacific and Union Pacific.

In discussing income matters such as these, the railroads often subtracted the mileage payments they made to PFE, from the dividend and compensation income received from PFE. Although this did reflect their net cash flow from PFE, and also in a sense reflected the net income from perishables, it was misleading in the following sense. The railroads would have had to make the same mileage payments if someone other than themselves owned the refrigerator cars in which the perishables moved, so the existence of the traffic itself required the mileage payments. But because PFE owned the cars, the railroads received revenue from both mileage and protective service tariff charges.

In 1958 the Car Hire Contract between SP and UP, setting the terms for their relationship with PFE, came up for renewal. The 1928 Contract, which had provided for "compensation" to SP for its disproportionate share of PFE load originations (averaging over 70% of all PFE loads in the 1927-58 period) had been revised somewhat in 1936 and renewed in 1942 and 1950. But many aspects of PFE's finances had changed. Car Service (mileage) revenue, about two-thirds of PFE net income in 1928, had risen steadily since, and by 1958 was over 96% of revenue. Protective service had been one-third of revenue in 1928, but after the ICC's 1941 decision requiring such revenue to accrue to the originating carrier and not to the car line (PFE), protective services provided less and less revenue.

Now UP wished to reopen the entire contract. Their basis was interesting. Instead of looking at load originations, they computed monthly earnings per PFE car; UP's much faster freight schedules meant that PFE cars earned more per month on UP than on SP. For 1959, these monthly numbers were $209 on UP, $152 on SP. But after extended negotiations lasting into 1960, SP declined to modify the contract basis developed in 1928 and 1936.

A new development for the PFE in the 1950's was the introduction of automated data processing equipment, a step preceding the installation of computers. In 1948 the

A comparison of the size of the PFE car fleet, in thousands of cars, and the annual carloadings along PFE's contract lines, in tens of thousands of loads. Note how well the two curves parallel each other. Graph by A.W. Thompson from PFE data.

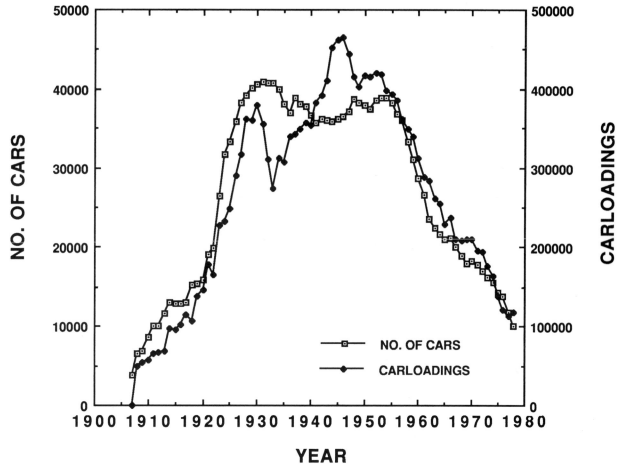

Southern Pacific contracted with IBM to research and install what was then the latest in IBM key-punch data processing equipment. This equipment speeded up such mundane functions as the production of consists and wheel reports at yard offices and soon spread to the Accounting Departments of SP and its subsidiaries, PFE included. The PFE Accounting Department reflected the changes with the addition of a Machine Accounts Bureau. By the early 1960's the Southern Pacific was researching a system that would eventually grow into its TOPS (Total Operation Planning System) system, and Union Pacific was preparing to make a similar installation. PFE followed suit with its own IBM 1401 computer and the establishment of a Systems Group within the Accounting Dept. that would later become the Data Processing Department.

There were also changes in the industries that PFE served. Increasing amounts of food were being processed rather than shipped fresh and this created demands for different forms and sizes of cars. The frozen food industry, growing since its inception in the 1920's, allowed shipment of much larger loads to market points but required lower-temperature refrigeration. In addition, food could be stored in much larger quantities for a longer time than had been previously possible.

Early frozen food shipments had been accomplished since the 1930's by refrigeration with ice plus 30 per cent salt, permitting car interior temperatures of 5 to 10°F. PFE had carried out the first coast-to-coast shipment of frozen food on Aug. 31, 1931, and in the 1940's was carrying half of all the frozen food shipped in America. But the turning point for this type of frozen shipment was the public acceptance of frozen orange juice, which had to be shipped at temperatures below what was accessible with ice and salt. As juice concentrates grew in popularity, mechanical refrigeration was necessary to ship at low enough temperatures. Chapter 9 describes PFE's development and early use of the mechanical refrigerator car in the early 1950's.

Along with these new demands, PFE had to serve its traditional customers with their loads of fresh fruit, vegetables and meats. These shippers, used to the flexibility of the 40-ton car, resisted the offers of larger cars. The PFE had been a rolling cold-storage warehouse for these people, who could divert a 40-ton car to the best market and be assured of a good price. There was too much risk in shipping a 70-ton car to a single market point which could suddenly become "soft" for that particular commodity. In addition, perishable shippers had for years adapted their methods of loading and bracing to the interior dimensions of a standard 41-foot car (33' 2-¾" inside length).

For the most part, however, through the 1950's the PFE relied upon its fleet of thousands of ice-bunker refrigerator cars of standard design. There was plenty of work for these

cars and a fine plant to support that work. Plummer knew his customers and he was well thought of by them. Within the PFE Plummer was known as an "ice man" through and through. He knew the ice-bunker car was the mainstay of PFE and he was going to stick with it. He did agree that mechanical refrigeration had a place in the PFE fleet, as evidenced by this statement in a paper he presented before the 41st Meeting of the American Society of Refrigerating Engineers in July, 1954, at Seattle, Wash., and published in *Refrigerating Engineering*:

"As for frozen foods – the transition is already underway. Somewhat slow, perhaps, but [it is] there. The reasons are obvious. The customers want it. And we have found that the zero temperature so urgently needed for frozen concentrates cannot be furnished with ice and salt."

In 1953 PFE had built its first 25 mechanical refrigerator cars at a cost of $21,200 each. In the same year the company built ice cars of the same size for about $13,400 per car. The difference in costs serves to demonstrate the much higher first cost of the mechanical cars over the "icers." Until 1957, PFE's mechanical reefers were used exclusively for frozen food, but the time was coming when these cars would be used for fresh produce also.

Other factors besides technology entered into the approaching end of the era of ice-bunker cars as the backbone of the PFE fleet. Labor costs had steadily risen since the advent of the unions and would rise at a greater rate with the strengthening post-war economy. The maintenance of facilities for the manufacture and delivery of ice to cars was very labor-intensive. Mechanization of icing was a partial answer. A mechanical car-icing machine was developed by Preco (the trade name for the Pacific Railway Equipment Co.), of Los Angeles, the developer and supplier of the air circulating fans applied to the PFE ice car fleet as well as supplying charcoal and alcohol-burning car heaters and other specialties to the industry.

The car-icing machine allowed one man to ice and, if necessary, salt an entire line of cars on either side of an ice deck. The primary advantage was the elimination of the icing crew. A car could also be iced faster, typically in less than a minute, but manual icing was often accomplished in two minutes per car or less. PFE's first mechanical icing machine was installed at Fresno in 1951. For more about this topic, see Chapter 13.

There was some dissension within the PFE regarding wholesale modernization of the fleet with mechanical refrigeration. Plummer knew his produce customers were happy with the ice cars and would resist paying higher rates for an entirely new fleet of more expensive mechanical cars.

In an effort to attract business for the larger cars, new

PFE not only designed and built modern cars, it carried out an intensive maintenance program to ensure that cars were always in first-class shape for delivery to shippers. One result of this philosophy was that shippers in PFE territory were often unhappy when a non-PFE car was spotted at their loading dock. Particular sources of complaint were smaller carlines, as well as New York Central's MDT and American Refrigerator Transit (ART), which evidently conducted less maintenance than did PFE or Santa Fe's SFRD. An illustration of this point is the following anecdote from the late A.L. "Pete" Holst (1898-1992), who managed Car Service Dept. operations in the Imperial Valley for a number of years (see Chapter 14). Although the story dates to about 1930, similar anecdotes are available for dates ranging from 1920 to 1960.

"Those Imperial Valley shippers never liked any of the MDT's, or the ART's, that we were getting. We'd load 'em if we had to, you know, in the melon rush. So they would squawk about 'em, and one time I told the boys in the Car Dept., 'Just keep storing those MDT's until you get enough to give everybody one.' I said, 'I'm sick and tired of getting all these phone calls, complaints about too many foreign cars,' not getting enough PFE's. So finally when we'd saved up all these MDT's, one day we spotted them on everybody's siding. We just painted the town white, you might say. [Many MDT cars were white.] And nobody squawked at all. They'd look across the street, and they'd think, 'Well, he's got all white ones too.' We got rid of all the complaints in one day, because there weren't any. Nobody made a phone call."

"incentive rates" were established, which offered lower costs per hundred pounds of lading, based on certain minimum loadings. These minimums were important. If accepted by shippers, they provided both a lower per-package cost to the shipper and also increased railroad earnings per car through heavier loading of the car. Indeed, incentive rates were in place for frozen food which were lower (per pound) than for ice plus salt refrigeration of the same cargo.

The Car Department people were in favor of more modern cars and had followed their 1952 development of cars for frozen food loading only, with technology which could serve both frozen food and fresh produce shippers. By 1957, Plummer as well as PFE's contacts with the perishable industry were noticing a change in attitudes, toward accepting produce shipments in mechanicals, and PFE began preparations to build mechanicals for produce.

In 1957 the PFE shops in Roseville, Colton and Los Angeles turned out the last of PFE's ice bunker refrigerator cars. Subsequent construction of cars, both by PFE and by its commercial builder after 1963, Pacific Car and Foundry, would be confined to mechanically refrigerated equipment. Clearly the reliance on ice refrigeration, dominant since PFE's founding, was beginning to fade away.

As had been done several times since 1920 (see Chapter 5), the 1957 cars were built by the SP Equipment Co. in PFE's facilities, using PFE employees. The reason was that SPE could purchase materials without paying sales tax, because the materials were to be used to manufacture cars for resale. PFE then took delivery of the cars at points outside California, saving (in 1957) more than $600,000 in state and city sales taxes.

During the 1950's PFE experienced a number of proposals by other car lines about changes in ownership. In

Construction of the first car of a new class in the PFE shops was always the occasion for a "car inspection" ceremony. In this photo, some 73 men are at Los Angeles in April, 1958, to examine PFE 300713, first of mechanical reefer class R-50-6 (see Chapter 9 for more details). An interesting detail here is that the new VP & GM, Charles Ahern, can be seen in the front row, beneath the left edge of the door opening, while his recently retired predecessor, K.V. Plummer, is fourth from far left. PFE photo, CSRM.

1952, Cudahy approached PFE about sale and lease-back of its cars; as the cars were not suitable for general service, nor did PFE need additional meat cars for its own use, nor was Cudahy's shipment territory convenient to PFE's shops, PFE declined. In 1953, essentially the same discussion ensued with Armour, with the same result.

Also in 1953, the Rock Island (CRI&P), whose contract with General American had ended, came to PFE about entering into a car contract similar to that of the Western Pacific, even expressing a willingness to buy up to 1000 new steel cars to lease to PFE. These would have been marked like the WP cars, that is, with PFE reporting marks, but with Rock Island medallions. The fact that the perishable rush in Rock Island territory was in the same months as PFE's, that hauls were generally short compared to typical PFE shipments, and that, again, PFE shops were remote from the Rock Island service area, were all negative factors. In addition, Union Pacific was strongly opposed due to the prospect of competing CRI&P joint routings with D&RGW via Ogden, or with SP via Tucumcari. The proposal was thus rejected.

Throughout the decade of the 1950's carloadings and revenues on the PFE gradually declined. As larger mechanical cars slowly began to replace the smaller ice cars, the total number of cars in the fleet dropped further. Some smaller mechanical cars, 40 instead of 50 ft. in length, were built in response to the anxieties of the old customers, used to the smaller cars, but they were never manufactured in significant quantities. It was clear that the 50-ft., 70-ton capacity mechanical refrigerator car was here to stay. Many of PFE's customers began to accept the larger cars as a fact of life, while others joined the trend to trucks.

INTERSTATE HIGHWAYS

Henry Ford's Model T, the car which would begin the Automobile Age in this country, was put on the road the same year PFE began operations, 1907. The automobile and its freight-hauling cousin, the motor truck, had been around before that year but the Model T gave the nation a real reason to begin the push for a highway system. Some sixty years later the results of that push would signal the end of dominance by the railroad industry of interstate haulage of perishables. What trucks lacked was a reliable and continuous system of long-distance highways suitable for rapid travel.

The U.S. Government had brought trucking under regulation by the ICC with the 1935 Motor Carrier Act which, however, carried a regulatory exemption applying to raw, unprocessed agricultural products. Even so, without good highways upon which to run, trucking posed no real threat to PFE's transcontinental produce business

until after 1955 or so, as the chart on p. 23 demonstrates.

Nationwide, railroad tonnage of perishables had steadily increased until the 1920's, when it leveled off at about 22 million tons annually, and began to decrease thereafter. The reason was trucking. In 1929 only about 15 per cent of all perishable shipments moving over 20 miles had moved by truck, but as early as 1936 it reached 44 per cent. Most refrigerator car operators felt this change keenly in the 1930's, but PFE, with its predominantly cross-country hauls, was insulated from the situation until the 1950's.

Although the Federal Government had been actively involved in the highway situation in the United States since 1893 when the Office of Road Inquiry, Dept. of Agriculture, was formed, the impetus to form an interstate highway system did not gain serious momentum until the end of World War II. Prior to 1944, emphasis was upon the development of a rural road system. The 1916 Federal Aid Road Act, better known as the "Good Roads Act," still had a rural emphasis, as did the Federal Highway Act of 1921. There was much building of highways between 1921 and 1931 but the Depression caused the diversion of funds to more pressing issues of national welfare.

Between the late 1930's and the 1950's there was more or less continuous competition between rural and urban highway interests which diluted the effectiveness of efforts to form an interstate system. President Roosevelt appointed a National Interregional Highway Committee in April, 1941. Its report, "Interregional Highways," gave the interstate highway system its present form. The report, submitted to Roosevelt on January 1, 1944, and transmitted to Congress shortly after, was incorporated into law and its route designations, which were retained in 1947 and 1955 legislation, are essentially those we see today.

Two additional factors lent major motivation to the formation of an interstate highway system. One was the entrance of people from the automotive industry into federal government service. The other was what was known as the "defense connection." The concept of an interstate highway system for defense purposes was first proposed as early as 1915. The Defense Highway act of 1941 and the Federal Aid Highway Act of 1944 set the proportion of federal funding for highways. In 1953 C.E. "Engine Charlie" Wilson, then president of General Motors, became Secretary of Defense under Eisenhower and this connection continued under Robert McNamara from Ford Motor Co. who served as President Kennedy's Secretary of Defense.

The Federal Aid Highway Act of 1956, also known as the Interstate Highway Act of 1956, was the key piece of federal legislation to make possible the interstates we know today. The name of the system was thenceforth known as the National System of Interstate and Defense Highways (bringing in the "defense connection" and justifying greater

Charles Ahern, VP & GM, 1958-1961

federal participation in funding). The 1956 legislation also raised the ratio of federal to state funding from 60-40 to 90-10 and even 95-5 in some western states. The funding came from user taxes on auto parts and accessories, motor trucks and parts, and petroleum fuels; automobiles themselves were not taxed.

The trucking industry, although it had come under ICC regulation with the Motor Carrier Act, continued to enjoy its unique agricultural exemption which allowed freedom in rate-making. With that freedom for perishable loads eastward, and the independent truckers' practice of cut-rate "return load" deals, the regulated railroad perishable industry had no means of meeting truck rates. As the interstate highway system took form, and particularly upon the system's practical completion by about 1970, the truckers had what they needed to compete with the PFE, challenging its dominance in intercity shipment of perishable and semi-perishable freight originating in its vast service area.

CHALLENGE IN THE 1960's

On February 28, 1958 K. V. Plummer retired from PFE. His illustrious career spanned the age of the ice cars, from the days of natural ice plants and thirty-ton cars to the advent of a fleet that was in the future to include highway trailers and seagoing containers as well as railroad cars, all refrigerated or heated by mechanical means.

Succeeding Plummer was Charles Ahern. He was a logical choice for the job, having worked side by side with Plummer during Plummer's time as VP & GM. Born on June 20, 1901, Ahern began his career with PFE as a traffic clerk in San Francisco on July 29, 1918. Until December 1, 1937, he held various car distributor positions, becoming General Car Distributor, San Francisco, on December 1, 1937. On June 16, 1944, Ahern became Superintendent, Transportation – Chicago, and reached the position of Assistant General Manager, San Francisco on February 16, 1945. Plummer had held the position of VP & GM for about two and one-half years by this time. On February 16, 1949, Ahern became Assistant VP & GM under Plummer. He moved into the top job at PFE on March 1, 1958 at a salary of $35,000 per year

Ahern was a formally-educated man, having attended Harvard, and he surrounded himself with educated people. He also stressed the value of education and training within PFE and organized training and development programs for PFE employees. He was considered a "pure" PFE man and was uniquely qualified for the top position at PFE by virtue of his coming up through the ranks at PFE and his long and close working relationship with Plummer.

Charles Ahern's tenure as top man at PFE was brief, being cut short by his untimely death on June 11, 1961. Though his time in office was short, his leadership was well-respected and effective.

Ahern was succeeded in office by Lewis D. Schley on June 16, 1961. Born on December 25, 1908, roughly one year after PFE began operations, Schley began his career with the Southern Pacific Co. in October, 1923. He held various clerical positions, becoming secretary and assistant to the President of Southern Pacific Co. on February 16, 1937. On July 7, 1947, Schley came to PFE as a secretary to Plummer, the VP & GM. On September 16, 1950, he became a contract and lease agent and on March 1, 1958, he became Ahern's assistant upon Plummer's retirement and Ahern's succession to the position of VP & GM. Schley received a salary of $37,500 per year upon his appointment to the VP & GM position. Schley had a Southern Pacific background like that of Plummer and therefore had good connections with the PFE parent which originated most of the perishable traffic.

Schley followed ably in the footsteps of Plummer and Ahern. He was actively involved in associations related to PFE and the refrigerated car industry. One of these was the Railroad Owned Refrigerator Car Committee (RORCC), a group consisting of representatives of all the railroads that operated their own refrigerator car lines. The RORCC met to solve many of the problems confronting the industry.

A trio of new UP GP20's, Nos. 714, 727 and 701, haul a long string of PFE ice refrigerators westward across 134th Street in Omaha. These engines were quickly renumbered to the 400 series to make room for the 700-series GP30's delivered soon afterward. Photo 68-407, UP Railroad Museum.

They worked toward standardization of freight refrigerator car features such as floor racks and load dividers, shared advances in design and location of refrigeration equipment and controls, and worked toward the technical advancement of freight refrigerators, looking into such things as liquid nitrogen refrigeration and controlled atmospheres

Lewis D. Schley, VP & GM, 1961-1973

to retard commodity spoilage in transit. Nearly all the refrigerator car operators came to accept such standardization through the RORCC in the 1960's, but there was one prominent exception: Santa Fe. Although an active member of the RORCC, Santa Fe went its own way on refrigerator car design and construction.

Lew Schley also took over a PFE that was looking at challenges and competition it had never faced before, chiefly from independent truckers aided by the agricultural exemption. The day when long-haul trucking was primarily large, unionized carriers was passing, and independent trucks, many of them one-man operations, were even more difficult competition. The same inroads from trucks that the railroads had faced with their short- and medium-haul traffic since 1925 had finally come to PFE, as the national highway network reached a level of quality that could support long-distance trucking of perishables.

In 1961, the year Schley took office as VP & GM, total car mileage was about 1.22 million. This was down from the postwar high of 1.69 million in 1953. Wartime mileage figures are not comparable because of the National Freight Car Pool which forced PFE to load cars other than its own. Mileage revenue, the amount PFE received for use of its equipment and its major revenue source reached a high of $65.9 million in 1954, the year after car mileage reached its high point. Mileage revenue for 1961 was $53.2 million. These figures do not reflect increases in PFE's operating costs in this period and are merely "raw" revenue figures.

The mileage rate for refrigerator cars had been set on May 1, 1960 at 4.35¢ per mile for all classes of cars: ice, mechanical and Ice Tempco (see Chapter 8). In 1965, the mileage rate was raised to 4.5¢ for ice-bunker cars and to

5.25¢ per mile for mechanical cars, the first recognition of these cars' cost.

Car mileage and mileage revenue were also affected by the changes in the car fleet itself. As the 1960's dawned, there was an increasing number of larger cars in the fleet, namely the 70-ton capacity mechanicals. In 1960 there were 2662 mechanicals, 9 per cent of a total fleet of 28,691; by 1970 the number of mechanical cars had increased to 12,450, or 68 per cent, of the total fleet of 18,289 cars. Notice that this was due both to increased numbers of mechanical refrigerators, and also to shrinkage of the total fleet as thousands of ice cars were retired.

The establishment of incentive rates for heavier per-car loadings helped the railroad industry as a whole, but was somewhat detrimental to PFE since its primary business was the rental of equipment on a car-mile basis and the provision of protective services. With increasing loads per car came a decline in total carloadings and thus a concurrent decline in mileage revenue to PFE. This had to be balanced against the retention of some parts of the business through the lower rates.

In November, 1961, PFE entered the era of Trailer On Flat Car (TOFC) service, which was to grow during the 1960's into a major operation. PFE's entry into TOFC service reflected the company's awareness of where rail transportation was going in the sixties. Against increasing competition from the trucking industry and stifling regu-

lation from the ICC, the railroad industry as a whole needed new methods of shipping. PFE's parent roads had themselves been involved in motor trucking on a local basis for years through their respective trucking subsidiaries. However, for regulatory reasons, development of cross-country trucking (and air freighting) by railroad companies was forbidden. TOFC provided a ready and logical answer, and PFE set out to apply it to perishables.

The problem of westbound loading came up again for the trailers as it had for the refrigerator cars. This time, a more successful program of westbound loadings was developed for refrigerated commodities and dry freight as well, to a large extent because PFE introduced the 13'6" high trailer to national TOFC shipping (see Chapter 10). By 1965, fully 98% of PFE's trailers were returning westbound with loads. But PFE's success would soon attract the attention of competitors in the railroad industry who were developing TOFC programs of their own.

With its entrance into the TOFC business and the additional loading flexibility this provided, PFE announced the formation of a new division, called Pacific Forwarding Express or PACFORD, on June 1, 1964. The purpose of PACFORD was to consolidate LTL (less than trailer load) shipments from various shippers into single trailers, move the trailers east on flat cars to a distribution point, and thence by motor carrier to the final destination. PACFORD was a means for PFE to offer service beyond its original

This photo encapsulates the PFE view of the past and the future, circa 1963: a PFE trailer in the foreground is being backed to a loading dock by a railroad-owned tractor (SP's subsidiary Pacific Motor Trucking), while in the background a long string of ice reefers stands at the ice deck – note the mechanical icing machine at right. Don Sims photo at Yuma, Ariz.

A pair of PFE's flat cars (reporting marks PFF) which were leased from SP descend the Roseville hump with PFE trailers. Although initially successful, PFE's trailer operations eventually became unprofitable. PFE photo, Oct. 1971, *Railfan and Railroad* collection.

ramp-to-ramp arrangement, in which PFE trailers were picked up and delivered by motor carriers; PACFORD essentially offered a door-to-door service to shippers.

The original distribution point was Chicago with distribution to any point within a 310-mile radius of that city. On October 26, 1964 PACFORD had expanded to include distribution points of Minneapolis, Omaha, Kansas City, St. Louis, Memphis, New Orleans, Denver, Dallas, Houston and San Antonio in answer to increased shipper demand for such service. As with Chicago, distribution to a radius beyond these cities was via motor carrier.

When PFE set rates for TOFC service they were set fairly low to obtain business. This became a problem, for even though costs rose, the ICC-controlled rates (per diem, not mileage, for TOFC) were difficult to change. Ironically, where PFE had struggled for years with regulated freight rates that could not be cut to meet the competition, they now were trapped with rates that were too low.

Perhaps the most disappointing factor was the discovery that most TOFC traffic in PFE trailers did not replace highway trucks, but was withdrawn from railcar traffic. Shippers got the flexibility of two, smaller loads on a single flat car with a single bill of lading, compared to a single, large reefer load. Since it cost more to provide TOFC service in PFE trailers than in PFE reefers (though rates did not reflect that fact), the operation clearly could not long continue. By 1967 rates were too low for an adequate return on investment, because competition, especially for

westbound loadings, had greatly intensified by that time.

Not only were competitors such as Santa Fe developing their own perishable TOFC programs, with resultant competition for westbound loads, but also the SP and UP were aggressively marketing TOFC for dry freight and this posed a particular problem for PFE's westbound loads; often the eastern customers would play PFE's parent roads against PFE itself for such traffic.

SP and UP also solicited the same westbound traffic in their own box cars, insulated or otherwise, competing directly with PFE's trailers. As mentioned, each owning line preferred to move westbound loads in its own cars or trailers, having no compelling reason to protect the revenue of subsidiary PFE at the expense of its own revenue.

To make matters even more difficult, in the late 1960's trucking companies such as XTRA also introduced 13'6" dry trailers, and these had more cubic capacity than did PFE's refrigerated trailers. When these bigger trailers were offered to shippers at rates equal to PFE's rate, the PFE westbound loadings disappeared rapidly. By the late 1960's, with many more competitors in the business, PFE faced severe economic as well as practical challenges in the rapidly changing climate of perishable transportation.

With westbound loadings shrinking below 50% and revenues after 1967 barely able even to pay costs, the handwriting was on the wall for PFE's effort to compete in TOFC service. The last batch of 100 trailers was purchased in 1968. The late 1960's saw the last of PACFORD operations, and trailer service was to cease a few years later. More about development of the equipment, and additional information about PFE's TOFC operations, are presented in Chapter 10.

In 1963, as described in more detail in Chapter 2, PFE underwent a reorganization to reflect its changing business, modifying its organization chart in several ways compared to what had been customary for decades.

Rising costs and aggressive competition were also squeezing the refrigerator car operations of PFE in the late 1960's, and other surviving refrigerator car operators felt the same effects. Rates on mechanical cars had been raised in 1969 to 5.8¢ and in 1971 to 6.3¢ per mile, but costs more than kept pace with revenues.

PFE's falling earnings as the 1960's dawned, with net (taxable) losses reported to the IRS for 1962 and 1963, had an effect on the financing of the car fleet. (In each of these years, PFE had a net income of over $4 million, but accelerated depreciation opportunities gave rise to tax losses.) By 1963, when PFE was ready to order the 1000 cars of class R-70-13 (see Chapter 9), it was realized by SP that PFE would not be able to take advantage of the 7% investment tax credit which the Kennedy administration had promulgated. Instead, SP proposed that it and UP

purchase the cars, enjoy the tax credit, and lease the cars to PFE at rates equal to ownership costs. For these 1000 cars, for example, the $28.76 million price tag implied a tax credit of over $2 million. PFE, with its net tax loss, would not be allowed to claim the credit.

For most of the rest of the 1960's, this process of railroad purchase of new cars, followed by lease to PFE, was continued. The initial leases were informally drawn, but in 1965 they were formalized under a "master lease" to avoid a new California sales tax on lease rentals. This was done to exempt both railcars and trailers covered by the lease.

In 1969, the capital shortage at PFE even led to the sale and lease-back of existing ice cars, in order to carry out needed reconditioning. SP and UP, acting through appropriately empowered subsidiaries (SP Equipment Co. for SP, and the Las Vegas Land and Water Co. for UP) each bought 200 cars for $800 each, then leased them back to PFE. For more on these cars, see Chapter 8.

More and more foodstuffs were being processed and did not need the protective service of a mechanical or iced refrigerator car. Greater numbers of "icers" were sent to the scrappers as they became obsolete. By 1970 there were only 5819 ice bunker cars in the fleet, a dramatic drop from the over forty thousand that PFE had in its heyday.

8500-HP gas turbine No. 19 heads west with a string of PFE ice cars, as the days of ice operations draw to a close. At left is the Council Bluffs ice deck with its mechanical icing machine, Dodge Park is in the right middle distance, and across the Missouri River is the Omaha skyline. Mid-1960's photo, no. M5200-1, UP Railroad Museum.

THE END OF THE ICE AGE

The mechanical refrigerator car fleet had been growing steadily since its inception at PFE in 1953, with tremendous growth in that part of the fleet in the 1960's. The mechanical car had become a true multi-purpose vehicle rather than one designed primarily for transport and protection of frozen foods. During the 1960's, the ice car became a smaller and smaller fraction of the fleet and the maintenance of ancillary facilities for bunker icing was no longer justified.

On September 2, 1973 PFE officially ended the ice age on its property. The National Perishable Freight Committee published Supplement 46 to Circular 5-L which located all icing stations of U.S. and Canadian rail carriers. All icing stations were eliminated on the lines of Southern Pacific Transportation Company, Union Pacific Railroad Company, St. Louis Southwestern Railway Company and San Diego & Arizona Eastern Railway Company, effective that date. The ice cars that did remain in the fleet were retained for shipments that were top-iced (called "top ice vegetable" or TIV cars) or body iced by the shippers themselves. A few such ice cars persisted on the equipment roster until 1981, abetted by older mechanical cars with their refrigeration equipment removed for TIV service.

LOSING MONEY - THE 1970's

In 1970 PFE posted its first net loss, in the amount of $111,574, a remarkable change from just 15 years earlier when PFE was still at its earning peak. Annual losses were to persist throughout the decade. Exempt trucking continued to make serious inroads. Even air freight became a competitor, in the transport of very delicate and perishable products such as strawberries which had in the past ridden in express refrigerators on the fastest passenger schedules. Though only the most valuable perishables went by air, it still represented a category of produce which PFE could no longer carry competitively.

There were also shifts in the kinds of products being loaded on the Southern Pacific and Union Pacific Railroads. Loadings from the SP were mainly in the fresh produce area. Union Pacific served a rapidly growing frozen food business in its Pacific Northwest area and was continuing to develop a year-round business for refrigerator cars, whereas loadings on the SP remained seasonal.

During this period it also became evident that the original rationale for a dedicated subsidiary to handle refrigerated perishable shipments was vanishing. Mechanical refrigeration brought about a simplification in handling shipments cross-country and there was no longer a need for a separate Refrigeration Department to operate and maintain a network of ice manufacturing plants and ice decks. With the advent of all-steel cars, stable insulation, and a mature mechanical design, the mechanical refrigerator was a reliable car. There was no longer much need for PFE's extensive shop facilities. The reasons for PFE's continuing existence as a separate operating organization were becoming fewer and fewer.

In 1971, a kind of public signal of these developments was sent as PFE replaced its age-old reporting marks on those cars which were owned by SP and UP, i.e. most cars purchased since 1963. The new markings were SPFE (for Southern Pacific) and UPFE (Union Pacific). Those markings would be the ones used when PFE split up in 1978, and would also permit per diem car charges in later years.

Yet PFE's predominance in the North American reefer business continued. In 1970, for example, PFE rostered over 12,000 mechanical refrigerators, over 56% of all mechanical reefers then in service and far more than any competitor (ATSF had about 3500 mechanicals in 1970).

Lew Schley retired on December 31, 1973. Schley had attained the top office in 1961, when PFE was still a major force, if no longer a dominant one, in perishable transportation. He led the company through a decade of shrinking business, with little or no regulatory relief from government agencies, contending also with increasing differences

A.E. Chiasson, VP & GM, 1974-1978.
(VP & GM, UPFE, 1978-1982)

Extra 8439 eases downhill from Donner Summit, eastward around Stanford Curve, in June of 1966. This "transition" consist contains both mechanical refrigerators and TOFC; even the locomotives reflect the change from F7 dominance of Sierra railroading, to the powerful new SD45 locomotives on the point. Richard Steinheimer photo.

in what the PFE's parents required of their shared subsidiary. Under him, PFE had done all it could, most notably with a worthwhile experiment in trailer shipment of perishables, which unfortunately did not succeed.

Succeeding Schley as Vice-President and General Manager of PFE was Armand E. (Ed) Chiasson. Born on Sept. 27, 1923, he had started with PFE as an iceman. Becoming a stenographer-clerk in Klamath Falls, Ore. on Sept. 21, 1941, and then Agent at Medford, he went on to be Car Distributor at Portland in Sept., 1950. In 1954 he became Executive Assistant to the VP & GM (then Plummer), reached AGM, San Francisco on February 1, 1963 under Schley, and took the office of VP & GM on January 1, 1974. He continued Plummer's tradition of involvement with shippers, serving as a Director of the United Fresh Fruit and Vegetable Association, the only VP & GM to do so. Employees considered him strict but fair. He was an

experienced operating man, but in these difficult times, careful financial management of PFE was essential.

PFE's financial numbers had been dropping. Losses became major in 1971, at $3.45 million. Over the next six years, losses varied from $2 to $5 million. In 1977, the last full year before PFE was split between UP and SP, the loss was $1.5 million; in 1978, it reached a high of $6.2 million.

Competition from trucks was severe in the 1970's, but making matters worse was the slippage in rail perishable service. Many railroads across the U.S. were undergoing very difficult times, and previously guaranteed perishable schedules were abolished or, worse, simply not adhered to. Delivery times to eastern destinations which were routine in the 1960's became both longer and less reliable in the 1970's. This accelerated the loss of business to trucks.

Not only had increased competition eroded PFE's business but costs of doing business had increased dramatically. Fuel prices were driven up by the 1974 Oil Embargo and now that the car fleet was virtually 100% mechanical, diesel fuel costs were a major factor. Fuel availability was another problem. PFE managers had to spend time over and above their usual duties locating reliable fuel supplies.

PFE, SFRD and other refrigerator car lines were trying to change their basis of car charges, from the time-honored mileage rate to a combination of mileage and time (or per diem). An additional problem was the inflationary spiral of the economy that would not end until after 1980. Since rates were still strictly regulated in the mid-1970's, neither PFE nor its parent railroads had any flexibility to raise or lower rates to suit competition or to keep pace with costs. Relief would not come until the era of deregulation, and for PFE, that would be too little and too late.

THE SPLIT-UP

On May 26, 1976 a joint meeting was held in Omaha, Nebraska among representatives of the Southern Pacific Transportation Co. or SPT Co, as SP's railroad operations were now called, the UP and the PFE, and a decision was made to proceed with a plan to divide the PFE into two separately owned and operated subsidiaries. Loading patterns on each of the parent railroads had changed to the point that each railroad's equipment and customer service needs had become vastly different. Along with these differences came differences in philosophies as to how service to shippers and receivers was to be rendered. One long-standing though unspoken difference was in fleet maintenance. Since the 1920's, UP had always been willing to

spend more on car maintenance than was SP. Now, as SP cut costs vigorously, that difference was increasing.

Both UP and SP released statements to the press as to the reasons for the decision to split up PFE. They were similar in making the following five points. First, overall PFE traffic had decreased drastically due to truck competition, not only due to interstate highways but through the agricultural exemption that permitted non-regulated truckers to be capricious in what shipments they would accept, the territory they would serve, and the rates charged (adherence to a published rate schedule was not required). None of these flexibilities were available to railroads or to regulated truckers, who had common carrier obligations.

Second, introduction of incentive rates, though helping to retain some perishable business, had driven virtually all smaller shipments to trucks. The average weight of a perishable shipment in 1958 was 34,000 pounds, while by 1977 it had risen to 80,000 pounds. Thus fewer reefers were needed for the traffic. Third, the transition from small farms to large agribusiness concerns led to better matches of crops to demand, thus stabilizing market prices and reducing the magnitude of harvest peak loadings.

Fourth and fifth, as mentioned above, produce storage techniques leveled demand for cars during harvests, and freezing and other processing led to spreading shipments more nearly year-round. All five of these reasons meant that the complementary harvest seasons along UP and SP rails, an important motivation early in the century for a fleet which could "follow the sun," had largely disappeared. Little real need or desire remained for joint ownership and operation of the PFE and its cars and facilities.

One of Southern Pacific's low-hood RS-32 (DL-721) Alco diesels heads a local train south out of Tracy, Calif., on Oct. 20, 1969, with a number of PFE reefers in tow.   John C. Illman photo.

The task of division was not easy for a company that had operated as a single entity for seventy years. As a first step a very detailed study was made of all facets of the PFE to be used in negotiations between the PFE's two stockholders. Outside appraisals were made of some of the PFE's physical plant (equipment and shop facilities), the outside firms being assisted by teams from the SPT Co. and the UP. The necessary plans were filed with the IRS and negotiations were begun with the labor unions representing PFE employees. In preparation for the split, UP incorporated "Union Pacific Fruit Express" as a wholly-owned subsidiary on Dec. 7, 1977, exactly 71 years after PFE's own incorporation by E.H. Harriman.

Management teams from SPT Co., composed of people from affected departments, and the UP, led by H.E. Grau, Assistant to the President, negotiated all aspects required for the division. On March 3, 1978 the announcement was made that PFE would be divided effective April 1, 1978.

To accomplish this, half of PFE's railroad equipment (by this time much of that half was already owned by UP and leased to PFE, as mentioned earlier and in Chapter 9) was conveyed to UPFE in return for the 50% of the PFE stock held by UP. Thereafter, PFE became a wholly-owned subsidiary of Southern Pacific. The PFE shops still operat-

Willam G. Cranmer, VP & GM, 1978-1982.

ing (Roseville, Tucson, Pocatello and Nampa) were conveyed to the railroads on whose lines they were located, although Roseville would be closed in 1980 and Nampa in 1982. Thus were PFE's once-vast shop facilities reduced to two, Tucson and Pocatello.

On the UP, the new Union Pacific Fruit Express commenced operation on April 1, 1978. Its Board of Directors was composed of senior UP officers, with John Kennefick, UP's President, as President of UPFE. UPFE was issued a contract to provide refrigerator cars and car distribution for UP and to inspect and service all perishable shipments on UP, and later also supplied new TOFC trailers of UPFE design. Separate financial statements continued to be prepared for UPFE, and the former PFE employees and union contracts were assigned to UPFE.

Within the SPT Co. the new PFE subsidiary retained both the name, Pacific Fruit Express Co., and also its traditional structure. To the extent that there continued to be a history of PFE after 1978, then, is almost entirely a story of the SP portion of it, although of course a thriving perishable business continued on UP under UPFE. The two companies continued to share cars as needed.

AFTER THE SPLIT – PFE ON THE SP

Ed Chiasson chose to accept the General Manager position with UPFE (retitled within about a year as VP & GM), and was replaced at PFE by William G. Cranmer, who had originally come over in 1948 as a consultant from IBM to aid PFE in setting up its mechanized data processing system. Cranmer joined PFE as an employee shortly thereafter, starting in 1951 as an assistant to the Auditor. He became Assistant Auditor on August 1, 1960 and by February 1, 1963 he was assistant to Lew Schley. He became VP & GM on April 1, 1978, the day of the split-off. In 1979 he was named President of PFE, a title not used for the operating head since 1913. His style was fast-acting and he was considered hot-tempered by some employees. He took command of the situation, bringing PFE back to the profit side of the ledger by determined cost cutting.

In 1979 PFE posted a net income of $5.4 million, the first positive net since 1969. By 1981 this had risen to $9 million. This was the best year of income since 1955 and was achieved despite a continuing decline in carloadings of perishable commodities. The 1980 net of $8 million represented a performance which the SPT Co. had not projected for PFE to reach until 1984. Several factors contributed to the income gain, most of them short-term cost-cutting measures.

There were changes in the physical and operational makeup of PFE which resulted in the cost reductions. The

SP switcher 2614, an SW-1500, backs a cut of PFE reefers through the streets of Watsonville, Calif., in May, 1981. Note the orange ends on SPFE 453821, a repainted class R-70-16 (see Chapter 9). A.W. Thompson photo.

Roseville shop was closed on January 1, 1980. The facilities were turned over to the Southern Pacific for their use as a car shop (see Chapter 11), and PFE was credited for the value of the property, a credit which was a significant contribution to 1980's net. The only remaining car shop now under PFE authority was Tucson, the most modern. All heavy repair and rehabilitation of PFE equipment was done at Tucson and that shop also took outside work on a contract basis. Although total work at Tucson was reduced to about one-half the volume of 1980, it still resulted in a contribution to net income of over $800,000. Light repair stations at Fresno and Watsonville were expanded. The former car and trailer conditioning yard at City of Industry, east of Los Angeles, was closed in 1974; the Los Angeles car shop had been closed in 1962.

Between the end of 1979 and September, 1980 the number of PFE employees had been reduced from 900 to 580. The maintenance budget was reduced, but at the same time Cranmer reported a reduction in the bad-order ratio from 8 per cent to under 1.6 per cent. This may have been achieved by allowing poorly-maintained cars to remain in service, because soon afterward, in-transit refrigeration failures began to be a problem. Cranmer also acknowledged in a September, 1980, presentation to SPT Co. that "overly enthusiastic" personnel reductions, particularly in the engineering staff, had contributed to an unacceptably high rate of in-transit MPS (Mechanical Protective Services, i.e. refrigeration unit) failures. The large reduction in maintenance expenditures was later judged to be a mistake.

Some adjustments were made in the rate structure to reflect repair costs, which helped increase revenue, and marginal improvements were made in equipment turn-around time. Utilization of the car fleet was improved and, after 1981, quality of repairs was increased, resulting in higher reliability of cars and refrigeration units. This was balanced with a need to keep maintenance spending within reason as shipments on PFE continued to decline.

In June, 1981, PFE made its last headquarters move, to 100 Valley Drive in Brisbane, just south of San Francisco.

Regulatory relief had come to the railroads in the form of the Regional Rail Reorganization Act of 1973 and the Railroad Revitalization and Regulatory Reform Act of 1976. The former was enacted to allow restructuring of the bankrupt railroads of the Northeast and the latter provided for greater flexibility in rate making. In 1978 the SPT Co. applied to the ICC for an agricultural exemption from regulation, similar to that enjoyed by the trucking industry; the application was at first denied but later granted. The ICC, for so long a rigid and uncompromising regulator of railroads, was finally in an anti-regulatory mood. Although the concept of deregulation of industry has been generally credited to the Reagan administration, deregulation of the railroads essentially occurred during the Carter administration, culminating in the Staggers Act, signed by President Carter on Oct. 14, 1980.

Economic conditions throughout the country were not good as 1980 waned, and were destined to worsen before they became better. The Reagan administration was ready to take office, but the country had experienced years of crippling inflation, coupled with slow economic growth, termed "stagflation." Another energy crisis in 1979 had further complicated things, particularly for industries like PFE, dependent upon petroleum fuels. Despite all this, the picture at PFE, for the moment, was a little brighter, thanks to energetic marketing and cost cutting.

END OF THE LINE - 1982-1985

Cranmer had predicted a net income of $15 million in the early 1980's but this was never achieved. He retired on May 31, 1982, at the age of 61, a somewhat early retirement but one to which he had been looking forward. There had been pressure brought from PFE's owner, Southern Pacific Transportation Company, to "make net" (income) or abandon the business. The SPT Co. had progressively involved itself in PFE's affairs and the incorporation of PFE into SPT Co's overall operation seemed imminent.

Cranmer was succeeded as head of PFE by Thomas D. Ellen on June 1, 1982. Ellen was born May 16, 1949 and had come from the General Executive Program of the Southern Pacific. He was educated at Massachusetts Institute of Technology, holding a graduate degree in civil engineering. He joined Southern Pacific in 1972 as a transportation assistant at San Antonio, Texas. and then held various positions such as assistant trainmaster, assistant terminal superintendent and assistant to the superintendent, all at Pine Bluff, Arkansas. Ellen's background on Southern Pacific was thus similar to that of many of the contemporary executives of the company, with a formal education and broad experience on the railroad. From March, 1977, through June, 1979, he was on assignment

Thomas D. Ellen, VP & GM, 1982-1985.

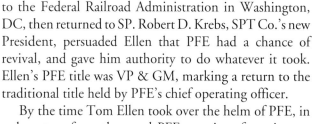

to the Federal Railroad Administration in Washington, DC, then returned to SP. Robert D. Krebs, SPT Co.'s new President, persuaded Ellen that PFE had a chance of revival, and gave him authority to do whatever it took. Ellen's PFE title was VP & GM, marking a return to the traditional title held by PFE's chief operating officer.

By the time Tom Ellen took over the helm of PFE, in a departure from the usual PFE practice of coming up through the ranks before taking the top job, SPT Co. had embraced the contemporary style of doing business in terms of profit and cost centers. Evaluation of each part of the organization was based on its contribution to the whole, both on a cost and a profit basis; department heads were given greater responsibility and authority for making this happen. Unprofitable segments were either changed or phased out of the larger organization.

On August 16, 1982 PFE took all responsibility for traffic functions relating to perishable and semi-perishable freight, specifically, marketing, pricing and sales, becoming a profit center for SPT Co. Although in the past PFE had appeared simply to be a car rental and operating organization, providing equipment and protective services to its contracting railroads, in actuality, it had been deeply involved in the marketing of its services to the perishable industry throughout its existence. The company had in many cases set the standards of perishable marketing, assisting its customers in obtaining the best prices through its extensive diversion and passing service and network of off-line agencies. It was true that PFE did not collect transportation nor did it set prices. The former was the duty of PFE's contracting railroads and the latter was highly regulated until the late 1970's.

During 1983, there was a considerable change in the organization of PFE. The details are described in Chapter 2, but the reorganization was intended to give PFE's Departments every chance to compete for business, as well as to be more consistent with the organization of SPT Co.

In late 1983 PFE took over the functions of Freight Claims and Loading Services for perishable and semi-perishable freight. Now all functions relating to the business of perishable freight transportation were under the authority of PFE except freight revenue accounting and transportation.

Many other changes took place in the short time after Ellen came to PFE, in an energetic effort to cut costs, regain perishable traffic and revive PFE's business. In 1982 PFE averaged 500 employees, but by 1985 this was down to 200, certainly an incredible reduction from the more than 5500 employees once on its payroll.

The old problem of westbound loading still plagued PFE. A market for the transportation of frozen foods from east to west for consumption and export was identified. Also, there was a market for transportation of frozen orange juice concentrate from Florida. Capitalizing on this business, however, depended upon other railroads' originating the loads. In some cases PFE trucked the commodities to places where it could be assured of loading in its own cars, such as Pine Bluff, Ark. and New Orleans. In the case of the Seaboard Coast Line (SCL), which controlled originating westbound loads in Florida and used Fruit Growers Express cars, this move forced negotiation to originate loads in PFE cars rather than risk losing SP's and PFE's business over SCL's rails altogether.

Other railroads were persuaded to accept PFE's rate structure, sometimes in return for concessions by PFE. Further marketing efforts targeted westbound loading of fresh commodities, beginning with shippers on the SP/SSW lines to avoid the complications of interlining. Florida and Texas grapefruit were shipped by PFE and marketed in California, a first for citrus markets there, and Colorado potatoes also appeared in California. This may have led to the anger that California potato growers expressed in their local press during those years. Loaded car miles, only 46% of total miles in June, 1982, neared 60% by late 1984.

Even with the marketing efforts, though, total carloads fell from 43,300 in 1979 to 25,500 in 1984 (compare this to the carloadings in earlier years shown on p. 23). With this decrease, even trimming of costs and staff to the bone within PFE, meant that the cost of doing business eliminated profits. The 1982 net income of $4.9 million declined in 1983 to $1.98 million. In 1984 net slipped again to the loss column with a loss of $175,000. Although not too significant a loss for a large subsidiary of a major corporation, it was a trend PFE's owner, Southern Pacific, did not want to see.

Conditions continued to deteriorate despite deregulation. Although PFE wanted to generate business and remain profitable, many of the railroads upon which it depended to reach the eastern markets or originate westbound business were placing indirect pressure upon PFE. For example, an eastern railroad charged PFE (through SP) a certain amount to haul its cars to destination which PFE in turn had to charge the shipper. With deregulation these rates varied widely and the "revenue requirements" of connecting railroads often priced PFE completely out of the market. Conrail's marketing group, for example, did not want any carloads that did not cover one hundred percent of long-run variable costs.

PFE also began to charge fees for things such as diversions, stops for completion of loading or unloading, and improper cleaning, which had been provided as part of PFE's complete service in the past. Now, economics dictated these fees as a way to capture revenues over and above

Union Pacific 9244 West, with some UPFE cars in its train, waits near Gibbon, Neb. in May of 1992 for an eastbound perishable block (at left of photo) which is racing for Council Bluffs. Wm. W. Kratville photo, courtesy UP Railroad Museum.

freight rates. Claims handling, long a sore spot between railroads and shippers, was speeded up.

In early 1983, a national union agreement with the railroads was reached, which included wage increases of about 40 per cent. This cost was passed on by the railroads to PFE, immediately raising PFE's costs and losing still more perishable traffic. In 1985, PFE tried to opt out of "national" union negotiations, even at the risk of a strike, but was unable to obtain the cost savings desired.

After consulting with Reebie Associates in the summer of 1983, PFE reinstituted PACFORD, with a different emphasis, in order to provide more flexibility for shippers in marketing their loads at forward points and for handling smaller shipments. In a way the new PACFORD was operating like the old "roller" concept in which a load departed unsold, and then utilized PFE's diversion and passing services and often PFE's knowledge of market conditions, to divert and sell at the most favorable location.

PACFORD provided for the storage of commodities in PFE cars for up to seven days and the loads were distributed to the most favorable markets by truck. This was all handled under a single transportation agreement. Under PACFORD, PFE became a customer of its owners to haul the cars to the forward points, and the customers dealt entirely with PFE (PACFORD) for service. The "new" PACFORD did not live up to expectations. Shippers resisted this apparently untraditional way of doing business, choosing to sell their loads at origin rather than at destination.

In the early 1980's, a position of Customer Service Manager was created to oversee customer relations. This was because "the customer is doing business with PFE/SP and should not be concerned with the technical problems of the way railroads go about producing transportation. We have made a concerted effort to let the customer know that he is doing business with us and we will take care of his door-to-door transportation needs." This quote, although from T.D. Ellen in June, 1985, could just as well have been made by Ken Plummer at the zenith of PFE operations.

By this time, however, the costs of providing perishable transportation had risen well above an economic rate of return on the investment in the equipment. This was true even using the depreciated "book" value of existing PFE cars, the newest having been built in 1971. The conclusion was much worse for an analysis using new cars; it was estimated that new cars in 1985 would cost $110,000 or more (the last new cars had cost $35,000). Labor costs were also adverse, being 35 to 50% above rates paid for comparable work by local industry.

Other technologies such as double-stack containers (COFC) were analyzed as possible ways to keep PFE in

business, but by the first half of 1985 the handwriting was on the wall. What perishable and semi-perishable freight business as there was on the lines of the SP could be handled along with all of their other freight business. Perishables no longer justified the existence of a separate operating subsidiary. In June of 1985, Tom Ellen wrote a 30-page memo for SP's D.K. McNear and D.M. Mohan about PFE's situation. The conclusion is worth quoting:

"In the final analysis, the perishable business is providing Southern Pacific with a contribution above marginal costs but does not cover capital costs even on a book basis. No further investment is justified as even intermodal technology does not generate adequate returns. This further suggests that there is not a technological solution to the railroad's lack of return in this business. The fundamental problems are service and the variable operating costs associated with producing that service, which overwhelm all other efforts to sell the business at more than it costs to produce it."

During the early fall of 1985 preparations were made to close the PFE's offices at Brisbane and transfer what was left to SPT Co.'s building at 1 Market Plaza (the old 65 Market St.), San Francisco. The Pacific Fruit Express Co. had, in effect, come "full circle" from its days with Southern Pacific Co. in the Flood Building.

All PFE's cars were dividended to SPT Co., and the Car Hire contract terminated, as of Oct. 31, 1985. PFE was thus no longer a car line. Many employees retired, took "buyouts" (early retirement), or stayed on with SPT Co. The PFE organization still existed within SPT Co. in 1991, headed by E.J. Morrisey, now titled "General Manager" (the title held by C.M. Secrist in 1907). All PFE traffic functions were moved to SPT Co.'s Marketing and Sales Dept., leaving 150 employees (under PFE's favorable labor and Worker's Compensation agreements) to perform car inspection and repair. All management functions were performed by SPT Co. personnel. These arrangements lasted until Union Pacific absorbed Southern Pacific on September 11, 1996.

To the historian, the end of PFE came with abolishment of its traditional ownership by UP and SP in 1978. In a way, though, the PFE is still around. The mechanical refrigerator cars it built in the 1960's still haul perishable loads for Union Pacific. But whatever the conclusion about its demise, there can be no question that Pacific Fruit Express set the standard in railroad refrigerator car operation for over seventy years, and during that time it was in all ways the greatest refrigerator car line in the world.

Senior managers of PFE gathered at the Palace Hotel, San Francisco, in the mid-1950's. Present were, left to right (front row, seated) Pete Holst, AGM San Francisco, CSD; G.P. Torburn, Gen. Supt., Car Dept.; Charles Ahern, Asst. to VP & GM; K.V. Plummer, VP & GM; Al Klaproth, AGM Chicago, CSD; Otto I. Larsen, AGM Omaha, CSD; and C.F. "Bus" Moody, Supt., Portland, CSD. (Middle row, standing) Joe Donnelly, General Traffic Manager, Chicago; E.F. "Gene" Gaebler, Chief Engineer; J.P. "Johnny" Ferron, Supt. Safety; Chuck Rowland, General Agent, New York, CSD;Robert F. McKee, Asst. Chief Engineer; Fred Garrigues, Manager, Personnel; Lewis D. Schley, Contract & Lease Agent; Bill Dreyer, Secretary to VP & GM; H.C. "Cookie" Morrison, Purchasing Agent; Bob Keating, Supt., Transportation, Chicago, CSD; and "Jimmy" Nolan, Traveling Agent for VP & GM. (Back row, standing) William G. Cranmer, Asst. to Auditor; Neil Cline, Asst. Manager, Purchasing; George Mountford, Traffic Manager, San Francisco, CSD; and Earl V. Hopkins, Asst. Gen. Supt., Car Dept. Three future VP & GM's are here as well as Plummer. CSD = Car Service Dept. George Shimmon photo 228874, courtesy Pete Holst.

2

COMPANY ORGANIZATION

This photo appears to depict a diversion office. The wall calendar, displaying the January page for 1920, is from the Graham-Reynolds Electric Co., a Los Angeles supply house, suggesting the location may be the Pacific Electric building. PFE photo, CSRM.

When the PFE was incorporated in 1906 and put into operation the following year, its organizational structure followed closely that of its parent railroads which not only followed business traditions of the era but were also heavily influenced by the top officer of both parents, E.H. Harriman. Management and supervisory personnel were chosen for their experience and for skills gained in a given area. Thus managers tended to rise within a single department.

Communication across departmental lines was generally held to upper levels of management. If, for example, a change in policy affected both the Car Department (rolling stock) and the Car Service Department (icing), whatever problems the change caused were solved at the head office and then handed down through the system to lower levels.

Typically, the labor forces had little to say about their working conditions until they were given a voice through union representation and this came in the 1930's, many years after PFE came into being.

The basic departmental structure of PFE, particularly its pattern of agencies, remained unchanged from 1907 until the 1960's, when more modern business practices began to come into the railroad industry and PFE's own business began to change extensively, as described in Chapter 1. Also, formally educated executives increasingly were replacing men who had come up through the ranks of the industry with little formal education.

This is the group photo for an ice plant managers meeting at Laramie, February 2-4, 1954. Shown here are, left to right, (front row) H.W. Barret, Tucson; Floyd Reneau; R.F. McKee; H.A. Shupe, Pocatello; W.W. Minkkinen, Modesto; Allen George; E.T. Quinn, Los Angeles; B.C. Ward; P.S. Toay, North Platte; D.F. Shuffler, Council Bluffs. Standing (back row) D.F. Briggs, Nampa; Chester George; Leroy Etzel; Floyd Warick; L.G. Schroeder, Colton; Claude Wilson; A.J. Scott, Las Vegas; C.L. Lovejoy, Fresno; George Jenkins; Carl Cramer; Ben Phillips; R.F. Jones, Ogden; C.M. Gerhart, Roseville; Mr. Wilson's secretary; R.G. Gilkison, Sparks; and H.A. Whitlock, Laramie. PFE photo, CSRM.

PFE underwent major reorganizations in 1962, at the split-up in 1978, and, on the SP side, in 1983, just before it ceased to be a car line and became only a minor subsidiary of the Southern Pacific Transportation Co.

For much of PFE's existence, its organization and the roles of its various departments were similar to those of the period 1949-1955, which is described here.

EXECUTIVE DEPARTMENT

The Executive Department was at the top of the PFE organization, formulating and executing policies affecting all aspects of its operation and serving as the main route of communication with the parent railroads.

In PFE's earliest years, the President was the chief executive officer of the subsidiary. In 1913, the title of Vice President and General Manager (VP & GM) was created for PFE's chief operating officer, C. M. Secrist. The title of President remained, but was held alternately by a director of each parent railroad, becoming a titular office rather than a managerial one. Also in 1913, PFE's headquarters were moved from Chicago to San Francisco.

Directly beneath the VP & GM were the Assistant VP & GM, an Assistant Treasurer (the Treasurer worked for the President in New York), and an Executive Assistant.

By 1953 a Superintendent of Safety had been added.

There were also Special Assistants to the VP & GM over the years assigned to various special or temporary projects.

The Manager – Personnel handled all labor contracts, negotiations and grievance procedures with the labor unions representing the various craft and clerical employees. In later years at PFE these came to number four: The American Railway Supervisors Association, representing supervisors below the rank of general foreman; The Brotherhood of Railway and Steamship Clerks (later Railway and Airline Clerks, BRAC) representing clerical and office personnel; the Switchmen's Union of North America (later the United Transportation Union, UTU), representing switchmen; and the Brotherhood of Railway Carmen, representing all carmen, apprentices, mechanics, laborers, and helpers at all shops and stores at outside points, which by far had the largest representation of all the labor unions on the PFE. The latter union's contract was administered until 1974 by the Car Dept., since it employed all PFE carmen.

The Contract and Lease Agent handled all contracts for ice supplied by outside concerns, contracts for ice decks not operated by PFE (of which there were many) and leases for land, facilities and office space not owned by PFE. These contracts and leases were maintained and updated by the Contract and Lease Agent.

While much of the car icing done by PFE was done at its own facilities by its own employees, there were many variations. PFE owned and operated some ice decks that were supplied by privately-owned local ice plants, while in other cases the contractor supplied both the ice and the icing service. Contracts for such services were drawn for a variety of terms and the duty for securing the best terms and maintaining the contracts fell to the Contract and Lease agents.

The PFE never had a separate law department, utilizing instead the law departments of its parent railroads for most legal matters. It did occasionally employ outside lawyers, for example on a large IRS case and on a large shipper suit involving equipment distribution.

Contract Lines Defined

In order to understand the overall PFE operation, a definition of who PFE served is needed. PFE was owned by the Southern Pacific Company and the Union Pacific Railroad. However, PFE served other railroads in the U. S. and Mexico under contract; except one, Western Pacific, which had a special relationship with PFE by virtue of the fact that it leased a small fleet of refrigerator cars to PFE, all of those U.S. railroads were subsidiaries of either of the two parent roads, SP and UP. These included the Texas & New Orleans, San Diego and Arizona Eastern, Pacific Electric, Northwestern Pacific, SP de Mexico, Visalia Electric, Petaluma and Santa Rosa, and Holton Inter-Urban, all SP-owned; and UP subsidiaries such as Yakima Valley Transportation Co. After 1936, nearly all UP subsidiary lines were merged in the parent Union Pacific.

After SP sold its Sud Pacifico de Mexico (SPdeM) subsidiary to the Mexican government in 1951, the Mexican railroads that had car contracts with the PFE were Ferrocarril del Pacifico, Ferrocarril Sonora-Baja California and Nationales de Mexico.

REFRIGERATION DEPARTMENT

The PFE-owned and operated ice manufacturing facilities were managed by the Refrigeration Department under a General Superintendent of Refrigeration. Two Superintendents - Refrigeration, one for all plants on the SP and the other for the UP, reported to the Gen. Supt.

It should be noted that the Refrigeration Department was responsible for the supply of ice and for icing cars at PFE plants, while Car Service Dept. personnel were in charge of icing at non-PFE facilities. In 1963 all ice plants came under the jurisdiction of the Car Service Dept., and the Ice Plant Managers reported to the AGM for the territory in which their plant was located.

CAR AND ENGINEERING DEPARTMENTS

In the earliest days of PFE, consulting engineers were engaged when needed, with major design projects for cars or buildings performed by the Union Pacific Mechanical Department, as had been agreed by SP and UP. In 1922, however, an Assistant General Manager (AGM) – Engineering was appointed, Harry T. Whyte, who was to serve in that capacity until 1945.

Initially, Whyte had responsibility for both structures and rolling stock, but in 1923, Luther Yates was appointed General Superintendent of the Car Department, separating responsibility for engineering and rolling stock that was to last for 40 years. In 1932, Lloyd E. Cartmill replaced Yates. In October, 1945, Whyte was succeeded by Eugene F. Gaebler as Chief Engineer, while in 1948, Cartmill was followed by G.P. "Gus" Torburn.

In this era, the Car Department handled all matters pertaining to the design, construction and repair of the car fleet, and the Engineering Department had charge of

Harry T. Whyte
AGM – Engineering
June 1922-Aug. 1945

Luther Yates
General Supt., Car Dept.
1923-1932

Lloyd E. Cartmill
General Supt., Car Dept.
Oct. 1932-Dec. 1947

Eugene F. Gaebler
Chief Engineer
Oct. 1945-May 1960

design, construction and maintenance of the fixed facilities of the PFE such as shop buildings, ice plants and office buildings.

The Car Department handled all centralized design work for refrigerator cars, and also was responsible for experimentation with new technologies such as mechanical refrigeration and trailer design and refrigeration. It also managed the car shops, each headed by a shop superintendent and his subordinates, and directed all car repair and rebuilding, as well as assembly of cars carried out in PFE's facilities (see Chapters 4 through 9). Light repair facilities (and later, trailer lots) were operated by Foreman-Inspectors. Technical aspects of purchase of cars from commercial builders were also the province of the Car Dept., although financial aspects were not.

Over the years there was some tension between the Car Department and the Car Service Department. The mechanical forces wanted to design and provide the best equipment available and keep up a high level of maintenance on the fleet. This sometimes conflicted with the needs of the Car Service Department, which wanted high-quality cars but also wanted fast turnaround and little delay in the shops in order to provide "OK" cars for shippers.

CAR SERVICE DEPARTMENT

PFE took care of operating, maintaining and servicing a refrigerator car fleet for the contract lines, who in turn billed shippers according to published tariffs for both transportation and protective services. PFE billed railroads for the mileage its cars ran over their lines, plus the cost of providing protective services (ice, salt and heaters when necessary) where provided. To this end, PFE had a large and well-run organization.

The operation was coordinated from above by the Executive Department, but PFE really got down to business at the Assistant General Manager level in the Car Service Department.

The Car Service Department as a whole took care of equipment distribution to loading points, enroute location of both loaded and empty equipment, return of equipment from offloading points, and provision of all protective services to cars while they were on the lines of Southern Pacific and Union Pacific. Many old hands on the PFE will also state that PFE people did a lot of the traffic and sales work for the railroads they served; it is hard to dispute this point, since PFE certainly maintained a close

Below is shown the 1953 organization chart for PFE. This chart, with only minor differences, could be used to illustrate PFE's organizational structure from the 1920's until 1962. From a PFE drawing, CSRM.

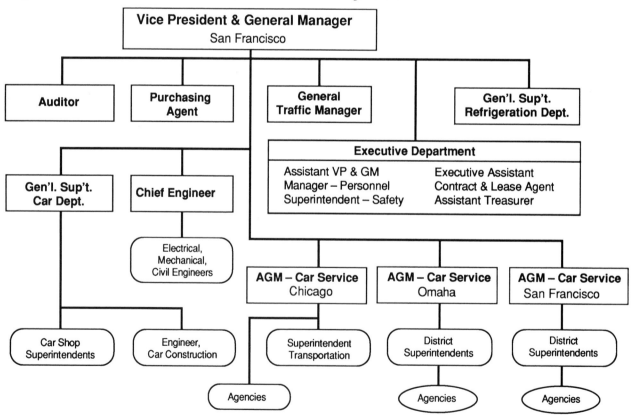

The new retop-icing machines and sub-deck of the Laramie icing platform are inspected by, left to right, Otto I. Larsen, AGM Omaha from 1946 to 1974, R.E. Drummy, and K.V. Plummer, VP & GM, in 1955. More about these machines is shown in Chapter 13. The car is PFE 60122. PFE photo, CSRM.

relationship to the agricultural industry which it served.

The Car Service Department was the heart and soul of the PFE operation and the public face of the PFE. Although the operation came under the authority of one department, the several elements of the Car Service Department are complex enough to warrant separate discussion. For instance, there were three Assistant General Managers' offices in three different locations, San Francisco, Omaha and Chicago, each of which served somewhat different purposes. The Chicago AGM's office was such a large part of the PFE operation that several of its bureaus are described in detail.

AGM San Francisco

The territory of the San Francisco AGM included all lines of the Southern Pacific and T&NO and their shortline connections, Western Pacific and the Mexican railroads that had car-hire contracts with the PFE. Since this was a vast amount of loading territory, the San Francisco AGM was concerned primarily with the distribution of empty cars to loading points and their blocking and dispatch eastward as rapidly as possible.

The key to PFE's operation, once the cars had been gathered by local freights and brought to marshaling points, was the "fruit block." These blocks of cars, often entire trains themselves, helped the PFE keep track of the locations of its shippers' loads and formed the basis of the diversion and passing service, which is described below. The San Francisco AGM, through the agency structure, oversaw the effort at the loading points within its territory.

Transportation Bureau. After 1960, the San Francisco office also housed the Transportation Bureau, the Superintendent of which reported to the VP & GM, an upgrade from former days when he reported to the AGM Chicago. Transportation's biggest job was allocation and distribution of empty cars within the "Western Territory" of the AGM San Francisco. It also helped collect empties from eastern unloading points, provided forecasts of needs for empties, and informed the various shops as to which incoming cars they would receive. The Superintendent of Transportation worked with all AGM offices to ensure rapid and equitable distribution of cleaned and serviceable empty equipment to active loading points.

AGM Omaha

The Omaha AGM took care of all Car Service matters on the lines of the Union Pacific except in southern

Supervisors of the Nampa Shop (Car Dept.) pose for a 1926 photo. From left to right, they are (back row) A. Williamson, C. Hamilton, G. Middlehurst, C.R. Simmons, and R.F. Nelson; (front row) P. Lownsdale, R. Howard, E. Botts, J. Foust, and W. Welbrock. PFE photo, CSRM.

California (west of Daggett, Calif.). The territories served by the Omaha AGM included much of what was termed "heater territory." During the fall and winter months many commodities had to be protected from freezing by use of heaters which were provided and serviced by PFE personnel while cars were on the lines of SP and UP.

At Council Bluffs, Iowa, all PFE heaters were removed from eastbound equipment and foreign heaters installed and vice-versa on westbound shipments under heater service. The mid-country location of this office also made it pivotal in distribution of returning empty PFE cars.

The two key points for distribution of PFE equipment were Kansas City and Green River, Wyoming; in later years distribution was handled from Kansas City and North Platte, Nebraska.

From Kansas City cars were sent via the Rock Island for the SP at Tucumcari, N.M. for use by the SP, UP or Mexican railroads in the Southwest. Empties coming via UP from Council Bluffs merged with the flow of empties via UP from Kansas City at Grand Island, Nebraska to supply UP, SP and WP in northern California and along the Overland Route.

The flow of empties to the UP in Idaho and the Pacific Northwest was governed by orders at Green River, Wyo. (later North Platte) covering deliveries to UP Idaho Division at Granger, Wyoming.

Cars for the SP in Oregon and for loading points in Utah and Wyoming were distributed directly from the cleaning tracks at North Platte.

Along with this critical distribution function, Omaha supervised much in-transit inspection, icing and, later, refueling, of refrigerator cars and trailers.

AGM Chicago

While no department of the PFE could lay claim to

being the most important, the Chicago AGM office came close. Chicago was the rail hub of the United States and was also the location of many of the major receivers of Western produce. And although many of PFE's loads terminated at Chicago, many more of them went through Chicago to destinations further east, and most of PFE's returning empty equipment came through Chicago. Additionally, it was a center of intercommunication between railroads. The AGM office here was at the heart of all the action.

The Chicago AGM's operation, through the network of fourteen off-line Agencies in the East, Southeast and eastern Canada, was concerned with not only getting loads to the proper receivers once off PFE's parent lines, but also rounding up the empty equipment and starting it back westward to be reloaded. Movement of these empties to the districts where they were most needed was the job of the Transportation Bureau, which was located in Chicago until about 1960, and then moved to San Francisco.

During peak growing and harvesting seasons PFE was servicing a greater demand for cars than even its great fleet could supply. Quick turnaround was the name of the game. When it could be arranged, the Agents tried to secure loads westbound in PFE equipment, but only if it did not hinder rapid return to the loading areas or interfere with loadings in the equipment of PFE's parent railroads.

The Chicago office was responsible for gathering information critical to PFE's billing process. PFE was paid on car mileage regardless of empty or loaded condition or which railroad carried the car to its destination. Railroads in turn charged the shipper for transportation and protective services according to tariff. Interchange and car movement records were kept by the Car Record and Mileage Bureau, records of protective services (ice, salt and heater) were kept by the Refrigeration and Heater Bureau and the Diversion and Passing Advice Bureau served the shipper with a means of knowing where his car was at all times and diverting it to a better market location when necessary.

Each of these bureaus was a part of the Car Service Department under the Chicago AGM, but the importance of each warrants giving a separate description of the duties and responsibilities of individual bureaus.

Car Record and Mileage Bureau. Chicago's Car Record and Mileage Bureau tracked the movements of all PFE cars loaded on PFE's contract lines. All interchange movements were recorded as well as actual mileage traveled by a car to its destination. This posting was done manually by Car Record clerks in large books set up by car series. The initial report was the loading report, followed by entries for diversions, transfers, out-of-line movements or any other information pertaining to the actual miles the car traveled, whether loaded or empty. On an average month in 1952 over one-quarter million entries were made for the movements of PFE's car fleet. Interchange records were kept for 375 different railroads. Mileage was computed from mileage charts, obtained from various sources and updated periodically. The interchange reports were used to prepare "car location statements" which were used to keep track of PFE cars on various foreign railroads and get them returned promptly to the loading areas.

Refrigeration and Heater Bureau. Protective service (provision of ice or heaters as necessary to protect a shipment) was another source of revenue for both PFE and the railroads it served under contract. PFE provided the service on the lines of Southern Pacific and Union Pacific as part of its overall Car Hire Contract. The railroads in turn billed shippers for the service. The Refrigeration and Heater Bureau in Chicago took care of keeping records for this service so billing could be made to the proper party. In the case of foreign lines billing for their service when a PFE car was off-line, PFE handled the charge on behalf of its

contract lines for shipments originated on those lines. This avoided the complication of a foreign line billing a PFE contract line directly for services provided off-line and was one more service PFE provided its contract lines.

Diversion and Passing Advice Bureau. To say the PFE operated in a dynamic environment would border on understatement. The PFE operation may appear simply to involve supplying refrigerator cars on a mileage basis, while the railroads in turn charged the shippers for hauling the cars to their destination. This straightforward task was made much more complex by the character of the perishable industry which was at the mercy of the economics of supply and demand at the receiving end of their products.

Produce prices fluctuated rapidly, much more rapidly than the transit time of a refrigerator car across the country. Consequently, much of the sale and purchase of perishable commodities was done after those commodities were loaded into cars and the cars had departed toward the eastern markets. Additionally, a given commodity often ripened all at one time in a loading area, before market conditions could be accurately determined.

Thus while market conditions were changing during the approximately seven-day trip eastward (including holds for diversion, inspection and service), shippers would often retain ownership of their loads until the best market could be found and the carload then sold. The PFE reefer fleet thus served as a giant rolling cold-storage warehouse. Changes in destination, ownership of the load and protective service were all provided for in the railroad tariffs.

To effect this marketing, it was essential that both shippers and receivers of perishables know the exact location of a given load at a given time. To this end the PFE maintained its Diversion and Passing Advice Bureau. When loads had been gathered at concentration points, as described in Chapter 14, they were consolidated into trains for the trip east; each train or large block of cars departing from a station was known as a "fruit block" or perishable block. The general term "fruit block" was used most generally and came from the early days of PFE when the company's primary cargo was California fresh fruit.

These fruit blocks formed the basis of information for the diversion and passing service; upon departure, complete information on each car in the block, such as shipper, consignee and protective service, was telegraphed to all relevant PFE offices for dissemination to those interested in the location and progress of the shipment. If a car was taken out of a block for any reason, such as held for diversion, wire advice of the change was telegraphed to all interested offices and to the Chicago Diversion Bureau as well. As the fruit blocks moved along the railroad, advice

Otto I. Larson
AGM Omaha
1946-1974

A.L. "Pete" Holst
AGM San Francisco
1949-1963

The Car Service and Traffic Departments worked with shippers. Here a number of shipper representatives are being shown features of a new "Giant" R-50-1 class car, PFE 100010, at Los Angeles in 1930. Those present are, from left to right, Frank Epperson, Traffic Manager, California Vegetable Union; C.L. Epp, Traffic Manager, Venice Celery District; L.S. Bechen, Traffic Manager, Peppers Fruit Co.; W.A. Salmen, Office Manager, Los Angeles Union Terminal Co.; J.W. Wolf, known as "Watermelon Joe," Sawdey and Hunt; George H. Corwin, Chief Clerk, PFE, Los Angeles; Jay T. Nash, Manager, Terminal Club; Jimmy Pease, Traffic Manager, Sawdey and Hunt; Jack Gorman, Traffic Manager, Emery and Kavanaugh and Fred R. Bright Co.; and at far right, C.E. Howard, General Agent, PFE. The R-50-1 class cars are described in Chapter 6. PFE photo, CSRM.

of their passing certain stations was also wired to all interested offices providing an almost up-to-the-hour record of the location of a shipment. Examples of these en-route activities are included in Chapter 15.

These passing advices were also given to Chicago. A shipper or receiver could contact a PFE agency for diversion of a car at any time if market conditions changed, the order being given to PFE by whichever party owned the load at the time. Loads were often sold and resold as they made their way eastward. When cars left the PFE contract lines the Chicago General Office took over the tracking and advising function, assisted by reports of departure of fruit blocks from interchange points with non-contract railroads. Chicago advised the Eastern off-line agencies of both PFE and the contract railroads who then notified owners of the shipments of their location and progress.

To accomplish this task the Chicago General Office maintained wire (telephone and teletype) circuits with many non-contract railroads as well as with SP and UP. A unique type of communication was the Western Union Chicago Pneumatic Tube service which was used to send paper telegrams, rather than the usual electrical signals, by air pressure to some Chicago railroads for retransmission over their circuits or for their direct use.

PFE's diversion and passing service was an important marketing tool for both PFE and its parent lines. Through the Chicago and Eastern offices' services to receivers the PFE was able to secure and solicit many routings and reroutings favorable to SP and UP which were originally billed as adversely routed.

District Superintendents and Agency Structure

The three AGM's who directed the Car Service Department had under them all the local Agents who dealt with shippers. The on-line AGM's in San Francisco and Omaha supervised District Superintendents, who in turn had charge over large territories. Beneath the Superintendents there were District Agents, usually in very busy or important areas, and beneath these Districts were the local Agents, some of which were seasonal. The on-line Car Service superintendencies were divided into seven districts. Their names and headquarters, along with locations of any District Agencies, were as follows.

Northwestern District – Portland. Territory was the

states of Oregon and Washington along lines of both SP and UP. District Agencies were located at Klamath Falls and Yakima. (Reported to both AGM San Francisco and AGM Omaha)

South-Central District – Pocatello. Territory was Montana, Idaho, Utah and stations along the UP in Nevada. The office of this district was in Ogden before 1955. District Agencies were at Nampa and Salt Lake City, and at Pocatello before 1955. (Reported to AGM Omaha)

Western District – Salinas. Territory was the coastal portion of California south to, but not including, San Luis Obispo. (AGM San Francisco)

Central District – Sacramento. Territory was inland California from Bakersfield north, and stations along the SP in Nevada. District Agents were at Bakersfield, Fresno, and Stockton. (AGM San Francisco)

Southwestern District – Los Angeles. Territory was southern California from San Luis Obispo south, and the states of Arizona and New Mexico and the city of El Paso, Texas. This district also included the West Coast of Mexico south to Guadalajara. There were District Agencies at El Centro, Guadalupe (later moved to Santa Barbara), Phoenix and Tucson. (AGM San Francisco)

Southern District – Houston. Territory was the states of Texas and Louisiana except the city of El Paso along lines of the T&NO. El Paso was considered the eastern terminus of the Pacific Lines of SP. District Agencies were at Edinburg and New Orleans. (AGM San Francisco)

Eastern District – Omaha. Territory was Nebraska, Wyoming, Colorado, and Kansas. This superintendency was eliminated by 1973 and integrated into the Omaha AGM office. District Agencies were at Kansas City and Denver. (AGM Omaha)

Off-Line Agencies – Chicago. Agencies located off of PFE's Contract Lines were for many years called either General or District Agencies, depending on their importance; these offices were usually located near the receiving end of PFE's eastbound perishable "pipeline" and dealt with consignees and foreign railroads. They reported to the AGM Chicago.

Locations of these Agencies were: Atlanta, Ga.; Boston, Mass; Buffalo, New York; Chicago, Il.; Cincinnati and Cleveland, Ohio; Detroit, Mich.; Minneapolis, Minn.; New York, N.Y.; Philadelphia and Pittsburgh, Penna.; St. Louis, Mo.; and Montreal, Que., Canada. By 1962, all the eastern agencies were termed General Agencies.

TRAFFIC DEPARTMENT

As mentioned before, PFE did not have a marketing or sales force for the purpose of originating business as did

Relations with the perishable industry were essential to PFE. This picture is from the *Imperial Valley Press*, reporting the "Annual SP-PFE Lettuce-Carrot Luncheon," held at the Eagle's Hall, El Centro, Dec. 18, 1956. Pictured are, left to right, Fuzzy Frizzell, Marty Wahl, Pete Holst, and Leo Ford. Photo courtesy Pete Holst.

traffic departments on railroads. Origination of traffic was officially the responsibility of the roads served by PFE. However, PFE's cooperative relationship and good connections with the perishable industry were important and were used to good advantage.

What PFE described as its traffic department was more of a claims and rate department than a sales department. Until the mid-1960's, this Department was under the authority of the General Traffic Manager (in earlier years the AGM – Traffic) in Chicago, with an Assistant Traffic Manager and a Supervisor – Claim Prevention, in San Francisco. The Traffic Department handled all rate, tariff and claim matters for PFE and furnished information on rates and tariffs.

The department also worked with the National Perishable Freight Committee to make favorable changes in the rules and charges outlined in the Perishable Protective Tariff, Division Sheet and Code of Rules. The NPFC was the rate-making body for all rail carriers of perishables. Its rules, adopted uniformly by its members, governed the methods and charges for carriage and protection of perishable commodities. The Traffic Department also handled information within PFE about claim prevention, and worked with the Car Dept. and shippers on this matter.

By 1972 the Traffic Department had been integrated into the AGM Chicago office and the San Francisco Traffic office was eliminated.

PURCHASING AND STORES DEPARTMENT

This department was headed by the Purchasing Agent, San Francisco, assisted by the Assistant Purchasing Agent, Portland and a staff of District Storekeepers. Although somewhat self-explanatory, this department had charge of providing all shops and facilities with whatever materials they needed to keep operating, from wood and metal for car construction to paper clips for the San Francisco office forces. The position of Assistant Purchasing Agent in Portland was needed because of the vast amounts of lumber that went into car construction, particularly in the days of wood-sheathed cars.

By 1967 the Portland position had been moved back to San Francisco. A District Store was maintained at each major shop location, headed by a District Storekeeper.

ACCOUNTING DEPARTMENT

In the 1940's and 1950's the Accounting Department was organized along conventional lines, headed by the Auditor, Assistant Auditor and Assistant to the Auditor. This office handled all accounts, payable and receivable, and tax matters for PFE.

It consisted of four Bureaus, each headed by a Chief Clerk: the Revenue Accounts Bureau, which collected all monies due PFE on car mileage, equipment leases, PAC-FORD bills (after 1964), and monies due PFE's contract lines for provision of perishable protective services; the Disbursements Bureau, which took care of paying all bills collectible from PFE; the Immediate Office, which handled and reported financial records, took care of taxes and settled compensation to PFE's parent railroads; and the File Bureau, which included the Mail Room.

THE 1962 REORGANIZATION

By 1960 a certain amount of modernization had come to railroad management. Traditional organizational lines which had prevailed for years began to fade as departments were changed and combined in efforts to cut costs and increase efficiency. The advent of machine accounting and computers meant the formation of new units to handle the operation and maintenance of the new technology.

In 1960, E.F. "Gene" Gaebler retired as Chief Engineer, and when the Car Department's G.P. Torburn followed in 1961, it was decided to combine the functions of the Engineering (buildings and facilities) and Car (rolling stock) Departments, returning to the system used prior to 1923. A major difference from 1923, however, was that Union Pacific no longer assisted with car engineering. Since 1946, it had been entirely PFE's responsibility.

The combined Department, which became the largest in the company, was called the Mechanical and Engineering (M & E) Department. Its new head was given the title of General Mechanical and Engineering Officer (GM &

EO). Earl V. Hopkins was promoted from Asst. General Superintendent of the Car Dept. to GM & EO. Robert F. McKee, Gene Gaebler's successor as Chief Engineer, became Assistant GM & EO.

The new M & E Dept. was divided into two sections, roughly along the lines of the old departments. An Assistant General Mechanical Officer, S.O. "Sarge" Littlehale, oversaw all matters pertaining to the equipment fleet and the car shops; an Assistant General Engineering Officer, W.R. "Bill" Carter, supervised all PFE facilities, including design and maintenance of the ice plants.

The engineering section staff consisted of four Engineers for civil, mechanical, electrical, and industrial engineering work. The mechanical section had six divisions which are largely self-explanatory: Engineer, Equipment Construction; Engineer, Equipment Maintenance; Engineer, Mechanical Refrigeration; Engineer, Planning and Control (a cost control position, also in charge of mechanical training); Chief Clerk, AAR Bureau (billing of off-line repairs to PFE equipment and PFE repairs to foreign equipment); and an Administrative Assistant. There were also two district maintenance engineers stationed at Roseville and Tucson. With Earl Hopkins' retirement on January 1, 1974, Bob McKee was promoted to GM & EO.

By 1963 the Executive Department moved the Superintendent of Transportation from the Chicago AGM office. The Superintendent of Transportation became a "bridge" type of office, reporting to the VP & GM on company-wide matters of distribution of empty cars to loading areas and working with the Car Service Department to secure the best equipment utilization. The PFE *Newsletter* of April, 1974 stated that a reduction in one day of turnaround of every car saved the equivalent of 400 new mechanical refrigerator cars, emphasizing the value of proper utilization of equipment.

G.P. Torburn
General Supt., Car Dept.
1947-1961

Earl V. Hopkins
General M&E Officer
Oct. 1962-Dec. 1973

By 1965 the Accounting Department had added a Systems Bureau, which wrote and maintained the programs used on PFE's computer. The Machine Accounting Bureau, under an Asst. Chief Clerk – Machine Accounts, was a somewhat later addition when PFE began using automated data processing equipment.

THE SPLIT INTO SPFE AND UPFE

With the division of the Pacific Fruit Express Co. into two separate entities in 1978, the "old" PFE essentially came to an end. The UP and SP (now operating as Southern Pacific Transportation Co., SPT Co.) organized their refrigerator car operations somewhat differently.

Union Pacific incorporated Union Pacific Fruit Express as a separate organization. It was headed by a General Manager, with an AGM – Car Service reporting to him, along with a Director of Administration, an Equipment Manager, and other functions, such as Shop Superintendents, Material Managers, a Director of Labor Relations, and so on. Cars continued to be marked "UPFE."

Southern Pacific kept the original name for its subsidiary, Pacific Fruit Express, and used the car reporting marks "SPFE." The subsidiary continued to operate as a separate entity, and at first its structure was simply the portion of the original organization which pertained to SP. However, changes were in store for what was left of PFE.

On both railroads, the employees continued to be on either UPFE or PFE payrolls, with corresponding union contracts, Worker's Compensation agreements, and so forth. Shops were still manned by PFE or UPFE forces, and separate financial statements were maintained.

The 1983 Reorganization

There were great changes in store from within PFE on the SPT Co. side of the ledger, as well as new influences from without. The departmental structure of PFE which had served it for seventy-six years was greatly changed by a reorganization in late 1982. At the time of the reorganiza-

tion, the departments were these: Mechanical and Engineering, Car Service, Transportation, Accounting, Data Processing, Industrial (Labor) Relations, and Executive. These departments performed the traditional functions commensurate with their titles.

The Car Service and M & E Departments were the core of PFE, one handling the provision of equipment and services to customers and the other handling the condition of the car fleet and facilities. These departments were to feel the greatest change, much to the chagrin of many old timers who had been with PFE most of their working lives. Three new organizations, called "Divisions," Fleet Management, Protective Service, and Mechanical, were created to handle the work of Car Service and M & E.

In brief, Fleet Management was set up to handle the movement, distribution and maintenance of the cars, with car hire (mileage and per diem) charges as its source of revenue. Protective Service was to provide that service, with protective service charges as its revenue. Mechanical was intended to be an independent car maintenance provider, with revenues from billings to the other divisions, and from non-PFE contract work at the shops.

Car Service, once the pride of the PFE organization, was eliminated, with most of its functions transferred to Fleet Management. All of the AGM, Assistant to the AGM and Superintendent positions, and their staffs, were eliminated. The great agency structure that had served PFE and

This road borders the old PFE shop area in Roseville. R. Church.

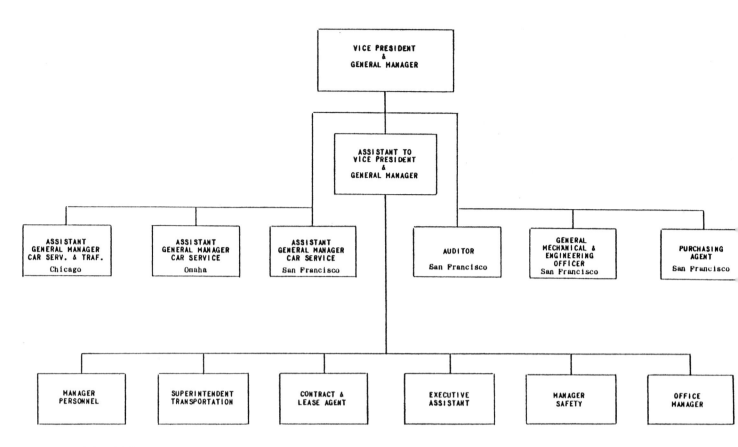

```
                    ┌─────────────────┐
                    │ VICE PRESIDENT  │
                    │       &         │
                    │ GENERAL MANAGER │
                    └─────────────────┘
                             │
                    ┌─────────────────┐
                    │  ASSISTANT TO   │
                    │ VICE PRESIDENT  │
                    │       &         │
                    │ GENERAL MANAGER │
                    └─────────────────┘
```

| ASSISTANT GENERAL MANAGER CAR SERV. & TRAF. Chicago | ASSISTANT GENERAL MANAGER CAR SERVICE Omaha | ASSISTANT GENERAL MANAGER CAR SERVICE San Francisco | AUDITOR San Francisco | GENERAL MECHANICAL & ENGINEERING OFFICER San Francisco | PURCHASING AGENT San Francisco |

| MANAGER PERSONNEL | SUPERINTENDENT TRANSPORTATION | CONTRACT & LEASE AGENT | EXECUTIVE ASSISTANT | MANAGER SAFETY | OFFICE MANAGER |

(Above) The 1972 organization chart, depicting only the highest level managers reporting to the VP & GM. The overall structure is much like that of 1953, shown earlier, and also of preceding decades. PFE drawing, dated September 1, 1972, CSRM.
(**Below**) Most industrial corporations conduct regular "safety awareness" campaigns as part of their safety programs, and PFE was no exception. This graphic, emphasizing that safety goes beyond hard hats, was used in the PFE *Newsletter* for December, 1972.

SAFETY STARTS JUST BELOW YOUR HARD HAT

DON'T MAKE YOUR HEAD JUST A HAT RACK; USE IT TO STORE AWAY YOUR SAFETY KNOW-HOW. WHAT'S UNDER YOUR HARD HAT PREVENTS INJURIES.

ALWAYS THINK SAFETY

its customers so well began a steady shrinkage which was to continue until the end of the PFE on the Southern Pacific, when only a very few local offices remained.

Shortly after the reorganization, Robert W. Terrill, General Manager of Protective Service, retired. When he could not be effectively replaced, that Division was merged into Fleet Management, which then handled provision of mechanical protective service, as well as car distribution, diversions, rate quotations, service monitoring and freight claims. Thus Fleet Management took on expanded duties from the old Car Service Dept. and absorbed the remnants of the Transportation Dept. It became a customer of the services that the Mechanical Division could provide, if such services could be not be found outside PFE for less money. The idea was to add the incentive of competition within PFE, to increase the profitability of the entire subsidiary.

The greatest change was in Mechanical. Duties of Mechanical would now be to handle equipment maintenance, and contract work with outside customers (begun in 1978 at Tucson Shop). In 1980, for example, Tucson performed major repairs on almost 1000 non-PFE cars. The old M & E Department was pared down drastically from its strength before the split-off. Since cars were no longer designed and built by PFE, many of the positions could be and were eliminated. The Equipment Engineer position was transferred to Fleet Management, leaving the General Mechanical Officer's position and Chief Clerk for the Mechanical Division.

The Mechanical Division was now a potential provider of service. Costs were strictly scrutinized and if lower prices could be found, Fleet Management was obligated to retain outside vendors. The Mechanical Division was thus in competition with vendors, adding further incentive for it to provide services at minimum cost. This was a new and very foreign position for the mechanical people, after years

of a tight "in-house" service, design and construction organization which always had the trust and confidence of every part of PFE and of its customers, despite cutbacks and changes in standards during the 1980's.

Along with the two new Divisions, there were four departments: Marketing & Sales, Accounting, Industrial Relations, and Executive. The new member of the list was Marketing and Sales, a signal that PFE would now handle origination of perishable traffic for its owner. One PFE Department, Data Processing, was eliminated on June 30, 1983 and both PFE's IBM 360 Model 30 computer and all data processing was taken over by the Southern Pacific.

PFE employees often organized sports teams for after-work activities. This is the 1928 Nampa Shop baseball team, posed before one of the cars they worked on. R.J. Church collection.

In the 1926-27 season, this was PFE's entry in the San Francisco AAU Industrial League (they finished fourth). The shirts were vertically striped maroon and orange with PFE shields. The manager on the left is Fred Garrigues; he is also shown in the photos which open Chapters 1 and 2. Photo courtesy Tim Walsh.

An award of safety plaques to Los Angeles ice plant and car shop supervisors is shown here in 1960. The second person from left is Earl Hopkins of the Car Dept., presenting the shop award, while Pete Holst, AGM–San Francisco (Car Service Dept.), second from right, presents the ice plant award with his left hand and the Vice President's 5-Year Award for the Southwestern District (1956-60) with his right hand. PFE photo, courtesy Pete Holst.

The 1983 plan was to judge each division by its profitability and output quality. Departments were viewed as service organizations to Divisions. By this time SPT Co. regarded all its subsidiaries as "profit centers," almost as separate businesses, and PFE tried to perform.

As described in Chapter 1, however, it was too late for the PFE to survive as a separate business and on October 31, 1985, many of its functions were taken over by its owner. The independent existence of the Pacific Fruit Express Company as a car line had ceased, and most of its work became the responsibility of Southern Pacific.

Even then, though, SP employees still called on PFE for car inpection and repair until the merger with UP in 1996. Since the merger, the various parts of PFE are now under single ownership again, and employees still refer informally to the organization as "PFE." In that sense at least, the tradition continues.

Part of PFE's extensive safety program was the organizational awards. Here the 1973 plaques (note how they've grown since 1960: see photo above) are presented in Pocatello on May 21, 1974, to shop, ice plant, purchasing and stores, and district office representatives. Third from right is AGM A.E. Chiasson, while at far right is R.F. McKee, GM&EO. UP Railroad Museum.

II

THE CAR FLEET

REFRIGERATOR CARS AND EQUIPMENT

Pennsylvania Railroad photo, Pittsburgh, 1949.

BY

ANTHONY W. THOMPSON

In this 1899 view, Wadsworth, Nev., still serves as SP's primary facility at the eastern foot of the Sierra Nevada. Its replacement by Sparks will come in 1904. On the third track from the right are a Fruit Growers car (left) and, next to it, a Continental Fruit Express car. Both are being used for transportation eastward of California fruit; and both represent formerly independent companies controlled by Armour Car Lines by 1899. Note the shipper's placard on the CFX car. These were quite common in the 19th century. Williamson collection, photo 11320, CSRM.

3

PFE'S PREDECESSORS

This car, built in May, 1892, in Peninsular Car Co. lot 632, is typical of cars built to be used in the produce trade before the advent of PFE. California Fruit Express was absorbed by Continental by 1901. Dan E. Nelson collection.

When the Pacific Fruit Express Company was incorporated in 1906, its purpose was to provide refrigerator cars to its two owners, the Union Pacific and Southern Pacific railroads. The refrigerator car was, at that time, already an established car type. Despite many misleading "historical summaries" published over the years, which typically describe the "invention" of the refrigerator car at dates after the Civil War, it is clear from White's summary in *The Great Yellow Fleet* (see Bibliography) that cargoes refrigerated with ice had been shipped in the 1840's, and that the essential feature of the 20th century refrigerator car or reefer, the end ice bunker, had been devised by 1860 and was accepted for construction by 1870.

The prolific inventors of the late 19th century were to invent many variations on the location of the ice supply in the car, and on the method of getting it into the car, but the end bunker proved to be the best design. Cars with this effective feature were soon used to ship meat, dairy products, fish, vegetables and fruit.

As early as 1867, before the Pacific Railroad's comple-

tion in 1869, a shipment of green California fruit was sent by express to New York with poor results, but in November, 1868, a consignment of grapes and pears from California was successfully shipped, partly by rail, in ventilated cars, effectively initiating the shipment of fruit from the west coast. During 1871, 115 carloads of fruit were shipped east. By the mid-1870's, meat and fruit shipments had become extensive. Much of this traffic was handled in cars of private car lines, which are further discussed below.

This chapter summarizes both the early designs and usage of refrigerator cars for produce traffic, and also the growth and dominating position of the Armour Car Lines between 1890 and 1906. The engineering practices used in design and construction of these cars is also relevant to the understanding of PFE's own cars, and are accordingly presented briefly.

By 1900, the technology of the ice refrigerator car had matured into a fairly standard form. Nearly all cars being built by that date had common features. Some of the technical aspects are discussed below, including insulation and

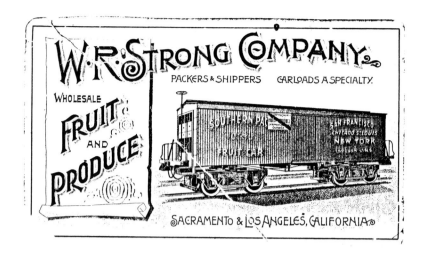

One of SP's 1883-type ventilated cars, shown in a label of the Strong Fruit Co. (original in color). The car is boxcar red. The passenger trucks, double hoses for straight air brakes, end ventilation openings, and end platforms with uncoupling lever and brake staff are noteworthy. The placard on the car side has a red diagonal stripe and reads W.R. STRONG COMPANY, FRUIT AND PRODUCE, SACRAMENTO and LOS ANGELES, CALIFORNIA. From CSRM collection.

brakes, as well as underframes. Prior to 1900, virtually all freight cars were built with truss-rod underframes.

SP and UP Fruit Cars

Though refrigerator cars date from before 1860, ventilated box cars came into use much earlier, and were widely used for produce, though not for meat and dairy products, by the end of the Civil War. As early as 1869, as shown in A.J. Russell photos, both the Union Pacific and Southern Pacific had constructed "fruit cars," which were ventilated box cars, equipped with small, adjustable doors in the sides and ends so that air circulation could be arranged to suit the cargo. These cars continued in use by UP and SP until the first years of the 20th century, when they were superseded by refrigerator cars. Other railroads, particularly in the southeastern part of the country, continued to use significant numbers of ventilated cars through the 1920's.

By 1880, enough crops could command the high price for shipment in passenger trains to justify special fruit cars for passenger service only. Thus both railroads began to add passenger-equipped cars, which were variously termed baggage, express or passenger fruit cars, to their rosters. At the same time, fruit cars for freight usage only were built.

A Central Pacific ventilated fruit car was exhibited at the 1883 Chicago Exposition, and its features were noted with approval; drawings were published in 1884 (see Bibliography). These cars, also shown in the 1884 *Car Builder's Dictionary*, were designed for both freight and passenger service, and had end platforms and passenger straight-air brakes (with two hoses between cars), with a vertical brake staff. Their Miller hook couplers were later replaced with knuckle couplers, as were the standard link and pin couplers on freight-only fruit cars. The latter cars were among the first UP and SP freight cars to receive air brakes, since they were used in relatively high-speed service along with the passenger-type fruit cars.

In the middle 1880's, both railroads purchased some refrigerator cars. The Central Pacific had constructed a reefer in its own shops in 1870, but now larger car orders

A ventilated fruit car of Southern Pacific design (called a "combination box car" by SP). Note the barred openings for ventilation on both sides and ends, and solid and barred side doors for the single door opening. The car shows a weigh date of Dec. 2, 1891, giving an approximate date to the photo. The lettering is the angular style characteristic of SP and CP at this time. Guy L. Dunscomb collection.

Table 3-1
SP and UP Cars Before 1900*

Car Type	Railroad†	1885	1890	1895
Baggage Fruit	CP, O&C	-	117	155
	UP	-	50	-
Freight Fruit	CP, SP	21	194	447
	SP CFFL	-	302	-
	UP	150	225	728
	UP CFFL	-	270	-
Refrigerator	CP, SP	83	-	33
	UP	150	452	426

*From freight *Equipment Registers*
†O&C = Oregon & California, SP subsidiary
 CFFL = California Fast Freight Line, 1890 only

were placed. Union Pacific obtained 25 Tiffany patent cars in 1883, and by 1885 both railroads listed both fruit and refrigerator cars, as shown in Table 3-1. Union Pacific in particular experimented with many of the patent car designs of the day, rostering by 1889 examples of the Wickes, Tiffany, Hamilton, Hutchins, Cook, and Goodell cars, descriptions of many of which can be found in *The Great*

Yellow Fleet and in articles cited in the Bibliography.

By the late years of the 19th century, a sliding door, similar to the "plug door" of contemporary practice, was in use to seal the cars, with sliding metal covers for the barred ventilation openings. But even with improvements, these ventilated cars were quite limited in their ability to deliver perishable produce in marketable condition. Refrigerator cars proved more dependable, even when their insulation was only needed to guard against extremes of heat or cold.

Before 1885, California fruit sold in the east primarily comprised peaches, pears, and table grapes. Oranges at that time came largely from Florida and Italy, while lemons came almost exclusively from Sicily. After 1885, however, western oranges and then lemons began to displace the European fruit. They also captured a larger market share than Florida citrus, despite the lower shipping charges from Florida. By 1895, imported citrus from Italy had become a small part of American consumption.

In December, 1885, about 1200 carloads of California oranges were expected to be shipped in 1886, and UP's General Agent in San Francisco, George Walts, urged the Union Pacific to cooperate with Southern Pacific in setting

This 1889-built ventilated box car is equipped for passenger service, with high-speed trucks and a second air hose for the signal line connection. In this view at Sacramento, the end ventilators are open, as is the plug door. Note that the large emblem is freshly painted, perhaps the occasion for the photo, while the far end of the car retains its original lettering. The photo is undated but cannot predate April 29, 1901, the reweigh date on the car. D.L. Joslyn photo, Signor collection.

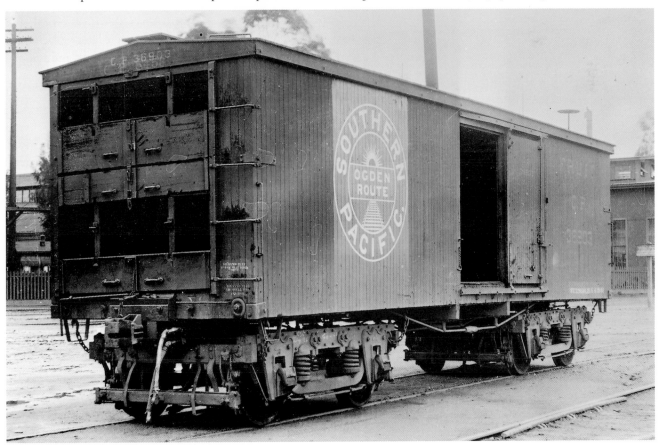

In this view dating from the early 1890's, UP locomotive 934 heads a solid train of California Fast Freight Line ventilated fruit cars. Location is thought to be Wyoming. UP Railroad Museum, photo 3-272.

a fast schedule via Ogden and Council Bluffs to secure the traffic. The competition for this traffic was the Santa Fe, already active in the California fruit trade, and SP's Sunset route to New Orleans. The UP and SP then organized the "California Fast Freight Line" and lettered their ventilated fruit cars (and also some other cars) accordingly. The result was that much fruit traffic did move on the joint Overland route. By 1895, the two railroads rostered more than 1800 cars in fruit service, although by then the Fast Freight Line was apparently no more.

Private Refrigerator Car Lines

Much of the early traffic in perishable products was carried in privately-owned refrigerator cars, that is, cars not owned by railroads. Railroads then, as now, tended to regard themselves as handlers of year-round, volume business. Specialized and expensive cars like refrigerators, which might

only be usable for one or two short produce seasons, were undesirable. The Georgia or Michigan peach seasons, then only 5 to 6 weeks, or the California cantaloupe season, about five weeks, could not provide enough revenue to pay for these cars. Thus private car lines, which could serve many different producing seasons in turn with the same cars, were able to manage the economics that an individual railroad could not.

There were some perishable shipments year-round, primarily meat and dairy products, and it might seem that this traffic would be attractive to the railroads. But their initial reluctance to buy refrigerators led the meat packing companies to operate their own cars. Thus even this year-round business was in the hands of private owners. Other seasonal cars, such as stock cars, and specialized designs like tank cars, were also primarily owned by private firms in the 19th century.

The earliest days of the long-distance shipment of meat

Armour car 3891 was evidently assigned to the Kansas City plant. This 1889 photo shows a light-colored car, though many of Armour's cars were darker colors, often green. The car has link and pin couplers and body-mounted brake beams. Pullman photo, neg. 790, Smithsonian Institution collection.

This 1885 view shows "fresh meat" car 5916, mechanically similar to car 3891, opposite page, in the typical Armour dark colors. Photo by Peninsular Car Co. (an AC&F predecessor), Detroit, courtesy Frank Ellington.

A Hammond beef car, built by Peninsular Car Co. at Detroit in 1895 or 1896, in lot 689. The style of paint and lettering is similar to that of the CFX car shown on page 57. Byron Rose collection.

employed stock cars, and animals were then slaughtered after arrival at the market city. As railroads began to acquire their own stock cars, and even to invest in stockyards, their reluctance to handle refrigerator cars of dressed meat increased. The Vanderbilt roads and the Pennsylvania Railroad were particularly noted for this hostility, often expressed in adverse freight rates, so that the Baltimore and Ohio, the Grand Trunk, and the Erie handled much of the meat business.

Gustavus Swift is usually credited with originating both large-scale shipment of dressed meat, and also the idea of a meat packer owning the needed refrigerator cars. After experimenting with leased cars, he commissioned the design of the "Swift-Chase" refrigerator car in 1878 and soon became not only the largest shipper of dressed meat from Chicago, but also the largest of the meat packers.

In the early 1880's, other packers, notably George Hammond and Philip Armour, also made large investments in refrigerator cars to handle their own meat. Armour was the quickest to imitate Swift's vertical integration, and became his strongest rival. By 1886, Armour controlled 24% of the cattle slaughtered at Chicago, to Swift's 31% and Hammond's 14%.

These three firms, along with Nelson Morris' company,

were known as the "Big Four" of the meat packing business, joined in the 1890's by Cudahy and by Schwarzchild & Sulzberger (which later became Wilson & Co.). Initially, they provided few or no cars for produce shipment, that being done on an irregular basis by the various fast freight lines. Meat cars had a number of specialized requirements, and except as experiments, were not suitable for produce shipment.

Armour soon became known as "just as good a railroad man as he was a butcher." He was the first, in 1883, to receive rebates from railroads for his meat shipments, and he followed Swift's lead in acquiring ice houses and icing facilities along his busiest shipment routes. The meat business soon expanded outside the Northeast to points west of the Missouri River and throughout the South. By 1890, the largest refrigerator car operation by far was Armour. Armour Car Lines provided not only meat cars for its own use, but also cars for fruit and vegetable service.

By the time Armour did so, there were already private car lines in the produce field. The first private car line organized just for produce appears to have been the California Fruit Transportation Company (CFT), founded in 1888 by inventor Carleton Hutchins, the fruit merchant F. A. Thomas and his son, and the Hubbard brothers. Soon

This string of cars has just been iced by the Continental Fruit Express crew on the deck (note CFX initials on the roof and sides of the building at left). Cars are posted with Earl Fruit Co. placards; Earl founded CFX. The nearest car is a Kansas City Fruit Express car, one of the many concerns which, like CFX, were absorbed into Armour by 1900. Neg. 11137, CSRM.

they were building cars, with a fleet reaching 600 by 1891.

But CFT's high rates soon caused others to enter the field. In 1891 their competitors included the Continental Fruit Express, founded by Edwin T. Earl, owner of California's large Earl Fruit Company; the Goodell Line, owned by the Porter brothers; the Kansas City Fruit Express; California Fruit Express; Fruit Dealers Despatch; and Fruit Growers Express (not directly related to the contemporary company of that name, which was not founded until 1920). The meat companies, however, brought great financial and organizational muscle to the fruit business, just as they had to the meat business. By 1895 Swift had absorbed CFT, while Armour absorbed all the others listed, along with about a dozen other small, private refrigerator lines.

Thus Armour came to dominate not only the business of shipping meat, but also produce shipment across the

United States. Since Armour had built or contracted for icing facilities at a number of locations to serve the meat trade, and had built car shops at Chicago, Fort Worth, Omaha, Kansas City, Memphis, Los Angeles, Sacramento and other points, there were efficiencies in providing produce service also. In 1900, Armour controlled about a third of all the private refrigerator cars in America.

The meat packers had experimented with car pooling and all had tried various rebate arrangements, common tactics throughout the railroad industry before passage of the Interstate Commerce Act in 1887. But Armour had the

(**Left**) The white cars of California Fruit Transportation, CFT, were familiar carriers of western produce during the 1890's. From 1890 *Equipment Register*. (**Below**) This 1899 view at Wadsworth, Nev., shows a CFX paint scheme different from the one which opens this chapter. To its right is an SP ventilated car. Stein collection, neg. 12433, CSRM.

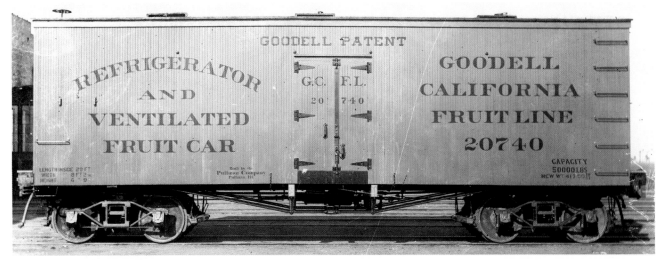

One of the Goodell Line cars, probably painted yellow with black hardware, built in October, 1894 by Pullman with patented Goodell features. Pullman photo, neg. 2781, Smithsonian Institution collection.

leverage to accomplish two other strategies. First, the exclusive contract was sought. This was a promise by Armour to route all their meat and produce cars over a particular railroad, if that railroad also contracted to use only Armour's refrigerator cars for on-line needs it could not serve with its own refrigerator cars (if it owned any). Second, through control of icing charges, large profits unconnected with freight rates could be realized. Among the examples uncovered in an ICC investigation were icing charges from Michigan to Boston, $20 in 1902 prior to implementation of an Armour contract with the Pere Marquette; after the contract was in force, the charges rose to $55. Many other examples of increases from 50 to 150% were also cited. Abuses like these led to the ICC and Supreme Court rulings described in Chapter 1, and eventually to the Hepburn Act of 1906, an important stimulus for the formation of Pacific Fruit Express by E. H. Harriman.

What was construction of these earlier refrigerator cars like? Air brakes and knuckle couplers were essentially standard by 1900, with consequences described below; the most notable design feature for reefers was the end ice bunker.

These end bunkers were important to effective cooling. They were arranged so that air could flow from the car's interior load space, through the mass of ice, thus cooling the air, and return into the car. This arrangement displaced earlier concepts in which the ice was in a sealed box, with only the box's exterior surface available to cool the air. Moving the air through the ice itself greatly increased the cooling surface and thus the efficiency of the car.

Although the first patent for a refrigerator car had apparently been issued in 1867, there were car building companies producing reefers before that date. In addition to ice bunker design, which was the subject of numerous patents, an important topic in the late 19th century was improved

This Armour fruit car is from the Kansas City Fruit Express subsidiary. AC&F photo, courtesy Frank Ellington.

The elaborate shaded lettering used on 19th-century Fruit Growers cars is shown here. This company was absorbed by Armour, but its name would be revived in 1920 by Armour's successor in the Southeast. AC&F photo, courtesy F. Ellington.

insulation. By the turn of the century, use of felted mats of cattle hair had replaced sawdust, ground charcoal, diatomaceous earth, and other primitive insulation materials. Some designs even tried to use numerous layers of "waterproof" paper (the 1876 Ayer refrigerator car used rubber sheet to reduce air leaks), with air spaces between, but air convection readily defeated such arrangements.

Dry air itself is indeed an excellent heat insulator, but only if it can be prevented from transferring heat by convection (the natural air circulation as warm air rises and cool air sinks). Prevention or minimization of the inevitable air convection is accomplished by forcing it to operate on a minute scale, with many fine fibers or cells. This is the principle behind felted hair insulation, and for other, familiar examples like goosedown, fiberglass, or plastic foams.

As refrigerator cars became more modern, they also came to be equipped with knuckle couplers and air brakes. Air brakes, adopted by CP and SP in the 1880's, became widespread in the 1890's and revolutionized railroading, not only through the great increases in safety which had largely motivated their adoption, but because they made possible the handling and braking of much longer trains. The obvious economics of operating longer and faster trains in turn drove the development of much larger locomotives between 1890 and 1910. The greatly increased draft (pulling) and buffing (compression) forces in these longer, heavier, and more strongly braked trains made the wood or truss-rod underframe obsolete. Steel underframes were the new standard of freight car construction by 1905.

Although nearly all freight cars after 1905 were built with steel underframes, truss-rod underframes continued to be part of refrigerator car construction because such cars were typically more lightly loaded than, say, box cars. More-

over, steel underframes were more costly; a refrigerator car already was two to three times as expensive as a box car to build, even with a truss-rod underframe, and many owners were reluctant to increase the cost further with steel underframes. As late as 1915 or so, all-wood refrigerator cars with truss-rod underframes were still being constructed, well after PFE had adopted steel underframes for all its refrigerator cars.

As is shown in Chapter 4, the new Pacific Fruit Express Company began to build modern refrigerator car designs, in all the senses just described, starting with its first class of cars in 1906. The same could not be said for many of the competitors of PFE. A number of them did not adopt steel underframes or other modern car features for a decade or more after PFE's founding.

Railroad Refrigerator Cars

Southern Pacific first signed an exclusive car contract with Armour in 1897, well before the period of Harriman control of both UP and SP, and the contract was extended in 1900. In July 1902, Southern Pacific purchased 150 cars to supplement the Armour cars which served the bulk of the western fruit business under contract to UP and SP, although in November of that same year, 1902, further extensions to the Armour contract were also signed. The 1902 reefers were rendered superfluous in 1906 when PFE was formed, and SP placed them in company service. By 1930 only 20 of these cars remained on the roster, and those were scrapped during and just after World War II.

Other railroad interests also were active in refrigerator car ownership. The New York Central had operated its Merchants Despatch Transportation organization since

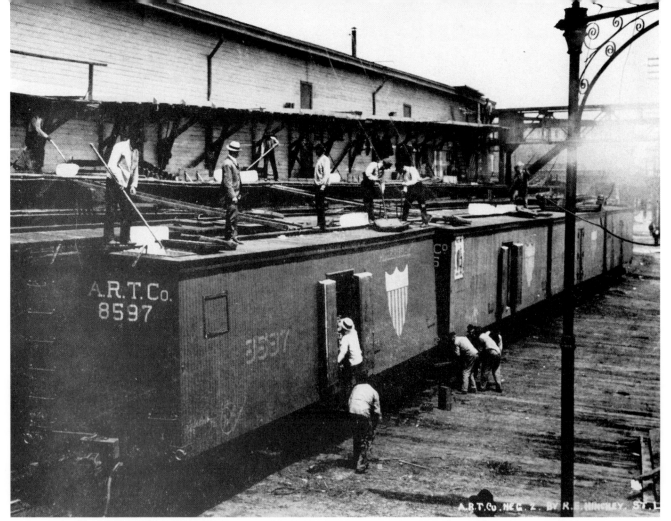

Icing cars of American Refrigerator Transit (ART) in St. Louis, in the last few years of the 19th century. Note the metal placard holder on the nearest car. AC&F photo by R.E. Hinchey, courtesy Dan E. Nelson.

forming it as a fast freight line in 1871, and by the end of the 19th century, had largely turned MDT into a refrigerator car operation. The Gould Lines, principally Missouri Pacific and Wabash, organized the American Refrigerator Transit (ART) in 1881, which continued to operate over their lines and associated railroads, such as Denver & Rio Grande Western, for many years. The Atchison, Topeka and Santa Fe began reefer operations in 1884, although ventilated cars outnumbered reefers until nearly 1900. A wholly-owned subsidiary, the Santa Fe Refrigerator Despatch (SFRD), was organized in 1902. Santa Fe even had a car contract with Armour for a few years after 1900. The Chicago, Burlington and Quincy organized its own operation, later called Burlington Refrigerator Express, in 1900. Great Northern followed suit in 1902, with its Western Fruit Express (WFEX). All of these, like PFE, were not strictly considered as private owners, since their ownership was entirely by one or more railroads. Because they were

(**Left**) SP's new 1902 refrigerator cars, Class CS-18, looked like this. Sides and ends were yellow. SP photo, neg. X-2136, Steve Peery collection. (**Right**) After 1909, SP discontinued use of the large railroad medallion, as shown in this photo from 1917 of an 1895 car. The 1911 safety appliances (see Chapter 4) have been installed. James Harrison collection.

This Wickes patent car was owned by MDT. It has link and pin couplers, but air brakes are installed for its body-hung brake beams. Note the red-white-blue stripes along the bottom of the body, an arrangement which MDT would still be using 60 years later. This and other photos in this chapter show how popular were curved lines of lettering in the late 19th century. Pullman photo, 1889, neg. 664, Smithsonian Institution.

In 1924, MDT organized a meat-shipping subsidiary called Eastern Refrigerator Despatch. This car, though somewhat modernized, remains essentially a 1903 MDT car, still with its original small door, truss rods, and arch bar trucks, as well as the signature red-white-blue stripes. UP Railroad Museum.

Beer cars, though painted like refrigerator cars, were really insulated box cars (note lack of ice hatches). This was one of only ten cars owned by Omaha Brewing. It was built by AC&F at St. Louis in 1899. It has link and pin couplers, and its air hose likely indicates it has air brakes. Byron Rose collection.

Typical equipment of the period for what was to be one of PFE's most energetic and effective competitors was this Pullman-built Santa Fe car of 1894, class Rr-D. It is a Wickes patent car, labeled for "bulk fruit" service, with link and pin couplers. Pullman photo, dated March 22, 1894, neg. 2677, Smithsonian Institution collection.

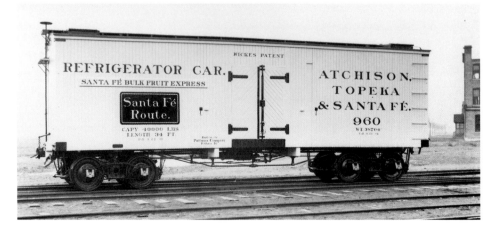

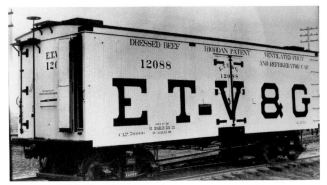

This 1890-built Riordan patent car of the East Tennessee, Virginia and Georgia (absorbed by Southern Railway in 1894) has link-and-pin couplers and unusual end ventilating doors. It is lettered for both dressed beef and fruit service, but was probably not used interchangeably for both. Dan E. Nelson collection.

A car built in 1917 but incorporating many features which were more like 19th century cars was this one for the Jacob Dold Packing Co., built by AC&F. Truss rods were at best obsolescent in 1917. Railway and Locomotive Historical Society collection, neg.11139, CSRM.

not themselves railroads (nor common carriers), their internal operations were not subject to the Interstate Commerce Commission, nor were they subject to, for example, the United States Railroad Administration (USRA) during the 1918-1920 period when the U.S. government, through the USRA, essentially operated American railroads.

These railroad-owned and directed car operations cut into the Armour Car Lines' western business very substantially, but Armour continued to serve other regions, particularly the southeast. When in 1919 the Federal Trade Commission directed Armour to sell its produce car lines as as an unfair advantage in the meat business, a successor was soon organized to fill the needs Armour had met.

In 1920, Henry Spencer, son of Samuel Spencer, founder and first President of the Southern, organized a company called Fruit Growers Express. As this was the name of a company absorbed by Armour in the 19th century, Armour's concurrence with use of the name was likely required. Spencer had the support of most eastern and southeastern railroads, notably the B&O, the Atlantic Coast Line, the Southern, and the Pennsylvania; others joined later. Some of the Armour car fleet was sold to FGE, as were many icing facilities, and Armour left the produce shipping business. FGE took over the operation of the Burlington's refrigerator cars in 1923 and GN's WFEX cars in 1926, although both lines continued to use their own name and emblem on their cars.

A few railroads, such as Northern Pacific, Bangor and

Aroostook (BAR), and Illinois Central, simply owned refrigerator cars as part of their freight car fleets, without creating a subsidiary organization to own and manage them. Others leased cars from private car leasing companies such as General American or Union Refrigerator Transit and added their own railroad medallion to the cars, whose reporting marks remained those of the leasing company. Among the railroads following this practice were the Nickel Plate, Milwaukee Road, and Gulf, Mobile & Ohio.

In later years, PFE was to establish fairly friendly relations with some of these organizations, such as MDT, FGE, BAR and ART, often arranging to use their cars in times of peak traffic on PFE, and reciprocating when PFE could spare the cars. SFRD, however, remained a bitter rival to the end of refrigerator car operations, and car sharing was most definitely not practiced between PFE and the Santa Fe. Each organization promptly returned empties to the other, even in times of car shortages.

These differences even extended to terminology. The practice of shipping unripened fruit in the 1880's led to calling fruit trains "green fruit blocks," a practice followed well past World War II by SFRD and some other lines. But it was discovered by 1890 that nearly ripe fruit traveled as well and was of much better quality to consumers. PFE reserved the term "green fruit" for deciduous tree fruits, and did not use the term for perishable trains.

Such differences may seem surprising, since the SP and the Santa Fe had cooperated in 1899 to make the tariff agreements which gave rise to the California Fruit Case (see Chapter 1), and W. A. Bissell, a Santa Fe assistant traffic manager, testified in 1907 that the two railroads had an unwritten agreement, in force since 1899, to share "equally in the citrus fruit traffic of southern California, scrupulously avoiding intrusion into the other's territory once the fruit has been picked." Santa Fe even approached SP and UP in 1919, as detailed in Chapter 1, and offered to form a joint refrigerator car operation. But those were contacts at a higher level. Those who worked for PFE and SFRD usually maintained a very distant relation with their rivals.

Table 3-2
Car Fleets in 1900

Car Type	Railroad	Cars
Ventilated	SP	804
	UP	758
	SFRD	538
Refrigerator	SP	188
	UP	404
	SFRD	1032

In this 1925 photo, car 2303 wears the 1909 PFE paint scheme, applied when the car was was rebuilt in 1916 at Sacramento. In 1927, this car will be rebuilt to R-30-2-13, with a new underframe and superstructure, and will finally be scrapped in 1940, still with the original car number and these trucks. For a number of years, PFE's Denver General Agency offices were in leased space in the building shown here. Hol Wagner collection.

4

THE EARLY WOOD ICE CARS

A "face in the crowd," one of over 3000 cars of class R-30-5, and a mainstay of the early PFE fleet. Car from Pullman's lot 5202, Pullman photo P-12893, Nov. 1, 1910, Smithsonian Institution collection.

It is customary to date the beginnings of the Pacific Fruit Express Company from its incorporation on December 7, 1906, when, as described in Chapter 1, it was formed as a jointly-owned subsidiary of the Harriman-controlled Southern Pacific and Union Pacific Railroads. Yet the essential feature of the new company, its refrigerator cars, had much earlier roots. The technical environment in which those cars originated was discussed in the previous chapter.

In 1904, when work began on the new car design which would be built for PFE, it had only been 10 to 15 years since the "modern" refrigerator car concept had emerged from the welter of exotic, complicated, and often inefficient or unworkable patent designs of the earlier period. John White's book, *The Great Yellow Fleet* (see Bibliography), presents that early engineering history in a clear and cogent fashion. One critical feature of the the "modern" design car was inclusion of ice bunkers at each end. Other features of modern cars were effective insulation, knuckle couplers and air brakes. As described in Chapter 3, air brakes had made much longer and heavier trains practical, thus motivating development of larger locomotives. By 1905, the wood or truss-rod underframe was obsolescent, with

steel underframes emerging as the new standard of freight car construction.

As is shown in this chapter, the new Pacific Fruit Express Company, with its progressive Harriman heritage, built modern car designs right from the outset, although many of PFE's fellow operators of refrigerator cars, both private car lines and railroads, were much slower to adopt modern car designs.

Classes R-30-1, R-30-2

That PFE's car concepts emerged well before the 1906 incorporation is evident from surviving drawings for individual car parts, some of which are dated as early as the first part of 1904. In PFE practice, once the design of the parts was finished, a "general arrangement" drawing of the entire car would be prepared. Such a drawing usually marked the completion of the design process. The general arrangement drawing for the first PFE car design, called R-30-1, is dated April 14, 1905, and carries drawing number C-746. That drawing does not bear the name "Pacific Fruit Express" but, like all mechanical drawings for the first 20 or so years of PFE's life, is labeled a "Common Standard" design. Moreover, the R-30-1 designation, which stands for **R**efrigerator, **30** ton nominal capacity, **1**st design, is an example of the Common Standard car classification system, implemented on the Harriman lines early in 1905, thus making the R-30-1 one of the first designs to receive this type of classification.

At this time, SP and UP owned very few refrigerator cars of their own, relying on the Armour car contract to satisfy shippers' needs for these specialized cars, nor had either road bought any such cars since 1902. Thus the 1904-05 drawings were clearly intended for a new Harriman operation, which became PFE. Certainly they represent design departures from the 1902 truss-rod cars.

As described in Chapter 1, Harriman knew in mid-1906 that the UP-SP refrigerator car contract would be terminated in six months. Construction of the first 600 PFE cars had been arranged well before that, however, with drawings, specifications, and an order sent to American Car and Foundry (AC&F) on December 20, 1905, prior to passage of the Hepburn Act, for future construction. The car specification was called CS (Common Standard) Specification 58, and it ran to quite a few pages, listing required materials, construction methods, and quality standards.

An order for 6000 additional cars was placed with AC&F on September 14, 1906, and announced in the railroad press of the day. Of these cars, 2000 were to be built at

AC&F's Detroit plant (lot 4590) and the balance at Chicago (lot 4591). The total, 6600 cars, was a huge one, apparently the largest single batch of refrigerator cars ordered in U.S. (and possibly world) history. It can be placed in perspective by noting that there then were, by Congressional testimony in 1905, about 56,000 refrigerator cars not directly owned by railroads. Moreover, this single batch of cars immediately made PFE the second-largest owner of reefers in North America, headed only by the Armour fleet of some 14,000 cars. But the day of the meat packers' dominance of refrigerator car ownership was waning. The day was not distant when PFE would be the largest refrigerator car owner in America.

A major part of PFE's new car fleet would be needed by summer, 1907, and construction of the first batch of 600 cars, AC&F's lot 4205, began in the same month as PFE began, December, 1906. About 320 of those cars were delivered by the end of that month.

Although AC&F began construction with the R-30-1 design, not all the new cars were to be of that design. During 1906, revisions to the R-30-1 design were being made, leading to design R-30-2. The general arrangement drawing for R-30-2, C-1126, was dated April, 1907, by which time construction was already underway on lots 4590 and 4591. By June, 1907, 1700 R-30-1 and 1900 R-30-2 cars, a total of 3600 cars, had been received by PFE. The balance of the 6600 cars were delivered from July to September,

R-30-2. Loading oranges at Claremont, Calif., in 1928. Though the underframe, door, and other details say "PFE," the photo has apparently been airbrushed for anonymity. Note the use of lug boxes and planks to support the roller tray. Sunkist photo, *Railfan and Railroad* collection.

Table 4-1
Numbers and Classes of Wood-Sheathed, New Cars (1906-1913)

Car Numbers	Number	Class	Built	Builder	Capacity*		Drawing
					cu. ft.	pounds	
1- 1700	1700	R-30-1	1906-07	AC&F	1964	50,000	C-746
1701- 4600	2900	R-30-2	1907	AC&F	1964	50,000	C-1126
4601- 4704	104	R-30-1	1907	AC&F	1964	50,000	C-746
4705- 6600	1896	R-30-2	1907	AC&F	1964	50,000	C-1126
6601- 7100	500	R-30-4	1909	Pullman	1921	50,000	C-1475
7101-10121	3021	R-30-5	1909-11	Pullman	1921	50,000	C-1531
10122-13219	3098	R-30-6	1912-13	AC&F	1928	50,300	C-1894

*Exclusive of ice (see text, page 73)

1907 (see Table 4-1). Average cost per car was $1614.

The new cars went into service as they were received, but as discussed in Chapter 1, there was in 1906 no PFE administrative, engineering or service organization. The SP and UP thus used the cars as they would any other freight car. But as soon as the PFE staff came into being, early in 1907, the organization took over refrigerator car operations, and began to grow steadily. Thereafter PFE had sole responsibility for its cars and their performance.

Design characteristics. These first two classes of refrigerator cars were interesting in a number of ways. As mentioned above, they were definitely "modern" cars, and have to be regarded as progressive for the era. The new cars had wood-framed superstructures, in which the vertical and diagonal members were bolted to castings at their ends, to minimize loosening and wear of the wood members in service. Steel tension rods paralleled the vertical posts to tighten the top and bottom sills. Oregon fir was specified for the tongue-and-groove sheathing on the sides, ends, roofs, interior lining, and floors. A relatively small side door, typical of the time, was used, 4 feet wide and 6' 1-¼" high. Insulation was in the form of two courses of ½-inch thick "Linofelt," a woven, paper-faced blanket of flax fiber manufactured by Union Fibre Co. In 1906, this insulation material was superior to the then-prevalent felt mats of untreated cattle hair.

The cars had underframes constructed entirely of pressed steel shapes, including pressed steel side sills. Although this underframe had some similarities to earlier pressed steel designs by Pressed Steel Car Co. and others, it was a distinct development by AC&F. It was a heavy and complex

R-30-1. The AC&F builder's photo of lot 4590, R-30-1 car 4685, built at Detroit on May 5, 1907. Note the Bohn Patent notation above the door for the 5500 lb. ice tanks. AC&F photo, Al Westerfield collection (from ACF Industries).

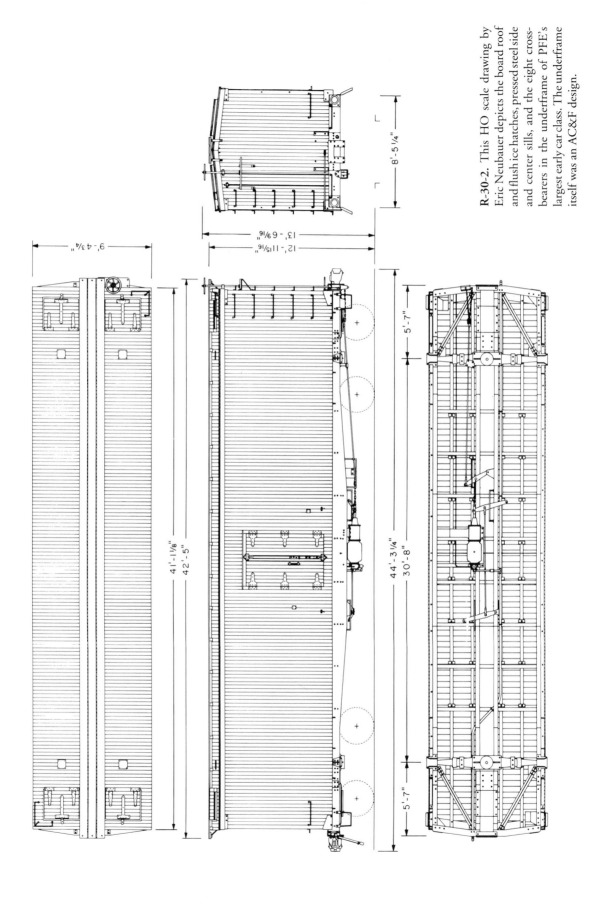

R-30-2. This HO scale drawing by Eric Neubauer depicts the board roof and flush ice hatches, pressed steel side and center sills, and the eight cross-bearers in the underframe of PFE's largest early car class. The underframe itself was an AC&F design.

R-30-2. AC&F's photo of R-30-2 car 2878, lot 4591, built at Chicago in July of 1907. The underframe and trucks have been whitewashed for the photo, but these parts were delivered with black paint. AC&F photo, Al Westerfield collection (from ACF Industries).

arrangement, with 8 cross-bearers riveted to the center sills. This underframe design was designated as a Harriman standard, and was first used by Harriman lines in 1902. It was applied to box, stock, flat, and furniture cars as well as to refrigerator cars. The underframe design itself, however, was an AC&F property; several non-Harriman roads also purchased cars with virtually the same underframe. Because of the side sill shape, PFE shop forces called these cars "possum bellies." Draft gear was typical of the time, with springs acting to absorb loads. Trucks were of arch bar design, with 4-¼" x 8" journals, and like all arch bar trucks, these proved to require extensive maintenance. These cars also established the length (over end sills) of about 41 ft. which was to be characteristic of nearly all PFE wood cars.

Among other features, these early cars also had ice hatches which were flush with the board roofs, that is, there were no ice hatch platforms. Hatch plugs were attached to the outer hatch covers with short lengths of chain. The bulkheads between the ice tanks and the car interior were of "Bohn Patent" design, using a metal "air syphon" which supposedly assisted air circulation. The "syphon" was a series of curved metal strips in the bulkhead which were thought to draw air from the car into the ice tank. This invention by John Ames had been awarded patent No. 625,309 in 1899. The patent rights were soon purchased by G.C. Bohn, and marketed through his Bohn Refrigerator Company or its subsidiary, the White Enamel Refrigerator Co., both of St. Paul, Minnesota.

There were two designs of these bulkheads, one of which was fixed in place, and the other which could be collapsed

into the car end. This provided more load space for cargo which needed insulation only, instead of icing, such as wine or nursery stock. The R-30-2 initially used the fixed bulkhead, but a few years later some of the cars were retrofitted with the collapsible or "convertible" bulkheads. Use of the various Bohn Patent devices carried a requirement to letter that fact on the car, which was done over the side door on these cars.

As mentioned, the class numbers of these cars, either R-30-1 or R-30-2, followed the parent roads' scheme, using the nominal capacity and design chronology. These cars had a 30-ton total capacity (25 tons payload and 5 tons ice); the "capacity" stenciled on the car side was the 30-ton value, in accord with standard practice. Externally identical to R-30-1, the -2 type had significantly larger ice tanks or bunkers, 146 cubic feet instead of the 118 cubic feet of the R-30-1. This was accomplished largely by decreasing the interior length between ice tanks by about a foot from the R-30-1, to 33' 2-¾" in the R-30-2. This exact interior dimension was to become the PFE standard, and years later, when the AAR finally released a design specification for a recommended (though not standard) refrigerator car, in 1940, its interior length was to be 33' 2-¾". Additional ice grates at the tank bottom were also included, probably for additional strength, from 9 oak bars in the -1 design to 11 bars in the -2. Starting about 1915, all surviving R-30-1 and -2 cars were gradually converted to a modernized ice bunker of 140 cubic feet capacity, and all the converted cars were classified as R-30-2's. By 1922, records showed no cars still listed as R-30-1.

R-30-1 (**Left**). Wood framing of R-30-1 cars, with notched wood carlines (transverse supports) ready for roof stringers. (**Right**). Waterproof "insulating" paper over outer insulation, ready for sheathing. AC&F photos, UP Railroad Museum.

A problem with loosening of the side sheathing appeared early, and starting in 1908 the cars were modified with a row of bolts along the lower edge of the car side to retain the sheathing. Another early change was in the arrangement of safety appliances (for example, grab irons). When built, the cars had rudimentary safety appliances, as was typical of the day. When the number and location of these appliances were standardized by amendments to the U.S. Safety Appliance Act in 1911, the cars were converted in a few years to the new arrangement, which was required by law.

Painting and lettering. When these cars were built, the paint schemes for the PFE cars originally followed the "Common Standard" (CS) for painting on the Harriman lines, called CS 22. The car colors were those which the SP and UP had adopted for the reefers they owned prior to the formation of PFE: sides, Color #8 (yellow with an orange tinge); ends, side fascia boards, and roof, Color #11 (a color

between tuscan and boxcar red); underframe, trucks, and all iron hardware, Color #13 (black). The side color, #8, was described by the words "refrigerator yellow." It was not a lemon yellow color; Color #8 was *mixed* from a yellow base with the addition of other materials. The painted car side was then finished with varnish coats, which probably added a brownish or orange cast to the painted color. The result was a light color, yellow with an overtone of orange.

Surviving paint chips for Color #8 at the Union Pacific Railroad Museum (see page 419) show a color resembling UP's "Armour Yellow" of today. Assuming for the moment that a 60-year old chip portrays a true color, comparison to Pantone chips showed an good match in sunlight with Pantone 143C, while under incandescent light the Color #8 chip lay between Pantone chips 129C and 130C. These Pantone colors cannot represent the varnished paint of the original cars, and, of course, fading, weathering or other effects are not included. On balance, UP Armour Yellow with a slight hint of orange would appear to be as good a

R-30-2. An early photo of R-30-2 4912, showing the post-1909 lettering arrangement, with owner's name and car number at the left of the car door. Close examination of the notation at the lower left corner of the car side indicates repainting at Colton in January, 1913, but the 1911 safety appliances have not yet been applied. PFE photo, CSRM.

R-30-1. Here the original PFE lettering arrangement is applied to a car for express service, drawn from AC&F lot 4205. The chalked lettering will be gold after the final Dark Olive paint is applied. (Freight-service cars had yellow-orange sides and red roof and ends). Photo H14-235, UP Railroad Museum.

match to the base color as we are likely to find at this date.

The same color arrangement just described, yellow-orange sides and boxcar red roof and ends, continued as the Common Standard scheme until 1922, with minor modifications in 1909 and 1911. In 1909, following a recommendation of the Master Car Builders (MCB), the car number and capacity data were moved to the left end of the car, while dimensional data were added on the right end. In 1911, the space beneath the side doors became Color #11 (boxcar red, which PFE and the other Harriman properties called "metallic"), instead of black. At this time, the slogan "UNITED STATES SAFETY APPLIANCES STANDARD," required by law for conforming cars, was added at the lower left corner of the car side. This required lettering was not eliminated until about 1925.

Passenger service. From the outset of PFE operations, a certain number of freight refrigerator cars were equipped for passenger (express) service with steam and signal pipes and rolled steel wheels, and were painted the Common Standard Color #1, Dark Olive, with gold lettering. Trucks were also olive; roofs were black. These cars were operated in passenger trains when used for time-value shipments. Car distribution and delivery was coordinated by Wells Fargo Express, and the cars were usually referred to in early PFE records as "Wells Fargo cars." Sketches 186-192 from PFE's Car Dept., for example, are so labeled and show arrangement of the passenger equipment. It appears that something in the range of 60 to 80 cars were usually in this service during 1910-1920, for example, and all were chosen from cars with one- or two-digit car numbers.

Whenever one of these express cars had to be withdrawn for heavy repairs, another car would be temporarily re-

numbered, and painted and equipped for express service. An example is car 6360, which was assigned to express duties in June, 1917, receiving the number of car 1 which was being rebuilt. In November, 1918, it was returned to freight work with its old number when car 1 returned to service. In 1923, 300 new 50-foot cars were built especially for express service, and all the freight-type cars returned to freight work and freight paint schemes. As described in the next chapter, R-30-2's numbered within 500-799 were gradually renumbered in the mid-1920's to other numbers within 1-6600 which had been vacated. This was to avoid duplication of the number series of the 50-ft. express cars, which was also 500-799 .

Service history. Throughout their lives, a few R-30-2's were modified by removing ice tanks, ventilators, and (if ever installed) floor racks. These cars were then used to ship beer in barrels, and occasionally bulk ice; essentially they were insulated box cars, and were in fact reclassified "RB" to reflect this. They were stenciled "Beer and Ice Refrigerator." There were typically about 80 to 100 such cars in service at any one time (83 in 1920). Once Prohibition began in 1920, however, their use was for ice only, though they retained the stencils. By 1930, only 10 cars remained in this service (and with this lettering).

The all-wood superstructures of these first cars were subject to considerable stress and wear, and most of the cars accordingly had to be entirely reconditioned in 1914-18. This program included replacement of most of the wood superstructure parts, new insulation and sheathing (still with retaining bolts along the bottom of the sides), and for many cars, reinforcing the bolsters and the center and side sills. An alternate arrangement of superstructure framing

R-30-1. This is PFE car no. 1, photographed at Nampa on September 19, 1928. This car was in passenger service from 1906 to 1923 (except during rebuilding), then returned to freight service. It was dismantled in 1936. PFE photo, Milton G. Sorensen collection.

appears to have been used on 2800 of these cars, numbers 3151-5950, and those cars did not have to receive the 1914-18 reconditioning. Difficulties with the cars, however, were not over in 1918. An internal PFE memo of the early twenties describes the R-30-2 underframe as "heavy, and of complicated and uneconomical design," and refers to problems with loosening and rivet-hole cracking in the many rivet joints of the design.

Accordingly, all the R-30-2 cars were rebuilt in 1925-28. This time, although over 2000 cars got new superstructures on their original frames, PFE also rebuilt 2500 of the cars with built-up steel underframes of the type then being

applied to R-30-13's. The nominal (payload) capacity became that of the replacement underframes, 30 tons, and entirely new superstructures were applied, which was evident, for example, in the taller doors of the newer design

Another change was that any remaining "Bohn Syphon" bulkheads were replaced with stationary, solid bulkheads. It had been found that an insulated bulkhead, with openings only at the top and bottom, gave more effective air circulation in the car. Rebuilding practices are presented in more detail in subsequent chapters, but the general intent was to produce essentially a new-equivalent car which met contemporary mechanical standards. When rebuilt in this

R-30-1. PFE 1128 after 15 years' service, photographed Oct. 3, 1920, as part of a damage claim documentation. Note the side sheathing bolts. In later classes, a light angle served this purpose. Wyoming State Archives photo, courtesy Terry Metcalfe.

R-30-2. PFE 12, rebuilt to class R-30-2-13 in February, 1928, and repainted at Los Angeles in August, 1935, poses for UP's photographer during 1938. Superstructure (except for the board roof), trucks and underframe are characteristic of the R-30-13 class. The paint scheme is that of 1925 (see Chapter 5). Neg. H12-254, UP Railroad Museum.

way, the cars received a sub-class designation, such as R-30-2-13. (This meant that they had been brought up to R-30-13 standards.) The cars also received the paint scheme current at the time (presented in the following chapter).

Over the next decade, nearly 1500 more of these cars were rebuilt to other, more modern classes, as discussed in subsequent chapters. But the remainder began to be scrapped in large numbers after 1934 when they came due for repairs which exceeded their repair cost limit ($250 in 1935). Retaining these cars in service would have necessitated their third reconditioning, almost surely exceeding the repair limit. Reduced traffic in the Depression also made these oldest cars less needed. Finally, the AAR was about to prohibit their arch bar trucks in interchange, a prohibition which finally went into effect in 1940. The cost of new cast-steel trucks and axles with 5" x 9" journals could have exceeded the repair limit if accompanied by even modest car repairs.

By 1939, no R-30-2 cars remained in service with their original underframes. Less than 2000 R-30-2's were still in service in 1940, and the class was down to a few dozen by 1947. The last three cars were dismantled in 1951, 1952,

and 1953. Some of these cars were sold to other users in the 1930's. One such sale was of 10 cars to the Southern Pacific for company use in local ice and meat service. It appears that two of these cars had not been rebuilt, while the rest were graduates of the 1924-28 rebuilding program. SP car numbers were SPMW 2049-2058. SP began to retire these ice cars in 1946, but it is not known in what year the last one was scrapped.

Classes R-30-3 through R-30-6

By 1908, PFE was beginning to need additional cars. The third car design, R-30-3, had a superstructure revised to incorporate the -2 ice tanks and an improved sheathing design, as well as many other, minor changes. The underframe, however, was the same Harriman design as on R-30-1 and -2. The general arrangement drawing for this car, C-1356, was dated 1 October 1908, and a complete specification, CS 58-B, was developed. But despite these signs that construction was expected, the R-30-3 was never built, possibly because of the underframe problems which were emerging with the existing cars. Instead, the improved super-

Icing cars at Evanston, Wyoming, about 1915. The open Bohn ventilators are of interest (note the hatch plugs lying flat inside the open ventilators). More than forty years later, the same ice tools and techniques would still be in use. Photo 17, Whitehead collection, UP Railroad Museum.

structure of the R-30-3 design was matched to a simpler steel underframe manufactured by Bettendorf, the combination being the R-30-4 design. This design was completed in April, 1909, and general arrangement drawing C-1475 and specification CS 58-C were prepared.

Design characteristics. The R-30-4 car had a somewhat different appearance from its predecessors because of the straight side sills, assembled from steel channel, and the distinctive underframe cross-bearers with **S**-curved ends. The underframe had a center sill which was slightly deeper in the center of the car than at the bolsters, fabricated from a single 18" I-beam, and with one-piece bolsters extending through the center sill. This underframe was a commercial product of Bettendorf, and although similar products were available from other suppliers, PFE was loyal to the Bettendorf design. This underframe had the same capacity as the Harriman underframe, nominally 30 tons (which continued to include 5 tons of ice in a loaded car).

The insulation thickness in this car was increased from 1" to 1-½", still of "Linofelt" material, in walls, floor and roof. Ice tank bulkheads continued to be the Bohn Patent stationary bulkheads. Most other major features of the

superstructure, draft gear and trucks were identical to the R-30-2 design.

That the R-30-4 design could be improved must have been evident, for only two months after completion of the R-30-4 design, the R-30-5 design was finished, and drawing C-1531 and specification CS 58-D prepared for it. Indeed, the first lot of R-30-5 was ordered at the same time as the R-30-4, as shown by Pullman's assignment of lot 5192 to the -4 cars, and lot 5193 to the -5's. It seems possible that design of the -4 class was an interim measure, perhaps for comparison to the -5 design. Certainly the two classes shared many new parts, whose drawings are dated in 1908. However, there were a number of internal changes in the -5 car. Steel ice grate bars were used for the first time, and smooth, galvanized sheet sides for the ice tank interiors replaced the vertical, 2-inch oak ribs of earlier ice tanks. The tank size was increased again, to 151 cubic feet. Cost per car averaged about $1400 for both R-30-4 and -5, well below the cost of the R-30-2's despite better superstructure construction in the later cars. Much of the reason was the simpler, lighter and cheaper underframe design.

An "alternative standard" ice tank was also designed, using the Bohn Patent "removeable" or convertible bulkhead.

R-30-4. The first car of 500 R-30-4's, 6601 has no grab iron or sill step at the left of the car side, as was true of all PFE cars prior to 1911. Photo is dated August 9, 1909. Pullman lot 5192, neg. P-11814, Smithsonian Institution collection.

This was not removed from the car, but could be raised up to the roof on hinges at its top, to permit use of the entire car interior when in ventilator or non-refrigerated service. Although the alternative ice tank had only 141 cubic feet capacity, it appears that all, or nearly all the R-30-5 class received these convertible ice tanks.

"Bohn Standard Ventilator" ice hatch covers were also applied to the R-30-5 cars. This cover was a sheet metal part which replaced the usual hatch cover, having louvers in the vertical end to direct air into the car when used as a ventilator. As described in more detail in Chapter 14, some kinds of produce were best shipped without icing, but with air flow through the car. This was accomplished by latching the hatch plugs partly open for "ventilator service." The hatch plugs continue to be the same wood

and canvas constructions as in previous cars. The surviving drawing for this ventilator hatch cover, C-1888, lists classes R-30-5 through R-30-10 as receiving it (see latter classes below).

Improvements in the -5 design, compared to the -4, may have been the reason why just 500 R-30-4's were built, compared to 3021 cars of the R-30-5 design; or perhaps only 500 fixed-bulkhead cars were needed. The first 105 R-30-5's were built in the fall of 1909, together with the R-30-4's. The construction of R-30-5 cars continued through 1910, with one design change. Hinged instead of chained hatch plugs were adopted for those cars. This change was recommended by the Master Car Builders in 1910, and PFE was quick to comply. The last few of a total of 3021 cars of this class were assembled in January, 1911.

R-30-5. Clearly shown in this builder's photo are the pre-1911 safety appliances on car ends, as well as the Bohn ventilator hatch covers. The date is March 15, 1910. Pullman lot 5193, photo P-12248, Smithsonian Institution collection.

R-30-6 (Above). Car 12808 depicts not only the 1911 safety appliance reform changes, but also the Bohn ventilators and their operating levers on the hatch cover sides. The legend over the door reads ICE TANKS OF THIS CAR CAN BE COLLAPSED GIVING FULL LENGTH LOADING FOR FREIGHT NOT REQUIRING ICING. AC&F photo, Al Westerfield collection.
R-30-5, R-30-6 (Below). PFE's drawing provides details of the Bohn ventilator design, including the round-end operating lever which opened and closed the end louvers. Note that the hatch plug can be raised up inside the hatch cover when the car is in ventilator service. Drawing by Eric Neubauer, based on PFE drawing, CSRM.

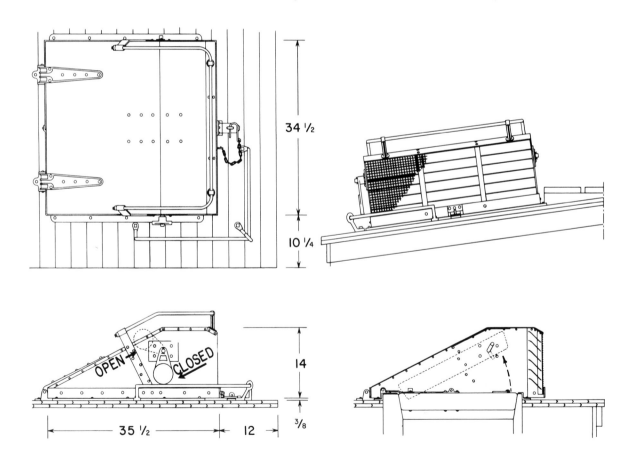

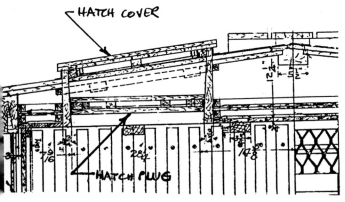

Hatch design. (Left) Part of a PFE drawing showing a cross-section throught the hatch opening, viewed from the car end. The hatch cover (top) and hatch plug (bottom) are separate. **(Right)** At the Evanston, Wyoming, ice deck in 1911, hatch plugs attached by chains are visible (Bohn ventilator in foreground). Wm. Kratville collection.

In August, 1912, a general arrangement drawing for a new car class, R-30-6, was completed as drawing C-1894, and specification CS 58-E was assembled. An order for 1098 cars had already been placed with AC&F in May, 1912, but construction was delayed until the drawings and specification were furnished. This first group of cars, AC&F lot 6666, was assigned to be built at the Madison plant. These cars cost about $1500 each.

It may be useful to point out the reason for ordering odd numbers of cars, e.g. 3021 R-30-5's or 1098 R-30-6's. All PFE authorizations for *additions* to the car fleet were round numbers, usually in thousands of cars. Any excess over a round number comprised "replacement" cars to maintain the size of the total PFE fleet, taking the place of wrecked or scrapped cars (though they had new car numbers, not the numbers of the destroyed cars.).

The R-30-5 design evidently had largely proven to be satisfactory, because few changes were instituted in the new design. This was PFE's first new car to incorporate the Safety Appliance Act reforms of 1911, though earlier cars were rapidly changed over to the new standards within a few years after 1911. Small changes were made in the installation arrangements for the insulation, and the insulation itself was changed to a new, treated felt material of cattle hair made by Johns-Manville and called "Hairfelt," which was more durable than the untreated hair products used earlier, and was also cheaper than "Linofelt." A more effective door closure was adopted as well, the Miner door latch, which had been patented on Aug. 23, 1910 by Calvin B. Patch and the patent licensed by the W.H. Miner Company. This closure, with minor modifications, was used by PFE until the end of wood car operations.

New castings were introduced for the joints among wood superstructure members, an important aspect of car durability, since the joints were the location of considerable wear in wood superstructures. These castings were shaped like pockets into which ends of the wood framing timbers were inserted and bolted. The Bohn ventilator hatch covers were again applied, as were Bohn "removeable" ice tank bulkheads. A minor rearrangement lengthened the interior distance between ice tanks to 33' 4-¼".

The first batch of R-30-6's in 1912, 998 cars, received the same wood Bohn convertible bulkheads (with metal syphons) as in previous designs, but the remaining 100 cars of lot 6666, as well as the two subsequent lots of 1000 cars each, 6936 (assigned to Madison but actually built at Chicago) and 6937 (Chicago), delivered in 1913, received all-steel Bohn convertible bulkheads. Like the preceding PFE cars, all these cars were delivered with arch-bar trucks, with some variations in truck design from class to class.

All three of these classes were painted and lettered as described above for the R-30-2 cars, with the yellow-orange sides, brownish-red roof and ends, and simple lettering with no railroad emblems or heralds. Like the R-30-2's, the R-30-4 and R-30-5 cars built before the Safety Appliance Act amendments went into effect in 1911 were quickly converted and relettered with the legend, "UNITED STATES SAFETY APPLIANCES STANDARD."

Service history. All three of these classes were structurally improved over the R-30-2, but it was still necessary to undergo reconditioning when they were about ten years old. The years 1920-25 saw virtually all the R-30-4, -5 and -6 cars reconditioned. The various designs of Bohn convertible bulkheads were replaced at this time with stationary bulkheads, since, as mentioned, the "Syphon" bulkheads were then known to produce less effective air circulation. The Bettendorf underframe was re-usable, but the superstructure durability was not much better than the "modified" R-30-2 superstructures had provided. Insula-

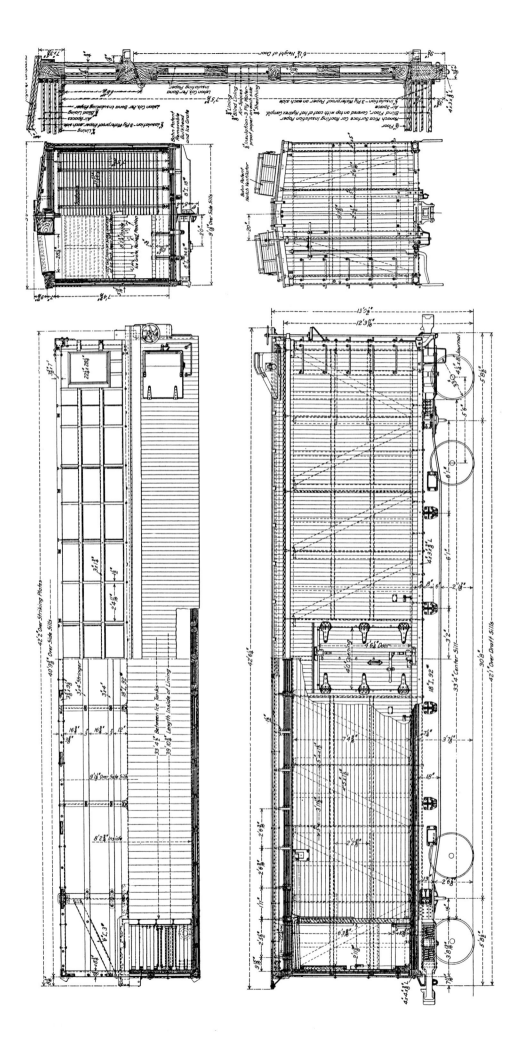

R-30-6. The general arrangement of the R-30-6 class, with Bettendorf underframe and Bohn ventilators. The underframe center sill was an 18" I-beam, reduced to 13" at the bolsters (after 1920, this bolster/sill dimension was 14"; see page 92). Both bolsters and cross-bearers were one-piece parts extending through the center sill from side sill to side sill. From *American Engineer*, May, 1913.

R-30-6. Another view of the -6 class, in a builder's photo dated March 19, 1913. AC&F photo, Al Westerfield collection, with permission from ACF Industries.

tion standards continued to rise during the years these cars were in their original state, and by the time of their rebuilding, they were obsolescent in terms of their refrigeration capabilities. Thus reconditioning was motivated both by wear in the wood superstructures, and also by the need for better insulation.

New superstructures and insulation extended the life and usefulness of the cars for another decade. But like the R-30-2 cars, they began to be scrapped when repairs which would have exceeded their book value came due after 1934. Scrapping was very heavy during 1934-37. Not only had traffic decreased due to the Depression, making these older cars expendable, but their arch bar trucks were on the verge of being prohibited in interchange. In addition to costs of new trucks, mentioned above, there was also a problem with obtaining cast-steel trucks with the correct center plate height, on these older cars, for AAR interchange requirements. All the cars were gone by 1950. Table 4-2 summarizes this history. A few hundred of these cars escaped scrapping during the 1930's, having been rebuilt to more modern classes, as discussed in later chapters. They then received a new car number and class.

An interesting detail on these classes is that 98 of the R-30-5's and two of the R-30-6's, 100 cars in all, were given 40-ton cast-steel trucks with 5" x 9" journals in 1929, at which time they were renumbered to 80001-80100. This was not a rebuilding, nor did capacity increase over the underframe's limit of 30 tons, and car classes remained the same. It may have been an experimental replacement of the cars' obsolescent arch-bar trucks.

In 1933-35, 41 of these re-trucked cars were sold to the California Dispatch Line (CDLX reporting marks). The average sale price per car was $1700, at a time when a new car would have cost twice as much, but PFE's repair limit for the cars was only $400. These cars were bought for use as wine tank cars. After removal of ice bunkers and hatches, six glass-lined tanks, of about 1000 gallons each, were installed, making them AAR mechanical designation TW.

In their new service, these cars were essentially insulated box cars containing wine tanks. Their CDLX numbers ran from 277 to 317, in order of delivery from PFE but unrelated to their PFE car numbers. CDLX leased these TW's to various California wineries, along with a varied roster of more conventional-appearing tank cars, and they contin-

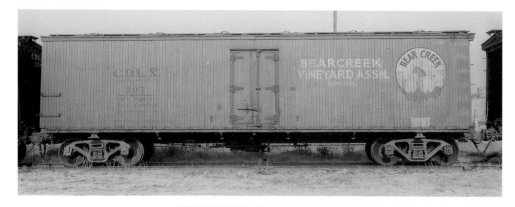

R-30-5. Car 307 was purchased by California Dispatch Line (CLDX) from PFE in 1934, when it had number 80019. It had been built as PFE 8423. W.C. Whittaker photo.

R-30-5. CDLX car 279 was operated for Italian Swiss Colony wineries. When sold by PFE, its number was 80071; originally it was PFE 7329. Photo at Oakland, Calif., Feb. 11, 1939, by W.C. Whittaker.

ued in service until the 1950's (the assets of CDLX were sold to General American around 1955). Two examples are shown in the accompanying photographs; both cars exhibit paint schemes which likely were vivid, but no information has survived about the colors used. Others of the 80,000-series cars were scrapped during the 1930's (trucks were reclaimed), so that by 1938 only 7 remained in this group.

Classes R-30-7 through R-30-10 (unbuilt designs)

The R-30-4, -5 and -6 classes of early cars with wood-framed superstructures did not have to be reconditioned quite as much as the R-30-1 and -2's, possibly because their more modern underframes were stiffer and the cast steel pocket elements in the superstructure framing were more

successful. However, despite the evident success of the R-30-5 and -6 car designs, there was clearly an interest in alternative designs during 1912-1914. Four of them were prepared in those years.

The first additional design, R-30-7, was completed in October, 1912, with drawing C-1917, and given specification CS 58-F. This design married the R-30-6 superstructure to the old pressed-steel Harriman underframe. This would have carried a weight penalty of 1500 pounds relative to the R-30-6, even though the design used the heavier and more complex superstructure of the -6 design, compared to the R-30-1 or -2. Given that problems had already become evident with the underframes of this type which were in service, it seems unlikely that new construction of -7's was contemplated. Instead, the R-30-7 design may have been intended for rebuilding the older cars. In fact, however, the

Table 4-2
Survival of Wood-sheathed Cars with Original Numbers*

Car Numbers	Class	Number of Cars					
		New	1925	1934	1940	1947	1950
1- 6600	R-30-1, -2	6600	6139	4171	1878	56	3
6601- 7100	R-30-4	500	480	440	6	0	0
7101-10121	R-30-5	3021	2860	2135	66	1	0
10122-13219	R-30-6	3098	2973	2788	37	1	1

*Decreases in numbers due to dismantling, wrecks, and rebuilding to other classes.

R-30-7 design was never used for either new or rebuilt cars, and when the Harriman cars were rebuilt in the 1920's, it was done to a different standard.

Almost as surprising as the R-30-7 concept are the three designs prepared in 1914. The R-30-8, whose general arrangement drawing C-2359 was dated October, 1914, was a Bettendorf underframe with a superstructure which had R-30-4 ice tanks, including 11-bar wood ice grates and fixed bulkheads. This was not a "throwback" to the earlier R-30-4 design, but was a modernized superstructure which had fixed bulkheads like those of the -4 cars. Among other things, this indicates that convertible bulkheads were not turning out to be necessary in all cars, and that the bulkhead conversion mechanisms in the R-30-5 and -6 cars were causing some maintenance headaches. Internal PFE memos of the period refer to repeated repairs being necessary on the convertible bulkheads, and they were finally removed from PFE cars during the 1920's. The fixed bulkheads, being a permanent part of the superstructure, also made a stiffer and thus sturdier car. PFE memos as late as 1927 continued to refer to this -4 design as a proven, durable one – referring primarily to the fixed bulkheads, not other details.

A companion design to the R-30-8 was completed at this same time, applying the R-30-8 superstructure to an AC&F "fishbelly" underframe (different from the "Harriman" frame) to create the R-30-9 design. These two designs were given specifications CS 58-G and 58-H, respectively. No cars using these -8 nor -9 designs were ever built. Finally, one more 1914 design was the R-30-10, the drawing for which, C-2389, was dated June 22, 1914. Like the -8 and -9 designs, it incorporated newly-designed castings for the wood superstructure members, and had a Bettendorf underframe with a superstructure like the R-30-5, with Bohn convertible bulkheads, Bohn ventilators, and a new design

In this 1917 photo at Spokane, Bohn ventilator cars are being iced on double track. A.W. Thompson collection.

of cork floor insulation. Its specification was CS 58-J, and like the other 1914 designs, was not built.

Although the R-30-10 design was not built, it was nevertheless an interesting and forward-looking design. Essentially, it was a modernized R-30-6, and a number of its features, like the new superstructure castings and the cork floor insulation, were to be used in subsequent designs. It should also be noted that even though none of the R-30-7 through -10 designs were built, the -8 and -9 *class numbers* (not the designs) were subsequently used for rebuilt cars of rather different design, as shown in the chapters on rebuilding. How close these four designs came to actuality is not known, though completion of a general arrangement drawing and a CS specification was normally an indication that construction was seriously intended. Economic conditions may have prevented construction of these designs; the nation slipped into a recession in the fall of 1913, and conditions worsened as the War in Europe in 1914 deprived the U.S. of many overseas markets. Whatever the reason, permission to place orders for these car classes was never given.

SP Mogul 1687 switches PFE cars at the Brawley, Calif., ice deck in 1911. All 3 classes then in existence are visible; the first car is an R-30-2, the second an R-30-4, the third and fourth cars R-30-5. Huntington Library photo, courtesy Donald Duke.

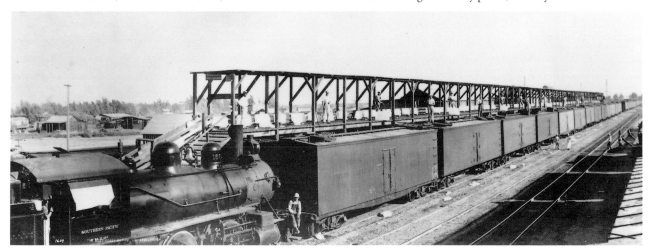

A view from the footbridge over the yard at Roseville, Calif., in 1928. The three long strings of reefers, mostly PFE in this photo, are on the cleaning tracks. Note the mixture of board roofs (pre-1920 cars) and outside metal roofs. Every car visible has the 1925 paint scheme, and some cars have "PFE" and car number stenciled on the ice hatch, a practice that never became universal. Note also that the galvanized roofs of some of the foreground cars aren't holding their paint well, a perennial problem with galvanized steel. If the photo looks familiar, it's because it was part of the inspiration for John Signor's dust jacket painting for *The Great Yellow Fleet*. PFE photo, *John Signor collection*.

5

PFE'S ROARING TWENTIES

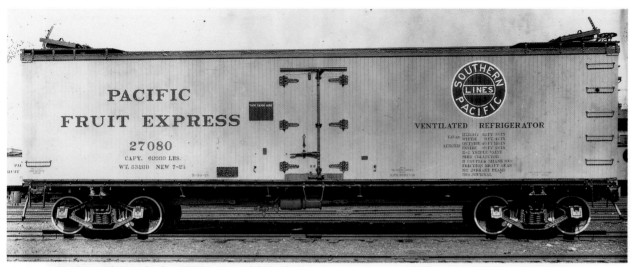

R-30-13. This car displays PFE's most widely-built design: a superstructure which was applied to nearly 20,000 cars, more than any other *total* refrigerator fleet. Pullman photo, neg. P-27257, Smithsonian Institution collection.

The preceding chapter covered the wood cars built before 1913. The result of that construction was a fleet of about 13,000 cars which were in every way competitive with other refrigerator car fleets. The cars were quite modern for their time, and already PFE's fleet was the largest in North America, surpassing the fleet of its nearest competitor, Armour. Although when the World War began in Europe in the fall of 1914, the American economy was at first depressed, within two years the effects of large orders for food and munitions by the Allies led to significant traffic increases throughout the country. At the same time, settlement and growth of the West was increasing. Accordingly, PFE began to need to add to its already substantial fleet. Advances in technology were at hand, and improved cars were possible. When the U.S. declared war on Germany on April 6, 1917, PFE had already begun construction of a new class of cars.

The U.S. government took over administration of the railroads to coordinate traffic during World War I, under the USRA (United States Railroad Administration). The USRA assumed control on Dec. 28, 1917, and relinquished that control on March 1, 1920. Non-operating subsidiaries like PFE were exempt from the USRA, and those 26 months of USRA direction of railroads affected PFE's car fleet only indirectly. Cars were pooled nationally for many types of

traffic, and the purchase of cars was controlled. It was not until late in 1919 that PFE received permission to place orders for more refrigerator cars. Upon the return to railroad management in March, 1920, a number of additional PFE car orders were placed. These are described below.

Class R-30-11

After a hiatus in car construction since 1913, a new car design was completed in January, 1917, with drawing C-2555. A severe national car shortage had developed in 1916, and PFE was planning to add to its fleet. This original design was called R-30-11, but after a limited number of cars had been constructed to the original plans and specification (CS 58-J), some minor improvements were made. Those first few cars were then re-designated as class R-30-11-½. The additional, much more numerous, modified design became the recipient of the designation R-30-11 (specification CS 58-K). All were ordered in January, 1917, with the AC&F portion of the order to be split between the Chicago and Madison plants.

Design characteristics. Several important advances were introduced in these designs and specifications. Both were based on the same general arrangement drawing, C-2555,

R-30-11. Although the body of 14209 looks much like earlier cars, many internal changes have been made. Trucks are Bettendorf cast steel. AC&F photo, Nov. 1917; Al Westerfield collection (from ACF Industries).

but there were a few differences between the two sub-designs, largely in hardware items, and trucks. The cars continued to have Bettendorf underframes. The trucks used on these cars are an interesting study. In 1915, PFE had adopted a Common Standard design of cast-steel 30-ton truck, a Vulcan (American Steel Foundries) pedestal design with separate journal boxes, though these side frames were not the kind which could accept the boxes of the older arch bar trucks (in contrast, for example, to the Andrews design). Yet during the 1917-18 construction of these new cars, that Vulcan truck was not used. Instead, arch bar trucks, much like those used on PFE's first cars in 1906, were applied to the R-30-11-½ cars. (Cast steel trucks were applied to these cars during the 1920's.)

When the next cars, the R-30-11's, were built, they received PFE's first cast steel truck side frames on new cars. They were a Bettendorf design resembling but slightly different than the later "T-section" design. Moreover, these trucks had larger axles and 5" x 9" journals, and thus were capable of 40 tons capacity, so car capacity became limited by the underframe. (Usually trucks, or more precisely, axles, determine freight car capacity. See Table 5-1 for a summary of these capacities, introduced by the ARA in 1920 as the basis for car capacity.) Later in the 1920's, some older cars with 4-¼" x 8" journals were converted to the 5" x 9" standard by installing new trucks, though these had to have special center plate height to match the old trucks. To quote a PFE document, arch bar trucks were "expensive to maintain," and were accordingly being replaced, though the cost of replacement and the non-standard center plate height prevented a major program of this kind for older cars.

Table 5-1
Axle Size and Car Capacity

Axle Code	Journal Size, inches	Nominal Capy., tons	Max. Weight on Rail,* lbs.
A	3-¾ x 7	20	66,000
B	4-¼ x 8	30	103,000
C	5 x 9	40	136,000
D	5-½ x 10	50	169,000
E	6 x 11	70	210,000

*Equals sum of "light weight" and "load limit" of car

There were a number of changes in the new superstructure. The -11 design incorporated the cork floor insulation of the R-30-10 design, replacing 1-½" of "Linofelt" or "Hairfelt" with 2" of cork. Cork had the advantage that it absorbed little water, and retained its structural integrity, important in a floor, even if wet. The cork was covered with a ¼" thick coating of an asphaltic waterproof compound, and the compound in turn was covered with a layer of mica-surfaced roofing paper. Over that was the 1-¾" tongue-and-groove wood flooring, with joints white-leaded. Two varnish coats were the final floor layer. Floor edges were also waterproofed to minimize water penetration into walls. Walls and roofs continued to be insulated with Johns-Manville's "Hairfelt."

As a result of joint tests in 1915-16 conducted by PFE and the U.S. Dept. of Agriculture (USDA), floor racks were installed in the R-30-11. A valuable increase in air circulation around the load, and thus in uniformity of internal temperature, was achieved by these racks, which

R-30-11. A step in the process of replacing a wheelset, with the sideframe ready to be replaced. Photographed at Nampa shop on March 12, 1930. PFE photo, Rich Hernandez collection, courtesy of Milton G. Sorensen.

were 4-⅞" high. That height was to remain standard with PFE for almost 20 years. These earliest racks were placed loose in the car, but soon were fastened in place with hinges (the racks lay on top of the wood floor). In 1918, PFE began to install these floor racks in older cars, and by 1922 nearly every PFE car in service had floor racks.

The ice tank bulkheads were fixed, and were of wood construction. The "Bohn Syphon" concept had been discarded. A solid bulkhead, with openings only at top and bottom, optimized air flow. Bulkheads were also insulated, to prevent freezing of lading nearest the ice tank. A heavy, galvanized wire screen basket was used to contain the ice itself. The ice tank walls continued to be lined with galvanized sheet metal, but ice tank construction was arranged so that a 1-⅝" air space on all sides, between the wall and the screen basket surrounding the ice, for air circulation. This design was called a "basket ice bunker."

This was PFE's first use of the basket bunker, a more efficient design because convecting air not only passed through the ice, but around the ice container itself. Cooperative tests in 1913-16 between the USDA and several car lines, including PFE, had shown the virtues of the basket bunker. Galvanized steel drip pans were used to line bunker bottoms. An improved door seal and latching arrangement was also adopted, although the door opening remained the size it had been with the previous five classes. The R-30-11 also retained the exterior board roof of the earlier cars.

The first cars built from these new designs were the 60 examples of R-30-11-½, built during 1917 by PFE in the Roseville shops. This was the first instance of cars being built new by PFE, instead of by a commercial builder, and reflects the growth of shop capacity and capability since 1906. The reconditioning of the R-30-1 and -2 cars in 1914-18, PFE's first such program, had also provided a pilot program in large-scale construction and assembly work on cars. It is possible that material availability problems of

World War I prevented acquisition of desired cast-steel trucks, causing these 60 cars to be built with arch-bar trucks.

Later in 1917 and 1918, 840 more cars were constructed, this time to R-30-11 design, and the cast-steel trucks were applied. This completed the 900 cars authorized to be built by PFE. The remaining 1800 R-30-11 cars were constructed by AC&F, starting in October, 1917.

Painting and lettering of these cars continued to look much like that of the earlier cars such as R-30-6 (see previous chapter), except that the car weight was deleted from car ends. Indeed, it is only the cast-steel trucks which provide an easy spotting feature to distinguish the as-built R-30-11's from earlier cars. Of the 2700 cars built for this class, 200 were considered "replacements" for earlier cars which had been destroyed, and only the remaining 2500 were considered additions to the fleet.

Service history. During the 1920's, the 60 cars of R-30-11-½ design were modified to bring them into compliance with the R-30-11 specifications, and by 1930 the former class, -11-½, was no longer listed in rosters. About two-thirds of the 2700 cars of R-30-11 were reconditioned with new superstructures in 1929-31, keeping their old numbers, and were eventually scrapped during 1945-55. The other one-third of the cars were rebuilt during the 1930's to other classes, as described in Chapters 6 and 7, below.

Classes R-30-12, R-30-13, R-30-14

As delivery of the R-30-11's was being completed in 1918, PFE stood on the threshold of an immense building program for cars. It has been asserted that this occurred in response to the growth in grape traffic occasioned by Prohibition. As discussed in both Chapters 1 and 14, produce loadings of all kinds, including grapes but certainly also including citrus, lettuce, and melons, did increase consid-

R-30-12. Among the early cars of R-30-12 was 17443. Note the cast steel Vulcan pedestal trucks, outside metal roof, and ice hatch platforms. AC&F photo, dated Aug. 6, 1920, Al Westerfield collection (courtesy ACF Industries).

Table 5-2
Numbers and Classes of Wood-Sheathed, New Cars (1917-1926)

Car Numbers	No. Cars	Class	Built	Builder**	Capacity cu. ft.	pounds	Drawing
13220-13279	60	R-30-11-½	1917	PFE	1924	50,800	C-2555
13280-14119	840	R-30-11	1917-18	PFE	1924	66,000	C-2555
14120-15919	1800	R-30-11	1917-18	AC&F	1924	66,000	"
15920-16919	1000	R-30-12	1920-21	SP Equip. Co.	1918	66,000	C-2788
16920-17219	300	R-30-12	1920	Mt. Vernon	1918	66,000	"
17220-17419	200	R-30-12	1920	PC&F	1918	66,000	"
17420-18019	600	R-30-12	1920	AC&F	1918	66,000	"
18020-18919	900	R-30-12	1920-21	Pullman	1918	66,000	"
18920-19619	700	R-30-13	1920	Haskell & Barker	1918	70,000	" *
19620-19919	300	R-30-13	1920	AC&F	1918	70,000	" *
19920-22519	2600	R-30-12	1922-23	Standard Steel Car	1918	66,000	C-2826
22520-23219	700	R-30-12	1922	General American	1918	66,000	"
23220-24719	1500	R-30-12	1923	Standard Steel Car	1918	66,000	"
24720-25719	1000	R-30-12	1923-24	General American	1918	66,000	"
25720-26219	500	R-30-12	1923	Mt. Vernon	1918	66,000	"
26220-26719	500	R-30-12	1923	Pullman	1918	66,000	"
26720-27219	500	R-30-13	1923	Pullman	1918	70,000	" *
27220-28249	1030	R-30-13	1923	PC&F	1918	70,000	" *
28250-28749	500	R-30-12	1924	General American	1918	66,000	"
28750-29649	900	R-30-13	1924	PC&F	1918	70,000	" *
29650-30449	800	R-30-12	1924	Pullman	1918	66,000	"
30450-31249	800	R-30-12	1924	Standard Steel Car	1918	66,000	C-3550
31250-31434	185	R-30-13	1924-25	PC&F	1918	70,000	" *
31435-32434	1000	R-30-13	1926	AC&F	1918	70,000	" *
32435-33434	1000	R-30-14	1926	General American	1918	70,000	"
33435-34434	1000	R-30-13	1926	PC&F	1918	70,000	" *
34435-35473	1039	R-30-13	1926	Pullman	1918	70,000	" *
35474-36473	1000	R-30-13	1926	Standard Steel Car	1918	70,000	" *
50001-52000	2000	(WP cars)	1923	AC&F	1918	70,000	–
52001-52775	775	(WP cars)	1924	AC&F	1918	70,000	–
500-799	300	R-E-1	1923-24	Gen. Amer., AC&F	2586	63,000	CB-20690

*with underframe dwg. C-2677   **PC&F=Pacific Car & Foundry

R-30-12. This General American builder's photo of the last car in their 1923 lot clearly shows the 1922 paint scheme. Trucks are Bettendorf "T-section." July, 1923 photo, UP Railroad Museum.

erably during the early 1920's, thus requiring additional car construction, but grape traffic was not the original stimulus for PFE's new car designs.

During 1918, design work continued on improvements to the R-30-11, as shown by numerous drawings for new parts with dates in that year. The Volstead Act was passed on October 28, 1919, and went into effect as the 28th Amendment to the Constitution in January, 1920. By that time, PFE had completed the design work which culminated in the general arrangement drawing for the R-30-12, C-2788, dated October 25, 1919. Orders for the first cars were placed at about the same time, prior to the end of the USRA period. There is no evidence this was anticipation of Prohibition's effects by PFE.

In the spring of 1918, the Car Committee of the USRA had adopted its seven well-known standard designs of box, hopper and gondola cars. During the remainder of 1918, six additional designs were also adopted, including flat, tank and caboose cars and, of interest here, a refrigerator car, although none of those additional designs was ever built by the USRA. The main features of the USRA refrigerator design (see Pennington and Winterrowd papers in Bibliography), many of which had emerged from USDA tests, were the inclusion of floor racks, basket bunkers, and insulated bulkheads, as well as increased insulation in sides and roofs and the use of cork in floors.

Every one of these features had already been adopted by PFE in the R-30-11 design, which predated the USRA standard. Moreover, PFE installed these features in its older

cars during 1918-1925. Other USRA car features, such as the heavy underframe with a 26"-deep center sill, were regarded by PFE as overdesigned (though Santa Fe and some others adopted it). As late as 1930, some authors were still urging attention by certain refrigerator operators to the main features of the USRA "Standard Refrigerator," but such remarks were certainly not directed at PFE.

Design characteristics. The 1919 PFE design for the R-30-12 incorporated many features of the R-30-11, including its Bettendorf underframe and ice tanks. A visible feature externally was the increase in side door height to 6' 8-⅛", replacing the 6' 1" or so which had been standard since 1906. Since the car height remained similar to older cars, the door reached much closer to the top of the

Proud of PFE's extensive use of their products, J-M shows an R-30-12 in this ad, though "Hairinsul" was introduced well after car 22520 was constructed.

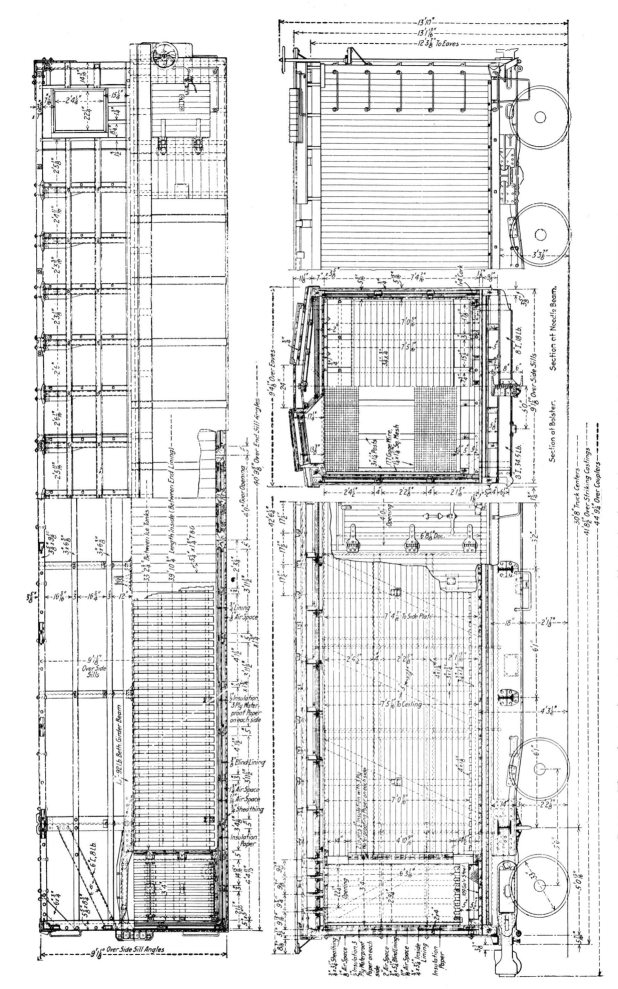

R-30-12. The car drawing shown in the 1931 *Car Builders' Cyclopedia*, which appears to be based on PFE drawing C-2826. Note the screen-lined basket ice bunkers, ice hatch plug and cover construction, and Bettendorf center sill and bolster arrangement. Reprinted with permission.

R-30-13. Here PFE 35199 has its frame whitewashed for the photographer, providing a good look at its "built-up" design. Pullman photo, 1926, Smithsonian Institution collection, courtesy Donald Duke.

car side, a distinctive spotting feature.

Roof insulation thickness was increased from 1-½" to 2" of "Hairfelt," and the roof was supported on steel carlines instead of wood ones. This was the first use of steel superstructure frame members in PFE cars. The original design also incorporated the same board roof as had been used since 1906, a roof which contained a waterproof lining between two tongue-and-groove layers, and was called an "inside roof." Early in the construction of the first R-30-12's, however, outside metal roofs were introduced (see below). A cast-steel, 40-ton Vulcan pedestal truck with separate journal boxes (not the 1915 Common Standard 30-ton design) was used for the 1920-built cars, but not for any later cars.

The R-30-12 superstructure design was eventually applied to nearly 20,000 cars, because it was also used for the R-30-13 cars. The R-30-13 specification consisted of the same superstructure, but on a new underframe design, called a "railroad design," as called out in drawing C-2677. The design itself dates from early 1919, but was not used until R-30-13 construction began in 1920. This new underframe continued to have the 30-ton capacity of the Bettendorf, but was constructed differently. Referred to as a "built-up" underframe, it was made by riveting stiffening angles onto flat pieces of plate, instead of the 18"-deep channel used for the Bettendorf center sill. It also had double center sills, 20-½" deep, in place of the single, heavier sill of the Bettendorf. This first batch of R-30-13's had Bettendorf cast-steel trucks.

The alternate-standard built-up underframe was adopted to permit more rapid production of new PFE cars in the early 1920's, without being limited by production rates of commercial underframes at Bettendorf. Produce traffic increased immensely in the 1920's, as discussed in Chapter 14, and PFE correspondence files from this period refer repeatedly to annual car shortages and the need to continue

to order more cars. Thus PFE built these two classes, -12 and -13, at the same time throughout the first half of the 1920's. The term "Roaring Twenties" is not only appropriate for the social and economic pattern of the times, but also for PFE's car production.

The 1920 production of R-30-12's has an interesting detail: the first 1000 cars in that year were built by the Southern Pacific Equipment Co., a first for PFE. The first 600 of these were built at Los Angeles, the rest at Roseville. It might be queried why SP was involved in PFE construction. In fact, the cars were built in PFE's shop facilities, by PFE personnel. It was done that way because tax and other financial reporting required that the costs of new-car construction be strictly segregated from repair or rebuilding expense. SP's Equipment Co., already in existence for similar purposes on the Southern Pacific, was a bookkeeping device to accomplish this cost reporting. The Equipment Co. purchased materials, paid "rent" for the work space in the form of 12-½% overhead, and paid the workmen, then "sold" the cars to PFE. This financial arrangement was to be used for PFE car construction for another 40 years. In later years, SPE also provided a means to avoid payment of California taxes, as explained in Chapters 1 and 9.

The cars cost about $4000, a controversial fact. To get this work, PFE had bid against commercial builders, and their bid of about $3100 per car was quite competitive. However, the actual cost was much higher, and this was remembered by UP and SP management. Comments about "PFE's 1920 cost overruns" appeared in correspondence for some time, and it was 1930 before PFE was again permitted to build any cars (see Chapter 6).

At the close of 1920, PFE's car roster had reached nearly 20,000 cars. This was fully double the fleet of PFE's nearest competitor, Santa Fe's Refrigerator Dept. (so named in March, 1920), and represented more than one in every five of all American non-railroad-owned refrigerator cars at the

R-30-12. Workmen apply outside metal roofs to PFE cars in production, 1922. General American photo, Jim Lekas collection.

time. The railroad-owned refrigerator fleet at the time was less than 60,000 cars, making a total U.S. fleet of about 150,000 cars. There was a sharp financial recession in 1921, accompanied by a drop in railroad traffic, and no PFE cars were constructed. But the superstructure features listed above for the new cars built during 1920, 3000 R-30-12's and 1000 R-30-13's, were being superseded.

Design modifications. During 1920-21, a number of design modifications were adopted, and put into use when construction resumed in 1922, with the changes reflected in a modified general arrangement drawing, C-2826. One such change was the adoption of Union's "Flaxlinum" insulation in place of "Hairfelt." Because so many of these sister designs, the R-30-12 and -13, were built during the 1920's (11,900 R-30-12 cars in 1920-24, and 7654 R-30-13 cars in 1920-26, as summarized in Table 5-2), the changes are worth some discussion.

An evident exterior change was the adoption of an "outside metal roof" as an "alternate standard" (a number of the 1920 cars had already received such roofs). Alternate standards sometimes were little used, sometimes treated as *de facto* standards; this one became universal for new

construction. In the early part of the century, there were a number of proprietary metal roof systems, as may be seen in the 1906 *Car Builders' Dictionary*. These were either "inside" roofs, in which metal sheets or roofing paper weatherproofing was installed between the wood tongue-and-groove outer roof and the inner roof, or "outside" roofs, in which a single tongue-and-groove roof was covered with sheet metal.

The famous "T-section" truck, applied to some 20,000 PFE cars. Initials of PFE and the builder (ASF) are cast into the sideframe. PFE photo, CSRM.

R-30-12. Construction of cars at the General American plant. (**Above**) Wood superstructure framing with steel tension rods can be seen here; note that the roof framing, including steel carlines and hatch casings, is a sub-assembly. June 30, 1922. (**Below**) Tongue-and-groove sheathing for roof and sides is being applied. Sheet metal for outside roofing is at right. July 14, 1922. Both photos from General American, Jim Lekas collection.

R-30-13. The 1925 paint scheme is clearly shown in these views of PFE 31911. The SP medallion is on the left side, as viewed from the brake end, and the UP medallion is on the right side. Note the cast metal trust plates above the left truck on each side. PFE photos, CSRM.

R-30-13. An end view of car 19918, one of the early cars of this class. AC&F photo, courtesy ACF Industries.

PFE used several patent roof products, including the "X.L.A. Flexible" and the "Murphy Type A" (Standard Railway Equipment Co. or SRE Co. products), and the "National Flexible Outside Metal Roof" from Chicago-Cleveland Car Roofing Co. Later the "Murphy Improved" roof (SRE Co.) came into use. Although the term "Murphy roof" has sometimes been interpreted as referring to a specific design of roof, the term was a trade name of SRE Co., supplier of several kinds of metal roofs, and the company applied the name to a variety of quite different roofs. About all these various roofs had in common is that they were metal roofs in which the joints were interlocked to minimize leakage. In the PFE roofs, flat, galvanized steel sheets were applied to the roof and the joints covered by 1" x 2" batten boards which were themselves steel-wrapped. The joints around the hatch openings in these roofs were soldered during installation.

A consequence of the use of these roofs was that a painted metal roof, when wet, was much smoother and more slippery than a wood-surfaced roof, and so wood "hatch platforms" were applied around each hatch to provide a safe working surface during icing or other work. Side views of such cars sometimes conceal the roof battens of the outside metal roof, but hatch platforms are usually quite evident. PFE experienced trouble getting paint to stick to the galvanized roofs, especially around hatches where the frequent wet-dry cycle caused paint peeling and then corrosion of the metal sheets. Shop records reveal that considerable attention was paid to maintenance and replacement of hatch frames and openings in the 1920's.

R-30-13. In later years, this class was "completely reconditioned," which meant that the wood superstructure was replaced in kind, and insulation replaced. This car was so reworked in July, 1937. R.H. McFarland photo, 1939, A. Menke collection.

In October, 1923, PFE adopted as an alternate standard the Bettendorf "T-section" truck, so called because the side frame had a **T** cross-section. This truck had already been used for the 1922 batch of R-30-12's, and was specified in 1923 for all new car construction. It was also used for rebuilds in the later 1920's. Until the ARA (later AAR) standard cast-steel truck with **U**-section side frames came into use in 1927, the T-section truck, which PFE purchased from both Bettendorf and American Steel Foundries (ASF), was applied to many thousands of PFE cars, and survived in such use into the 1950's.

Under most freight cars, railroads found that the T-section sideframe was prone to fatigue failure at the inside corners near the truck bolster and near the journals. But with cars usually loaded well below the 40-ton truck capacity, PFE had good service experience with these trucks, and in the 1940's when the AAR first proposed that they be banned from interchange, asked for and received extensions for their use. In 1945, for example, PFE felt they could not replace all T-section trucks in service until 1953. Shop directions explained how to inspect, "re-normalize" (which means to anneal at 1500-1600° F., remove from the furnace to cool in air), and return the sideframes to service, if no cracks were found.

A less visible change than the new roof, but important for car performance, was PFE's 1920 adoption of friction draft gear. Almost since the introduction of knuckle couplers in the nineteenth century, draft gear had consisted of various arrangements of springs to absorb pulling and buffing forces, thus cushioning the run-out and run-in of slack in the train. However, springs merely stored the slack motion, and when the forces on the spring lessened or reversed, much of the motion was released again among the cars. Thus train forces were only temporarily absorbed.

The development of friction draft gear was intended to counter this, and absorb motion by means of friction between wedges and plates inside the draft gear. Moving the draft gear in one direction did not result in a "back force" in the opposite direction, releasable on reversal of forces; instead, reversal of motion required additional friction, again absorbing forces. Shocks and forces on the car lading were considerably reduced, as was wear and tear on car structures. In 1921 PFE also made another performance advance, adopting as standard a coupler centering device, to reduce wear on draft gear.

A new design of ice bunker bulkhead was introduced in 1925 which was all steel, replacing wood bulkheads used earlier. PFE used Equipco's product. In 1925 and 1926, PFE began to change its insulation materials. In 1925, a board form of insulation called "Insulite," ½" thick, was installed on the sub-floor, under the cork, making a total floor insulation thickness of 2-½". In 1926, a similar board material called "Celotex," ⅜" thick, was added to roofs and floors, increasing their insulation thickness but more importantly replacing a layer of shiplap siding used as a blind lining between insulation layers. This not only eliminated a construction expense, but also reduced air leaks within the insulated walls and roof. Fiber insulation was changed to "Hairinsul," a product of Johns-Manville which was essentially an improved "Hairfelt." These changes, together with other minor design improvements, meant that R-30-13 cars built in 1925 and 1926 followed a new general arrangement drawing, C-3550.

The 3300 R-30-12's ordered in 1922 comprised 3000 additions to the fleet and 300 cars considered as "replacements." The 1923 orders totaled 5030 cars, of which 30 were replacements. The 1924 construction was 3185 cars, with 3000 additions and 185 cars as replacements. For

Table 5-3
Survival of Wood-sheathed Cars with Original Numbers*

Car Numbers	Class	Number of Cars						
		New	1934	1940	1947	1950	1958	1962
500-799	BR-1	300	298	298	289	287	118	46
13220-13279	R-30-11-½	60	46	40	35	12	5	0
13280-15919	R-30-11	2640	1966	1830	1581	694	210	11
15920-18919	R-30-12	3000	2942	1866				
18920-19919	R-30-13	1000	980	631				
19920-26719	R-30-12	6800	6697	4196				
26720-28249	R-30-13	1530	1510	989	3389**	284	5	0
28250-28749	R-30-12	500	496	335				
28750-29649	R-30-13	900	888	597				
29650-31249	R-30-12	1600	1581	1106				
31250-32434	R-30-13							
32435-33434	R-30-14	5224	5165	4558	2012	131	2	0
33435-36473	R-30-13							
50001-52775	(WP cars)	2775	2726	2682	2599	916	0	0

*From freight *Equipment Registers*.

**This group had comprised 9720 cars in 1940.

1926, 5000 additions and 39 replacements were built. It will be noted that authorizations for additions were round numbers in thousands of cars, and the balance of the orders was the "replacement" cars (though they had new car numbers, not the numbers of the destroyed cars). Prices per car, which had averaged $3900 in inflated 1920, were about $3100 for the improved cars in the 1926 orders.

Also in 1926, the R-30-14 class was introduced, with a total of 1000 cars built. The R-30-14 design, though essentially an R-30-12 design, including the Bettendorf underframe and based on drawing C-3550, had a separate specification, 58-N. Among the differences with these cars was an experiment in 500 of the cars with a new insulation material, "Quilted Dry Zero" by Johns-Manville, which used the natural fiber kapok, and the first use of steel grating for the ice tank bottom, replacing the 11 steel bars used

Car interiors. (Left) Handtruck loading of oranges into R-30-11 15808 in a 1928 photo. The pre-cut bracing for the load leans against the doorway on the right. Loading methods are described in Chapter 14. Sunkist (California Fruit Growers Exchange) photo at Placentia, Orange County, Calif.; *Railfan and Railroad* collection. **(Right)** Interior of PFE 12, an R-30-2-13 whose varnished wood lining and floor racks are evident. Note also the screened opening in the fixed bulkhead. UP Railroad Museum, no. 60-622A.

since the R-30-4. Externally, however, the R-30-14 was indistinguishable from the R-30-12. The cars of classes R-30-11, -12, -13 and -14 had essentially identical dimensions, for example, the exact same cubic capacity, 1918 cubic feet. This arose in response to shippers' desire for standard car interior dimensions, permitting pre-cut bracing for loads (see photo, facing page, and Chapter 14).

Painting and lettering. The PFE standard paint scheme, changed only in minor ways since 1911, was modified on Dec. 10, 1920, to reflect the adoption of outside metal roofs. The lettering arrangement and side and end colors of the 1911 scheme were retained (see summary, pages 418, 419), but the modification specified that the roof surface would be Color #13 (black) if the roof were metal. Since outside metal roofs had just been adopted by PFE for new construction, this paint change affected only new cars. Older cars usually retained their wood roofs, which continued to be entirely painted the original boxcar red color.

Continuing in the black color were all iron parts on the car side (door hinges and latch bars, grab irons, etc.) and trucks and underframe, for black was the preferred color for metal parts. On metal-roof cars, the remaining wood areas of the roof (the ice hatch platforms and the running boards), as well as the ends, and the side and end fascia boards, continued to be boxcar red. In October, 1923, PFE adopted metal sheathing for ice hatches as an alternate standard, again for new cars, and metal-sheathed hatches, if applied, also became black at that time. Car sides continued as Color #8, yellow-orange.

PFE's overall paint scheme and lettering arrangement, with no railroad emblems or heralds on the cars, had remained largely the same since its 1906 beginnings. But all that changed in 1922. It began with lettering changes adopted on January 19, 1922, in which the road name was spelled out in 9" letters, and car numbers were 7" high. End lettering was increased to 6" high. Dimensional data on the right half of the car side were also rearranged in 1922 and reduced to 2" height. Car end hardware was now red.

In February, UP President Gray and SP President Sproule agreed, on the basis of an SP proposal (SP drawing SF-3732, Jan. 5, 1922), "to recommend, on account of the advantage in advertising, that a Union Pacific shield should be placed on one side, and Southern Pacific medallion on the other side of new PFE cars." This new paint scheme, with the SP herald applied toward the B or brake end and the red-white-blue UP shield with the diagonal "Overland" slogan on the other, became official on March 1, 1922. Shop records show that the new paint scheme began to be applied in April, 1922. By 1925, PFE had applied railroad emblems to over 15,000 of the 19,900 cars which did not originally have them, and no emblem-less cars

remained in service as of the end of the year 1928.

In 1925, dimensional data were changed again, this time reducing the amount of information (in accord with an ARA recommendation). At the same time, the lettering was also changed on the left side of the car, from the 1922 arrangement which was much like that of 1911, to a more modern form with 9" PFE initials, 7" road name, and 5" car number. Black stripes, 1" wide, were added above and below the initials and car number. The PFE car class was shown to the right of the door in 4" letters.

The medallions at the right end of the car side continued as in 1922, with the UP herald being 3' 2-½" wide, that of the SP 3' 9". From 1922 until 1936, the UP emblem contained the words "UNION PACIFIC SYSTEM" in the blue field at the top, but the word "SYSTEM" was discontinued after Jan. 1, 1936, when UP absorbed its various subsidiaries. Also, the 6" end lettering used during the 1920's was reduced to 3" for new cars in 1928, although older cars and rebuilds sometimes kept the larger lettering, throughout the 1930's and into the period after World War II. See page 418, Appendix, for additional information.

It should be recognized that the PFE shops painted a great many cars during the 1920's, not only when rebuilding took place but whenever even minor repairs were done. For the years 1920-29, an average of 4736 cars, exclusive of rebuilds, was painted per year; for 1925-29, the average was near 6000 cars per year. These numbers were in accord with PFE's internal recommendations that cars should be repainted every 5 to 7 years. Both from these numbers and from the separate statistics on addition of emblems, for example, it is certain that by 1929, no pre-1922 paint schemes were still extant.

The 1922 paint scheme, which included railroad emblems or medallions, caused many thousands of older cars to be repainted. Here a workman stencils the SP medallion at Los Angeles in 1922. PFE photo, CSRM.

During the same period, cars were very frequently washed. From March, 1923, when car washing statistics first appear in the monthly PFE shop record (PFE Forms 865), until the end of December, 1929, an average of more than 12,000 cars was washed per year, over one-third of the average car fleet in those years. The most notable year was 1929, in which fully 21,304 cars were washed, when the fleet size was about 40,000 cars. It was true that refrigerator cars became very dirty in service, but it was also true that the average PFE car in the 1920's was washed one to three times between repaintings.

A point to note is that the cars with capacity limited by the underframe, rather than by the trucks, had capacity data stenciled differently. For the 5" x 9" journals, for example, the sum of light weight and load limit would normally be 136,000 pounds (see Table 5-1). The R-30's, though, had light weights of around 54,000 pounds. The corresponding load limit, 82,000 pounds, would have exceeded the underframe capacity. Thus the car's actual load limit, such as 70,000 pounds, had a star stenciled next to it, to indicate a limit not controlled by truck journals. Starred load limits must not be changed when cars receive new light weights upon re-weighing.

Service history. There were 20,554 cars built in classes R-30-12, -13, and -14. As noted, the 554 "odd" cars in this total reflect PFE's intent to "physically replace" destroyed (wrecked or dismantled) cars. During the 1930's and 1940's, most of the R-30-12's and -13's were rebuilt to other classes, as discussed in later chapters, and then received new class designations as well as new car numbers. Some 3350 cars of R-30-12 which had not yet been rebuilt were scrapped under their own numbers during 1947-49. Essentially none of the R-30-13's survived under their own numbers to be scrapped; about 550 of the 7654 cars of the class were

destroyed (wrecked) while bearing their original numbers, and all the rest were rebuilt. The R-30-14's had the same Bettendorf underframe as the -12's, and nearly all were scrapped in 1948-51, still with their original numbers. See Table 5-3 for survival information on all these classes.

Express Refrigerators

As mentioned in the previous chapter, PFE had in its early years used regular freight refrigerator cars, equipped for passenger service, to serve as express refrigerators. In 1923, the first specially-built express reefers were constructed, and all the R-30's returned to freight service.

There were 300 of these new cars, numbered 500-799, and the design was shown in drawing CB-20690, dated December, 1922. The first 200 were built by AC&F, the balance by General American, all during 1923-24. (Incidentally, the remaining R-30-2's with original numbers in the 500-799 range were given lower or higher numbers over the next few years, taking the numbers of destroyed cars elsewhere in the 1-6600 series, to prevent confusion.)

Design characteristics. The new express cars were of typical round-roof design, exactly 50 feet over end sills, and had flush ice hatches (no platforms) when built. They were equipped with 8-ft. wheelbase Commonwealth trucks, and a fairly deep center sill. Typical passenger service buffers were used on the ends. When built, they were classified as R-E-1 (Refrigerator-Express). They were PFE's most expensive cars up to this time, $6650 each.

The cars were leased and operated at first by American Railway Express, the 1918 successor to the Adams, American, Southern, and Wells Fargo express companies. In 1929, 86 railroads combined to purchase the assets of American, and reorganized it to form the Railway Express

Pacific Fruit Express Co., Oct. 3, 1923
A.C.& F. Co., Lot #9547, Neg. 30062-B-2

Express. This builder's photo shows both the original roof configuration, without ice hatch platforms, and also the original lettering, on car X-534. Note lack of end lettering. AC&F photo, dated Oct. 3, 1923, from the Jeff Winslow collection.

Express. At Stockton, Calif., on Sept. 9, 1951, PFE 726 hasn't been rebuilt. Ice hatch platforms, end fascia, curved end lettering, and drain chutes are clearly visible. W.C. Whittaker photo.

Agency. At this time, PFE's express car lease was reassigned to REA; the ARE lettering on the car sides was replaced by REA's, and the "X" dropped from the car number. Two years later, in November, 1931, the lease was terminated, the cars were returned to PFE, and the express company name was removed from car sides, though REA continued to direct the operation of the cars through its express pool.

The REA car direction meant that shippers desiring an express refrigerator called REA, not PFE, to have one spotted on their siding. PFE, however, maintained and iced the cars, and collected mileage charges. PFE's cars, like the express cars of a number of other owners, were voluntarily placed in a pool for operation by Railway Express, and SP, UP, or PFE had to obtain REA's approval to withdraw cars, e.g. for milk shipments. Table 5-4 lists the REA pool for 1953, to show how this supply of express cars was provided.

An interesting detail about the 50-ft. cars is that the original design shown in the earliest version of drawing CB-20690 did not have the roof shape which was eventually built. Instead, the first design had roof ends which matched those of a "Harriman" arched coach roof, so that the roof had a curved end shape when seen from the side. However, no cars were ever built this way. A conventional cylindrical arch roof was used instead (see photo, above).

Service history. In their original condition, without ice hatch platforms, the cars were usually iced at passenger stations (the earliest air-conditioned passenger cars, and some dining cars, were also supplied with ice through roof hatches). As the practice grew more common of operating solid blocks of express cars, the preferred icing arrangement was to use regular icing platforms, as was done with

freight refrigerators. Accordingly, all the cars were equipped with ice hatch platforms during the early 1930's, to make icing operations safer. At the same time, side and end grab iron arrangements were changed to conform to freight car practice. This meant that grab iron rows were replaced with ladders, end grab irons were relocated, and the Miner lever hand brakes were moved from low on the car end, to the normal freight location near the top of the end. These and other changes are depicted in drawing CB-21804, dated August, 1930.

These cars were built with all-wood superstructure framing. However, because they had buffers to restrict slack

Table 5-4
Express Car Pool Operated by Railway Express, 1953

Car Owner	Reporting Marks	No. Cars
ACL	ACL	49
ATSF	ATSF	73
CWRD†	KCS	25
GN	GN	203
NC&StL	NC&StL	10
PFE	PFE*	149
PRR	PRR**	358
SAL	SAL	18
REA	REX	595
Gen. American	REX	750
CWRD†	REX	274
	Total	2504

*Prior to rebuilding 83 50-ft. cars and adding 50 freight refrigerators to pool
**Includes 76 bad-order cars, to be repaired
†Central Western Refrigerator Despatch (Chicago Freight Car Leasing), converted troop sleepers

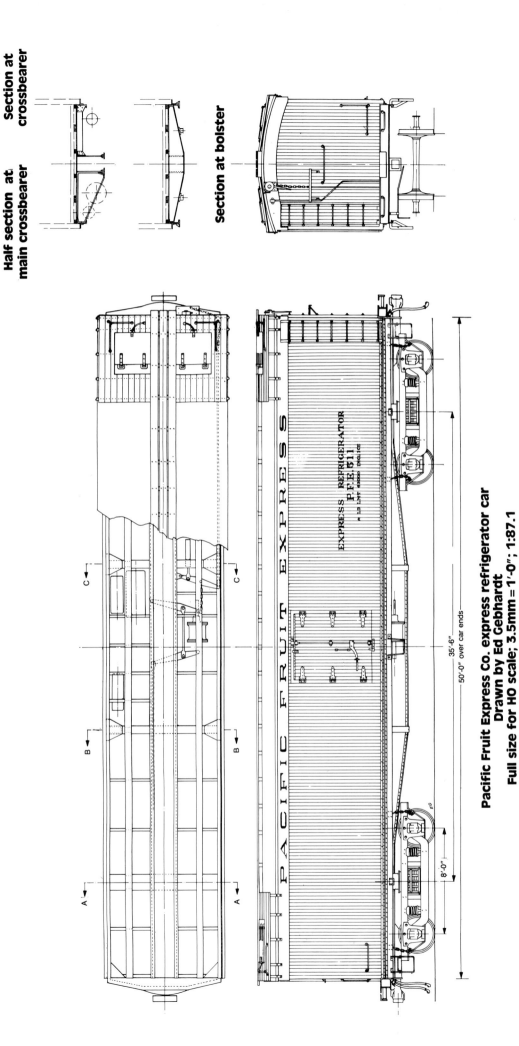

Section at crossbearer

Half section at main crossbearer

Section at bolster

PACIFIC FRUIT EXPRESS

EXPRESS REFRIGERATOR
P.F.E. 511
A LD LMT 65000 ENGLICE

35'-6"

50'-0" over car ends

8'-0"

Pacific Fruit Express Co. express refrigerator car
Drawn by Ed Gebhardt
Full size for HO scale; 3.5mm = 1'-0"; 1:87.1

BR-1 (express). This drawing shows the express cars as they appeared after the early 1930's modifications, with ice hatch platforms, safety appliances like those of freight cars, and PFE lettering with no express agency lettering. This general appearance continued until the 1950's. HO scale drawing by Ed Gebhardt, reprinted from *Railroad Model Craftsman* with permission.

Express. (Left) Details of the express car end with new ice hatch platforms and post-1930 safety appliance changes, when the Miner lever hand brake was still in use. PFE photo, CSRM. **(Right)** Rebuilding with steel frames at Nampa in 1954. These are welded frames, as was standard after 1950 (see Chapter 7). Loyd Furnace photo for *Idaho State Journal*, Milton G. Sorensen collection.

action, were primarily operated in passenger trains which had much less slack motion anyway, and were rarely loaded anywhere near capacity, it was the early 1940's before these cars required a general overhaul. About 100 of the express cars with the most severe problems were overhauled at the Los Angeles shop during 1942-46. At about this time, the cars were reclassified BR-1. The most visible consequence of this and later overhauls was the replacement of the Miner lever hand brake with power brake wheels like those being applied to freight refrigerators at that time, although complete new interiors and insulation were also applied. New AAR type E couplers were installed on any cars still having the original "Sharon" couplers. In 1949-50, an additional 75 cars were overhauled at Nampa, leaving over 100 cars still in need of work.

For 1950, the *Equipment Register* shows 287 of the original 1923 50-ft. cars still on the roster, though only about half were considered by PFE to be in active service. By that time, many cars were in need of heavy repairs and were of obsolete design. PFE's Car Department evaluated the entire fleet, and recommended that those in worst shape be dismantled; others were chosen for program heavy repairs (see Chapter 11). In 1952, 55 cars (37 of which had been overhauled in 1942-46) received program heavy repairs at Nampa, and over 50 more were scrapped. But in 1952, a controversy about inadequate REA supply of express cars arose with shippers, as also discussed in Chapter 8. Part of PFE's response was to convert 50 of the standard 40-foot R-40-10's for passenger service in 1953, reclassifying them as BR-40-10 (see Chapter 8). When supply problems continued in the 1953 season, however, plans were made to modernize some of the 50-foot cars.

In 1954, 83 of the 50-foot cars were rebuilt at Nampa. Table 5-5 lists numbers of the rebuilt cars. In this rebuilding, the cars were stripped down to the underframe and a new superstructure built, including steel framing. Also, the insulation thickness was increased, Preco electric fans were applied (no fan shaft), and steel channel side sills were added. (More details on car fans may be found in Chapters 7 and 8.) Any cars still having the Miner lever hand brake (by now an AAR "non-approved" brake) received power brake wheels. The most visible change was that the new side fascia boards on most of the cars were very narrow. The original fascias were 50-ft. lengths of 10"-wide clear redwood, a material not available at any price in 1954. When possible, the removed redwood was salvaged for tool boxes and other use in the shops. The new fascia material was fir.

This rebuilding, combined with additional scrapping, left the 50-ft. express fleet comprising just 138 cars in 1955. In the late 1950's, the unrebuilt cars reached the end of their lives and began to be scrapped, soon followed by the rebuilds. By mid-1962, the express fleet was down to 46 cars, and in December, 1963, only 18 remained. In one sense, these were very long-lived refrigerators, some surviving for 40 years in service.

Table 5-5
Express Refrigerators Rebuilt in 1954

500	549	589	631	666	700	737	754
503	555	592	632	670	714	740	757
506	558	594	640	672	716	742	761
510	560	596	641	678	718	745	764
511	561	598	644	681	721	746	771
528	563	601	647	683	726	747	780
532	568	616	648	685	731	748	784
534	569	620	658	686	732	750	796
539	579	621	664	696	733	751	798
545	586	624	665	699	734	752	799
548	587	626					

Express. An example of the rebuilt express cars, with narrow fascia. Note the fan symbol. F.C. Smith photo at PFE's Los Angeles shop at Taylor Yard, on Feb. 12, 1955. Stan Kistler collection.

In addition to their traditional place among passenger head-end consists, these express cars were operated in solid trains, using rider coaches instead of cabooses to permit higher speeds. Whenever a new crop began to be harvested, the first shipments brought (and still bring) a high price. Thus the first week or two for any crop might see that harvest moving in express reefers, in addition to crops with all-season priority, such as Idaho cherries, Oregon salmon, and California strawberries. These cars were also used for milk shipments along the west coast, and for various other cargos. For example, flowers were shipped in them to midwestern cities twice a week on the Golden State route, which was operated jointly by SP and Rock Island.

Painting and lettering. When new, the express cars were painted a dark brownish-green. This color, designated Color #1 in CS Standard 22 for painting, and named "Dark Olive," was used by both UP and SP for heavyweight passenger equipment until the 1950's, and was definitely different than Pullman green. Lettering was gold leaf, with the car number preceded by an "X." The underbody and roof were black, as were side hardware and the metal-sheathed body corners. Trucks were the same color as the car body, a dark olive which in the form of truck enamel was Color #2. When delivered, the cars had no end lettering, but reporting marks and car numbers were added to the ends (curved along the fascia) in the 1920's.

It appears from shop records (PFE Forms 865) that about half of these cars had had the ARE side lettering replaced by REA lettering by the time the lease was terminated in 1931. Thereafter, the painting diagram shows that no express company designation appeared on the cars, and car numbers no longer included an "X." In the early 1930's, when the *Daylight* train was briefly pearl gray in color, some of these cars were painted the same color, with the roof, side hardware, fascia and corner posts black. But like the heavyweight *Daylight* cars, these were soon repainted Dark Olive when the gray proved too subject to road dirt.

The 83 rebuilt cars of 1954, and gradually many of the other 50-foot cars, received a new paint scheme in which the lettering, Dulux Gold in color, was arranged more like that on freight refrigerators, and a fan symbol was painted on the car side. The narrow fascia board no longer carried the company name. The car side and end color remained Dark Olive, though trucks were black. Although many SP and UP head-end cars, including three of SP's express box cars, received the standard 1950's passenger two-tone gray paint used by both railroads, this scheme was never applied to the express refrigerators.

Western Pacific cars

In addition to the tens of thousands of cars owned by PFE in the 1920's, there was also a group of less than three thousand cars which had PFE reporting marks but which PFE did not own. These cars were owned by and bore the medallion of the Western Pacific Railroad, which in turn leased the cars to PFE. The background of this lease is described in Chapter 1. It is interesting to backtrack slightly in time for a moment and consider the details of this Western Pacific relationship. WP's formation of a subsidiary "Western Refrigerator Line" on Jan. 1, 1923, was accompanied by preparation of a drawing for the lettering of the expected WRL cars. At the same time, however, PFE was strenuously opposing the WP being allowed to "advertise" its own refrigerator organization. Drafts of the agreement between PFE and WP had, by March, 1923, a provision that the cars would be lettered just as other PFE cars, except that the medallion or herald of the WP could be placed on the cars.

The final agreement had not been signed, however, when AC&F began production of the cars for WRL. Since the cars were built expressly to be operated as part of the PFE fleet, the WP had the full cooperation of PFE in building these cars, mostly R-30-13 duplicates. Exactly 146 of the cars were built and painted for WRL, then sent west to Roseville to be accepted by PFE. In light of the pending agreement, PFE repainted them into PFE livery before they were put into service. (This is shown by agreement between the builder's records and the Roseville shop records: the number of cars built at AC&F in each month agreed exactly with the number of WP cars repainted at Roseville, month by month!) Thus although an interesting paint scheme had been devised by WP, cars made just one empty trip from Missouri to Roseville in that scheme. Starting with car 50147, all subsequent cars were lettered for PFE at the factory.

The agreement between PFE and WP specified that WP would provide as many cars as its proportional share of the traffic. The initial order for cars in 1923 was for 2000 cars, followed by 775 more in 1924, reflecting an adjustment in the car calculation. PFE set aside the 50001-52775 series for these cars, and they were maintained (and reconditioned or rebuilt) by PFE just like the other cars.

The cars were built with all-wood bodies using PFE's blueprints for the R-30-13 design, which is to say PFE's superstructure drawing C-2826 and the riveted underframe drawing C-2677. Some individual car record cards (PFE Form 120) denote WP cars as "R-30-12," suggesting that some fraction, perhaps as many as 200 cars, had the Bettendorf underframe of the -12 design. The remainder, a large majority of the total WP car ownership, had built-up underframes, that is, were R-30-13 duplicates.

One of the few features of the WP cars which did not duplicate PFE practice was in the choice of a proprietary outside metal roof. WP specified the Hutchins roof on the first order for 2000 cars, a roof used on some WP box cars. Although generally similar in design and appearance to other metal roofs of the period, a spotting feature for this roof is that it had 12 narrow, formed-metal battens between hatch platforms instead of the 10 flat battens characteristic of SRE Co. or Chicago-Cleveland metal roofs. The second, 775-car WP order specified SRE Co. roofs, in conformity to PFE's preferences.

In one of the last orders for PFE's R-30-13's, Pullman built four replacement WP cars, to replace cars destroyed in service (numbers 50329, 50349, 50984 and 52017), although all the other WP cars were AC&F products. Thereafter, it was decided that destroyed cars need not be replaced.

Painting and lettering. The paint scheme of the WP cars was essentially identical to that of all PFE cars. The most visible exception was the railroad medallion. They were painted with square WP "Feather" medallions in place of SP or UP heralds, though metal emblems (see next chapter) appear never to have been used on the WP cars. They also displayed no class numbers, and were always simply listed in PFE rosters as "WP cars."

The color of the WP cars was always the same as other PFE cars of the time, so after being painted PFE's yellow-orange when new, the WP cars became light orange in 1929 when the other cars were changed (discussed in next chapter). Also in 1929, WP medallions were made smaller, 45" square, to be consistent with the UP and SP ones.

WP Cars. This historic photo shows the first of the WP cars, renumbered within weeks to PFE 50001 at Roseville after a trip across the U.S. in the yellow and black WRL paint scheme. AC&F photo, courtesy ACF Industries and Ed Hawkins.

WP Cars. (Above) A portrait of PFE 50601, showing the PFE paint scheme applied after the WRL painting was discontinued. (Below) An end view of 50601. Both AC&F photos, May 23, 1923, Al Westerfield collection.

These WP emblems were entirely black and white, without the red feathers as were used on the emblems applied to WP steam locomotive tenders.

After 1938, the WP cars began to be reconditioned, at the time that the PFE's other R-30-13 cars were rebuilt. Although the differences between reconditioning and rebuilding are discussed in a subsequent chapter, it may be noted here that the WP cars received new all-wood superstructures and had their original outside metal roofs reinstalled if in acceptable condition. By this time, PFE considered the all-wood design obsolete, and was replacing the framing in its own superstructures with steel. WP, however, declined to bear that expense. The reconditioned cars were characterized by a change in interior dimensions, just like PFE's other rebuilt cars, with a new cubic capacity of 1988 cubic feet. Scrapping became heavy in 1947, and by 1950 only 114 of the un-reconditioned R-30-13 duplicates remained, out of a total of 916 WP cars still in service. Of those 916, many were stored unserviceable. This remainder of the WP fleet was finally rebuilt in 1953-54, as described in Chapter 7.

Throughout their life, the WP cars carried PFE reporting marks, were listed under PFE in freight *Equipment Registers*, and were under PFE's operating direction. This meant that PFE directed the cars to shippers (WP cars were freely mixed in the PFE fleet, and were neither preferentially returned to WP rails, nor segregated for WP's shippers). PFE also collected mileage payments. Maintenance

WP Cars. After reconditioning at Los Angeles in April, 1939, PFE 52273 looked like this at SP's Bayshore Yard, near San Francisco, in the summer of 1939. Note that the car at right is PFE 15919, the last member of the R-30-11 class. R.H. McFarland photo, Arnold Menke collection.

of the cars was PFE's responsibility, as was engineering and construction, in PFE shops, when the cars were rebuilt (at owner WP's expense). Finally, when the cars became surplus in the 1950's, they were formally "returned to WP for disposal," but physical dismantling was largely done by PFE at Roseville, without the cars visiting WP rails one last time. WP did retain a few of the cars for company ice service, as shown in Chapter 7.

By 1927, when construction of new R-30 cars finally ceased, the PFE fleet exceeded 38,000 cars. As Table 5-2 shows, car orders for this great fleet growth were divided among a number of builders. Notice that the two largest classes together, R-30-12 and -13, comprise over 19,000 cars, which exceeds the size of any other owner's *total* car fleet at the time. Not only were there all these new cars, but most older cars had been upgraded. The entire PFE fleet, far larger in total than that of any other operator of refrigerator cars (Santa Fe rostered less than 19,000 cars in 1930; American Refrigerator Transit owned about 12,500 cars), was, for its day, modern and well maintained. Yet PFE was ready for further modernization, aimed at greater car capacity, better insulation, and further upgrading of older cars. Those advances are the subject of Chapter 6.

WP Cars. PFE 52473 is from the second WP batch. The only external difference is the Standard Railway Equipment Co. roof on this batch, compared to the Hutchins roofs on the first batch (see facing page). AC&F photo, dated May, 1924, courtesy ACF Industries, provided by Ed Hawkins.

This view of an R-30-13 car receiving a steel superstructure frame illustrates a key part of PFE rebuilding practice which began in 1928: the steel superframe. The car shown, however, is being reconditioned with the welded frame which was not used until 1947. Stacked at left are pre-cut angle iron pieces ready for installation. Cars were being moved to the left in this view as rework continued. Photo at Los Angeles Shop by Richard Steinheimer, December, 1950.

6

NEW DIRECTIONS

R-50-1. A sterling example of the work PFE's higher-capacity cars were designed to do. Wine barrels are being unloaded at San Francisco in this 1938 photo. The SP medallion is vitreous enameled steel sheet, and car 100323, painted in Los Angeles in April, 1934, had last been weighed at Fresno in February, 1938. W.C. Whittaker photo.

From its inception in 1906, PFE had been a forward-looking organization in freight car design, although the preceding chapters make it clear that most of the successive car designs represented relatively small advances over their predecessors. This kind of evolutionary change is a dependable engineering philosophy, quite appropriate for an organization like PFE, which ordered cars in the thousands. But in 1927, this approach began to change. Despite having much the largest, and arguably the most modern fleet of refrigerator cars in North America, PFE initiated work on more innovative car designs. In this chapter, the design of higher-capacity refrigerator cars is presented.

The new designs which resulted were of several kinds. One kind was to enlarge the capacity of the cars in pounds, with a new 40-ton standard car to replace the 30-ton standard in use. The second was to make cars with larger volume capacity (as well as larger pound capacity), in the form of 50-ton cars which were longer. The third was to modernize the superstructure design with steel instead of

wood framing, and thereby eliminate the primary location of wear of refrigerator cars in service. All three represent a turning point in PFE technology, in the character of the car fleet, and also in the programs of rebuilding. Before these new trends had gone very far, the Depression intervened, and additional changes (most notably an increase in car rebuilding, as opposed to new car purchase) took place after 1936. The post-1936 period of rebuilding is described in the subsequent chapter.

Class R-40-1

Although a full carload of most kinds of produce weighed less than the nominal 35-ton capacity of the newer R-30 cars (when loaded as full as permitted for minimum air circulation around the load), some lading, such as citrus or potatoes, could reach the car capacity. Moreover, as 40-ton trucks were largely standard under PFE cars, a 40-ton underframe to match the trucks seemed appropriate. The

first design which was prepared was the R-40-1, whose general arrangement drawing, C-4200, is dated 1926. Its specification, no. 65, was the first not to form part of the long series of CS 58 sub-specifications of R-30 cars dating back to 1905, each of which had a letter denoting the sub-specification, such as CS 58-K.

There are several surprises in the R-40-1 design. A 5-ft. door opening was used, in contrast to the 4-ft. door opening used by PFE on all other car classes from 1906 to 1950. What is most interesting about this 5-ft. door is that it was a standard of the Santa Fe's SFRD (which after 1920 stood for Santa Fe Refrigerator Department), but used by almost no other refrigerator car operator. The end appearance adds to the intrigue, as it is a near-duplicate of SFRD's Rr-5 (and successors through Rr-9 and Rr-11) class cars. The Rr-5 was built in 1927, with the same **W** corner post and recessed upper end as the R-40-1. Was PFE trying out a few Santa Fe design features? were SFRD drawings perhaps borrowed?

The actual explanation is that the design was PFE's own experiment. The PFE designers were interested (as was SFRD) in the 1924 ARA box car design, which had a very similar end arrangement, as a possible basis for a more modern refrigerator car. The R-40-1 design used the ARA standard 40-ton steel underframe, and also the ARA-design steel superstructure framing, both unique usages in PFE annals. It was also the first PFE class to use the newly-adopted ARA 40-ton truck sideframe design. The first PFE versions of this truck were produced by Columbia Steel.

UP's President Carl Gray, pleased with the performance of steel-framed box car superstructures, warmly endorsed PFE's proposal of a trial for this approach. It was estimated to add only $300 to the roughly $3000 price of an R-30-13 car. The trial, then, was the reason for the design, not borrowed ideas from SFRD. Moreover, PFE's R-40-1's

R-40-1. The first and second members of this 89-car class are shown here, in broadside and end views. PFE photos: side view, S. Peery collection; end view, CSRM.

were being built by PC&F at almost the exact same time that SFRD's first cars of this design, the Rr-5, were being built by Pullman and AC&F. The ARA and AAR Car Committees, incidentally, never settled on a *standard* design for refrigerator cars, though in 1940 they were to issue a list of *recommended* features in such cars.

Just 89 R-40-1's were built by PC&F during 1927, another of PFE's "replacement car" orders, rather than a fleet addition. Few of the R-40-1 design details were

Table 6-1
Numbers and Classes of Wood-Sheathed, New Cars After 1926

Car Numbers	No. Cars	Class	Built	Builder	Capacity cu. ft.	Capacity pounds	Drawing
36474-36562	89	R-40-1	1927	PC&F	1918	78,200	C-4200
36563-37562	1000	R-40-2	1928	Pullman	1918	80,000	C-4470
37563-38562	1000	R-40-2	1928	PC&F	1918	80,000	C-4470
38563-39062	500	R-40-4	1930	PFE	1918	78,500	C-5000
100001-100400	400	R-50-1	1930	PC&F	2349	101,000	C-4890
200001-200100	100	R-70-2	1932	PFE	2612	122,000	C-5450

repeated in subsequent PFE cars; instead, PFE went on to design its own 40-ton underframe and steel superstructure framing. Thus the R-40-1 design, though an interesting experiment, was for PFE a dead end. The R-40-1's survived with original numbers until they began to be scrapped during 1948-54.

Classes R-40-2, R-40-3

In 1928, design was completed of two possible successors to the R-40-1 class. The two designs were given the designations R-40-2 and R-40-3. Both designs had the superstructure of the "improved" R-30-13, shown in drawing C-3550, with wood superstructure framing. However, the two designs had different underframes. The R-40-2, with general arrangement drawing C-4470 and specification no. 66, introduced a new underframe, built up like the earlier R-30-13 underframe, but with larger dimensions in the center sill and bolsters, and with enlarged attachment arrangements to the center sill for both cross-bearers and draft gear. The R-40-3 had a Bettendorf-like underframe, with a single center sill fabricated from an I-beam. As events proved, the -2 design was chosen for construction, and PFE never built any of the Bettendorf-like 40-ton frames. The R-40-2 underframe design is also interesting in that it not only offered greater capacity than the 30-ton frames, but was lighter in weight than either the Bettendorf or built-up 30-ton designs. This clearly represents better design through improved understanding of underframe performance. It also resulted in a lower price than the R-30-13's, to $2820 per car.

The exchange of correspondence in late 1927 to identify the number of cars to be built was similar to what had occurred throughout the 1920's. The months of August, September and October were PFE's peak carloading period, and during this time, 15,000 to 25,000 foreign-line cars were loaded each year (out of a total of 90,000 to 115,000 cars loaded in those months). This provided a

R-40-2. A string of freshly painted, yellow-orange R-40-2's outside Pullman's plant in 1928. The superstructure is the same as that used for the R-30-14. Pullman collection, Smithsonian Institution.

"cushion" against market fluctuations, in that PFE's own cars were 100% utilized, but shippers were vociferous in their preference for PFE equipment. In addition, PFE worried about future years in which foreign cars might be less available due to bumper crops in their home areas. In 1928, the decision was made to add 2000 cars to the fleet to help protect traffic.

This R-40-2 class is noteworthy in that the two lots of cars built in 1928, see Table 6-1, happen to have straddled a significant change in brake gear. The first 1000 cars, built by Pullman, had the new power brake wheels, in which a horizontal brake wheel shaft was attached to a gearbox to provide mechanical advantage in setting the hand brakes. The second 1000 cars, built at PC&F, were PFE's last new cars with the vertical brake wheel shafts which had been standard on PFE cars since 1906 (and indeed on nearly all other freight cars in North America prior to 1928). But PFE did not suddenly adopt the power brake wheel. As with many innovations, PFE had already tested this idea thoroughly, having first applied earlier versions of power brake wheels to five of its cars in 1923. The test equipment was serviced and inspected regularly, and found to perform well.

The lettering scheme of these cars continued to be what it had been in the latter days of R-30-13 construction, as described in the previous chapter, the 1925 arrangement of lettering and railroad emblems. Sides were a yellow-orange, with boxcar red ends, ice hatch platforms, and running boards, and black metal roofs, underframes, and side hardware. The railroad emblems were stenciled on the car side with paint. But in 1928, the railroad medallions or heralds began to be manufactured as pieces of sheet steel,

R-40-2. This HO scale drawing shows details of the R-40-2 cars, though the side view incorrectly locates brake cylinder and levers. Drawings by Julian Cavalier and Robert Hundman, courtesy *Mainline Modeler* and *Railroad Model Craftsman*.

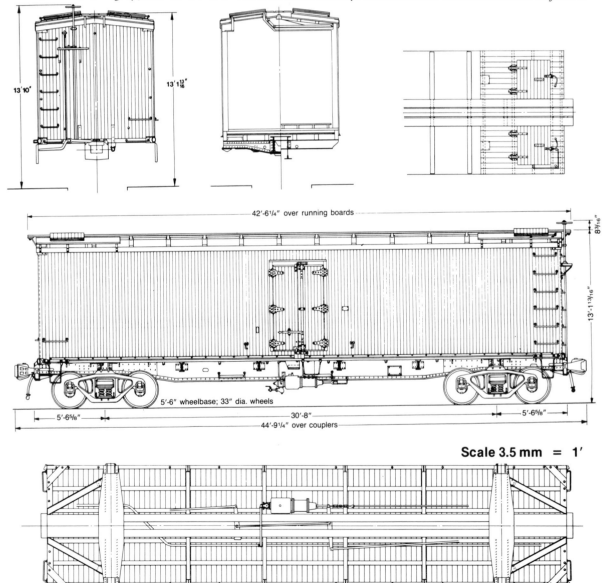

R-40-2. (Above) One of the PC&F cars ("B" end is at left). PC&F photo, Steve Peery collection. (Below, left) A shipment of 40-ton underframes about to leave PC&F's plant for Roseville. Note the wide bolster cover plate in contrast to the 30-ton underframe shown in the previous chapter. (Right) Another PC&F shipment, this time on a flat car. Two photos, PC&F, courtesy R. Hundman.

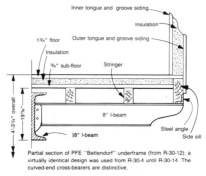

decorated with vitreous (porcelain) enamel. These enameled metal medallions were then screwed to the wood car sides. The R-40-2 cars were apparently the first to receive these medallions. In about 1937, however, the metal medallions began to be removed, and stenciled paint on the car side was re-instituted. The heavy metal sheets had a distressing tendency to fall off in transit, posing a real hazard to persons or objects along the right-of-way.

By the end of the 1930's car records show that most cars had had the metal heralds replaced, often at a time which did not coincide with other shop work. This emphasizes that removal was not merely cosmetic but had safety implications. A few of the enameled metal heralds survive today as treasured finds for the knowledgeable collector.

Rebuilding. As mentioned in the previous chapters, PFE

had been reconstructing its older cars since at least as early as 1914, in order to return deteriorated cars to service. This had generally meant a re-use of the old underframe (except for the 2500 new frames applied to R-30-2's), and a new superstructure which was essentially like that being applied to the new cars of the day. But by 1928, a more extensive rebuilding program began. In this program, a new, higher capacity underframe would be applied, together with the customary new superstructure, thus making the car virtually a "new" car (some items of car hardware might be re-used), except that cars which originally had board roofs usually retained them. In recognition of the considerable modernization, a new car class and a new car number were assigned when cars were rebuilt in this program.

This program to both rebuild and increase capacity of cars began in 1928, with most work done during 1929-30.

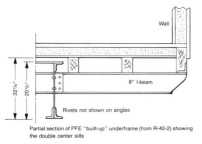

Cross-sections of Bettendorf 30-ton (**Left**) and the railroad-design 40-ton underframe (**Right**), illustrating the double center sills of the latter. From a drawing by A.W. Thompson, courtesy of *Railroad Model Craftsman* magazine.

R-40-2. An R-40-2 rebuilt from PFE 8752, PFE 70102 has retained its original board roof, which in turn means that it still has no ice hatch platforms. D.L. Joslyn photo, Sacramento, 16 July 1936, G.L. Dunscomb collection.

R-40-2. End view of rebuild 70067 at Roseville in 1944. Note metal medallion and metal roof. PFE photo, CSRM.

There were 1443 cars from the R-30-2 class rebuilt and re-classified to R-40-2. As described in Chapter 4, these were R-30-2 cars which had not received new, 30-ton built-up underframes in 1925-28. They were renumbered into the 70,000 series, in which they were intermixed with R-40-4 rebuilds (see below). All these cars received the same built-up 40-ton underframe and, if the original board roof was in good condition, it was retained. Otherwise, a new, outside metal roof was installed. As just mentioned, there also were 2000 *new* R-40-2 cars built in 1928. In this case, then, unlike later practice, these rebuilt cars were given the same classification as a group of new cars.

Because the R-40-2 cars had wood superstructure framing, they needed to be rebuilt within 10 years. Many were reconditioned (including steel superstructure frames) in 1938-41, or were reconditioned after World War II, as described in the next chapter. By 1950, all cars with the original (unrebuilt) numbers had been scrapped. In some cases, the R-40-2 underframes were salvaged for re-use in rebuilding.

Class R-40-4

An important change in PFE car design was introduced with the R-40-4: steel framing for the car superstructure became standard, following the experiment with the R-40-1 class. Steel-framed refrigerator cars were not a new idea, with the Pennsylvania Railroad's R7 cars having been built in 1913; but those cars, which essentially were a refrigerator version of PRR's X23 box car, had the framing on the car *exterior*. The conventional view among refrigerator car operators in the 1920's was that metal framing would lead to unacceptable heat conduction and warming within the superstructure, so no cars with internal steel frames had been built (other than a few experiments).

Improved insulation techniques, particularly the use of board insulation and of continuous insulation blankets which extended around the car interior from door post to door post, made it possible to overcome the heat conduction problem and proceed with steel-framed cars. PFE completed the R-40-4 superstructure design, including

R-40-4. Brand-new PFE 38995. Note the metal medallion and the ladders replacing the grab iron rows typical of PFE cars since 1906. PFE photo, CSRM.

R-40-4. The left side of one of the new cars at Roseville. PFE photo, CSRM.

steel framing different than the R-40-1, and addition of another course of board form insulation to bring wall insulation to 2-¼" thickness, with drawing C-5000 on Feb. 25, 1930. The specification was no. 68. This was also PFE's first new car class, except for the R-40-1 experiments, to have side and end ladders instead of grab iron rows (a change recommended by the ARA at that time).

In late 1929, a request for 1500 new cars had been prepared by PFE, and it was approved by UP. As had been happening for ten years, UP was willing to approve a bigger car order than SP; in 1922, for example, a request for 5000 cars was trimmed to 3000. This time again, SP was opposed to so large an order, and the AFE which had been issued for 1500 cars on Feb. 1, 1930, had to be modified for just 500 cars. With the Depression beginning, this was, in hindsight, prudent, but none of the correspondence about this order gives any hint that hard economic times were foreseen.

The design also included an additional waterproof asphalt floor covering, which was applied over the floor and three inches up the car sidewall. This was added because of increasing use of "top ice" with vegetable shipments, in which either packages of ice were placed atop the load or shaved ice was blown onto the load. Either way, considerable meltwater resulted inside the car, and the new floor design was intended to cope with this. When the water -

Table 6-2
Numbers and Classes of Rebuilt Cars (1928-1936)

Car Numbers	Number of Cars*	Class**	Rebuilding Dates	Capacity cu. ft.	pounds	Drawing
13220-15919 ⎤ 19920-22519 ⎦	619	R-30-4	1930-31	1918	66,000	C-5000
19920-28749	6	R-30-8	1931-34	1918	66,000	C-5300
18920-36473	4	R-30-8	1931-35	1918	70,000	C-5300
70001-71272	1272	R-40-2	1928-30	1918	80,000	C-4470
71273-71300	28	R-40-4	1928-30	1918	77,800	C-5000
71301-71358	58	R-40-2	1928-30	1918	80,000	C-4470
71359-71400	42	R-40-4	1930	1918	77,800	C-5000
71401-71428	28	R-40-2	1928-30	1918	80,000	C-4470
71429-71500	72	R-40-4	1929-31	1918	77,800	C-5000
71501-71585	85	R-40-2	1928-30	1918	80,000	C-4470
71586-71953	368	R-40-4	1929-31	1918	77,800	C-5000
71954-72353†	400	R-40-8	1931-32	1974	70,000	C-5300
80101-80150	50	R-40-6	1935-36	1948	75,200	C-5200
90001-91021	621	R-30-8	1931-32	1974	66,000	C-5300
90001-91021†	400	R-40-8	1931-32	1974	70,000	C-5300

*total R-40-2 cars, 1443; total R-40-4 cars, 510
**sub-class designations such as R-30-12-8 omitted here for simplicity
†cars renumbered from 71954-72353 to 90001-91021 in Sept.-Oct. 1935.

The final step of an insulation test: the car sheathing is removed and the insulating material is examined for deterioration. Here an R-30-9, in test for 5 years, has been opened at Roseville to reveal its batts of "Stonefelt" in good condition. PFE photo, July 21, 1942; CSRM.

proof floor was found to be successful, the cork floor insulation was replaced with blanket material like that used in walls and roofs, which was more efficient than cork, provided it could be kept dry. A secondary benefit of this new floor design was that cars could be washed out as part of cleaning, without a long drying period before re-use. Car cleaning before delivery to shippers is described in more detail in Chapter 11.

Another improvement was the adoption of better door sealing arrangements, important since air leakage around doors could significantly affect load temperatures. One part of this change was the concave door stile. The stile fitted against a convex door jamb, with the jambs having

LaFlare patented spring padding to ensure a tight fit. The door top and bottom sealed against a rubber cord attachment. With all these changes, the cost per car was just under $2790, less than had been paid for the R-40-2's, with their wood superstructure frames, just two years earlier. The cost reduction was partly because suppliers cut prices as the Depression worsened.

PFE also took the opportunity to conduct further experiments with insulation when these cars were built. The 500 cars constructed were built in two groups at PFE's shops, the first 350 at Roseville and the last 150 at Los Angeles. Among these, the first 50 had "Balsam-wool" in roofs and walls, the next 225 had "Flaxlinum" in roofs and walls, and the last 225 had "Dry-Zero" in roofs and "Hairinsul" in the walls. "Balsam-wool" was made from wood fiber; "Dry-Zero" used the natural fiber of kapok, which is resistant to water absorption (the reason for its use in naval life vests) in addition to its insulating properties. Of this list, the "Balsam-wool" and "Flaxlinum" were less successful. Neither material was used subsequently.

These experiments illustrate the great interest in insulation materials, by PFE and other refrigerator operators, as the 1930's dawned. Older forms of insulation were becoming obsolete, while many new ideas were being put forward. Typically, PFE tried a number of these ideas by installing the proposed insulations in new cars (such as the R-40-4 trials just described) or in older cars selected for test, operating them for a time, then pulling off the sheathing and inspecting the insulation.

In December, 1937, PFE examined a group of ten cars, with a variety of insulation materials installed, which had representative service records. The purpose was to examine PFE's list of approved insulation materials, and to remove approval of those which were obsolete or performed poorly, while making recommendations about future usage of these materials. Of some 14 insulation types considered, only a few were to be retained on the approved list. These included "Hairinsul," particularly when panels were covered with burlap rather than paper; mixtures of hair and jute fibers; "Dry-Zero," the kapok fiber insulation; and a

Table 6-3
Numbers of Wood-sheathed Cars with Original Numbers*

Car Numbers	Class	New	1934	1940	1947	1950	1958	1962	1965
					Number of Cars				
36474-36562	R-40-1	89	88	88	85	59	0	0	0
36563-38562	R-40-2	2000	1980	1950	557	0	0	0	0
38563-39062	R-40-4	500	498	493	483	477	340	18	3
100001-100400	R-50-1	400	400	395	111	2	0	0	0
200001-200100	R-70-2	100	100	100	100	99	34	0	0
200101-200120	R-70-3	20	-	20	20	19	18	9	0

*From freight *Equipment Registers*

R-40-4. (Left) Exterior of the side-bunker car, with tank vent on end and triple hatches on each side. (Right) Car interior; one side bunker is at the left of the picture, a portion of the other is visible on the right. Both photos, PFE from CSRM.

relatively new material, fiberglass. Actually, this first test was a so-called "fiberglass wool" having short fibers. It was not successful, being too prone to compaction and damage by water absorption. Soon, however, the more modern, long-fiber type of fiberglass was available, and it was found to perform well.

Other insulation ideas tried by PFE included thin, parallel sheets of stainless steel, called "Ferro Therm;" lightly crumpled sheets of aluminum foil, made into panels and called "Alfol;" fiber mixtures, such as a 50-50 combination of cattle hair and redwood fiber; and several mineral wool materials with trade names like "Rokflos" and "Stonefelt."

Painting and lettering. Because of the age of surviving paint chips and lack of color photographs, there has been some dispute over the color of PFE car sides in the early years. As described in Chapter 4, it appears that a varnished or orangish "Armour Yellow" is a close match. But whatever the exact color of the "refrigerator yellow" prior to 1929, the color was changed to a distinct light orange early in that year. Car record cards (PFE Form 120's) show the new orange (page 419) being applied as early as February, 1929. The R-40-4 cars, and the R-50-1's described below, were the first new cars to be painted orange.

The new color was designated Color #8-A, and simply named Orange. One story is that the color was intended to portray the citrus cargo often carried by PFE. Within a short time, the color was renumbered #8 instead of #8-A, so care is necessary in checking records. The color was virtually identical to SP's *Daylight* orange (Pantone 152C). The SP Passenger Department was hardly the source of the color, however; this was seven years prior to introduction of the red/orange scheme on the *Daylight* trains. Indeed, it seems likely that SP deliberately chose PFE's already-standard color. This new PFE color, or very similar colors, remained in use until the end of PFE in 1978.

Within a very few years, a great many PFE cars were repainted orange. In fact, shop records show that during

the five years 1929-1934, a total of 47,606 cars were painted at PFE shops (excluding rebuilds). Since the fleet only totaled about 40,000 cars at this time, it seems safe to state that essentially all cars were orange by the end of 1934. PFE issued a Supplement No. 1 to Mechanical Instruction No. 30-F-3 in 1930 to retain the old color, re-designated Color #8-B, to touch up repaired cars; but interviews with PFE employees indicate that this was rarely done. Instead, the whole car would be repainted in the new color. Individual car cards confirm this report.

As mentioned in Chapter 5, PFE cars were frequently washed in this period. Except for Aug.-Dec., 1931, when washing was suspended due to the Depression, about 15,000 cars were washed annually from 1930 to 1936.

Service history. After the construction of 500 new R-40-4's in 1930, it might have been expected that additional orders for these modern cars would be forthcoming. But with the Depression deepening, no additional new cars of the R-40-4 design were ordered. Instead, a number of older cars, drawn from R-30-2 through R-30-6, were rebuilt to this R-40-4 standard. Table 6-2 shows that these 510 R-40-4 rebuilds were intermixed with the R-40-2 cars in the 70,000 series. Like the R-40-4's built new, these rebuilds, with their steel superstructure frames, lasted through the 1950's before extensive scrapping took place.

One of the most interesting of PFE's experiments in this period was car 71586, a 1930 test of the concept of ice bunkers on the car side instead of the end (see Rice article in Bibliography), with the bunker shape being an inverted "**L**." The car also was equipped with brine tanks to retain meltwater, and each tank had its own vent. There was a bunker on the right side of the "B" end, or BR location, and one diagonally opposite, in the AL corner. Three roof hatches fed each bunker. In several years of tests, the car was found to have problems with temperature uniformity, and it was rebuilt with standard bunkers in January, 1942.

In addition to the R-40-4 rebuilds just discussed, 619 R-30-11 and R-30-12 cars were also rebuilt during 1929-31

with the steel-framed superstructure of drawing C-5000, but retaining their original 30-ton underframes. These cars were reclassified as R-30-11-4 and R-30-12-4, meaning that they were upgraded to current -4 standards. They retained, however, their original car numbers and, if they had them, board roofs. Inasmuch as some 450 cars of the 1909-built R-30-4 class were still in service at this time, some confusion may have arisen with the use of this subclass. PFE, however, retained sub-class designations such as this until about 1945.

The R-40-4 new and rebuilt cars, with their steel superstructure frames, lasted very well in service. None had to be rebuilt, although all surviving cars were reconditioned in 1958-59, receiving new insulation and mechanical improvements. Many cars remained in service into the 1960's.

Class R-40-6

PFE set up an additional rebuilding class of R-40 car in 1930, with general arrangement drawing C-5200, dated Oct. 10, 1930. The superstructure and underframe were essentially those of the R-40-4, but internal racks were included for egg loading. The original request in March, 1931, was for 500 of these cars to be built new, and 300 additional ones to be rebuilt from older cars. When the design was finally implemented in 1935-36, only 50 cars were converted, using R-30-11, -12 and -13's which needed rebuilding. As no new cars or additional rebuilds of this design were ever constructed, it can be presumed that PFE's egg traffic was small. Scrapping began in the mid-1950's; all were gone by 1959.

Class R-40-8

In 1931 PFE modified further its rebuilding standards with the R-40-8 design, as shown in drawing C-5300, dated April 8, 1931, and specification no. 71. Thus rebuilding continued with application of this new sub-class, -8, to 400 cars, essentially the successor to the R-40-4 rebuilt design. These R-40-8 cars, which were rebuilds of cars in classes R-30-2 through R-30-6, were initially num-

bered in the 71954-72353 series, but in September and October, 1935, the whole R-40-8 group was moved into the series 90001-91021. In that series, they were thoroughly intermingled with 621 R-30-11-8's which were simultaneously being rebuilt, using the R-40-8 modernized superstructure with steel framing, but re-using the original 30-ton underframe.

For the former R-30-11 cars, the most visible aspect of the change was the addition of an outside metal roof and

(**Above**) A portrait of the Simplex truck, taken at LA Shop on a hazy Aug. 15, 1935. Behind lurks one of SP's workhorse 2-10-2's of class F-4. (**Below**) A snubber of the spring-replacement type, in this case made by Simplex. Note the wedges. Load application would be vertical. PFE photos, CSRM.

A Simplex spring-replacement type snubber in place in a 40-ton truck. PFE photo, CSRM.

taller doors. Another detail of interest: some of these 40-ton rebuilds were not lettered as rebuilds, but as new cars. This reflects the car's having received a new underframe. Otherwise, given the ARA rules on recording car history in the lettering, the original built date would have been stenciled on also. Many, though apparently not all of these cars received the enamel metal medallions when rebuilt.

Trucks and snubbers. Forty of the R-40-8 cars received experimental trucks in 1932, new National Type B's on 20 cars, and on 20 others the unusual-looking Simplex design. PFE also applied Simplex trucks to at least four R-40-4's during the 1930's, in a quest for a truck which was easier-riding at high speeds. Among the R-40-8's known to have had these trucks at one time are 90412, 90469, 90715, and 72281 and 72302 (prior to renumbering into the 90,000 series). Part of the idea behind the Simplex truck was to combine cylindrical and elliptical (or leaf) springs. The leaves rubbed against each other when deflected, absorbing some vertical motion as friction. This also prevented resonant motions in the truck as a whole.

It is reported that these trucks delivered a good high-speed ride only when maintained carefully. Dirt and rust between the spring leaves varied the frictional resistance. Even so, the trucks were still regarded as "in test" in 1941, and several cars survived after World War II with these trucks installed.

A related topic to the Simplex trucks is spring snubbers. PFE was aware, as was most of the railroad industry, that harmonic oscillation of truck springs in service could give rise to large, often rhythmic, superstructure motions or "bounce." One early effort to reduce this effect was the spring snubber. Analogously to friction draft gear, the idea was to cause absorption of motion in friction devices. The leaf springs in the Simplex truck, and in other trucks of the day which combined coil and leaf springs, were intended to provide the same friction, but the spring snubber had internal wedge or shoe surfaces for this purpose.

Starting in 1931, PFE began to apply commercial snub-bers, which were simply inserted in place of one of the springs in each truck, and by 1940 many thousands of cars had these devices. Some designs of snubbers were installed within the spring group, making them difficult to see. The 40-ton truck, for example, had a group of either four or five springs per sideframe, one or two of which were paired inner and outer springs. It was soon realized, however, that the spring-insert type snubber was not the best answer.

After World War II, better arrangements were devised. For PFE's post-war new cars, a snubber device within the bolster, as described in Chapter 8, was preferred. The spring-replacement type snubber, however, continued to be used extensively in truck upgrades during the 1950's, and also continued in service in older PFE trucks. No other method of improving the "ride" of cars was as simple and low in cost.

Service history. Most of the surviving members of the R-40-8 rebuilds were scrapped during 1955-59. Between the R-40-2, R-40-4, and R-40-8 rebuilds, then, over 1500 cars from R-30-1 and -2 were rebuilt in 1928-32. The -8 design ceased to be used because the deepening Depression had caused traffic declines, exacerbated by loss of some of PFE's heavy grape traffic when Prohibition was repealed in Dec. 1933. By the time traffic did increase and money was available, new designs had been prepared.

Class R-50-1

In 1927, as mentioned above in regard to the R-40-1 design, PFE had been exploring cars of larger capacity. One part of this experiment was the R-50 design of 1929. This design combined a longer car body, 47 feet, with a larger truck capacity and a 27"-deep "fishbelly" under-frame of riveted, built-up design. The general arrangement drawing for R-50-1, C-4890, is dated July 31, 1929. The 400 cars were ordered in October, 1929, and delivered by PC&F in January, 1930, following specification 67. These larger cars cost nearly $3900 each, about one-third more that the contemporary R-40-2, despite being only 15% longer. The main difference was the heavier insulation.

Interest in a car with larger cubical capacity had arisen as early as 1926, when certain classes of traffic in the Northwest, packaged such that conventional reefers could not be conveniently loaded, began to be lost to the Northern Pacific and Great Northern. It was not until 1929 that UP, whose rails served the Northwest, and PFE were able to persuade the SP to approve construction of larger cars. The R-50 cars were designed with higher volume capacity, for such cargo as barreled loads (for example, wine), preserved fruit, cured fish, and nursery stock, and were nicknamed "Giants" by PFE.

Design characteristics. The thicker insulation in the R-50-1 was an effort to help equalize temperatures within the load, given the relatively weak air circulation arising from convection. The usual ice bunker length in the rest of the fleet of 41-ft. cars was about 4 feet, giving an ice bunker capacity of around 140 cubic feet. But the R-50-1's had larger bunkers, just over 5 feet in length and 163 cubic feet capacity, evidently to provide more cooling for the longer load space. The cars were delivered in orange paint and with the porcelain enamel medallions described above.

Perhaps their most remarkable feature was the "Bohn Ventilator" hatch covers, an item not used by PFE since the R-30-6's of 1913. It appears that they were chosen to provide a "weatherproof" ventilator for the cargos of these cars. By the 1940's, these ventilators would be removed from all PFE cars, including the R-50-1's, in the interests of standardization. Convertible bulkheads of a "gate" design, which swung back against the side walls when not in use, were installed in these cars. Although PFE had not installed convertible bulkheads in new cars for many years, they were specified for the R-50-1 because of the intended loads, many of which, like wine, required an insulated car but not refrigeration. These bulkheads proved hard to handle, and were later replaced with fixed bulkheads when the cars were rebuilt.

Service history. Almost as soon as these cars were delivered, the frozen food trade began to make its needs known for adequate refrigerator cars, as discussed further in connection with the R-70-2 class, below. Three of the new R-50-1 cars were rebuilt in July and August, 1931, with a variety of very thick insulation arrangements: 6" to 8" insulation in roofs, floors, sides and ends. The roofs were all "Hairinsul," while floors, sides and ends were mixtures of "Hairinsul" and "Celotex" board. These cars, 100260, 100264, and 100350, evidently were used to reach a final design on the R-70-2 insulation. One of them also was used for PFE's first frozen food shipment, from Portland

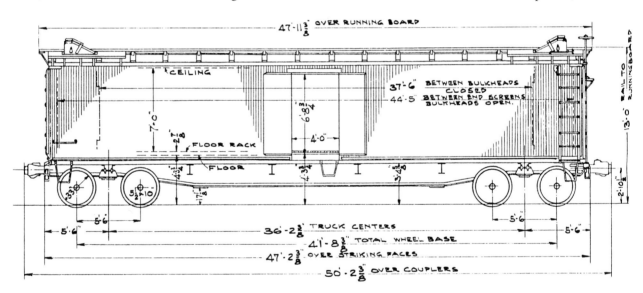

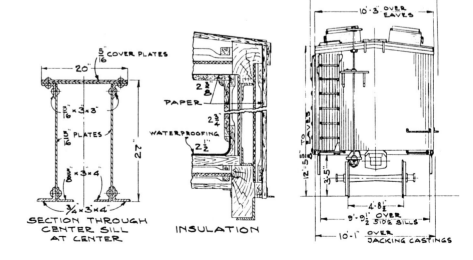

R-50-1. The PFE diagram for the class, which is much more of a scale drawing than most PFE diagrams. Side and end views clearly show the Bohn ventilators. Dimensions and built-up construction of the deep center sill of the underframe are also shown. PFE.

R-50-1. The "B" end of this class, shown on PFE 100368. Note the metal medallion. Photo from PFE, CSRM.

to Boston on Aug. 31, 1931, accompanied by PFE officials including K.V. Plummer, future VP & GM. These three cars then continued in service, often used for frozen food, for a number of years. In 1938, 10 additional R-50-1's were also rebuilt with very thick insulation and plywood side sheathing. This may have been an experiment; in 1941, nine of these 10 cars were among the cars rebuilt to R-50-3 and -4, while the tenth car, 100298, seems to have been part of the first R-50-5 rebuilding in 1945. Those rebuildings are covered in Chapter 7.

The R-50-1's were initially successful in service and were kept very busy. A request for expenditure was submitted by PFE in March, 1931, to build 200 additional cars of the same design as the R-50-1, but this was denied by SP and UP. Later in the 1930's shippers tended to redesign pack-

aging for conventional car sizes. By the time PFE had the capital to consider more cars of this size, the need had decreased, and they were not repeated.

By 1940, the wooden superstructures of the R-50-1's were in need of rebuilding, and gradually the entire class was reworked with thicker insulation, as described in the following chapter, and the cars became primarily used for frozen food.

Classes R-70-1, R-70-2, R-70-3

At the end of the 1920's, as the infant frozen-food industry began to ship a sufficient volume of its product to require rail transport, PFE took an interest. After design studies and the tests of insulation thickness, mentioned

R-50-1. The class portrait which appeared in the *Car Builders' Cyclopedia*. The UP medallion has been "burned in" during printing because the negative was dense. The Bohn Ventilators are clearly visible. PFE photo, CSRM.

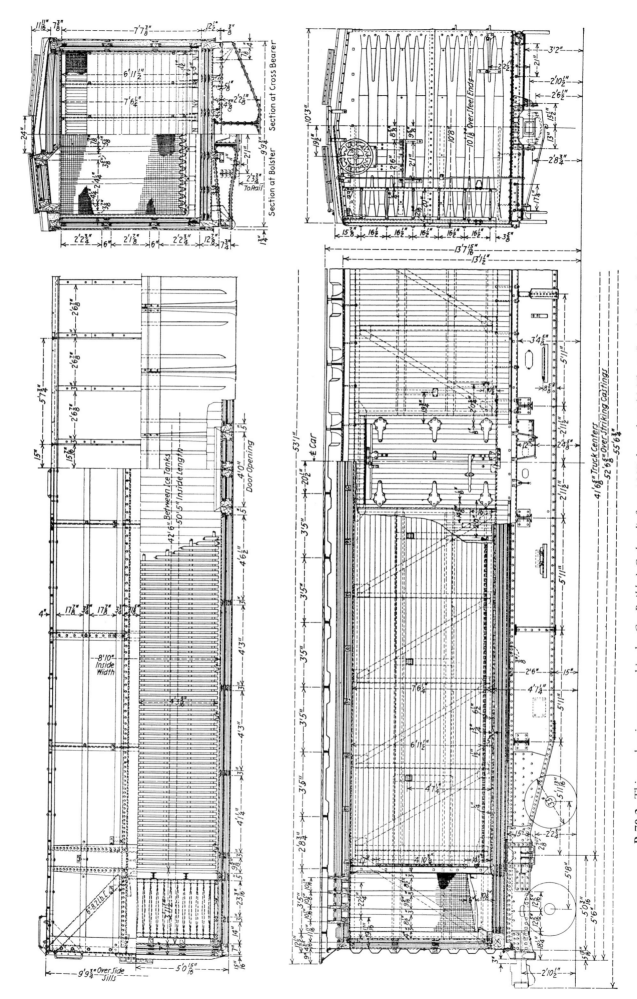

R-70-2. This car drawing appeared in the *Car Builder's Cyclopedia* from 1937 through 1946. The 30" underframe depth is clearly shown, along with the screen-lined basket bunkers and steel ends and roof. Reprinted with permission.

above, PFE's request for 200 additional R-50-1's of March, 1931, was modified and resubmitted in October as a request for 200 cars of 52' length with extra-heavy insulation. It was known that the Great Northern and Santa Fe each planned to order 100 frozen food cars, and it was felt essential to be able to compete for this business. For both financial and competitive reasons, SP and UP approved 100, not 200, of these cars in February, 1932.

Meanwhile, design work on component parts for a frozen food car had been underway in 1930 and 1931. With guidance from experience with the three R-50-1 cars which were heavily insulated, drawings were prepared for two new car designs, each for a 52-ft. long car of 61 tons capacity. Both designs had the same underframe, a riveted, built-up type with a deep "fishbelly" shape. Possibly derived from the earlier R-50 underframe, which was 27" deep, the R-70 underframe was 30" in depth. This made the R-50-1 and R-70 classes the only PFE cars equipped with fishbelly underframes. Trucks were assigned with 6" x 11" journals to provide the needed capacity, as can be seen in Table 5-1.

Both designs, called R-70-1 and R-70-2, had a steel-framed superstructure, and had about triple the insulation thickness of earlier cars, which was necessary for the intended frozen food service. Both also had tongue-and-groove (T&G) siding, as was standard in that era, and had wood ice hatch platforms and running boards.

The two designs had important differences, however. The R-70-1 had wood-sheathed ends as well as sides, all T&G, and had a wood roof sheathed with an outside metal roof. It looked like an elongated version of the R-30, R-40 or R-50 cars of the day. Its general arrangement drawing, C-5410, is dated Nov. 5, 1931. The R-70-2 design was significantly different. It had a roof which was all steel, with riveted ribs and flat, raised panels between the ribs. This roof, called a "Murphy Solid Steel Roof" by its maker, Standard Railway Equipment Co., was new to PFE, and

PFE adopted the name, "solid steel roof," for this and later usage of these roofs.

Also new to PFE were the Dreadnaught ends of the R-70-2 design, of the early 4-4 rib pattern. This means a two-piece end, with four ribs on each piece. These ends did not have an internal "**W** corner post" (see Chapter 8), and thus had a sharp corner. They also differed from later ends in that a separate end sill, fabricated from channel, was attached to the bottom of the end. Even the ARA Type E couplers were new to PFE. The R-70-2 drawing, C-5450, was completed on Jan. 28, 1932.

The R-70-2 design was chosen for construction, probably because of its more modern character. As provided in

R-70-2. **(Below)** Brand-new PFE 200071 shows off its 52' 6" length, deep center sill, and enamel railroad medallion. Neg. 14-265. **(Above)** The Dreadnaught ends had channel end sills. Note the "One Hand" logo on the Universal hand brake. Neg. 500.057. PFE photos, UP Railroad Museum.

R-70-2. A "Super-Giant" in later years, with the 1946-48 paint scheme. The lighting here makes the "sharp-corner" Dreadnaught end very evident. Also visible are the hatch platforms and the underframe construction. The car is at Kansas City in 1949, loaded (according to the side placard) with frozen food. G. Sisk photo, Charles Winters collection.

specification no. 73, 100 cars were built at PFE's Los Angeles Shop. Car delivery commenced on July 1, 1932, and was completed on Sept. 7, 1932. At nearly $4300 each, these were PFE's most expensive freight reefers to date.

Being even longer than the R-50-1 cars, which were called "Giants," these R-70's were nicknamed "Super-Giants" by PFE. A copper-bearing steel was used for the roof, for corrosion resistance. Like the outside metal roofs before it, and like later solid steel roofs, the roof was galvanized for additional corrosion resistance. An interesting detail is that the steel superstructure frames were built by Consolidated Steel, though earlier steel-framed cars had had these parts built in PFE shops. In the depth of the Depression, this might have been an effort to spread the work, but more likely was done to avoid having to increase shop forces, already trimmed to the bone, to build these cars. Later cars had steel work done by PFE again. The cars had steel ladders rather than grab irons, and the floor and lining T&G, like that for the exterior sides, was specified as Oregon fir. Floor rack height was increased to 6-½", and ice bunker capacity to 175 cubic feet, to assist with maintenance of low and uniform temperatures.

When the R-70-2's were built in 1932, with the first solid steel roofs on PFE cars, all parts of those roofs were painted boxcar red. Sides were the light orange color introduced in 1929. Enameled medallions or heralds for SP and UP were applied, the last new PFE cars to receive them; the UP herald still had the word "SYSTEM" in the field at the top. The painting diagram for these cars, C-5430,

is dated Nov. 1931, and shows all these changes from then-prevailing practice. At this time, the older outside metal roofs of earlier cars continued to be black until at least 1935, but the exact date when those roofs also began to be painted all red is not known. It was apparently between 1935 and 1940.

Steel wheels. There had been an interest at PFE in the question of using steel car wheels, instead of cast iron wheels, in the 1920's. This culminated in the initiation of a large test application in 1928. The new R-40-2 class had been chosen for the test, and of the last 500 cars built by Pullman, 100 cars were delivered with cast-steel wheels, 200 with wrought steel "multiple-wear" wheels, and 200 cars with wrought steel "single-wear" wheels. (The "wear" designation indicates whether the tread is heavy enough for re-machining when wear becomes excessive. A single-wear wheel is discarded when excessively worn; a double-wear wheel can be re-contoured once; and a multiple wear wheel several times.) In 1932, these 500 test cars were joined by new R-70-2 cars, all of which had steel wheels, the first half with wrought multiple-wear wheels and the second half with cast wheels.

By 1936, PFE decided (as did many railroads at the time) that the extra dead weight and cost of multiple-wear wheels was not cost-effective, compared to single-wear wheels. The same conclusion was later reached about double-wear wheels, relative to single-wear wheels, after testing them on R-40-10's. But by 1940 it was clear that steel wheels,

R-70-2. Car 200096 late in its life has cracked and streaked plywood sides, mechanical car fans, and integral ice hatches (the hatch platforms have been removed). The paint scheme is that of 1952. V.W. Davis photo at Sidney, Nebr., in 1957.

whatever their wear designation, were superior to cast iron. They had longer life, reduced maintenance costs and time out of service, and fewer defects such as brake burns and shelled spots on the treads. In December, 1941, steel wheels would be adopted as standard for new and long-life rebuild cars, although these wheels continued in short supply for 15 more years.

Service history. In 1939, a slightly modified design called R-70-3 was built as a 20-car order, with construction at the Los Angeles shop. Aside from a modernized ice tank, integral hatch plugs and covers, and plywood interior sheathing, the design was much like the R-70-2 and simply represents an extension of that class. The last five cars of this order, 200116-200120, received plywood exterior sheathing. These cars cost nearly $6000 each, significantly more than the R-70-2 cars had cost.

In 1949 and 1950, the R-70-2 cars were all given general overhauls. This included addition of metal running boards, integral ice hatches (and removal of the ice hatch platforms), plywood lining and air flues, new car fans, and "Spring Control Packages" in place of the coil springs delivered with the trucks. In the years after World War II, a number of the R-70-2 cars, when receiving heavy repairs, were also given "Harborite" plywood side sheathing. As discussed in the next chapter, though, this plywood was not very successful, and some cars later had T&G sheathing re-applied.

By 1957, both the R-70-2 and surviving R-50 cars (now rebuilt to R-50-5), heavily insulated for frozen food and thus routinely using high proportions of salt in icing, were showing severe corrosion damage as well as deterioration of age. Consideration was given to rebuilding them in kind, or rebuilding them with all-steel superstructures.

But just as they had already ceased to carry frozen food,

as mechanical refrigerators came into the fleet (see Chapter 9), their usual 1950's cargos of beer, packaged goods (especially in cans), wine and nursery stock was now shifting to the more heavily insulated mechanicals and to insulated boxcars. They were particularly limited in shipping of canned goods and beer, as palletized shipments would not fit conveniently into their narrow 8' 8" interior width, due to the insulation thickness (insulated boxcars were often 9' 4" wide inside), and shippers disliked the narrow 4-ft. door width.

Thus the 1957 decision was to scrap the remaining 111 R-50-5 and 93 R-70-2 cars. Both the R-50 and R-70 classes described in this chapter would have to be termed successful, however, judging by their long lives, even though there was always a limited number of them, compared to the overall PFE fleet.

By the end of 1930, PFE's car numbers had reached 39062 in the series which had begun in 1906 (some of those cars, of course, had now been rebuilt), together with 298 express reefers, 400 cars of R-50-1, and 2744 surviving WP cars. Shop records show that as of Sept. 30, 1930, 1043 of the original PFE cars had been sold, destroyed in wrecks or scrapped. Ignoring cars being held for heavy repairs or scrapping, the total PFE fleet on 9-30-30 totaled 41,261 cars, the all-time peak. The nearest competitor, Santa Fe, rostered only 18,291 cars in 1930. Yet much of PFE's immense 1930 fleet was old, such as the more than 12,000 surviving cars of R-30-6 and earlier classes, built in 1913 or before. The older cars not only were mechanically deteriorated, but also contained relatively thin insulation of obsolete materials. The great challenge was to replace or modernize these cars, with a worsening Depression in progress. How this challenge was met, during and after the 1930's, is described in the next chapter.

Freshly rebuilt R-50-5's with plywood sides star in this publicity shot, posed at Nampa in the summer of 1946, just before PFE adopted its 2-medallion paint scheme. Note the consecutive car numbers and the restfully posed workmen. Motive power for this string of cars was engine 9046, one of UP's 9000-series 4-12-2's. UP Railroad Museum.

7

REBUILDING THE FLEET

R-30-13-9. Typical of PFE's largest group of reworked cars, car 98126 was photographed at Washington, DC, in the summer of 1940, shortly after its reconditioning at Roseville in April of that year. The trucks and underframe are those of the original car, R-30-13 34627, built in 1926. Car 98126 would remain in service until 1962. Ernest Stephan photo, NB-01135, courtesy Kalmbach Memorial Library, NMRA.

As an introduction to PFE's rebuilding practices, a general description was given in the previous chapter. Here we continue with rebuilding after 1936, a time when very large numbers of older cars were continued in service by repair and replacement, as well as upgrading, of the mechanical car parts. A table of these rebuildings, including a few car groups discussed in Chapter 6, is shown as Table 7-1, with physical characteristics listed in Table 7-2.

During the early and mid-1930's, there was an extended and lively exchange of correspondence between the Presidents of the SP and the UP, and the Vice President and General Manager (VP & GM) of PFE, expressing the views of their mechanical staffs. The subject was the question of whether scarce funds were best spent on new cars, or on thoroughly rebuilt cars with steel superstructure frames like the R-40-4 and R-40-8 cars rebuilt during 1930-32, or whether a more modest extent of car refurbishment would be the best approach. As the time neared for purchase of the first all-steel cars, the R-40-10 class (Chapter 8),

another proposal was made: to build all-steel superstructures on the old frames. Cost estimates were that the R-40-10's would cost $3300 each – when built, they actually cost $3700 each – while rebuilds with all-steel superstructures would cost about $2400 each to rebuild, re-using the old underframe. Reconditioning, a less extensive version of rebuilding, was estimated to cost $1600 per car. (Recall from the previous chapter that the last new, steel-framed cars, the R-40-4's, had cost $2790 each in 1930.)

The all-steel rebuild design, which according to an unconfirmed report was designated R-40-7, but for which drawings either were not prepared, or have not survived, was considered to be less attractive because of the underframe re-use. Not only would these frames not be new, and thus of shorter life expectancy, but many of the cars which needed rebuilding had 30-ton underframes. PFE was not willing to make as large an upgrade as an all-steel superstructure, and be limited to 30 tons capacity. At this time, then, the all-steel rebuild idea was discarded. The Santa Fe's SFRD

Table 7-1
Numbers and Classes of Rebuilt Cars (1937-1955)

Car Numbers	Rebuilding Class	Dates	Number of Cars	Capacity		Drawing
				cu. ft.	pounds	
60001-62500	R-30, -40-18	1942-43	2500	1988	70,000	SK 1000
62501-63500	R-30, -40-19	1944-45	1000	1988	70,000	SK 1100
63501-65920	R-30, -40-21	1945-47	2420	1988	70,000	SK 1100
65921-68532	R-30, -40-24	1947-48	2610	1988	70,000	2000
73001-76554	R-30, -40-16	1940-42	3554	1988	70,000	SK 990
79995-79999	R-30-12-17	1940	5	2132	70,000	C-7500
85001-85100	R-30-9, -16*	1937-41	100	1988	70,000	SK 617
85101-85275	R-30-9	1944-45	175	1988	70,000	SK 617
91022-98718	R-30, -40-9	1938-40	7694	1988	70,000	SK 617
99001-99052	R-30, 40-15	1939-55*	52	1500	–	SK 961
100036**	R-50-1-2	1940	1	2 x 1240	90,000	C-7604
100401-100475	R-50-1-4	1941	75	2530	101,000	SK 825
100476-100500	R-50-1-3	1941	25	2530	101,000	SK 825
200121-200125	R-70-4 (new)	1940	5	2820	122,000	2300
200301-200375	R-50-5	1945-47	75	2557	95,000	SK 825
200379-200587	R-50-5	1945-47	209	2557	95,000	SK 825

*See text for numbers and conversion dates of individual cars

**Two-compartment car

Fe's SFRD did follow that course, and rebuilt a great many of its cars with steel superstructures on larger-capacity USRA underframes.

Work on a test car for the PFE reconditioning concept was done at Roseville, car 91022. Not only was the car a satisfactory one technically, the cost was estimated, and later confirmed, to be only $1400 per car when the work was done on large numbers of cars. This procedure was then selected for the next large car renewal program, for by

the mid-1930's, there were quite a few cars in need of upgrading and modernization.

This internal debate about rebuilding was also occurring throughout American railroading in the mid-1930's. In 1936, *Railway Age* reported that for every car being purchased new, there were three older cars being rebuilt. Yet economic analyses of the period showed that the shorter life of rebuilt cars, typically 10 years instead of the 20 or more years' life of a new car, made rebuilding

R-30-12-9. The test car for the large reconditioning program of R-30 and R-40 wood cars is inspected at Roseville in June, 1936. Of the two men in the center, the one on the left is Horace Giddings, PFE's VP & GM at the time. On his left is his assistant, K.V. Plummer, who would become VP & GM in six years. Warm weather has brought out straw hats. PFE photo, CSRM.

in addition to perpetuating in service a smaller, relatively heavier, and less capable car. The reason for rebuilding, of course, was that the required investment was half or less of the cost of a new car. With capital funds scarce in the Depression, rebuilding provided more serviceable cars per dollar. Like many other car owners, PFE chose to rebuild a considerable number of cars after 1935.

Testing programs. From the beginning in 1906, PFE was interested in technical advances and in new commercial specialties for refrigerator cars, and conducted tests with its own cars to try these designs in service. Several of these test programs have been described in earlier chapters. Among the important tests for the cars of this chapter was a series of tests on car fans.

A variety of methods to circulate air inside a refrigerator car, some of them rather complex, had been tried by PFE since C.A. Richardson's fan design received patent 1,643,471 in 1927. The benefit of air circulation was greatly improved temperature uniformity within the car. Several sample fan installations and test runs with various produce cargoes had produced inconclusive results during the 1930's. But with the advent of improved commercial fan hardware in 1938, PFE commenced a new and detailed test program.

Several patent fan designs were installed in PFE cars and placed in service. These included the earliest Preco (Pacific Railway Equipment Co., Los Angeles) design, with 5-3/8" diameter "squirrel cage" fans; an improved Preco design with 6-3/4" fans; an Eventemp "wind motor" design, in which the car's motion through the air drove the fans, which were located in ducts below the interior ceiling; and a Moorman design of paddle-wheel fans with vertical shafts, driven mechanically by belts from the truck axle. All worked well in tests, though the Preco had the advantage of being easiest to install with convertible bulkheads, and to operate under pre-cooling conditions (the Eventemp had to have electric motors clamped to each of the four wind motors atop the car). About the time PFE concluded its tests in 1940, Preco's improved Van Dorn fan design was patented, and soon became the first type of fan adopted as standard for PFE cars.

The PFE rebuilding program. Before presenting individual car class histories, it is appropriate to give a summary of what PFE meant by rebuilding. PFE began in 1914 to extend the life of its cars by reworking them. After 8 to 10 years of service, the superstructure of wood cars had to be repaired or replaced. Even with the "pocket" castings for wooden superstructure framing, the frame members loosened in service, causing the car to "weave" when moving. This further damaged the framing, as well as damaging the insulation and opening air leaks in the car structure. As Mary Pennington said in 1919 of cars which had been in service, "we know that the floor and the trucks will start off several inches ahead of the roof when the pull comes." By the time such cars came into the PFE shops for rebuilding, they were called "good morning" cars by shopmen. Earl Hopkins described how they behaved: "When the switch

Eventemp "wind motor" fans (cloth wrapped prior to test), installed in R-50-1 car 100260, one of the "thick insulation" test cars described in Chapter 6. The wind motor drove fans in ceiling ducts. A wire to a temperature-measuring thermocouple is visible on the roof. Photo at Sacramento, 1938, by PFE, CSRM collection.

engine would stop them in the yard, the cars would bow 'good morning' to you, rocking back and forth."

In PFE's early years, such cars were reconstructed with new superstructures which still had wood framing. The R-30-1 and -2 cars, as mentioned previously, had to have new superstructures during 1914-18 and 1925-28, and underframes were replaced on many of these cars in the later campaign. Though subsequent classes required less frequent rework, classes R-30-4 through R-30-6 all received new superstructures at least once by 1927. Accordingly, more than 15,000 new superstructures had been applied to reworked PFE cars as of 1927. Yet all these cars received wood superstructure frames, and only the 2500 cars of R-30-2-13 constituted what was later called "rebuilding."

It was the PFE Car Department's estimate that the 8 to 10 year life of cars with wood superstructure frames could be extended with steel superstructure frames (called "super frames") to an expected life of 10-15 years. The 1935 problem was the more than 20,000 R-30-12 and -13's, now over 10 years of age and overdue for rebuilding.

In PFE parlance, there were two kinds of car rework.

"Rebuilding" meant stripping the car literally down to the center sill (even bolsters, frame cross-members, draft gear and trucks were removed, and only sometimes re-used), and then starting over. As PFE employees said, "We jacked up the car number and ran a new car under it." Essentially all wood parts were replaced, while steel parts were re-used only if they were of modern design and in good shape.

The opportunity was also usually taken to update or modernize the car. After 1930, a steel superframe would be installed. This was a frame of light steel angles, stiffened by the remainder of the car structure. Thus the tongue-and-groove siding would be pulled off, the steel frame installed, and new insulation and siding applied.

The second kind of rework, after 1930, was called "reconditioning." This meant superstructure replacement, either renewing wood structural members in the superstructure or (after 1949) upgrading with steel framing instead, and installing new insulation, but not stripping the car down to its underframe. As described below, this was done for the R-30-9 and the Western Pacific cars in the years up to 1940.

Table 7-2
Characteristics of Rebuilt Cars

Car Number	Rebuilt Class	Original Class(es)	Equipment*; Structure**
13220-22519	R-30-4	R-30-11, -12	S; SP&B, OMR, KC
19920-28749	R-30-8	R-30-12	S; SP&B, OMR, KC
18920-36473	R-30-8	R-30-13	"
60001-62500	R-30, 40-18	R-30-12 to -14, R-40-2	RF, C, SI, IH; SP&B, SSR&E, AB
62501-63500	R-30, 40-19	R-30, R-40	RF, C, SI; SP&B, SSR&E, AB
63501-65920	R-30, 40-21	"	F, C, SI; SP&B, SSR&E, AB
65921-68532	R-30, 40-24	"	"
70001-71585	R-40-2†	R-30-1, -2	S; WP&B, OMR or WR, KC
71273-71953	R-40-4†	R-30-2 to -6	S; SP&B, OMR or WR, KC
73001-76554	R-30-16	R-30-12 to -14, R-40-2	SI, IH; SP&B, SSR. (fans, brakes varied).
80001-80100	–	R-30-5	original superstructure
80101-80150	R-40-6	R-30-11 to -13	S; SP&B, OMR, KC; egg loading
85001-85100	R-30-9	R-30-11 to -14	S, SI; WP&B, OMR, KC; meat service
85101-85275	"	"	"
90001-91021	R-30-8	R-30-11	S; SP&B, OMR, KC
90001-91021	R-40-8	R-30-1 to -6	S; SP&B, OMR, KC
91022-98718	R-30, -40-9	R-30-11 to -14, R-40-2	S, SI; WP&B, OMR, brakes varied
99001-99050	R-30, -40-15	R-30-12	WP&B, OMR, AB; dry ice service
100401-100475	R-50-4	R-50-1	S, IH; SP&B, SSR&E, AB
100476-100500	R-50-3	R-50-1	F, C, IH; SP&B, SSR&E, AB
200301-200375	R-50-5	R-50-1	F, S, SI; SP&B, SSR&E, AB
200376-200378	R-50-1	R-50-1	F, C; SP&B, SSR&E, AB
200379-200587	R-50-5	R-50-1	F, S, SI; SP&B, plywood, SSR&E, AB

*F=circulating fans; S=stationary ice bunkers; C=convertible ice bunkers; SI=stage icing; RF=retrofit (electric) fans; IH=integral hatch cover and plug.

**P&B=posts and braces of superstructure (W=wood, S=steel); siding all tongue-and-groove unless otherwise noted; OMR=outside metal roof; SS=solid steel (R=roof, E=ends); handbrakes all horizontal-shaft; brake gear KC or AB

†See Table 6-2 for individual car number groups

R-30-12-9. This car, PFE 91022, began the -9 reconditioning program. It was the prototype for the thousands of cars reconditioned with wood superstructures during 1938-40. After 1945, the designation of the class would be simplified to R-30-9. End lettering is 7" high. PFE photo at Roseville, June, 1936, CSRM.

It might be asked why such extensive work as rebuilding was conducted, when a new car would technically be very little different. The answers were cost, as mentioned, and the tax consequences. Rebuilding which could be classified as "replacing" the car's function was an expense, thus deductible from income. But new construction, or "improvements" to car function, were capital expenditure and not deductible. There was a formula for distinguishing "replacements" from "additions and betterments" in AAR Rule 112, and PFE's correspondence files on Rule 112 bulge with documents and reports.

Eventually, around the end of 1948, the IRS (Internal Revenue Service) decided that if rebuilding achieved a renewed car life of 15 or more years, the car had to be treated as new, thus as a capital expense. The IRS made its own determination of the expected car life in a particular rebuilding program. Among the car rebuilders hit with tax bills was PFE, which paid nearly $12 million in back taxes and interest dating from 1944 (see Chapter 1). Rebuilding of cars from the center sill up stopped rather abruptly on most railroads, as it did on PFE.

Cars being rebuilt typically received most mechanical improvements in current use on new cars. From the outset of rebuilding, this was manifested in at least two ways, as follows. First, the icing equipment was improved; and second, other mechanical parts of the car were modernized. In the first category would be included addition of fans, stage icing equipment, or convertible ice bunkers. "Stage icing" used a grate which could be swung into place to permit filling just the top half of the ice bunker, for certain commodities, cooler weather or shorter trips. "Convertible ice bunkers" were stowable to permit use of the entire car interior for cargo when icing wasn't needed, a fairly common practice for canned goods and other lading before the advent of insulated box cars. In 1947, for example, fully 20% of car loadings in reefers comprised canned goods.

The second category, "other mechanical improvements," would include brake gear modernizations, new safety appliances, and occasionally addition of a new underframe. Usually, though, re-use of the old center sill meant that "30-ton" Bettendorf underframes continued to have 30-ton capacity. After about 1930, all rebuilds were given horizontal-shaft brake wheels in place of the old style vertical-shaft ones. (The 1931 *Car Builders' Cyclopedia* shows that the same change was taking place in new car construction for all freight cars at about the same time.)

Class R-30-9, R-40-9

The test car mentioned above, 91022, was the first of the R-30-9 and R-40-9 cars. In 1938-40, a time when funds did not permit any additional, new all-steel cars to be purchased, this -9 program was to include a great many older cars. The cars which were given this "reconditioning" instead of rebuilding, that is, a lesser process to extend service lives, were given the sub-class -9 as as suffix to their original class numbers. After 1945, the classification was simplified to R-30-9 or R-40-9, depending on whether they were rebuilt from cars of classes R-30-11 through R-30-14, or were from R-40-2. Note that this means that underframes among the -9 cars included 30-ton Bettendorf (from R-30-11, -12, or -14), 30-ton built-up (from R-30-13), or 40-ton built-up (from R-40-2).

These cars were not modernized like the -8's which preceded them, as Table 7-2 shows, for they retained allwood superstructures and their original underframes. The first cars reconditioned also retained their original KC brakes. They did receive ladders to replace the rows of grab irons characteristic of most original R-30 cars, and also new power brake wheels and cast steel truck sideframes if needed,

R-30-12-9. Car 94300, the test car for PFE's extensive subsequent use of plywood for external sheathing. The recently introduced "repack" outline may be noted. Photographed at Los Angeles, June, 1938. PFE photo, CSRM.

but further modernization, as would have been done in rebuilding, was not done in this reconditioning program. The cars did receive floor racks increased in height to 6", as was usual after 1936. The numbers for these cars were in the series 91022-98718, comprising 7694 cars in all. Most of the -9 cars received standard ice tanks of 10,000-pound capacity, but cars numbered 96524-98718 had a larger, 11,500-pound tank applied. Either way, the cubic capacity for cargo was increased from the original 1918 cubic feet to 1988 cubic feet.

Two interesting experimental cars are included among the R-30-9 class. Both had plywood interior lining, a first for PFE, and both also had plywood exterior sheathing on the sides. This was PFE's pioneer use of plywood for car exteriors, a product of Harbor Plywood of Chicago and Hoquiam, Wash., called "Harborite," and it was the basis for later use of this material on other rebuilds (see below). Unlike other -9 cars, both also had steel superstructure

framing. Other features of the two cars were different, however. One was car 94300, completed in 1938, which had a Viking solid-steel roof and was the first rebuild to have an "integral" ice hatch, that is, a single piece incorporating the functions of hatch covers and plugs. This car's original number was 16084, an R-30-12 built in 1921.

The second experiment was car 96522, originally 21508, which was given extra-heavy insulation in 1939 for test purposes. About 1950, this car was renumbered 296522 and used both for frozen food and for insulated-load cargo such as canned goods. Ten other experimental cars, 93519-93528, tried out "Alfol" foil-bonded reflective paper as an outer insulation layer. This worked well, and was used in many later car classes.

With car 94300's ice hatch covers performing well in service, cars in the group 95737-98718 were given the same type of integral ice hatches. No hatch platforms were

R-30-9. Experimental car 94300, constructed at Roseville in 1938. (**Right**) This was the only car PFE ever built with plywood *ends* as well as sides. (**Below**) The car also had a Viking roof, the only one ever installed on a PFE car, and was the first car to receive the formed-metal Equipco one-piece hatch plug and cover, which became standard for both rebuilds and steel ice cars in 1940 (see next chapter on steel cars). Both photos, PFE from CSRM.

The ice hatch and platform being applied to PFE cars in the 1930's looked like this. The hinged hatch plug can be seen below the wood hatch cover. PFE photo, CSRM.

R-30-9. Outside metal roof of a -9 car (92508) in 1957. The wood-sheathed hatches retained on later -9 conversions needed no platforms because slate granules were added in the roof paint. The reporting marks and car number are stenciled near the car center. V. Davis photo at Gering, Nebr.

used with these hatches, because slate granules were added to the roof paint to make it "skidproof," as had been done on the R-40-10 cars the previous year (see Chapter 8). This roof treatment also made it possible to gradually remove ice hatch platforms on other cars, although separate plugs and covers often remained.

Painting and lettering. These cars received the current paint and lettering described in the previous chapter, with orange sides and boxcar red roof and ends. The only change from the previous chapter is that the word "SYSTEM" was omitted from the UP shield after 1935.

In March, 1938, a distinctive feature of PFE ice car lettering was introduced, in the form of Car Dept. sketch 619. This was a pair of rectangles outlined on the car side,

to serve as a location for recording journal repacking dates (a very early predecessor of today's "repack stencil" design). The photo of car 94300 shows an example.

These cars received painted medallions or heralds, if they had previously had enamel ones (see Chapter 6).

Service history. During the late 1930's, PFE rebuilt 79 cars of R-30-11, -12, and -13 to R-30-9 standards, i.e.

R-30-12-9. Car 97680 at the Stockton ice deck on July 13, 1941. The car has the underframe and trucks it received when built in July, 1922 as car 20028, but the ladders and formed-steel integral ice hatches are new features; it was "completely reconditioned" at Roseville in April 1940, still with the original T-section Bettendorf trucks, and a stenciled medallion. W.C. Whittaker photo.

Interior of a meat car, showing the ceiling "meat rails" for hanging of the meat hooks which are stored along the wall. The car shown is a later class, but the interior arrangement was standard. PFE photo, CSRM.

reconditioned, but these were equipped with meat rails. They were identified by receiving a different number series, 85001-85100. In this series, 21 other cars, 85060-85080, were actually R-30-16's with steel roof, steel superstructure frames, and AB brakes (the -16 rebuilds are described below). An additional 175 cars for meat service, numbers 85101-85275, were added, also as R-30-9's, in

1944-45. Much of the meat traffic in PFE territory was carried in meatpackers' cars, and PFE records indicate that packers used PFE equipment as "overflow" when they did not have enough of their own cars. This accounts for the relatively few cars equipped for meat service in a company serving UP and SP's extensive cattle territories.

In the late 1940's, cars 97409-97413 were equipped with Preco Model D-3 fans, but this 5-car experiment was never extended to other -9 cars. Car fan usage and applications are discussed in more detail later in this chapter and in Chapter 8.

Starting in August, 1949, the R-30-9 and R-40-9 cars were reconditioned again, this time receiving steel superstructure framing to extend their lives. At a cost of about $1400 per car, 1000 cars were scheduled to be redone in 1949, 1750 in 1950, 3000 in 1951, and about 1500 in 1952. Starting in 1950, the superframes were welded instead of being riveted. Work was finally completed in December, 1953, by which time 6287 of these cars had been given steel superframes.

Some -9 cars received plywood sheathing in the 1949-51 period, though the usual T&G (tongue and groove) siding was later restored; for discussion, see class R-40-24.

An interesting detail is that 50 of the cars received a different experimental application of plywood external sheathing. As was mentioned in Chapter 6, the "Harborite" plywood was already proving less than satisfactory, and an additional alternative to T&G siding was desired. This new type of sheathing had its face grain in the vertical direction, rather than horizontal as in "Harborite," with

R-70-4 (Above). Although representing a class discussed later in this chapter, this photo is the only one known which illustrates the experimental plywood sheathing with horizontal grooves. Photo at Roseville in 1950. R-40-9 (Left). Here the inner insulation has been installed in a continuous doorpost-to-doorpost piece. More insulation will be added outside the riveted steel frame before sheathing the sides and ends. PFE photos, CSRM.

R-30-9. Car 98444 with integral Equipco hatches, in the 1949-51 paint scheme (see Chapter 8), with side hardware and corner steps orange. The side sill and center step, black in this photo, became orange in 1951 when the SP herald was returned to its traditional location, toward the "B" end of the car. Original car number was 27380. G. Sisk photo, C. Winters collection.

the hope of minimizing warping and seam opening. What made it distinctive is that horizontal V-grooves, 12" apart, were routed into the outer ply to relieve surface tension and prevent checking. Accordingly, the cars appeared superficially to be sheathed with 12" longitudinal boards. It was asserted by PFE that these grooves presented a "streamlined appearance." One car known to be in this group was

95707, as well as the 5 cars of R-70-4 described later in this chapter. Presumably this material was no more successful than "Harborite," as the application was not repeated.

With their new steel superframes, the -9 cars served an additional 15 years or so, generally surviving longer than other rebuilt classes. The last of the class was retired in 1966, by which time few other rebuilds were in service.

R-30-9. This car is in the shop at Roseville to have side sheathing repaired (note boards with chalked "x" marks). Integral hatch and metal brake step (these steps replaced wood boards in 1939) are visible, and side and end hardware details are clearly shown. This car was numbered 31349 when built in 1925 as an R-30-13; reconditioned in 1940, it would be scrapped in 1958. PFE photo, March 25, 1944, CSRM.

R-30-15. A string of the first dry ice cars, here with class numbering for R-30-10, soon changed to -15. Note the 4-hinge door, unusual in PFE practice. The white notice boards at the left of the car side read "RETURN TO MOSQUERO." PFE photo, CSRM.

Class R-30-15, R-40-15

The shipment of dry ice as cargo required a heavily insulated car, but since the cargo refrigerated itself, ice bunkers, hatches, and floor racks were unnecessary. The earliest PFE dry ice cars were obtained by converting a few R-30-9 cars, by removing floor racks and ice grates and adding heavier insulation, but without the interior partitions of later, specially-built cars. In 1937, cars 93028-93030 were so converted to serve a dry ice plant at Wellington, Utah; in 1938, car 94519 was similarly modified; and in 1939, car 92736 also was converted for the same use. As soon as a sufficient number of R-30-15's had been rebuilt, these older conversions were returned to general service.

The first PFE cars built especially for dry ice service were a group of 15, numbered 99001-99015 and classed R-30-12-15 (AAR designation LRC). Initially assigned to subclass -10 in PFE records and so lettered on the first cars rebuilt, the subclass was soon changed to -15 when it was realized

that use of 40-ton underframes for these cars would duplicate the new steel car class, R-40-10. These cars were rebuilt from R-30-12's, 6 in May and 3 each in August and November of 1939, all at Roseville, and the last 3 at Los Angeles in June, 1940. This first group retained the wood superstructure framing of the original R-30-12's. A second batch of 10 R-30-15 cars was converted in April, 1943, and 5 more were added in May of 1944. Both these groups of cars had steel ends, and the second group had steel running boards. Both groups also had steel superframes and solid steel roofs, as did all subsequent dry ice cars.

Another group of 10 of these cars was converted from R-30-16's (see below) in June, 1947, and thus had wood-sheathed ends and (briefly) wood running boards. The final batch of 12 cars was added in May of 1955, making a total of 52 of the -15 cars. Most of the latter two batches were R-40 rather than R-30 cars. All the -15 cars had extremely thick insulation, typically 17" in sides and ends, 13" in the roof, and 13" in the floor, all fiberglass. They also

R-40-15 . One of the last batch of dry ice conversions. Wood external sheathing was retained on ends, since loads were not heavy enough to require the stiffer steel ends. Note legend, "DRY ICE SERVICE." PFE photo at LA Shop, May 5, 1955, CSRM.

R-40-15. This view of car 99044 shows the internal bulkhead and door for one of the dry ice compartments. In this publicity photo, the model holds a thermometer above a block of dry ice. UP Railroad Museum.

had interior partitions with loading doors in them, and the internal bulkheads were also heavily insulated.

To repeat, these cars did not use dry ice as a refrigerant, but were for shipping of bulk dry ice. They were used primarily to service the plant at Mosquero, New Mexico, where a carbon dioxide gas well field supplied a dry ice manufacturing plant. Although most of the cars were la-

beled "RETURN TO MOSQUERO," some were unlabeled and were used for other shippers of dry ice. They continued to be used until about 1960, by which time mechanical refrigerator cars of adequate refrigeration capability were available for whatever rail shipments of dry ice were made.

Experimental Paint Schemes

During the 1930's PFE experimented with several variations on its standard paint scheme. Although none were adopted for general use, nor even were retained for long in service, they are most interesting footnotes to PFE history.

The first of these seems to have been the "curved corner" scheme of 1936. Records are incomplete, but at least 22 cars are known to have been given this scheme. Although it is a "streamlined" design, consonant with the thirties' fascination with such ideas, it was apparently only applied to older cars with arch-bar trucks, rebuilt R-30-5 and -6 cars. A variation on this scheme, applied to only one car, is the "script" scheme, in which the owner's name was spelled out in script lettering. Applied in June, 1938, to car 14760, it was removed by October, as was the curved corner paint on all the other cars.

In October, 1937, a scheme was tried which omitted the medallions of the two railroads, substituting a "slogan" arrangement. Whether this was a thought for Depression painting economy, by eliminating the several colors of the SP and UP medallions, or an attempt at introducing a

(Left). The "curved corner" scheme of 1936, on an R-30-6-11½ car. The upper corners of the car side are boxcar red, the lower ones black. The remainder of the car is the standard PFE paint and lettering of the time. PFE photo, CSRM.

(Right). The one car which received the "script" scheme, and evidently retained it for only a few months. The scheme is the same as the "curved corner" one except for spelling out the owner's name in script. PFE photo, CSRM.

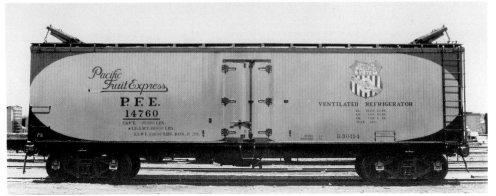

The "slogan" scheme, applied experimentally to car 93218 but never placed in revenue service. Car sides were the usual orange. PFE photo at the east end of the paint shed (steel shed in background), Roseville, October, 1937, CSRM.

The "stripe" scheme of 1941, which was applied only to the 5 cars of R-30-16 which received steel ends. The cars were repainted orange within a few months. The stripes were boxcar red. PFE photo,

slogan on PFE cars, is not known. Apparently, though, this scheme never went into revenue service. After being photographed at Roseville, the car was repainted within a week or so, and returned to service.

Finally, a scheme with 3" horizontal stripes near the top and bottom of the car body, boxcar red in color, was applied to the 5 cars of R-30-16 (discussed next) which received Dreadnaught ends in addition to steel roofs. These were soon reclassified to R-30-18. This "stripe" scheme apparently remained on the cars for several months before being repainted when -18 conversions began in early 1942.

Class R-30-16, R-40-16

PFE had found the steel roofs of the R-70-2 and R-40-10 cars entirely satisfactory. Starting in 1940, therefore, wood or outside metal roofs were no longer rebuilt in kind

by PFE. After that date, all rebuilt cars received structural steel roofs identical with those on the new cars of the time. PFE called these "solid steel roofs." The first group to receive them was the 3554 cars of sub-class -16, converted in 1940-42 from classes R-30-12 through -14 and including R-40-2, though that class was only about 10 years old. When rebuilt, these cars had the -16 sub-class added to their original car class.

As Table 7-2 shows, the steel-framed superstructure was wood-sheathed on both sides and ends. The new 6" floor racks were used. This group of cars was rebuilt during a time of considerable change in engineering practice. For example, 10 cars were given convertible ice bunkers (75643-75652), and the last 2357 cars received AB brakes in place of the original KC gear (74198-76554), as AB brakes became PFE's standard for rebuilds. Five cars were also given steel Dreadnaught ends as a test, cars 75648-75652, and these

R-30-16. Car 74781 being iced at Albina (UP's yard in Portland, Ore.) in 1948. The solid steel roof is just discernable. Rebuilt in May, 1941, from car 23168, 74781 retains its original Bettendorf underframe and T-section trucks, although AB brakes have been applied. It was repainted in 1947 to the two-medallion scheme shown. PFE collection, CSRM.

R-30-16. A pair of -16's at Salinas in 1957, rather grimy but clearly showing the combination of wood-sheathed ends and solid steel roof which made this class unique on the PFE roster. E. Mohr photo.

were effectively the prototypes for the following R-30-18 class (see photo of 75652 in the experimental "stripe" scheme). One hundred cars (74096-74195) received plywood side sheathing and lining, an extension of the trial on the two R-30-9 experimental cars, 94300 and 96522.

Of particular importance, 500 cars (76005-76504) were given Preco mechanical air circulating fans, Model G-2, the first PFE cars to have them. As mentioned earlier, it is an indication of how closely PFE was following development of car fans that they were prepared to test the new Preco (Pacific Railway Equipment Co.) product as soon as it was available. William E. Van Dorn's patent on this invention

was issued on Sept. 10, 1940, and within months PFE was installing them on -16 rebuilds.

Service history. In the early 1950's, the 50 cars of the group 76505-76554 received Equipco fans as a test, but no further systematic retrofit applications of fans were made to R-30-16 cars. Instead, cars were given fans from time to time, without an explicit upgrading program or any discernable pattern in car number groupings. Most of these were Preco overhead electric fans. In the fall of 1954, following the usual service period of about 15 years for steel-superframe cars, a program of general repairs to the survivors of the -16 class was begun, permitting these cars to remain in service. But as the fleet shrank in the 1960's, they underwent wholesale scrapping, completed in 1966. The last R-30-16, car 74583, was donated in 1967 to the Rio Vista Museum in California, where (at this writing) it survives, complete with original Bettendorf underframe.

Class R-30-18, R-40-18

In 1942, completion of work on the -16 cars was followed by the start of a new series of rebuilds which were all given not only the modernizations listed in Table 7-2, but (most visibly) Dreadnaught steel ends in addition to solid steel roofs. Clearly the 5-car experimental group in R-30-16 which received these ends was considered a success. The ends on those -16's, and on the -18's, had "**W** corner posts," giving them a rounded exterior corner, unlike the early style Dreadnaught end with a sharp external corner, as used on the R-70-2, for example. All the -18's also received the now-standard AB brakes, adopted in 1940.

Unlike the -16 cars, the 2500 cars of -18 all received convertible bulkheads. Their 6" floor racks were of the herringbone design adopted in 1940. However, they did retain wood sheathing over steel framing on the sides. The R-30-12-17 cars, described later in this chapter, were al-

ready completed, so the next available sub-class for these cars was -18. These cars were assigned to the 60,000 series, a series which eventually included 8830 cars by the end of 1948. As Table 7-1 shows, these cars were not only the -18 class, but also the succeeding -19 and -21 versions of both R-30 and R-40. The latter two classes are simply listed in PFE rosters as "converted from various R-30 classes." All three classes were similarly rebuilt, with minor exceptions described below. The -18 cars held up well in service, receiving general repairs and electric car fans in 1953-54, and surviving into the 1960's.

Class R-30-19, R-40-19

The first of the rebuilds to have steel grid running boards was the -19 class of 1000 cars. Otherwise, this class was very

(**Below**). A test of the one-piece Equipco hatch cover and a Holland "hatch closure device" (the dark "latch bar"), here in place on a galvanized outside metal roof. Note that neither the roof nor the replaced boards on the car end have yet been painted. These hatch covers became standard for both new car construction and also for rebuilds, including the last group of R-30-9's. PFE photo at Roseville, Nov. 10, 1939, from CSRM.

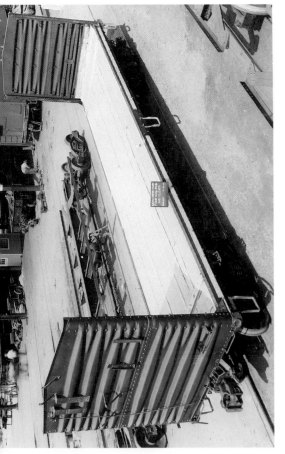

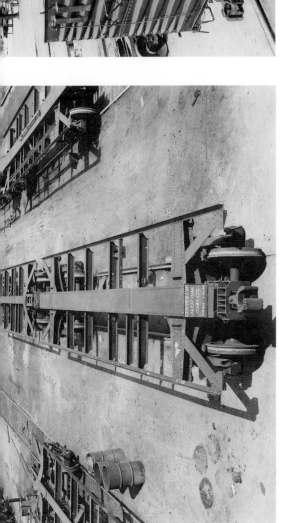

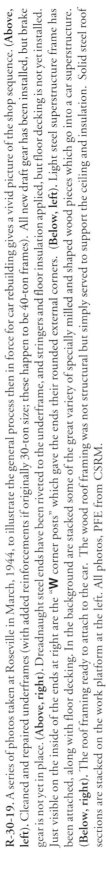

R-30-19. A series of photos taken at Roseville in March, 1944, to illustrate the general process then in force for car rebuilding gives a vivid picture of the shop sequence. (**Above, left**). Cleaned and repaired underframes (with added reinforcements if originally 30-ton cars, these happen to be 40-ton frames). All new draft gear has been installed, but brake gear is not yet in place. (**Above, right**). Dreadnaught steel ends have been riveted to the underframe, and stringers and floor insulation applied, but floor decking is not yet installed. Just visible on the inside of the ends at right are the "**W** corner posts" which gave the ends their rounded external corners. (**Below, left**). Light steel superstructure frame has been attached, along with floor decking. In the background are stacked some of the great variety of specially milled and shaped wood pieces which go into a car superstructure. (**Below, right**). The wood roof framing was not structural but simply served to support the ceiling and insulation. Solid steel roof sections are stacked on the work platform at the left. All photos, PFE from CSRM.

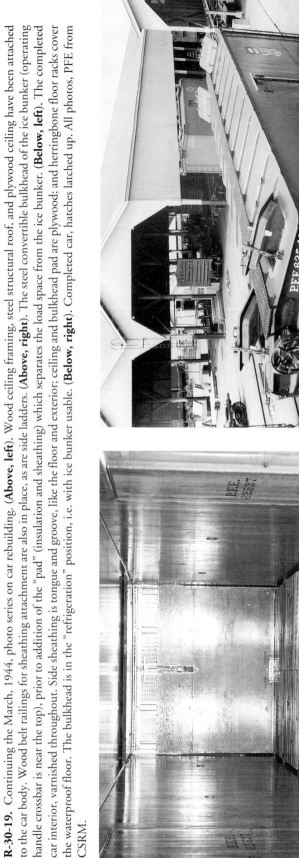

R-30-19. Continuing the March, 1944, photo series on car rebuilding. **(Above, left).** Wood ceiling framing, steel structural roof, and plywood ceiling have been attached to the car body. Wood belt railings for sheathing attachment are also in place, as are side ladders. **(Above, right).** The steel convertible bulkhead of the ice bunker (operating handle crossbar is near the top), prior to addition of the "pad" (insulation and sheathing) which separates the load space from the ice bunker. **(Below, left).** The completed car interior, varnished throughout. Side sheathing is tongue and groove, like the floor and exterior; ceiling and bulkhead pad are plywood; and herringbone floor racks cover the waterproof floor. The bulkhead is in the "refrigeration" position, i.e. with ice bunker usable. **(Below, right).** Completed car, hatches latched up. All photos, PFE from CSRM.

R-40-19. Completed car 62537, photographed on March 25, 1944, after completion of rebuilding at Roseville. Each car required about two weeks to be rebuilt. PFE photo, CSRM.

similar to the preceding -18 class. A complete set of photographs was taken at Roseville on March 25, 1944, as the work on this class was beginning. Some of these are presented here to illustrate how complete a car renewal was accomplished in rebuilding.

It may appear surprising that PFE's rebuilding continued, essentially unabated, during World War II, and moreover continued to apply steel superstructure frames and steel roofs and ends to the cars. It was mandatory for railroads generally during the war to retain in service virtually every car which could be coupled into a train. PFE not only discontinued "all voluntary retirements and dismantlings" in May, 1942, to keep older cars in service, but limits of repairs were also set aside, and all cars which needed them were to receive general or heavy repairs, including the ap-

R-40-19. A clear view of the Dreadnaught end applied to this class, as well as to -18 and -21. PFE photo, CSRM.

plication of steel superstructure frames. This applied even to the R-30-2-13 and other old car classes. Other improvements, such as better insulation, AB brakes, and modern ice bunkers, were also continued.

The PFE fleet was considered essential to the war effort by the War Production Board, and PFE was able to obtain needed materials, other than certain critical steel alloys and some rubber and other special materials, throughout the war. On the other hand, as discussed in the next chapter, PFE was not given permission to buy new, all-steel cars during the war. A new car consumed too much steel.

During World War II, car washing was considerably reduced, as were most non-essential operations. The years 1937-42 saw an average of nearly 19,000 cars washed annually, but in 1943-45, only about 7000 cars were washed each year.

In the early 1950's, the -19 cars began to receive Preco overhead electric fans. They also received general repairs in 1954-55. Like the -16's and -18's, their steel superstructure frames permitted them to remain in service until the fleet underwent major shrinkage in the 1960's. The last car of the -19's, as with the other 60,000 series cars, was retired in 1966.

Class R-30-21, R-40-21

The class which followed -19 was the -21 of 1945-47, which was essentially the same as cars of the preceding -18 and -19 classes, although a major difference in performance was achieved with car fans. Installation of mechanical fans began with the -21's, using such a wide range of Preco and Equipco models that an experiment was presumably being conducted. However, this also marked the beginning of

R-30-21. This photo of PFE 64668, rebuilt in March, 1946, at Colton, shows the 1942-46 paint scheme with its deeply-indented Union Pacific medallion, no longer including an "Overland" slogan. PFE photo, UP Railroad Museum.

PFE's large-scale fan installation. In the early 1950's, the -21 cars had their mechanical fans replaced with Preco Model AA-19 electric fans.

It is interesting that although the initial shop order for work under class -21 specifications was written in 1945 to convert 2000 cars, this was evidently extended, and eventually 2420 cars were rebuilt (numbered 63501-65920) by September, 1947. The next month the class -24 program began. A few of the -21's received new 40-ton underframes permitting a change (if necessary) from R-30 to R-40, in cases where the original underframe was too corroded, cracked or distorted to re-use, but the great majority of these rebuilds continued to ride on their original frames. As with preceding rebuild classes having steel super frames, these cars remained in service until the mid-1960's.

There is also said to have been a proposed R-40-22 design at war's end, for steel side sheathing to be applied to

PFE rebuilds, but it was never implemented. A number of other refrigerator car operators carried out such rebuilds, for example SFRD, but PFE never did. As discussed earlier in this chapter, such a design had also been considered in the 1930's but was rejected as too expensive in light of the use of an older underframe.

Painting and lettering. In June of 1946, part way through the -21 rebuilding campaign, PFE adopted a modified paint scheme in which the medallions of both railroads were painted on each side of the car, with the SP medallion closest to the car door. The UP shield was also re-shaped, with somewhat less side curvature. Thus cars of the -21 group were built with two paint schemes, depending on when they were completed. It appears that the new scheme was introduced at about the time car 65100 was completed.

R-30-21. This portrait at Los Angeles Shop of PFE 65150 in August, 1946, shows the two-medallion paint scheme adopted in June, 1946. Note that ice bunker, fan and stage icing information was now in 2-in. lettering at upper left. PFE photo, CSRM.

In the years 1942-47, inclusive, about 25,000 cars (including about 6400 rebuilds) were painted in PFE shops. Together with 6000 new steel cars delivered in the same period, this means that over three-fourths of PFE's total fleet had already lost pre-1942 paint schemes, that is, with UP "Overland" medallions, by the end of 1947.

Class R-30-24, R-40-24

The next rebuild class was the -24 design, which was very similar to the preceding -21 design except that the car ends were changed to the "improved Dreadnaught" design at or about the start of -24 rebuilding. Preco Model FG-41 or FK-2 mechanical fans were applied.

The most visible external differences of the -24 class were its "improved" ends, with small ribs between the large ones to increase stiffness, and its plywood external sheathing. As early as 1938, when R-30-9 car 94300 was built, the potential of plywood had been recognized as a simpler sheathing method for refrigerator cars. The -24 design, however, was PFE's first large-scale use of it. These rebuilds cost about $6000 each, at a time when new steel R-40-25 cars were costing $7225 each.

The material specifications in the shop orders for rebuilding of the -24 class specify "Harborite" exterior plywood (see section on R-30-9 class) for car sides. The old underframe, whether a 30-ton or 40-ton underframe, was re-used, as on earlier rebuilds. The plywood attachment along the side sill was a light angle, identical to that used on tongue-and-groove (T&G) sides. Surprisingly, the PFE diagram for this class makes no mention of plywood siding (though diagrams for other classes do so).

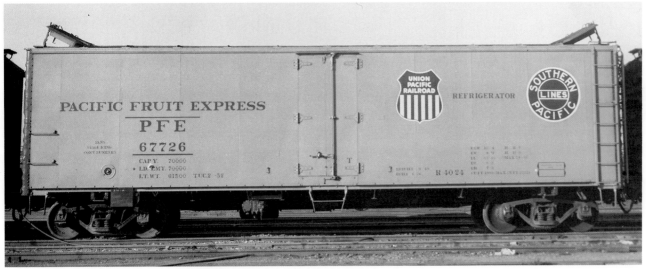

R-40-24 (Above). Repainted at Tucson in February, 1952, PFE 67726 shows off its plywood sides and the 1952 paint scheme, with the black-white UP medallion. The car has mechanical car fans. W.C. Whittaker photo, Oakland, March, 1952.

R-30-24. One of the -24 cars which received T&G sheathing as a replacement for plywood in the mid-1950's, car 66073 was photographed at Salinas in 1957. Note that a few sheathing boards have been repainted (probably replaced) subsequent to the original painting. This car originally was PFE 34281, an R-30-13. E. Mohr photo.

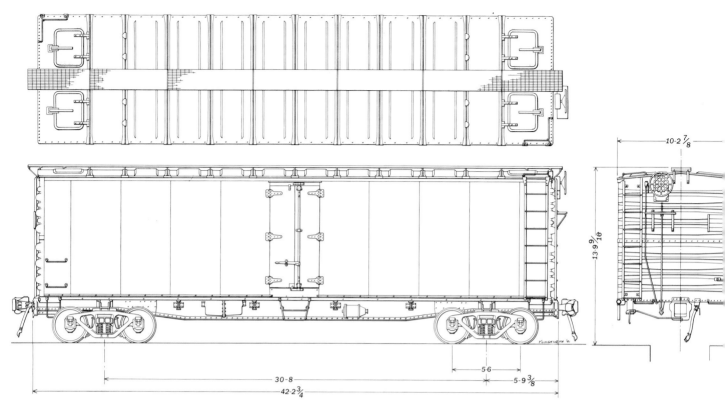

R-40-24. This HO scale drawing of the plywood-sided design was made by Chuck Yungkurth from PFE blueprints. The fan control box and fan location are not shown because they differed for diffferent makes and models of fans. Ajax brake gear and Apex running board shown but other makes of specialties were also applied. The last rebuilds of this class had diagonal-panel roofs.

In the 1960's, many PFE rebuilds received the Gothic lettering typical of that period, especially the fan-equipped classes. Here PFE 67312 exhibits the 1960-61 scheme (see Chapters 8 and 9) and T&G siding replacing its original plywood. This car's original number was 31933, an R-30-13 built in 1926 by AC&F, and was rebuilt in July, 1948. Bob Lorenz collection.

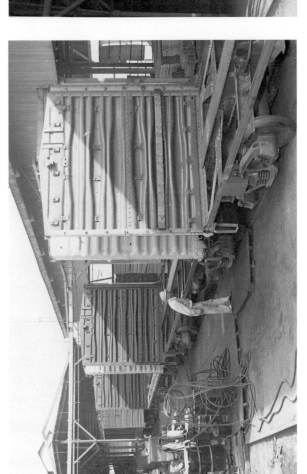

R-40-24. This series of photos was taken at Colton Shop on Oct. 19, 1948, by a Southern California Edison Company photographer and provided to PFE. **(Above, left).** After stripping cars down to frames, stiffening was applied and any needed repairs were made. Note new triple brake valve beneath the side sill. **(Above, right).** The many specially shaped and drilled wood pieces needed for car superstructures were mass produced in the wood shop. **(Below, left).** Primer-coated "improved Dreadnaught" ends have been riveted to refurbished and stiffened frames. Fan control boxes and the "**W** corner posts" are visible. **(Below, right).** Freshly painted 67886, with its plywood sheathing and two-medallion paint scheme, is ready for service. All photos, PFE collection, CSRM.

R-30-9. Car 91593, rebuilt from R-30-13 27942 in 1937, received plywood sides in 1948 and was repainted in this 1952 paint scheme in May, 1953. Ends remain T&G. V.W. Davis photo, 1956, at Gering, Nebr.

The plywood sides were not entirely successful, tending to curl in service, thus opening the joints between sheets, and to peel. After 1955, the plywood was no longer repaired, but instead the entire car side was re-sheathed with T&G siding. Shop directions in fact specified that removed plywood was not to be saved even if in good condition. The number of cars which received T&G replacement sheathing is not known, but a number of -24 cars were photographed with T&G replaced sides.

Photos also exist showing a few cars from classes R-40-8, R-40-9, and R-40-21 with plywood sides (including cars 64771, 68453, 91593 and 94242), presumably cars which were in the shop for sheathing replacement during the period of enthusiasm for plywood, but how extensive such application was has not been determined. Car photos are apparently the only surviving record of a particular car's siding material at a particular time. Other plywood applications are discussed elsewhere in this chapter.

Near the end of the -24 rebuilding, PFE began to use the diagonal panel roof, also used for the new R-40-25 class then being built. Exact car numbers are not known, but it appears that the last 200 or so cars had such roofs.

The R-40-24 cars marked the end of major rebuilding programs on wood cars by PFE, as noted above. However, smaller reconditioning and upgrading projects, some already mentioned, such as the addition of steel superframes to the -9 cars, continued thereafter.

During the -24 program, a general arrangement drawing was prepared in 1947, dated Oct. 2, 1947, for a new class of rebuilds, the R-30-25, similar to the -24 cars with wood sheathing and steel roof and ends. Before they could be undertaken as follow-ons to the -24 program, however,

rebuilding ceased for the tax reasons mentioned earlier. The -25 class number was used instead for the new steel cars, discussed in the following chapter, which were built in 1949-50.

R-50 REBUILDS

The 1930-built R-50-1's began to need rebuilding by 1940. In addition to a single experimental rebuild, the R-50-1-2 described next, 100 of the original 400 cars were rebuilt during 1941 with steel ends like those being applied to R-30 and R-40 rebuilds.

Class R-50-1-2

An interesting variation on the class, and clearly an experiment, was the R-50-1-2 car, numbered 100036, which was rebuilt from an in-service R-50-1 in March, 1940 at the Los Angeles shop. Drawing C-7604, dated Aug. 1940, shows it with eight hatches. This was a two-compartment car, with individual doors for each compartment, evidently intended for use with smaller loads. (Load dividers would later serve this purpose in a more flexible manner.) It also had overhead ice bunkers, a design feature discussed below. Although shippers found the car interesting (see Bibliography), in PFE's eyes it was clearly not a success, or at least not worth repeating, since only the one car was constructed, and it was off the roster by 1944.

Classes R-50-1-3, R-50-1-4

The following year, 1941, 100 of the R-50-1's were

R-50-1-2. A rare service shot in Los Angeles: the car was only used for about four years. Photo 13743, UP Railroad Museum.

rebuilt with steel roofs and ends, as well as steel superstructure framing and "integral" (one-piece) hatch plugs and covers, that is, like the R-30-18's. Of these, the first 75 were classed R-50-1-4 and had stationary bulkheads; the following 25 were classed R-50-1-3, and were given convertible bulkheads as well as air circulating fans. These 100 cars were also renumbered to 100401-100500. (In about 1945, these sub-class numbers were dropped, and these cars were then classed R-50-3 and R-50-4.)

Class R-50-5

During 1945-47, the remaining 284 of the original R-50-1's were rebuilt, this time to class R-50-5. These were being converted for frozen food service, to supplement the R-70-2 cars (see previous chapter), and accordingly their 5-inch insulation, already double the thickness of most cars of their vintage, was replaced with 7 inches of new insulation, and they were given improved doors and ice tanks. The first 75 cars, rebuilt in 1945, had stationary bulkheads, stage icing, and fans, as well as steel roofs and ends. These ends were the round-corner "early" Dreadnaught style.

These cars also were equipped with an internal latticework "lining" intended to assist air circulation. Ordinarily, when cargo was loaded flush with the walls, air could only move above and below the cargo, and there was also a possibility of heat conduction from the wall into the load. Later, the new R-40-23 steel cars would replace these hori-

R-50-1-2. (Left) The plywood-side, two-compartment car with 5-4 Dreadnaught ends (slightly different than the 4-4 ends shown earlier in this chapter). (Right) The car first had 16 roof hatches for its overhead bunkers (it was redone in 8-40 to have just 8; see photo above). Hatches were in pairs, as shown by the open pair at the near end of the roof. PFE photos, CSRM.

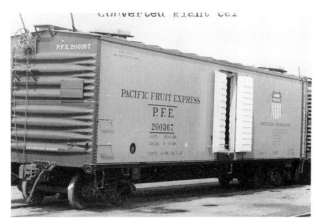

R-50-5 (Left). The **W**-corner post steel ends and thick door linings are evident in this 1945 Nampa photo. **(Right).** PFE 200375 here displays the internal lattice framing (predecessor of the side-wall flue) to provide better air circulation. Herringbone floor racks and fixed bulkheads are also visible. PFE photos, CSRM.

zontal strips with plywood to form a sidewall "flue" for the same purpose.

The balance of the cars received "Harborite" exterior plywood rather than tongue-and-groove siding, with 100 cars completed in 1946 and the balance in 1947. As with other classes, this plywood was not a great success, and a number of the cars later had T&G siding re-applied. In later years, many R-50-5's had electric fans added.

When rebuilt, the R-50-5's received new car numbers. The T&G-sheathed cars became 200301-200375, and the plywood cars became the 200379-200587 series. The "in-between" cars were the thick-insulation R-50-1 rebuilds: 100260 became 200376, 100350 became 200377, and 100264 became 200378. These R-50-5 cars thus joined the R-70-2 cars as part of the 200,000 series, now identified as a frozen food series. They were finally scrapped in the late 1950's when, as described in the previous chapter,

both the frozen food and other cargoes migrated away from ice cars, to mechanical cars or to insulated boxcars.

Overhead ice bunkers: Classes R-70-4, R-30-12-17

In 1940, PFE undertook experiments with overhead ice bunker cars. The cars were a mixture of rebuilds and new cars. The R-50-1-2 car has already been mentioned; preceding it in the summer of 1940 were 5 rebuilt cars of class R-30-12-17 (described below). The new cars were especially interesting. The 1939 construction of the R-70-3 class, little modified from R-70-2, was described in the previous chapter. The next year, 1940, a much different car design was built as R-70-4. The 5 cars of this order had overhead ice tanks with 10 ice hatches, five on each side. Built at Los Angeles for about $6000 each, these were an experiment to test out the overhead tank idea, continuing

R-50-5. The last of the T&G-sheathed rebuilds to R-50-5, at Nampa in 1945. The deep underframe, inherited from the original 1930 construction, is evident, as is the round black fan shaft location on the car side. PFE photo, CSRM.

R-70-4. The left side and "B" end of car 200121. The plywood sides, 4-4 steel ends, and particularly the 5 hatches on each side of the roof are evident. The underframe is essentially that of the R-70-2 design. PFE photo, CSRM.

PFE's innovative thrusts described in the preceding chapter. Much of the construction was based on PFE's close monitoring of Canadian experience with this design, including a series of very detailed reports in the PFE archives of the construction of 50 Canadian Pacific overhead bunker cars of wood-sheathed design with 8 roof hatches, cars 289940-289989, in 1938. The overhead bunker design had an extensive history in Canadian practice.

Tests in the 1930's, particularly in Canada, had shown that cars with overhead ice tanks provided good temperature uniformity in loads, and could use less ice (see for example, the Lentz-Cook and Townshend articles in the Bibliography). Some writers, such as White in *The Great Yellow Fleet*, have even asserted, regarding adoption of overhead ice tanks, that American railroading interests "resisted mightily" on economic rather than technical grounds. Paid on a mileage basis, they had no incentive to invest in a better-performing car. Does the record support this charge? Why, in light of Canadian construction of over 3000 cars of this design, did U.S. operators such as PFE remain unimpressed by the temperature uniformity provided by overhead ice tanks? The record shows that there were a number of technical reasons.

These reasons can be divided into three groups. First and most important, the end-bunker car was capable of faster cooling of warm loads of produce, a factor which was also to delay the replacement of ice bunker cars by mechanical refrigerators for produce. (The R-70-4 was designed for frozen food, not produce.) The Canadian ownership total of over 7000 refrigerator cars, 4000 of them end or side bunker cars, was equipped 100% for meat

Icing a car with overhead ice bunkers, here with salt additions being monitored. The car is a Fruit Growers Express (FOBX) 50-ft. car. CSRM collection, neg. 248.

R-70-4. An interior view of the overhead ice tanks. The plywood ceiling panels under the drip pans have been dropped down on the left. PFE photo at Los Angeles on Jan. 8, 1940, CSRM.

service, and only occasionally used for produce. Moreover, when produce was shipped in Canada, the end-bunker cars were ordinarily specified.

A second group of reasons was related to the operational differences between overhead and end ice tanks. It was more difficult to ice and salt overhead tanks, as the usual process of chopping blocks in the hatch opening, and using a long bar to settle and compact the ice in the tank, was much more prone to tank damage with these shallow overhead tanks. Filling the tanks went much more slowly, a concern with long trains of reefers, even when crushed ice was used. Finally, if the tanks leaked, brine fell onto the load; moisture condensed on the tanks and dripped onto the load in spite of "drain pans;" and these tanks considerably raised the cars' center of gravity. And the overhead bunker cars cost more to build and to maintain. The Canadian

overhead ice bunker cars, incidentally, were all equipped with brine tanks for meat service, something not done in most U.S. experiments with this car design, as American operators (other than packers) were primarily interested in produce or frozen food shipment.

The third reason relates to particular Canadian conditions. As W. T. Pentzer of the U.S. Dept. of Agriculture pointed out in discussing the Lentz-Cook paper (see Bibliography), "much of the Canadian traffic in perishables [mostly meat] is for export, and the cars may wait several days to a week for unloading at the port. Under these circumstances, the overhead bunker car provides somewhat more uniform temperatures than fan cars standing without fans operating. This is not an important consideration in the United States." (Lentz and Cook concurred.) This raises an important point: car fans.

As mentioned earlier, PFE actively conducted experiments with methods to circulate air around the load, another means to make the car interior temperature more uniform. Their first experiment with essentially commercial fan designs occurred in 1938. It was not until the Van Dorn patent fan was marketed by Preco in 1940, however, that a commercially successful design was available. PFE, like other American refrigerator car operators, found fans to be a more satisfactory answer to temperature uniformity for their predominant traffic in produce. The Canadians had difficulties in snow or icy conditions with fans, and accordingly preferred overhead bunkers.

A related issue is heater service in cold weather. Normal practice was to place heaters in the end bunkers, and the resulting convective air flow, especially if augmented by fans, was effective. With an overhead bunker, there was no good place for heaters (Canadian cars had them permanently mounted under the floor, a weight penalty U. S. operators

R-70-4. An overhead view, showing the hatch opening pattern and the steel roof. Note the precooling shed in the background. PFE photo at Los Angeles on Jan. 8, 1940, from CSRM.

R-70-4. In 1949, PFE tested a new insulation material, "Isoflex," with alternate layers of corrugated foil and fiberglass, here being installed in the floor. This test led to usage in mechanical refrigerators, which were primarily loaded, like the R-70-4's, with frozen food. PFE, CSRM.

were reluctant to pay). Thus even in cold weather, produce service was better accomplished with end bunkers which were equipped with fans.

PFE did conduct a number of test runs with these cars, but did not repeat the R-70-4 design, although the cars remained in service through the 1950's as part of PFE's frozen food fleet. In 1949, the cars were retrofitted with Equipco air circulating fans, and were reconstructed to add end bunkers to the overhead ice bunkers. At this same time, they also received horizontally-grooved plywood sheathing, as discussed earlier in this chapter in connection with the R-30-9 cars, and illustrated for car 200121 on pages 134 and 255. A test of "Isoflex" insulation was also made. As described in Chapter 9, this became the standard insulation in mechanical refrigerators throughout the 1950's.

As already shown, PFE rebuilt a single R-50 with overhead bunkers and two compartments, the R-50-1-2 100036, shown above, and designed an overhead-tank car of more conventional size, which was intended for produce service. This was prepared as drawing C-7500, dated June, 1940, for an R-30-12-17 car which had a similar appearance to the R-70-4, but on a standard PFE 41-ft. car body, with 8 ice hatches, steel roof and ends, and wood side sheathing. The weight of the overhead ice tank arrangement can be seen from the light weight of these cars, 64,400 pounds, compared to the R-30-18's, which also had steel roofs and ends but weighed just 57,700 pounds. This extra 4700 pounds, being at the top of the car, was the source of the concern about center of gravity. Just 5 of these cars were rebuilt from R-30-12's in late 1940, numbered 79995-79999; two of them, 79996 and 79998, had 16 hatches instead of 8. As with the R-70-4, PFE conducted extensive

experiments, but never repeated the design. All the -17 cars were retired in the early 1950's.

As this summary makes clear, PFE was not initially "hostile" to the overhead bunker concept. Instead, they built eleven cars, of three different sizes, to test the idea, and maintained the cars in service for some time. The technical findings cited above, however, were adverse to the overhead ice bunker, particularly since car fans proved equally adept at making lading temperatures more uniform, but with fewer drawbacks. American refrigerator car service conditions were significantly different than Canadian ones, and different in ways which militated against the overhead ice bunker design. To assert that overhead bunker cars weren't built in the United States out of managerial stubbornness is to ignore the technical record.

Western Pacific Cars

An important part of PFE's car rehabilitation was the work done on part of the Western Pacific car series. By 1950 only 114 of the cars remained un-reconditioned. But the condition of the WP cars was deteriorating. When reconditioned in the 1939-40 period (Chapter 5), they had received new wood-framed superstructures with a life expectancy of only about 8 years.

By 1950, a substantial number were being scrapped (officially, "returned to WP"); some were retained by WP for company use. Among these were 38 cars which were converted to ice service in 1951-52. At the WP Sacramento shops, the ice bunkers and floor racks were removed from the cars; some cars also lost the ice hatches. They were numbered MW 7021-7058, with maintenance-of-way paint schemes (silver with black lettering after the early 1950's). They remained in service until the 1970's.

In early 1952, PFE notified WP that the remaining cars needed extensive work, if, as PFE desired, the cars were to be kept equivalent to PFE's own cars. Again WP requested a minimum expense project. PFE agreed to recondition 900 of these cars, at a cost of $10 million. When the work was carried out in 1952-53, it developed that only 899 cars

WP cars. A "returned" car from PFE service, as it later appeared in WP ice service. W.C. Whittaker photo, 1954.

153

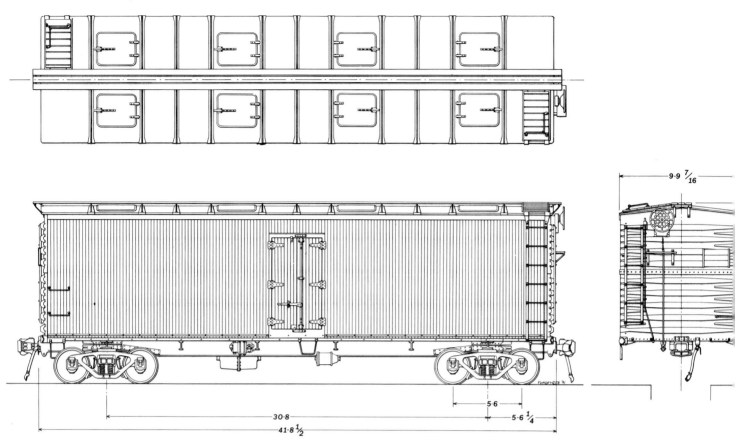

R-30-12-17. Shown here in an HO scale drawing by Chuck Yungkurth, this was a 5-car class of experimental overhead ice bunker cars, of 41-ft. or "standard" length (PFE's terminology). As noted in the text, two of the five cars had 16 instead of 8 hatches in the roof; none had end ice bunkers. The underframe is a 30-ton Bettendorf, inherited from the original R-30-12 construction.

PFE ice service cars were typically older cars demoted from revenue service. In the 1955-60 period they often were R-30-16's, as with the two cars at left (PFE 74796 and 73822), but other cars were used too, such as R-30-8 91665 at right. The photo illustrates that these cars didn't always receive lettering to denote their assignment. PFE 91665 has only 1-inch white lettering to the left of the car number to indicate its service. UP photo 40123, July, 1957, Riverdale (Ogden) yard, PFE collection, CSRM.

WP Cars. The first of the 899 reconditioned WP cars, photographed at Roseville in June, 1952. A dummy "fan plate" indicates the presence of electric fans. PFE photo, CSRM.

could be found in good enough shape to be worth reconditioning. This time the cars did get steel-framed superstructures, and Preco Model AA-15 electric fans with dummy fan plates like those on the R-40-26 steel cars. PFE had set aside car numbers 55001-55900 for these reworked cars, though the highest number used was 55899.

At that time, PFE would have preferred to rebuild the cars with solid steel ends and roofs, but, at owner WP's direction, instead had to repair and re-install the existing wood ends, wood ice hatches with obsolete hinged plugs, and outside metal roofs. Such roofs were also re-applied to PFE's own R-30-9 cars during 1949-53. Thus the external

appearance of the WP cars remained much the same as when they were built. More significantly, their technical characteristics remained typical of the late 1930's, rather than of the 1950's rework dates.

As expected, this rework only extended life of these cars by about 7 years. After the demise of the wood car fleet, PFE supplied its own ice and mechanical cars to WP under terms of a revised car agreement. As described in Chapter 1, the series of agreements between WP and PFE came to an end in 1967, when WP gave the minimum notice required to terminate 44 years of car agreements and signed instead with Fruit Growers Express.

WP cars. Car 55759 in service, showing the hinged plugs and wooden hatch covers, wood-sheathed ends, and edge of the outside metal roof, all features superseded on PFE's own rebuilt cars, except for R-30-9. Photo by Herman B. Miller, NB-10223, courtesy Kalmbach Memorial Library, NMRA.

Table 7-3
Numbers of Wood-sheathed Cars with Original Numbers**

Car Numbers	Class	Number of Cars					
		New	1934	1940	1947	1950	1958
1- 6600	R-30-1, -2	6600	4171	1878	56	3	0
6601- 7100	R-30-4	500	440	6	0	0	0
7101-10121	R-30-5	3021	2135	66	1	0	0
10122-13219	R-30-6	3098	2788	37	1	1	0
13220-13279	R-30-11-½	60	46	40	35	12	5
13280-15919	R-30-11	2640	1966	1830	1581	694	210
15920-18919	R-30-12	3000	2942	1866			
18920-19919	R-30-13	1000	980	631			
19920-26719	R-30-13	6800	6697	4196			
26720-28249	R-30-13	1530	1510	989	3389*	284	5
28250-28749	R-30-12	500	496	335			
28750-29649	R-30-13	900	888	597			
29650-31249	R-30-12	1600	1581	1106			
31250-32434	R-30-13						
32435-33434	R-30-14	5224	5165	4558	2012	131	2
33435-36473	R-30-13						
36474-36562	R-40-1	89	88	88	85	59	0
36563-38562	R-40-2	2000	1980	1950	557	0	0
38563-39062	R-40-4	500	498	493	483	477	340
50001-52775	(WP cars)	2775	2726	2682	2599	916	0
100001-100400	R-50-1	400	400	395	111	2	0
200001-200100	R-70-2	100	100	100	100	99	34

*This group had comprised 9720 cars in 1940.

**From freight *Equipment Registers*

The important thing to be kept in mind about rebuilds is this: they comprised many thousands of cars after 1935. Table 7-3 has been constructed to furnish some idea of the numbers of wood cars which retained their original car numbers in later years. But if one looks only at the surviving members of the original R-30 classes, as in Table 7-3, a misleading impression is gained of the rate of attrition of the fleet. In fact, when PFE ended its rebuilding programs in December, 1948, shop records (Forms 865) showed that a grand total of 45,561 cars had been rebuilt by the company, some two or even three times in their lives, since 1907. More than 15,000 cars had also been reconditioned in the same period of time.

These wood-bodied cars had been rebuilt, had received new car numbers in the 60, 70, 80 or 90,000 series as well as new class numbers, and remained in service. This is how it was possible for there to be as many as 14,000 wood cars in service as late as 1958, 30 to 40 years after they had been

Early PFE intermodal? No, just a surplus WP car converted to other use, here on a road move. C. Winters collection.

Table 7-4
Survival of Rebuilt Cars*
(Principal Rebuilt Classes Only)

Car Numbers	Class	Number of Cars						
		Rebuilt	1950	1955	1960	1962	1965	1968
71273-71953	R-40-4	510	488	474	179	17	2	0
90001-91021	R-40-8	1021	960	728	235	17	3	0
91022-98718	R-30, 40-9	7694	7181	6642	708	100	13	1
99001-99100	R-30, 40-15	52	40**	39**	43	34	0	0
85001-85275	R-30-9, -16	275	218	52	6	0	0	0
73001-76554	R-30, 40-16	3554	3436	3219	1383	754	569	2
60001-62500	R-30, 40-18	2500	2455	2427	1639	236	14	1
62501-63500	R-30, 40-19	1000						
63501-65920	R-40-21	2420	5958	5853	4863	2341	387	3
65921-68532	R-40-24	2610						
200301-200587	R-50-5	287	279	278	181	71	8	0

*From freight *Equipment Registers*
**Not all cars in class rebuilt before 1955

A view of the car repair tracks at PFE's Los Angeles Shop, along the west edge of SP's Taylor Yard. The shop crane is carrying the top half of a Dreadnaught end for re-application to a car being repaired, of class -18, -19 or -21. The car superframes are the new welded design adopted in 1950. These cars are most likely R-30-9's getting new superframes, a project in progress at the time of the photo (also see Chapter 11, and opening photo, Chapter 6). Richard Steinheimer photo, December, 1950.

Table 7-5
Proportion of Wood-sheathed Cars, by Year

	1934	1938	1940	1944	1947	1950	1958
Total Car Fleet*	40608	38426	37265	35921	36245	38434	33090
Number of Steel Cars	–	4695	4683	5658	6637	14554	19130
Per Cent Wood-Sheathed Cars	–	88.0	87.4	84.3	81.7	62.1	42.0

*Includes rebuilds

built. By that time, in fact, virtually all such cars carried class designations other than the ones they were built with, as is evident from Table 7-1 and from the discussion of individual classes in this chapter and in Chapter 6.

This complication with the rebuilds leads one to ask the further question: how many cars in the PFE fleet continued to be wood-sheathed in the years covered by Tables 7-3 and 7-4? Table 7-5 has accordingly been constructed to emphasize the proportion of the PFE fleet which was wood-sheathed, by subtracting the steel cars from the total car fleet. Although the 60,000-series rebuilds had steel super frames, they are lumped in with the other rebuilds and original cars. A related question is the survival of the rebuild classes themselves, as the PFE fleet shrank during the 1960's. That history was presented in Table 7-4.

Painting and lettering. The paint schemes applied to rebuilt cars were those current at the time of the rebuilding. It is worth repeating that during 1915-1942, most cars were repainted every 4-6 years, so that paint schemes tended to remain current. Although painting frequency was reduced in 1931 and during most of World War II, the 1945-52 period was a busy one in the shops.

In those eight years, more than 45,000 cars were painted in total. Since 8000 new cars were delivered in the period, and the fleet only averaged about 38,000 cars, it should be

clear that older paint schemes were rare by 1952. Certainly few pre-1942 paint schemes (UP shields with "Overland" slogans) were still extant on wood-sheathed cars. Any earlier schemes were certainly extinct, and even the pre-1946 "single medallion" paint schemes were becoming rare.

During 1953-55, another 22,000 cars were painted. The pre-1949 paint schemes were being eliminated, and photos from 1955 or so confirm that virtually every PFE car in that period had the "black-white" two-medallion scheme. It must be remembered that PFE cleaned and inspected every working car several times a year in its own shops (see Chapter 11), inasmuch as the average car made

Clearly shown in this unusual view are the formed steel grate bars at the bottom of a PFE ice tank, and the metal screen of the "basket bunker" (see Chapter 5). Typical of 1920's practice, such a bunker would be modernized in rebuilding. A.W. Thompson collection.

As long as it was possible to do so, and well after AAR deadlines for replacement, PFE reworked its T-section trucks and kept them in service. PFE photo, CSRM.

R-30-9 (Left). With the outside metal roof removed, the pressed steel carlines (transverse members) are clearly seen. Above them are the longitudinal wood roof supports. These carlines were PFE's first use of steel superstructure parts, in 1919. They are still in service here in car 94663 at Los Angeles on Oct. 30, 1941. PFE photo, CSRM. **R-40-21 (Right).** A roof view of a freshly-rebuilt car at Roseville in 1944. This car originally was 36811, an R-40-2. In the background at left are an express reefer and an R-30-8 car in for repair, while at right is a partially resheathed R-50 car which awaits painting. PFE photo, CSRM.

about ten revenue trips a year, and passed through a PFE shop after each trip; and paint schemes were readily kept current if that was management's wish.

In the post-war period, PFE continued to wash car exteriors, averaging almost 11,000 cars per year during 1945-48. Labor costs caused washing frequency to decrease sharply in 1949, and remained at about 2000 cars annually until 1955. At that time, PFE requested funds to construct a mechanical car washer, to replace the hand labor used since World War I for this task. The request unfortunately brought the car-washing practice to the attention of Southern Pacific's blunt-spoken President, D.J. Russell, who not only denied the request, but exclaimed, "You're never going to wash a goddamn freight car on my railroad." Car washing declined sharply, and soon thereafter was halted for good. The only cars washed in later years were in the course of repairs or repainting.

Also in the early 1950's, an asphalt emulsion began to be applied to the ends of wood-sheathed cars, duplicating the practice begun about 1940 on steel cars. This was either boxcar red in color in some cases, or was painted that color. The asphalt coating on the ends, like that already in use on roofs, was believed to be resistant to water penetration and thus to corrosion and deterioration of the car structure.

After February, 1949, PFE cars began to be stenciled near the center of the roof with reporting marks and car number, presumably for the convenience of icing crews. This is visible in the photo earlier in this chapter of the roof of car 92508, as is the granular material in the asphalt coating (applied to all rebuilt cars after May, 1940, and to all shopped cars after Oct. 1949). The roof lettering, how-

ever, never was extended to all cars, and its application seems to have been discontinued about 1952.

A final note on car painting relates to the interpretation of photographs. The photo above shows a car of R-40-21, freshly completed at Roseville. In accord with standard practice, the roof is boxcar red with slate granules sprinkled into it when wet, for skid resistance, while the ends are the same color over an asphalt emulsion (standard on steel ends from the early 1940's). The lighting makes it look like the roof is a lighter color, but note that the upper surfaces of the end ribs also look lighter in color. The light scattering from the slate granules is part of this effect, and most PFE car roofs which were photographed from a low angle after the introduction of the granules in 1940 have this lighter color appearance.

Until the 1960's, as discussed in the next chapter, ice cars continued to have red roofs. The steel frozen food cars (see next chapter) at first were given light gray roofs, which were soon changed to aluminum paint, but that paint color was not officially applied to ice car roofs until 1962. Some color photographs show ice cars prior to 1962 with aluminum roofs and black ends, colors which later became standard. Other photos appear to show other combinations, such as red roofs/black ends, black ends/black roofs, and others, which might reflect a car partly painted in accord with the scheme specified for mechanical cars (see Chapter 9), which was aluminum roof and black ends, or merely a dirty roof. Since PFE generally adhered closely to official painting directions (particularly before about 1955), such examples are rare. Even in 1962, when the specifications were changed, the vast majority of PFE ice cars still had red roofs and ends.

A familiar sight to travelers on California's U.S. 101 highway is this view from the overcrossing of the SP Coast Line at Camarillo. Here it's the summer of 1956, and Alco's DL701 (RS-11) demonstrators 701, 701A, and 701B, already purchased by SP and bound for Los Angeles, are overtaken by a train of PFE reefers loaded with Santa Maria vegetables or citrus from Santa Barbara and Ventura Counties. All hatches are latched up in "vent" or ventilation position. Don Sims photo.

8

THE STEEL ICE CARS

R-40-10. The first big order for steel reefers was PFE's R-40-10 class, 4700 cars strong. This photo of PFE 42225 was used in PFE publicity as well as by several of PFE's suppliers in their own advertising. PFE photo, CSRM.

The preceding chapters summarize the history of Pacific Fruit Express "wood" refrigerator car classes, the very successful steel underframe-wood superstructure type of design which had been followed from 1906 until 1930. Yet by 1930 this design was obsolescent. As discussed in Chapter 6, steel framing of wood superstructures was introduced in 1930 with the R-40-4, while 1932's R-70-2 class (designed in 1931) represented a further transition toward an all-steel car, with its steel roof and ends. It might be thought that an all-steel reefer was imminent; many thousands of all-steel boxcars had been built for U.S. railroads by 1930.

It must be recognized, however, that all-steel *refrigerator* cars for ordinary freight service did not exist at this time in North America. As late as 1929, no all-steel refrigerator cars had been built, except a very few experiments or cars in express service (see Sweeley and Dietrichson articles in Bibliography). Much of the reluctance to build such cars stemmed from the belief that the heat conduction, and thus heat losses, of steel external sheathing might be exces-

sive. Advances in insulation, however, were to demolish this concern after 1930.

Design work for an all-steel car was undertaken by PFE in late 1930. The underframe, the engineering details, and many aspects of external appearance of this design reflect PFE's awareness of contemporary work toward the 1932 ARA steel box car design, work on which began in 1929. (ARA and AAR committees worked for over a decade on refrigerator car designs, but none was ever adopted as standard.) Many drawings of car parts for this new PFE car, and even the painting diagram, are dated 1931 or 1932. But in the depths of the Depression, a new car order was out of the question. The beginning of the steel car era on PFE had to wait until financial conditions eased in 1936.

Class R-40-10

Between 1932 and 1936, additional design work was done on the all-steel car. The insulation arrangements, for

R-40-10. The final car of the batch of R-40-10's built by SPE Co. at Roseville (a second batch of 300 cars was built by PFE at Los Angeles). Several shop foremen and supervisors pose with the new car, which clearly shows its sharp-cornered "early" Dreadnaught end. PFE photo, CSRM.

example, were revised several times, last in 1934. Finally finances permitted car orders. Expenditure of $10 million for 3000 cars was announced by PFE in January, 1936. But prices turned out to be higher than expected, and when orders were placed in April for class R-40-10, the $10 million bought only 2700 cars, at about $3700 each. This class followed general arrangement drawing C-5800, dated July 15, 1936, and specification no. 74.

The first 700 of these cars were to be built by the SP Equipment Co., an initial 400 being constructed at Roseville, the balance at Los Angeles. The remaining 2000 cars of the same class were ordered from commercial builders. Delivery began in August and was completed in November. A second set of orders followed in November, 1936, for 2000 more cars, at $200 more per car, for delivery early in 1937. The builders are shown in Table 8-1. These were the first significant commercial orders in North America for all-steel ice reefers, and at 4700 cars, represented one of the largest single classes of such cars ever built.

Design characteristics. These cars were of riveted design, with "standard" or prewar-style 4-4 rib Dreadnaught ends. These ends had the sharp corners typical of the early end design. They were slightly taller than the wood cars at 13' 4-⅝" to the running boards. Like most steel cars built in the 1930's, they had wood running boards. An internal detail is that the cars had "stationary ice bunkers," that is, conventional fixed bunkers like most R-30 cars. These cars had rectangular steel hatch covers, and the hatch plugs were separately hinged, like the plugs of earlier PFE cars.

The R-40-10's had no placard boards on sides or ends, but had small route card boards on the side sill, just above the left bolster. That location for route card boards continued into the early 1950's.

The R-40-10's were the first new standard cars with an increase in insulation thickness to 3" in walls and 3-½" in roof and floor. They were also PFE's first new cars to incorporate fiberglass insulation, which was used in the floor of most of the cars. The side, end and roof insulation was "Dry Zero," which soon led to problems. The natural fiber insulation in this material was kapok, and was quite flammable.

In normal refrigerator service, of course, the main concerns with insulation material were air circulation and resistance to moisture, not fire. But drains from the ice tanks

R-40-10. The National Type B truck, in a 1935 photo at Los Angeles. In the background is PFE 32631, a rarely-seen R-30-14. PFE photo, CSRM.

would occasionally clog or freeze up, and carmen might use torches or other sources of heat to break the clog. When this ignited the kapok, a hot fire was started inside the car walls, which as can be imagined was very difficult to extinguish. Soon after these cars went into service, then, stenciled messages appeared at the car corners, warning workmen. The stenciling read, "AVOID IGNITING INSULATION - DO NOT USE CUTTING TORCHES OR FIRES FOR THAWING DRAIN PIPES OR MAKING REPAIRS."

High-strength steel was used for the center sills, a PFE first. Floor rack height was increased to 6" in these cars, giving better air circulation under loads. Floor rack height was a compromise in air circulation patterns, since the higher the floor rack, the larger the reservoir for cool air at the floor, and the warmer the top of the load would be, when the car was under refrigeration. But in the winter, the lower the floor rack, the sooner the bottom of the load would be subject to freezing, if protective heater service was not in use. PFE concluded after many tests that 6" represented about the best compromise in height.

Most of these cars had conventional-appearing "AAR" trucks, but some of the Pullman-built cars had National Type B trucks (cars 41701-41900 and 43201-43400). PFE had operated these trucks since 1932 (they were first built in 1931), initially on R-40-8 rebuild 90355. PFE retained the Type B trucks in service until 1951, after which they were gradually replaced with National Type C-1 trucks, but did not purchase Type B trucks for any other cars.

In addition, 400 cars delivered by General American had "Barber stabilized" trucks (41201-41400 and 44201-44400). The Barber stabilizer was internal to the truck bolster and hence not readily visible. This stabilizer, which damped lateral motions, was patented by the Standard Car Truck Co. It was available in Standard's own trucks, and

Table 8-1
Numbers and Classes of Steel Ice Cars (1936-1957)

Car Numbers		Class	Built	Builder	Drawing	Capacity		Equipment**
						cu. ft.	pounds	
40001-	40700	R-40-10	1936	SPE Co.	C-5800	1988	82,000	REF, S, SI
40701-	41200	R-40-10	1936	PC&F	"	1988	82,000	"
41201-	41700	R-40-10	1936-37	Gen. American	"	1988	82,000	"
41701-	42200	R-40-10	1936	Pullman	"	1988	82,000	"
42201-	42700	R-40-10	1936-37	AC&F	"	1988	82,000	"
42701-	43200	R-40-10	1936-37	PC&F	"	1988	82,000	"
43201-	43700	R-40-10	1937	Std. Steel Car	"	1988	82,000	"
43701-	44200	R-40-10	1936-37	AC&F	"	1988	82,000	"
44201-	44700	R-40-10	1936-37	Gen. American	"	1988	82,000	"
44701-	45700	R-40-14	1941*	PC&F	C-7485	1988	80,000	REF, S, SI
45701-	46200	R-40-20	1945	Gen. American	C-8810	1988	78,000	REF, C, SI
46201-	46700	R-40-20	1945	Mt. Vernon	"	1988	78,000	"
46701-	46702	R-40-20	1945	Consol. Steel	"	1988	78,000	"
46703-	47202	R-40-23	1947	AC&F	C-9803	1988	80,000	F, C, SI
47203-	47702	R-40-23	1947	Gen. American	"	1988	80,000	"
47703-	48202	R-40-23	1947	Pullman	"	1988	80,000	"
48203-	48702	R-40-23	1947	PC&F	"	1988	80,000	"
2001-	5000	R-40-25	1949-50	SPE Co.	C-10000	1988	80,000	F, S, SI
5001-	6000	R-40-23	1947	Mt. Vernon	C-9803	1988	80,000	F, C, SI
6001-	6500	R-40-23	1947	AC&F	"	1988	80,000	"
6501-	7000	R-40-23	1947	Gen. American	"	1988	80,000	"
7001-	7500	R-40-23	1947	Pullman	"	1988	80,000	"
7501-	8000	R-40-23	1947	PC&F	"	1988	80,000	"
8001	10000	R-40-26	1950-51	SPE Co.	2500	2011	80,000	EF, S, SI
10001-	11700	R-40-27	1957	SPE Co.	3500	2022	80,000	EF, C, SI
11701-	11800	R-40-28	1957	SPE Co.	3500	2022	80,000	EF, C, SI
200126-	200200	R-70-5	1952	SPE Co.	2900	2742	133,000	EF, S, SI
200601-	200700	R-70-5	1953-54	SPE Co.	2900	2742	133,000	"

*Aluminum cars 45698 and 44739 built by PFE in 1946 and 1947, respectively.

**Equipment: F=mechanical fans, as built; RF=retrofit fans; EF=electric overhead fans, as built;
   S=stationary ice bunkers; C=convertible ice bunkers; SI=stage icing.

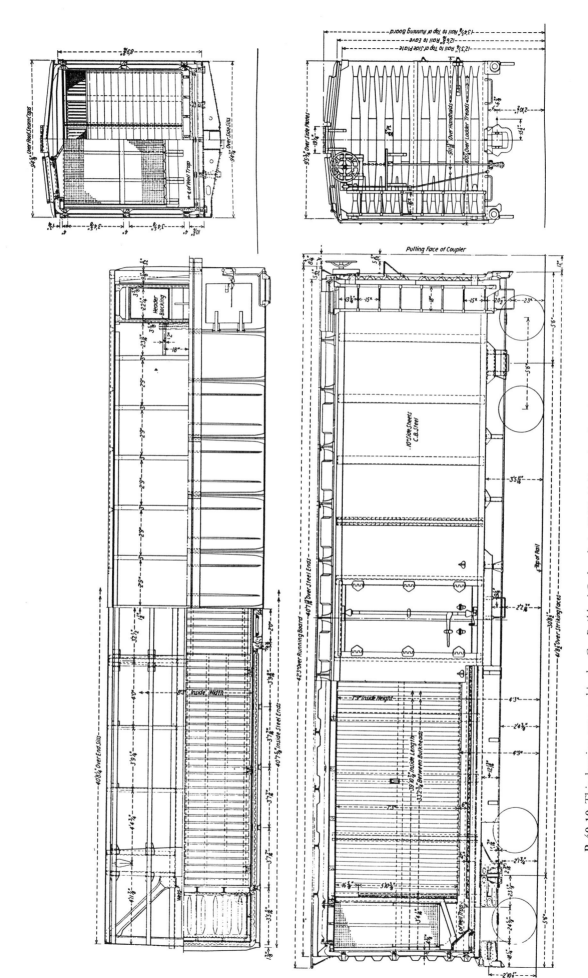

R-40-10. This drawing appeared in the *Car Builders' Cyclopedia* in 1937, 1940 and 1943. The rectangular Holland hatch covers, wood running board, and lack of any placard boards are clearly shown. Reprinted with permission.

R-40-10. A Miner C-2-XB snubber installed in the center of a 40-ton spring package (a 40-ton sideframe typically contains 4 or 5 springs). Courtesy Simmons-Boardman.

was also supplied for use in the products of other truck makers. Barber devices were used for several other PFE classes, including R-70-2, R-40-24 and R-40-25. All R-40-10's had spring snubbers within their spring groups; all but 500 were the Miner C-2-XB design, with the balance being Cardwell.

As mentioned in Chapter 6, PFE began testing steel wheels for its cars in 1928. By 1936, PFE decided to test double-wear wheels on 500 R-40-10's, 41201-41700, as a compromise between single-wear and multiple-wear wheels. But by 1940 it was clear that single-wear steel wheels were superior. Although such wheels were adopted as standard in 1941, availability problems during 1942-48 meant that only part of each order for new and rebuilt cars during that period received steel wheels. It was not until 1950 that all cars of a particular class could be given single-wear steel wheels.

Painting and lettering. When the first steel cars were delivered in 1936, the paint scheme was the same as what it had been for the R-70-2's of 1932: orange sides, boxcar red roof and ends, and black hardware. The 1922 arrangement of medallions was still in use, including the "Overland" slogan on the UP shield, although the word "SYSTEM" was omitted from the shield after January, 1936. For the steel cars, medallions were stenciled on rather than applied as metal sheets, and of course there was no fascia board to paint. Photos and painting diagrams show also that the "tabs" along the side sill, covering the ends of underframe members, were painted black, and that the space beneath the side door was no longer painted a color which contrasted with the sides. In August, 1942, the "Overland" slogan was dropped from the UP shield.

Express cars. In the summer of 1952, the Railway Express Agency was experiencing a serious shortage of express refrigerators. Shipments in these cars had tripled since 1945, yet car supply was restricted; the REA had built no express cars for a number of years. A letter at that time from the California Grape and Tree Fruit League to UP and PFE, among others, stated that the 1952 express shipments would have been double what they actually were, had enough express cars been available. It was proposed by PFE that 50 freight refrigerators be equipped for express service, and the UP offered to supply Chrysler and Symington-Gould high-speed trucks. This truck offer was attractive, not only because it would cut the cost of converting cars in half, but because the steel supply in 1952 was such that a minimum of six months would be needed to receive new cast-steel

BR-40-10. PFE 901, freshly painted Common Standard Color #1, Passenger Dark Olive, with Dulux Gold lettering, has yet to be weighed in this photo at Los Angeles in 1953. A "fan plate" symbolizes the presence of electric fans. This car has the Chrysler trucks. PFE photo, CSRM.

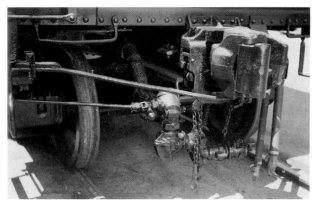

BR-40-10 (Above). The arrangement of the steam line connectors, signal line, and angle cock on the express car conversions. This PFE photo was taken at LA Shop on May 18, 1953. CSRM.

BR-40-10 (Above). The Symington-Gould "XL" truck in a builder's photo. Note "pedestal" design with separate journal boxes. Courtesy Simmons-Boardman. **(Below)** The FR-5 Chrysler truck. CSRM.

passenger trucks. The difficulty raised by PFE, however, was that some railroads were known to restrict operation in passenger service of cars equipped with Chrysler trucks.

The cars selected for conversion were 50 R-40-10's which had been overhauled in 1951 (24 cars) and 1952 (26 cars), at which time they had been given electric fans (discussed below) and Apex steel grid running boards. Now, in the spring of 1953, they also received steam and signal lines, upgrading of brakes for passenger service, marker light brackets, and trucks with passenger axles and high-speed friction bearings. The cars retained their Type E freight couplers rather than being given tight-lock couplers. The 50 cars were reclassified as BR-40-10 and were painted Common Standard Color #1, Passenger Dark Olive, like the older 50-ft. express cars, and received Dulux Gold lettering.

The trucks used are an interesting story. They were Chrysler FR-5-D (cars 901-925) or Symington-Gould Type XL (cars 926-950). All 50 pairs of trucks were purchased from the UP, which had reclaimed them from a test program on the high-speed S-40-10 cars in its stock car fleet when roller bearing trucks were applied to those cars (by 1950, over 600 UP stock cars had received roller bearings). The Chrysler sideframes, which were marketed by Symington-Gould, superficially resembled the conventional AAR design, but they also had additional snubbers at the bolster ends. Some 50 railroads were queried about acceptability of these two kinds of trucks for passenger service. Of those, only ACL, Canadian National, Grand Trunk, GM&O, L&N and Wabash objected to both truck types. REA concluded that these few roads refusing the cars would not materially affect operation of the express pool, and approved the trucks.

By 1961, the need for express refrigerator cars had largely disappeared. In that year, all 50 of the BR-40-10 cars were returned to freight service. They received sets of conventional freight trucks, and were repainted into the then-

BR-40-10. The second half of the steel express car group had Symington-Gould trucks, as shown in this photo of PFE 933. V.W. Davis photo, Sidney, Nebr., 1957.

R-40-10. (Above) Though much like the varnished 1928 car interior shown in Chapter 5, sheathing here is vertical. Lining was plywood in subsequent classes. Load is stacked as high as good air circulation permits. "Dick" Whittington photo for PFE. **(Right)** Icing an R-40-10. Note latch irons and wood running board. Both photos, CSRM.

current orange paint scheme. They even were renumbered to their original freight numbers. As summarized in Chapter 5, the 50-ft. wood express reefers were also being scrapped at about this time.

Service history. In 1939, PFE decided to test the new steel-grid running boards then being introduced. Five R-40-10 cars were selected, 41136, 41479, 43522, 43770, and 44214, and the running boards were installed at Roseville. They were successful, and by 1941 all PFE's cars being rebuilt, and also the next class of new steel cars, R-40-14, were to receive these running boards. It was not until 1944 that the AAR adopted as recommended practice, that running boards on new cars be of materials "other than wood."

General repairs to the R-40-10's began in October, 1950. During the next three years, most R-40-10's were retrofitted with various models of Preco and Equipco overhead fans. The Equipco fans were mechanically driven by a flexible shaft, but the Preco units were electric fans of a design similar to those used on the R-40-27 cars (see below). Steel running boards and stage icing grates were also added to those cars at that time. When fan bearings in this system overheated, it was sometimes possible to ignite the kapok insulation, and these "fan fires" were very troublesome. The best remedy was good maintenance on the fan mechanism.

In 1963, general repairs were needed again. Some 150 R-40-10's received new floors and ice tanks, while about

200 other cars were converted to top ice vegetable (TIV) service. This was service in which crushed ice was blown over the load (for a number of different types of vegetable loads). When so converted, the car was stenciled near the door with "FOR TIV/DLO SERVICE ONLY" (top ice vegetable/dry loading only). Most such cars had the ice bunker bulkhead walls converted to end walls, and hatch covers bolted closed; if the bunkers remained operational, ice ordinarily was not then loaded in the bunkers. This provided a cool, damp shipping environment without actual refrigeration. When the TIV conversion was done, the cars were renum-

R-40-10. A test of an Apex steel running board in 1939, at Roseville, showing the hinged hatch plugs and Holland covers. PFE photo, CSRM.

R-40-10. The appearance in later years, with the 1952 paint scheme, electric fans (note fan box at left bolster), placard boards, and steel grid running boards. E. Mohr photo, Salinas, 1961.

R-40-10 (Above). The FCP converted the -10's it purchased to bunk cars in 1964. FCP photo.

bered within the then-vacant 30001-34700 numbers by the simple expedient of changing the first digit of the car number from 4 to 3.

All the R-40-10's were scrapped by 1970, except a few cars sold to buyers like Ferrocarril del Pacifico; FCP converted them at Guadalajara to (insulated) bunk and other work cars. The original paint scheme is said to have been silver with a green stripe, but other stripe colors are reported in later years.

Classes R-40-12, R-40-14

The R-40-10 cars were an immediate success. PFE made a few design changes to improve the car, and prepared drawing C-6500 and specification no. 74-A in 1938 for an R-40-12 class. A sheet for the diagram book and a lettering drawing, C-6568, were even prepared. However, economic conditions in 1938 were not as good as expected, and PFE ordered no new cars in 1938 or 1939. Meanwhile, engineering improvements continued to be designed. A new general arrangement drawing, C-7485, dated Oct. 2, 1940, and specification 74-B, were prepared for a class incorporating those improvements, R-40-14. These cars were ordered at the end of 1940, and 1000 cars were delivered by PC&F in 1941.

Design characteristics. The external appearance was much like the R-40-10, except formed steel Equipco integral hatch covers and steel grid running boards were applied, and placard boards were used. These cars marked PFE's first use of "integral" hatch covers in a new car. Integral hatch covers incorporated the hatch plug and the cover into a single unit, with a sponge-rubber sealed closure. The ends, though superficially still prewar 4-4 Dreadnaught ends, incorporated the new "**W** corner post," and hence had relatively rounded corners. This was PFE's first use of this type of end. The cars cost about $4500 each in 1941.

In 1941, PFE was also beginning to install "convertible ice bunkers," which were bunkers capable of being stowed against the car end to permit use of the whole car interior for cargo, when icing was not required. The design was easier to handle than the "gate" bulkheads used in the R-50-1's. These bunkers were applied to rebuilt cars of the period and in the new R-40-14 class. PFE's return to this

The **W**-section corner post design of 1940, which caused Dreadnaught ends to have a much more rounded external corner. *Railway Mechanical Engineer*, July, 1940.

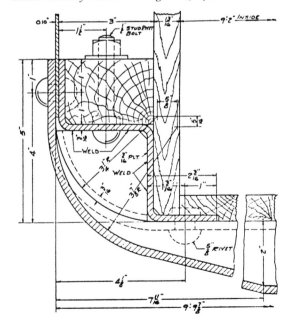

168

R-40-14. The "B" end and left side of a new car at PC&F's Renton, Wash., plant, on a rainy November day in 1941. PFE photo, CSRM.

bunker design indicates in part the increased use of refrigerator cars for un-iced cargo such as canned goods (which in later years would be shipped in insulated boxcars), as well as continuing use with produce loads which were un-iced or ventilated. The interior lining was plywood, PFE's first use of this material in a new car, although over 200 rebuilt cars had already received this type of lining.

Service history. In the early 1950's, PFE began to retrofit Preco Model AA-3 electric overhead fans to R-40-14 cars, a process completed by 1958. These overhead fans had no fan shafts visible, nor fan control boxes below the car side. As with the R-40-10, with which they shared "Dry-Zero" insulation, fan fires were sometimes a problem after fans were installed. Although 150 R-40-14's received

general repairs in 1963, all were gone by 1970.

Classes R-40-15, R-40-20

PFE made a few changes in designing a subsequent all-steel car class, the R-40-15, as shown in specification no. 74-C. The drawing for this class, C-8401, is dated Mar. 12, 1942, and orders totalling 2000 cars were placed in May, 1942, with three builders. Because of the war, however, the government had assumed control of the production of new railroad equipment on April 4, and War Production Board (WPB) authority was required to proceed with a car order. Such authority was denied to PFE, and the order was cancelled the next year. By the time orders could be authorized in 1944, a new design had been prepared. Thus

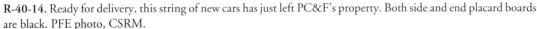

R-40-14. Ready for delivery, this string of new cars has just left PC&F's property. Both side and end placard boards are black. PFE photo, CSRM.

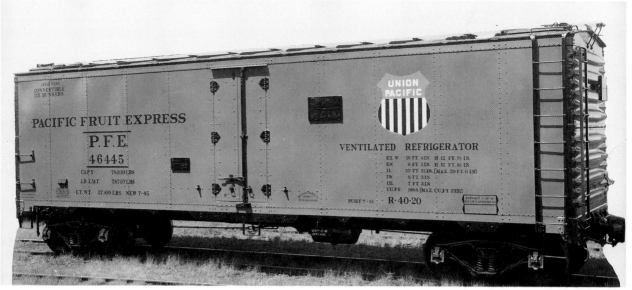

R-40-20. The right side of a new R-40-20, showing placard board location. Note the shape of the UP medallion adopted in 1942, the first time it had been applied to a new PFE car. Mt. Vernon Car Co. neg. M-178, for PFE, CSRM.

the R-40-15 class number was never used for steel cars (it was used for dry ice cars, Chapter 7).

The next class, R-40-20, was a minor change from the R-40-14 (intervening class numbers were used for rebuilds, as covered in the previous chapter). The drawing for this class, C-8810, is dated Jan. 20, 1944, and the cars were ordered in May of that year. PFE carried on its car rebuilding with steel roofs and ends, despite wartime restrictions on steel availability, because the WPB felt PFE's handling of foodstuffs was essential to the war effort. Orders for new cars, however, only began to open up in 1944. The first order for 1000 R-40-20's was delivered from January through April, 1945, with the war still in progress. The price per car was about $5300.

One visible appearance difference was that placard boards were relocated, compared to the R-40-14. Probably the most noteworthy technical progress was the use of fiberglass

wool batts in the sides, ends and roof of these cars, replacing the earlier kapok or hair products, the first new cars to have all-fiberglass insulation (except floors). Trucks for this class were all Barber Stabilized "AAR"-design trucks from four makers, ASF, Buckeye, Scullin Steel, and Columbia Steel.

An interesting detail about this class is that the last two cars, 46701 and 46702, were built by Consolidated Steel, a World War II shipbuilder looking for post-war work (they also built a pair of cars for the Santa Fe's SFRD). Consolidated must have been unsuccessful in the freight car business, for their name does not reappear in later records as a car builder. After a merger with Western Pipe and Steel, forming Consolidated-Western Steel, however, they

R-40-20. Arrangement of car end, as shown in a Mt. Vernon builder's photo, neg. M-180, for PFE. CSRM.

R-40-20. An example of the slate granule roof treatment. Here the galvanized running board is yet to be painted. PFE cars did not enter service with unpainted running boards except for an occasional replacement board. Photo 500.037, UP Railroad Museum.

R-40-20. Bolsters and side sills of many of the steel car classes were reinforced in the 1950's, as depicted in this photo of PFE 46679 at North Platte, Neb., in February, 1967. Also note fan box below side sill, to left of door. The white dot over the "PFE" on the car end was the indication of a fan-equipped car. Frank Peacock photo.

continued to manufacture car specialties. These two cars were an experiment using higher-strength steel for the car sides, permitting a thickness reduction from the usual 0.100" specified for open-hearth (OH) mild steel, to 0.067" with a low-alloy steel. Although riveting these sides and keeping the sheets flat was a problem, PFE was sufficiently satisfied to use this material for the next steel ice cars, the R-40-23.

"Herringbone" floor racks were introduced with the R-40-20 class. These racks had the floor slats at a slight diagonal, about 15 degrees, away from perpendicular to the car side, whereas earlier floor rack slats had been perpendicular to the side walls. This seemingly minor detail is a good example of PFE's design refinements. Hand trucks could be moved over the herringbone racks more smoothly, and crates did not tend to snag or bind in the racks, since their edges were no longer parallel to the gaps between the slats in the racks. At this time, PFE floor racks were still of all-wood construction.

Service history. In 1950, the R-40-20's were upgraded by addition of Preco Model FM-2 electric fans. These avoided the mechanical problems of the drive machinery from the car wheel, and were the same as the fans on the then-building R-40-26 cars. They had external shafts and fan controls in a box below the car side, at the bolster. In the middle 1950's, the shafts below the car side were removed, and overhead electric fans installed instead. Fan fires were not a problem in this car class due to the use of fiberglass insulation. In 1963, general repairs were applied to a number of the surviving cars; 200 received new floors and ice tanks, as well as replacement electric fans. All were scrapped by 1970.

Aluminum cars

Not long after the delivery of the R-40-20 cars, an addition was made to the history of the R-40-14 class, when two of them underwent an intriguing conversion. In September, 1946, PFE finished construction at Los Angeles of an experimental car which had an all-aluminum superstructure, made from material furnished by Reynolds Aluminum. Even the running board, floor rack slats, hatch covers, brake wheel, and most of the ice tanks were aluminum. The underframe, however, was steel, except for aluminum side and end sills; safety appliances were also steel, as aluminum was not permitted for those parts.

The first car, numbered 45698, had been one of the 1000 R-40-14 cars built in 1941, and officially was "rebuilt." The entire superstructure and nearly all the underframe members were entirely new. The finish was clear lacquer over bare metal. In October, 1947, PFE completed a second, virtually identical aluminum car, this time constructed of Alcoa's metal, and numbered 44739. As with 45698, the number of a dismantled car was used. PFE was very proud of these cars, and they were used in a tour around the West to publicize PFE's post-war modernization for shippers and customers.

Although built in 1946 and 1947, the two aluminum cars were classified with the 1941-built R-40-14's, having the same dimensions, cubic capacity, and mechanical arrangements as others of that class, except that the aluminum cars had fans for internal air circulation. The significant feature, though, was the light weight, which was nearly 10,000 pounds less than all-steel cars.

For these experimental cars, it is known that the aluminum companies provided some subsidy of the cost. Thus, in considering any additional orders for aluminum cars, the weight saving, together with the better corrosion resistance and other advantages of aluminum, had to be measured against the markedly higher cost of aluminum compared to steel. L.E. Cartmill, General Superintendent of PFE's Car Dept., stated in a 1947 letter that "Reynolds Metals...realized a test was involved, and therefore furnished their material at a reduced price. However, it is our opinion that if purchased on the market the price would have been prohibitive, and probably will be for years to come."

There were a few problems in service with galvanic corrosion wherever steel and aluminum parts were in close proximity, particularly in car 45698. Performance of 44739 was considered better, evidently due to better separation of aluminum and steel. Although it is stated in *The Great Yellow Fleet* (p. 156) that "the two cars just did not stand up under the ordinary abuse experienced in switching or road haul service," both cars lasted over 15 years in service.

R-40-14. The first aluminum car, with fan motor installed for an exhibit at Los Angeles. Even journal box lids are aluminum. Note black paint on steel parts and the end placard board. "Dick" Whittington photo for PFE, CSRM.

The 45698 was destroyed in a wreck on the Burlington at Stratton, Nebraska, in May, 1962, while 44739 was scrapped in 1966. Scrapping of the steel R-40-14's had begun by that time. Thus, as with other aluminum experimental cars, service durability was not one of the problems.

These two reefers remained in their natural aluminum color all their lives. It has been reported that PFE's shippers called the aluminum cars "the white elephants," presumably because of their color and rarity; there is no indication that operating performance was deficient. (A puckish employee even stenciled "white elephant" on the cars in the 1950's, to the irritation of K.V. Plummer; it was soon removed.) But by 1949 an article in *Railway Age* on "Postwar Refrigerator Cars" (see Bibliography) made no mention of aluminum for car construction. Moreover, additional aluminum refrigerator cars were not built. All indications are that cost was the reason. Today, aluminum's weight saving has led to renewed interest for freight cars.

Among the many distinctions enjoyed by the aluminum cars is that they were the first new PFE cars to receive air circulating fans. In 1941, PFE had begun to install mechanical floor fans (initially in rebuilt cars, as described in the previous chapter) to increase air circulation within the car and give a more even temperature for the load,

R-40-14. The second aluminum car, this time constructed of Alcoa instead of Reynolds material. The long side sill is the only major difference from PFE 45698. PFE photo, CSRM collection.

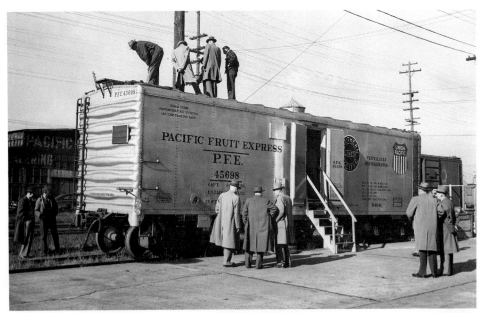

R-40-14. On tour for shippers (and sometimes open to the public), PFE 45698 is being very thoroughly inspected from all sides in this scene at Yakima, Wash., in Dec. 1946. PFE photo, CSRM.

whether the car was being cooled or (as in very cold weather) warmed with charcoal or alcohol burners to prevent freezing. The fans were driven from a rubber wheel which was turned by pressing against one car wheel on each truck.

To permit operation of these fans when the car was standing (for example, during pre-cooling), the fans also had a shaft connection on the car side, called a "fan shaft," by which the fans could be driven from an external power source. That source could be a direct mechanical drive, but more usually a small electric motor was attached through a V-belt to a separate pulley sheave on the fan shaft. These are sometimes misidentified as "fan controls." For the car classes which had fan controls accessible on the car side, such controls were under the side sill (see drawing, next page). Both the fan shaft and controls were located over the truck at the lower left of each side of the car.

R-40-14. John L. Hays, UP agent at Walla Walla, Wash. on the right, poses with a shipper before the placard inside 45698 describing the various advantages of the aluminum reefer design. UP Railroad Museum.

Apparently the first car to be painted in the 1946 paint scheme, adopted in June, is this R-40-10. The occasion may have been replacement of some side sheets toward the right of the car side, which are very rippled for this class. Roseville, July, 1946; PFE, CSRM.

Two further distinctions for these cars, though discussed in more detail below, should be mentioned here. First, they were the first new cars to be lettered in the 1946 "two-herald" paint scheme. For the first time, the medallions (sometimes called heralds) of both of PFE's parent railroads would appear on each side of the car. An additional distinction is that these two cars pioneered PFE's use of the "improved" Dreadnaught end (see photos), a design with both narrow and wide end ribs. As explained for R-40-23 cars, this design had greater stiffness than the earlier end, such as used on the R-40-10.

Class R-40-23

The largest class of PFE steel ice cars, and the only American order for steel refrigerator cars to surpass the R-40-10 order, was the post-war R-40-23. The specification was 74-G, and the general arrangement drawing, C-9200,

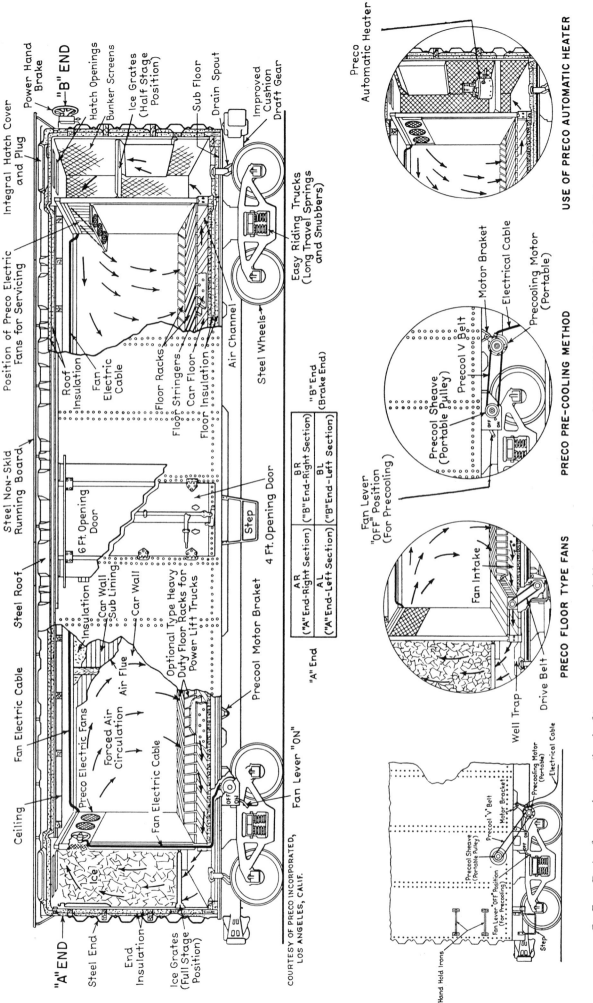

"B" END

Power Hand Brake

Integral Hatch Cover and Plug

Hatch Openings

Bunker Screens

Ice Grates (Half Stage Position)

Sub Floor

Drain Spout

Improved Cushion Draft Gear

Position of Preco Electric Fans for Servicing

Roof Insulation

Fan Electric Cable

Floor Racks

Floor Stringers

Car Floor

Floor Insulation

Air Channel

Steel Wheels

Easy Riding Trucks (Long Travel Springs and Snubbers)

Steel Non-Skid Running Board

6 Ft. Opening Door

Step

4 Ft. Opening Door

"A" End		"B" End (Brake End)
AR ("A" End-Right Section)		BR ("B" End-Right Section)
AL ("A" End-Left Section)		BL ("B" End-Left Section)

Ceiling

Fan Electric Cable

Steel Roof

Insulation

Car Wall Sub Lining

Car Wall

Optional Type Heavy Duty Floor Racks for Power Lift Trucks

Precool Motor Braket

Preco Electric Fans

Forced Air Circulation

Air Flue

Fan Electric Cable

Ice

Ice Grates (Full Stage Position)

End Insulation

Steel End

"A" END

Fan Lever "ON"

COURTESY OF PRECO INCORPORATED, LOS ANGELES, CALIF.

Preco Automatic Heater

USE OF PRECO AUTOMATIC HEATER

Motor Braket

Electrical Cable

Precooling Motor (Portable)

Precool Sheave (Portable Pulley)

Precool V Belt

PRECO PRE-COOLING METHOD

Fan Lever "OFF" Position (For Precooling)

Fan Intake

PRECO FLOOR TYPE FANS

Well Trap

Drive Belt

Electrical Cable

Precooling Motor (Portable)

Precool "V" Belt

Motor Bracket

Precool Sheave (Portable Pulley)

Fan Lever Off Position (For Precooling)

Hand Hold Irons

Step

Car Fans. Design for a modern ventilated refrigerator car, as recommended by the refrigerator car comittee of the United Fresh Fruit and Vegetable Association. The composite car drawing at top shows both swinging and sliding (plug) doors, with fixed ice tank bulkheads Note that diagonal floor racks are shown. The car's left end shows "full stage" icing and overhead electric fans, while the right end shows half-stage grates in place. The small drawings show, from left to right, the original arrangement with a pulley sheave on the car side (**far left**); the later arrangement with a pulley sheave below the car side an electric generator (**mid-left and mid-right**); and the use of an automatic heater for cold-weather service (**far right**). See text for more detailed description. Courtesy of Preco, Inc.

was dated Feb. 15, 1946. Orders were placed in May, 1946, for 2000 cars, followed by additional orders in August for 3000 more. Since numbering these 5000 cars consecutively would have carried them into the 50,000 series, already in use for Western Pacific cars (discussed in Chapters 5 and 7), the last 3000 were numbered 5001-8000. This meant, of course, that the earlier R-30-2, -4, and -5 cars which had formerly occupied those numbers were gone (rebuilt or scrapped) by this time.

These 5000 cars were distributed in lots of 1000 among five builders, AC&F, Pullman-Standard, PC&F, General American, and Mt. Vernon Car Co., because builders were very busy, and because steel allocations were still a problem during 1946 and 1947. Car delivery began in January, 1947, with some of the Pullman-Standard cars, and continued through October, when the last of the Mt. Vernon order arrived. Cost was about $7650 per car.

Design characteristics. The R-40-23's were the first entire class to be built new with fans (Preco Model FG-36), to have welded underframes, and to have "improved Dreadnaught" ends. The R-40-23 had a 3-3 style of that type Dreadnaught end, which was introduced by Standard Railway Equipment Co. in 1945 to provide increased stiffness through deeper corrugations. The cars were also taller than earlier classes, 13' 7-⅜" tall at the running board. An additional inch of insulation in sides, ends, roof and floor was also included in these cars, following the details established in the aluminum cars. This was Gustin-Bacon's "Ultralite" fiberglass. However, "Hairinsul" continued to be used in floors because of its resistance to moisture deterioration.

This was the only PFE ice car class to be built with high-strength steel instead of OH mild steel side sheets. The new steel sides only needed to be two-thirds as thick as OH sides, and saved about 4,000 pounds, but the lower corrosion resistance of this steel was later to prove an operational headache. There was considerable interest at and after the end of World War II in reducing refrigerator car weight, as in the aluminum cars described above (for this viewpoint, see Hallmark letter, Bibliography.)

Another important feature of these cars was side-wall flues. These were "blind" plywood walls along the sides of the car, spaced one inch inside the car wall and open at top and bottom, to assist vertical air circulation at the car sides. This feature permitted loading against the flue without fear

R-40-23. The first of 5000 cars. The "improved" model of Dreadnaught end is clearly shown, and the Morton running board is evident. AC&F photo (Lot 3075) for PFE, July, 1947, CSRM.

been practical in earlier cars because they would have exaggerated harmonic truck motions. But the new R-40-23, with its ASF A-3 "Ride Control" trucks, overcame this problem, as mentioned in the previous chapter, by using an internal spring snubbing device in the truck bolster (not externally visible like the retrofitted ones used earlier), thus preventing the truck as a whole from developing harmonic motions. These truck design advances were standard on subsequent PFE cars, and for truck replacements. Truck bolster snubbers became an AAR requirement for all new freight cars in the U.S. after Jan. 1, 1956.

Painting and lettering. The R-40-23's were also the first class of new cars delivered in the 1946 paint scheme. In June, 1946, the paint scheme was changed significantly for the first time since 1925. The emblems of both railroads were then applied to both sides of the cars. Otherwise, the color scheme was unchanged, and side hardware continued black in this scheme. An important detail of the 1946 scheme is that it called for the SP medallion to be toward the car center, nearest the door, on each side. (Note that this means the two sides were identical.) One reason this is interesting is that PFE painting diagrams from 1922-46, and from 1951 until PFE was divided between SP and UP in March 1978, specified that the SP medallion was to be at the B or brake end of the car, thus making the two sides non-identical.

After the 2-emblem paint scheme was introduced in 1946, placard boards were placed on the left side of the door. This was done for the new R-40-23 cars, and boards in the same location were retrofitted fairly rapidly to the earlier steel car classes. Placard boards were painted black until 1949; they were 16 x 26 inches in size.

Service history. During the 1950's the -23 and earlier classes began to develop bolster and side sill cracks. Begin-

R-40-23. Roof of General American car with the round-hole Morton running board and the 1½-in. white "dot" over the "F" in PFE, designating a car equipped with fans. PFE, CSRM.

of heat transmission from the wall, as well as better air circulation and equalization of temperature throughout the load. They were well accepted in service by shippers, showed good performance in tests, and were used on all subsequent ice cars.

The R-40-23's were widely touted by PFE as "easy riding" cars. This was due to the use of long-travel springs, providing better cushioning. Such long springs had not

R-40-23. A broadside view of a month-old car, in October, 1947. Note the fan shaft and control box at lower left, "igniting insulation" warning below grab irons, and cast metal trust plate at upper left. W. C. Whittaker photo.

R-40-23. A car from the Aug. 1946, orders, covering some 3000 cars. Mt. Vernon Car photo, courtesy Steve Peery.

R-40-23 (Above, left). In this construction photo, the interior insulation is ready to be sheathed with plywood. AC&F photo for PFE, CSRM. **(Above, right)** Convertible ice bunker being swung parallel to sides; next it slides back to wall. Note opening of sidewall flues at top of wall. "Dick" Whittington photo for PFE, CSRM.

R-40-23. (Below, left) Interior view with bulkhead in place. Note herringbone floor racks. **(Below, center)** Ice grates being set at bottom of bunker for "full stage icing." Ice hatches above are open, with drains below grates. **(Below, right)** Same ice grates as in center photo, but now being set for "half-stage icing." Hatch opening at top. "Dick" Whittington photos for PFE, CSRM.

ning in 1957, reinforcements were applied to those parts, and underframe diagonal braces between the bolster center and car corner were added. By 1963, over 9000 steel cars of classes R-40-10 through -25 had been so repaired. Earlier in this chapter is a photograph of an R-40-20, showing the side sill reinforcement.

The R-40-23 class was the object of a number of experiments in later years. For example, PFE had experimented with use of a small diesel engine to drive fans even when the car was not running, converting one R-40-26, 8131, in August, 1959, and a second, 8130, in October. In 1960-

R-40-23 (Above). First of the production Ice Tempco cars, 20002, with Preco "Cargotemp" equipment. Inside the open engine compartment are the air-cooled diesel engine and alternator which powered the electric car fans. The thermostat box on the car side is open. **(Below)** Cranking to start the diesel engine. Preco photos at Los Angeles in December, 1960; CSRM.

61, 1000 R-40-23's were converted to powered fans, using an improved version of the equipment in car 8131 (which was then renumbered to 20001). The equipment was called "Ice Tempco" (temperature control), with three different types of units from Preco and Equipco being used. The cars were then renumbered to 20002-21001. Car 8130 became 21002. The cars all retained just a single ice bunker at the "B" end, but in 1962-63, ceiling ducts were added to the cars in an effort to improve air circulation.

The small diesel units were a major maintenance headache, however, and also became notorious for their orneriness in starting, since they had to be hand-cranked. Their removal began in 1965 and was completed about 1970. Several hundred of the cars were re-converted to conventional ice bunker service, with the "Tempco" units removed, and renumbered again, this time into the 35,000 number series. By that time, ample numbers of large R-70 mechanical reefers were available, and many shippers were reluctant to accept the smaller size and door width, and poorer temperature control, of an ice car, even if it had continuous fans.

In 1965, 239 of the R-40-23's were converted to top-ice vegetable service, and renumbered to the 36001-36500 series. These and other renumberings are summarized in Table 8-2. The same year, 800 other -23's received heavy repairs.

Also in the summer of 1965, PFE initiated an experiment with liquid nitrogen as a refrigerant. A commercial arrangement called "Polarstream" had been devised for this purpose, and PFE converted 15 of the R-40-23's to this use at Roseville, giving them 6' sliding doors and renumbering them as 1001-1015. Though repeated experiments and trial shipments were conducted with these cars, the temperature control and rate of liquid nitrogen consumption was never fully optimized. In 1968 the cars were reconverted to top ice vegetable service and renumbered to 36501-36515.

A few of the R-40-23 class continued as ice refrigerator

R-40-23. After removal of the Tempco equipment, these cars kept their electric fans and rejoined ice bunker service. This very dirty example, PFE 35085, was photographed on Sept. 4, 1970, at Granger, Wyo., by Frank Peacock.

R-40-23. An overall view of an Ice Tempco car in the 1961 lettering scheme (discussed later in this chapter), with silver roof and black ends. Freshly outshopped in April of 1961, and photographed in front of the precooling deck at Los Angeles, the car has yet to have its light weight measured. PFE photo, CSRM.

R-40-23. One of the "Polarstream" liquid nitrogen cars, 1013, with its 6-ft. sliding door conversion. PFE photo.

cars, either with ice bunkers or in one of the top ice versions, until the end of ice service in 1972 and beyond. In 1972 there were still 445 of the original 5000 cars on the roster.

Class R-40-25

The steel car class which followed R-40-23, the R-40-25, was very similar. It was designed in 1947, and one of its significant changes was a return to OH steel side sheets, since neither the corrosion problems of the R-40-23's nor the cost could be justified for the weight savings achieved with the thinner steel. The new class was described in speci-fication 74-H and drawing C-10000, dated Aug. 20, 1947. (This drawing, incidentally, was among the last to be prepared by Union Pacific designers in Omaha and consequently bearing the "C" prefix of a UP drawing. PFE's Car Department engineering was transferred to San Francisco during 1946-48, and thereafter drawing numbers no longer had "C" prefixes.)

The companion design, specification 74-J, described an otherwise identical car with high-strength steel sides, which was not built. The OH-side cars built to specification 74-H cost $7225 each.

The R-40-25 cars were numbered in the 2001-5000 series when delivered by SP Equipment Co. between February and September, 1949. The first 1500 cars were assembled at Los Angeles, the next 500 at Colton and the rest at Roseville. The major visible difference from the -23 class was the diagonal-panel roof on the R-40-25; they had Preco Model FK-6 mechanical fans. The R-40-25's also saved costs with stationary ice bunkers.

Painting differed slightly from the preceding -23 class. In January, 1949, just before delivery of the R-40-25's, the ladders and grab irons on the car side, the door hardware, and the corner steps, were specified to be painted orange instead of black on all PFE cars. Since the earliest days of PFE, all side hardware (door latch bars and hinges, grab irons, ladders, steps) had been black. However, the center sill step and the side sill "tabs" remained black (until 1951),

R-40-25 (Above). First of this 3000-car class is inspected at Los Angeles in 1949. Though very similar to the preceding R-40-23's, these cars had diagonal panel roofs (not visible here), and side hardware and placard boards were no longer black.

(**Below**) Brand-new 2600 at Los Angeles, May, 1949. For this and later classes, trust plates were replaced by stenciled information at the upper left of the car side, and the "igniting insulation" warning was still used. The PFE shops underbid commercial car builders in 1948, by more than $1000 per car, to obtain this construction job. At photo center, VP & GM K.V. Plummer, in the dark suit, has his arm around the shoulder of Jim King, LA Shop Superintendent. PFE photos, CSRM.

R-40-25. Here workmen prepare to attach end sills to welded underframes at Los Angeles as PFE undertakes its first assembly of steel cars since the R-40-10's of 1936. These frames were virtually identical to the design used under the R-40-23. PFE photo, CSRM.

Table 8-2
Renumberings of PFE Steel Ice Reefers

Original Numbers*	New Numbers*	Class	Cars	Date	Remarks
5001-8000	1001-1015	R-40-23	15	1965	LN$_2$ conversion [A]
2001-5000	12001-15000	R-40-25	575	1965-67	Load height increased [B]
8001-10000	18001-19999	R-40-26	265	1965-66	Load height increased [B]
46-48000,5-8000	20002-21001	R-40-23	1000	1960-61	Conv. to ice tempco
40001-44700	30039-34690	R-40-10	216	1965	Conv. to TIV + vent [C]
10001-11700	30001-31700	R-40-27	98	1971	Conv. to TIV [C]
11701-11800	31701-31800	R-40-28	2	1971	Conv. to TIV [C]
20002-21001	35002-36000	R-40-23	140	1966	Ice tempco removed [D]
46-48000,5-8000	36001-36500	R-40-23	239	1965-66	Conv. to TIV [C]
1001-1015	36501-36515	R-40-23	15	1968	Conv. to TIV from LN$_2$ [A,C]
2001-5000	60001-60999	R-40-25	90	1970	New foam floors [E, F]
8001-10000	61001-61999	R-40-26	109	1970	New foam floors [E,F]
2001-5000	65001-65999	R-40-25	90	1970	New foam floors [E,G]
8001-10000	66001-66999	R-40-26	110	1970	New foam floors [E,G]
2001-5000	82001-85000	R-40-25	85	1963	Meat rails added
10001-11700	190003-190502	R-40-28	454	1971-72	Conv. to TIV, new doors [C]

*Not all numbers used in some series

Notes:　[A] The "Polarstream" liquid nitrogen (LN$_2$) car experiment

　　　　[B] Interior height increased from 7'4" to 7'10", new floors and insulation added

　　　　[C] TIV (top ice vegetable) conversion involved decommissioning ice bunkers. Thereafter, cars could be used for top icing, but were not refrigerated by means of bunkers.

　　　　[D] Ice tempco units removed, cars restored to 2-bunker ice service

　　　　[E] New foamed-in-place floors added (see Chapter 9), cars rebuilt to extend non-mechanical car services. Part of SPE Co. / Las Vegas Land and Water, LVLW, lease (see Chapter 1).

　　　　[F,G] F = LVLW lease on behalf of UP, G = SPE Co. lease on behalf of SP

R-40-25. In 1968-70, the lives of some of these cars were extended by program repairs, and they were sold to SP and UP subsidiaries and then leased back. Here one of the cars sold to Las Vegas Land & Water Co. is seen at Dallas, Tex. on June 17, 1970. The paint is touched up only where repairs occurred or for relettering. Frank Peacock photo.

as they had been since the R-40-10 cars. This discontinuation of a separate trim color must have greatly reduced the labor of car painting, though it made for a somewhat less elegant-appearing car. The same kinds of paint scheme simplifications were also being applied to refrigerator cars of other owners during this period.

As had been the case since about 1940, PFE coated the roofs with a red asphalt compound, sprinkled when wet with "slate granules," to withstand corrosion and to make a non-skid roof surface. The roof color was still close to boxcar red. After 1949, small commodity card boards were also added to the left of the door (see photos of R-40-25 and -26 for location).

In 1963 about 85 of the R-40-25 cars were converted to meat service and renumbered by adding an "8" in front of their original car number. In 1965-67, about 575 more R-40-25's were given heavy repairs, including thinner, foam-insulated floors which permitted increased loading height. These roomier cars were renumbered by adding a "1" in front of their original car numbers.

In 1968-70, another 180 R-40-25's were given heavy repairs, including floor insulation which was foamed in place with polyurethane foam, and renumbered into the 60,000 series. These renumberings are shown in Table 8-2. This repair effort was performed to extend top-ice (TIV) service a few more years. Since PFE did not have the resources to pay for these repairs itself, the cars were sold to SP Equipment Co. (acting for SP) and the Las Vegas Land and Water Co. (acting for UP) and then leased back by PFE, as described in Chapter 1. By the end of ice service in 1973, only 500 of the -25 cars remained on the roster.

Class R-40-26

During 1949, PFE designed a new car with a 6-ft. door opening, and a "plug door" closure. Increasing use of fork lift trucks by shippers led to the need to change the 4-ft. standard door, in use by PFE since 1906 and standard for refrigerator cars on nearly all American railroads. The general arrangement drawing was number 2500, and the specification was no. 74-K, both dated August, 1950. Between July, 1951 and May, 1952, these plug-door cars were delivered as class R-40-26. The cars were built by SP Equipment Co., 8001-9175 at Los Angeles shop, the remaining 825 cars at Colton shop. They cost about $8650 per car.

Design characteristics. The R-40-26 design was most visibly different in the installation of a plug (sliding) door. The Youngstown door which was specified, however, was no novelty to PFE. In 1946, a test program had been initiated to try four different door designs, applying them to R-40-10's, and the cars with those doors remained in service for a number of years. The Youngstown was the final choice, and PFE was to remain satisfied with Youngstown doors for many thousands of later cars.

This was also the first class to be built new with electric overhead fans, Preco Model AA-2. The fan location at the

One of the R-40-10 cars used to test sliding doors, in this case a bottom-hung Youngstown design installed in April, 1947. Note that the door hardware is painted black, a practice not used with the R-40-26 cars which were built with this type of door. PFE photo, CSRM.

R-40-26. This was the first class to use metal slats on floor racks since the two aluminum cars. Stringers remained wood. UP Railroad Museum.

R-40-26. The brake end and left side of the first car of this class, 8001, on the occasion of its inspection at Los Angeles in July, 1951. PFE photo, CSRM.

top of the car was thermally more effective, but until the advent of alternator-powered electric fan equipment from Preco in 1950, this location had not been considered feasible by PFE. The electric operation also eliminated several shaft bearings of floor-level mechanical fan equipment, which, as discussed above, were prone to overheat and cause car fires. Alternators were driven by shafts from car axles.

The R-40-26 cars are interesting as a transition between mechanical and all-electric fans, as an external shaft was still installed below the lower left edge of the car side for pre-cooling (see fan arrangement drawing). This shaft, called an alternator shaft, accepted a pulley and V-belt to drive the alternator, rather than the fans themselves, to pre-cool the car. There was also a circular "fan plate" on the R-40-26, about the size and at the location of the earlier fan shafts. This plate was so that workers at loading locations

would have a visual indication, similar to the mechanical-fan cars they were used to, of the presence of fans. In the mid-1950's, the original fans were replaced with an all-electric system, Preco's Model AA-3, which meant no shaft on the car side. It was replaced by an electrical receptacle for pre-cooling, as on later cars.

The -26 class was the first to use floor racks with metal slats (rack stringers remained wood) to carry lift trucks. Insulation was entirely fiberglass, for the first time in PFE practice. Both these innovations were widely used later.

As has been mentioned, PFE began testing steel wheels for its cars in 1928, and adopted them as standard for new and rebuilt cars in December, 1941. However, the difficulty of obtaining steel wheels during and immediately

R-40-26. The inspection party for car 8001. A portable motor has been connected with a fan belt to the alternator shaft below the car side. The gentlemen with the vest in the center of the front row is VP and GM K.V. Plummer; the man in the suit at Plummer's left is Earl Hopkins, who was Engineer, Car Construction; the man in the dark jacket near the right front is Jim King, the long-time shop superintendent at Los Angeles; and at extreme right is G.P. Torburn, General Superintendent, Car Department. PFE photo, CSRM.

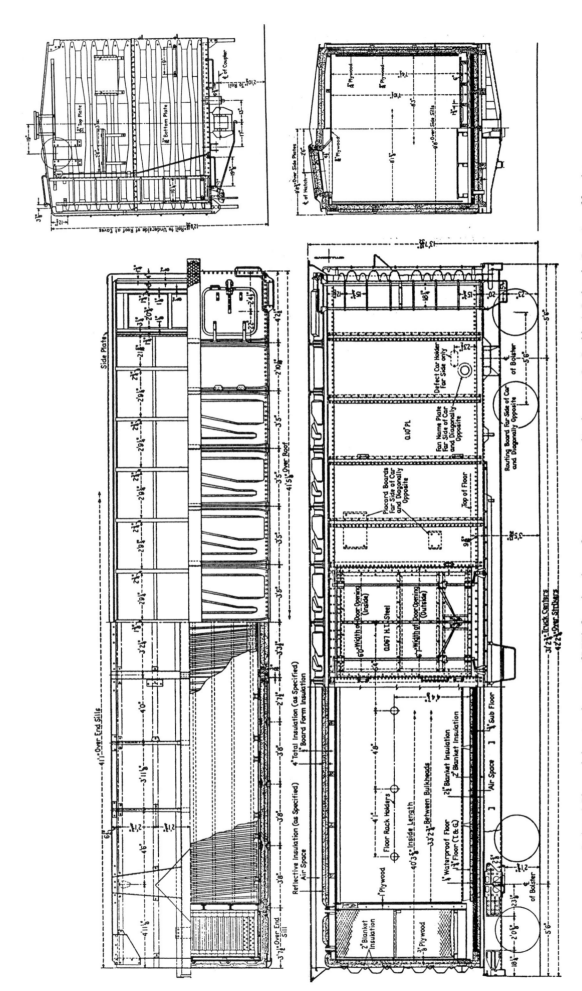

R-40-26. Plan and elevation drawings of PFE's first plug-door refrigerator car appeared in the 1953 *Car Builder's Cyclopedia.* Location of fan plates on diagonally-opposite car corners, diagonal-panel roof, and herringbone floor racks are all shown. Reprinted with permission.

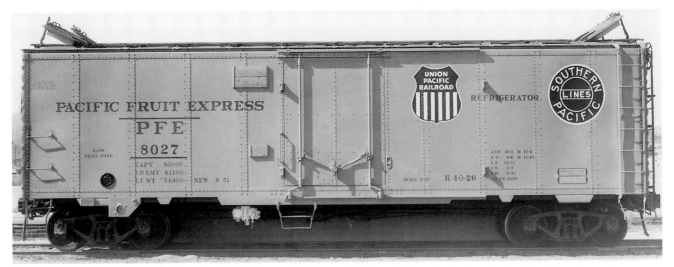

R-40-26. A fine portrait of the left side of car 8027. There is a black metal "fan plate" where fan shafts had been located on earlier cars. This class has its alternator shaft in the control box below the side sill. The "igniting insulation" warning is still stenciled on the car, despite the fiberglass insulation of -26, to maintain PFE's concerns on this topic. PFE photo, CSRM.

following the war delayed the desired process of converting the fleet. It was not until 1952 that the steel wheel supply permitted significant replacements for older cars. The program then installed steel wheels on 1500 cars in 1953, 2500 cars in 1954, and 3000 cars in 1955. Together with new car construction, this meant that about half of PFE's cars had steel wheels by the end of 1955. The wheel program continued through to 1959, at 500 to 1000 cars yearly. In combination with scrapping of older cars, and the specification of steel wheels on all new cars, this program led to conversion of virtually the full PFE fleet to steel wheels by 1960.

Painting and lettering. The R-40-26 cars were the first to be delivered in an altered paint scheme from the 2-herald scheme of 1946. After June, 1950, the two railroad medallions were still painted on each side of the car, but now the Union Pacific shield was black and white, instead of the traditional red, white and blue. In addition, the word "RAILROAD" was added to "UNION PACIFIC" at the top of the UP shield, and a narrow white rim was added around the shield, matching the white rim on the SP emblem. These changes were undoubtedly made to reduce inventory and labor costs of painting.

R-40-26. One of two cars used to test the Ice Tempco concept (the other was 8130) in 1959. PFE photo, CSRM.

In June, 1951, a further change was to paint side sills and all steps orange, and more visibly, to restore the SP medallion to its traditional location at the B end of the car. This latter change was supposedly made to return to the situation in which switch crews could tell the B end of the car in switching shop tracks without seeing the end itself, just by observing the heralds. An alternate explanation has been suggested, that SP officials requested the change after noting that open doors on a car in the 1946 scheme would cover the SP emblem on both sides. The change, in any case, restored the B end location of the SP herald which had been in use since 1922. The new R-40-26 cars exhibited all these changes.

In March, 1952, the horizontal lines above and below the reporting marks ceased to be an AAR recommended practice, and PFE, like many railroads, removed them from its lettering diagrams. The following year, PFE ceased to

R-40-26. A view showing the plywood interior sheathing, floor racks, and high fan location. PFE photo, CSRM.

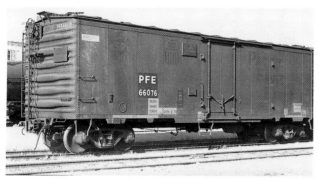

R-40-26. PFE 66076 is one of the TIV cars leased from SP Equipment Co., an SP subsidiary, as noted in the small white rectangle above the grab irons. Granger, Wyo., Sept. 4, 1970, Frank Peacock photo.

use periods between the letters "PFE" in the reporting marks, ending a practice begun in 1925. All these changes are documented in lettering diagram C-9861.

One detail to note on PFE cars, particularly in photos of cars in service, is that the station symbols applied when cars were re-weighed and re-stenciled were often those of the major PFE shops. These were Roseville, Calif. (symbol **ROS**), where the largest shop was located; Tucson, Ariz. (symbol **TUC**); Los Angeles (**LA**); and Nampa (symbol **NA**) and Pocatello, Idaho (symbol **PO**). In addition, SP and UP shop symbols were frequently seen, such as Oakland (**OAK**), Omaha (**OM**), Houston (**HO**), Ogden (**OG**), and so forth. Another detail is that all the R-40 steel cars had trucks with 5" x 9" journals, so that the sum of the "load limit" and "light weight" was always 136,000 pounds, the capacity of the journals in a 40-ton conventional truck (see Table 5-1).

Service history. Although the R-40-26's served in their original form for many years, they too began to undergo conversions as the 1960's approached. One of the first of

these was to serve as test cars for the "Ice Tempco" concept, discussed earlier in relation to the R-40-23 class. This might suggest that the R-40-26 cars were being considered for Ice Tempco conversion, but only the R-40-23's were actually converted. In the early 1960's, some of these cars received underframe reinforcements. At the same time as the R-40-25's received foam insulation and increased loading height, so did 265 R-40-26's, and they were then renumbered by adding a "1" in front of their original car number.

In 1969-70, about 130 cars were given heavy repairs and new, foamed-in-place floors, in order to extend their lives in TIV service. Like the R-40-25's repaired at the same time, they received new numbers in the 60,000 series after being sold to SP and UP subsidiaries and leased back.

Class R-70-5

As frozen food business increased after World War II, PFE's fleet of R-70-2 and R-50-5's, described in Chapters 6 and 7, was hard-pressed to carry the traffic. Accordingly, a modern steel car for frozen food service was designed. The general arrangement drawing was 2900, dated Sept. 1951, and the specification was 74-L. When authority was first requested for these cars in 1950, 100 overhead bunker cars were planned. In 1951, as mechanical refrigeration looked increasingly practical, it was decided to build 25 of these as mechanically-refrigerated cars (see next chapter) and the balance as conventional end-bunker cars.

The first 75 cars were built in May-July, 1952. During Dec. 1953-Feb. 1954 PFE added 100 more. These cars were 53 feet long (43'6" inside) with straight side sills and considerably thicker insulation than conventional steel ice cars, and had 6-ft. plug doors, fans, and conventional ice bunkers of 350 cubic ft., as in the previous R-70 ice cars. These cars averaged about $13,400 each. They had the

R-70-5. The left side of the first R-70-5, car 200126. Although already close to obsolete when it was constructed, it was designed for easy conversion to mechanical refrigeration. The car had Preco overhead electric fans, thus the fan plate. The roof is light gray, the standard for the earliest mechanical cars, also being built for frozen food in 1952. PFE photo, CSRM.

orange sides and boxcar red ends of contemporary ice cars, but had a light gray roof, the same color being applied to the then-new mechanical cars. The light gray was presumably to minimize heat absorption. It had been known since the 1920's, however, that heat absorption by paint depended far more on how dirty it was, than what color it was. (See Hukill's 1932 article, Bibliography.) PFE's own tests had found similar results, though with the end of the steam era approaching, it may have been felt that painted roofs would not get dirty as quickly.

In recognition of their size, the new cars were called "Supers" by PFE, an analogous nickname to the earlier R-50 "Giants" and R-70 "Super-Giants." However, the day of ice plus salt refrigeration for frozen food was ending, as much more capable mechanical refrigeration, described in Chapter 9, came into use by PFE and other refrigerator car operators. Accordingly, these cars were not in much demand, and in 1955 they were rebuilt at Roseville with mechanical refrigeration units, to achieve lower and more consistent temperatures. They then were retained in service as frozen food cars.

In rebuilding, the ice bunker at the B end was removed, and in place of the A-end bunker, a 7-ft. mechanical compartment was installed. This left the car interior length the same as it had been in its ice-car version. The cars were also renumbered when rebuilt, with the first group changing from 200126-200200 to 300388-300412 and the second group from 200601-200700 to 300413-300512. The mechanical cars were originally used only for frozen lading, and all were being numbered into the 300,000 series. The cars were not renumbered in order within each group, but merely as rebuilding was done. Subsequent history of these cars as mechanical refrigerators is presented in the next chapter.

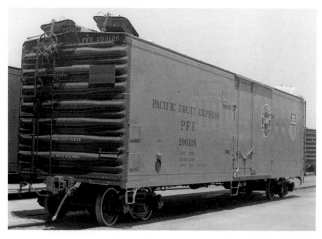

R-70-5. Arrangement of the brake end. Note the "igniting insulation" warning. PFE photo, CSRM.

Class R-70-6

In 1950, PFE purchased 12 overhead ice bunker cars (10 ice hatches in the roof) from American Refrigerator Transit. These were obtained to supplement the R-50-5 and R-70-2 ice cars which were primarily used for frozen food service at that time. These were unique in PFE's history because the cars were purchased used. Under ART ownership, these cars carried AMRX reporting marks, and numbers 1000-1011. They were purchased for $8,500 each, at a time when new ice cars of the same type and size with conventional ice bunkers (the R-70-5) cost about $13,400 each. Originally built in 1946 as an experiment by ART and used in meat service, they were purchased by PFE in 1950 for frozen food only. They arrived in September, and after meat rails were removed, they were classed R-70-6 and numbered 200225-200237.

In 1954, they were converted at Roseville to mechanical

R-70-6. One of the ART cars in its original paint at St. Louis in 1949. The next year all 12 of these cars were sold to PFE, which simply removed meat rails and repainted them. Note the original-style 5-4 Dreadnaught ends. Neg. 600009, UP Railroad Museum.

refrigeration, as described in the next chapter, and they retained their unusual (for PFE) 5-ft. swinging doors, duplicated only in the 89 cars of R-40-1 design.

Classes R-40-27, R-40-28

The 6-ft. width of the plug door of the R-40-26 and R-70-5 cars was well received by shippers, who were increasingly using lift trucks to load and unload cars. Compared to the 4-ft. width which was standard for hinged doors on reefers, six feet was a real improvement. But inspection of shipments posed a problem, both to open the entire six-foot width to let cold air out, and the weight of such a large door. With a hinged door, it was convenient to open just one of the two-foot halves.

With this in mind, PFE experimented with combination door arrangements during the 1950's. At least two design ideas were tried on older cars. One idea was a "triple" door, each section of which was the conventional ice-car width of 2 feet, with two sections hinged together as a sort of folding sub-door. The other idea was to combine the sliding or plug door of the -26 cars with a 2-ft. hinged door. The former idea was tried on R-40-10 41010, and the second idea was installed on R-40-26 9974.

Evidently the sliding plus swinging door design was the preferred answer. Drawing 3500 and Specification 74-Q described the 1700 cars of class R-40-27, assembled from January to August, 1957, the first 350 at Roseville, the next 600 at Colton, and the last 750 at Los Angeles. In these cars, a new four-foot wide Youngstown plug door was mated with a 2-ft. hinged door, retaining the six-foot door opening of the -26 but adding the inspection convenience. But shippers desired an even wider door, and accordingly, the companion class, R-40-28, had a two-foot hinged door at the right of a *six*-foot plug door, making a total door opening of 8 feet. The same drawing and specification 74-R applied to this class as for R-40-27, indicating that the door design was the only difference

between the two classes. Cars of either class cost about $12,300 each. Built at Los Angeles by the SP Equipment Co. in July, 1957, the small class of only 100 cars of R-40-28 was PFE's last acquisition of ice refrigerator cars.

The overhead electric fans on these two car classes were various Preco and Equipco models, most of which had no external fan or alternator shafts at all. For fan operation when the car was standing, by electrical rather than mechanical means, an electrical receptacle was provided on the car to accept an extension cord. There was therefore no provision for the V-belt drive of the earlier cars, and thus no external shaft on the car side, for most of these cars. As mentioned above, this same type of overhead fan was also retrofitted to many of the earlier R-40-10, -14, and -20 cars during the 1950's. The R-40-26's likewise had their alternator shafts replaced with electric receptacles for pre-cooling.

Painting and lettering. Although the R-40-27 and -28 cars were lettered when built in the 1952 scheme used on the R-40-26's, with the reporting mark periods and stripes removed, they and many other repainted steel ice cars were soon to receive the new PFE "Gothic" paint scheme, adopted in April, 1960. This scheme simplified the railroad medal-

(**Left, below**) The tryout of the 3-piece door design on R-40-10 41010. (**Above**) The triple door in the full-open position. With the left segment closed, the center segment could be opened to fold over the left segment to give a 4' opening, as on conventional ice cars. PFE photos, 1954, CSRM. (**Right, below**). The sliding plus swinging door system prototype, tried out on R-40-26 car 9974. PFE photo at LA, Feb. 1955, CSRM.

R-40-27. The first of the Colton batch of these cars, showing the paint scheme (unchanged since 1953) and the door arrangement – note that the sliding door moves to the left, rather than to the right. Electric fans are denoted by the circular symbol above the truck. PFE photo, February, 1957, CSRM.

lions by stenciling them in black on the orange car side, eliminating white paint in the heralds. The medallions were also moved to the left of the car door, with large Gothic letters spelling out "PACIFIC FRUIT EXPRESS" to the right of the car door. All other lettering also became Gothic rather than Roman style. In this scheme, the car sides remained orange and the roof and ends (for ice cars) remained boxcar red.

In March, 1961, the paint scheme was changed slightly, with the SP medallion revised to have a Gothic "SP" in the center of the design. The photographs earlier in this chapter of the Ice Tempco and Polarstream cars of class R-40-23, illustrate the 1961 scheme.

In April, 1962, painting directions were revised to specify black ends and aluminum paint for roofs of ice cars, as was already standard for the mechanical refrigerators. At the same time, wood sheathing of car interiors, varnished since 1906, began to be painted light gray. In 1965, as

(Below) The original Gothic lettering scheme of April, 1960, here shown on the first production Ice Tempco R-40-23. The spotting feature is the "circle and bar" SP medallion. Red roofs were standard for ice cars, but this car has a silver roof. "Dick" Whittington photo, PFE, CSRM.

R-40-28 (Below). An HO scale drawing from *Railroad Model Craftsman* magazine, by Julian Cavalier. The diagonal-panel roof is visible. Reprinted with permission.

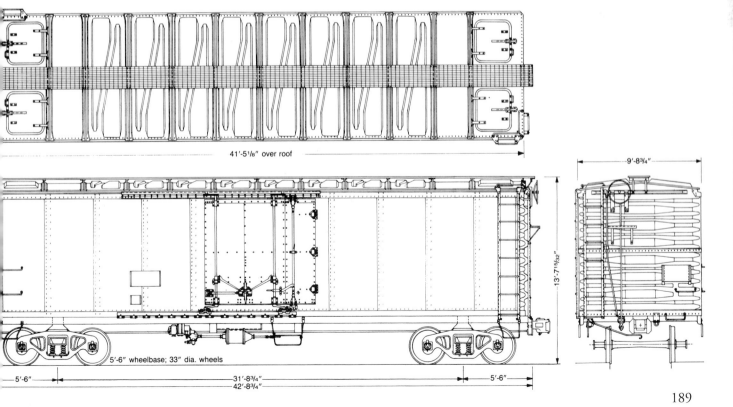

41'-5⅛" over roof

13'-7⁵/₃₂"

9'-8¾"

5'-6" wheelbase; 33" dia. wheels

5'-6"   31'-8¾"   5'-6"
42'-8¾"

R-40-28. An October, 1965, photo of the second member of this class at Tucson. The sliding door is larger than the one on the -27 car; otherwise the two classes were very similar. This photo basically shows the 1961 paint scheme, plus the black rectangle for the reporting marks, introduced in 1965, and the 1962 aluminum roof paint and black car ends. PFE photo, CSRM.

discussed in the chapter on mechanical refrigeration, PFE added a black rectangle so the reporting marks could be stenciled in white, for better visibility when the car was dirty. The photo of R-40-28 11702 shows that scheme. Although PFE did not paint cars very frequently during the 1960's, a substantial number of the ice cars did receive the various versions of the Gothic scheme in that decade. But even at the end of ice service in 1972, ice cars could still be found with pre-1960 Roman lettering schemes.

Service history. Five of the R-40-27's were chosen for an experiment in conversion of ice cars to mechanical refrigeration, by mounting diesel engines, alternators, and refrigeration equipment similar to that used in refrigerated trucks on the "A" end of the car, and removing both ice bunkers. These conversions are described in more detail in Chapter 9. When the experiment was terminated, the cars

R-40-27. An end view showing the roof and the latch hardware on the hatch bottom which permitted the hatch to be locked from the inside to prevent theft. Neg. 470-9-20, UP Railroad Museum.

were returned to TIV service and re-numbered.

These last two classes of ice cars naturally survived to a relatively late date in service. Table 8-3 shows the pattern of car survival under the original numbers. These newer cars were also given various conversions, as shown in Table 8-2. In 1971, 100 of the R-40-27 and -28 cars were converted to TIV cars, in which the ice bunkers were decom-

Table 8-3
Numbers of Steel Ice Cars with Original Numbers*

Car Numbers	Class	New	1955	1962	1965	1968	1972	1975
40001-44700	R-40-10	4700	4495	4079	2761	552	20	0
44701-45700	R-40-14	1000	977	943	749	179	1	0
45701-46702	R-40-20	1002	982	964	778	243	3	0
46703-48702	R-40-23	2000	1975	1566	1531	974	82	4
5001-8000	R-40-23	3000	2953	2220	2171	1389	108	1
2001-5000	R-40-25	3000	2977	2898	2613	1895	569	34
8001-10000	R-40-26	2000	1995	1937	1850	1552	753	44
10001-11700	R-40-27	1700	-	1667	1640	1614	1572	1275
11701-11800	R-40-28	100	-	97	96	92	86	69
200126-200200	R-70-5	75	75	0**				
200601-200700	R-70-5	100	100	0**				

*From freight *Equipment Registers*
**Converted to mechanical refrigeration (see Chapter 9)

R-40-27. Icing a string of -27's with machines dispensing salt (left) and crushed ice (right); see Chapter 13. Both Specification 74-Q and the painting diagram specify "freight car red" roof paint, and a color version of this photo confirms that coloration. That these cars appear to have lighter color roofs is probably because of light scattering from the slate granules, as discussed in the previous chapter (page 159). Neg. 55-203, UP Railroad Museum.

missioned and hatches bolted closed, so that only top icing of lading could be accomplished. The cars were then renumbered by changing the first digit of their original car number from "1" to "3." The next year, 450 more cars were similarly converted, but this time they were renumbered into the 190,000 series. By this time, 1972, ice bunker service was ending, and PFE collected all remaining TIV cars into a single number series, 190,000, to facilitate record-keeping and car distribution and also to match the then-current 6-digit numbering applied to all mechanical cars.

Though the R-40-28 cars of 1957 were PFE's last ice-cooled cars, ice refrigeration continued in use by shippers. During the 1960's, this use decreased for three reasons. First, mechanical refrigerator cars were taking over more and more perishable shipments, as described in Chapter 9; second, the railroads were losing business to trucks; and third, fresh produce shipments were decreasing as a fraction of the food business, as freezing, canning and other processing of food increased. Graphs in Chapters 1 and 14 show how severely PFE's carloadings declined after 1955, making the PFE car fleet oversize for its traffic. Accordingly, ice cars were scrapped whenever extensive repairs were needed.

Other cars were converted to different service. As de-

scribed earlier in this chapter, some ice-bunker cars were assigned to "top ice service" or TIV, in which crushed ice was blown over the load but no ice was placed in the bunkers. This kept produce cool and damp without ice deck services. Even after ice refrigeration service was discontinued in 1973, some of the ice-bunker cars continued in use as ventilators, that is, with the hatches latched open to circulate air through the car as it moved. This is the reason the PFE roster contained a few TIV cars as late as 1980. Crops like onions, grapefruit, oranges and dates required ventilation in cool weather rather than refrigeration.

This point, incidentally, demonstrates that reefers with hatches latched up, often described in photo captions as empties, were more likely being used as ventilators. Although it is true that empties were occasionally moved with the hatches open, possibly to dry the interior, standard practice for empties being returned from the east was for hatches to be closed. Icing dock and cleaning yard crews throughout the West were instructed to close the ice hatches on empty PFE cars. The only empty cars ordinarily moved with hatches open were cars released from PFE shops, to air out any odors from shop work.

The ice cars were displaced from their traditional use in produce service by mechanical refrigeration, as described in the following chapter.

Yet another eastbound perishable block, made up of PFE mechanical cars, heads uphill on June 13, 1974, at Curvo, Utah, milepost 931 on the Salt Lake Subdivision, at an elevation of 6546 feet above sea level, near the top of the eastbound grade into Wyoming. Overhead, a trio of SD40-2's heads a westbound down the hill toward Ogden. This eastbound line is relatively new, having been laid in 1916-17; the westbound line is the original 1869 UP alignment. UP Railroad Museum.

9

MECHANICAL REFRIGERATORS

Two members of PFE's most numerous class of mechanical refrigerator cars, 455118 and 455171, stand at North Platte in 1966. The R-70-16 class numbered 2000 cars. Only Santa Fe, among all other refrigerator car owners, owned as many mechanical cars in *total* as this one PFE class. UP Railroad Museum, photo 47420.

Ice refrigeration was considered adequate for rail transportation of perishables in 1950, but efforts to design and successfully operate refrigerator cars which were cooled by mechanical means had a long history in North America before 1950. That history has been well summarized by John H. White in *The Great Yellow Fleet.* However, few car designs prior to World War II enjoyed much success. There were three reasons for this, when mechanical reefers were compared to the ice reefers of the time: lack of a compelling business reason for mechanical refrigeration, lack of a dependable, proven refrigeration system, and the substantially higher cost of a mechanical car. This situation is discussed in articles by Hulse and others (Bibliography).

The business reason for mechanical refrigeration began to emerge in the years immediately after World War II. To understand it, since White's history is much less complete on this topic, we must look back to 1930. In that year, the infant frozen food industry could give its age as 6 years, dating from Clarence Birdseye's pioneering development of commercial food freezing in 1924. From seafood, the

industry had moved to vegetables and fruit, and in 1930 shipped some six million pounds of frozen food. That total included several dozen railroad carloads (in 1930 the total of all types of refrigerated rail shipments in the U.S. was over 1.5 million carloads).

Yet frozen food was becoming an accepted part of the American menu, and this new traffic source spurred Pacific Fruit Express and the Santa Fe Refrigerator Department (SFRD), during 1930-32, to be among those who responded with new refrigerator cars. They built some ice reefers of conventional design but with very heavy insulation, 5 to 8 inches thickness, compared to the 2 to 3 inch thickness in typical cars of the time. PFE's first R-70 ice cars for frozen food are described in Chapter 6. Lading to be shipped in such cars would be frozen and brought to a temperature near 0°F. before loading. Ice refrigeration with salt additions of 30% could maintain temperatures of 5 to 10°F. for a few days, when starting with a large mass of frozen lading. (Although the laboratory freezing temperature obtainable with a 30% salt solution is about -6°F., the average tem-

R-70-7. PFE's first mechanical refrigerator car, car 300001, developed entirely by PFE engineers. Design work for this car was in progress at the same time as similar work at Fruit Growers Express. PFE photo, CSRM.

perature in a loaded refrigerator car was naturally higher.) As early as 1932, PFE alone moved over a hundred carloads of frozen food, with steady increases thereafter.

Although this approach to shipping frozen food did work, under these conditions it was marginally satisfactory. The problems arose when shipping times extended beyond a few days, or when uneven temperatures developed within the load due to the weak air circulation typical of ice refrigeration. Food researchers found that maintaining temperatures below 0°F. greatly extended storage life, and shippers began to demand such temperatures. These problems became more evident after World War II. Shipments of frozen food continued to increase, as public acceptance of this type of food product increased and as the technology of freezing a wider variety of foods was perfected. As an example, about 10,000 carloads of frozen food were shipped in 1945; by 1950, the number had risen to 34,000. More serious, however, was the success of frozen orange juice among consumers after World War II. The problem here was that the juice concentrate had a low freezing temperature and accordingly needed to be shipped at temperatures of 0° to -10°F. Such temperatures were beyond the capability of ice refrigeration.

As these performance demands for lower and more consistent temperatures emerged, a number of refrigerator car operators started serious experimentation and development of mechanical refrigeration systems. This started first with Fruit Growers Express (FGE). Florida oranges, being less

suitable than California ones as table fruit, were correspondingly more available to be used for juice. The dominant supplier of reefers in the southeast was (and is) FGE, and they led the development of the modern mechanical reefer. Starting with 25 experimental cars which entered service in 1949, FGE rostered 175 cars by 1952. PFE and Santa Fe each began their mechanical fleets in 1952, Santa Fe's initial order being 30 cars.

All three of these companies communicated technical findings with each other, though Santa Fe designs differed in some respects from those of FGE and PFE. In particular, Santa Fe used less insulation, larger refrigeration units, and a smaller engine compartment. PFE regarded their own configuration as better. As mentioned in Chapter 1, PFE executives frequently cited rumored advances by Santa Fe as a means of justifying their own proposed construction or improvement requests, referring of course to the need to provide "competitive service." There are indications that Santa Fe people did the same with rumors about PFE's work. This continued into the 1960's. On the other hand, PFE worked closely with FGE, frequently exchanging engineering personnel and information. Design improvements at one company often showed up promptly in the other company's cars.

The earliest post-war mechanical cars were built with gasoline engines directly driving refrigeration compressors. Among other things, this meant that on-off cycling of the compressor to meet a thermostat setting involved stop-

Table 9-1
PFE Mechanical Reefer Roster

Car Numbers	Cars	Class	Built	Builder†	Length	Drawing	Notes
100001,100002	2	R-40-29	1957	PFE, Roseville	42' 7"	-	3,11
100003-100502	500	R-40-30	1958	SPE, Los Angeles	41' 9"	4000	1,12
101001-101005	5	R-40-27	1956/61	PFE, Roseville (CV)	41' 7"	6679	18
300001-300025	25	R-70-7	1952-53	SPE, Roseville	51' 7"	2700	13
300026-300125	100	R-70-8	1953-54	SPE, Roseville	51' 7"	3000	15
300126-300137	12	R-70-6	1946/54	ART/PFE, Roseville (CV)	51' 7"	2600	5
300138-300337	200	R-70-9	1954-55	SPE, Roseville	51' 8"	3200	14
300338-300512	175	R-70-5	1953/55	SPE, Roseville (CV)	51' 7"	2900	15
300513-300712	200	R-70-10	1956	SPE, Roseville	51' 8"	3600	4,16
300713-301212	500	R-50-6	1958	SPE, Los Angeles	51' 8"	4300	16
301213-302212	1000	R-70-12	1960	SPE, Los Angeles	52' 2"	4800	17
400001-400025	25	R-70-11	1961	SPE, Los Angeles	52' 2"	5100	2,16,22
450001-451000	1000	R-70-13	1963	PC&F	56' 10"	6000,6300	20
451001-452000	1000	R-70-14	1964	PC&F	56' 9"	6400,6500	21
452001-453500	1500	R-70-15	1965	PC&F	56' 10"	6400,6500	22
453501-455500	2000	R-70-16	1966	PC&F	56' 9"	7200	21
455501-456000	500	R-70-17	1967	PC&F	56' 9"	7000	23
456001-456500	500	R-70-18	1967	PC&F	56' 9"	7100	20
456501-456900	400	R-70-19	1968	PC&F	56' 9"	7500	22
456901-458100	1200	R-70-20	1969	PC&F	56' 9"	7900	21
458101-458700	600	R-70-21	1969	PC&F	56' 9"	8700	23
458701-459300	600	R-70-20	1970	PC&F	56' 9"	8700	20
459301-459400	100	R-70-22	1970	PC&F	56' 9"	8700	20
459401-459500	100	R-70-23	1970	PC&F	56' 9"	8700	23
459501-460100	600	R-70-24	1971	PC&F	56' 9"	8700	20
460101-460700	600	R-70-25	1971	PC&F	56' 9"	8700	23

†(CV) means conversion of existing ice car class. See text for details.

EQUIPMENT NOTES

Power Plant - Detroit Diesel 2-71 unless noted

1. Witte   2. Deutz

3. Witte (100001), Deutz (100002)

4. Witte (300513-300547), balance Detroit Diesel

Refrigeration Unit

11. Equipco* (100001), Carrier (100002)

12. Equipco*(100003-100027), Trane (100028-100327), Carrier (100328-100502)

13. Frigidaire (300001-300014), Trane (300015-300025)

14. Frigidaire (300138-300287), Carrier (300288-300337)

15. Frigidaire   16. Carrier

17. Trane (301213-302201), Carrier (302202-302212)

18. Transicold (101001), York (101002, 101003), Thermo-King (101004, 101005)

* These units replaced with Carrier by 1964.

Underframe

20. Hydra-cushion underframe

21. 1st half of order, Hydra-cushion

22. 2nd half of order, Hydra-cushion

23. Keystone underframe

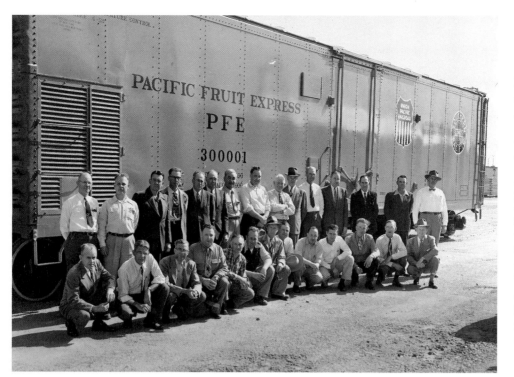

R-70-7. The car inspection ceremonies for the first mechanical car at Roseville. PFE personnel from all over the system are present, along with ART representatives (left 3, back row). The kneeling gentleman in the hat at the right end of the first row is Earl Hopkins, at the time PFE's Engineer, Car Construction, who oversaw assembly of this car. The wrinkled side sheet above the louvers may indicate some difficulties in final assembly. PFE photo, CSRM.

start engine cycles or operation of a clutch. It was soon realized that better reliability was achieved using a small diesel engine to drive an alternator, thereby providing electric power for the compressor. This arrangement is analogous to what is done on diesel locomotives. The small diesel could run continuously, independent of refrigeration needs, a reliable and relatively economical procedure. Either type of equipment, however, was capable of providing the reliability and relative economy which had been absent before World War II (see White's book, and the articles on mechanical refrigeration in the Bibliography).

In the decade 1953-1963, construction of mechanical cars by PFE reveals interesting patterns of experimentation with mechanical equipment, insulation, car size, and car body design. In many cases, multiple sources of equipment were used in a single class. In later years, this was often done to spread orders among competing suppliers, rather than provide a "jackpot" order to one. In earlier years, however, the practice also offered a chance to operate different equipment under comparable conditions, to identify the best machinery, as well as to avoid production capacity limitations at some suppliers. As shown below, the various PFE

car classes can be divided by both design and appearance into "early," "transition," and "late" groups.

Class R-70-7

In early 1950, PFE began design and development work for mechanical refrigerator cars. During 1950, PFE had received authorization for 1951 construction of 2100 new ice refrigerators, 2000 R-40-26 cars and 100 R-70-5 "super-insulated" cars for frozen food. Early in 1951, it was decided that mechanical refrigeration looked sufficiently promising to construct cars for test, and the order for 100 50-ft. ice cars was modified to assign 75 cars to ice refrigeration, and the balance of 25 to PFE's first mechanical refrigeration. A further modification to the order was to design the R-70-5 ice cars so they could be readily converted to mechanical refrigeration, should that prove desirable. The construction contract was dated in June, 1951.

This pioneering mechanical design, drawing 2700, was originally planned for construction in the spring of 1952, along with the 75 ice cars. It soon became apparent that the suppliers of the refrigeration equipment would be delayed

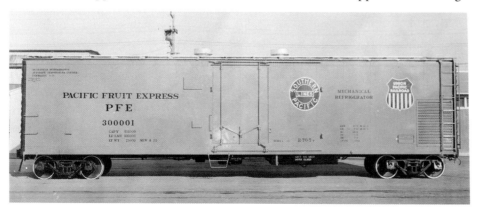

R-70-7. The right side of car 300001 (the left side is shown on page 194). In this view from April, 1953, the plain paint scheme adopted in 1952 is clearly shown. What appear to be roof vents are on an adjacent building. PFE photo, CSRM.

Table 9-2
PFE Mechanical Reefer Characteristics

Car Numbers	Class	Capacity*		Doors		Notes
		Load	Cubic	Width	Height	
100001;100002	R-40-29	67,000; 73,000	2113	6'	7'-3"	A,J,M,Q
100003-100502	R-40-30	80,000	2380	6'	8'-2"	B,H,J,M,Q
101001-101005	R-40-27	73,000	2207	6'	7'-5"	A,P
300001-300025	R-70-7	130,000	2912	6'	7'-3"	L,M,P
300026-300125	R-70-8	30,000	3032	6'	7'-3"	J,N,P
300126-300137	R-70-6	130,000	2848	5'	6'-7"	C,K,N,P
300138-300337	R-70-9	130,000	2738	6'	7'-3"	H,J,N,P
300338-300512	R-70-5	80,000	2507	6'	6'-8"	J,N,P
300513-300712	R-70-10	130,000	3085	6'	8'-0"	L,N,P
300713-301212	R-50-6	89,000	3026	6'	8'-0"	G,J,M,P
301213-302212	R-70-12	120,000	3174	8'	8'-6"	D,H-K,M,N,R,T
400001-400025	R-70-11	120,000	3472	8'	8'-6"	H,M,R,T
450001-451000	R-70-13	130,000	3989	8'	8'-7"	G,H,K,N,S,T
451001-452000	R-70-14	130,000	4022	9'	8'-8"	G-N,S,T
452001-453500	R-70-15	130,000	4042	9'	8'-8"	G-L,N,S,T
453501-455500	R-70-16	130,000	4042	9'	8'-8"	E,G,S,T
455501-456000	R-70-17	130,000	4022	9'	8'-8"	O,S,T
456001-456500	R-70-18	130,000	4022	9'	8'-8"	E,O,S,T
456501-456900	R-70-19	130,000	4050	9'	8'-8"	O,S,T
456901-460700	R-70-20/25	130,000	4050	10'-6"	8'-8"	O,S,T

*Thousands of pounds (load) or cubic feet (cubic). Some cars differed in capacity - see *Equipment Registers.*

EQUIPMENT NOTES

Doors - Youngstown sliding (plug) door unless noted.

A. 4' sliding + 2' swinging   B. Superior sliding   C. Swinging

D. Mixed Youngstown and Superior   E. Some Landis (see text)

Running Boards, Hand brakes - when known

G. Gypsum running board   H. Equipco brake   J. Ajax brake

K. Universal brake   L. Miner brake   M. Morton running board

N. Apex running board   O. No running board

Car Body

P. Riveted side sheets   Q. Welded, smooth sides   R. Welded, outside post

S. Riveted, outside post   T. Load dividers

in delivering units, and construction dates were postponed to December, 1952. Delivery dates continued to slip, and the cars were not actually assembled at Roseville until mid-1953. Each car cost $21,200.

The cars were assigned class R-70-7. As with previous PFE nomenclature, this meant **R**efrigerator, **70** tons nominal capacity, **7**th chronological design. These earliest cars received letter suffixes on their class numbers to indicate the refrigeration units installed, either R-70-7F or R-70-7T, for Frigidaire and Trane. The class totalled 25 cars, numbered 300001-300025, although originally the numbers were planned to have been extensions of the existing "frozen food" number series, i.e. 200126-200225.

All 25 cars were powered with Detroit Diesel model 2-71 (2 cylinders, each of 71 cubic inches displacement) 34-hp engines and 400-gal. fuel tanks. This diesel was one of a family of General Motors engines, available with various numbers of cylinders, which had been proven in World War II landing craft. It was to become the industry standard for refrigerator cars. The first fourteen PFE cars had Frigidaire refrigeration units and were completed in May, 1953; the last eleven had Trane units, delivery of which delayed construction until September, 1953. Car ends were the contemporary "improved" Dreadnaught design.

This class was also interesting because it was the first PFE class to have a "closed" air circulation pattern, with a

R-70-5. Photos of this class, converted from ice cars (see Chapter 8), are rare. E.J. Ott found car 300411 at Baltimore on May 7, 1964, a few years before conversion to meat service. Howard W. Ameling collection.

sealed load space. Refrigerated air was delivered into a wide, shallow plenum above a false ceiling. From there it flowed down through flues comprising the entire side wall, emerging into a space under the floor before returning to the refrigeration unit. There was no need for floor racks. The fact that the cold air didn't flow through the load space meant that heat extraction from a warm load such as fresh produce would have been quite slow, although it was an efficient arrangement for pre-frozen loads.

The low interior temperatures placed a premium on control of condensation moisture and inertness of insulation. PFE used glass fiber batts and a proprietary product called "Isoflex K-20," which had alternating layers of glass fiber bonded to aluminum foil vapor barriers (photo, page 153). Isoflex's president, T.F. Elfving, published a very interesting paper on this topic, including applications to PFE mechanical reefers (see Bibliography).

Classes R-70-5, R-70-6

It had been true since the 1930's that PFE had rebuilt its existing cars to obtain better performance. In 1954 and 1955, this process was also applied to mechanical refrigerators. In 1955, the 175 ice cars of class R-70-5 were converted to mechanicals. Ice bunkers were removed and Detroit Diesel-Frigidaire equipment installed. They were already heavily insulated, but were given new roof sheets at the hatch locations, as well as interior changes to permit

"envelope" air circulation. Drawing 2900 shows these changes. In 1968, 100 of these cars were fitted with meat rails and renumbered (renumberings are shown in Table 9-3, below). In the 1970's, many had their mechanical equipment removed. They were then assigned to TIV (top ice vegetable) service (see Chapter 8).

These cars were preceded in 1954 by a set of very interesting car conversions, unique in PFE's history because the cars were purchased used. In 1950, PFE obtained twelve cars from American Refrigerator Transit which had overhead ice tanks. A photograph is included in Chapter 8. These cars were AMRX numbers 1000-1011 when with ART, which had built them in 1946 for meat service. The only change by PFE, other than repainting, was removal of the meat rails, and they entered frozen-food service as class R-70-6. Like all "early" cars, they were about 14'6" tall at the running board, a full foot taller than the tallest ice cars.

In 1954, they were converted at Roseville to mechanical refrigeration with Frigidaire units powered by Detroit Diesel. The drawing for this work was 2600. The car roofs were simply given a 42" x 96" patch where the hatch openings were, but entirely new interiors, including insulation and floors, were installed. The exterior sides and ends remained as they had been built (except adding louvered openings for the mechanical units), as did their unusual (for PFE) 5-ft. swinging doors. They retained their R-70-6 class but were renumbered 300126-300137. In 1963 they received foamed-in-place urethane floor insulation.

R-70-5. In this photo at Roseville, Calif., car 390351 (originally 300351) reveals its conversion to TIV service. Frank Peacock photo, May 11, 1973.

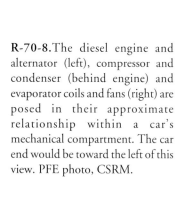
R-70-8. The diesel engine and alternator (left), compressor and condenser (behind engine) and evaporator coils and fans (right) are posed in their approximate relationship within a car's mechanical compartment. The car end would be toward the left of this view. PFE photo, CSRM.

Classes R-70-8, R-70-9

In January, 1953, before the R-70-7 cars had even been built, PFE requested authority to build 200 more such cars to follow up the experimental R-70-7 class. The reason given was that frozen food loadings had doubled since 1948. Cautiously, the UP and SP modified the request to a quantity of 100 mechanical cars and 100 additional 50-ft. ice cars (the second complement of class R-70-5).

At first, internal documents referred to all these cars as continuations of the preceding car classes (R-70-5 and R-70-7), but modifications to the -7 design led to a new drawing, no. 3000, specification 74-M, and class R-70-8. During March-May, 1954, these 100 additional cars, which were externally of very similar design to the R-70-7's, were assembled at Roseville (numbers 3000026-300125). They

all had Frigidaire refrigeration units powered by Detroit Diesel engines, since this was felt to be the most reliable combination of equipment among the various designs then on the market.

Like all the "early" cars after R-70-7, the two ends of the cars were different. The engine compartment end (always the A or non-brake end) was a conventional (pre-War type) Dreadnaught end, while the other end was an early improved Dreadnaught. The reason for this was that only the B end had to resist shifting of the load. At the A end, that task was taken up by an internal, corrugated bulkhead. Thus the A end could be the earlier, less-stiff end design. These ends were certainly not in production at Standard Railway Equipment Co. by the date these cars were built, so they were either surplus ends, or a special order, and may have been less expensive.

R-70-8. The first car of the class, car 300026, is posed at Roseville with the mechanical refrigeration equipment in the foreground (a better view of the equipment is shown at the top of this page). PFE photo, CSRM.

R-70-9 (Above). Car 300242, built in April, 1955, poses at Kansas City in 1958 in a Charles Winters photo. R-70-8 (Below, left). The B end of car 300026, showing lettering and improved Dreadnaught end. PFE photo, CSRM.

The most evident external difference from the -7 cars was the arrangement of ventilating louvers on the mechanical compartment. Both the large louvered areas, and the long individual louvers on the -7 were reduced considerably on the -8 and following classes. In addition, small vertical louvers were used on the right side of the car in R-70-8 and later cars.

Then came the 1954-55 group of 200 R-70-9 cars. The slightly changed design is shown on drawing 3200 and in specification 74-N. This time, the first 150 cars received Frigidaire refrigeration units, while the last 50 were given Carrier units, still with the same Detroit Diesel engine. Clearly the R-70-7 design philosophy was proving effective, as each of these classes was very similar, despite differences of detail. The R-70-9's, like the -8's, cost about $20,500 each.

In later years, 140 of the R-70-9 cars were converted to meat service, and then in the 1970's, cars from both R-70-8 and -9 were demoted to TIV service (see Table 9-3).

Class R-70-10

In 1955, PFE requested authority to build an additional 2000 ice reefers. The response from UP and SP was that part of the order should be for mechanical cars, and the agreement finally was that 1800 ice cars were built (classes

R-70-9. In this photo at Sterling, Colo., car 250312 (originally 300312) is in meat service. The panel at left reads "RETURN TO COUNCIL BLUFFS." The engine compartment vent panels are replacements. Frank Peacock photo, July 25, 1971.

R-70-10. Very similar to its predecessor classes, car 300624 is shown when new at Roseville, April, 1957. The vent stack above the engine compartment is evident. PFE photo, CSRM.

R-40-27 and -28) with the other 200 cars being the last cars of PFE's "early" cars, class R-70-10. These had some changes in equipment compared to prior classes, as shown in drawing 3600 and specification 74-P. All received Carrier refrigeration units, and the first 35 cars received Witte opposed-piston diesel engines, the first use of this type by PFE. Witte engines were built by U.S. Steel's Oil Well Supply Division. The balance of the order, 165 cars, received the usual Detroit Diesel 2-71 engine. They cost an average of about $21,500 when constructed at Roseville, February to May, 1956. The -10's were the first to be 15 ft. tall at the running board (earlier mechanicals were 14'6").

All the "early" PFE mechanical cars had riveted sides, 400 gallons fuel (usually as a 200-gal. tank on each side), two end styles, fiberglass insulation, and conventional solid-bearing trucks. PFE also briefly leased an EMD experimental reefer in 1957, numbering it 301000 while in service.

Painting and lettering. When the first mechanical cars were built in 1952, they received the paint scheme then current, the 1950's PFE scheme (see Chapter 8), with Roman lettering and both railroad medallions or emblems painted in black and white on each side of the car. The significant difference from the ice cars was that the roofs were painted a light gray on the first 25 cars, then aluminum from 1953 onwards. Until 1956, silica sand was sprinkled on this paint when wet, to make a skid-resistant surface. Car ends were coated with a black asphalt emulsion. The ice cars were receiving red asphalt on roof and ends in this same era. The car sides were light orange.

In this 1952-60 period, the refrigeration unit installed in the car was identified in 1-inch letters at the upper left corner of each car side, as may be discerned in the photos. Accordingly, the refrigeration units are identified with the corresponding car numbers for pre-1960 classes in the car roster, Table 9-1.

Class R-40-29

During the mid and late 1950's, mechanical car fleets of most reefer operators continued to grow apace with the growth of the frozen food market. Produce shipments, however, which did not require mechanical refrigeration as preferred shipping temperatures were in the range 35-45°F.,

R-70-10. Car 300562 shows its right side as well as the 1970 paint scheme in this 1975 photo near Luckenbach, Texas by Frank Peacock.

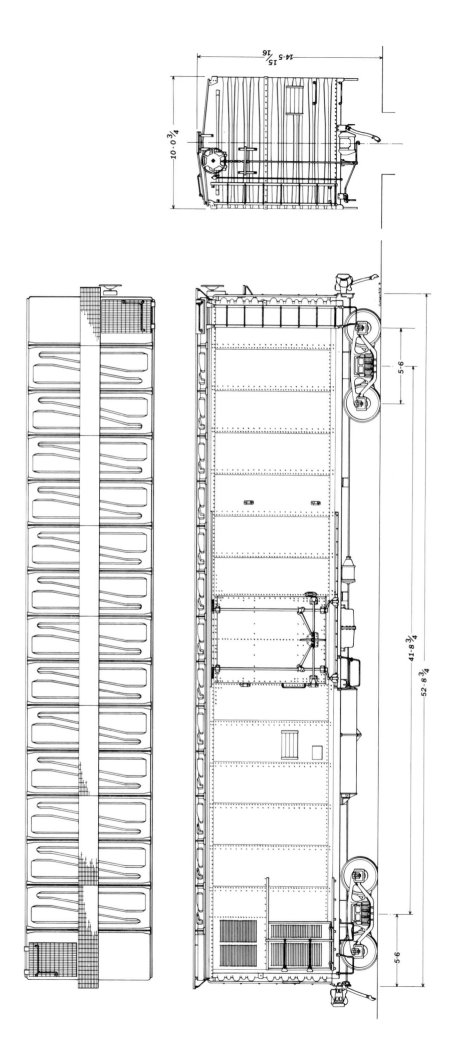

R-70-10. This HO scale drawing by Chuck Yungkurth shows the appearance, features, and major dimensions of this "early" PFE class.

R-40-29. The pioneer 40-ft. mechanical car, shown at the time of its inspection at Roseville in September, 1957. Note the 2-piece door, a 4-ft. sliding door and a 2-ft. hinged door, exactly like the door design of R-40-27. PFE photo, CSRM.

were falling steadily as trucking rates undercut the regulated rates imposed on the railroads (see Chapter 1). The ice fleets, therefore, ceased adding new cars and cut back on refurbishing as well. Yet ice was a significantly cheaper refrigerant, and had the ability to cool a warm load rapidly.

Shipment of produce in mechanical reefers thus had to await two developments. One was wider use of precooling by shippers, so that produce was loaded into the car at about the desired transit temperature, making rapid cooling capacity unnecessary. The second and more important, for those loads which did require rapid cooling, was development of "all-purpose" cars. Once again, Fruit Growers Express led the way with this car type, and demonstrated its worth during 1954-57.

These cars had wide-range thermostats so that cars could be used interchangeably for the temperature ranges for produce or frozen food, and had a "semi-envelope" air circulation pattern, in which cold air traversed the ceiling, descended through the walls, and entered the load space through the floor rack slats, returning at the top of the end wall. This air movement through the interior meant that produce loads could be effectively cooled after loading. It finally began to look as if mechanical cars could take over all of the reefer trade.

In 1957, the last PFE ice cars, class R-40-28, were ordered (see Chapter 8), concluding a tradition that extended back to PFE's beginnings in 1906. The 40-ton capacity car, with its 33-ft. inside length between ice bunkers, was a suitable size for many produce shippers (for a forceful presentation of this view, see the 1951 Kelley article in Bibliography), and PFE accordingly tried out designs for mechanical cars of this size. They were the first of what can be classed as "transition" PFE mechanical cars.

These cars were developed to handle produce shipments, as well as frozen food. It is important to remember that

although the mechanical reefer was accepted almost immediately for frozen food, in the early fifties there continued to be a debate as to its utility for non-frozen shipments (see Plummer, Ransom and Henney articles, Bibliography).

The PFE transition period began with two experimental cars, both designated R-40-29 and externally identical. Car 100001 received a Witte diesel engine driving an Equipco refrigeration unit, while 100002 had a Deutz (German) diesel powering a Carrier unit. The air-cooled Deutz engine would have been an attractive unit, since it dispensed with radiator, cooling fluid, and some bulk and weight. But experience showed that the engines, although beautifully made, were noisy and, worse, were unable to deal with temperature extremes in service.

These cars had 500-gal. fuel tanks in the engine compartment, rather than twin tanks slung under the car, as on earlier mechanical reefers. The bodies were welded with a slender external post. Like all PFE's "transition" cars, they were of semi-envelope design. This meant using the first floor racks in PFE mechanical cars. As in the late ice cars, these racks had wood stringers and metal slats.

Class R-40-30

The following year, 1958, 500 additional 40-ton cars were constructed by the SP Equipment Co. (SPE) at Los Angeles, classed R-40-30. The initial proposal by PFE for 1958 construction was for 3000 more ice cars. This was changed a few months later to 500 50-ft. and 2500 40-ft. mechanical cars. The final authorization by UP and SP was for 500 of each size, with no new ice cars.

For these 40-ft. cars, smaller mechanical equipment could be used. Instead of the usual 34-hp diesel power plants, an 18-hp Witte was selected, with 12-½ kw instead of 15-kw generators applied. The first 25 cars, starting with

R-40-30. The first of 500 cars, PFE 100003 shows the differences from the R-40-29 predecessor class. A a 6-ft. sliding door, of double-post Superior design, and a return to riveted side sheets, was chosen for the production cars. PFE photo, CSRM.

100003, had Equipco refrigeration units; the next 300 had Trane units; and the final 175 received Carrier refrigeration. The first 25 cars were a tryout for "fresh" lading only, with 32 - 70°F thermostats, but the remaining 475 cars pioneered "all-purpose" 0 - 70°F. thermostats. These cars, along with the R-50-6 class, also pioneered roller bearing trucks for PFE cars, using Buckeye, Symington and Scullin sideframes. The average price per car was just under $19,000.

The R-40-30 class was also used for insulation experiments. The floors were foamed in place with polyurethane foam, a first application for PFE, in 24 of the cars, and the last car, 100502, had all insulation in floor, sides, ends, and roof foamed in place. This car was examined in May, 1962, and the insulation found to be in excellent condition. On this basis, PFE began to use polyurethane foam in later cars. All the R-40-30's had 6" insulation in floors and walls and 8" in the ceiling.

This class, together with the R-40-29's, was numbered in the 100,000 series, previously used for R-50-1 cars. By this time, however, all the R-50's so numbered had been rebuilt and renumbered, as described in Chapter 7.

In the early 1970's, the surviving cars of this class had their mechanical refrigeration equipment removed, and they were assigned to service as TIV cars. As with all such cars, their AAR classification became RB (for "bunkerless" refrigerator), and the second digit of their car numbers changed from zero to nine (see Table 9-3).

Class R-50-6

Also in 1958, 500 cars of an intermediate size, nominally 50-ton capacity (actually 89,000 pounds), were built as class R-50-6. They were to be the only PFE mechanicals built new with nominal 50-ton capacity (body design was the same as the R-70 cars, but 50-ton trucks were used). The cars were intended for lighter loads, such as produce, which is usually much less dense than frozen food. Although the cars initially had "fresh" thermostats, which

R-40-30. Shown here is PFE 190075 after its conversion to TIV service and renumbering into the 190,000 series. Frank Peacock photo at Rock River, Wyo., on Aug. 28, 1978.

R-50-6. The only class of nominally 50-ton PFE mechanical reefers, these were designed for produce, which was a limitation in later years. Mechanical compartment door is open for inspection. PFE photo, CSRM.

could be set within the 32° to 70° F. range, they later received all-purpose thermostats with a -10° to 70° F. range. The refrigeration equipment and all other mechanical features, however, were identical to other PFE mechanical cars, to ensure interchangeability.

Built by the SP Equipment Co. at PFE's Los Angeles shop like the R-40 mechanical cars, with extensive use of welding, they all received Carrier refrigeration units driven by Detroit Diesel engines. They were numbered 300713-301212. Each car cost about $22,500.

One important detail in this class is that the last five cars of the class received experimental applications of load dividers. These dividers were useful to shippers, as they permitted discontinuance of the wood bracing formerly used to prevent load shifting (see Chapter 14). The installations were a success, and PFE was to use these dividers in all

subsequent car classes. All-metal floor racks were also tried in this class, but were never repeated in a later class.

Like the 40-ft. mechanical cars, they were to fall victim to lack of suitability for general use by the 1970's, and with their thinner insulation, were less effective as "all-purpose" cars. They might have been usable as meat cars, but there were numerous other classes, as shown in Table 9-3, which were also available and were converted instead. The R-50-6 cars were converted to TIV service in the early 1970's and like other TIV's, renumbered with a nine as the second car number digit (see Table 9-3).

Class R-70-11

The smaller cars just described, of classes R-40 and R-50, were the last of their kind to be built. When construc-

Table 9-3
Renumberings of PFE Mechanical Reefers

Original Numbers	New Numbers	Cars	Class	Date	Remarks
100001-100502	190001-190502	464	R-40-30	1972-73	Converted to TIV (see Chapter 8)
101001-101005	34701-34705	5	R-40-27	1968	Mech. equip. removed (see Ch. 8)
200196-200337	250196-250337	133	R-70-9	1973	See next entry
300196-300337	200196-200337	140	R-70-9	1963	Meat rails added
300338-300512	200338-200512	100	R-70-5	1968	Meat rails added
300026-301212	390026-391212	681*	several*	1972-74	Mech. equipment removed, for TIV
400001-400025	350001-350025	25	R-70-11	1967	Load dividers removed
451001-454500	351001-351179	179	R-70-14/16	1982-84	Load dividers removed
301213-302212	351213-352212	1000	R-70-12	1968	Load dividers removed

*Most cars (265) from R-50-6; other classes were R-70-5, R-70-8, R-70-9, R-70-10.

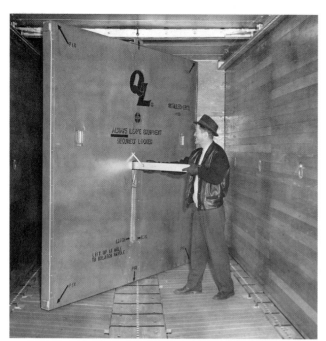

R-50-6. An Evans load divider, installed in PFE 301208. This is the "single-bulkhead" type (most divider designs had two bulkheads), with tracks in the floor and at the top and bottom of the side walls. PFE photo, CSRM.

tion of new cars resumed in 1960, all subsequent cars were to be of R-70 classes. The first two such classes, R-70-11 and -12, were built in 1960-61, and concluded the PFE "transition" era. They also shared a unique spotting feature for PFE mechanical cars, a diagonal outside brace on each side of the door. Both classes were built by PFE through the SP Equipment Co. (see Chapters 1 and 5), the last cars so built, and were of welded construction throughout. They

also were the first classes to use rigid foam "board" insulation, installed as sheets and blocks of foam material.

General arrangement drawing 5100 and specification 77 described this class. All the R-70-11 cars had 5" rigid urethane foam board insulation in the floors, but the remainder of the car insulation was chosen from a variety of materials. There were several groups of insulation combinations for the walls and ceilings. The first 5 cars had urethane foam boards, 5" in walls and 7" in the ceiling; the second 5 had K-20 Isoflex (glass fiber plus aluminum foil), also 5 and 7"; the third 5 had polystyrene foam boards, 5 and 7"; and the last 10 had a combination of 3" K-20 Isoflex and glass fiber batts, 2" in walls and 3" in the ceiling. Clearly, the R-70-11's were an experimental class, for insulation as well as for other features.

The R-70-11 class, like the first 25 R-40-30's and all the R-50-6's when they were built, had a "produce" or fresh thermostat, only able to be set in the range 32 to 70°F. As with the other "transition" cars, it is evident that PFE was searching for a good mechanical design for produce shipments. Equipco load dividers were installed, and the 500-gal. fuel capacity was in tanks hung under the car, as it was on all subsequent cars. Like the R-40-29, all these cars had Deutz engines initially.

The R-70-11 was the first PFE class to have a cushioned underframe. The first 15 had "Super-cushion" underframes, the other 10 the SP-developed "Hydracushion" design. Delays in selection and purchase of these underframes delayed construction of the R-70-11's until 1961, after the R-70-12 class was completed.

For ready identification, these cars were numbered into

R-70-11. Car 400016, one of just 25 experimental cars in this class, was photographed prior to weighing at Los Angeles shop, with pre-cool shed behind, in 1961. Note the "outline" SP medallion in this 1960 paint scheme. PFE photo, CSRM.

Seen here are "double-bulkhead" style Equipco load dividers. (**Above**) Note the floor and ceiling tracks for the dividers, which are independent on each half of the car. (**Below**) Each bulkhead could be rotated against the wall if not needed. PFE photos, CSRM.

a new 400,000 series when built. But by 1964, with the newest cars of 57-ft. length numbered in the 450,000 series, some confusion developed. The 50-ft. R-70-11's were then renumbered to 350001-350025 (see Table 9-3).

Painting and lettering. In April, 1960, PFE adopted a new lettering scheme, with the name spelled out in large Gothic letters on the right end of the car side, and with the two railroad medallions at the left end. The medallions, or heralds, were in "outline" form, done entirely in black paint on the orange car side, and the SP herald was toward the B end on both sides. Note that the UP herald no longer had a black field at the top, as it did during 1952-60. The refrigeration unit was no longer identified in this scheme, but the legend "MECH REFRIG" was placed in the upper left corner of the side, with the date of installation of that unit (which might be later than the built date) underneath. Also at this time, the AAR type designation, RPL for R-70-11, began to be included with the capacity data block.

Class R-70-12

Where the R-70-11's can be regarded as experimental, the R-70-12's, 1000 strong and thus by far PFE's largest class of mechanical cars to date, were intended as a new "standard car." Drawing 4800 and specification 78 described the cars, which cost about $25,000 when assembled at LA in 1960, largely from vendor's components.

The cars were intended for construction starting in late 1959, but the steel strike of that period delayed start-up of the assembly line, and the first car was not completed until April of 1960, with the other cars following throughout the rest of the year. Shown on the following pages are some of the construction photos from that assembly line.

All the R-70-12's were insulated alike, with 7" rigid foam in the floors and K-20 Isoflex plus glass fiber batts in walls and ceilings. They also had all-purpose thermostats.

The diesel engines were either Witte (700 cars) or the usual 2-71 (300 cars), this time in a "power package." This package was purchased by PFE from a vendor, such as Stewart and Stevenson, or Emerson, which in turn had first purchased the GM 2-71 diesel and then had assembled engine, generator and associated equipment onto a chassis which was ready to install in the refrigerator car. This chassis arrangement was designed for quick and easy exchange of units when a package failed in service.

The R-70-12's were given four different brands of load dividers. Installed in these 1000 cars were 25 sets of Evans dividers, and 325 sets each of Pullman, Preco, and Equipco dividers. These early-model dividers were removed in 1968, however, and the cars renumbered by changing the second digit of the car number from zero to five (see Table 9-3).

R-70-12. In this photo, the outdoor primary assembly area at Los Angeles is shown, with purchased floors and underframes receiving the prefabricated sides and ends. Very visible in this photo is the internal bulkhead (far end of each car), reminiscent of the corrugated ends used in the 1930's, at what will be the A end of the car, separating the mechanical compartment from the load space. At the right of the photo, mechanical and ice cars are undergoing repairs, also outdoors. PFE photo, neg. N5902-30, CSRM.

As with many of PFE's cars which had been assembled by SPE Co., the R-70-12's were "delivered" to PFE at places outside California, such as Yuma, Arizona or Klamath Falls, Oregon. This avoided payment of California sales tax on the cars, since they remained the property of SPE until title was transferred to PFE outside California. The cars thus made their first trips empty, on route to their delivery location. Only upon PFE's acceptance of title did they enter revenue service. This was, incidentally, a perfectly legal procedure.

During the 1958-1962 period, PFE converted most of the older "closed" interior cars, classes R-70-5 through R-70-10, to semi-envelope design. Fan capacity was increased, and floor racks (now changed from metal slats on wood stringers, to wood slats on metal stringers) had to be installed. By 1965, every R-70 car was an all-purpose car.

R-70-12. Workmen at Los Angeles are preparing to set the pedestal truck frame onto the roller bearings of this 70-ton truck. ASF, Buckeye, National C-1, and Barber products were used. A few more trucks remain to be assembled. PFE photo, CSRM.

Ice car conversions

When the last ice refrigerators cars, classes R-40-27 and -28, were built in 1957 (Chapter 8), they were designed to be "constructed in a manner to permit conversion to mechanical refrigeration should such a development occur during the life of the equipment." In 1959, it was decided to try such a conversion with R-40-27 car 11124, which was given an underfloor direct-drive mechanical refrigeration unit made by Trane and powered by American Marc, and renumbered 101001. Early in 1960, a second experiment was tried, with a Witte engine-generator set installed underneath car 10462, also a -27, with an electric York refrigeration unit installed in one former ice bunker. This car was renumbered 101002 (see photo, page 422).

In the fall of 1960, a second York electric test unit with a Witte engine was installed in car 11445, which was renumbered to 101003. Also that fall, an additional car was selected for conversion like the first one, with all equipment under the car, this time in car 10739 which became 101004. The Trane-American Marc hardware on 101001 had been having service troubles with engine overheating and compressor failures, and a Deutz engine and a Carrier refrigeration unit were planned for 101004. Delays in equipment delivery postponed this conversion until summer, 1961. These conversions cost about $8500 per car.

In the spring of 1961, a fifth experiment was planned, with a Detroit Diesel engine and a generator underneath the car once again, but with a Carrier refrigeration unit installed in the side walls of the car to permit the full 40-

R-70-12. On this page are part of a series of construction photos taken during assembly of this class at Los Angeles shop. Roof trusses were added when cars came inside the rebuild shed. The truss frames are open to permit air flow through them, toward the load space. PFE photo N5902-45 at Los Angeles, CSRM.

R-70-12. The diagonal-panel roof sections are welded in place, completing the basic car body structure. Note the assembled running board ready for application. PFE photo, N5902-14, CSRM.

R-70-12. The final step in construction, painting the new, 1960 PFE emblem. Note that the metal stencil has locating channels to fit over the ribs, thus ensuring a consistent location for lettering. PFE photo, neg. N5902-29, CSRM.

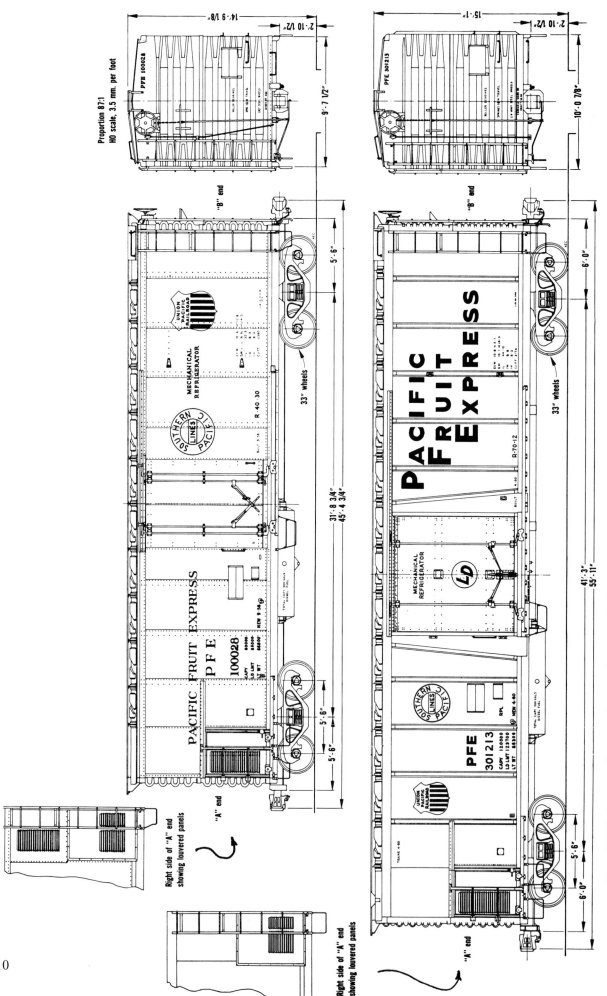

Proportion 87:1
HO scale, 3.5 mm. per foot

Right side of "A" end showing louvered panels

Right side of "A" end showing louvered panels

Two of PFE's "transition" cars are shown in this HO scale drawing by Allan E. Craig, R-40-30 at top and R-70-12 below. Although the dimensions and features of the drawing are accurate, the lettering is not. The SP and UP heralds should be reversed on the R-40-30 so that the SP herald is toward the B end, and on that car, both heralds should be reversed in contrast, that is, white lettering on black backgrounds (see photo, page 204). Also, the original magazine caption described an incorrect color scheme. The actual scheme had light orange sides, with black ends and underframe, and silver roof. Reprinted from *Model Railroader* magazine.

R-70-12. This was the last PFE class to have "regular" Dreadnaught A ends. PFE photo at Los Angeles, CSRM.

R-40-27 (Below). One of PFE's experimental nose-mount conversions of an ice car to mechanical refrigeration, here using Thermo-King equipment. Note the car end was moved inwards after ice bunker removal, with grid walkways above. None of these experiments was deemed successful. PFE photo, CSRM.

foot inside length of the car to be available for loading. Car 10232 was to became 101005. By summer, the Detroit Diesel had arrived and was installed in 101004 along with a Carrier side-wall unit, while delays in delivery of the Deutz engine for 101004 led to transfering it to the 101005 project. When a decision was made to remove the unsuccessful Trane-American Marc equipment from 101001, the Carrier-Deutz set-up was installed instead in car 101001, and car 10232 remained in service as an ice car.

In 1962, the 101005 conversion, now using car 10198, finally took place, using a Detroit Diesel 2-71 engine and a Thermo-King refrigeration unit. These various underslung equipment experiments were moderately successful, and in 1962, PFE made a budget request to convert 500 ice cars to mechanical, using equipment like that on 101005, but financial stringencies at that time precluded the program. Subsequent requests were not made, probably in part because further testing was less encouraging.

Starting in 1965, PFE experimented with a different conversion of ice cars to mechanical refrigeration, following drawing 6679, using "nose-mount" units on the car end. For this conversion, the end was moved inward about 20" to permit the external mechanical units to fit the car body. Two of the experimental cars had their units replaced with trailer-type units from Transicold and Thermo-King, in cars 101001 and 101004. The side-wall Carrier refrigeration units in those cars had not proved to have adequate capacity. In 1968 the nose-mount and under-slung units were removed and all five cars converted to "top-ice vegetable" service (see Chapter 8) and renumbered to 34701-34705, among the remaining ice cars.

Like other refrigerator car operators, PFE ultimately found these ice car conversions not economical. No ice car owner made significant numbers of such conversions, though many experiments were tried. Insulation in the ice cars was suitable only for produce, the air flow pattern was "open," and it was not cost-effective to add features such as load dividers, 6-ft. doors, or cushion underframes which shippers were beginning to expect. Perhaps most important, the flexibility of "all-purpose" cars was preferable in a climate of declining produce shipments.

Class R-70-13

In 1963, car construction resumed with a new design of larger cars, nominally 57 feet in length. This length was chosen to achieve an inside length for cargo of 50 ft., the same as then standard for regular and insulated box cars. The first of these was R-70-13, with general arrangement drawing 6302 and specification 82. The initial specification, dated April 20, 1962, was for 500 cars; when a second batch of 500 was added to the order in November, 1962, minor changes resulted in specification 82A. These and all subsequent cars built for PFE were constructed by Pacific Car and Foundry at their Renton, Wash. plant.

Within PFE, there was strong sentiment to continue the production of new cars in company facilities. Costs were competitive, quality control was good, and complete oversight of car construction could be maintained. But the parent railroads, particularly SP, felt that the commercial builders deserved support. Moreover, the closure of the Los

Angeles shop in 1962 greatly reduced PFE's capacity to assemble cars; had the R-70-13's been built by PFE, it would probably have been at Nampa, where cars had not been assembled previously. The final "compromise" which PFE accepted from the UP and SP was to build one class, the R-70-13 cars, at PC&F as an evaluation. This turned out, however, to be a permanent change in the source of new cars; PC&F was to build all subsequent new PFE cars.

As described in Chapter 1, the R-70-13 cars were the first which PFE did not purchase itself. Instead, they were purchased by the parent railroads, SP and UP, and then leased to PFE. Although initially a financial device, this arrangement was to continue throughout most of the remaining history of PFE. The R-70-13's cost $26,800 each.

The R-70-13 inaugurated PFE's "late" style mechanical cars. Observers have tended to regard all these later cars as "cookie cutter" designs, and there was indeed some similarity among them. All had outside-post sides, with the side sheets riveted to the posts. This type of construction simplified and improved the application of insulation to the cars. They also had identical A and B ends, unlike the preceding PFE mechanical reefers. These cars marked the first use on new PFE car classes of double-wear steel wheels, after over 20 years of considering single-wear wheels as standard. Interior capacity was about 4000 cubic feet.

This class also inaugurated a change in safety appliances. The cars had short ladders, instead of grab irons, at the car corners which did not have full-length ladders. As

R-70-13. The first of PFE's classes to be built at PC&F since the R-40-23's of 1947, these 1000 cars had outside-post bodies with riveted side-sheet attachments. UP Railroad Museum photo 45501.

the end view shows, there was a steel-grid step above the coupler on both ends, and a horizontal grab iron above it.

Other car features continued to change. For example, the R-70-13 was the last class to have a diagonal-panel roof. It was also the last to have relatively conventional insulation. All 1000 R-70-13's had foamed-in-place floor insulation, 450 cars had foamed ends, and 100 were completely foamed, all with polyurethane foam. The balance of the insulation was fiberglass or foam blocks. The all-foam car was about 800 pounds heavier than an all-fiberglass car of the same insulation thickness, but the insulation was more efficient. PFE calculated that 5" of foam (the thickness used) was the equivalent of 7" of fiberglass. Installation of 7" fiberglass batts would weigh about 800 extra pounds, which is to say that equivalent insulation weighed the same, but foam was thinner. In addition to the efficiency just mentioned, this foam was easy to install, filled insulating spaces fully without any seams, did not pack or settle, did not absorb odors, was very moisture-resistant with its closed cells, permitting thinner insulation without moisture barriers, and adhered to the inside of steel walls, greatly reducing corrosion and eliminating interior asphalt coatings.

The R-70-13 was the last class to have the 8-ft.-wide door with unsupported vertical locking bars. This type of mechanism was satisfactory in an 8-ft. door, but was less

R-70-13. The A end shows the short ladders, coupler step, and grab iron. PFE photo, CSRM.

Table 9-4
Numbers of Mechanical Refrigerator Cars with Original Numbers*

Car Numbers	Class	Number of Cars						
		New	1965	1970	1975†	1975‡	1980†	1980‡
100001-100502	R-40-29, -30	502	497	474	0	0	-	-
300001-300025	R-70-7	25	25	25	25	0	-	-
300026-300125	R-70-8	100	99	95	55	0	-	-
300126-300137	R-70-6	12	12	11	0	0	-	-
300138-300337	R-70-9	200	199	54	17	0	32**	0
300338-300512	R-70-5	175	174	39	3	0	-	-
300513-300712	R-70-10	200	199	191	0	0	-	-
300713-301212	R-50-6	500	493	485	203	0	-	-
301213-302212	R-70-12	1000	989	966	0	0	-	
450001-451000	R-70-13	1000	997	977	471	467		442
451001-452000	R-70-14	1000	999	976	481	⎡	464	⎡
452001-453500	R-70-15	1500	-	1472	715	⎣1190	697	⎣1148
453501-455500	R-70-16	2000	-	1976	975	961	951	932
455501-456000	R-70-17	500	-	496	0	475	0	472
456001-456500	R-70-18	500	-	496	491	0	476	0
456501-456900	R-70-19	400	-	396	384	0	100	0
456901-460700	R-70-20/-25	3800	-	-	2070	1683	1841	1611

*From freight *Equipment Registers*. For renumberings, see Table 9-3.
†SP owned, leased to PFE (SPFE reporting marks), or PFE owned.
‡UP owned, leased to PFE (UPFE reporting marks).
**Some meat cars returned to general service (see Table 9-3)

R-70-13. The diagonal panel roof of this class is depicted here, as is the lacy appearance of the Apex running board. The exhaust stack is visible at the far left corner of the roof. PC&F photo for PFE, CSRM.

ers, 300 sets each from Preco and Evans, and 400 from Equipco. Pullman's dividers had evidently been found wanting. In most succeeding classes, dividers were from some combination of Preco, Evans and Equipco.

The -13's inaugurated the 400,000 series numbers, emblematic of the 4000 cubic foot capacity. As a final distinction, in 1961 the SP medallion was changed to its modern design, with a Gothic "SP" in the center; R-70-13 was the first class to be painted with this new emblem.

Classes R-70-14 and R-70-15

With the development of PFE car production at PC&F with the R-70-13, and satisfactory performance of many features of that design, PFE was ready to continue with new features and improvements in mechanical refrigerators. The 1000 cars of R-70-14 of 1964 followed drawings 6200 and 6400 (SP cars) or 6500 and 6700 (UP cars) and specification 85. The next year, 1500 cars of class R-70-15 were ordered from the same drawings and specification 88.

Class R-70-14 began the usage of a peaked roof with small, straight ribs between the large ones. Like the previous roof designs, this roof was supplied by Stanray (1963's new trade name for Standard Railway Equipment Co.). It was simpler to manufacture and had even better stiffness than the diagonal panel roofs used on earlier cars.

Doors were also changed. In the face of continued shipper demand, a still wider, 9-foot width was adopted in the R-70-14. On this larger door, exterior horizontal supports for the locking bars appeared on the (usually Youngstown) style doors used. The insulation was all foamed-in-place polyurethane in the R-70-14 and succeeding classes.

effective in the wider doors of subsequent PFE classes. The makers of the Youngstown doors originated a new door mechanism in class R-70-14.

The R-70-13 cars received load dividers from three mak-

R-70-14. This was the first class with the ribbed roof and a 9' door. UP Railroad Museum photo 45998.

Previously, a smooth side wall, with an air flue behind it for air circulation, had been standard construction with wood internal lining. A new fiberglass liner of PFE design was installed in the -14 and later cars (and in trailers, Chapter 10), with sinusoidal wavy grooves for both air circulation next to the load, and also for prevention of wedging or snagging of cartons into the grooves as the load shifted. Earl Hopkins, GM&EO of PFE at the time, was assigned the patent for this invention, although, as he pointed out, it was hardly a lucrative patent. By this time, few others in North America were buying mechanical reefers, and such an innovation was of little benefit outside PFE.

In most respects, R-70-15 was very similar to the R-70-14. One external difference was a change in the exhaust stack for the diesel engine. PFE had long used a T-shaped stack with a square top tube aligned with the long direction of the car. But the R-70-15's had a new kind of stack: a straight stack with a spring-loaded cap, like those used on construction equipment and other small diesel engines. The new-style stack was used for all subsequent cars.

Painting and lettering. Car roof paint for mechanical cars was aluminum from 1953 until 1964. In that year, an experiment was tried with the R-70-14's, with the last 500 cars of the 1000-car order given white roof paint. Starting with the R-70-15 class, this color became standard for PFE mechanical reefers. In subsequent years, earlier classes of cars, when repainted, also received white roofs.

From 1960 onwards, PFE reefers carried door lettering which indicated the presence of load dividers (a large LD in a circle), as well as the legend "MECHANICAL REFRIGERATION," arranged variously from year to year. The accompanying photos give examples. There were also slogans

Typical roof view showing the ribbed roof construction of the PFE car classes R-70-14 through -19. PFE collection, CSRM.

indicating the cushion underframes, and this topic has the following sidelight.

The SP-developed "Hydra-cushion" underframe was a fine performer, but was said (outside the SP, at least) to require excessive maintenance. Partly for this reason, and partly because of a dispute about whether royalties would have to be paid for use of the underframe on UP-owned PFE cars (UP owned no other Hydra-cushion cars), UP directed that its part of each PFE car order have devices other than Hydra-cushion. PFE maintenance records reveal little difference in upkeep for the two types of cushioning arrangements; what small difference did exist was that the Hydra-cushion mechanism needed *less* maintenance.

In UP-owned cars of classes R-70-14 and -15, the cushion devices were located at the end of the car (the "Freight Master" design), but thereafter were underframe-type designs, usually Keystone. This is relevant to paint schemes because the car door either was labeled with the legend "HYDRA-CUSHION" or with "CUSHION UNDERFRAME." These distinctions can be made from Table 9-1.

R-70-14. This wavy plastic liner was introduced in class R-70-14 to permit better packing in the car (although this particular photo is the interior of a car from R-70-17). This patented PFE design was intended to prevent packages from wedging into the grooves, and thus be damaged in switching. Note the Preco load dividers against the end wall, and that floor racks still have wood slats. PC&F photo for PFE, CSRM.

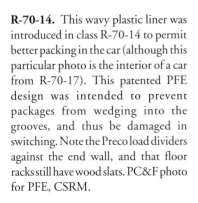 

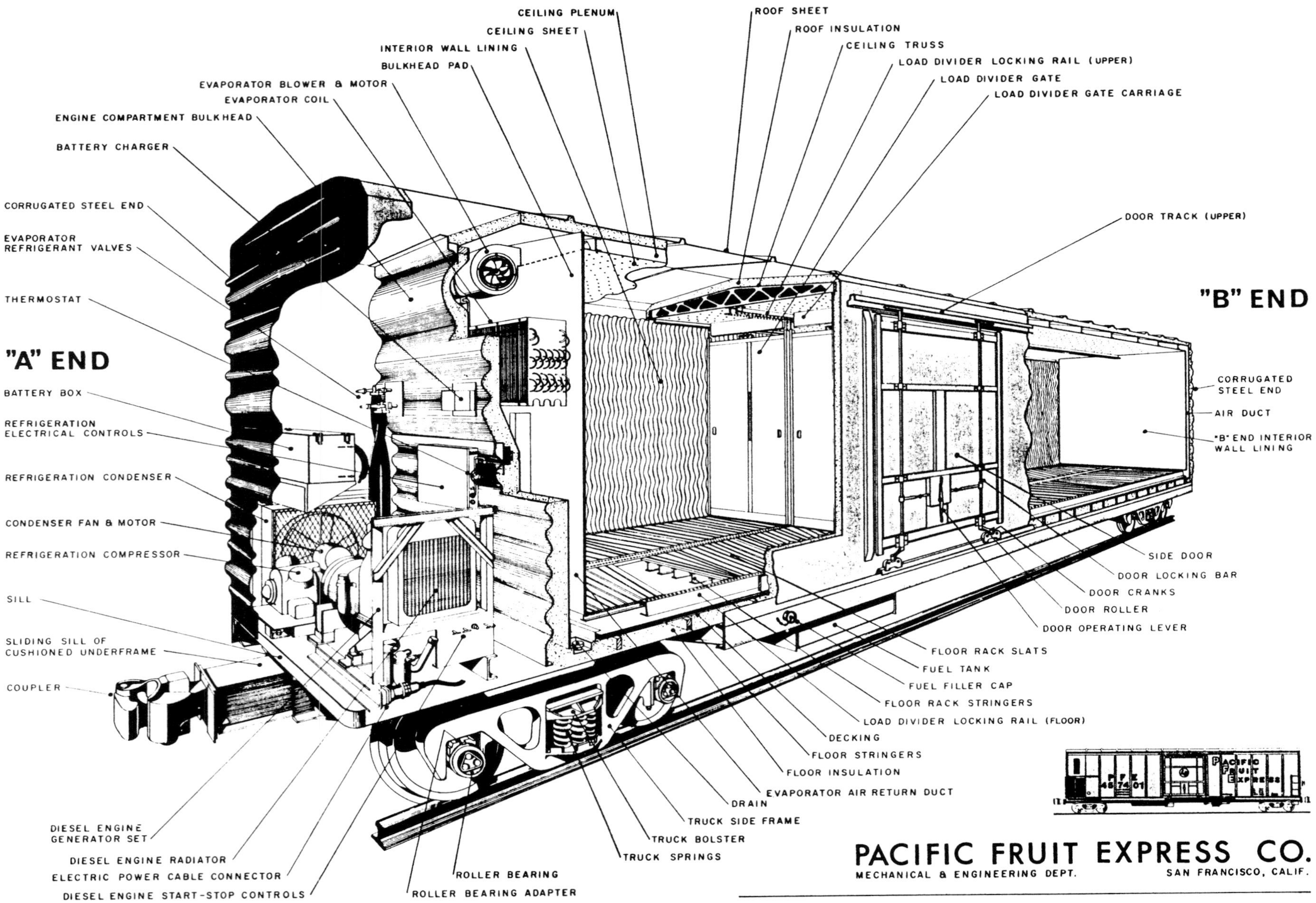

"B" END

CORRUGATED STEEL END

AIR DUCT

"B" END INTERIOR WALL LINING

DOOR TRACK (UPPER)

LOAD DIVIDER LOCKING RAIL (UPPER)

LOAD DIVIDER GATE

LOAD DIVIDER GATE CARRIAGE

CEILING TRUSS

ROOF INSULATION

ROOF SHEET

CEILING PLENUM

CEILING SHEET

INTERIOR WALL LINING

BULKHEAD PAD

ENGINE COMPARTMENT BULKHEAD

BATTERY CHARGER

CORRUGATED STEEL END

EVAPORATOR REFRIGERANT VALVES

THERMOSTAT

EVAPORATOR BLOWER & MOTOR

EVAPORATOR COIL

"A" END

BATTERY BOX

REFRIGERATION ELECTRICAL CONTROLS

REFRIGERATION CONDENSER

CONDENSER FAN & MOTOR

REFRIGERATION COMPRESSOR

SILL

SLIDING SILL OF CUSHIONED UNDERFRAME

COUPLER

DIESEL ENGINE GENERATOR SET

DIESEL ENGINE RADIATOR

ELECTRIC POWER CABLE CONNECTOR

DIESEL ENGINE START-STOP CONTROLS

ROLLER BEARING ADAPTER

ROLLER BEARING

TRUCK SPRINGS

TRUCK BOLSTER

TRUCK SIDE FRAME

EVAPORATOR AIR RETURN DUCT

DRAIN

FLOOR INSULATION

FLOOR STRINGERS

DECKING

LOAD DIVIDER LOCKING RAIL (FLOOR)

FLOOR RACK STRINGERS

FUEL FILLER CAP

FUEL TANK

FLOOR RACK SLATS

DOOR OPERATING LEVER

DOOR ROLLER

DOOR LOCKING BAR

DOOR CRANKS

SIDE DOOR

PACIFIC FRUIT EXPRESS CO.

MECHANICAL & ENGINEERING DEPT.   SAN FRANCISCO, CALIF.

MECHANICAL REFRIGERATOR CAR
CUTAWAY ILLUSTRATION

R-70-15. The 9-ft. doors were designed for cargo handling by fork lift truck. Here PFE 453257 is being loaded with crates of celery. Photo 470-9-11, UP Railroad Museum.

Class R-70-16

R-70-15. A view of the B end. PFE photo, CSRM.

The fact that all the late cars had cushioned underframes as well as load dividers was one reason why the cost of a single car would rise to about $35,000 by 1970. It was becoming increasingly hard to pay such capital costs from the produce rates maintainable in the competitive atmosphere of the 1960's, with its free-wheeling trucking industry and inflexible railroad rate regulation.

Although the PFE design of mechanical cars was mature by the time the R-70-16 was ready to be ordered, a few external changes continued to be made, as listed in specification 90. During production of the R-70-16's, in accord with a change made in freight cars generally in 1966, installation of running boards was discontinued, and the end brake wheel was moved to a low position on the car end. At least the first 1000 cars of the -16 class (the Hydra-cushion portion of the order) did receive Gypsum running boards, and apparently about 100 cars of the second 1000 in the order did also, before installation was discontinued.

The discontinuance of running boards was a safety meas-

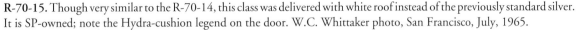

R-70-15. Though very similar to the R-70-14, this class was delivered with white roof instead of the previously standard silver. It is SP-owned; note the Hydra-cushion legend on the door. W.C. Whittaker photo, San Francisco, July, 1965.

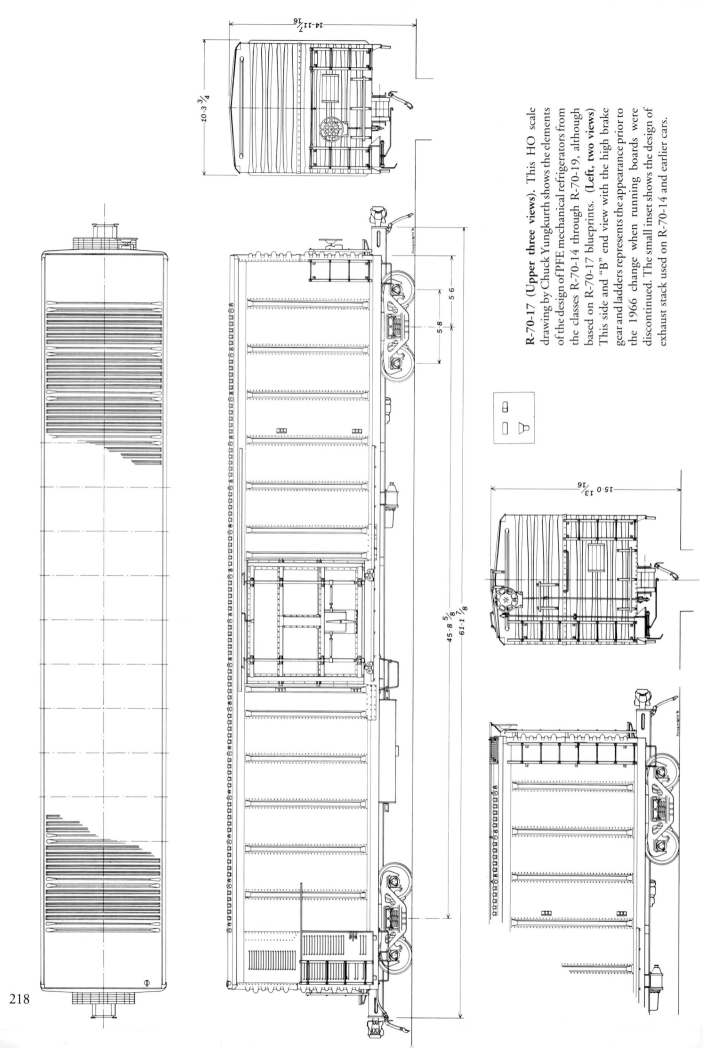

R-70-17 (Upper three views). This HO scale drawing by Chuck Yungkurth shows the elements of the design of PFE mechanical refrigerators from the classes R-70-14 through R-70-19, although based on R-70-17 blueprints. **(Left, two views)** This side and "B" end view with the high brake gear and ladders represents the appearance prior to the 1966 change when running boards were discontinued. The small inset shows the design of exhaust stack used on R-70-14 and earlier cars.

R-70-16. The car sides of this class looked much like the preceding -15 cars. During assembly of the second half of this order, however, use of running boards was discontinued. As a result, ladders were shortened, as shown on this UP-owned car. The black rectangle for the PFE initials also began with R-70-16. PC&F photo for PFE, CSRM.

ure, and car owners were instructed to remove them from older cars as well as to cease applying them to new cars. Running boards were removed only gradually from older cars, however, and as late as 1977 PFE was still applying for, and receiving, permission to postpone removal of running boards from older cars.

Of the 2000 cars of R-70-16, 200 were equipped with Landis "Leverless" doors, with internal locking bars and a chain drive arrangement for operating the locking bars. These doors, shown in the photograph below, were applied to cars 454401-454500 in the SP order, and 455401-455500 in the UP order. The Landis doors evidently offered no advantages over the usual Youngstown doors, since the only application on any other PFE class was to part of the R-70-18 order (see below).

When the -16's were built in 1966, a black rectangle was added to the paint scheme; the reporting marks and number were then white, a change for greater visibility on dirty cars. This rectangle, adopted in the fall of 1965, was also applied to older cars, and remained in use until 1970.

Classes R-70-17 through R-70-19

These last classes of the peaked-roof body design were quite similar, and continued to reflect the leasing of cars to PFE from the two parent railroads. All the -17 cars, as described in specification 93, had Keystone underframes and were UP-owned cars, while the -18 class followed specification 94, was all equipped with Hydra-Cushion frames and was leased from SP. Both classes were built in 1967, 500 cars each. This was the first time the underframe disagreement had resulted in separate classes of PFE cars, instead of merely two groups of cars in the class.

Other than the underframes, classes R-70-17 and -18 were virtually identical. They were the first PFE classes to be built entirely without running boards, and with short ladders at all corners and lowered brake gear. One distinction which the R-70-18's shared with the -16's was the Landis doors: 250 cars of R-70-18 received these doors (456001-456250). In later years, some cars received Youngstown replacement doors. With the R-70-17 class, the older

R-70-16. The unusual cars in this class were the 200 cars with Landis doors, one of which is shown here. The first half of this class had running boards and full-height ladders, as illustrated on this SP-owned car. The large hydraulic cylinder centered under the door is part of the Hydra-cushion mechanism in the center sill. PC&F photo for PFE, CSRM.

R-70-17. Typical of all of PFE's last three classes of peaked-roof cars, the left side of car 455947 is shown here at Renton. PC&F photo for PFE, CSRM.

"chevron" shaped door operating mechanism was replaced with a rectangular latch arrangement.

This purchase of 1000 cars in 1967 followed PFE's plan for fleet acquisition, of 1000 or more new cars per year to replace the old ice cars, which were being retired even faster than mechanicals could be built. But financial stringencies (primarily an unexpected surge in inflation) in the following year, 1968, led to a marked change. Not only was it necessary to acquire only 400 cars, well below the 1000 cars PFE had requested, but for the first time in several years the cars were acquired and financed directly by PFE rather than the railroads.

This purchase also gave rise to a slightly different method for satisfying the insistence of UP and SP on different underframes. This time, 400 cars of a single class, R-70-19, were built, but to two specifications rather than one. The UP version was 98, the SP one 99. Later, when PFE's assets were divided between the two railroads, SP's share of R-70-19, the Hydra-cushion cars, remained lettered PFE (not SPFE), reflecting the financing arrangement.

The two parent railroads intended to make up for the small 1968 purchase of PFE cars by going above 1000 cars

per year subsequently. However, these additional cars were to be of a different car body design.

Classes R-70-20 and R-70-21

When the first of these classes was built, the R-70-20's of 1969, PFE had nearly reached its final car design. When the second batch of orders for -20's were completed in

R-70-18 (**Above**). One of the cars with Landis doors. The operating wheel is visible near the bottom of the door. PFE photo, CSRM.

R-70-18 (**Left**). Here is a typical appearance of a car in service, with the 1971 addition of SPFE reporting marks, photographed at Laramie, Wyo., on April 2, 1972, by Frank Peacock.

220

R-70-19 (**Above**). Although not a PC&F builder's photo, this is a typical right-side view; builders may have preferred to photograph the side with a smaller vent screen. UP Railroad Museum neg. 48945. **R-70-18** (**Left**). An end view of this class, typical of the late peaked-roof cars with lowered brake gear and shortened ladders. PC&F photo for PFE, CSRM .

1970, the last general arrangement drawing, 8700, was used, with specification 100, and continued to be used for each class until R-70-25, the last new PFE car class. By the time the R-70-20's were ordered in 1969, PFE's fleet of over 8000 mechanical refrigerators was not only the largest in North America, it was more than double the size of any other owners' fleet.

The 1000 or more new cars per year that PFE had estimated would be needed through the 1960's had largely been satisfied by UP and SP agreements on car purchase, until the 1968 acquisition of only 400 cars (R-70-19). Fleet needs were reassessed early in 1969 by PFE, and it was concluded that traffic would require buying 1200 cars in 1969 and again in 1970, then 1600 cars per year in 1971 and 1972, until needs would fall to 700 cars in 1973. Purchase of these 6300 mechanical cars would have been a huge financial demand, totalling close to $200 million. Neither UP nor SP nor PFE could likely afford it.

The alternative was to cover some traffic needs by retaining former ice cars, as well as older mechanical cars which had refrigeration equipment removed, as TIV cars. It was believed that as many as 4000 TIV cars could be usefully kept in service and reduce demand for mechanicals. As shown earlier, this TIV alternative was in fact carried out during 1970-74 (see Tables 8-2 and 9-3).

Some new mechanical cars did have to be acquired. The first ones, R-70-20, the complement built in 1969, were in fact the desired 1200 cars, split between Hydra-Cushion and Keystone underframes.

The roofs of these classes are an interesting detail. From R-70-20 onwards, a shallow, slightly-flattened, round arch roof was used. This late roof style has caused some confusion because of the shape of the car ends. When seen from

R-70-20 (**Bottom left**). The standard 70-ton Barber S-2 roller bearing truck used on R-70-20 and most other PC&F-built classes. PC&F photo for PFE, CSRM.

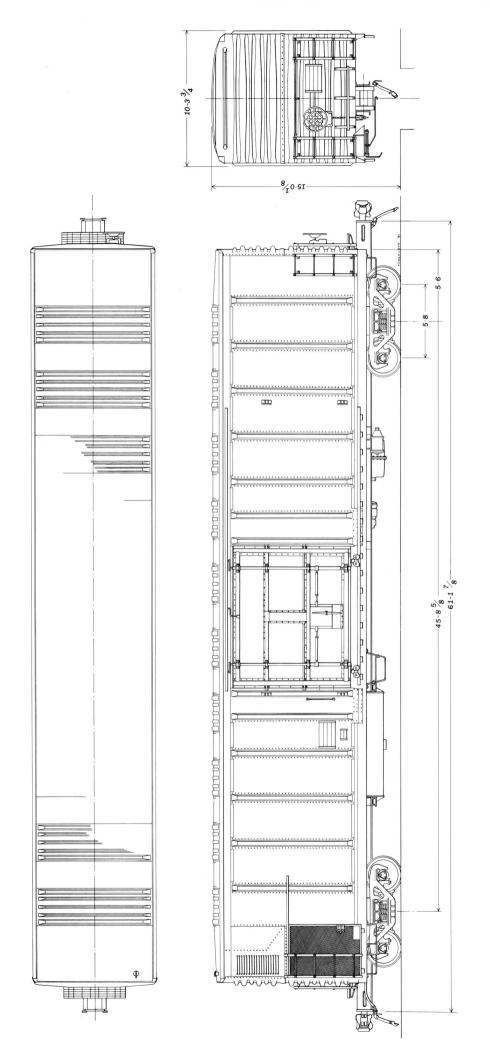

R-70-20. The final PFE car design, as drawn by Chuck Yungkurth in HO scale. In subsequent classes, through R-70-25, only the roof rib pattern would change, to an arrangement with the three small ribs in each roof panel.

SPFE 460039

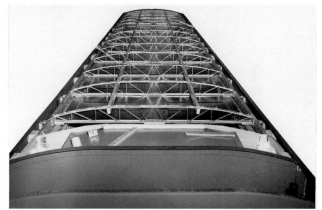

Roof construction of PFE's late-style cars, R-70-21 and later. (**Above**). The structural part of the roof is these trusses, which are open because cold air passes through them to reach the ceiling and side wall air passages. Over these trusses was formed a plywood covering, then foam ribs and insulation were applied before installing the roof cover. (**Left**). An endwise view of the final roof contour, showing the round roof arch and the ribs in each panel. PC&F photos for PFE, CSRM.

the end, the roof appears to be a "flat" roof (with a small slope along each edge), but these contours are faired into the round shape within a single roof panel.

The 1969 batch of R-70-20 cars had a roof with alternating ribbed and ribless panels, at first with slender ribs between the three medium ones (see photo, next page),

then with medium ribs only (see drawing), but the 1970 batch, and all subsequent classes, had the arrangement shown in the photograph at left, with ribs in every panel. This outer roof skin plays a minor structural role, but is primarily an outer weather seal.

The sliding or plug door size was enlarged again, reaching 10' 6" (see Table 9-2) in the R-70-20 and succeeding classes. The key to successful use of such large doors was the advent of foam insulation, which helped to reduce door weight to manageable proportions.

The first complement of R-70-20 had SP and UP halves. The second complement of these cars in 1970 was again 1200 cars in size, but now the SP and UP orders were separated by car class, with the UP version being called R-70-21, similarly to the division of classes R-70-17 and -18. The one new introduction in the -21 class was the ABD

R-70-20. Typical of the late cars, PFE 457632 here exhibits its left side (most PC&F builder's photos are right side), with the new "outline" PFE initial letters in the Gothic PFE logo at right. PC&F photo for PFE, CSRM.

R-70-20. A typical end view. Note the flat segment at the top, which was not reflected in the shape of most of the car roof. PC&F photo for PFE, CSRM.

brake lettering; these brakes were introduced in 1967 and used thereafter for all PFE cars.

Painting and lettering. The R-70-20 cars were painted much the same as the preceding R-70-19's, with two major exceptions. The R-70-20 cars introduced a new style with initial "outline" letters in the name on the right end of the car side. These letters had a black outline around a white interior. Secondly, all car doors were lettered "CUSHION UNDERFRAME," regardless of the type of underframe which was installed. The -20's were also the first class to have ACI (Automatic Car Identification) labels added to them as new cars. Many older cars also received ACI labels within a short time, as this system went into use on American railroads. Within a decade, the difficulty of keeping the labels clean enough to read would doom the system, and thereafter ACI labels gradually disappeared from PFE cars.

Classes R-70-22 through R-70-25

After purchase of the 2400 cars in classes R-70-20 and R-70-21, PFE had nearly finished its acquisition of new cars. There were, however, to be four more small classes

R-70-20. The earliest roof rib pattern, with two small ribs between the medium-size ribs. A.W. Thompson photo.

built. For the most part, these cars followed exactly the specification and drawing for R-70-20. In the R-70-23 and -25, UP introduced Type F interlocking couplers to its cars, although SP continued to specify the Type E, but there were virtually no other changes. All these last car classes cost about $35,000 each.

With the R-70-22 class in 1970, the black reporting mark rectangle was discontinued, and 14" black numbers and letters were used instead. The contrast in the UP shield was reversed during assembly of class R-70-24.

As described in Chapter 1, the leasing of cars to PFE by the parent railroads, UP and SP, had been begun in 1963. In 1971, it was decided to identify ownership with the reporting marks on the cars themselves. Thus PFE's last

R-70-20. An increase in door width to 10' 6" meant a heavy door, but improved suspension was supposed to make it still a "one-man" door. UP photo 973-4-2, CSRM.

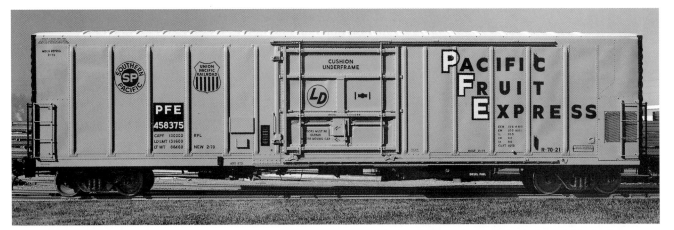

R-70-21 (Above). This only lettering difference between R-70-20 and this class was the ABD brake legend (the brakes themselves were introduced in 1967). **R-70-22 (Below).** One of the Hydra-Cushion classes, eventually destined to wear SPFE reporting marks. The newly-adopted 14" reporting marks are evident. PC&F photos for PFE, CSRM.

R-70-23 (Above). This class was entirely owned by UP. Except for the underframe, though, its mechanical design and lettering arrangements are identical to R-70-22. Also, like R-70-22, it was a class of only 100 cars. **R-70-24 (Below).** This is PFE's 10,000th car built by PC&F. The hydraulic cylinder for the Hydra-Cushion underframe of this SP-owned car can be seen below the door. Note the reversal of contrast in the UP medallion. PC&F photos for PFE, CSRM.

R-70-25. This was to be PFE's last group of new cars, and it fell to UP to own all 600 cars in the class. PFE photo, CSRM.

two classes, R-70-24 and -25, were delivered with the reporting marks, respectively, SPFE and UPFE, for the two railroads' portions of the Pacific Fruit Express car fleet. At the same time, older cars also began to be relettered to reflect their lease status; in a few years all the affected cars, as shown in Table 9-5, were relettered.

In 1975, car ends began to be painted the same orange as the car sides. From then on, black ends on some earlier

Table 9-5
UP - SP Reassignments

Reporting Marks	Car Numbers	Class
SPFE	450001-450250	R-70-13
UPFE	450251-450500	R-70-13
SPFE	450501-450750	R-70-13
UPFE	450751-451000	R-70-13
SPFE	451001-451500	R-70-14
UPFE	451501-452000	R-70-14
UPFE	451001-452750	R-70-15
SPFE	452751-453500	R-70-15
SPFE	453501-454500	R-70-16
UPFE	454501-455000	R-70-16
UPFE	455501-456000	R-70-17
SPFE	456001-456500	R-70-18
UPFE*	456501-456700	R-70-19
PFE	456701-456900	R-70-19
SPFE	456901-457400	R-70-20
PFE	457401-457500	R-70-20
UPFE*	457501-457600	R-70-20
UPFE	457601-458100	R-70-20
UPFE	458101-458700	R-70-21
SPFE	458701-459300	R-70-20
PFE	459301-459400	R-70-22
UPFE*	459401-459500	R-70-23
SPFE	459501-460100	R-70-24
UPFE	460101-460700	R-70-25

*Some cars of this series initially marked UPRX

cars were repainted also, although even cars in service today often have not been repainted. The last change was the use of reflective white "Scotchlite"™ reporting marks and numbers. This seems to have begun in 1975, but was only applied to part of the fleet; one can still spot cars with orange or black ends having black reporting marks. At the same time as the reflective reporting marks were introduced, consideration was also given to adding railroad medallions in the "Scotchlite"™ material. Union Pacific was interested in returning to a red-white-blue emblem, and, loath to take a back seat to UP's colors, SP officials designed a version of their emblem with the same colors (color image, page 425). Alas, costs proved too high, and this potentially handsome change was never made.

Throughout the sixties, scrapping of the ice cars (see Chapters 6, 7 and 8) continued at a rate much greater than

R-70-24. This photo marked the delivery of car 460000. Understandably proud of their joint contribution to producing 10,000 mechanical refrigerators, PC&F's General Manager R.J. Salathe looks on as PFE VP & GM L.D. Schley, center, shakes hands with PC&F VP B.C. Jameson. PC&F photo, June 2, 1971, courtesy E. Hopkins.

R-70-24. This 1977 photo shows a test application of a paint scheme with orange sides and ends, white roof, "Scotchlite"™ reporting marks, Consolidated Lubrication stencils, and no railroad medallions or heralds at all. Although the concept was developed in anticipation of PFE's split-up, it was never used. PFE photo, CSRM.

the 1000 or so new mechanical cars being purchased each year. Accordingly, the fleet shrank substantially in numbers (though of course the capacity per car had increased), as shown in Chapter 1, to reflect the great drop in PFE's carloadings. Even so, it was not until 1969 that more tonnage was shipped by PFE in mechanical reefers than in ice bunker cars. The shipping situation was greatly different in another way, too. As Pete Holst, with many years' experience in PFE's Car Service Dept., put it, "They didn't load as many of those mechanical cars in a month as we did in a day, back in the thirties." The railroads' inability to compete on shipping rates for perishables, largely due to regulation but also due to labor and capital costs and management rigidities, was taking its toll (see Chapter 1).

Even when new car construction ceased in 1971, PFE continued to search for better technology. In 1973, they awarded a contract to Garrett AiResearch to develop a gas turbine power plant for mechanical cars, using a closed

Brayton cycle. Though tests were promising, this type of power plant was never chosen for installation in PFE cars.

In March 1978, PFE ceased to operate as a jointly-owned property of UP and SP, and the assets were divided among the two owners. The remaining ice or mechanical cars built prior to 1963, nearly all of which were in TIV service by 1978, remained part of SP's PFE property. Table 9-5 lists the assignments of reporting marks among the "late" PFE cars. Most of these reporting marks had been changed during 1971-73, so the 1978 change-over was largely a bookkeeping one. Among the cushion underframe cars, SP received those with Hydra-cushions.

Any older cars previously owned by PFE and conveyed to the new UPFE, as well as a few cars previously owned by UP, already marked UPFE, were temporarily given UPRX reporting marks. Some were scheduled to be converted to uses such as bunk cars or company service. Within two years, all UPRX cars were either transferred to UPFE own-

(**Right**) The Garrett candidate power plant for modernizing PFE mechanicals, an idea never put into service. From left, Earl Hopkins, Bob McKee, "Sarge" Littlehale, and Bill Cranmer. PFE photo, courtesy E. Hopkins. (**Below**) The design for the SP color medallion (shown in color, page 425). Note reversal of contrast from SP medallion in actual use. PFE drawing.

R-70-23. One of the UPRX cars, with orange ends and lube stencils but retaining both railroad emblems, photographed at Cheyenne on Aug. 3, 1979, by Frank Peacock.

ership, or renumbered as UP maintenance cars. There were no UPRX cars in the *Equipment Register* by 1980.

As summarized in Chapter 1, UP incorporated UPFE as its reefer subsidiary, while SP maintained PFE as a separate car line until October, 1985, when all cars were transferred to SP. A small vestige of PFE remained, still listed in the SP telephone book as "Pacific Fruit Express," whose only duties were car inspection and repair.

After the Split-Up

Details of painting and lettering after 1978 are beyond the scope of this book, but a few general comments can be made. SP's PFE operation experimented with an orange

At least three designs of "stick-on" panels were used on SPFE cars to cover up the UP medallion, as shown here. This was never done to all cars, and both UPFE and SPFE orange cars can still be found with original pairs of medallions. (**Bottom**). Note the fading paint of the added "S" in SPFE. Photos at Watsonville Junction, Calif., Dec., 1991, first two by Jim Providenza, bottom by A.W. Thompson.

paint scheme which would have had no railroad medallions at all, but finally adopted the simpler expedient of simply covering the UP medallion with a "stick-on" panel bearing the new slogan, "Perishable Freight Experts." There were apparently three versions of this panel, one with upright, white-filled outline initial letters, and two with slanted "speed lettering." Both the latter had orange-filled outline initial letters, with a "fat letter" and a "skinny letter" version. In March, 1981, PFE began to repaint SPFE cars into an all-white scheme which looked much like the all-orange scheme with no railroad medallions (previous page) but had an all-white car body. In 1983, cars began to be painted with large orange initial letters.

With the 1985 change to SP ownership of the cars, the SPFE reporting marks were retained. In the 1990's, a simpler scheme appeared, with a small SP medallion in color, either red, blue or green. The shop at Tucson reportedly had no system for assigning these colors; the shop painted blue medallions one day, red ones the next.

On the Union Pacific side, an initial experiment with lime green paint (see page 425) was rejected, and cars which needed repainting were given the UP's usual Armour Yellow color, with the spelled-out name, "Union Pacific Fruit Express," to the right of the door, even retaining a smaller version of the outlined white initial letters used by PFE since 1969. In 1988, UP began to use a simplified scheme, omitting the spelled-out name and with the UP shield moved to the right of the car side. Subsequently, a smaller UP medallion came into use. As UPFE no longer has a paint shop, all painting is done by contractors.

UPFE added a class R-70-26 to their fleet, comprising cars inherited from ART in the 1982 Missouri Pacific merger. These cars were built by PC&F in 1967, lettered with ARMN reporting marks and car numbers 851-921, and in 1968, cars ARMN 953-1019. They had 9' doors and peaked roofs, with GM 2-71 diesel engines and York refrigeration equipment. When rebuilt by St. Louis Refrigerator Car Co. in 1981, they were relettered to ARMN 756000-756099. Upon UP's takeover, they became car numbers 461001-461100. Mechanical equipment of some

R-70-20. The first SPFE all-white scheme, adopted in 1981, which unfortunately showed rust and dirt badly. Watsonville Junction, Calif., Dec. 1991, A.W. Thompson photo.

Starting in 1983, PFE painted a few cars into this scheme, with black-outlined, orange-filled initial letters "PFE" on a white body. This is an R-70-19 which was renumbered after load dividers were removed (see Table 9-3). Color views of this scheme are on pages 406 and 410. W.C. Whittaker photo, 1983.

R-70-20. The first UPFE paint scheme, with Armour yellow sides and ends, white roof, and large UP medallion to the left of the car door. East Oakland, Dec. 1991, photo by A.W. Thompson.

R-70-21. UPFE followed its first "spelled out" scheme with this plainer yellow scheme, retaining the large medallion. George Cockle photo, Council Bluffs, May 11, 1989.

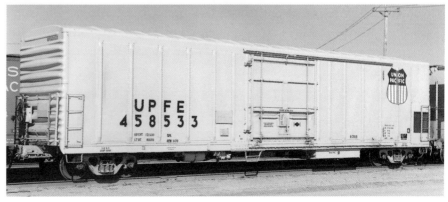

(**Left**) Refueling a mechanical reefer, class R-70-18 with a Landis door, at Roseville, 1971. This ordinarily simple task became a major headache during the various Oil Embargo shortages. Here, a local dealer dispenses the fuel; at some locations, PFE did the refueling itself. PFE photo, CSRM. (**Right**) This is the later white scheme for SPFE cars. SP medallions may be red, blue or green, varying from day to day. The graffiti were added later. Watsonville Junction, Dec. 1991, A.W. Thompson photo.

of the cars has been changed to match that of UPFE cars.

In the 1990's, UP was rebuilding some of the deteriorated mechanical cars (what once would have been "reconditioning," Chapter 7, now qualifies under AAR rules as rebuilding). Rehabilitated cars received new car numbers (these have extended upwards from 461401). Cars more extensively reworked and upgraded received both new numbers and a new class. The new classses R-70-27 to R-70-30

occupy numbers 461101-461391. Today, therefore, one can spot much different UPFE car numbers and classes than the original PFE series shown in Table 9-1.

But the longevity of mechanical cars is such that it is still possible to see examples of some orange schemes used before 1978, although the fleet is steadily becoming all yellow. Even from a car fleet standpoint, then, PFE lives on in the form of its last paint schemes on refrigerator cars.

R-70-25. The most recent UPFE scheme has included this much smaller UP medallion, located on the right half of the car side, as was the large medallion (see previous page). This is a rehabilitated and renumbered car. East Oakland, January, 1992, A.W. Thompson photo.

(**Left**) The days of partial repainting after repair work did not end with the demise of tongue-and-groove car siding. This photo of UPFE 455255 shows a single repainted panel at Council Bluffs on April 27, 1991, in a George Cockle photo. (**Right**) Some ex-PFE cars were assigned to UP company service and renumbered accordingly. Here an R-40-30 has been so assigned by UP. It looks like it's in the midst of either being cleaned, or having grime applied. Milton G. Sorensen photo, Nampa, April 1984.

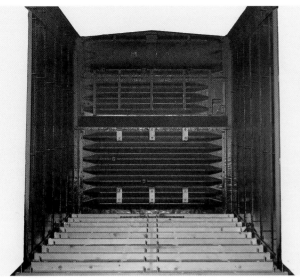

(Above) An interior view of an R-70-18 car under construction. The same "corrugated" internal bulkhead at the A end of the car as in the R-70-12 cars shown earlier in this chapter are evident. PC&F photo for PFE, CSRM.

(Above) A workman foaming insulation in place at the A end. This was far faster, cheaper and more effective than blankets of various fibers. PFE photo, CSRM.

(Above) When a door needs repair, the entire door is usually exchanged with a repaired one in the shop, rather than delay the car by working on the door. A Clark lift truck is acting as a crane for this door. PFE photo, Roseville, 1970.

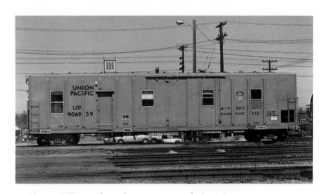

Some UP cars have been converted to maintenance use, as in this bunk car, painted UP's MOW green and still lettered R-70-13. Yes, that's an air conditioner over the door. Nampa, April 9, 1967, Milton G. Sorensen photo.

(Left) The dirty door on SPFE 454060 is clearly a replacement in this Chuck Yungkurth photo at Binghampton, New York, 1980.
(Right) With the advent of white car body paint, it was inevitable that a white door would show up on an orange car, as here on 456017. A. W. Thompson photo, Watsonville Junction, December, 1991.

A piggyback train of perishables heads eastward up Weber Canyon behind an A-B-A set of Union Pacific EMD DD35 locomotives, the only railroad able to field such a set, since no one else owned both A and B versions of this 5,000-horsepower locomotive. All this power is to keep these PFE trailers on a fast schedule over the Wasatch Mountains. The train is just above Echo, Utah, in this 1965 view; the flatcar is PFF 835182, class F-70-30, while both trailers are PFE's "removeable-bogie" design, the forward one PFC 145140, an RCM-40-1, 12'6" high, and the trailing one PFC 130243, an RC-40-4, 13'6" tall. UP photo, courtesy Ed Chiasson.

10

FLAT CARS AND TRAILERS

As darkness falls on Cotton Belt's yard in East St. Louis, all-white PFE trailers of class RC-40-8 await pickup. Orange PFF 835937, a class F-70-31 flat car from ACF, carries the two nearest trailers. Don Sims photo, 1968.

Throughout the 1950's, greatly increasing portions of the produce business were being captured by trucks, as explained in Chapter 1. Moreover, many railroads were beginning to operate their own trucking subsidiaries for local pick-up and delivery from freight houses. Piggyback movement or TOFC (trailers on flat cars) for long-distance trucking was becoming established as well by 1960. To PFE officials, it seemed natural to consider extending their fresh produce operations into refrigerated trailers. To be sure, as described in Chapter 9, general-purpose mechanical refrigerator cars were being tested in the late 1950's, which potentially could take the business of carload produce shipments away from ice cars. But trailers had the advantages of smaller loads, suitable for many customers with smaller produce sales, and of quick pickup and delivery. The only lack was an appropriately sturdy refrigerated trailer which could offer performance consistent with PFE's existing standards. Thus the PFE mechanical

designers, now expert on diesel-powered refrigeration, set out to create such a trailer.

The refrigerated truck or trailer had been around since the 1920's, and shipment on railroad flat cars, requiring significant improvements in both the trailer body and in the refrigeration system, was already being established. SP's trucking subsidiary, Pacific Motor Trucking (PMT), was operating refrigerated trailers in piggyback service in 1958. But PFE wanted a better air circulation pattern, similar to that in refrigerator cars, to ensure successful shipment of perishables. In addition, rugged, high-performance refrigeration equipment was regarded as essential, and PFE personnel worked with the manufacturers to produce new products which could meet these requirements. PFE, incidentally, usually referred to them as "vans," rather than trailers.

Although at least some PFE managers were opposed to the idea, PFE also acquired flat cars to accompany its new

F-70-21. This flat car betrays its SP parentage by retaining SP's slogan and car number series. The trailers with their underslung mechanical units and cylindrical fuel tanks are RTM-40-1's, PFT 120002 and 120004, built by Fruehauf in 1961. Photo 1261-1-4, UP Railroad Museum.

trailer fleet. Ironically, when PFE had attempted to begin acquisition of insulated boxcars in the early 1950's, in order to hold its "dry" traffic which previously had been moving in un-iced refrigerator cars, the parent railroads had informed PFE that its business was perishables, period. If insulated cars were a new business category, UP and SP would handle it themselves. The concept was thereby established that PFE's only role was to provide equipment for lading which required protective services.

Thus it was naturally expected that flat cars, without any capacity for "protective services" themselves, would not be appropriate for the PFE fleet. But UP and SP needed the additions to the car supply, and PFE was directed to add flat cars to its roster. Most PFE flats were leased, although one class was purchased. Since there was never any belief that PFE's trailers and flat cars could be kept together (and indeed they didn't stay together), this acquisition was simply regarded as a kind of PFE contribution to the piggyback equipment pool.

The first flat cars in PFE service were cars already in existence, which were leased from the UP and SP. Thereafter PFE acquired new cars, though in parallel with the practice in mechanical refrigerator cars (see Chapter 9), after 1963 the cars were purchased by the parent railroads and, upon construction, leased to PFE. This later meant that when trailer operations eventually were discontinued, the flat cars could be easily returned to the parent roads.

The 85-ft. flat cars

The first group of flats came from UP and SP, and specifications 80 (UP cars) and 81 (SP cars) were issued on Jan. 2 and Jan. 5, respectively, in 1962 to describe the cars.

All were 85-foot cars which had been previously built in the 1959-1961 period and were leased to PFE by the parent railroads. These leased flats arrived during Dec. 1961-Jan. 1962. Given PFF reporting marks, the 310 cars were painted boxcar red when first in PFE assignment. At least in the case of the cars leased from SP, it appears that only the reporting marks were changed upon transfer to PFE. The SP car number series (513,000) was retained, as was the slogan "TRAILER – FLATCAR SERVICE" in italicized Gothic letters, which SP used on its piggyback flats at the time. All these cars had ACF retractable hitches, with bridge plates applied at the A-L and B-R corners of the cars for "circus-style" loading. When substantial numbers of PFE's own flat cars began to arrive in 1963, these leased cars were returned. Most went back to SP and UP between Sept. 1963 and Feb. 1964.

In June, 1962, PFE took delivery of the only flat cars it was ever to own itself, 50 cars of the F-70-1 class purchased from ACF. These cars were essentially duplicates of SP's F-70-21 cars, and had the same side sill member, a deep channel higher than the car deck. Sides were painted orange like the refrigerator cars, with boxcar red ends. The ACF Model A collapsible hitch, with its screw mechanism designed to be operated by a power wrench, was applied.

The F-70-1 class followed specification no. 81. One interesting detail of this specification was the requirement for curve radii which the cars could negotiate. The cars were specified to be capable of a 180' radius uncoupled, and to be capable of a 375' radius coupled to a short car. The short car described was a Pennsylvania Railroad N-5 cabin (caboose) car, just 30' 7" long. Whether ACF kept such cars at its plant for tests, or if PFE conducted any tests with borrowed PRR cabins, is not known.

F-70-1. This photo of PFF 830010 shows the wood riser boards beside the retractable hitches (required for truck axles to clear the 9" height of the retracted hitch during circus loading), white "non-skid" surface, lever hand brake, and orange side rails. This class was soon leased to MDT and then to SP. AC&F photo, PFE collection, CSRM.

During the late 1960's, the 85' F-70-1's were leased to MDT, enabling PFE's flat car fleet to become entirely 89' lengths, and in Sept. 1970, the lease was transferred to SP as trailer operations by PFE began to wind down. SP renumbered the F-70-1's as 513650-513699.

The F-70-1 cars brought the PFE fleet to 360 flat cars, which, at two trailers per car, was a capacity of 720 trailers. At that time, PFE owned just 425 trailers, though more were contemplated. This numerical comparison is not too important, however, since, as mentioned, it was not expected that PFE flat cars would necessarily be used to carry PFE trailers. Most photographs from the late 1960's show railroad-owned flats and, increasingly, Trailer Train cars, under PFE trailers in service.

Classes F-70-30, F-70-31

There were two classes of 89' flat cars in PFE service, the F-70-30 cars built by General American, and the F-70-31 cars from ACF, specifications 84 and 91. The former group comprised 800 cars, more than all other PFE flats combined, while the latter class was 250 cars. They were delivered between 1963 and 1966. All were of similar design, with slender side sills and a sheet-metal attachment

Table 10-1
PFE Flat Cars (marked PFF)

Class	Numbers	Cars	Builder, Date	Drawing	Notes
F-70-2	53700-53799	100	Pullman, 1959 (UP lease)	6F-20000	D,F
F-70-3	53815-53899	85	ACF, 1959 (UP lease)	C-14631	D,F
F-70-17	513026-513050	25	ACF, 1960 (SP lease)	-	D,F
F-70-21	513051-513200	150	Bethlehem, 1961 (SP lease)	6F-20050	D,F
F-70-1	830000-830049	50	ACF, 1962	6F-20060	C,D,F
F-70-30	835000-835099	100	Gen. American, 1963	6F-20070	A,E,G
F-70-30	835100-835199	100	Gen. American, 1964	RF-20375	B,E,G
F-70-30	835200-835299	100	Gen. American, 1965	RF-20380	A,E,G
F-70-30	835300-835799	500	Gen. American, 1965-66	RF-20365	A,E,G
F-70-31	835800-836049	250	ACF, 1966	RF-20600	B,E,F,H
		1360			

A. First half of order leased from SP, balance from UP

B. First half of order leased from UP, balance from SP

C. PFE-owned cars, leased to SP after 9-70.

D. 85' over end sills   E. 89' over end sills

F. ACF trailer hitches   G. General American hitches

H. Car 835936 converted to 3-container diesel power unit in 1967 (hitches removed); dwg. EF-20822

F-70-30 (Above). The orange body of the GATC cars had the badge plate for name and reporting marks toward the B end on both sides of the car. (Oct. 1963). These were essentially the General American G-89 design. GATC photo, CSRM.

F-70-31 (Below). The ACF cars had side-sill "tabs" over the ends of center sill braces, and only a single sill step at the car center, unlike the three side-sill steps on F-70-30's. They also had ACF screw hitches. ACF photo, Aug. 1966, CSRM.

F-70-30. (Left, below) The first of the 89' cars had all-orange bodies, with dark gray running surfaces, a 4" orange stripe on the right side of the deck, and GATC automatic hitches. Oct. 1963. GATC photo for PFE, E. Chicago, Ind., CSRM.

F-70-30. (Right, above) The 1965 batch had black ends and lighter gray color across the entire "non-skid" car top. July, 1965. GATC photo for PFE, E. Chicago, Ind., CSRM.

F-70-30. Fabrication of these cars simply involved welding the various sub-assemblies onto the massive center sills. GATC photo, 1963 for PFE, CSRM.

for lettering, steel decks flush with side sills, bridge plates, roller bearing trucks, and orange paint. All classes had lever handbrakes, orange like the car sides on the early F-70-30's and then black on later cars; all cars also had an orange stripe along the right side of the deck. All these cars, from 1963 to 1966, cost about $16,000 each. One minor

variation: the F-70-31 cars of 1966 received the black background square, on which white reporting marks were stenciled, which was also being applied to refrigerator cars at the same time (see Chapter 9). All these cars were purchased by SP and UP, then leased to PFE, and were so listed in rosters and diagram books. PFE operated them with PFF reporting marks. When PFE trailer operations began to be terminated, all were returned to their owners. Returns took place between 1969 and 1974.

TRAILERS

Broadly speaking, there were two groups of PFE trailer classes, RT and RC; either one could also have an "M" suffix, such as RTM, for a meat-service trailer. The PFE trailer roster is shown in Table 10-2. The RT (**R**efrigerated **T**railer) units were conventional trailer designs, with diesel engines and refrigeration units mounted under the body, and their reporting marks were "PFT."

The RC (**R**efrigerated **C**ontainer) units are especially

Table 10-2
PFE Containers and 40-ft. Highway Trailers

Class	Numbers	Quantity	Builder, Date	Notes
NRC-1	101-150	50	Trailmobile, 1964-65	M
RT-40-1	110001-110180	180	Strick, 1961-62	N
RTM-40-2	110181-110205	25	Fruehauf, 1962	N,P
RT-40-4	110206-110455	250	Trailmobile, 1967	N
RT-40-5	110456-110705	250	Timpte, 1967	N
RT-40-2	115000-115089	90	Trailmobile, 1965	N,S
RT-40-3	115090-115097	8	Brown, 1965-66	N,S
RTM-40-1	120000-120200	200	Fruehauf, 1961-62	N
RTM-40-3	125001-125100	100	Timpte, 1968	N,T
RC-40-1	130001-130020	20	Strick, 1962	Q
RC-40-4	130021-130250	230	Fruehauf, 1964	Q
RC-40-5	130251-130550	300	Fruehauf, 1965	Q
RC-40-2	135001-135150	150	Fruehauf, 1963	Q,T
RC-40-3	135151-135200	50	Timpte, 1963	Q,T
RCM-40-2	140001-140200	200	Strick, 1965	Q
RCM-40-1	145001-145200	200	Strick, 1964	Q,T
RCM-40-3	140201-140205	5	Timpte, 1965	Q
RC-40-6	160001-160300	300	Trailmobile, 1965	Q
RC-40-8	160301-160550	250	Trailmobile, 1966	Q
RC-40-9	160551-160800	250	Timpte, 1966	Q
RC-40-7	165001-165200	200	Timpte, 1965	Q,R,T
		3308		

M. 24-ft. container (side doors on 1965 units, NRC 113-150)
N. Bottom-mounted engine, refrigeration unit, and fuel tank
P. Purchased from Bud Antle Co., 1962
Q. Nose-mounted engine, refrigeration unit, and fuel tank
S. Overall height 13'0"
R. Side door
T. Overall height 12'6"

The "Flexi-van" design received extensive testing and use by the New York Central. Here a trailer is being removed from a flat car by means of the "turntable" mechanism attached to the flat car. As the trailer slides from the turntable, it will have a bogie attached. None of PFE's fleet had the turntable mechanisms. New York Central photo, A.W. Thompson collection, 1961.

interesting, because they were based on Strick's "Flexi-Van" design. It seemed to PFE that a container-like trailer body, removable from the wheel assembly or bogie, would make sense for perishable shipments. Such a container had to have its refrigeration equipment mounted on the nose, rather than under the body, and that arrangement was characteristic of the RC trailers. Today, containerization is an accepted part of railroading, and containers on flat cars (COFC) are a common sight. But in 1961, when PFE began design of a Flexi-Van system for perishables, it was clearly ahead of its time. The PFE container-trailer concept for perishable traffic was not successful during the 1960's, in the sense of achieving little use of the equipment for containers *per se*, instead of use as trailers only. The sliding tandem-wheel assemblies did permit adjustment of load over the axles. The bogies had different numbers than the trailers, with "PFB" reporting marks, for record-keeping purposes; those numbers are not tabulated here. The RC and the RCM classes all had "PFC" reporting marks.

PFE also tried containers alone, that is, containers which did not have their own refrigeration unit and were not designed to be attached to bogies for highway service. Instead, the containers were placed on frame trailers for highway delivery. They were intended for use with shipments requiring insulation, to and from Hawaii, on board ships. Eastbound, canned pineapples were the intended lading, while it was hoped that general westbound freight could be carried through to Hawaii. Designed for use on Matson Navigation Company ships, these containers were nicknamed "fishybacks" by PFE employees. The idea, however, never received extensive usage. Matson, which had pioneered Pacific container shipping in 1958, operated containers which it owned itself, along with removeable-bogie refrigerated truck trailers, and Matson used them in preference to PFE's containers. Fresh pineapples were also shipped in Matson's containers, with on-board refrigeration. PFE was unsuccessful in developing other uses for the 24' containers. It is worth pointing out

Here Matson removeable-bogie 24' containers, painted white with red lettering, are loaded on PFE's only "powered" flat car, PFF 835936, with a load of fresh pineapples. A motor-generator set on the car powered container refrigeration units. PFE photo, CSRM.

NRC-1. The concept with PFE's insulated containers was exactly like today's containers, namely to move them over the highway on frame trailers. Only 24 feet long, their capacity limited their use. PFE photo, CSRM.

that in 1964-65, when these containers were built, standardization of container sizes was several years in the future, and PFE chose the 24' size solely in collaboration with Matson (which continues to use 24' containers). Three of the 24' containers, either PFE or Matson, would be loaded on an 85' flat car.

Because of the rate structure in which railroad car shipments of trailers on flat cars were included, it was not possible to compete with trucking rates on the traditional refrigerator car basis, in which cars usually returned empty westbound. Instead, sources of westbound loads would have to be identified, and trailer design would have to be compatible with such loading. As indicated in the accompanying comments by A.E. Chiasson, this was an important source of PFE's choice of trailer height, 13' 6". At this time, all trailers in the east, and many in the west, were 12' 6" high, and the new height was to cause some problems with routing east of the Rockies.

The first trailers

The trailer era began for PFE with a design of a 40' trailer, given specification no. 79 on Apr. 24, 1961. Strick and Fruehauf were chosen to build the first two groups of RT trailers in 1961-62, with Fruehauf chosen for the meat version. (At this time, Strick was a division of Fruehauf Corp., although separately managed and operated.) In addition, 25 trailers designated RTM-40-2 were purchased from Bud Antle Co., a major produce shipper, by taking over an order already under construction at Fruehauf. The final part of this first batch was the initial group of RC units, built by Strick in 1962 from specification no. 83.

Additional trailers arrived steadily during 1963 and 1964. The 200 1963 deliveries were RC-40's, while 200 RCM-40's and 230 RC-40's came in 1964. For this equipment, PFE issued specifications as detailed as for refrigerator cars, but did not issue drawings. At the end of

RC-40-1. The first batch of removeable-bogie trailers exhibit their nose-mount refrigeration units and the typical smooth-side Strick trailer design. Fuel tanks are below the refrigeration units. UP photo 44679, PFE collection, CSRM.

Recollections of Ed Chiasson:

"Well, on the 13'6" trailers. the whole country, particularly east of Chicago, was all 12-6 then. So the story was that to support trailer on flatcar equipment, we had to have a two-way haul, just like a trucker. Railcars were normally a one-way haul until we got into the bigger mechanicals, with the load dividers, and we could get the two-way haul. The ice bunker car was a wet car, and just not suitable for a two-way haul. With the trailer, the two-way was necessary for the economics of it. The logical thing was to attract quality traffic, to get the consolidators to load these trailers back. They had westbound traffic that was in boxcars, and the boxcar wasn't that suitable for this quality traffic, in expedited service. With a trailer at destination, a trucker could dray it right out and get it to the customer, so the trailer was the logical equipment.

At the start, when we were going to establish the piggyback service out of the perishable loading areas in California, going eastbound, we were going to key it into certain destinations, such as Chicago, Philadelphia, and New York, that had westbound quality traffic. A lot of that traffic was moving in regular dry freight trailers, and we wanted to put it into our trailers. There was more traffic, greater demand, than the available trailers at that time. I was assigned the job of going to Philadelphia to meet with a Mr. Forgash, who was President of U.S. Freight, the largest forwarder in the United States and one of the owners of Trailer Train, about utilizing our equipment.

We sat all day in the meeting, and came to the conclusion with a large receiver of perishables there in Philadelphia, that he could take so many trailers a week, and Forgash agreed that he would load so many trailers a week back west. So after a day's meeting, we had accomplished what we came to do, to have the two-way haul on our equipment, under an agreement. Forgash was a very progressive type of fellow; maybe some of the others would have been reluctant to make that agreement, but he was not that way.

So he made the commitment to re-load as many trailers as we could get to him, and he was also interested in the cubic capacity, because the refrigerated trailer naturally has less cube than the dry freight trailer, with the insulation and equipment. The other thing was that they shipped light, bulky things like paper napkins, that were very light weight, light density, so he needed all the cube he could get. At the end of the day, it was all agreed, and everything was ready to sign on the dotted line, and I sat there a minute and started to think, and I wondered what size trailer he thought we were talking about, because that had never come up in the conversation. He hadn't said anything about that, and I thought, well, gee, practically everyone else in the world is building 12 foot 6 trailers, practically the whole country's 12-6 except for a few western states that are 13-6, and there's even a few low underpasses in the west. So there at the end of the day, I asked the question, 'Are you considering that these trailers will be a standard height, an outside height, of 12 foot 6, or 13-6?' He answered, 'Well, 13 foot 6, of course.'

And that was his answer, 13-6, disregarding all problems, which sometimes you have to do. I knew we were heading for 12-6 [on our trailers], his answer was 13-6, and I knew a lot of people said we had to have 12-6, you couldn't operate with 13-6. I went back to the hotel that night and took a piece of hotel stationery, and I wrote to Charlie Ahern. He was VP & GM then. I told him we had about reached the agreement, because in those days you didn't make phone calls and that, like we do today, but I said the agreement was about fixed for a 13-6 trailer. Well, he had the foresight to go along with it, and immediately we put together the package requesting 13-6 trailers. All they were waiting for was the recommendation, and it was approved, and that was the way we went.

We did have the problems of operating them in some cities, and even on certain rail lines in the Northeast. Some of the Northeast railroads couldn't handle them, due to tunnel clearances and all. One big problem we had, which we had not anticipated, was on the westbound section of the Union Pacific, where the Aspen Tunnel couldn't handle 13-6, and that was where all these trailers had to go west. But already they would handle auto rack cars which are higher than 12-6, they'd haul them around on the other line, and put them back in the train after they got around the tunnel, which was costly. That led to lowering of the track in Aspen Tunnel, to handle 13-6 trailers and auto racks, and it was a more efficient operation."

RCM-40-2. PFE removeable bogies. Nearest the camera is the front end, with the adjusting mechanism and air brake connections. PFE photo, CSRM.

RC-40-2. Trailer PFC 135078 was built by Fruehauf in 1963. (**Left**) Nose appearance includes orange Thermo-King unit with fuel tank immediately below, and ventilation doors. (**Center**) Rear door also has ventilation openings. (**Right**) Interior view shows vinyl "finger ducts" at top and open flooring. PFE photos, CSRM.

1964, the insulated (non-refrigerated) containers, class NRC, began to be delivered. They were all aluminum except for a steel frame, and insulated with 2" of foamed-in-place polyurethane. The first trailers cost about $12,000 each, with costs rising to $14,500 by 1968.

Some aspects of the overall appearance of trailers, particularly side sheathing, was at the builder's discretion, and it is possible to recognize the products of Timpte, say, or Fruehauf, by side sheathing and other details. Fruehauf used a closely-spaced rib design of sheathing, while Timpte's sheathing had wider rib spacing. Strick usually produced smooth-side trailers in this period.

The later trailers

When TOFC perishable shipments were established and began to be truly sucessful, PFE invested in hundreds of additional trailers (specification list in Appendix). There were 1095 units delivered in 1965, more than the total number of trailers delivered before then. These were all RC or RCM units, except 90 RT-40-2's from Trailmobile. In 1966, 500 RC units were delivered; in 1967, 500 RT's arrived. The last 100 trailers were delivered in 1968.

Trailers continued to have design features strictly specified by PFE, including foam insulation, "finger ducts" of fabric on the ceiling, sidewall flues, and "open" flooring for air circulation. At the time, these were advanced features for refrigerated trailers. External appearance continued to be that typical of each trailer manufacturer.

Painting and lettering. The early trailers all had black lettering on a natural aluminum trailer body, with an orange stripe around the body. The SP and UP medallions were painted on each side of the trailer, with the SP

RC-40-4. Interior details of PFE trailers included (**Left**) aluminum T-flooring with its air circulation holes and (**Right**) load-restraining bars in some units. Note wavy plastic lining, discussed in Chapter 9. PFE photos, CSRM.

medallion toward the left end of each side. The two sides were not identical in arrangement, however, because the reporting marks and legend were arranged differently. The legend, "TEMPCO-VAN SERVICE," was lettered at the lower rear of each side, and the reporting marks were at the forward end. As the 13'6" height of most PFE trailers was non-typical, a sizeable warning about the height was lettered on front and rear in earlier days, but after 1965 this lettering was smaller.

In 1965, some trailers received white backgrounds to the railroad medallions, although trailer sides continue to be natural aluminum. In 1966, the entire bodies began to be painted white, with the same black lettering and orange stripe applied. Initially, mechanical units were painted aluminum. They began to be orange in 1964, and some in the late 1960's were a grayish blue color.

Atmosphere control. The rate of ripening of fruits and vegetables depends on the availability of oxygen in the atmosphere surrounding the produce. By reducing the oxygen content, ripening is retarded. In the 1960's, two concerns offered atmosphere control to shippers, Tectrol (a division of Whirlpool Corp.) and Oxytrol (a division of Occidental Petroleum). The trailer or mechanical reefer was tightly sealed and the air inside replaced with an atmosphere lower in oxygen and higher in nitrogen and carbon dioxide. This service was not offered by PFE (the shipper contracted with Tectrol or Oxytrol for it), but the refrigerated vehicle had to be equipped to accept the devices of the atmosphere control system, primarily the inlet and outlet vents for replacing the atmosphere.

Beginning in 1965, PFE began to equip RC trailer classes for this service. Those so equipped were re-numbered. By 1967, over 300 Tectrol trailers (assigned to the 150,000 number series) and 120 Oxytrol trailers (170,000 number series) were in service.

RCM-40-2. This Strick-built trailer clearly shows the 1965 change to white backgrounds for the railroad medallions. Strick also applied a rather square Gothic lettering which was not in accord with PFE's lettering diagrams. PFE photo, CSRM.

RC-40-7 (Below). PFE's highest-numbered new trailers, built by Timpte in 1965, had side doors and were only 12'6" high. Typical Timpte "wide-spacing" ribbed sheathing is evident. PFE photo, CSRM.

RT-40-4. Some trailers had only the sides white, like this Trailmobile-built unit; the nose is natural aluminum (other classes were entirely white). Like all RT classes, it has an underslung mechanical unit. Wayne Fergason photo for PFE, Longview, Tex., May, 1967, CSRM.

242

NRC-1 (Above). One of the 24-ft. containers being loaded at San Francisco onto a Matson ship, 1965. The aluminum containers experienced severe corrosion in the marine environment. UP Railroad Museum, photo LAC40-115.

RC-40-5. Here PFC 130366 is ready to leave the customs area at Nogales, Arizona, in 1966. The tractor in this photo appears to be a 1947 model Peterbilt (constructed in Oakland, Calif. at that time) with the usual "West Coast" long mirrors. John Signor collection.

RC-40-5. This SP-owned Autocar tractor is loading flat cars circus-style at Phoenix. The distinctive diagonal corner of the Fruehauf trailer is evident. As was typical in later years of PFE TOFC operation, a Trailer Train flat is being used. SP photo N7519-2.

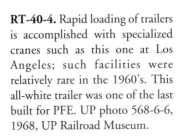

RT-40-4. Rapid loading of trailers is accomplished with specialized cranes such as this one at Los Angeles; such facilities were relatively rare in the 1960's. This all-white trailer was one of the last built for PFE. UP photo 568-6-6, 1968, UP Railroad Museum.

243

Refrigerated trailers were loaded much as were reefers. (**Left**) Lettuce is loaded by hand, using a roller tray, into one of PFE's first trailers, PFT 110008, at Salinas in 1967. SP photo N6544-4. (**Right**) Forklift trucks could enter PFE trailers on the aluminum floor. Here crates of celery are being loaded into PFC 130203. The pallets will be left behind to save space. PFE photo, CSRM.

F-70-30. Just as PFE trailers often rode on non-PFE flat cars, so PFE flats were used for other trailers. Here at Binghampton, New York, in 1968, PFF 835186 carries a single Pacific Intermountain Express trailer (PIE would merge with Ryder in 1983). Chuck Yungkurth collection.

Service history. By 1967, though new trailers were still arriving, it was becoming evident that the economic tide was running against PFE's trailer operation, as described in Chapter 1. The economic life of a trailer body was only 5 to 10 years, and it was already clear that additional new units, or replacements for the older trailers which were wearing out, would be justifiable only for specific traffic. Thus the 1968 RTM-40-3 units, PFE's last, were bought on the basis of loadings at Spencer Packing's Schuyler, Neb., plant. By 1970, trailer operations were declining steadily. From a high of over 3000 trailers, by the end of 1972 the fleet had fallen to 1700 units, and a year later to barely 1000.

Some of PFE's trailer fleet was scrapped as it wore out, but the great majority was sold as part of the business decision to leave the trailer operation. A few hundred trailers were sold to other users, most notably the Ferrocarril del Pacifico, and a few were sold as cold storage units. The trailer weight, arising from rail service requirements, was heavier than what most truckers wanted for highway service, thus limiting any resale prospects.

Most of the surplus units ended up being sold to Fruehauf at Oakland, Calif. Fruehauf removed the bogies which were in useable condition, and reconditioned them for resale or installation under new trailers at a discounted price. It is reported that SP and UP obtained a credit for each PFE bogie reconditioned, but records do not show if these credits were ever used toward new Fruehauf trailers for either railroad. Fruehauf advertised and sold the boxes (bodies) for farm and other business storage, without refrigeration units. SP also kept some boxes for storage.

The refrigeration units, though sturdy and well-maintained, were regarded as overbuilt by some trucking interests, and not interchangeable with their existing equipment. Though sales were slow, many of the salvaged refrigeration units were eventually sold to parties interested in used units, or scrapped, but PFE retained a few for parts.

PFE had done its best to compete with the trucks which were sapping its lifeblood. It had introduced well-designed TOFC equipment and service, brought interior air circulation and foamed-in-place insulation to the trucking industry's attention, and made the 13'6" trailer acceptable in national TOFC service. But in essence, PFE could not overcome the problem of regulated rates and competition for westbound loading, as summarized in Chapter 1. Thus a promising effort failed in little more than a decade.

III

OPERATIONS

SHOPS ICING FACILITIES
WESTERN PERISHABLES PFE IN ACTION

Jim Morley photo, Roseville.

BY
ROBERT J. CHURCH

This scene in the Los Angeles Shop's Heavy Repair Yard shows many different repair activities. The chalk markings indicate work to be done on each car, many of which have been removed from their trucks. The car at far right, PFE 85012, is an R-30-9 with a white rectangle stenciled "EQUIPPED FOR MEAT SERVICE" (see Chapter 7). The Ice Manufacturing Plant is in the background. Richard Steinheimer photo, December, 1950, DeGolyer Library.

11

CAR SHOPS

Colton. The heavy repair tracks are busy in this mid-1950's view, with light repair tracks in the background and the Colton Ice Manufacturing Plant and pre-cooling track behind. PFE photo, CSRM.

When PFE commenced operations in early 1907, the company was in the process of receiving 6600 new refrigerator cars, and for a time, light running repairs were all that were needed to keep this fleet operating. Along with the purchase from Armour Car Lines of some of that company's icing facilities, PFE also officially took over Armour's western car repair shops on Oct. 1, 1907.

These shops were constructed as early as 1899, when Armour began building its own fleet of nearly 5,000 cars to operate in the California fruit trade. The Armour shops that PFE purchased were all in California: at Sacramento, Los Angeles, Riverside, and Colton. Armour had designed these shops to handle light repair work only, as they did all heavy and general repairs at their larger eastern shops.

As business for PFE steadily increased, the fleet size grew rapidly with new car orders to meet demand. Within a few years a need also emerged for heavy and general repairs to the original car fleet, so in 1909, PFE began a program to upgrade and enlarge its car repair capabilities. The shop equipment at Riverside was transferred to Colton, where a

modernized shop had been built one year earlier adjacent to the new ice plant.

The shop at Sacramento was transferred that same year to Roseville, alongside the new ice manufacturing plant that had been constructed in the Southern Pacific's newly completed classification yard. During late 1926 and early 1927 PFE's shops at Roseville were again relocated, to a new site just to the west, near Antelope. This new facility allowed for needed expansion. The PFE car repair shop at Los Angeles, adjacent to the SP's Taylor engine terminal, was also enlarged and modernized as conditions demanded.

As federally-developed land reclamation and irrigation projects in eastern Washington, Oregon, and Idaho began producing perishable shipments for PFE, it was deemed necessary to locate a repair shop in the district. In May, 1926, a completely new shop for heavy and general repairs was opened in Nampa, Idaho. A light repair shop and car cleaning yard was also activated at Pocatello at that time.

Extensive development of land and the growing of perishable commodities along Southern Pacific lines was also

Removal of thousands of tons of ice in cars returning from the east was a major job at PFE's initial inspection and cleaning yards. These three views show the procedure at North Platte. Left photo, PFE; lower two, photos 30909 and 30912, UP Railroad Museum.

taking place in the Southwest. New irrigated croplands were springing up west of Tucson, in the Salt River and Yuma Valleys of Arizona, along the west coast of Mexico, in the Coachella and Imperial Valleys of California, and the Lower Rio Grande Valley in Texas. Backhaul of empties that had been serviced and cleaned at Colton became uneconomical. To ensure the supply of cars in first class condition to these expanding agricultural areas, a new shop was required at a more central point. In 1928, that shop was built in Tucson, to accommodate the need for light repairs, painting and car cleaning.

At the far southeastern end of the system, car service needs were also met. The 4.4-mile Huey P. Long bridge, for highway and SP double tracks across the Mississippi River, was completed in 1935. In that year PFE moved its light repair and car cleaning facilities that had been in the SP's Algiers yard on the west side of the river to East Bridge (New Orleans). These repair yards did initial inspection of returning empties, and conditioned cars for loading in the

vicinity of New Orleans and points to the west, including much of Texas and some points on the Cotton Belt.

On the UP, a major car inspection and cleaning yard was set up at North Platte where many returning cars had their ice bunkers initially cleaned and de-iced. As a result of experimentation started in 1943, PFE installed a hot water system to wash out bunker and top ice remnants. A 15,000 gallon storage tank provided water that was heated by the ice manufacturing plant's three steam boilers. Sufficient hot water was available to supply 40 gallons a minute to each of five hose outlets which accommodated 40 cars: 20 each on adjacent tracks. With 100 ft. hoses, the workmen could either enter the car doors to remove body ice, or reach the top to clean the car bunkers. The water, 190° F., was directed on the ice dregs, and quickly melted them. Cleaning generally took from 5 to 25 minutes per car. North Platte in 1959 removed 41,175 tons of body ice and 58,939 tons of bunker ice from cars moving into the Idaho territory for potato and onion loading.

The PFE's primary operations divided naturally into three main geographic areas, and car service and maintenance also took place in these same three areas: (1) the Idaho-Northwest area into which dirty empties moved principally over the UP from Council Bluffs and Kansas City through North Platte to car shops in Pocatello and Nampa for servicing, (2) the northern California area into which dirty empties moved principally over the UP-SP via Ogden to Roseville Shops for servicing, and (3) the southern California-Southwest area into which dirty empties moved principally over the SP through El Paso to the Tucson Shops or the Colton and Los Angeles Shops. See map, page 432.

The peak loading season in Idaho ran from September through April, while in northern California it was from May through October. Thus, car volume was up in one area when it was down in the other, so these two areas complemented each other. The peak loading season in the Southwest was in May, June and July, thus generally corresponding to the peak period in northern California. Peak months for PFE as a whole were September and October, with August slightly lower. This very wide diversity in car requirement work loads necessitated full and efficient use of each shop's capacity and manpower.

During the peak loading season work would shift to the light yard for light and heavy running maintenance to expedite placing as many cars back into service as possible. The heavy yard output decreased and a backlog of heavy repairs would usually collect. Most of this work had to wait and was handled during the off-peak season.

To maintain maximum usage of the shops, and at the same time reduce the rapid increase in backlogs during the peak season, heavy repair cars were often routed selectively to shops having the lighter work load at a given time. Heavy repair cars were known as such based upon routine inspection reports of westbound empties. Initial inspections were done at eastern points as soon as the empties reached UP or SP rails, and reports of needed repairs were immediately forwarded to the car's destination shop.

The Car Dept. maintained a "lookout list" at all shops and inspection points. Cars destined for program repairs, i.e. to the entire car class, or candidates for a class rebuilding program (see Chapters 6 and 7 for a description of car rebuilding), were identified from this list and routed to the shop at which the work would be done. PFE could thus quickly collect and work on desired groups of cars.

Upon arrival of a returning empty car to any of the major repair shops, the car was immediately given a complete and thorough inspection. This inspection was standard for all the shops and was done by a team of five men, one of whom was a light repair foreman. It was accomplished in accordance with the diagram shown next.

Inspector 1, the recorder, listed all defects on PFE Form

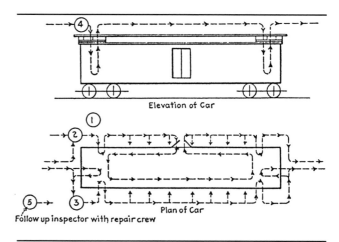

courtesy *Railway Age*, 1929

59, called a "door card," and marked all defects with chalk. Inspector 2 checked draft gear, trucks, underframes, sides and ends and the side doors. He also entered the body of the car and inspected the interior. Inspector 3 was equipped with a coupler height gauge and inspected all draft gear, couplers, and examined the trucks, underframe, sides and ends of the car on the opposite side from Inspectors 1 and 2, marking defects in chalk. Inspector 4 had a short-handled broom and checked the ice tanks, hatch covers, plugs and all roof fixtures, tested hand brakes, and swept down the walls of the ice tanks and the tops of the ice grates. He also removed all rubbish (it was common at eastern warehouses and terminals for trash to be thrown into empty cars).

Inspector 5, the light repair foreman, directed and advised the team, and coordinated repairs and materials. He passed judgment on any work or defects found, and if the car was judged a heavy repair, it was moved to that yard. The car inspection was made in advance of the repairmen, the car inspection teams usually starting work about 30 minutes before the repair crews came on shift. When repairs were completed, the foreman sealed hatches and doors, and applied a tag stating the car was ready for service. Every attention given the car on the "door card" was checked and signed by the foreman. These cards were collected daily at the shops and sent to the Car Department Office in San Francisco. Information from the "door cards" was placed on the car's 5" x 7" Mechanical File Card (see Appendix for examples), PFE Form 120 (Form 78-1 after 1930), called a "car card," enabling PFE to keep full records and statistics on problems that could develop for a given car class.

To balance the heavy repair work loads between Nampa and Roseville, dirty westbound cars were classified for repairs at Council Bluffs or North Platte cleaning and inspection yards. The heavy repair candidates were then cut out by the UP at Laramie or Green River and routed into Roseville from November through March, and to Nampa from April through October. Cars needing heavy repair coming

Table 11-1
Classifications of PFE Repairs

Light Running Maintenance (LRM)

This designated those cars placed in the Light Yard by the railroad and OK'd for loading the same day they were received. The detention time on these cars was one day. The work done on such cars consisted of:

- Car cleaning with washing, de-icing or de-odorizing as necessary.
- Thorough inspections by a team of inspectors moving along the track.
- Repacking and COT&S (Clean, Oil, Test & Stencil) as required.
- Air test.
- Truck and underframe repairs that could be completed without uncoupling and separating the cars, and could be completed during the one day detention period.
- Body and superstructure repairs that could be completed during the one day detention period.
- Fan repairs and replacement.
- Journal inspection and oiling.
- Mechanical refrigeration repairs and preventive maintenance that could be completed during the one day detention period, such as periodic inspections, oil changes, engine changes, and calibration of instruments.

Heavy Running Maintenance (HRM)

This designation covered those cars requiring repairs that were either:

- So extensive that the repair could not be completed during the one day detention period in the Light Yard,
- So located that it was necessary to uncouple the car and separate it from adjacent cars.

These were repairs that could be completed in two or a maximum of three days' time. Such cars were switched out and set back to the Heavy Yard when the railroad removed the Light Yard OK's. Shop manpower was scheduled to keep this group of repairs on a current basis in order to keep the maximum number of cars active.

Heavy Repairs (HR)

This designated the group of cars including heavy wrecks and all cars that required extensive stripping and replacement of parts of the car body or underframe. All of these cars required more time than the Heavy Running Maintenance cars and were worked separately to avoid blocking the HRM tracks.

Program Heavy Repairs (PHR)

These were cars scheduled as a group for general repairs on the basis of age and condition. In this operation deteriorated parts of the car were replaced, design deficiencies corrected, and the cars modernized to the extent economically justifiable. This work was normally similar on all cars in the group and was performed on a "production line" basis.

Roseville. A spring replacement is in progress using this specialized vehicle in the light repair yard. The fourth car down on the left is a visitor from ART. Photo N-2383-3, Southern Pacific.

in via the southwestern route were sent to either Colton or Los Angeles, or to Roseville, again depending upon the work load of these shops.

Shop operations were separated into four classifications by PFE and were based on work methods, not on repair costs as was true with standard railroad or AAR designations. The four classifications were: Light Running Maintenance (LRM), Heavy Running Maintenance (HRM), Heavy Repairs (HR), and Program Heavy Repairs (PHR), as described in Table 11-1.

All the PFE shops operated under the "unit system" of shop control. This system was adopted in 1926. The unit system was predicated upon the principle that if the labor cost of one operation was $50 and another $100, there must be twice the labor involved in the latter case, and that a definite relation existed between the labor cost of the two operations. The unit system did not incorporate material cost at all, being purely a labor pattern. While this structure was not infallible, it served as a barometer in connection with shop operation and automatically regulated many practices which would never have received attention if such a system had not existed. It also served as a basis by which the output of one shop or department was measured against another. An example of a daily report is shown below.

The unit system readily indicated when shop forces should be increased or decreased and was a means of telling whether the organization was in balance with the work on hand. It served to show the company if it was receiving a dollar's worth of work for each dollar paid in payroll. When the slack season of the year arrived, requiring a reduction of forces, it protected the efficient workman. The management was responsible for results; therefore they kept men in their forces who produced results.

Prior to the adoption of the unit system by PFE it was found that identical work varied in cost among the shops. This system highlighted these differences and stimulated analyses which, in some instances, resulted in changes of method and in cost reduction, while in other instances the differences remained because they were justified. The system made known each shop's record and this promoted "friendly" competition between the shops.

Classification of shop work under the unit system was

SP Bulletin

Daily Unit Report from Shops to General Office

Roseville Shop, October 7, 1929

No. Cars		Units Each	Total
8	Heavy repair cars OK'd...............	170	1,360
4	General repair cars OK'd...............	314	1,256
235	Light repair cars OK'd................	14	3,290
	Paint repair cars OK'd................	50	
	Rebuild repair cars OK'd.............	482	
	Total No. Units		5,906
	Total Man-Days Worked	332	
	Average Units Per Man	17.79	

(Signed) Superintendent

developed as a result of this careful analysis and study of records of labor and material costs. In 1930, for example, the classification "general repair cars" included all cars for which the labor cost amounted $100 to $250, excluding rebuilt cars. "Heavy repair cars" included all cars for which the labor cost of repairs amounted to more than $250.

The cost of repairs in accordance with the classification varied with respect to individual cars. However, on the average, there were no appreciable fluctuations in costs. The success of this system depended upon the judgment of the inspectors and foremen in setting proper classifications for the various cars repaired, and experience of the PFE showed that the shop organization established the classification of repairs with surprising accuracy.

Annual routine car maintenance, excluding general repairs, did not vary appreciably whether the car was two years old or 20 years old, except for the fact that the company endeavored to have wood cars repainted every five years. Shop records (Forms 865) show that this generally was done, except in the worst of economic times. Annual maintenance cost averaged from $300 to $350 per car in 1949.

General heavy repairs were undertaken from one to three times during the life of a car with the objective of keeping the car in service until such time that the end of the service life of the repaired body coincided with the service life of the trucks and underframe. In other words, a wood sheathed car could be kept in service as long as a steel sheathed car by periodic general repairs if the underframes and trucks were of similar design to stand up in service.

The periodic need for general repairs varied with the type of car and the cost also varied considerably, regardless of whether cars were modernized at the time of repair. In the late 1940's cars with wood superstructure frames and wood sheathing required general repairs after 8-10 years service and the labor and material cost per car would run around $1600. Wood sheathed cars with steel superstructure frames required general repairs after 10-15 years service and cost from $1000 to $1200 per car. Steel sheathed cars would require general repairs after 15 or more years service, and repair of these cars would run from $2000 to $3000. The service life of a car depended on what type of service it was in, and the repair cost varied, according to the type of underframe, insulation, floor and roof construction, and the amount of corrosion of all metal parts.

The Car Department would determine the number of cars to be rebuilt in a given year and then allocate those rebuilds to its major shops according to each shop's capability. For many years Tucson was light car repair only, and did not really enter into even heavy car repair until the early 1950's. The other four major shops did all the rebuilds, and the annual output figures over the years were generally the following: Roseville, 35%; Los Angeles, 30%; Colton,

Los Angeles. Prior to reconditioning of these R-30-9 cars (see Chapter 7), the superstructures are being stripped. Reusable wood and hardware items were salvaged. Richard Steinheimer photo, 1950.

20%; Nampa, 15%. An example in 1926 shows the number of cars rebuilt were: Roseville, 573; Los Angeles, 468; Colton, 321; and Nampa, 106, for a total of 1468 rebuilds.

Cars undergoing complete rebuild of the superstructure were switched to the dismantling or stripping track

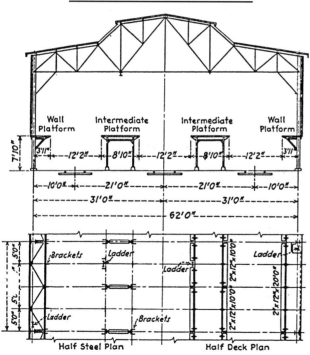

Roseville. Wall and intermediate platforms in car shop, from *Railway Mechanical Engineer*, February, 1930.

where the entire superstructure was removed. As much material and hardware as possible was reclaimed and sorted. The underframe and trucks were then repaired and upgraded if needed. The underframe was then switched into the main erecting shed. The layout of this shed was much the same in all the shops, normally having at least 3 tracks.

There were different stations on each track at which certain operations were done. The various operations were: wooden subsills and floors applied; wooden superstructure, including ceiling of car, applied; outside course of insulation, siding and hardware applied; roof applied; inside courses of insulation, the lining and the side doors applied; bulkheads, ice tanks, floor racks and door packing applied. Some of these operations are shown in Chapter 7. After leaving the erecting shed, the car was given an undercoat of paint and two finish coats in the paint shed.

Before World War II it was common practice to direct an owner's refrigerator car "home" for repairs at their shops and loading on the owner's lines. Because of the extremely heavy movements of freight throughout the country during the war, refrigerator cars were pressed into general service, as described in Chapter 1, and refrigerator car "pooling" was conducted. Consequently, in the 1943-47 period, comparatively larger numbers of "foreigns" passed through PFE shops. The existing standard AAR code of rules was extended to cover refrigerator car repair methods and billing of costs to the owner company. This was the "Code of Rules Governing the Condition of, and Repairs to, Freight

Roseville (**Above**). Needed repair parts were brought to each car in the light repair yard by a "trailer train." (**Below**) Truck repairs were made at the "Hot Spot" fixed car jack, where the car could be lifted and the truck changed out. All three photos, PFE from CSRM.

and Passenger Cars for the Interchange of Traffic," issued by the AAR's Mechanical Division.

Repair and maintenance of a refrigerator car fleet that reached a maximum number of 41,261 cars in September, 1930, and that still numbered 38,925 cars at the beginning of 1954, provided PFE with its own unique set of logistical problems. Major railroads had long used a "One Spot System" for the average freight car repair, wherein all work on that car was done at a single "spot" to which the car was moved, and all materials were brought to that location.

Refrigerator cars, due to the nature of the traffic, were and still are required to be maintained inside as "Grade A" cars. There are no "rough loaders" in an interchange reefer fleet. (Ice service cars used locally were another question; just ask anyone who ever loaded one!) This requirement always demanded more extensive body maintenance and repairs than as with a standard freight car passing over a railroad "one spot."

The variety of materials for a refrigerator car was much larger. Beyond normal freight car materials such as trucks,

brakes, etc., were the requirements for maintenance of ice bunkers, drains, grates, gasketed hatch plugs, bulkheads, floor racks, door hardware and accessories, insulation, fan and electrical materials, mechanical refrigeration units and materials, and fueling and oiling facilities.

Gross volume of cars also made the "one spot" operation of a light repair yard impractical for PFE. It was not uncommon for Roseville to OK in excess of 700 cars, or for Tucson to OK in excess of 500 cars, in a single day shift from the light yard. It would have been impossible to have run all these cars through a single spot.

At the PFE shops, westbound dirty empties were brought into the light repair yard. Long strings of cars were worked on by crews moving down the line of cars. Repair parts were brought to the cars by truck or by a parts "trailer train." Cars moving into territories where they received loads requiring heater protection during transit were de-iced and dried.

In 1948, PFE developed the "Hot Spot" system for truck repairs, originally to accomplish the rapid change-

Roseville (Left). This straddle carrier moved entire truck assemblies to any point in the repair yard. PFE photo, 1958, CSRM. Watsonville Junction (Right). PFE mechanical reefer service shed, 1985. R.J. Church photo.

out of "T" or "L" section Bettendorf side frames that had been prohibited in that year by the AAR from interchange service (though PFE requested and received extensions on this deadline until at least 1953). A given track in the heavy repair yard had a designated "spot" where permanently placed car jacks would lift a car, allowing for quick wheel set changes, side frame changes, or spring changes. Wheel set changes were done quite regularly, especially with cast iron wheels which wore beyond limits more quickly than other truck components. By the mid-1940's the cast iron wheels were being replaced with cast steel wheels, and the cast iron wheel became illegal on all interchange cars on January 1, 1969.

This system worked well for ordinary truck repairs, but by the late 1950's, the modern trucks with built-in snubbing devices were coming in for repairs in increasing numbers. By this time, 90% of the PFE fleet had steel wheels, and experience showed that by the time steel wheels required changing, the major truck members also required overhaul. In addition, due to faster train speeds and other changes in freight train handling, maintenance requirements were much more rigid.

A new truck repair system was adopted in 1958 whereby a straddle-carrier transported the truck from under the car to a truck repair station. Trucks of like design that had been previously reconditioned were immediately placed under the car. This interchange could be done at any point in the heavy repair yard by use of air jacks and standees. The method thus alleviated the bottleneck created by the congestion of cars awaiting heavy truck service at the "hot spot." Cars could be segregated and classified as to type and amount of work while on the transfer track.

The period between 1947-1949 saw a critical undertaking by PFE to establish systemwide repair and upgrading programs for its existing car service facilities, from simple car cleaning yards to the major shops. This was not just to cope with the increased size of the car fleet. Years of use had taken their toll on the shops. A survey was done by the Car Service Department and funds were allocated to complete all necessary facility repairs and upgrading to make the work conditions more efficient and safe.

One of the biggest problems contended with was deterioration of track, and drive and workways in the initial inspection yard and light repair yard. This was caused by the fact that these areas were continually immersed in melting runoff water. Thousands of tons of ice were dumped from incoming cars, and the cars were then steam cleaned. This runoff would rot ties and undermine pavement and concrete to the point that work conditions were unsafe and intolerable. The upgrading program overcame the difficulty to some degree, but this water was always a problem.

As the mechanical car fleet grew, so did PFE's development of facilities to repair and maintain the diesel and refrigeration units. Defective units were replaced with reconditioned and rebuilt units which were on hand, rather than consume time with repair inside the car.

Fueling and lubrication requirements of the mechanical units had to be dealt with. Fuels and oils were either purchased from and distributed by local dealers under contract, or at some shops, purchased in bulk and distributed by PFE forces. In July, 1974, the Roseville Shop's diesel oil vendors pumped 1,202,736 gallons into mechanical cars in the LRM yards (see page 230). This operation kept six trucks occupied in full-time delivery service.

Programmed repairs were set up to handle servicing and maintenance of the hydraulic cylinders on the mechanical cars with Hydra-Cushion or Freight-Master cushioned underframes. It was found that more repair was required for the Freight-Master underframe cars.

The following is a description of the six major car repair shops within the PFE system. The explanation of departments and management pertains to all the shops.

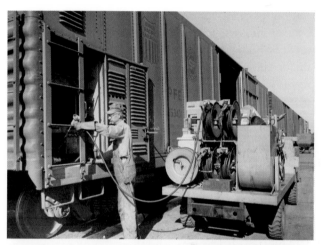

(Above) Fan repair truck (note "PFE – SAFETY" emblem) at Roseville, early 1950's. PFE 200121 is discussed in Chapter 7. (Left, above) Mechanical refrigerator power packages (engine-generator sets) to left, compressor units to right, for R-70-12's at Los Angeles, 1960. (Left, below) Power package crane truck; note the corrugated bulkhead inside the engine compartment. (Below) Diesel engine service vehicle. All photos, PFE, CSRM.

(Right) Journal box oiler at Los Angeles, 1950. The car is an R-30-9, which is about to be light weighed, as ordered by the card tacked below the car number. This car's load limit is not calculated from the light weight, but is set by underframe capacity, thus the star by that item. Richard Steinheimer photo.

(Below) Chevrolet panel truck purchased for mechanical refrigerator car repairs and servicing, Los Angeles, May 15, 1956. PFE photo, CSRM.

Nampa. This photo of the car rebuild shop appears to date from the mid-1920's. Note wood roofs of cars on center track, with a waterproof layer being applied between two layers of tongue and groove roofing on the second car. Track on right has cars with outside metal roofs. PFE photo, CSRM.

NAMPA GENERAL SHOPS

This plant was considered by many in the Car Service Department as having the best layout of track plan and buildings of all the PFE shops as experience gained from the earlier built shops was incorporated into it. PFE had announced in June, 1924, its willingness to build a new shop complex in Nampa if the city would provide the land site at a cost to the city of approximately $45,000. The Nampa Chamber of Commerce took up the challenge

Nampa. Lumber mill shop interior, where rough lumber was cut and milled to shape for the many specialized pieces in a wood refrigerator car. The belt-driven equipment is all electric powered. L.J. Young photo for PFE, CSRM.

immediately, raised the funds to purchase 101-½ acres, and deeded the land to PFE on July 15, 1924. The new shops, officially opened on May 5, 1926, added 18 buildings and 5 miles of new track to the UP yard.

The description of the buildings, which was typical of the set-up of all the PFE major shops, is as follows. **Main shed**, where all heavy work was done; **air brake test shop**, where necessary repair and rebuilding of the air brake equipment was done; **boiler house**, which supplied heating for all buildings through a system that utilized hot water in pipes and radiators, (reported to have been the largest such heating system of its kind in the world when installed in 1925), and steam for air compressors and fire pumps housed in the boiler house; **stores and office building**, for administration and parts storage; **mill building**, where rough lumber was cut and milled to size for repair work; **milled lumber building**, to store various lumber that had been cut to size and shape until required for use; **insulation storage building**, for the considerable amounts of insulation required; **locker and wash room**, for employees' use; **paint building**, where purchased paints were stored and mixed; **tin shop**, which had all equipment to repair and construct galvanized iron work used in the ice bunkers; **reclaiming building**, where considerable materials and parts were recycled; **machine shop**, for machining and mill work on metal parts, wheel sets, etc.; **welding shop**, for repair of metal parts; **storage shed**, for tools, heavy jacks, etc., used in the yards; and the **incinerator**, which burned refuse removed from cars and shavings and sawdust from the mill.

The Nampa Car Shops underwent major reconditioning and repair in 1947. Many tracks were relocated to improve the flow of cars going through for repairs, as the work load had increased beyond the limits of the original layout. Repaving was done in most areas between work tracks.

Nampa's main function was repairing heavy defect cars and doing rebuild modifications to units and equipment. No new cars were ever built here though PFE was prepared to move a projected 1961 new car program to Nampa until it was decided to contract out the car order to Pacific Car & Foundry in Renton, Wash.

After the March, 1978, UP-SP split of PFE, Nampa continued to repair UPFE equipment until December, 1982, when the UPFE closed Nampa entirely. The wreck work and program work were transferred to the UPFE car shops at Pocatello and is still performed there by UPFE personnel. With the exception of light running repairs performed by UP personnel while the cars are under load on Union Pacific trackage, UPFE personnel perform all of the maintenance on the UPFE car fleet.

Nampa. Material storage yard for rough cut lumber and other materials. Lumber mill shop is at right with sawdust pipe going to incinerator in background. PFE photo, CSRM.

Nampa (Right). New shop tracks 2 and 3 are being laid by PFE's contractor, Morrison-Knudsen, in this May, 1928 photo. At left are the car shops. PFE photo, Milton G. Sorensen collection.

Nampa (Below). Part of the shop crew poses for a group photo from the 1930's, on some unrecorded occasion. Nearly every man wears a hat, and the hats alone are an interesting study in this view. PFE photo, CSRM.

Pocatello. This view of the light repair shops and car conditioning yard was made from the roof of the ice manufacturing plant, looking west. UP photo.

Pocatello Light Repair Shops

PFE initially had a small repair complex in the Oregon Short Line yards. The first major facilities here were built between 1925-27 in conjunction with PFE's decision to establish complete car servicing in Idaho for the Northwest territory. Pocatello did most light repair and car cleaning duties on westbound dirty empties that had not been cleaned at North Platte.

The PFE shops and trackage were moved and totally upgraded in 1949 in conjunction with Union Pacific's removal and relocation of its trackage to build a new retarder type classification yard. The new plant was directly across from the icing deck and was able to handle the increasing demands of the Idaho Falls and Twin Falls districts, which could average in the winter months as high as 270 cars daily, and could reach on any day a maximum as high as 370 cars. The old PFE yard had a capacity of only 113 cars,

while the new shops had sufficient trackage to repair 340 cars.

Pocatello was also PFE's only car shop on the system where Carrier Protective Service (CPS) heaters, at first charcoal and later alcohol, were installed in bunkers of all standard refrigerator cars prior to being placed for loading in the winter months. During the period from November 1st through the end of March, an average of 40,000 CPS heaters (2 per car) were installed at Pocatello to protect winter shipments of potatoes and onions. These units could burn for about 24 hours before having to be refueled.

Pocatello would handle annually up to 50,000 LRM cars and 1500 HRM cars. They also supplemented Nampa if that shop became backlogged with HR cars, sometimes doing as many as 350 HR cars a year. In 1957 PFE installed facilities for the maintenance of mechanical cars here instead of Nampa as Pocatello was the gateway to the important loading areas of Idaho and the Northwest territory.

Pocatello. The paint shop is in the foreground in this view, with the light repair yard and PFE ice manufacturing plant and ice deck in the right background. UP photo.

Roseville. The original Roseville Shops built in 1909 were at the south side (left in this photo) of the ice plant. These shops operated until 1927, when the new shops were built to the west at Antelope. SP photo.

Pocatello is still active and is now the only shop operated by UPFE. Other locations where UPFE has pretripping operations for their mechanical fleet are: Hinkle, Oregon; Ogden, Utah; Stockton, California; and North Platte, Nebraska.

ROSEVILLE GENERAL SHOPS

The huge plant at Antelope, just west of Roseville proper, was opened in 1927. The original shops were built in 1909 adjacent to the ice plant in the SP Roseville yards. The area covered by the shops at the Antelope site was roughly 108 acres, and construction cost was about $3,000,000. The yard incorporated 24 miles of tracks, providing working capacity for 1517 cars. The longest track was 1.7 miles.

Procedures were divided between light or running repairs performed on the south side of the yard, and heavy repairs, rebuilding or new car building on the north side. Separating the two areas was the row of shop buildings consisting of the wheel shop, wood mill, car rebuild shed, finished lumber storage, insulation storage, locker rooms, tin shop, machine shop, steel construction shed, paint shed, annealing furnace, incinerator and main offices.

The light repair yard was made up of six tracks up to 6,500 ft. in length. Through the late 1940's to the late 1950's the Roseville light repair yard handled some 95,000

cars annually. During the peak shipping period in northern California, 600 to 700 cars were conditioned daily. The HRM yard would service up to 2700 cars a year while 1500 cars received heavy repairs annually along with any new car construction programs being undertaken at the same time. Car capacities in 1930 are shown below.

Car Capacities of Various Units at Roseville Shops			
	No. of tracks	Spacing on centers	Space allowed per car	No. of cars
Light repair tracks......	7	20 ft.	45 ft.	723
Waste ice track.........	1		45 ft.	134
Heavy repair tracks.....	6	20 ft.	100 ft.	118
Rebuilt tracks	3	20 ft.	75 ft.	68
Paint tracks	4	20 ft.	55 ft.	65
Strip track	1	20 ft.	50 ft.	21
Total car capacity				1,129 cars

Purchasing, storing and disbursing materials were handled by the purchasing and store department under the supervision of the purchasing agent. The material sections were grouped into five divisions in 1930, each division under a section storekeeper who maintained necessary stock records on standard ARA, later AAR, stock-book forms. The store department handled the delivery of all materials to the mechanical department. Mechanization was instituted and utilized wherever possible. Auto trucks and Fordson tractors with trailers were used to deliver the materials. The 1930 inventory of material carried ranged between $600,000 and $800,000.

Roseville. In this view of the west end of the shops, looking west toward Antelope, the light repair and car conditioning tracks are on the left, heavy repair tracks on the right, and the supply storage area in the center. PFE photo, CSRM.

The shop personnel consisted of the following: the superintendent, a general foreman, two assistant general foremen, rebuild foreman, light-repair foreman, blacksmith and machine shop foreman, painter foreman, planing mill foreman, welder foreman and scrap-reclaim foreman. The shop employed a minimum of 240 workmen, with up to 860 men at peak periods, all Car Dept. employees; the Stores Department employed another 140. Total payroll

in 1930, both departments, was in excess of $4 million.

PFE's first special shop for handling repairs and overhaul of mechanical units was installed at Roseville in 1955-56. By 1960 the company was operating 2,500 mechanical reefers and the shops had been substantially reorganized to handle the work associated with these cars and (later) the trailer fleet. The refrigeration shop had a total floor space of 5,100 sq. ft. It was divided into the following work areas:

Roseville. An eastward view in August, 1964. The wide shed, right rear, is the paint shop, with the steel shed to its left. SP photo.

Roseville. In the summer of 1949, brand-new R-40-25's are spotted in front of the paint shed for touch-up work on the trim and lettering of these freshly painted cars. The 3000 cars of this class were all built by PFE, 1000 of them at Roseville (see Chapter 8). The steel shed is to the right in this westward view. SP photo N-1810-4, courtesy Steve Peery.

engine overhaul area, refrigeration overhaul and repair area, electrical repair, fuel injector repair, cylinder, piston and blower repair, test room, drying room, and lube-oil testing area. The shop was equipped with a 3,000 lb. overhead crane. During the peak six-month shipping season, up to 56,000 cars and trailers were cleaned, serviced and repaired.

Throughout the history of the PFE repair facilities, the Roseville Shops consistently handled the most cars on an annual basis, whether in light repairs or new car construction. It was PFE's most important shop facility.

On January 1, 1980, the Roseville PFE Shops were transferred to the SP and became SP's Reconditioning and Maintenance Center (RAMAC) Shop, where heavy freight car repair and rebuilding has been done. At the same time, SP discontinued all its heavy car repair in LA. All SPFE heavy car repairs were then handled at Tucson.

PFE 1. This is the Roseville shop loco as it appeared in later years. The loco had been decorated with raised heralds, a very small amount of streamlining, silver stripes and star, and even a PFE wing above the cylinder. Note that the saddle tank is shorter on the air pump side. Photo, Al Phelps, Feb. 2, 1948.

PFE 1. This is nearly the original appearance of this Baldwin-built (1928, bldrs. no. 60680) 0-4-0 ST. Note the cut-out alteration to enlarge window on engineer's side. The locomotive was equipped for one-man operation. SP Roseville locomotive shops handled all repairs on this engine, which was PFE's only owned steam engine. Retired in March, 1953. Photo above by D.L. Joslyn, Guy Dunscomb collection.

PFE leased SP or UP power on occasion. SP 4-6-0 2248 was leased, from 2/24/49 to 3/10/49, at Roseville; SP 2-8-0 2664 was leased, Roseville, 3/11 to 3/19/49. Leases possibly took place when steam loco No. 1 was in for shopping.

PFE 1 (second). This GE 44-ton loco, built in Aug. 1950, for the Pine Flat Dam Contractors, was purchased in Feb. 1953 by PFE to replace steamer No. 1 at the Roseville Car Shops. This loco also carried both the SP and UP heralds. The unit was retired in 1966, and was subsequently sold to the International Mineral and Chemical plant in San Jose. Jim Lekas photo, March 7, 1959.

PFE 1023. In 1966, an Alco S-3 became the Roseville Shop switcher. This ex-SP Alco 1023, built 1951, replaced second 1 at Roseville in 1966. The paint scheme is PFE orange, with black lettering and black and white stripes. Al Phelps, July, 1977.

(Left) Car cleaning involved clearing drains and, if necessary, ensuring that all ice and dirt was out of the bunker. Here a workman uses a ball-peen hammer to encourage draining. Note the numerous staples on the car side, souvenirs of previous placards, and the heavy corrosion on the truck sideframe. Richard Steinheimer photo at Los Angeles, December, 1950.

(Below) The layout of Roseville Shop, showing both 1960's and earlier facilities, in a partially schematic arrangement. Track numbers and capacities included. Redrawn from PFE charts, UP Railroad Museum.

Building Key

A. Wheel shop
B. Test cell (1960's)
C. Car wash
D. Woodworking mill
E. Rebuild shed (later Repair Shed No. 2)
F. Finished lumber storage
G. Insulation storage
H. Tin shop
J. Machine shop (later Mechanical Refrig. Shop)
K. Steel construction shed (later Shed. No. 1)
L. Paint shed (later Shed No. 3)
M. Wood chip incinerator
N. Truck overhaul shop
P. Air brake shop
Q. Main offices
R. Fabrication shop
S. Scale
T. Trailer area (1960's)
V. Parts cleaning
W. Maintenance center (1960's)

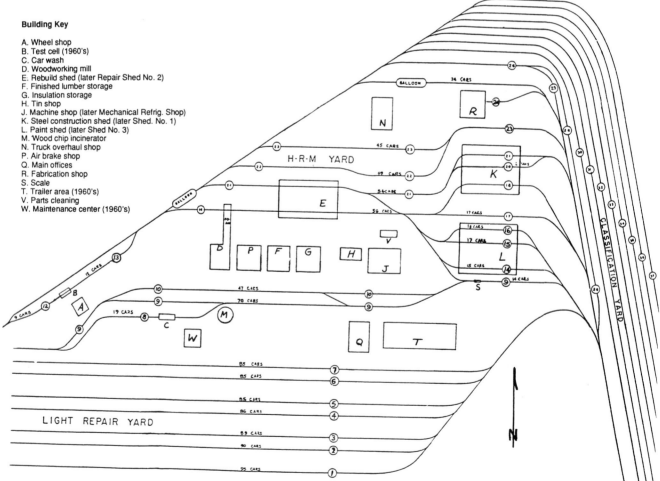

Los Angeles. Behind the open-air lumber storage is the south end of Mill No. 1, with the rebuilding shed beyond. Heavy repair yard is at left, icing tracks and ice deck at right. This view, looking north, dates from about 1950. PFE photo, CSRM.

LOS ANGELES GENERAL SHOPS

This facility began as one of the light repair shops originally purchased from Armour. These early shops became inadequate in a short time. In 1914 PFE abandoned the old site and established its General Shops on land adjoining its Ice Manufacturing Plant which greatly increased efficiency. It was continually upgraded to meet increasing demand for conditioned cars in the area. The buildings incorporated all the departments for wood and metal fabrication and painting as described earlier.

The site of the Los Angeles shops comprised about 12 acres on which slightly over seven miles of repair tracks were laid. There was sufficient capacity to accommodate approximately 250 cars in the light repair yard and 250 cars in the heavy repair yard. There were normally around 450 men employed in the repair yard, shops and stores. The main shed used for building and rebuilding car bodies was 600 ft. long, contained three tracks, and could accommodate 36 cars in various stages. On each of the three tracks there were six stations, and at each station there was ample room for two cars properly spaced for efficient handling.

Cars were spotted in the yard by a switcher. PFE did not have an owned switch engine here, so the switching duties were handled by an SP engine and crew. During rush season the tracks had to be switched once or twice daily to handle the volume of cars. Cars were moved in the work shed by tractors.

This shop could handle everything from light running maintenance to new car building. It was second only to Roseville in new car construction, but because Tucson and Colton shared the light and heavy running maintenance for cars distributed to the southwest, the annual numbers for LRM totalled only around 40,000 while the HRM totalled around 1200 cars.

At Southern Pacific's request, the Los Angeles PFE Shops were closed in early 1962. The SP used some of the PFE land at Taylor to expand its own diesel locomotive shops, but retained some of PFE's buildings and sheds for car repair use until 1980.

In February of 1962 a new million-dollar facility, for light repair only, was completed for icers, mechanical cars, and trailers on a 23-acre site just a few miles east of Los Angeles in an area called City of Industry. This was the replacement for the old LA Shops.

City of Industry facilities were set up to handle 100 to 125 cars per day in LRM and about 14 cars per day in HRM. This yard only handled repairs, cleanings and bad order cars originating in the Los Angeles area. The complex remained active until December 31, 1980, when the property was turned over to the SP.

Los Angeles (Above). A view between Mill No. 1 (at left) and the lumber shed, showing piles of specially cut wood parts used in car rebuilding, with repair tracks beyond. The background shows smog, though that word was not in general use when this photo was taken in December, 1950. Richard Steinheimer photo, DeGolyer Library.

(Below) Layout of the shop in 1957, with PFE trackage shown dashed in this SP drawing, courtesy Alden Armstrong. Taylor Yard (SP) facilities at top, ice plant at right (south).

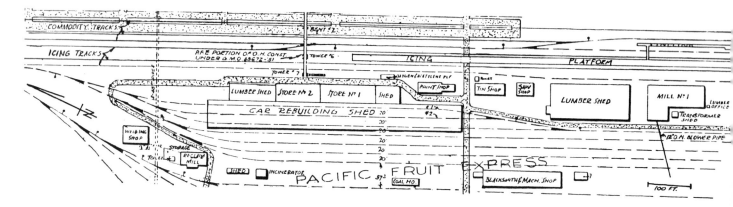

LA Shop Vignette by Richard Steinheimer, December 1950.

Los Angeles. The rebuilding shed (**above**) was used for heavy car work or new car construction. Note the permanent scaffold supported from the roof. Cars undergoing heavy or program repairs often had the car body removed from the underframe. After trucks and underframe were repaired, the body was returned to the underframe and attention given to the superstructure, either with complete or partial replacement. Reclaimed material was re-used wherever possible. The car was then moved by a tractor to the initial spot in the rebuilding shed.

Each of the three tracks in the shed had six stations: subsills and floors; superstructure; outside insulation and siding; roof application; inside insulation and doors; bulkheads, ice tanks and floor racks. When the car left the roofing station, it was given a coat of paint, then two more coats were applied outside the shed, followed by stenciling. The car was inspected, air tested, doors sealed, and sent to a loading territory.

Major repairs usually required lifting or separating the body from the frame, as in the view of a welder working on the draft rigging attachment of R-30-9 meat car 85071 (**below, left**); note the studs along the bottom of the superstructure which accomplish the attachment to the frame. Small rubber-tired tractors were used to move cars within the shops (**below, right**), as with this rebuilt car which is ready for paint. The location is the south end of the rebuilding shed. Three photos, Richard Steinheimer.

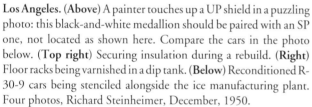

Los Angeles. (**Above**) A painter touches up a UP shield in a puzzling photo: this black-and-white medallion should be paired with an SP one, not located as shown here. Compare the cars in the photo below. (**Top right**) Securing insulation during a rebuild. (**Right**) Floor racks being varnished in a dip tank. (**Below**) Reconditioned R-30-9 cars being stenciled alongside the ice manufacturing plant. Four photos, Richard Steinheimer, December, 1950.

Los Angeles. The views on this page show the last new cars constructed by PFE in its own facilities, 1960. (Left) The R-70-12 mechanical cars were constructed partly outdoors. Workmen are erecting sides, with roof panels on flatcars in the background. Five PFE photos this page, CSRM.

Los Angeles(Above). This frame for an R-50-6 has had fuel tanks, brake cylinder and reservoir applied, and is now being flipped over to place on trucks. 1958 photo.

(Below). The 25-ton shop crane at LA Shop. Most shops had similar cranes, often used for light switching.

Los Angeles (Above). Spray painting was not a finesse job. Man on car top shields roof from overspray.

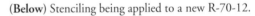

(Below) Stenciling being applied to a new R-70-12.

Colton. Car shop facilities are in the foreground and the ice manufacturing plant is in the center of this aerial view, with SP's original Colton freight yard behind. The SP turntable and engine facilities are at left, and stockyards are visible just above the ice plant in this view. PFE photo, CSRM.

COLTON GENERAL SHOPS

On January 25, 1908, PFE's Los Angeles representative A.M. Mortensen confirmed that the company had appropriated $400,000 to purchase land and build a new modernized car shop and ice manufacturing plant at Colton. PFE secured a nine-block section of land lying between Eleventh St. and Mount Vernon Ave. on the south side of the SP tracks. On this property were built the ice plant, precooling plant, icing platforms, and the car shops. The new shops had all the usual departments and buildings for a standard PFE general repair shop.

In 1912 a steel car shed over the heavy repair work area, 50' x 400', was built to protect workmen from summer heat. An enclosed paint shop, with four tracks, 74' x 496', was constructed in 1925 to allow Colton an output of eight cars per day, or about 2400 cars painted per year. PFE policy in the 1920's was to try and repaint wood cars every five or six years, and as shown in Chapters 5 and 7, this was accomplished in all but the worst of economic times.

In its 50 years of operation, this shop handled all classes of repair, rebuilds, and at the same time performed about 20% of the new car construction in the 1930's and 1940's. In 1958, there were 244 employees in the car department and 50 men in the stores department.

The post-war urban sprawl that occurred in the Los Angeles Basin and San Fernando Valley brought about a diminished agricultural output as farmlands were buried under houses and asphalt. During the same period the need for refrigerator cars in Arizona was greatly increasing. Car repair ceased at Colton on April 15, 1959, and the entire shop complex and stores department were completely closed down by August, 1959. All major repair duties on westbound empties were assumed by the Tucson Shops.

Colton. Layout of PFE Car Repair Shops and yard in 1929, from *Railway Age.*

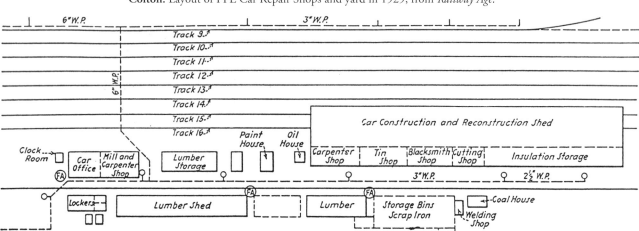

270

Colton. Car bodies were removed from frame and trucks on these heavy repair tracks. Note removed sheathing on superstructures in background. Southern California Edison photo, Oct. 1948, PFE collection, CSRM.

TUCSON GENERAL SHOPS

These shops were opened in 1928 to enable PFE to direct conditioned cars to the Imperial Valley, the Salt River Valley and to western Mexico, without having to backhaul from Colton or Los Angeles. Prior to that time a small service yard was maintained, but all material had to be shipped from PFE's shops in California. Originally the new Tucson repair shops performed car cleaning services, light repair, and painting in a five-track yard. Two additional tracks were added in 1934. In 1937 the light repair yard was improved when paving was provided for the wide working alleys and better drainage was installed. Light repair work was mechanized by extensive use of automotive equipment.

In 1943, the SP reopened its wheel shop in Tucson, principally to furnish wheelsets for the PFE shops. Prior to that time, PFE's and the SP's wheel requirements at Tucson had been furnished by the SP's El Paso Shops. El Paso continued to furnish the railroad with its wheel needs after 1943. PFE exchanged nearly 6000 pairs of wheels at this shop in 1944.

The light repair work load increased so that by 1958 an annual total of 70,000 cars were handled with a monthly peak of 11,000 cars. The repair yard had been expanded to eleven tracks by 1954. The PFE's first schooling in mechanical refrigeration for repairmen was held here in 1953. To meet the increasing demand for repair of this type car, it became necessary to utilize more mobile units,

SCHEDULE OF BUILDINGS		
1	Paint Shop	30 x 40
2	Blacksmith and Machine Shop	30 x 60
3	Mill Building	30 x 60
4	Insulation and Lumber Storage	30 x 60
5	Office and Store	30 x 90
6	Toilet and Locker Room - Tool House - Brake Shop	30 x 75
7	Pump House and Well	14 x 14
8	Water Tower (Proposed Location)	
9	Hose Reel House	6 x 8
10	Septic Tank	7 x 17

Tucson. This drawing shows the layout of the light repair yard and shop in 1929. From *Railway Age.*

Southern Pacific Co. Right of Way Line ---

Light Repair Yard - P. F. E. Co.

22'   5,640 = 120 Cars

44'   5,076 = 108 Cars

22'   4,747 = 101 Cars

44'   4,136 = 88 Cars

22'   3,901 = 83 Cars

℄ Track to face of buildings

271

Tucson. This paint shed was where much of PFE's car painting was done, due to Tucson's climate. PFE photo, CSRM.

such as Kalamazoos. Vans were also used on outside calls for repairs at loading areas such as Wilcox, Nogales, Red Rock, Picacho and Maricopa.

The geographical relationship of Tucson to other PFE shops was such that movement of heavy repair cars to either Roseville or Nampa was uneconomical. Subsequently, in conjunction with the projected closure of the Colton Shops, Tucson was upgraded in 1958-59 to handle all types of heavy car repair. This program included building of various new structures, extension of some existing tracks and the addition of Tracks 12, 13, and 14 to meet the needs of a major facility.

Effective thereafter, all cars westbound through the El Paso gateway were stopped and conditioned at Tucson. The land area covered by the yards and various repair and maintenance buildings, machine shops, foundry and paint line was 1-¼ miles in length.

Climatic conditions at Tucson were the most favorable of any major PFE shop for volume car painting. Accordingly, a new, modern automatic painting facility with a capacity of 5000 cars per year, or 20 per work day, was developed there in 1966. Incoming cars going through the paint line were prepared first by getting a spray cleaning with chemical detergent and steam. The cars moved through each step of the entire process by means of a cable connection.

Upon completion of cleaning, the cars entered a drying chamber, after which any masking was done, such as the grill of a mechanical car's refrigeration unit. The car next traversed a chamber where grit blasters removed rust and loose paint. In a third chamber, the car was phosphatized and undercoated, and the underbody painted. The sides, ends and roof were painted in the fourth chamber, and in the last room, heat lamps dried the car before it moved to an open shed for lettering. As of 1959, Tucson handled all periodic repainting of PFE cars. Thereafter, the other shops only did painting required because of repairs, the paint crews utilizing properly equipped mobile paint units. In 1975, PFE converted from oil-base to water-base paints.

During PFE's operating zenith in the early 1950's, Tucson was second only to Roseville when it came to annual work loads, averaging above 70,000 LRM cars, 2,000 HRM cars and 1,050 HR cars a year.

After the UP-SP split-off of PFE in 1978, the Tucson plant became the centralized repair facility for the entire SPFE car fleet, and remained in that role into the 1990's.

PFE 1048. This shop engine was PFE's second at Tucson. The first, an ex-SP switcher, served from 1964 to 1968, and was replaced that year by former UP 1048, an EMD NW-2. When PFE was split up, this unit was retained by SP for SPFE use. Paint scheme is white and black. PFE photo, 1981, CSRM.

An aerial view, looking east, of the Tucson Shop complex in the early 1960's. The ice deck and SP yard are at left. The large circular structure near top center is an incinerator, screened on sides and top, called the "circus tent." PFE photo, CSRM.

On the pond at Evanston during a harvesting operation of natural ice. Rafts of partially cut ice blocks are being floated through a channel in the ice sheet toward the ice house, where they will be split into individual blocks, 22" square, and moved into the storage gallery. UP Railroad Museum.

12

NATURAL ICE PLANTS

Donner Ice Company facility at Donner Creek. Drawn by R.J. Church from sketch on cover of *Sierra Heritage* magazine.

The complexities of providing the services for which the PFE Company was established were monumental. The venture that Harriman initiated on December 7, 1906, to capture a larger share of the growing business of moving western fruit and produce to eastern markets, required a vast network of repair and icing facilities to ensure refrigeration, heat, or ventilator requirements as regulated in the tariff specifications.

The fledgling attempts by the early railroads to move perishables began before the completion of the first Transcontinental Railroad. By the time that historic link had its opening ceremonies at Promontory on May 10, 1869, both the Union Pacific and Central Pacific had small numbers of ventilated boxcars. The two railroads used these cars to move fruit and vegetables locally, but foreign market (cross country) shipments in this type car inherently led to too much spoilage.

Insulated and ice-cooled cars had been developing with various designs dating back as early as 1842. But in the 19th century, the initial investment cost for railroads to enter into the ice refrigerated car business was substantial, and because there was no way of predicting the growth potential of the budding western agriculture, the railroads

couldn't know if enough revenue would be generated to offset such costs. The heaviest use of ice refrigerator cars during this period was by meat packing companies such as Swift and Armour, and most western railroads and California shippers contracted with those private companies for cars to move their loads of produce to the eastern markets.

The PFE parent lines did recognize the increasing demand by Western perishable producers for cars to adequately ship their products, and the railroads made cautious attempts to serve the perishable business. Both Union Pacific and Central Pacific owned over 100 cars for produce service, ventilated box cars as well as refrigerator cars, by 1885 (see Chapter 3), although much California produce was shipped by private car lines at that time.

The expanding California orange industry and aggressive competition from the Santa Fe prompted both UP and CP railroads, in an endeavor to secure the hauling of this fruit, to furnish more refrigerated cars. Although the two roads slowly increased their ownership of ice refrigerator cars before 1906, both relied primarily on car contracts with Armour to serve this traffic. Chapters 1 and 3 discuss this early period in more detail.

Along with providing the refrigerated car service came

the need for ice to fill the bunkers. The ice available before and at the turn of the century was mainly what nature provided (see Chapter 13 for early history of manufactured ice). The harvesting and storage of winter ice was certainly not a new concept, but private rail car operators had to develop a dependable network of ice storage and servicing stations along their western routes.

It was a fact, though, that there was no real organization for the handling of transcontinental shipments. When the Pacific Fruit Express Company was formed, only a loose-knit network of small natural ice plants existed along the lines of the Southern Pacific and Union Pacific. A few were owned by the railroads, but most were either owned locally or in some cases by the meat packers, principally the Armour Car Lines. These plants were in areas where winter was severe enough to form thick ice on harvesting ponds.

The locations of all the PFE owned natural ice plants that, as explained below, the company either built, purchased from its parent railroads, purchased from local owners or Armour were: Donner Creek Ice Co. at Donner Lake, California; Carlin, Nevada; North Powder, Oregon; Payette and Montpelier, Idaho; Evanston and Laramie, Wyoming; North Platte, Nebraska, and Council Bluffs, Iowa. PFE's purchase of the Armour facilities went into effect on October 1, 1907, and PFE also contracted with other private or parent-railroad owned facilities to provide icing services throughout PFE territory.

The company immediately developed plans to enlarge some of these natural ice plants (NIP), and it initiated the building of huge ice manufacturing plants of its own. These natural ice plants were phased out as ice manufacturing plants were built, so by 1936, PFE had only three remaining: North Powder, Carlin, and Laramie.

Donner Natural Ice Plant (NIP). Originally operated by Armour and purchased by PFE in 1907. Its ice pond was located on Donner Creek just below the outlet of Donner Lake, at the site of the present Donner Party State Park, about 2-½ miles west of Truckee, California. The Truckee region had become the largest ice-producing district on the Pacific Coast by the late 1800's. At that time, most of the ice used from southern Oregon to the Southwest came from the Truckee Basin. Besides Donner Lake, there were many other private artificial ice ponds along the nearby Truckee River, with more than 26 different ice production companies harvesting and shipping the ice by rail. At Truckee, PFE had an icing platform with 21 car capacity where re-icing of all eastbound and any westbound shipments was done.

The ice storage house, or gallery, at Donner had 12 uninsulated rooms. It was common practice to pack saw-dust around and over the top of the ice to prevent meltage, but PFE soon stopped that practice as the sawdust would clog the drains in the ice cars. There was a large mess hall, blacksmith shop, tool sheds, office and sleeping cabins.

The ice was shipped in box cars to supply the icing platform at Truckee, and also to loading points at Newcastle, Sacramento, Stockton, Winters, and other points where perishable freight originated. The private ice industry along the Truckee River continued to supply the ice requirements for all of northern California.

The Donner ice storage house was destroyed by fire in 1910. It was full of ice and the partitions burned between the rooms, leaving pyramids of ice standing. The storage house was never rebuilt and operations at Donner ceased. Ice was secured for the Truckee icing platform from the Union Ice Company ponds in the Boca area. Icing at Truckee was discontinued after the Sparks ice manufacturing plant was built in 1920. PFE's Donner property was sold in 1922 to The Native Sons of the Golden West and is now part of the Donner Party State Park.

TRUCKEE RIVER ICE EMPIRE

The high Sierra ice business in the Truckee River Basin was actually an outgrowth of mining conditions in the Comstock Lode surrounding Virginia City. This rich silver mining area was south of Reno, on the Nevada side of the Sierra slope. Geologically, the eastern side of the Sierras in this area is volcanically active. By the 1870's, the tunnels of the Comstock mines had been driven deep into the earth, and the problem of working in the intense heat became as important a factor as the extraction of the ore.

The quantities of underground hot water and the high temperatures encountered constantly increased below the 1000-foot level. In the Yellow Jacket shaft the temperature of the rock in a dry hole on the 3000-foot level was recorded at 167 degrees. The rock facing was constantly sprayed with cooling water. The miners at the deeper levels worked only in shoes, head protection, gloves, and breechcloth. They glistened in the candlelight as their bodies were cooled with water from hoses. Test drill holes would often strike steam vents or hot water deposits necessitating a change in direction. No other mines in the world had encountered such heat and such flooding or scalding water conditions.

Both the California and Consolidated Virginia Mines had tunnels with temperatures of 140 degrees at the 1850 foot level. These companies allocated a minimum of three gallons of iced drinking water and 95 lbs. of ice to be consumed by every miner working the deeper levels in an eight hour shift. The half fainting men constantly chewed ice fragments to cool their parched throats. It took four

Truckee Basin ice was shipped to many loading areas in California where it was stored for later use. Here in San Jose, PFE cars are being iced from horse-drawn wagons in a very rudimentary manner. Whitehead collection photo 12, UP Railroad Museum.

men to do the work of one under these conditions. The mules working these tunnels were also given ice water to drink five to six times each shift and their lips and heads were rubbed with ice as well.

In the beginning, before the mines hit levels necessitating the use of large quantities of ice, the ice and snow-ice supply business was carried on by the Virginia City Ice Company that had established itself in the early 1860's. They made ice by packing snow in storage cellars. Their first ice pond was built on an alkali mud flat, but the product was considered undesirable because of the bad taste. A second pond was constructed at Joy Lake, but inconsistent winter temperatures still necessitated an area to produce clear, thick ice.

Even before the Dutch Flat-Donner Lake toll road was completed in 1864, the Donner area of the Sierras was found to be ideal for the very best ice production. Horace Hale had been cutting ice off Lake Angela near the present day Donner Ski Ranch much earlier. In 1866 John Friend and W.E. Terry went into the Boca area to log ties for the Central Pacific. They built a small dam across the Little Truckee River to form a 30-acre mill pond. The natural lake ice was harvested that winter, and the business so rapidly developed that a second pond was built the following year. By 1872, the business was expanding so that they formed the Boca Mill and Ice Company.

Because cost of transportation by wagon was high, the ice industry in the Sierra did not really flourish until the completion of the Central Pacific through the area. Then tons of ice began moving to the big cities on the coast. At this time the Comstock mines had not reached the depths where heat demanded extravagant use of ice. Refrigerant demands for food in Virginia City were met by freight wagon from Reno, as the transcontinental line's railhead had reached there in 1868. When the Virginia & Truckee

Railroad was completed from Reno to Carson City in 1872, the Comstock mines had reached the levels with extreme heat. Most of the ice needed was now brought in by rail from the Truckee River Basin. The mines were now using about 10,000 tons annually in various ways.

The newly expanding ice industry utilized the construction camps left behind by the railroad as it proceeded across Donner Pass. The first ice house, which held a capacity of 8,000 tons, was built at Camp Twenty, later named Boca. Six ice houses 250 feet long were constructed with steep roofs to shed the deep winter snow. The walls were three feet thick and were filled with the oldest sawdust obtainable for insulation, as it would pack down tighter.

The Truckee River ice empire rapidly extended from Tahoe City to Verdi. Ice ponds appeared all along the river: at Polaris, Prosser Creek, Bronco Creek, Boca, Iceland, Farad, Floriston, Gray Creek, and Verdi. By 1880 the ice companies had the capacity of producing 60,000 tons of ice per year. The industry was so important that the Central Pacific constructed several ice storage houses and loading docks for speedy loading of ice into box cars for shipment to the demanding public. Nearly a third of the ice went to the San Francisco area.

The primary ponds were at Boca, Prosser and Iceland, but so many small companies had started along the Truckee River that competition was almost disastrous in 1882. During the summer of that year many of the companies incorporated under the name of the Union Ice Company. The company's main function was to distribute the ice harvest and establish uniform prices for the various outlets in the cities. Soon the organization realized it should also control the ice ponds, so by 1891, the Union Ice Company began acquiring direct control of the harvesting ponds and ice houses. As the years went on, the Union Ice Company would become the largest to serve California.

Carlin. The original ice storage gallery on the SP, with horses pulling cutting plows or blades. UP Railroad Museum photo 500.009.

By 1907 the natural ice facilities located at Boca, Prosser and Iceland had a production and storage capability of 100,000 tons, and the Union Ice Company controlled the entire industry in the Truckee Canyon. The company provided much of the ice used by the new PFE company's contracted icing facilities in California's Central Valley.

The Truckee River natural ice ponds gradually gave way to the Union Ice Company's mechanical ice manufacturing plants built in the local areas of need. The Boca ice ponds were the last to close down, and that was not until 1927. A local business that developed and flourished by meeting the unique needs of the Comstock mines, that also gained markets throughout the West by use of rail transportation, and the business that spawned the Union Ice Company had finally come to an end. (Material from PFE *Newsletter*)

Carlin NIP. Regular icing station until 1951. Location: almost midway between Sparks (283 miles to the west) and Ogden (209 miles to the east), on land between the Southern Pacific and Western Pacific yards.

The construction of the PFE ice harvesting plant at Carlin was started in 1907. The original six-room ice storage gallery was built in the SP's Carlin yards, but the first ice pond was built at Tonka, in the Humboldt River canyon seven miles east of Carlin. The ice was to be loaded in box cars for transportation to the Carlin ice house for storage. The house and pond were finished by fall, and the ice harvest was anticipated with the winter's cold, but as it turned out, no ice was stored that year.

The pond was filled and ice began building up. Before the first harvest, though, the levee gave way from the pressure of the ice. The slope of the levee on the inside was constructed too steeply, and the expanding ice could not crawl up the slope, thus causing its collapse one afternoon when the temperature rose above normal. Then flooding destroyed the pond the next two successive years. Ice had to be shipped

to Carlin from the Donner and Evanston plants during those three years.

In 1910, PFE purchased an additional 50 acres and built a new 25-acre pond between the SP and WP tracks adjacent to its ice house on the SP side. At that time PFE also had a small 6,000-ton ice storage house and icing platform alongside the Western Pacific tracks. PFE forces filled the WP ice house, but originally the WP used their own men to re-ice their trains. In the 1920-22 period the WP, with varying agreements, had contracted PFE to do all of their car icing for their refrigerator service (PFE eventually did all car repairs too), but in 1922 the Western Pacific constructed its own 10,000-ton storage house and ice pond at Carlin.

During World War I, under the USRA, the two railroads shared paired track operations on their parallel lines between Weso (Winnemucca) and Alazon (Wells), Nevada. That practice was discontinued in March, 1920, but in August, 1924, the two lines resumed the joint trackage rights (see Chapter 1). In that same year the PFE ice storage house and their operations on the WP were moved to the SP side of the pond as both roads' westbound trains now operated over the SP to Alazon, and re-icing was done at the PFE platform on the SP line. In 1923 PFE increased the pond to 33 acres, and by 1927, it had been enlarged to 50 acres to meet growing requirements.

This lake was originally formed by impounding the waters from Maggie Creek that flowed into the basin, and by adding any additional water as needed by pumping from the Humboldt River. Pumping was first by means of a single gas pump and eventually after 1919 by three electric centrifugal pumps. The lake was about 3200 ft. long by 600 ft. wide and had a depth of 3 to 5 feet at the time freezing weather came, usually in December. Crop estimates for the annual harvest were: 10" thick ice – 34,596 tons, 15" thick ice – 51,890 tons, 20" thick ice – 69,184 tons (twice the thickness yielded twice the tonnage). The storage house had a total of 16 rooms, 50 ft. by 100 ft., and could hold nearly 55,000 tons. Excess ice was either shipped to other locations or stored outside, covered with insulative tarpaulins and used first.

The freezing ice would be crystal clear, and each freeze showed in distinct layers. Nights with a minimum temperature of 23 degrees below zero would account for layers 3 inches thick, and from there, the layers would taper off to ½ inch or less, depending on the temperature, each layer as clearly defined as rock strata.

It was necessary to continually scrape off any snow which fell on the ice as it acted as an insulative blanket, preventing further freezing. Originally this was done by horse-drawn plows and later by small trucks equipped with chained tires and front mounted plows.

The ice harvest, or cutting, started when the ice was frozen to the required thickness, or to as thick as Mother Nature would provide. The plant manager would make the decision to "open the pond" to start the harvest. This was usually in early January. The normal harvest was a period of about three weeks, and from 160 to 200 men were employed. As PFE's wages were higher than most, transient workers usually flocked into the area when ice harvesting began.

First, a straight line was surveyed across the pond in both directions and was marked with a groove by means of a small machine that looked like a cultivator, initially horse drawn. The first cut in each direction was done by hand. Then a horse-drawn cutting plow with a 22" guide that slid along the first cut was drawn across the pond. The cutting plow would make two or three passes to make a cut to the required depth. Each "plower" had to provide his own horses, and received $2.50 per day for his team and $2.50 a day for his own 10 hours work. The "plowers" would start their work day earlier than the rest of the ice crew to get a head start.

Later, in 1919, power saws appeared, usually a four-cylinder gasoline engine with a circular lumber sawblade hooked up behind. The power saws had a guide to follow the previously marked grooves and cut the ice to a depth of 9 to 10 inches, throwing a stream of ice chips out behind for 30 feet or more.

Men called the "face-spudders" followed each saw, several cuts behind, and with a heavy steel spade-like "splitter" bar and with regular measured strokes, divided the ice into long strips of two cake widths. These strips were roped and floated, drawn by horses, to the channel entrance. At the channel other "spudders" broke the large ice raft into 8, then 4, 2, and single blocks.

The channel led to an incline chain conveyor where the ice was caught on wooden bars and conveyed up the incline to the ice storage building which was called the "gallery." The gallery's 16 rooms were filled simultaneously and the gallery incline chain conveyor could be raised as the level of ice filled the rooms.

Each man had his specific job so there was no wasted effort from the time the cake left the ice field until it was stored. Mounting the incline, the blocks were swept clean of snow and loose ice by an adjustable brush. At the top, the blocks were moved along the adjustable conveyor deck where men with "picaroons" kicked them off into appropriate rooms. Men inside, "switchers," caught the blocks and moved them to the parts of the room being filled. PFE stored the blocks on edge, thus each layer in the storeroom was always an even 22 inches high. Storage on the top or bottom side of each block would have produced an uneven layer due to irregular thickness of the natural ice.

This work went on 10 hours every day until the harvest was completed. A good day's run was 3000 tons, or 6,000,000 pounds cut and stored. Each cake of 14 inch thick ice weighed 225 lbs, which meant the handling of about 26,667 cakes a day or over 44 cakes per minute. A

Carlin. Motorized ice saws were introduced around 1919. This view of Carlin in the early 1920's shows three such gasoline-powered units. By this time, the ice storage gallery had been much expanded, to 14 rooms. PFE photo, CSRM.

Snow had to be plowed off the ice daily to keep the rate of freezing as high as possible. Snow would act to insulate the ice from colder air. All six photos, UP Railroad Museum.

When the pond was "opened," the surface was first marked with lines apart. This gas-powered marking machine replaced a horse-drawn

A gasoline-powered ice saw in action. These replaced horse-drawn cutters after 1920.

A raft of ice cakes is being pulled by one man to the incline. When reaches the ice house, the raft will be split further.

Men called "spudders" at the channel to the incline broke up the ice raft into single blocks.

Inside the gallery, "switchers" sent the blocks of ice in rotation to me with "pickaroons" who stacked the ice on edge.

60,000 ton harvest involved cutting and handling into and out of storage of more than one-half million cakes of ice!

Eventually there were two large storage galleries with a total of 60,000 tons capacity. The original building was increased to 14 rooms by 1921. A second gallery, a few hundred feet to the west, would ultimately total 12 rooms (two of which were the storage rooms brought over from the WP side), and was built between 1923 and 1928. This huge plant also incorporated a two-story building with a dining room and kitchen on the bottom floor and bunk-rooms on the second floor. There were also three other bunkhouses, a machine shop, blacksmith shop, other storage buildings, and offices.

The island type icing platform, lengthened in 1921, '26, '27, and '29, to handle traffic increases, was eventually 80 carlengths (3520'), roofed, painted gray. There was a 6-car loading and a 2-car unloading platform. A 12-carlength section of the main platform burned in 1945 and was rebuilt.

Carlin was a re-icing stop for all eastbound and west-bound loads. Over 60,000 cars were re-iced here annually, each car averaging 1500 to 2000 lbs of ice, requiring between 50,000 to 55,000 tons annually. In addition, 5000 tons were provided for Southern Pacific's Salt Lake Division Stores Department, passenger trains, and station requirements.

The 1945 fire also destroyed several rooms of the ice storage gallery which housed 32,000 tons of the total 60,000 ton capacity. To protect the limited storage and supply, Carlin was discontinued as a regular icing station from October 1 to April 15 of each year. Nonetheless, PFE had to ship in 6 to 8000 tons each year. By 1948, the pond at Carlin had been reduced to two smaller ponds, one 25 acres, and one 10 acres. Better train performances by the SP brought about by dieselization and other improvements decreased the necessity of Carlin, as trains could run Sparks-Ogden without needing re-icing. The main Carlin ice storage house burned in 1950, and icing there was discontinued shortly afterward in 1951. In 1952 heater and ventilation services were also discontinued.

The late A. L. "Pete" Holst began work for PFE in 1917 loading ice in Roseville, and rose through the ranks of the Car Service Dept. In 1949, he became Assistant General Manager, the number two position in PFE, and retired from that position in 1963, culminating 45 years of service. His memories are a priceless view of PFE's early days.

Recollections of Carlin by Pete Holst:

"Well, I started to work for PFE in May of 1917, in Roseville. I worked a month on the ice deck, and then went to the Stores Department and worked the balance of the summer of '17 there. When business dropped off, I was laid off. Then a job came up at the ice plant for a timekeeper clerk, and I worked in the ice plant office until 1918.

Several boys in Roseville and I went to Stanford University and the Student Army Training Camp that was there during WW I. We were soon let out after the Armistice, though. On the way back home I stopped in the PFE office at San Francisco. Assistant General Manager McClymonds gave me a long tale that I had to come back to the PFE. He said he needed me to go to North Powder, Oregon, for the ice harvest. I told him I was planning to go duck hunting with one of my buddies. He said, 'Fine, we don't need you until the first of January.'

I came back, with lots of ducks, and stopped in at Roseville to give my old plant manager some birds, and he said, 'Where in hell have you been?' He said that San Francisco had been on the phone every day. 'Jack Lorenz was supposed to go to Carlin as timekeeper for the ice harvest, but he's in the hospital, and you're supposed to be in Carlin.'

So, I caught a train east and landed in Carlin the next morning, Christmas Day. Twenty below zero, and it never changed, day after day. That was the damnedest cold winter I ever put in! Oh, it was a good place for an ice harvest, and things happened all the time during the harvest. New Year's morning, the men all struck. See, most of the crew there were shipped in from Ogden, Sacramento and San Francisco, and we couldn't depend on 'em at all. They wanted time and a half for working that holiday. Well, in those days PFE never heard of time and a half. So, I was paying 'em off for the time in December and that first six hours of January, probably about 150 of 'em. Well, with our system of timekeeping, that was one hell of a job.

They pumped the water into the pond at Carlin from the Humboldt River, about a quarter of a mile away, until they got the pond three to five feet deep. We had men fall in it, and horses too, but they'd always get out. That winter was the worst, because we not only had strikes, but problems with the river pumps. They'd lose their prime, and always in the middle of the night. One week, Jack Matthews, the agent there, and I had already made two night hikes at one or two in the morning through the snow to the river. Boy, that intake pipe was about ten feet down in the water and you had to pull it up, take all the bolts off and plug it up with mud, and then ease it down in there again to prime it to start and get it going.

Well, the third night the watchman came and told us,

281

North Powder. This view shows the plant after its 1910 upgrading. The salt storage room is at the near end of the ice deck, and the pond and incline are at the left. Whitehead collection photo 1, UP Railroad Museum.

'All hell's broke.' When we got down there to the river, we found that the piston on the big pump had let go and went right through the end of the head of the cylinder and out into the river! It was a gasoline engine and it had a lot of history. They would ship it to Brawley in the summertime to power the deck there and then back to Carlin in the winter. We were not half through the harvest, and in two days the ice would be on the ground as we'd have no water under it. I'd have to pay off the crew again until we could get the pump fixed.

Matthews got the trainmaster out of bed and got his speeder car, as we had no telephones then between Carlin and San Francisco. They went to Elko, and he phoned an order for wiring and electric motors for the pumps from the San Francisco office. We had to generate our own electricity at Carlin at that time, too. We used a Bessemer gas engine that had been on display at the San Francisco Fair in 1915, and another old engine that generated power for the ice deck. It was five days before we had the new electric motors set up, and then it took three days of pumping to lift the ice off the bottom. Anyway, we filled the ice house that winter, and I went back to Roseville. That was my breaking in on the ice harvest business.

Come ice harvest the next year, and back to Carlin I went. The winter of 1919 was good, but the winter of '20, though fairly cold, was not the 20 below zero that was needed to produced good thick ice. We never liked to open a pond [start the harvest] until we had, say, at least twelve to fourteen inches of ice. We cut all our ice at 22 inches square with whatever thickness we could get from nature. We were the only ones that did that, as the Union Ice Co. at Boca and all the rest of the private companies cut theirs 22 by 28 inches.

It got a little colder for a couple of nights, and I went out and measured only nine inches of ice. That was the best I could get for days. I told 'em, 'We've got to open this thing or we're not going to get a harvest.' I went out the next day and fudged a half an inch a day. The second day I said, 'We got ten inches and we've got to open.' We opened the pond and cut every inch of that ice, and got only about two-thirds of the rooms full. We never got another freeze of any kind that year."

North Powder NIP. Regular icing station. Location was between La Grande and Baker, Oregon, near the Powder River on the main line of the Oregon, Washington Railway & Navigation Co. (OWR&N), a subsidiary of the UP. This was originally a significant PFE icing station for all the Pacific Northwest's fruit and vegetable shipments eastbound. The plant also furnished carload lots of ice for other PFE ice stations to the west.

The first facilities were built here in the mid-1880's by private shippers. They had considered a natural ice plant at Meacham, Oregon, to the west, but chose North Powder because it had temperatures considerably lower. Comparison records kept during the winter of 1883 showed February temperatures in Meacham at 38 below zero, while North Powder registered –61 °F on the same day, cold enough for plenty of ice!

In 1910 PFE upgraded the North Powder plant with a new 15,000-ton storage gallery that had a single track platform on one side and loading/unloading dock and conveyor on the pond side. A major portion of the plant was destroyed by fire in July, 1937. With the construction of PFE's new icing platform and facilities at La Grande in 1937, the Company, in 1938, decided to sell the North Powder property rather than rebuild. This left Carlin and Laramie as the only active natural ice plants.

Payette NIP. Regular icing station. Location on the main line of the Oregon Short Line (OSL), a UP subsidiary. This PFE plant, acquired from Armour in 1907, furnished some of the initial icing for the early agricultural and fruit districts developing in western Idaho including those along the New Meadows Branch, the New Plymouth and Emmett Branch, and the Burns and Brogan Branches in eastern Oregon.

The ice was secured from the Payette River and a small pond. Between the pond and the storage house was a 20-ft. high embankment. A wood incline was built, and horses were used to drag two blocks of ice at a time to the top of the ridge, where the blocks were then slid down a chute into the small storage house. PFE continued operating this plant even after the company purchased the ice manufacturing plant at Nampa in 1921. Ice was harvested to supplement the Nampa plant for a short time, but use of the facilities was stopped in 1923. The 29-acre property was sold to the Palumbo-Arata Fruit Co. in 1930 for $3000.

Recollections of Pete Holst:

"I put up ice at Payette two winters. The ice harvest there would take a long time because of the layout. The old guy that ran the place had first managed the ice pond at Donner. He came from Bath, Maine, and he was running the Donner Ice Company when PFE took it over from that Armour outfit. He was a character though. Blinn was his name, W.D. Blinn. He came to Donner before 1900. He'd tell all about those guys going into Truckee. Truckee was real wild in those days. He told me that in Truckee he'd get the payroll from D.O. Mills, the banker in Sacramento, and the paperwork was just beyond him entirely. He said, 'Mills would send me a sack of twenty-dollar and ten-dollar gold pieces, and that's what I paid off the workers with.'

PFE sent him to Carlin when they built that whole layout there. After a few years, they sent him to Payette. The Armour outfit had a little ice house and an agent's house there that we took over. What a character he was! He'd tell stories about when they built the Oregon and Washington line, the OWR&N, you know, and he was a meat hunter for 'em. He went out and killed deer and antelope for meat in the work camps. After that road was done, he came down to California and worked out of Santa Barbara building the SP's new line up the coast, shooting goats over on the island, Santa Cruz Island, for meat for the crews.

The agent's house at Payette had one room that was Blinn's office, a big bare room, you know, and some other rooms for him and his wife. He got married when he was about 70 years old, see, to his childhood sweetheart back in Maine. She had been a schoolteacher all her life.

That old Yankee, now he limped when he walked, and one night I said, 'How come?' Well, he took his shoes off and showed me. He said, 'I had corns on all those toes and they got to hurting like hell, so I took a chisel and cut 'em off after I first stuck my feet in the ice pond and froze 'em up.' He'd go over to the wood stove, and up in back of it he had a ten-inch file, and he'd sit there and file his fingernails. That's the kind of character he was."

Montpelier NIP. Regular icing station. Located on the OSL main line. This PFE plant on the eastern Idaho border was constructed in 1915 to provide re-icing for eastbound OSL trains routed via the Pocatello-Granger line, for any westbound shipments as required, and for loads originating in the Blackfoot-Idaho Falls area. PFE had been operating an obsolete ice storage house in Pocatello with ice shipped

Montpelier. This natural ice plant was about a mile from town. (**Above**) The bunk house, eating hall, shop and storage sheds were at the back of the plant by the pond, which is dry in this summer view. (**Below**) From trackside can be seen the plant manager's house, and the ice deck and storage gallery. Apparently an eastbound fruit block is due, as stacks of burlap-blanketed ice line the entire length of the deck. Both photos, PFE from CSRM.

Evanston. In the 1915 era after PFE added additional storage galleries, the plant looked like this. The bunk cars may have been used to house men during the ice harvest. UP Railroad Museum photo 500.000.

in from Humphrey to re-ice trains up to that time.

There was a 25-carlength single platform, an ice storage house, and a short loading/unloading deck. The ice pond was immediately adjacent to the back side of the platform. The facility was supplemental after the Pocatello ice manufacturing plant went into service in 1922, and was abandoned in 1933, as trains could run Pocatello-Laramie with minimal claim hazard.

In 1945 a small ice storage house and platform facilities were reinstalled here to ice potato shipments originating north of Pocatello during the season from August 20, to October 10, to avoid congestion in the Pocatello yard. In 1950 the Union Pacific completely modernized their Pocatello yards, and the new yard could easily handle all traffic. The reefers from the north could be iced there, and in that year Montpelier was retired.

Recollections of Pete Holst:

"The ice plant at Montpelier was a mile out of town. I know how far that was because when I first got there, I'd stay at the hotel in town. I'd catch a ride out with a couple of fellows that lived in the country. They'd pick me up in their sleigh and we'd drive out past the stockyards. I'd have to stay out there some evenings and check how much ice we'd run, and make out the wires to send to San Francisco. I'd have to walk the tracks back to town. After my wife arrived, we lived in the agent's house next to the plant. At Montpelier, the first power ice saws we had were electric, and we dragged big electrical cables all around the pond."

Evanston NIP. Regular icing station. PFE first leased the harvesting ponds, storage plant and icing platform that were originally built in 1897 by the UP. Evanston is on the UP main line east of Ogden, near Wyoming's western border. It had two connecting ponds, covering ten and thirteen acres each. The ponds were adjacent to the tracks just two blocks east from the center of town. By 1901 there were six storage galleries. PFE added three more in 1909 to bring the storage capacity to 35,000 tons.

Temperatures here in winter were severely low enough, 35 to 40 degrees below zero, that a foot-and-a-half of ice could form in just 20 days. The ponds could be harvested

Evanston. The ice deck in use, around 1911, with the Bohn ice hatch covers evident (see Chapter 4). Wm. W. Kratville collection.

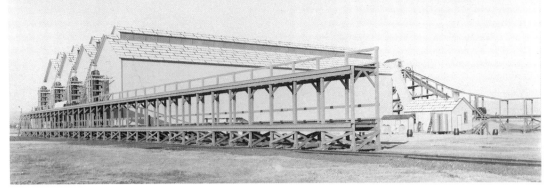

Laramie. The original 1906 natural ice plant at Laramie, built by UP. UP Railroad Museum photo 500.003.

three or four times each season, and more than 100 men were employed during these operations. After sufficient ice was placed in storage from each day's harvest, the remaining ice was shipped to Ogden by a special train a day. An agent was kept there year-round to also ship stored ice to Ogden or other PFE plants. It was standard procedure for all these plants to supplement each other as local surplus or shortages demanded.

In 1920, the winter at Carlin was mild, causing a harvest of only a nine-inch thickness. This didn't nearly fill the storage houses, so the Carlin harvesting crew was moved to Evanston, where severe temperatures there had produced more than one harvest and enough ice to fill Evanston's storage galleries plus Ogden's storage house. Carlin obtained an additional 10,000 tons of ice shipped in by rail.

This plant was abandoned in 1921, when PFE opened its ice manufacturing plant in Ogden. The ice ponds were still harvested for some time by private business for home ice box service and soft drink bottling operations. A fire finally destroyed several ice houses and the UP tore down the remaining buildings and ice deck.

Laramie NIP. Regular icing station. This original PFE facility was actually built on the high Wyoming plains by the UP in 1906 and served as the major re-icing station for shipments east out of Ogden or Idaho. (Prior to that time the UP used its own Ice Transfer Plant at Cheyenne as its re-icing station.) There were two connecting ponds, 20 and 33 acres, and the normal severe winters guaranteed at least two harvests, each harvest lasting three weeks.

Horse-drawn cutting equipment allowed for only 800 to 900 tons cut and stored daily. Favorable weather for harvesting at Laramie was very limited and it was necessary to take advantage of it. In 1922 the introduction of gasoline field saws permitted the normal contingent of two hundred

workmen to cut and store 2,500 to 3,000 tons of ice each eight-hour workday. The cakes were the standard 22 inches in width and length, the thickness varying as to the freeze.

The ice storage gallery was doubled in size in 1909. Additional ice storage rooms were built to increase capacity to 25,000 tons in 1920, along with a new 55-carlength island type icing platform.

In 1923 flood waters from a rampaging Laramie River devastated these ice storage buildings. A new ice storage house was built, and as its capacity was increased over the years, it became what is believed to be the largest ice storage gallery in the world, eventually being 900 ft. long, 108 ft. wide, and 34 ft. high. It would eventually have 16 huge rooms that could store a total of 71,000 tons. Thousands of additional tons were often stockpiled outside, covered by heavy tarpaulins for insulation. In 1946 two such stockpiles were stacked outside, each measuring 100 ft.

Laramie. Flood damage to the storage house in 1923. Whitehead collection photo 20, UP Railroad Museum.

Laramie. The new facilities, built after the 1923 flood, remained on the north side of the UP main line. PFE photo, CSRM.

Laramie. This 1924 view shows the additional storage galleries which had been added. PFE photo, CSRM.

long, 45 ft. wide, and 22 ft. high. A season total could exceed 80,000 tons of ice.

By 1929 the icing platform was 80 carlengths and roofed. This was replaced with a new 85-carlength icing platform and top icing sub-deck in 1946.

With the ever-present winds of the Laramie Plains, the workmen there felt the ice cleats they strapped to their boots were not only for safety and leverage, but were more to keep themselves from being blown off the pond!

Laramie was converted to an ice manufacturing plant in 1951, as described in Chapter 13, making it the last natural ice facility in the PFE system, and since PFE was the largest refrigerated car operator, Laramie was undoubtedly the last natural ice plant of its size in the country and probably the world. The old Laramie ice storage house later became a

timber shipping plant and was still in use as late as 1978. An interesting fact is that the winter of 1951, the year the new plant went into operation, was the first winter in the history of the natural ice plant that a cover of ice failed to form on the ice pond.

North Platte NIP. Regular icing station on the UP main line. Originally built by UP in 1896 and leased by PFE, was subsequently enlarged to have 18 rooms with a storage capacity of 40,000 tons and a 1540' platform, making it the largest ice storage gallery in the world in the 1918 era. (By 1923 Laramie surpassed North Platte's storage capacity to become the largest storage gallery.) The storage rooms followed the early design of the UP and were without insulation, resulting in heavy shrinkage. Ice was secured for

Laramie. Construction scene of new galleries at Laramie from the pond side. The platform with the railing running the entire length carried the chain that moved the ice to the different storage galleries. All rooms were filled to a given level, then the entire platform was raised, until the rooms were filled to the top. PFE photo, CSRM.

Laramie. Here the "spudders" are splitting up an ice raft into single blocks. Note saw-cut marks on the ice, and workers' pickaroons. Photo 7052-2, UP Railroad Museum.

Laramie. The two men on the stools, called "switchers," are directing the blocks to the men stacking the ice coming into the room on the incline. PFE photo, CSRM.

the shipping season by harvesting ice from a pond and from the nearby Platte River. The natural ice plant was phased out by the early 1920's when an ice manufacturing plant was built here.

Council Bluffs NIP. Regular icing station. Natural ice harvesting facilities were established here in the early 1890's by Armour and other meat packers to ice carloads originating just across the Missouri River at the growing Omaha stockyard and slaughterhouse operations. The facility was purchased from Armour in 1906 to allow PFE icing without

depending upon foreign line icing and higher charges.

There was an ice pond in the Missouri River bottom land adjacent to the storage house. Additional ice was also harvested from Seymour Lake in Omaha and shipped by carload for storage at the Council Bluffs facility. Ice may also have been shipped from more distant points. The plant was converted to an ice manufacturing plant in 1921.

The Council Bluffs plant completed the chain of early PFE natural ice harvesting, storage, and transfer plants that stretched eastward from central California and the Pacific Northwest.

North Platte. The Union Pacific ice house at North Platte which was leased to PFE at its 1906 startup, shown about 1918. Photo 500.012, UP Railroad Museum.

(Above) These two views show loading of river or pond ice directly into boxcars for shipment to ice storage houses on the main line. Location is unknown but possibly is along the Platte River in Nebraska. UP Railroad Museum.

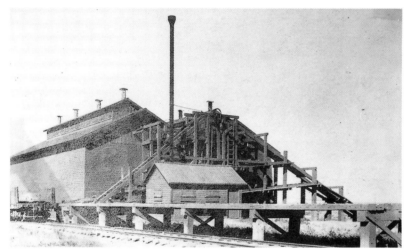

(Left) Rare view of 1905-era ice storage and transfer plant on UP. Note absence of ice deck, with transfer deck only. Location unknown. Wm. W. Kratville collection.

(Opposite page) Union Pacific's 1909 list of ice storage houses in Nebraska, Kansas, and Colorado. Note that PFE furnished most of the houses with ice. President's Office correspondence file, UP Railroad Museum.

North Powder. The summer ice gang, carrying their tools, getting set for the Fourth of July parade, 1914. Note the elegant vest on the dog. Whitehead photo 14, UP Railroad Museum.

UNION PACIFIC RAILROAD COMPANY

SUBJECT: -Putting up ice - winter 1909-10.

FILED WITH AGREEMENT
AUDIT NO. 11694

Omaha, Nebr. Dec.4, 1909. IN REPLY PLEASE REFER TO

U. P. R. R. Co.
Agreement
Audit No. 13868

Mr. J. Van Rensselaer,

Superintendent, Pacific Fruit Express Co.

Dear Sir:-

Replying to your letters of November 3rd and 24th in regard to putting up ice: The filling of Union Pacific Railroad ice houses at various points should be handled as follows:

Co.Bluffs	Pass.Yd.House	1500	Tons mountain ice	PFE furnish; UP fill
"	Frt.Yd.House	1900	Tons mountain ice	PFE furnish; UP fill
Omaha	Lower Yard Hse	1000	Tons Cut Off Lake	U.P. furnish and fill
"	6th Street Hse	1200	Tons mountain ice	PFE funish; UP fill
"	Union Sta. Hse	1900	Tons mountain ice	PFE furnish; UP fill
Gr.Island	Passgr.House	700	Tons mountain ice	PFE furnish and fill
"	B&M Xing House	2000	Tons mountain ice	PFE furnish and fill
Columbus		1500	T Gothenburg Ice	PFE furnish; UP fill
Kearney		550	T Gothenburg Ice	PFE furnish; UP fill
Lincoln		700	Tons Valley ice	U.P.furnish and fill
Beatrice		500	Tons Valley ice	U.P.furnish and fill
Denver	House No.1	300	Tons Mountain ice	PFE furnish; UP fill
"	House No.2	1800	Tons mountain ice	PFE furnish; UP fill
Shar.Sprgs.	House No.1	850	Tons mountain ice	PFE furnish; UP fill
Hugo	House No.1	800	Tons mountain ice	PFE furnish UP fill
Sterling	House No.1	400	Tons mountain ice	PFE furnish; UP fill
Oakley	House No.1	260	Tons mountain ice	PFE furnish; UP fill
Armstrong		6000	tons	PFE furnish; UP fill
Juc.City		2500	tons	PFE furnish; UP fill
Solomon		300	tons	PFE furnish; UP fill
Salina		1300	tons	PFE furnish UP fill
Plainville		260	tons	PFE furnish; UP fill
Harrison		180	tons	PFE furnish; UP fill
Leavenworth		260	tons	PFE furnish; UP fill
No.Platte	House No.1	1755	tons mountain ice	PFE furnish and fill
"	House No.2	2540	Tons mountain ice	PFE furnish and fill
"	House No. 3	2313	Tons mountain ice	PFE furnish and fill
Cheyenne	House No.2	1421	Tons mountain ice	PFE furnish, UP fill
"	House No.3	450	tons mountain ice	PFE furnish, UP fill
Sidney		1050	Tons local ice	UP furnish and fill
Rawlins		1200	Tons mountain ice	PFE furnish; UP fill
Evanston		100	Tons local ice	PFE furnish and fill

---- Ice from Gothenburg or other Nebraska Division points.

At all points not shown in the above statement the ice should be furnished and put in the houses by the Pacific Fruit Express Company's forces, and at all P.F.E. Houses located atpoints shown in the above statement, the furnishing of ice and filling to be on the same basis as I have shown for the U.P.R.R. houses.

A skilled engineer works steam on his big 4-8-2 locomotive, an Mt-3 built in SP's own shops, as he eases a Salinas reefer block to the ice deck "spot" in Roseville in 1947.

13

ICE MANUFACTURING
AND
ICE TRANSFER PLANTS

Colton IMP. This view, looking east in about 1920, shows the ice storage room, cooling towers (right), and precooling shed (at left) of one of PFE's busier ice manufacturing plants. PFE photo, CSRM.

In its first few years of operation PFE had to depend almost entirely upon the existing ice plants of its parent railroads or commercial companies for its ice requirements. It did build the company's first ice manufacturing plants at Roseville (1908) and Colton (1910), but about 80 per cent of the ice it used was purchased from commercial concerns, and a very large portion of that was natural ice harvested from ponds. The first successful ammonia compression machines were introduced by C.P.G. Linde of Germany and David Boyle of the United States during 1873-75, but commercial application of these new forms of apparatus to manufacture ice did not gain wide acceptance until the turn of the century.

In 1907 the PFE handled 48,902 carloads of perishables, 50 percent of which were given refrigeration service requiring 250,000 tons of ice. By 1921 PFE's volume of perishables had increased to 170,000 carloads, of which 70 percent moved with ice in the bunkers and required a total

of 1,600,000 tons of ice. Within its first decade PFE's demand had exceeded the supply of commercial ice.

During the World War I period the production and distribution of perishable shipments received a considerable stimulus. Because of various reasons, including the impossibility of securing the necessary materials for construction purposes, this increase in traffic was not met by a corresponding increase in icing facilities. At the war's end, the parent railroads deemed it advisable for PFE to own and operate all main line icing facilities to insure more economical and prompt handling, and the company adopted an aggressive plan to build its own Ice Manufacturing Plants (IMP).

Early in 1920 PFE received authority to proceed with a construction program which contemplated an expenditure of approximately $4 million for new and enlarged ice plants and icing facilities. A standard layout plan and design for buildings was adopted and construction was

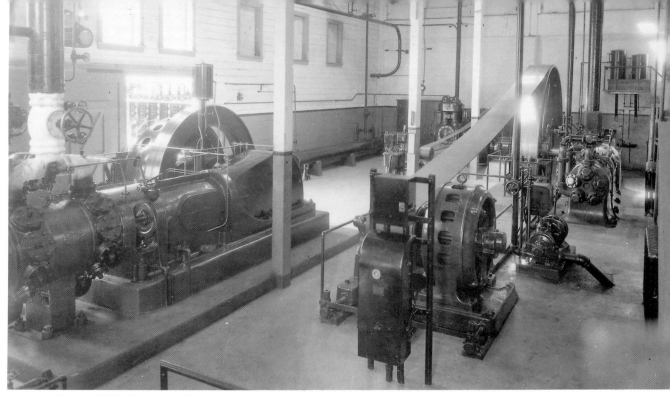

Nampa IMP. The original Harris ammonia compressor and the No. 1 well pump. In 1958, New York compressors were installed. PFE photo, CSRM.

started on several plants as soon as the foundation drawings were prepared. This action was taken to prevent delays that would have occurred if startup had been held off until final plans and bidding from all contractors were complete. An example of the dispatch with which the work was handled: ground was broken at Council Bluffs on March 21, 1921; the plant was placed in operation on Aug. 1st.

Reinforced concrete was used almost exclusively throughout these plants, including the pilaster and curtain wall construction. The insulation for the storage rooms was two to three inches of waterproof "Lith," faced with two inches of cork. The "Lith" insulating material was a product of the Union Fiber Co., Winona, Minn. The wall

construction of cork plus "Lith" had a heat transmission of less than 0.9 B.T.U. per sq. ft. per day per degree difference in temperature. Application in thickness varied as to the climate in which each IMP was built.

With the exception of four steam-driven plants (Roseville, Las Vegas, Tucson, and North Platte), all ammonia compressors were electrically operated. The flooded system was adopted as standard for all freezing tanks. Tank coils were split transversely in the center, each coil half being provided with a separate feed. Agitators were provided to insure proper circulation of the brine in the freezing tanks, and electric hoist and power-driven cranes were installed. All cans were refilled automatically at the ice

Filling ice cans (North Platte, left) and typical tank room floor with can hoist (Nampa, right). UP Railroad Museum.

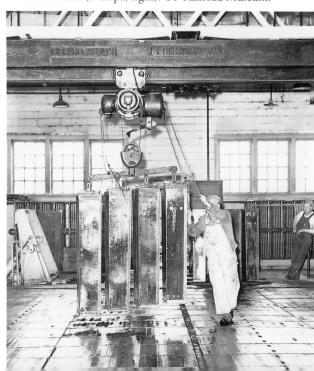

292

Laramie IMP. In these views, the new ice deck is under construction. Standard bents are being assembled (left) and erected (right) in April, 1946. They were placed on PFE's typical 11-ft. centers. PFE photos, CSRM.

dump location. The standard PFE 300-lb. ice block inspired a sign in many ice houses: "That block of ice is bigger and tougher than you. Watch it. Safety First." The incline elevators as well as the elevating and lowering machines and conveyors were of PFE's own design. The size and capacity of these new plants varied in accordance with seasonal ice demands of each location.

By the mid-1920's, PFE had constructed or purchased 18 such plants in the United States that could produce 5560 tons daily and had a combined storage capacity of 330,900 tons. The company also had an IMP built at Empalme, Mexico, and the Laramie IMP was built in 1951 to replace the natural ice harvesting facility there. Roseville was the largest of all PFE plants, known as the largest of its kind in the world, having a daily manufacturing capacity of 1300 tons, and a storage capacity of 53,000 tons.

Icing requirements continued to rise as new and expanding croplands opened up in the west, originating spiraling numbers of car loads. In 1923, PFE used 1.9 million tons of ice. Business had increased so by the year 1929, that the bunkers of PFE reefers consumed 2.3 million tons of ice. By 1939, annual ice consumption was down to 1.23 million tons, but this was not due to a decrease in shipments. Rather, it could be attributed to faster train movements which allowed for more efficient icing services. The "reefer blocks" were moving further before the need to re-ice, so less ice was required.

The annual loadings grew from the relatively meager 48,902 cars in 1907, to 339,336 carloads in 1936, and continued to expand each year until 1952, when PFE experienced its greatest (excluding war years) annual number of carloads, 420,392 shipments handled. In that year the company operated 18 ice manufacturing plants (some plants had been sold), owned and operated 51 icing platforms and contracted with nearly 50 private ice companies to provide protective service. Ice consumed in 1952 was 2,500,000 tons. It was not until 1953 that two icing

platforms, Fresno and Los Angeles, had mechanical icing machines installed, so those millions of tons of ice were delivered to ice bunkers by backbreaking manual labor.

Mechanical icing afforded considerable savings in labor and cost. A machine with 5 men was capable of initially icing 30 cars in 45 minutes, whereas the manual method required at least 20 men. Estimated annual savings in cost at a platform with the mechanical icing machines was around $40,000. It was the enormous amounts of labor and cost that led to the installation of these machines at other major icing decks (Table 13-1).

Efficient ice delivery was from icing platforms at car height. Only a few emergency icing stations did not have such a deck, and at these points ice was delivered by truck and elevator. PFE had a standard platform design that had been developed over the years (see drawing, next page), but it was commonly modified to suit local conditions. Platforms ranged in length from a few cars to over 100 cars, and were either single sided or island type. PFE's icing decks were built in multiples of 44 feet, which was the coupled length of a 41-ft. ice refrigerator car.

These platforms were frame structures, generally 14 ft. high, many with a shelter roof, and a width of 14 ft. on a island platform. Single platforms ranged in length from 5 car lengths (220 ft.) to 50 car lengths (2200 ft.). Island platforms ranged from 20 car lengths (880 ft.) to 100 car lengths (4400 ft.) or more. Icing platforms that had mechanical icing machines installed in 1953 or later ranged in length from 3300 ft. to 5064 ft.

The single deck serviced cars on one track only, while the island-type platform had a track on each side. A platform that was categorized as having double track capability meant that it had two parallel tracks, either on one side of a single platform or on both sides of an island platform. Ice was slid on boards over the inside row of cars to the cars on the outer track. Thus two rows of cars could be iced simultaneously by the same crews on the same side

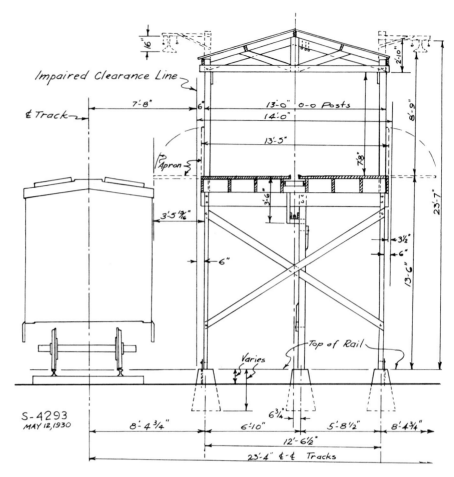

(**Right**). Standard Impaired Clearance Island Icing Platform with Roof and Wide Apron. This design was the basis for many PFE locations, though usually with significant modification. Decks in California *not* following this design were Roseville, Los Angeles, Colton and Watsonville Junction. From PFE drawing S-4293, UA-22-A AFE files. UP Railroad Museum.

S-4293
MAY 12, 1930

Material Specification

Foundation – concrete pedestal
Bays – 11' centers
Posts – 6" x 6" (3 per bay)
Caps – 4" x 12"
Joists – 3" x 12"
Fascia – 2" x 10"
Deck – 2" x 10" plank
Braces – 1" steel rod diagonal stabil-
  izers every 4th bay, 1 each side
Apron – 2' or as required
Paint – gray (see page 419)

Table 13-1
Mechanical Icing Machine Installations

Location	Platform, car lengths	No.	Type	In Service
Ice Manufacturing Plants				
Colton - Loma Linda	75	2	Preco single end	June 15, 1954
Council Bluffs	100	2	Preco single end	West 60 car lengths (c/l), March 1, 1956
				East 40 c/l, April 20, 1956
Fresno	75	2	Link Belt single end	East 34 c/l, May 7, 1951
				West 41 c/l, June 6, 1952
Laramie	100	3	Preco single end	April 27, 1955
Los Angeles	30	1	Preco single end (cable)	June 23, 1953*
Ogden-Riverdale	110	3	Preco single end	August 1, 1954
Roseville	80	1	Preco single end	April 13, 1956
		1	Preco double end	
	110	2	Preco single end	April 13, 1956
		1	Preco double end	
Ice Platforms				
Kansas City	100	2	Preco single end	June 1, 1954
Yuma	23	1	Preco single end (cable)	May 19, 1954
	108	1	Preco double end	East 66 c/l, May 1, 1956
Nampa	55	1	Preco single end	1960 (machine originally at Laramie)

*Original machine transferred to Yuma; 2nd machine in service March 15, 1954

Summary of equipment	No.		No.
Link Belt single end - overhead trolley	2	Preco single end - overhead trolley	15
Preco single end - cable type	2	Preco double end - overhead trolley	3
		Total	22

Spokane ITP. This view of the newly rebuilt single-track ice deck in February, 1955 clearly shows details of standard construction after 1946 (no center post). Typical timber sizes are listed next to the diagram, facing page. PFE photo, CSRM.

of the deck, but this was rarely done at PFE platforms.

Most railroads did not use roofs on icing platforms, but PFE used them at many locations to provide shade to reduce ice meltage, shelter for the icing crews and protection against snow for heater service operations. Ice shrinkage or melting tests made on platforms showed a variation from 2.6 per cent meltage at the roofed Colton ice deck to 21.2 percent shrinkage at the Yuma platform which did not have a roof. These tests also indicated that aprons and ice blankets reduced ice shrinkage as much as 22 per cent. The amount in dollars saved by preventing shrinkage with a roof was indicated in figures from ice issues at Laramie. From May to September 1945 inclusive, Laramie issued 83,849 tons, having a value of $503,094; therefore a 1 percent shrinkage equated to a $5,030 loss per year.

In 1946, PFE was planning to upgrade the platforms at Houston, El Paso, and Graham Yard in Los Angeles. By then the rising cost of building roofs in these warm climates was deemed unjustified when compared to the savings in ice shrinkage. The expense of a roof on a 70-carlength platform was estimated at $34,000. It was recommended that all new platforms proposed in locations where snow protection was not needed be built without roofs, but with structure construction designed so a roof or mechanical icing machines could be added in the future. Burlap ice blankets were used to reduce shrinkage. Short sections of roof were only built to protect machinery.

Fresno IMP. PFE's first mechanical icing machine, installed in May, 1951. Ice is delivered to the machine by the original deck chain. PFE photo, CSRM.

Colton IMP. Icing platform showing the blue flag lights. Some platforms had small semaphores instead of lights (see Council Bluffs photo, page 400). Note ice service car, one of a fleet of 45 old wood cars used to transfer ice to Loma Linda and Coachella. PFE photo, CSRM.

Railroad and PFE rules required that trains on which men were working be protected at each end by blue flags or lights. To accomplish this it was necessary to assign men to place the blue flags before starting service and remove them after service was completed. Beginning in 1952, PFE installed electrically operated "blue flag" signal systems on all major platforms. They consisted of signals, one at each end of the deck, for each track, and used green, yellow and red lights. Some had a short semaphore arm blade to aid daytime visibility. These lights were operated by push buttons located at 10-carlength intervals along the platform. They showed the light color in both directions so that PFE deckmen and railroad forces beyond the ends of the platform could see the signal color at all times.

When PFE started up, the ice at most of the early facilities was moved by hand, from the storage rooms and along the deck. PFE soon mechanized this process with a conveyor chain. Ice was delivered to the island-type platform through a tunnel and incline conveyor, or from an overhead bridge at least 24 ft. above the track to clear movement of cars to and from the deck. Standard platforms were 14 ft. wide with a reversible conveyor running the entire length. Lugs on the conveyor were spaced 5 ft. apart and the speed of the chain was 186 ft. per minute. This gave a capacity to deliver 37 standard 300-lb. blocks or 5-½ tons per minute.

A "delivery" for a given train would be sent from the storage house to the deck, where deckmen would first slide the ice blocks off the conveyor chain. The edge of the platform was equipped with "aprons," a hinged section of planking that could be dropped down onto the near edge of the car and hatch to be iced. A short "icing board" was used to scoot the ice to the far ice hatch.

At times it was necessary to have three or four deliveries

Roseville IMP. Ice delivery coming down retarder elevator from bridge onto platform from winter storage room. Ice already on deck is covered with burlap blankets, awaiting train arrival. PFE photo, CSRM.

Coachella ITP. Filling ice bunkers, two men to a car. The clerk on the ground is chalking either the car's outgoing yard track and train assignment, or date and hour iced—but not "graffiti"! Don Sims photo, 1951.

stockpiled on the deck at once to handle the volume of multiple train arrivals during prolonged hot spells when fruit or vegetables were maturing at a fast rate. On heavy requirement days, the larger plants would issue from 2400 to 3000 tons of ice daily.

The Car Service Department divided the icing stations, either owned or contracted, into seven districts: Northwestern, South-Central, Western, Central, Southwestern, Southern and Eastern. To appreciate the magnitude of producing or receiving and dispensing millions of tons of ice and salt into the bunkers of thousands of carloads annually, all PFE icing stations are listed here and the contribution of each to the system is noted.

The list of stations following the description of each district is a summary of essential statistics pertaining to each location as taken from PFE, owner railroad, and other records. The time frame is 1952-53 but is otherwise noted for ice facilities that may have been obsolete by that time. This will indicate the network as it existed during the height of PFE activities. Major modifications and expansion of stations are listed. Undoubtedly most icing stations were upgraded to some degree over the years, and some had been downgraded by this date.

NORTHWESTERN DISTRICT – SP, UP

The Northwestern District jurisdiction on the Southern Pacific started at Alturas and Black Butte, California, and extended north to Portland, Oregon. The Portland connection was made with the Union Pacific over whose lines PFE operated to Seattle, Yakima, Spokane and Huntington. Total trackage, including branch lines, was 2,120 miles. In addition, the UP had equal rights on the Camas Prairie Railroad which it owned jointly with the Northern Pacific. The SP also operated and jointly owned with the Great Northern, the 65-mile Oregon, California & Eastern that ran east out of Klamath Falls.

Principal crops originating on this district are potatoes, tree fruit, frozen foods, onions, berries, and miscellaneous items in that order. Potatoes originate in the Klamath Basin area of south central Oregon on the SP, and from central Oregon and the lower Columbia Basin of Oregon and Washington on the UP. Tree fruits come from the Rogue River Valley of southern Oregon, the Hood River Valley in northern Oregon, and the Yakima Valley of central Washington. Frozen goods originate throughout the district.

KEY: Facilities listed are from 1952-53 records. Figure following facility name indicates tons of ice issued, 1952 season. Facilities obsolete by 1952 also included in listing and so noted. ITP = Ice Transfer Plant. IMP = Ice Manufacturing Plant. See fold-out map of PFE system facing page 433.

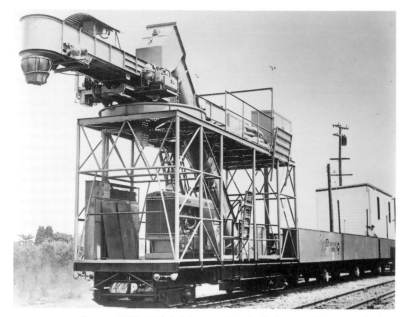

Eugene ITP. Mobile icing machine, built for use at Eugene only. It ran on an adjacent track to the cars, and carried its supply of ice in trailers. A car could be iced in 2 to 3 minutes. Left, R.J. Church collection; right, *Railroad and Railfan* collection.

At the height of PFE operations in the late 1940's and early 1950's, perishables originating in the Northwestern District ranged from 28,000 to 30,000 cars annually for both the SP and UP and their feeder lines. Of this total, approximately 11,500 cars moved each year under refrigeration, 4,200 under heater service, and the rest under ventilation. The larger part of the perishable tonnage of this district was highly competitive with the other railroads, so these figures do not represent the total crop production shipped from the area.

The Northwestern District is credited as being among the first in pioneering the shipment of frozen foods by rail. Starting with a very few carloads in the early 1930's, by 1970 over 5000 carloads, or approximately 20 per cent of all PFE frozen food shipments, originated in this district. The main commodities shipped frozen were potatoes in various forms, corn, peas and berries. PFE used heavily insulated ice bunker cars for these shipments from 1932 until mechanical refrigerators arrived in the mid-1950's.

District headquarters were at Portland and included the Superintendent and Assistant Superintendent plus a day shift diversion force Monday through Saturday to handle diversions and advise of shipments coming north in Roseville Blocks and of shipments coming from the east.

Northwestern District – SP

Brooklyn-Portland ITP. (8923) [figure is tons of ice issued-1952 season] Regular icing station. Located south of SP lumber yard and car repair sheds. PFE had island-type platform, built in 1922, 561' long, 13 carlength each side, no roof, painted gray. Small 20' x 60' ice storage house, frame construction. Ice furnished by contract.

This station also cleaned cars needed for loading on the SP at Portland and nearby points in the Willamette Valley.

Icing was performed by PFE. A large number of cars were initially iced here for frozen food loading.

Icing, at Portland and East Portland (2,118), was mainly initial icing of empties for loading at packing sheds, and the reicing of loads awaiting delivery. These services were performed by private contractor on the team and industrial tracks by truck. Railway Express Agency car icing was done at the Portland Union Station if necessary by truck, under contract.

Eugene ITP. (2,465) Regular icing station. PFE single-side ice deck, 13 carlengths by 1953, with one 10' x 15' ice storage room on the deck, 10 ton capacity. Ice purchased under contract, delivered by truck. No machinery to elevate ice. Mobile icer (see photos above) installed 1958.

Icing done for shipments moving via Eugene when originated at stations south of Eugene and destined to Coos Bay; Clackamas to Eugene except Salem and Albany; north of Medford to Eugene except Roseburg. PFE performed all icing.

Recollections of Pete Holst:

"We installed a different type mobile icing machine at Eugene about 1958. That was one of my ideas, instead of building a new deck, you know. The main office came out with this idea to put in a new longer ice platform and install icing machines there, but icing business was slowing around the system by then and justifying the expense was a big concern. I'll never forget, sitting in the bar at the Biltmore Hotel with the engineer from Preco, and we drew pictures and ideas on paper until we came up with this mobile icing machine deal.

It had a gas engine that ran and propelled it, and it pulled along a load of ice in a trailing car and ran on rails next to the row of cars to be iced. A conveyor lifted the ice

Hood River ITP. This deck was used to service fruit shipments, primarily apples and pears, from the Hood River Valley and west. PFE photo, CSRM.

up to the mobile's deck where it was crushed and put into the cars. It worked fine, and we didn't have an expensive ice deck in Eugene to tear down when they decided they didn't need it."

Albany ITP. Emergency icing station. PFE contracted all services through Albany Ice & Cold Storage. Icing performed at a 5-carlength, single platform by ice company for loads originating in local area.

Roseburg ITP. Emergency icing station. PFE contracted with Douglas Ice & Storage Co. for all services. They could manufacture 40 tons of ice daily and performed icing on a 4-carlength, single platform.

Medford ITP. (11,447) Regular icing station. PFE owned 7-carlength extension of private ice company's deck. Ice purchased under contract. Ice company owned 13-carlength platform of which 6 carlengths were island type, making possible a total of a 26-car spot. All icing performed by ice company on loads of pears, peaches, apples and other produce that originated in the Rogue River Valley. An agent was kept here during the pear season and the heater season. Pears movement to eastern market all moved via Klamath Falls and Alturas.

Klamath Falls ITP. (12,874) Regular icing station. Location: half mile south of SP freight house on SP land, west side of yard. PFE single platform built 1925, originally 2420' long, 57 carlengths, icing track on east side, painted gray. Ice was purchased from private contractor and stored in contractor's building alongside PFE deck. Forty carlengths of the deck were retired in April, 1958.

The Klamath Basin could annually generate over 6000 cars of potatoes which moved during winter months under heater service. During these months, the agent at Tulelake, Calif., handled installation of heaters for shipments loaded on the Modoc Line in California. Empties for refrigerated loading on the Modoc were iced at Klamath Falls. PFE performed icing. There were also four potato loading sheds on the Oregon, California & Eastern which PFE agents handled.

Northwestern District – UP

Albina-Portland ITP. (6706) Regular icing station, except for shipments routed via Hinkle or loads destined north of Portland. Located 250' east of UP Dock No. 1. It was not possible for the owner roads to share a common icing facility in Portland, so in 1923 PFE constructed this platform. Prior to its completion, UP cars requiring icing were switched from Albina to the East Portland team tracks where ice was delivered to them by trucks. Specifications: single platform 341' long, 8 carlengths, no roof, ice house 10' 4" x 48' 6", frame construction, 32 tons storage, and a 1 car unloading spot. Ice was secured under contract. Albina did initial icing for frozen food loads and cleaning of cars for local requirements (icing photo, page 139).

Seattle ITP. (2,041) Regular icing station. In 1921 PFE originally built a five car, single icing platform, salt house, unloading platform, incline conveyor, ice storage house and office in the Argo Yard. Ice was purchased locally in carload lots to protect vegetables trucked into Seattle which originated some PFE business. As loadings increased, the local ice companies, who were also shippers, installed their own platform facilities at loading points that were served by PFE's competitive lines, so they could furnish iced empties where shipments originated. PFE felt that because of these conditions it was not economical to own and operate its own facilities.

In 1934 PFE retired its property and secured services from the Ice Delivery Co. which also furnished labor and trucking. Ice was also contracted from Rainier I & CS Co., San Juan Fishing and Packing Co., and Booth Fisheries Corp., for initial icing of shipments originating at their respective sheds and plants.

Hood River ITP. (7,025) Emergency icing station. Built in 1925 to meet seasonal demands as local growers association facility was inadequate. Location: east of Hood River bridge on land owned by UP. PFE single-track platform, 10 carlengths, two car ice unloading platform under deck, roofed, painted gray. Ice storage building 39' x 99' x 29' high, frame construction, 2,300 ton capacity.

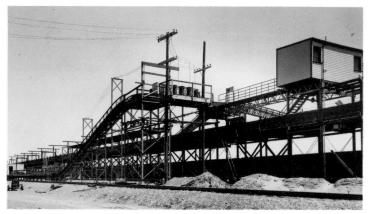

Hinkle ITP (Left). The office, ice house, ice unloading platform (foreground), and delivery system to deck, in 1951. Neg. 32525, UP Railroad Museum. Rieth ITP (Right). This island platform, shown in a January, 1948, view, was replaced by Hinkle in 1951. UP photo for PFE, CSRM.

Ice furnished by contract from Hood River Apple Growers Association which owned small ice manufacturing plant and an additional 10-carlength platform adjacent to PFE deck. The Apple Growers Association operated and furnished labor for both facilities.

A seasonal agency at Hood River was maintained from September 15 until the end of March to handle distribution, diversions, the few shipments under heater service, and to supervise icing of PFE fruit loads originating from the Hood River Valley. At the height of rail shipments in the early 1950's, about 1150 cars of apples and 1850 cars of pears were handled annually by PFE from this point.

Hinkle ITP. (12,724) Regular icing station. Location: north side at east end of the new UP yards 28 miles west of Pendleton. PFE island-type platform with no roof, 1,320' long, 30 carlengths; 4 car unloading dock. The ice storage house was 13'4" x 48', constructed of concrete blocks, and was capable of holding 37 tons.

Ice for Hinkle was secured by contract from Stadelman Ice Co. in The Dalles, Oregon, and occasionally from other commercial ice companies when necessary.

Hinkle was the regular icing station for eastbound loads, and was one of the most modern PFE facilities, having been activated September 2, 1951, for all traffic. It was established by the UP as a terminal in lieu of Rieth, Umatilla, and Wallula, due to the construction of the McNary Dam at Umatilla which raised the water level of the Columbia River for about 50 miles upstream. This completely inundated the site of the PFE ice manufacturing plant at Wallula. With the opening of Hinkle, the plant at Rieth was also discontinued. Besides handling initial icing for loadings in the vicinity, Hinkle cleaned a considerable number of returning empty cars, between 6000 and 8000 annually.

Reith ITP. Regular icing station until 1952. Location: in UP yard opposite railroad turntable. PFE first owned single track platform, 7 carlength and small storage house built in 1916 with gas powered incline. In 1925 it

was replaced with a new island-type platform 15 carlengths, no roof, which was eventually lengthened to 1001' long, 23 carlengths each side, painted carbolineum. Ice storage house was under east end of deck, 12' x 120', 60 ton capacity with electric powered incline, as OWR&N Co. had electric power brought into its roundhouse in 1924. Services performed by PFE. Retired in 1951 with construction of McNary Dam and new facilities at Hinkle, Ore.

Wallula IMP. Regular icing station until activation of the new plant at Hinkle in 1951. Prior to that time, Wallula had PFE-owned ice manufacturing plant that could produce 65 tons daily, with 7187 tons storage capability. PFE also had a single track platform, no roof, 671' long, 14 carlengths, no unloading track; closed 1952.

Milton-Freewater ITP. (720) Emergency icing station. Supplied initial icing as required during prune, onion and pea season. Services contracted.

Yakima ITP. (17,971) Regular icing station. PFE island-type platform, 23 carlengths, single car unloading spot. Ice secured under contract from Artificial Ice & Freezer Co. PFE performed labor. Ice storage house had 7000 tons capacity.

Yakima Valley was the heaviest produce area served by the Union Pacific in the Northwestern District. When weather conditions allowed ideal crop production, about 2,600 cars of apples and 500 cars of pears originated here annually. Initial icing was done on traffic brought in by the Yakima Valley Transportation Co., an electric line serving the fruit districts around Yakima. Also, some cars were initially iced for loading at lower valley points.

Zillah ITP. (1,061) Emergency icing station. Yakima Fruit Growers Association had ice manufacturing plant, 40 tons daily, storage house of 4,500 tons capacity and a 5-carlength double icing platform. Freight and REA shipments originating in the vicinity were iced under contract for PFE.

Wallula IMP. Retired in 1952 when backwater from the McNary Dam covered the UP yard and this facility with about 25 feet of water. UP photo for PFE, CSRM.

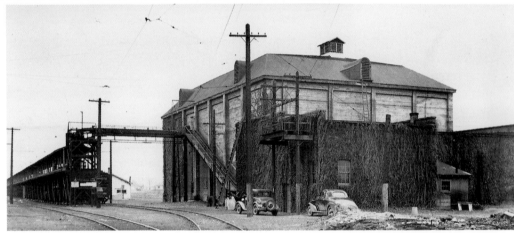

Yakima ITP (Right). The concrete storage house, crossover bridge to the deck, and island platform in 1948. Note overhead wire of Yakima Valley Transportation (a UP subsidiary since 1909). UP photo for PFE, CSRM.

Grand View ITP. Regular icing station. Location: across from UP depot. PFE owned single platform, 220' long, 5 carlengths, 30' x 50' ice storage house, 1 carspot loading/unloading dock. Facilities painted gray. Icing performed on originating loads. Station listed as active in 1940's, not listed in 1953.

Walla Walla ITP. (6,976) Emergency icing station. PFE contracted with Walla Walla Meat & Cold Storage Co. that had the capacity to produce 42 tons of ice daily, store 600 tons, and owned a 10-car single track platform. They supplied initial icing service for REA and freight originating in the Milton-Walla Walla district.

Spokane ITP. (624) Regular icing station from mid-June to mid-September, each year. OWR&N built original ice house here in 1896. PFE owned single track platform, 8 carlengths. Ice was secured from Empire Cold Storage that was delivered by truck. PFE performed labor.

Riparia ITP. Regular icing station. Location: 200' west of OWR&N (UP) depot. PFE owned single platform, 222' long, 5 carlengths, built on a curve with impaired clearance, 8' x 40' ice storage room. Listed in 1929 records. Icing done on shipments originating in area and coming in from the Camas Prairie Line through Lewiston, Idaho.

La Grande ITP. Emergency icing station. PFE owned island-type platform, 1144' long, 26 carlengths, roofed, with 15' x 22'6" ice storage house at east end of platform, painted gray. Also provided initial icing of some local loads. Retired in 1949 as faster train schedules from Reith, Ore., to Nampa, Ida., made re-icing unnecessary.

SOUTH-CENTRAL DISTRICT – UP

The South-Central District jurisdiction encompassed trackage totally owned by the Union Pacific. Its western terminus was Huntington, Oregon, on the old Oregon Short Line. The railroad swings through western and southern Idaho, closely following the Snake River and its bordering fertile crop lands. These farmlands were reclaimed from semi-arid sage covered desert around the turn of the century by government irrigation projects.

The Payette, Malheur, Weiser and Boise Rivers flow

La Grande ITP. A 1948 view of this 26-carlength facility prior to its retirement in 1949. UP photo for PFE, CSRM.

through and irrigate the productive farm land of the Treasure Valley, and this area along with the croplands adjacent to the Snake River Basin around Twin Falls, Rupert, Blackfoot, Idaho Falls, and Pocatello, produced thousands of carloads of potatoes, onions and other vegetables, fruits, dairy products and meats annually. By 1930, 35,027 carloads were shipped out of Idaho alone and the business kept growing. The bulk of the movement, potatoes and onions, was during the winter months, so heater service was provided, while ice service was necessary in the spring and fall.

The district extended on through Pocatello to Ogden, and south on the Salt Lake Route to Las Vegas. The South-Central District main offices were at Pocatello, where all diversions and shipment advisories were handled.

Huntington ITP. Obsolete after Nampa was activated. OWR&N originally built two ice storage houses, 3250 ton capacity, and deck, 6 carlengths, in 1898; was leased to PFE at its start up.

Nampa IMP. (56,827) Regular icing station. All eastbounds iced except for shipments originating west of Huntington, Oregon, icing for westbound shipments received from connections at Wells, Nevada, or originating on UP between Pocatello and Nampa. Initial icing for loads originating on the the branches that the Payette NIP had handled, plus the Stoddard, Wilder, and Homedale Branches.

PFE owned an ice manufacturing plant, gained by purchasing an existing plant in 1921, which could produce 180 tons daily, and store 33,200 tons. Ice required in excess of PFE plant production was secured from Terminal I&CS Co. that could produce 460 tons daily, had storage of 900 tons, and had an overhead conveyor from their plant to the PFE platform. PFE owned an island-type platform, 55 carlengths, 2 carspot loading/unloading dock.

In 1930, 5396 cars were iced initially, and 7,759 cars were re-iced, totaling 35,097 tons issued. In 1944, because of increased demand, a new island platform, 18 carlengths, with a lower deck for top icing, was built adjacent to the original deck. Nampa was the hub of PFE activities for eastern Oregon and western Idaho. A mechanical icing machine from Laramie was installed in 1960.

Boise IMP. Emergency icing station. PFE contracted services from Boise Cold Storage Co. which could produce 60 tons daily, store 2000 tons. The ice company owned a single track platform, 3 carlengths, and performed all labor, including icing REA cars on passenger trains when required at the depot, by truck.

Pocatello IMP. (35,023) Regular icing station. Location: west of depot across from roundhouse on UP property. PFE owned ice manufacturing plant built in 1922, produced 125 tons daily, storage capacity 18,300 tons. PFE owned two platforms, an 85-carlength island-type platform for eastbound trains (originally 55 carlengths), a

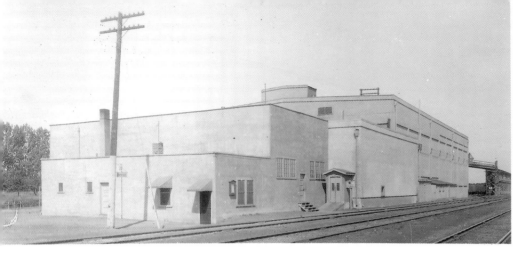

Nampa IMP. (Left, above) The new 18-carlength double deck platform with retop icing platform on lower level, June, 1949. **(Right, above).** Old PFE wood ice cars were used as bunkhouses for icing crews, both here and at other major icing facilities. Both photos, PFE from CSRM. **(Below).** Looking northwest, the 55-carlength island platform and 18-carlength retop deck are visible. The first section of train 18, the eastbound *Portland Rose*, glides by on the main line. Note the express reefer behind the FEF-1 4-8-4 in this 1947 view. Nampa Car Shops are at top left. UP photo 17494.

7 carlength single platform for westbound icing, with a single-spot dock for ice loading and unloading. In 1960 an additional 968-ft., 20-carlength extension was built adjoining the east end of the existing icing dock. Initial icing was also done for loads generated on the Twin Falls Branch, the Idaho Falls area, and the southern end of the Butte Line.

The original icing facility here was built in 1885 by the Oregon Short Line, and for a while the ice that was issued was for most of the originating shipments on the entire OSL. The early ice storage house eventually had a capacity of 12,000 tons. The natural ice stored was collected from private company ponds located at Humphreys, Idaho, on the Butte Line. PFE upgraded the facility when it took over, and continued to utilize it until the IMP was built.

Ogden IMP. (73,174-SP, 62,433-UP) Regular icing station. Ogden had multiple decks on both UP and SP as eastbound and westbound trains bunched here from all the radiating routes. It was a regular icing station for the SP except for shipments received from the D&RGW or delivered to the UP. Ogden was also a regular icing station for the UP except for shipments delivered to the SP. Both roads re-iced trains continuing on their lines at the facilities in their respective yards.

PFE's original ice manufacturing plant at the SP yards was built in 1921 after the ice transfer plant burned in 1919. It had the capacity of 375 tons daily, storage space

Ogden ITP. Original ice storage galleries and ice deck, with PFE's early R-30-1 and -2 cars. Ice was brought in by carloads from the Carlin and Evanston NIP's. Re-weigh dates on cars date the photo to 1910. PFE photo, CSRM.

Ogden IMP - SP. These three ice decks were located on Southern Pacific's line. This 1947 view shows two large elevators to the south. PFE photo, CSRM.

for 10,500 tons in the winter storeroom, 3300 tons in the daily storeroom, and 800 tons in the dock storeroom. Adjacent to the plant were two island-type platforms, No. 1 being 2,893' long, 66 carlengths, No. 2 being 3,113' long, 70 carlengths. There was a 1 carspot loading dock on the back track and a 15-carlength double track loading dock with the ice coming through from the daily storage house. In 1943, 33 car lengths were added to each platform to accommodate 100-car perishable trains.

Prior to 1954, at the UP's Ogden-Riverdale yards,

PFE owned an ice transfer plant and island platform, 105 car lengths. The storage house had a 500-ton capacity. In 1954, this facility was completely upgraded to become the most modern type of ice manufacturing plant in the PFE system.

The new plant utilized the latest type group ice harvest design, in which standard cans holding 300 lbs. of water were suspended from grids in tanks containing low temperature sodium chloride brine. Four huge tanks each held 1600 cans, 40 rows of 40 cans each. Individual cans were

Ogden-Riverdale IMP - UP. (Left, above) Ice plant and cooling towers. **(Right, above)** The salting machine on the 105-carlength ice deck is visible partway down the deck. **(Left, below)** Forty cans of ice have just been dumped. Note automatic can filler pipes above the cans. **(Right, below)** Tank room floor with overhead crane used to lift 40 ice cans. All photos, July, 1957, PFE, CSRM.

Salt Lake City ITP. The Utah Ice & Storage Co. manufacturing plant with the WP-D&RGW deck adjacent. The conveyor bridge brought ice to PFE's 14-carlength deck in the foreground (and right). PFE photos, CSRM.

11" x 22" x 51", and produced an ice cake about 10-½" x 21-½" x 42" long.

The refrigeration system was a departure from the previous ice freezing plant practice inasmuch as centrifugal compressors were used that cooled the brine external to the freezing tanks. The refrigeration machines each consisted of a compressor, condenser, brine cooler and allied auxiliaries. Brine from the freezing tanks was pumped through the cooler of the refrigeration machine and back to the tank where it was circulated between the cans of freezing ice by propeller agitators.

This plant was capable of producing over 4750 cakes of ice daily, or more than 700 tons. The freezing plant was fully automatic and capable of starting and stopping without attendance by an operator. The only personnel regularly required was a crane operator to pull the ice cans from the freezing tanks, and an engineer on day shift to perform routine maintenance.

A bridge conveyor took the blocks over the ice tracks to the island platform, which was a mile long, accommodating 110 cars on each side. Three Preco mechanical icing machines, installed in August, 1954, during the upgrading, delivered the ice to the cars.

PFE also contracted with the Utah Ice & Storage Co. that could produce 50 tons daily. They had a single track, 3 car platform. Icing of Railway Express cars in passenger trains was performed with PFE-owned ice lift trucks and employees at the depot as required. Solid blocks of REA cars were run along the PFE ice platforms and handled expeditiously.

Salt Lake City ITP. (9,221) Regular icing station for shipments originating at Salt Lake or received from connections east, south and west of there, except those moving in UP San Bernardino Perishable Specials, and all westbound shipments, except those which were iced at Ogden.

PFE owned a 14-carlength double platform and secured ice from Utah Ice & Storage manufacturing plant adjacent to the deck. Services performed by ice company employees. Some icing also done by them at passenger depot. Western Pacific reefer blocks were iced by Denver & Rio Grande Western through their contract company.

Provo IMP. Emergency icing station. PFE contracted with Utah Ice Co. into the mid-1950's to do needed services here.

Milford ITP. Regular icing station. Location: south of eastbound yard of LA & SL (UP). PFE owned single platform, 1100' long, 25 carlengths, no roof, painted gray, ice storage house 13' x 118', frame with asbestos-sheet exterior. Retired 1950.

Las Vegas IMP. This end of platform, with ice delivery for incoming train, was single track. SP photo, Steve Peery collection.

Cedar City ITP. Emergency ice station for carloads originating locally. PFE owned 4-carlength double icing platform. UP owned 2-carspot unloading platform. Ice was shipped in from the PFE plant in Las Vegas, and icing was performed by PFE employees sent there as required. Obsolete by 1952.

Moapa ITP. Emergency icing station. Location: across from depot next to freight house on UP land. Ice platform 131' long, 3 carlengths, built on old ore dock. No storage house, 1 carspot unloading dock that also served freight house. Obsolete by mid-1930's.

Las Vegas IMP. (5,482) Regular icing station. PFE-owned plant could produce 115 tons of ice daily, and storage for 5700 tons. In November, 1904, the Armour Car Lines entered into a refrigeration contract with the San Pedro, Los Angeles and Salt Lake Railroad (later the LA & SL portion of the UP), and Armour erected an artificial IMP and storage house. It was listed as PFE-owned by 1910, and it is probable that this plant was purchased from Armour shortly after PFE operations were set up. By 1943 PFE had a 34-carlength platform, of which 21 carlengths were single track, and 13 carlengths at the east end were island type, allowing servicing of originating and through traffic at the same time. A roof protected 200' of the platform opposite the ice plant for protection of heaters and charcoal stored there for heater service in the winter. Icing performed by PFE employees.

WESTERN DISTRICT – SP

The Western District comprised the California coastal area south from Arcata, which is just north of Eureka, to San Luis Obispo. This district's territory along the central coast was one of PFE's highest carload-generating areas and originated 88,463 carloads of perishable traffic in 1952. Eighty-five percent of the loadings occurred in the Salinas, Watsonville, King City area, and approximately half of the shipments from this area were straight carloads of lettuce. The remainder of annual carloads comprised nearly every type of edible vegetable.

The district's superintendent headquarters at Salinas supervised General Agencies at the following shipping territories: San Francisco territory which included North Bay or what was generally known as the Northwestern Pacific territory, Oakland and Alameda territory, San Jose territory, which was served by the SP and WP, and the Watsonville-Salinas territory.

Santa Rosa ITP. (12,856) Regular icing station. PFE owned island-type platform, 20 carlengths, 9 car unloading spot, with a 75-ton storage house. Icing requirements of the NWP and Petaluma & Santa Rosa Railroad were taken care of at this focal point. Most ice was purchased locally, with some shipped in by rail from Visitacion during peak loading periods. Local ice company also had a single side platform, 4 car capacity. PFE operated its own deck July 1 to October 1, and the ice company performed any icing during the off season.

San Francisco-Mission Bay ITP. Original facility in San Francisco, 16th and Kentucky St., was an 8-carlength platform, 20' x 20' unloading platform and a 32' x 10' x 10' ice storage house on leased property. Retired in 1924 when Visitacion IMP was built.

Visitacion IMP. (8,368) Regular icing station. Location: south end of Bayshore freight yards, on west side. PFE owned the plant, built in 1924, with 90 tons daily production capacity, 2300 tons storage capacity, island platform of 10 carlengths, 3-carspot unloading/loading track. Ice stored at this plant was also to protect partial requirements at the Santa Rosa ice deck. During the ice shipping season, a maximum of ten carloads of ice a day originated from this station.

Visitacion IMP. This unusual (for PFE) concrete deck was built in 1924. Timber decks were preferred for ease of repair and modification. Note also the brick ice manufacturing plant and storage room, and corrugated metal roof on the icing deck. Located at the south end of SP's Bayshore Yard near Brisbane, the ice storage room still exists. PFE photo, CSRM.

Watsonville Junction ITP. This ice crossover bridge could deliver ice to the deck (center) from the ice storage room (beyond incline, not room with windows) or move ice from unloading deck (left) to deck or storage room. Feb. 1930, PFE photo, CSRM.

Icing was primarily to incoming destination business of meat and packing house produce for San Francisco, and pre-icing of empties for frozen food loading. During the year, 2 to 5 cars were initially iced per day, and the cars re-iced averaged below 10 per day. Discontinued in 1955.

Santa Clara ITP. (26,204) Regular icing station. PFE contracted all services. PFE built its own single-track platform here in 1928 to eliminate practice of icing cars at San Jose and to make room in San Jose for SP yard expansion. Originally 30 carlengths, it was at 15-car capacity by 1952, adjacent to Security Warehouse & Cold Storage Co. which furnished ice, salt and labor. Under contract in this area were 10 other cold storage plants with a total capacity of handling 1,200 cars.

Icing was done for shipments originating in the Santa Clara Valley and the territory from and including San Francisco, Oakland, Stockton, and Fresno, to and including Watsonville Junction, except did not apply to shipments iced or re-iced elsewhere after loading in territory just described nor to shipments of fresh or green vegetables moving in "Salinas Vegetable Blocks" to Roseville.

San Jose IMP (WP). Regular icing station. PFE contracted with Union Ice Co. for all services required for loads and initial icing of traffic generated on the Western Pacific in this area. Ice company had island-type platform, 7 carlengths, produced 50 tons ice daily, storage for 90 tons, single spot unloading dock.

Watsonville Junction ITP. (119,455) Regular icing station. PFE owned an island-type platform, 30 carlengths. PFE upgraded its own deck over the years as business, which increased beyond its expectations, grew. Ice was contracted from Union Ice Co. that could produce 500 tons daily and store 3000 tons. The ice company had a travel gantry with a movable platform extension to the PFE platform giving a capacity to ice 20 additional cars.

Icing was done on all loads here except for shipments of fresh or green vegetables originating on the SP Coast Line from King City to Gilroy, including the Santa Cruz, Monterey and Hollister Branches, when the cars were to move via Nevada, Utah, or north to Oregon and points beyond. Those loads could move to Roseville for initial or re-icing when necessary for operating conveniences.

There were also four other private ice plants in Watsonville that were under contract with PFE and could handle at their small platforms a total of 22 cars.

Salinas ITP. (16,468) Regular icing station. All icing at this point was done by local ice companies under PFE contract. Cars iced were those loaded at packing houses located on the property of those companies. There were 14 private ice manufacturing plants in the Salinas area with a production capacity of approximately 2900 tons daily.

Soledad ITP. PFE owned a 15-carlength single platform, built in 1930 at request of lettuce shippers; retired 1935 for insufficient utilization. Timber and materials reused at El Paso.

CENTRAL DISTRICT – SP, WP

The Central District incorporated the vast Central Valley of California. The northern end of the great valley is known as the Sacramento Valley and the southern end is the San Joaquin Valley, named for the major rivers that drain these respective fertile croplands. The district's jurisdiction extended from Gerber at the north end to Bakersfield in the south and across the Sierra Nevada Mountains to include Sparks and Carlin, Nevada. The main Superintendent Offices were at Sacramento, with General

Salinas ITP. This 1962 view shows some of the vast facilities here. Produce sheds are at right with crossover bridges and conveyors moving boxed produce to cars in foreground. Beyond the center row of mechanical and ice cars are two of the Union Ice Company's vacuum cooling chambers, where either rail cars or trailers could be placed to remove field heat (see Chapter 14). At left is the Union Ice Co. icing platform with a mechanical icing machine. Since the ice supply was contracted from a manufacturer, PFE considered this an ITP. E.R. Mohr photo.

Agencies at Roseville, Modesto, Fresno and Bakersfield.

The Central Valley is one of the richest and most diversified agricultural regions in the world. It contains three-fifths of California's farm land and produces almost every kind of agricultural crop. The principal perishable crops produced in this valley are cantaloupes, grapes, tree fruit, oranges, potatoes, tomatoes, peppers, asparagus, lettuce and onions. In 1968 this district originated 46,051 shipments on the SP and its short-line connections.

Red Bluff ITP. Prior to Gerber IMP being built in 1924, this was the designated regular icing station for all north and southbound shipments during months of March to November inclusive, when considerable volume was moved by the northern lines. The SP abandoned Red Bluff as a freight terminal in 1919, and through trains had to stop

and switch the icing platform, causing delay. Ice was secured by carload from Ashland.

Gerber IMP. (4,263) Regular icing station. PFE-owned IMP plant, built in 1924, could produce 75 tons daily, storage held 2000 tons, single platform built in 1921, 12 car capacity, no roof. PFE did icing as needed on trains from Ashland to avoid claims account of long run from there to Roseville, and on loads originating from the surrounding fruit growing areas. Southbound shipments moving through from Klamath Falls went on to Roseville, and northbound shipments from Roseville or Marysville were not stopped here. Closed in 1954.

Marysville IMP (SP). Emergency icing station. PFE contracted services from National Ice Co. to perform icing

Gerber IMP. Two rows of ice cars sit alongside the deck in the early 1950's. John Signor collection.

Portola ITP. This photo from about 1915 shows ice from boxcars on an elevated track being used in refrigerator cars. At this time, PFE owned the deck. WP, still under D&RGW control, was using Rio Grande cars for the ice transfer from Gulling. Whitehead photo 15, UP Railroad Museum.

as required. National a had single-track platform, 4 cars.

Marysville ITP (WP). Regular icing station. Operated by Western Pacific. The railroad owned a single track platform, 6 carlengths. There was no ice storage house. Ice was shipped by rail from Sacramento and stored on a one carspot unloading track. Icing done on all eastbound shipments not iced at Sacramento, and on loads originating in the local area.

Yuba City ITP. On the WP-owned Sacramento Northern Railway. Ice was trucked from National Ice Co. in Marysville. WP owned a single 6-carlength platform. Ice company performed all service.

Chico IMP (Sacramento Northern Railway). PFE contracted with Union Ice Co. that had a 40 ton daily production, 60 ton storage capacity, single platform, 2 carlengths. Ice company performed icing on shipments originating locally.

Portola ITP. Regular icing station. Single 24 carlength platform owned by PFE, 12 car unloading dock. Ice here was originally secured from a small natural ice pond and storage house owned by a lumber company at Gulling, just a few miles east of Portola, and delivered to the reefers from a 5-carlength platform at Portola. PFE lengthened the platform in 1912 and contracted to buy all the ice in 1918 to better insure dependable delivery to Portola.

Gulling was operated only a few years as PFE decided to either ship in ice from Sacramento or obtain it by carload from Reno contractors. The Portola ice deck was sold to the WP in 1924 under a revised contract with PFE. Re-icing was done on all east or westbound loads so requiring, and for those westbound shipments going north on the Keddie-Klamath Falls "High Line."

Recollections of Pete Holst:

"I went to Gulling in 1920. Supt. of Refrigeration Phillips said he had a nice summer job for me. He said, 'We bought an ice house full of ice, and you go up and take it out.' I got a fella from Wallula and we started with one or two cars a day. I'd work switching each ice block inside the car as it came down the chute from the house. You had to grab it and throw it across the rough floor to place it. We mostly used refrigerator cars, so the ice wouldn't melt. After you got one layer in, it got rougher to switch the next layer, not like in a house. It was summer, see, and it didn't slide so good as cold ice. I worked my butt off in there, but I learned to switch right and left-handed. The WP local would come in there to pick up the loads and leave off empties, then go on to Loyalton to work the lumber mill. But they'd make it a full day. The trainmaster was always calling, 'That crew been up there yet?' Hell, I didn't tell him they were fishing at the creek. I had my English Setter up there as the mountain quail hunting was good. I kept my gun against the ice house when I was moving ice, and when they came out of the creek I'd pick 'em off."

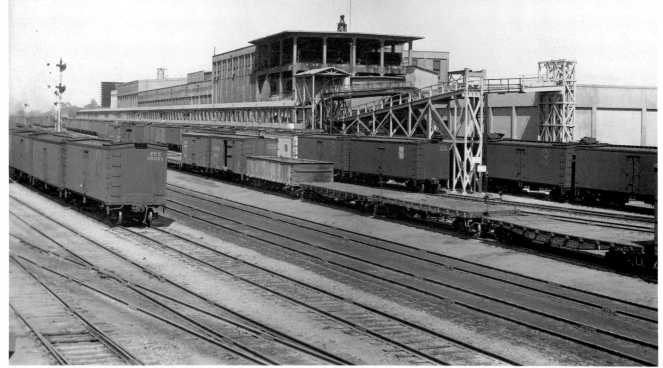

Roseville IMP. This is the north side of the plant in 1925, showing the deck used to pre-ice cars. It could handle 50 cars on each side, and was originally used for pre-cooling. The dark-shadowed building is a roofed condensing tower. The darker ballast tracks with the semaphore signals in the center are the SP main line. PFE photo, CSRM.

Roseville IMP. (288,982) Regular icing station. This PFE-owned ice manufacturing plant was unequivocally the largest such plant in the world. Its record-holding output was the capacity of 1300 tons every 24 hours, and a storage capacity of 52,000 tons.

Icing was done on all loads originating from the Central and Western Districts heading east and north, and re-icing on westbound trains. Initial icing of empties for: loading at points east of Roseville to Colfax, Lodi grape areas including Central California Traction lines, asparagus and pear loading in the River Delta Territory, Placerville Branch, Marysville-Dantoni area, and territory west of Roseville to Winters and Napa Junction.

The original ice plant, No. 1, was built in 1908 and had a daily production capacity of 250 tons. Initially two single-track platforms were used, one on each side of the plant. The 60-carlength deck was used to re-ice incoming through trains which pulled alongside.

The shorter 24-carlength platform employed a new process that was placed into operation on October 9, 1909: the intermittent precooling of incoming fresh loads. Such loads could have field heat of 70 to 80° F. To cool the commodity, cold air was blown into the car through the doors, circulated over and around the load and drawn out the bunker hatches by means of heavy canvas ducting. The car temperature could be dropped to 40 degrees in two hours with precooling, then the car bunkers were iced. This process lessened considerably the amount of ice needed at the first re-icing station.

The perishable business was soon to become the single most important commodity handled through the Roseville yards. In the 1921 season, a record occasion (up to that time) saw the Roseville plant place 1600 tons of ice in the bunkers of refrigerator cars in a single day. During September of that year, 37,726 tons of ice were issued by the plant to ice 13,525 cars.

Roseville IMP. Sections showing fans and air ducts of the 1909 pre-cooling plant. From *Railway Age Gazette,* 1910.

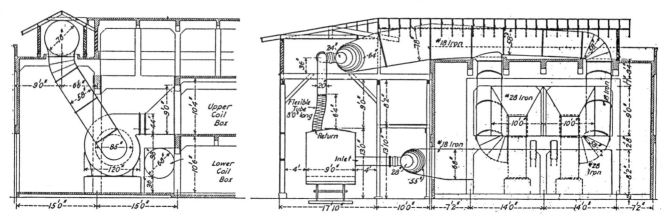

Roseville. This view looking toward the ice plant was taken during the process of moving the PFE shops in 1927 (old foundation and lumber in foreground). The string of wood-roofed Southern Pacific stock cars is interesting; it includes a group of T&NO and predecessor lines (Houston & Texas Central, Morgan's Louisiana & Texas) cars. PFE photo, CSRM.

Roseville IMP. This is the compressor room of the 1924 addition. Roseville, Las Vegas, Tucson and North Platte were the only steam-driven plants, all converted later to electric. PFE photo, CSRM.

In 1924, PFE commenced work on a $780,000 expansion program for the icing facilities. Ice Manufacturing Plant No. 2 and two new island-type platforms, replacing the original decks, were constructed and placed in service by June, 1927. This additional ice plant brought Roseville's capabilities to the figures mentioned above. The precooling apparatus was torn out, as by this time precooling was done by the shipper using various methods at their packing sheds.

The two new decks, one used for pre-icing, could handle 100 cars, 50 each side. The other, the re-icing deck, could handle two 78-car trains. These two decks were increased in length around 1950, the pre-icing deck to 80 cars each side, and the re-icing to 110 carlengths.

During the peak years in the early 1950's, Roseville iced between 90,000 to 100,000 cars annually, with total ice issues each year being around 285,000 tons. Of that figure, 61 per cent was used during the months of July, August, and September. Five million pounds of salt were used annually to provide specified load temperatures.

The facilities employed over 400 men at the ice plant

Roseville, 1959. Jim Lekas photo.

and platforms during these peak months when cars were hand iced. Manual re-icing, with a deckman and a barman at each car end, could take as little as one minute per car.

In 1956, the 80-carlength pre-icing platform received two Preco Mechanical Icing Machines, and the 110-car re-icing deck received three of the Preco machines. Eight to ten 100-car trains would be iced daily at the plant, using in excess of 3500 tons of ice.

By 1961, the mechanical car fleet began making inroads on decreasing the plant's ice requirements. The annual production was down to 150,000 tons issued, with 3.9 million pounds of salt used to pre-ice 9,216 cars and re-ice 66,790 cars. The annual totals continued to decrease. By the end of the 1972 season, the plant, valued at $1.8 million in the mid-1950's, became idle. It was demolished in 1974, marking an end to a remarkable era.

Colfax ITP. (4,539) Regular icing station. Location: on land leased from the SP west of their enginehouse. PFE owned a single platform, built in 1926, 878' long, 20 carlengths, painted gray, built on a slight curve with impaired clearance, ice storage house was 32' x 12' x 8' at platform level at the west end, 2-carspot unloading dock.

Cars to be loaded at Colfax, Auburn, and Newcastle were given initial icing at Roseville and then re-iced at Colfax during the sixty-day green (deciduous) fruit shipping season. Regular icing for shipments cooled in cars by shipper at this station. Ice used was normally shipped in from PFE ice plant at Sparks, thus utilizing westbound empties. All services performed by PFE. In the 1950 season 1,054 cars were serviced.

Sparks IMP. (44,167) Regular icing station. Location: on PFE-owned land, platform on leased SP land. Main buildings were erected by PFE in 1920: an addition to the compressor and tank rooms was erected in 1924, along with a bunkhouse, blacksmith shop, cookhouse, dining room and well house. Rated manufacturing capacity was 330 tons daily, winter storage 19,562 tons, daily storage 150 tons, dock storage 150 tons. Island-type platform, roofed, 3784' long, 86 carlengths, with double track capacity.

The original 1920 platform extended west of the plant and was 55 carlengths. In 1924, a 19-carlength platform was added to the east end, and in 1926 an additional 12 carlengths was added, again to the east end. Re-icing done on all traffic, including shipments moving to or from the northwest via Alturas on the Modoc Line. Icing performed by PFE employees.

Interviews with SP employees indicate that PFE at Sparks-Reno used a car similar to the one described under "El Paso Plant," page 326, to re-ice express reefers on passenger trains, but that is the only reference found.

When icing was discontinued at Sparks, the plant was sold, and William Harrah's immense collection of antique automobiles has been exhibited in the old ice storage house.

Hazen ITP. Six carlength single platform constructed in 1925 to do initial and first re-icing of shipments of cantaloupes originating in the Fernley-Fallon districts, thus eliminating time and ice loss of cars coming for these shipments that had previously been serviced at Carlin. Retired in 1938.

Sacramento ITP (SP). (12,523) Regular icing station. Location: in SP lumber yard between 8th and 9th Street on SP land, across main line and thirteen yard tracks from Consumers Ice Company's plant. PFE owned island type platform, built 1928, 1100' long, 25 carlengths, no roof, painted gray. Ice company had a 7-car single platform. Ice contracted from Consumers and transported to PFE platform via steel conveyor bridge, 224' long, crossing over the SP tracks. Icing done for shipments cooled in cars by shippers at Sacramento and cars iced for local loading. Icing performed by PFE employees.

Sacramento IMP (WP). Regular icing station. Location: west side of WP freight yards in south Sacramento, across from railroad's general shops. PFE contracted all services from Consumer's Ice Company (became National Ice Co. in mid-1950's). Plant could manufacture 97 tons of ice daily, store 7500 tons. Island-type platform, 24 carlengths, with double row icing capabilities on the outside tracks. PFE originally owned the ice deck, but sold it to the WP in 1924, and contracted to have PFE cars iced. This was the main icing facility for traffic generated in the area and loads brought in on WP and the Sacramento Northern. Re-icing of loads heading for Salt Lake that were not iced at Stockton was also done.

Stockton ITP (SP). (10,619) Regular icing station. Location: on land leased from SP 3 miles south of passenger station. PFE owned a single platform, 881' long, 20 carlengths, no roof, painted gray. The ice storage house was at the north end of the platform between tracks, 122' x 13', with 3-carspot unloading.

Most ice used was shipped in from the PFE Modesto IMP. Cars were given initial icing at Stockton for loads originating on the Stockton, Terminal & Eastern, the Oakdale Branch, and some points on the SP's west side valley line. Regular icing for shipments afforded transit privileges at Stockton, also for shipments cooled in car by shippers at this station. Icing was performed by PFE.

Stockton ITP (SP). Ice storage house and 20-carlength deck, Nov. 1945. PFE photo, CSRM.

Stockton IMP (WP). Regular icing station. PFE contracted all services with Valley Ice Co., whose roofed platform (photo, page 133) had double-track capability with 42-car capacity. Plant could produce 450 tons of ice daily, store 11,000 tons. This was the major WP icing station for shipments generated on its lines in the Delta area and those loads originating on the Tidewater Southern and Central California Traction. Initial or re-icing of shipments east to bypass Sacramento was done here.

Tracy ITP. (14,883) Emergency icing station. Cars were iced at Tracy for loading in surrounding territory during peak season to relieve PFE's Modesto and Stockton plants. Icing was done by Tracy Ice Co. There was no platform; icing was done with escalator trucks owned by the ice company. Ice from the Tracy Ice Co. was also utilized by the WP at Carbona in a similar fashion.

Modesto IMP (SP). This view from the east shows the interchange tracks of the Tidewater Southern. PFE's deck can be seen on the west side. PFE photo, CSRM.

Brentwood ITP. (6,255) Emergency icing station. PFE contracted with Union Ice Co. to perform all services as needed during peak season to provide relief for Stockton and Modesto. Ice company had single platform which accommodated 6 cars. Ice shipped in by truck to 100-ton storage house.

Modesto IMP (SP). (21,519) Regular icing station. Location: ½-mile north of SP depot, on east side of yards and Highway 99. PFE-owned plant purchased for $292,000 from Valley Ice Co. in 1927 with capability of 400 tons daily production, storage of 9,400 tons, island platform on north end of plant, 1303' long, 29-car capacity on west side, 17-car capacity stub track on east side, with double track icing capability on each side, 1 carspot loading dock.

Icing done for shipments cooled in cars by shippers at this station. Empties were iced for loading at points from Lathrop to Merced, inclusive on the east side line, and generally points on the west side line from Tracy to Mendota. Shipments originating Merced and north were re-iced at Modesto. PFE performed icing.

Modesto (Tidewater Southern/WP). Regular icing station. PFE contracted with Union Ice Co., which had a single platform, 2 carlengths, for service as needed for originating loads on the TS that were not iced at PFE's facilities.

Fresno IMP. (186,306) Regular icing station. PFE owned and constructed ice manufacturing plant completed in 1928, cost $788,455, with rated capacity of 630 tons daily production, 42,000 tons winter storage, and 760 tons in the dayroom storage. Island-type platform, 3300' long, 75 carlengths, with double track icing capability, both sides.

Initial services here were contracted with the Valley Ice Co. In 1921 PFE and Santa Fe jointly purchased the Valley Ice Company's plant at Calwa in south Fresno. To meet the needs of the two railroads an additional 10,000-ton storage room was built and 25 carlengths added to the island platform. In 1925 the Santa Fe asked PFE to sell them its half of the plant so the Santa Fe could expand it to meet its requirements, which exceeded its half share.

Fresno IMP. The newly constructed plant is seen in this aerial view, showing the storage room, crossover bridges, and 75-carlength platform. Fresno received PFE's first mechanical icing machine in May, 1951. 1928 PFE photo, CSRM.

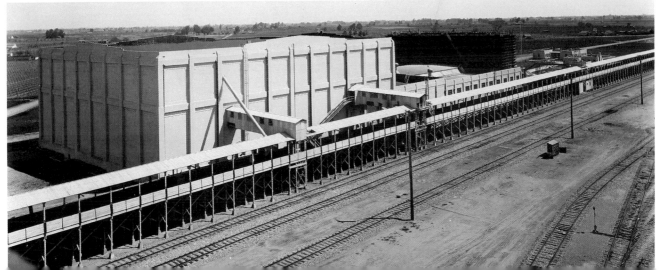

Bakersfield IMP. PFE built the plant in 1922. This view predates 1925. PFE photo, CSRM.

PFE was happy to comply, as its ice demands also exceeded its half share of the Calwa plant's production. During the years of joint ownership PFE had to have 40,000-60,000 tons of ice shipped in annually to augment its needs. This, coupled with Southern Pacific's plans to construct a new yard in Fresno at Muscatel, some 4 miles north of Calwa, made the sale, and construction of a new PFE plant in the modern yard advisable. Extensive negotiations ended with an agreement and sale in late 1927.

Fresno was the first PFE icing station to receive mechanical icing machines. Two Link-Belt model FK mechanical icing machines were installed, the east end machine in May, 1951, and the second, west end unit in June, 1952. Record days of ice issued by these two machines were: August 2, 1955, when 883 cars were serviced, 3554 tons of ice issued; and June 16, 1957, when 782 cars were serviced, 3512 tons of ice issued.

During 1961, Fresno manufactured 153,837 tons of ice, serviced 50,909 cars at the icing deck, issued 179,614 tons of ice to car bunkers along with 1549 tons of salt. This was the major icing station in the San Joaquin Valley. Icing done except on northbound shipments for movement via Merced to Stockton, Sacramento, Roseville and beyond, which had been iced at Bakersfield. Empties were iced for loading on the Porterville Branch, on the west side line as far north as Los Banos, and south to Famoso. PFE performed all services.

Exeter - Rocky Hill IMP (Visalia Electric Railroad). Regular icing station. PFE contracted with Rocky Hill Ice Co. which had a 5-car single platform and provided initial service for loads originating on the VE.

Hanford IMP. Regular icing station. PFE contracted with Hanford Ice Co., which serviced both SP and AT&SF loads. Initial icing for loads originating on the Coalinga Branch. Ice company had a 6-car platform, performed all services.

Bakersfield IMP. (78,052) Regular icing station. To eliminate contracting services from Union Ice Co. as was

done initially, PFE built its own ice manufacturing plant, completed in May, 1922 at a cost of $261,345. Capable of producing 320 tons daily, winter storeroom capacity of 8700 tons, daily storeroom capacity of 300 tons, island-type roofed platform, originally built with 33 carlengths, extended an additional 23 carlengths in 1947, for a total length of 2396', and had double track loading capability on both sides. Roof removed by 1952; electrical "blue flag" system installed in May, 1958. Ice furnished for empties for Edison territory, Arvin Branch, south to Tehachapi, and during most of the year, as far north as Delano. Icing performed by PFE.

SOUTHWESTERN DISTRICT – SP

The Southwestern District covered a large area embracing the territory bounded on the north and west by San Luis Obispo, Mojave, and San Diego, California; and on the east and south by Las Vegas, Nevada; Tucumcari, New Mexico; El Paso, Texas; and Nogales, Arizona. The lines serving this territory were Southern Pacific, 2846 miles of trackage; Union Pacific, 542 miles; Pacific Electric Railway, 204 miles; and the San Diego & Arizona Eastern, 196 miles.

In addition, this district supplied refrigerator cars to the Southern Pacific Railroad of Mexico or SPdeM (Mexican-owned as Ferrocarril del Pacifico after Dec. 21, 1951) for perishable loads. This line extends 1,071 miles into Mexico from Nogales to Guadalajara, and originated about 9000 cars of perishables yearly. These shipments entered into the United States through Nogales, Arizona.

Los Angeles was headquarters for the district. The main office force averaged 38 employees. Shippers and receivers got 24-hour diversion service, because the SP agent at Taylor Yard handled the diversions when the PFE main offices were closed. During 1952 the Los Angeles offices handled 100,525 diversions; the entire district handled 204,454.

Except for four facilities in the Los Angeles and San Diego area (one had been retired by 1953), all PFE icing

Los Angeles IMP. The compressor building and condensers loom above a string of cars which appear to be candidates for rebuilding. Note the Bohn ventilators and deteriorated roof on car in foreground. PFE photo, CSRM.

stations in this district were on the lines of the Southern Pacific.

Guadalupe IMP. (12,819) Regular icing station. Location: west side of Puritan Ice Co. plant one-half mile south of SP depot. PFE owned a 485' single platform built in 1928, 10 carlengths, no roof, painted gray. Ice contracted from Puritan Ice Co. and the ice company performed all service.

Operations in the Santa Maria Valley were centered at Guadalupe. In the early 1950's, shipments numbered nearly 12,000 cars annually. Guadalupe also had a vacuum cooling plant for removing field heat from lettuce and celery loads.

Oceano ITP. (3,532) Regular icing station. Cars loaded locally were iced by contracted ice company with escalator truck. There was no platform.

Santa Maria IMP. (8,060) Regular icing station. Location: on the Santa Maria Valley Railroad that connected with the SP at Guadalupe. PFE contracted with Santa Maria Ice Co., which had a production capacity of 250 tons daily, 2700 tons storage, single platform, 7 carlengths. Santa Maria had a vacuum cooling plant to remove field heat from car loads.

Santa Barbara IMP. (20,101) Regular icing station. PFE contracted ice and icing services from the Puritan Ice Co. PFE owned the island-type platform, 15 carlengths. Icing done except on eastbound shipments iced at Guadalupe, Oceano or Santa Maria; westbound shipments except those iced at Los Angeles. Furnished iced empties for loading in Santa Barbara and Goleta areas.

Oxnard IMP. (34,342) Regular icing station. PFE contracted ice and icing services from Union Ice Co. that had 300 tons daily production, 500 tons storage, island platform, 12 carlengths. Icing was done for shipments originating at Oxnard, received from Ventura County Railway, or for Santa Paula and Ojai branches.

Los Angeles IMP (SP). (50,795) Regular icing station. Earliest facilities were in SP's River Station yard, a 20-carlength single platform ITP, retired in 1924. The first IMP, located in Taylor Yard adjacent to PFE car shops, was erected by PFE in 1913, 60-ton daily production capacity, 500 tons storage. Later upgrading gave a production capacity of 300 tons daily, 13,000 tons storage. The icing platform was 30 carlengths, island-type with double track capability, 8-car loading/unloading dock. Precooling facilities for cooling citrus shipments were located on two 13-carlength single icing platforms, allowing 26 cars to precool at once. The precooling plant was retired in April, 1961. A single Preco Mechanical Icing Machine was installed on the long deck in June, 1953.

Los Angeles IMP. Preco car icing machine, installed June 23, 1953. PFE photo, CSRM.

Oxnard IMP. PFE owned the 12-carlength deck, which was operated by Union Ice Co. All but four aprons have been removed to accommodate the new icing machine. The sign says "Danger from falling ice" in both English and Spanish. Note the "electric blue flag" lights and 40' steel REA cars behind deck. Don Sims photo.

This facility handled westward (northbound) shipments, and eastward shipments originating in the San Fernando Valley, Santa Ana, Fillmore and Canoga Park. Eastward shipments previously iced at Santa Barbara, Oxnard, or Bakersfield passed through to Colton or Loma Linda. Heater service was comparatively light in this area and consisted chiefly of charcoal heaters for winter protection of banana carloads originating at the shipping docks at Los Angeles Harbor. In July, 1950, initial icing was done on 1162 cars, re-icing was done on 1352 cars, and 640 cars were pre-cooled at this plant.

The PFE Car Service Department also operated three other platforms in the Los Angeles area, as follows (one, Watson, was retired by 1952).

East Los Angeles Yard ITP (UP). Regular icing station. Original 15-carlength PFE-owned deck was adjacent to Federal Refrigeration Co. plant which furnished ice and services. In 1934 PFE retired that platform and built a 10-carlength single platform, 25-ton ice storage house, salt house and office, in the LA&SL's East Yard which serviced all UP inbound loads for holding, and some origination outbound shipments. Ice furnished by carload

from the LA IMP. In July, 1963, facilities were built here to handle servicing of mechanically refrigerated trailers which amounted to over 15 per day.

Watson ITP (Pacific Electric). Records show that PFE approved construction of a 10-carlength single icing platform, incline and ice unloading platform and ice storage room at Watson in 1943. Prior to that time banana shipments loaded into cars at the Port of San Pedro were moved from the docks by the Harbor Belt Railroad to the Pacific Electric at Wilmington, and then to Thenard for weighing, following which they were moved to PFE's ice deck at SP's LA Taylor Yard. Fruit Dispatch Co. had considerable number of claims due to overripe conditions as cars were not being iced until 8 to 20 hours after loading. This facility allowed icing just a short time after loading. Ice purchased from commercial firm. Retired by 1952.

Graham ITP (PE). (7,634) Regular icing station. PFE owned island-type platform, 25 carlengths, operated June to November. Most icing on the Pacific Electric was handled here plus banana shipments coming in from the Los Angeles Harbor District.

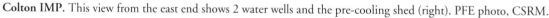

Colton IMP. This view from the east end shows 2 water wells and the pre-cooling shed (right). PFE photo, CSRM.

Colton IMP. (**Left**) The newer precooling shed is seen in this 1954 view with a string of five freshly repainted R-40-23 and -25 steel cars. (**Right**) The cold air return ducts were attached to the bunker hatches. The brine-cooled air was blown through a large duct that fitted into the car side door. Depending on the load, field heat could be eliminated in 2 to 8 hrs., e.g. grapes were faster than oranges (see Chapter 14). Both photos, PFE from CSRM.

Chula Vista ITP (San Diego & Arizona Eastern). Regular icing station. PFE contracted with Union Ice Co. which had 100 tons storage, ice trucked in, with single platform, 12 carlengths, and an island platform, 15 carlengths. Icing company performed services for between 2000 and 2100 cars of perishables each year that originated on this portion of the SD & AE.

San Diego IMP (SD&AE). Regular icing station. PFE contracted with Union Ice Co. which produced 90 tons daily, 900 tons storage, had single platform, 6 carlengths. Icing done for shipments eastbound to El Centro.

Colton IMP. (79,530) Regular icing station. Original PFE plant purchased in May, 1908, from Armour at a value of $7,087. It had a 200-ton daily production capacity, 16,000 tons storage. An entirely new ice manufacturing and precooling plant was completed in June, 1910, with a capacity of 500-ton production daily, 28,000 tons winter storage, 780 tons daily dock storage. The old Armour facilities were abandoned in June, 1912.

By 1915 PFE had three single platforms, all with mechanical conveyors: 20 carlengths, 21 carlengths, and 19 carlengths. The 19-car track could precool also. In 1947 there was a new island-type platform built, 15 carlengths, and a precooling island platform, 7 carlengths. Thus 33 cars could be precooled at once. Precooling was normally done on citrus loads only. Total capacity at all decks was 104 cars. A severe windstorm in 1949 blew off 170 ft. of the precooling shed roof and the entire shed over No. 6 platform was dismantled. Precooling operations were shut down in the late 1950's.

Colton IMP. Looking east, the original precooling sheds are at center. A portion of the PFE car shops are seen at right and in the background. Mott Studios photo for SP, John Signor collection.

Loma Linda ITP. This view shows the newly installed Preco mechanical icing and salting machines on the deck in June, 1954. SP photo, John Signor collection.

In 1952, there were 24,175 cars iced, and 7,523 tons of ice were shipped to the Coachella icing platform during June and July for grape shipments. Cars were initially iced at Colton for loading on the Redlands and Riverside Branches of the SP. It also serviced cars loaded on the UP and PE from Los Angeles and San Bernardino and furnished ice for other icing stations in the area. Winter crew averaged 40 in number and increased to 140 in June and July. An aerial view of the entire facility is on page 270.

Traffic originating locally did not tax the maximum plant capacity, but trains from the west, often as long as 100 cars, far exceeded the capacity of the short track and ice deck layout. Such long trains were taken to the yard and icers doubled over to the ice deck, or the train was taken directly to the ice deck and the hangover doubled over to another ice deck or to the yard. Since UP also used this deck, the SP would often find part or all of the deck occupied when their trains arrived.

The lack of adequate facilities to service trains at a single spot caused much delay to both railroads' operations. Elapsed icing time, start to completion, to ice a train could range from as little as fifteen minutes to as long as three hours. When practical, through SP trains were consequently directed on to Loma Linda for icing.

At Colton, after icing, the cars were assembled into "Colton Blocks" for movement eastward in trains that could have as many as 101 cars. These priority trains were usually assigned timetable, or manifest, train numbers and were often run in many sections at peak seasons.

Loma Linda ITP. Located ¾-mile east of the Colton Plant parallel to SP main line along the Santa Ana River. This facility was built to relieve the bottleneck at Colton. PFE owned the island-type platform, 3300' long, 75

carlengths. Ice was delivered by SP to an unloading spur located southside and parallel to icing platform. Unloading platform was 25 carlengths, 1128'. PFE had 45 ice service cars (old wood icers) assigned to Colton-Loma Linda transfer. Each car usually carried 164 blocks of ice that were produced at the Colton IMP for that station.

The platform was equipped with two Preco Mechanical Icing Machines and two mechanical salt machines in June, 1954. Ice from the unloading platform went up an incline conveyor, to a crossover bridge and onto the loading deck. This station performed re-icing on through trains.

Coachella ITP. (10,485) Regular icing station. PFE owned an island-type platform, built in 1949 to replace the old deck at Indio which was retired that year. It was on a curve of approximately 30 minutes, 20 carlengths, 880' long, no roof, 27 tons storage in a frame structure 12' x 33' that was built at platform level on east end. Ice brought in from Colton by rail. Icing done on all westbound cantaloupe loads (50 to 60 carloads daily) originating from the Imperial Valley, and on originating loads from the Coachella Valley during June and July grape shipping season. Grape shipments, 1121 cars in 1952, were principally moved by express cars. PFE performed icing.

Brawley ITP. (69,886) Regular icing station. PFE originally owned a single platform, 11 carlengths, built in 1911. Island-type platform built in 1925, 925' long, 20 carlengths, roofed, no ice storage, and the single platform lengthened to 21 carlengths. Ice brought in by PFE ice service from Colton. Icing for shipments originating at Brawley or vicinity performed by PFE according to operating convenience at peak of shipping season.

El Centro ITP. (Above) This 1921 view shows PFE's 10-carlength deck at left, prior to the new island-type 20-carlength facility that replaced it in 1923. At right is ice company's deck. (Below) The Imperial Ice Company (a subsidiary of Southern Sierras Power Co., later part of Southern California Edison) furnished all the ice to PFE's decks. 1923. Both photos, PFE from CSRM.

PFE also contracted with Imperial Ice Co. which produced 330 tons daily, had 30,000 tons storage, and had an 18-carlength single platform adjacent to PFE's platform. They performed simultaneous service in peak season and performed all services for Brawley in the off season.

From the 1920's on Brawley was one of the heaviest loading points on the PFE system. Some 115 men at Brawley, and 60 men at Calexico and El Centro, working in 12-hr. shifts, were employed in icing operations. These men were engaged in pre-icing cars until 2 PM. After that time, the loads began to come in for re-icing until 2 AM, when the last loads were put in trains. Both Brawley and El Centro had cook and bunkhouses that were used around the clock by icing crews during cantaloupe season. During the peak loading seasons, carload ice was shipped in from every location in southern California where ice could be obtained. The combined icing facilities in the area would dispense 150,000 tons or more of ice. See Chapter 14 for more on Imperial Valley operations.

Arizona Eastern had operating rights). PFE performed icing during shipping season and the ice company in off season.

There was also a vacuum cooling plant at this station, and two vacuum cooling plants in the Holtville area, all installed in the early 1950's. During the 1952 season, 6041 lettuce cars, or 43% of the total lettuce movement from the area (14,064 cars) were processed through the vacuum cooling plants at these locations, and this greatly reduced ice consumption.

El Centro ITP. (30,534) Regular icing station. PFE owned two platforms. The early 5-carspot platform, against the wall of the Holton Power Company's ice manufacturing plant that had 200 tons daily production and 20,000 tons storage, was replaced in 1915 with a 10-carlength platform. A new island platform built in 1923, parallel to the SP's main line and adjacent to the original deck, was 978' long, 20 carlengths, as a crossover conveyor bridge took considerable space at the south end. Both platforms roofed, painted gray. The ice company (Imperial Ice and Development after 1916) furnished and stored all ice.

El Centro was the initial icing station for shipments originating in the vicinity; for shipments, principally cantaloupe, cooled in the car by shippers; and for shipments originating on the Tijuana & Tecate Railway (the rail line south of the Mexican border over which the San Diego &

Calexico ITP. (1,092) Regular icing station. PFE owned an island-type platform, 15 carlengths, no ice storage facility, 4 carspot unloading dock. PFE performed icing on melon shipments awaiting connections at this station, May through August, and also provided manpower at private ice docks contracted to service PFE cars.

Rico ITP. (4,426) Regular icing station. PFE owned the island-type platform, 20 carlengths, located on the Holton Interurban Railroad that ran between El Centro and Holtville to the east. PFE performed icing according to operational needs.

Yuma IMP. (71,860) Regular icing station. There were two PFE-owned platform facilities in Yuma. Ice was purchased from the adjacent Yuma Ice & Cold Storage Co.

Yuma IMP. This 1934 view, taken from PFE's 34-carlength deck, shows the Yuma Ice and Cold Storage plant and PFE's 100-carlength deck. PFE photo, CSRM.

plant that had 250 tons daily production, 34,000 tons storage. There was a 100-carlength island platform for through trains and loads, and a 23-carlength island platform used exclusively for initial icing of empties for local originating loads in the Yuma Valley and Somerton areas (15,000 cars in 1952). There was a 10-carspot unloading dock, and vacuum cooling plant for precooling lettuce.

The second facility was in the SP's East Yard, had a single track, 5-carspot loading platform with a 10-ton storage house, 1 car unloading dock. It was used primarily for initial icing for local shipments and servicing westbound loads if needed.

The peak season was in June and July, 42,000 tons of ice being issued in June alone. At the peak cantaloupe season as many as 350 empties were initially iced daily, and of course, re-iced. This was in addition to main line and Imperial Valley trains that were all re-iced at Yuma.

In May, 1954, a Preco single-end Icing Machine was installed on the 23-carlength island platform. In June, 1956, the longer 100-car platform received a double-end type Preco Icing Machine.

Phoenix IMP. (19,331) Regular icing station. PFE contracted for ice from Crystal Ice Company that had 250

Yuma IMP. A severe fire on the night of August 10, 1949, burned the salt house and 250 ft. of the platform. Here a crew from an SP steam engine fights the fire with a hose connected to the locomotive injector. PFE photo, CSRM.

Tucson IMP. The former Santa Cruz I&CS plant that PFE purchased in 1920, with PFE's original 35-carlength ice deck. The plant was steam powered at the time. On the foreground spur, in the photo center, is an SPMW "icing car" with roof platform used for reicing express cars at the depot just east (right) of this view. Car paint schemes indicate date is about 1925. PFE photo, CSRM.

tons ice production daily, 7000 tons storage capacity. PFE owned an island-type platform, 36 carlengths, 5-carspot unloading dock. Regular icing for shipments cooled in car by shipper, and initial icing for loads originating in the Salt River Valley district which extended 40 miles west to Dixie, and to Queen Creek, about 40 miles to the east. The ice company performed all services.

Mesa IMP. (18,563) Regular icing station. PFE contracted ice from Crystal Ice Company which could produce 150 tons daily, store 14,000 tons. PFE first owned 10-carlength platform that was replaced by an island-type platform, built in 1927, 20 carlengths, 2-carspot unloading dock. Ice company performed icing services. A vacuum cooling plant was also at Mesa for precooling field heat from lettuce loads.

Tucson IMP. (45,769) Regular icing station. PFE owned two facilities at Tucson for icing cars. The ice manufacturing plant, originally the Santa Cruz Ice & Cold Storage Co. located near downtown Tucson, that PFE purchased in a 1920 contract, eventually had a capacity of 260 tons daily, with storage capacity of 22,500 tons. The plant manufactured 45,769 tons of ice in 1952, issued 12,091 tons for initial icing, 18,695 tons for re-icing, and loaded 12,520 tons in cars for shipment to other PFE locations.

Santa Cruz Ice had a 13-carlength platform. PFE immediately constructed a new 35-carlength island platform. Around 1945 PFE built a 70-carlength island deck with a 10-carlength unloading platform in the large SP freight yard (see aerial photo, page 273). The other plat-

form was in the SP's yard near the depot, which had a 20-ton storage capacity, a single platform, 5 carlengths, and a 1-carspot unloading dock.

Icing performed by PFE at both facilities. Westbounds were only iced if shipments originated west of El Paso. Eastbounds were iced as follows: shipments of grapes, melons, and potatoes originating east of Beaumont, California; shipments originating in Eloy-Casa Grande district of Arizona; shipments originating in Mexico; shipments destined to points intermediate to Tucson, El Paso, or Nogales; and shipments for delivery to connections at Deming, New Mexico.

Nogales, Arizona IMP. (3,617) Emergency icing station. Originally PFE owned an icing platform, 29 carlengths, 100 tons storage, and for many years PFE did icing and all ice came from Tucson. At times, tomato loads would run over 100 cars daily calling for icing at Nogales. By 1952, icing at Nogales was contracted with the Citizens Utilities Co. which had a 20-ton daily production capacity and storage for 800 tons. Their platform was single, 6 carlengths, 1-carspot loading/unloading dock. Ice to the PFE deck was transferred under the track via a tunnel conveyor from the ice plant.

Facilities were for emergency icing only. All loads of Mexican cantaloupes, frozen shrimp, and other commodities were re-iced at Nogales, Arizona, if required; however, the regular icing station for the traffic from Mexico was Tucson. Top icing was done on peas and cantaloupes when requested by the shipper. In 1952, 1204 cars were bunker iced, and 260 top iced. Ice company performed icing and all services.

Empalme IMP. This was PFE's only facility in Mexico, with somewhat untypical concrete ice deck supports. This plant pre-iced and re-iced all PFE shipments going north from the productive agricultural areas of Mexico's west coast. John Signor collection.

PFE IN MEXICO – SPdeM

The first shipment of Mexican produce exported to the U.S. in PFE equipment through the Nogales gateway was in 1916. In the early years of PFE operations, the Agent's offices were located in Nogales, Sonora, Mexico, and during the civil difficulties in Mexico in 1927 it was necessary for PFE to walk a tightrope between the adversaries in order to keep PFE cars moving.

The west coast of Mexico originated approximately 9000 cars of perishables annually, primarily tomatoes, cucumbers, peppers, melons and peas. The refrigerator cars were furnished at Nogales, Mexico, to the Southern Pacific of Mexico (sold to the Mexican government in 1951) by PFE under contract. PFE also had Car Hire contracts with National Railways of Mexico and Ferrocarril Sonora-Baja California. PFE was well known in Mexico and when shippers asked for "carro amarillo" the agents knew they wanted a PFE "yellow car," long after PFE cars became orange in color in 1929. Large crops of fruits and vegetables were moved through all border gateways, but Nogales and Laredo were the most important for West Coast and Central Mexico produce. The shipping season was normally from about December 1 to June 1.

The loading area in Mexico extended from Empalme, 260 miles south of the border, to Mazatlan, 734 miles from Nogales. The heaviest loading territory was around Sinaloa

and Culiacan, a distance of 600 miles from the U.S. PFE maintained an agent in Guadalajara to forward loads north that originated on the National Railway of Mexico. PFE's only icing facility in Mexico was at Empalme.

Empalme IMP. Regular icing station. In the late 1920's, PFE built, owned and operated an ice manufacturing plant that was sold in the early 1950's to the Pacific Railway of Mexico. It had an island platform, 15 car-lengths, one side being a spur and the other a through track, for a 30-car capacity at one time. PFE performed pre-icing for cars sent south to the growing areas for loading. The cars would return in blocks for re-icing and dispatching north to Nogales. Tucson also shipped many carloads of ice south to supplement the Empalme plant.

On arrival at the border, all cars from Mexico were placed on team tracks in Nogales, Sonora, Mexico. After necessary inspections were made by U. S. Dept. of Agriculture and Customs officials, the Transcontinental Freight Bureau, and interested buyers and brokers, the cars crossed into the U. S. in accord with crossing diversions filed with the PFE. These diversions were processed and given to the SP in Nogales, Arizona, for handling. During the heaviest shipping period of the season, February and March, as many as 200 cars were cleared daily at the border.

El Paso ITP. This is the 100-carlength island platform built in 1948 that also had a top-icing deck below. Here workmen demonstrate the five Link-Belt retop icing machines, creating an atypical snow storm. PFE photo, CSRM.

El Paso ITP. (79,827) Regular icing station. This point was one of PFE's busiest main-line stations, and facilities here grew with the need. PFE contracted ice from the Globe Ice Co., which had production capabilities of 300 tons daily, storage of 21,000 tons, and a loading/unloading dock 29 cars long. Original 25-carlength (c/l) island platform was built in 1920, and a 45 c/l extension was added in 1928, for a total of 70 carlengths. This platform was opposite the Globe plant.

In 1948 PFE built a new 100-carlength island platform, three miles from the Globe facility. The old deck at the Globe plant was retired and a replacement 15-c/l platform built there. The new 100-c/l platform could provide bunker icing and retop icing. The lower level had 5 Link-Belt retop icing machines, each one being equipped with a 4" hose that could deliver one ton of ice per minute.

All eastbound perishables from Southern California, Arizona, and Nogales routed via SP and its connections moved through El Paso and were serviced there. The yard office and icing facilities were on a 24-hour basis throughout the year. During 1952, 36,321 bunker icers, using 64,868 tons, were serviced and 3281 cars were retop iced, using 8,660 tons. Salt issues were quite heavy, 7013 cars being salted, using 2,668,505 lbs.

A fleet of old wood ice cars was assigned to ice service to transfer the ice from the Globe plant, the three miles to the 15-carlength unloading dock adjacent to the new main platform. This operation entailed loading and unloading close to 50 cars per day during the busy season. It was also necessary during the heavy summer season to augment

El Paso ITP. Ice was fed into the Link-Belt machines through trap doors from the ice deck above. The machines rode along light rails on the retop deck. PFE photo, CSRM.

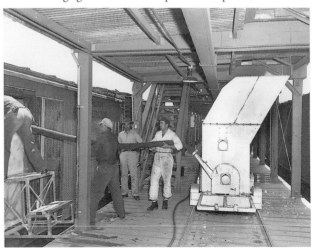

El Paso ITP. (Left) Here the crossover bridge from the unloading deck is shown. Note the trap doors on right that allowed ice to be dropped to the retop deck (see photo, previous page). The sign for the old Hotel Cortez is just visible at far left. PFE photo, CSRM.

(Below) The "Jumbo Car" used to re-ice express reefers at the passenger depot. It may have been rebuilt from a 50-ft. automobile car. These Polaroid photos are the only known views of SPMW 602. PFE photos, CSRM.

Globe's ice supply with carload ice from other points. Yard storage of 500 tons was maintained at the platform year-round to serve as an emergency supply.

Express car icing, except solid trains, was performed in a unique way by PFE at the SP depot. A 60' car with a platform, an "ice deck on wheels," and referred to as the "Jumbo Car" was used for this service. It was loaded with ice at the main platform and switched to await incoming passenger trains. One complete express car, plus one end of each of the two adjoining cars could be iced from the "Jumbo" at one time. The "Jumbo" would then be moved along the parallel track to the next set of hatches. Solid express trains were routed directly to the main platform.

In addition to the servicing performed at the platform and depot, heater inspections (821 cars in 1952) and the icing of westbound perishables were done at the SP (T&NO) Alfalfa Yard, eight miles from the PFE platform. A specially designed truck, complete with lift conveyor, was used for these icings. Manpower was sent out when required from the regular platform crew.

This practice was established in April, 1953. Previous to that date, westbound icers were switched from Alfalfa Yard to the main deck. All westbound trains were made up at Alfalfa Yard. During the cooler winter months, west-bound empties had hatches opened here to vent position to aid in ice removal by melting the ice enroute to Tucson. In the hot summer months the ice melted on its own.

The regular online business was augmented by approximately 500 carloads of Mexican perishables received annually at El Paso from connections at Juarez across the border.

A 1964 building program upgraded and expanded the mechanical refrigerator car servicing facilities here to meet the increasing demand.

El Paso ITP. Toward the end of express reefer operation, icing was done by truck and "Jumbo" icing cars at PFE facilities were retired. The trailer carries a conveyor to raise the ice to hatch level. PFE photo, CSRM.

Recollections of Pete Holst:

"PFE had standard plans for single or double track ice decks, and sections of it were all standard, though it would be modified to fit specific requirements such as restricted clearance or curvature. In the spring of 1920 I had gone to Tucson with Superintendent of Refrigeration Phillips to upgrade the old ice manufacturing plant we had just purchased there. Phillips practically ran PFE as he had the say in everything that went on inside the company. Anyway, we got Tucson pretty near working, and here comes another telegram, 'Go to El Paso and buy all material needed for a new icing platform there.'

We had a track problem in El Paso. There was no room to build a two-track island platform and keep the SP's double-track main line open. For years after they'd always ask me, 'How come the cross joints in El Paso are all cut diagonally?' I'd say, 'There's a story behind that.' We had to build the platform that way to get one side working until we could put the track in on the other side. We had to move two tracks in order to do it without getting on top of the SP's main line.

We had about twenty car lengths of the new platform all set up, and the bents were all raised and nailed together, just temporarily, see, before we started to bolt them. Then the SP came through with a train that had a carload of scrap that had been picked up at the mines out in Bisbee. Some of that load was sticking out on the side, and it hit that new row of bents, and I'll never forget that thing, just like a string of dominoes, the whole platform went down. I'll tell you, there's a lot of things I've seen in this outfit. By the time I got out of there that summer, I was quite a purchasing agent!"

Tucumcari IMP. Special icing station. PFE contracted with Tucumcari Ice & Coal Co. to service special car shipments originating near Mosquero on the Dawson Branch that ran out from Tucumcari. The company had a single 2-car platform.

Near Mosquero were carbonated wells from which carbon dioxide for dry ice was produced. PFE maintained a complement of specially rebuilt and equipped cars for dry ice, which after 1939 were a separate class (see Chapter 7). These cars had no ice hatches, since the load refrigerated the car, and were provided with extremely thick insulation to retard meltage or sublimation of the product. Yearly shipments were between 400 and 450 carloads.

SOUTHERN DISTRICT – T&NO, StLSW

The Southern District jurisdiction covered the entire Texas & New Orleans subsidiary of the Southern Pacific. The western end of the territory was Del Rio, and it extended south to Edinburg and Brownsville, and east to New Orleans. The district functioned under a General Agent, District Agent, and four Agents, all of whom were supervised by the Superintendent located at the General Offices in Houston. Southern Pacific's main routing connected with the St. Louis Southwestern Railway (Cotton Belt) at Corsicana and Shreveport. This district also extended on the StLSW to where that road connected with the Memphis and East St. Louis gateways.

A General Agency was established by PFE in Houston in 1917; however the Southern District did not come into existence until 1927 when the Southern Pacific completed its lines into the Rio Grande Valley and Brownsville. A rough triangle between Houston, Galveston and Corpus Christi, plus its extension into the Lower Rio Grande Valley, comprised the boundaries of approximately 1300 miles of lines operated by the SP. Most of these lines were originally constructed to serve the huge cattle ranches, but the development of the fertile lands for agriculture changed the character of operations. In 1928, a PFE District Agency

A typical scene in southern Texas in 1946. This is the daily train from Brownsville to Victoria, trundling through an unidentified small town. The motive power for train 352 is T&NO 2-8-2 No. 755 with a water car supplementing its modest-size tender. T&NO photo, courtesy Don Hofsommer.

was set up at Harlingen, Tex., and about that same time, an ice manufacturing plant was built at Edinburg.

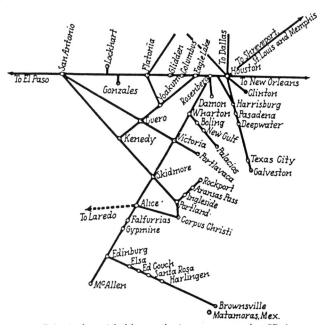

Principal perishable producing areas on the SP in southern and southeastern Texas. *Railway Age*, 1940.

These principal Texas growing areas, where almost every known vegetable, except artichokes, is cultivated, was apportioned by the SP and PFE into four districts to meet the varying needs of the shippers. Crops varied in each of these districts as well as climatic and harvest periods.

District No. 1 included the lines between Houston on the northeast, San Antonio on the northwest and Beeville on the south. District No. 2 followed the line of the Texas-Mexican and portions of the SP between Corpus Christi

and Laredo. District No. 3 extended from Beeville south, including the Corpus Christi territory, to the northern boundary of the Lower Rio Grande Valley. The fourth district comprised the 23 by 75 mile Lower Rio Grande Valley which was and is one of the richest and most fertile agricultural territories in the country. The SP had about 25 per cent of the track mileage in the Valley and records indicate that PFE handled about 25-30 per cent of the perishable traffic from these districts. With the advent of mechanical refrigerator cars and trailers (TOFC), that figure went up to 47 per cent, or 6800 carloads in 1969.

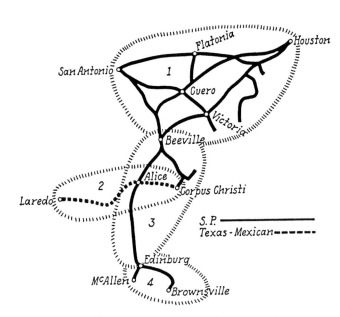

SP perishable districts in Texas. *Railway Age*, 1940.

The Valley operations center was at Edinburg in the northwestern corner of the district. The reserve of empty

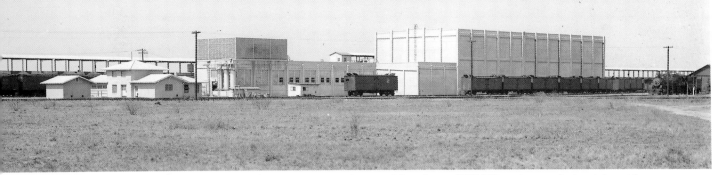

Edinburg IMP. This is the new plant shortly after its construction in 1927. Note the small T&NO engine terminal at right, with two locomotives (the one on the left is M-4 Mogul 459) ready for their next asssignment. Angel Studio photo for PFE, CSRM.

reefers was kept there. There were 13 loading points located in this area, the largest being at Elsa, which could annually generate loadings of 2500 cars or more. Other important loading points along the SP were Edcouch, Santa Rosa, and Los Fresnos.

Loading in the Valley was done at night, and requirements for empties from the north were distributed to the loading points by two trains daily, each of which made the round trip between Edinburg and Brownsville, setting out empties and picking up loads. During heavy seasons, additional trains were frequently operated, but no standby power was kept at Edinburg, since the need for additional power could always be determined in advance, and locomotives would be sent down from the division point at Victoria, 211 miles north of Edinburg.

When loads were brought into Edinburg during the night, they were consolidated into trains in two classifications, one for the north Texas gateways and the other for the Shreveport gateway, to simplify the switching at Victoria, where the lines of these two routings diverged. Northbound trains out of Edinburg were filled out with perishables at Alice, where the Texas-Mexican cars were delivered to the SP, with Skidmore and Wharton being other important points where cars were added to the trains. Over 3500 cars of citrus fruit and 4800-5000 cars of vegetables would be generated annually out of the Valley. In general, because of the climatic conditions in this area, operations were organized on a basis of a fairly constant flow of traffic throughout the year.

Officials of PFE made a survey of the Cotton Belt when SP took control of that road in 1932 to see if there was enough production to make up contract "deals" to furnish cars. It was found that comparatively few loadings originated on line. The biggest business was the rose plant shippers in the area around Tyler, Texas. No contracts were drawn up, but as an SP subsidiary, the PFE cars were there when the StLSW asked for them.

Del Rio IMP. (9,659) Regular icing station. PFE contracted with Central Power and Light Co. for ice. They had 48 tons daily production capability, 75 tons storage. There was a 45-car single platform; ice company owned 20

carlengths, PFE owned 25 carlengths, 3 car loading/unloading dock. Icing performed by the ice company.

San Antonio IMP. (4,188) Regular icing station. PFE contracted ice from Southern Henke Ice Co. that could produce 1200 tons daily, store 1260 tons, had 10-car single platform, 1-carspot unloading/loading dock. Bunker re-icing done here on westbound shipments from the Rio Grande Valley, and on eastbound shipments except those originating west of Del Rio and destined to Hearne or Houston or points beyond. Retop icing done when requested by shipper regardless of origin. Icing performed by ice company.

Hearne ITP. (11,690) Regular icing station. Located at east end of railroad yard. PFE owned a single platform built in 1929, 45 carlengths, 2-car unloading/loading dock. Ice storage house had 65 tons capacity, salt house 32 tons, both under platform. Re-icing of eastbound shipments from El Paso. Icing done by PFE. Storage house gone by 1953 and all ice brought in by rail. Mechanical refrigeration service facilities built here in 1968.

Houston ITP. (9,085) Regular icing station. Located in T&NO Englewood Yard. PFE contracted for ice from Southern Ice Co. PFE owned an island platform, 45 carlengths, had storage house with 100 tons capacity. Ice was transported in cars from ice plant to ice deck. Unloading/loading dock, 5 carlengths. Icing done by PFE.

Skidmore ITP. Regular icing station. PFE built island-type platform here in 1927 to meet refrigeration requirements of new territory south of Falfurrias, 30 carlengths, roofed, with 120-ton ice storage house, 5-carspot unloading/loading dock. Obsolete by 1950.

Edinburg IMP. (7,081) Regular icing station. PFE originally built this ice manufacturing plant in 1927. It had 145 tons production capability, 17,000 tons storage. There was an island platform, 30 carlengths, roofed, 2 carspot unloading/loading dock. PFE subsequently sold the plant in 1937 and contracted ice from the Edinburg Ice Co.

(probably the company that bought the plant), and icing services were done by that company. Icing was done on originating loads from the Lower Rio Grande Valley, mainly vegetables and citrus fruits; grapefruit, the famous Texas Ruby Red, was a major shipment.

Brownsville IMP. Emergency icing station. PFE contracted services from Central Power & Light Co. which had a small 50-ton production capacity, no storage, island platform, 10 carlengths.

Galveston ITP. Located in T&NO yard south of scale house. PFE built a single platform, 10 carlengths, no roof, in 1935. Constructed to render proper icing service for incoming banana shipments. PFE contracted for ice. Facilities last used in 1942, and retired in 1951, as initial icing and re-icing for Galveston was then done at Houston. Obsolete by 1952.

Beaumont IMP. (553) Regular icing station. PFE contracted all services from Morgan Ice Co. that had single 3-car platform. Icing done on all shipments moving via Rockland Subdivision, and emergency icing for other traffic.

Lake Charles IMP. Emergency icing station. PFE contracted from Service Ice Co. that had 90-ton daily production, 100 tons storage, single 2-car platform. Icing done for shipments originating on the De Riddle Branch.

New Orleans-Avondale ITP. (6,345) Regular icing station. PFE contracted with City Ice Service which had 300 tons daily production capability, 3200 tons storage, island platform, 5 carlengths. PFE built a 10-carlength single platform in 1935. Icing done for all traffic only if required, except no icing on traffic routed via Cotton Belt moving through Houston. Ice company performed service. PFE retired the ice deck in August, 1969.

Dallas IMP. Emergency icing station. PFE contracted for services as needed from Pure Ice & Cold Storage which had 20 tons daily production capacity, 180 tons storage, single 8-car platform. Ice company performed services.

Fort Worth. (441-T&NO, 47-StLSW) Regular icing station. PFE had short-term ice contracts. No platform. Icing done with escalator trucks owned by ice company.

Tyler (StLSW). (7,081) Emergency icing station. PFE contracted local services as required.

Pine Bluff (StLSW). (9,945) Regular icing station. Icing done at StLSW ice platform. Ice was purchased from local ice companies.

East St.Louis (StLSW). (8,091) Regular icing station. StLSW owned the platform, ice purchased from local ice company.

EASTERN DISTRICT – UP

The Eastern District comprised stations entirely on the Union Pacific lines extending across the vast great plains area, into the "Heart of the Midlands." The district's western end was at Green River, Wyoming. It stretched south to Denver, Colorado, with eastern terminals at Kansas City, Kansas, and Council Bluffs, Iowa. Omaha was the location of the district's main offices.

Being situated at the source of the world-famous midwestern corn-fed beef, most of the PFE "deals" here were with the major meat packing companies of the nation and many large independent packers. Between 60 and 65 percent of the originating loads in this district were meat and packinghouse products, followed by frozen foods, which accounted for nearly 20 percent of the total shipments from the district.

One of the most unique unloading/loading points situated on the Union Pacific line is in this district. It is the Mid-Continent Underground Storage Warehouse at Bonner City, Kansas. This is a series of manmade caves developed in limestone formations by quarrying opera-

A string of PFE reefers is eased into the Mid-Continent warehouse at Bonner City, Kan., by UP 2-8-0 No. 201. UP Railroad Museum photo 00357-12.

Laramie IMP. This view shows the new artificial ice manufacturing plant built in 1951 (foreground) and the huge ice storage gallery that was still utilized. UP Railroad Museum, photo 34527.

tions. The immense natural limestone deposit has been mined since the early 1900's with the limestone rock being used for railroad roadbeds as well as in the construction industry.

The mining is done by the room and pillar method, whereby large rooms are excavated from solid rock with about 20 percent of each room's area left intact in the form of giant pillars supporting the solid rock roof. Around 1950 it occurred to various companies quarrying the limestone that the rooms could be used as storage chambers, particularly since the inside temperature remains at a constant 55° F., year-round.

Industry has found many uses for the caves, from manufacturing, to office space, to record storage. Five of the caves are refrigerated and serve as public storage facilities for foodstuffs. These warehouses provide an excellent mid-country storage of rail shipments of frozen foods, fresh fruits and vegetables, meats, eggs and dairy products, and dressed poultry for subsequent forwarding to any section of the country.

The Mid-Continent Company's facility is one of the largest and has 13.3 million cubic feet of freezer, cooler and dry storage space. It is accessible at ground level throughout to railroad cars, supplemented by tractor-trains and lift trucks. The railroad tracks and unloading platforms can accommodate 22 cars at one time within the cave. During 1974 Mid-Continent handled 2256 PFE cars in and out of the cave storage.

Green River ITP. Emergency icing station. This plant apparently became obsolete around the time the new Laramie IMP went into operation in 1951. It was listed active in 1950 records, but was not listed as an icing station in 1953. Original icing platform and natural ice house here were built by the UP in 1906 at the west end of the yard. PFE operated the platform under lease.

In 1930 the UP rearranged the Green River Yard and

requested PFE to move the icing facilities to conform with the new yard layout, and to locate at the east end of the yard as the greater amount of icing was in connection with westbound perishables handled on the rear of trains. PFE built, at a location about one mile east of the passenger station on the south side of the UP main line near the point where Bitter Creek flows into the Green River, a single platform, 220' long, 5 carlengths, no roof, painted gray, 20' x 52' 60-ton storage house with salt storage house under 3 bays of the icing platform.

Two heater and charcoal/alcohol storage houses were also located here as heater protective service was always the prime duty of this station for eastbound loads heading across the high plains country in fall and winter. These duties were performed even after the icing services ceased.

Laramie IMP. (104,155) Regular icing station. Laramie was always one of PFE's most active icing stations and was the largest on the entire UP system. Until 1951, Laramie was the site of PFE's largest natural ice plant (see Chapter 12).

The PFE facilities (both the NIP and IMP) were located about 1-¼ mile west of the UP bridge over the Laramie River. In 1951, PFE's Vice President and General Manager, K.V. Plummer, announced a million-dollar upgrading project to convert Laramie to a modern ice manufacturing plant. The main reasons for the decision were the high labor cost of handling the ice harvest, unpredictability of the annual harvest, and the necessity of shipping 40,000 tons of manufactured ice annually from other plants to supplement the local harvest.

Construction began in April, 1951, and was completed by fall. The new construction included installation of refrigeration equipment in the existing ice storage rooms built in 1923 and the erection of a single story 96' by 180' reinforced concrete building to house modern ice manufacturing equipment. Newly designed ice conveyor deliv-

"New 300-lb. ice blocks manufactured at Laramie serve as chairs, table and floor for Shirley Whitlock, left, and Judy Houtz. The 28° F. temperature in the ice storage room helps them beat the July heat. They are, of course, knitting socks for the Wyoming winter" (from PFE's press release). UP Railroad Museum, photo 070752B.

ery facilities for moving ice from storage to the platform were also installed.

The new plant had the capability to manufacture and store sufficient ice to handle re-icing for the 70,000 cars that halted there annually. The plant could produce 420 tons of ice daily, had winter storage for 39,000 tons, daily storage space for 800 tons. The ice requirements at this station during the peak season in August and September exceeded 1000 tons daily. Nearly 200,000 gallons of water were required per day during this period to produce ice.

The island-type platform, 85 carlengths, roofed, had been built in 1947 and was used as such until 1955. In that year the platform was lengthened an additional 880', and the entire 4620' deck, 105 carlengths, was remodeled, including removal of the roof, to accommodate three new Preco mechanical Car Icers. The Preco icing machines operated on 40 lb. rails the full length of the platform.

The upper platform also had three salt lorries with a capacity of 5 tons of salt each. These ran along behind the Preco icers to add salt as specified per car. The sub-platform or retop deck accommodated retop ice blower machines and salt storage. The 105-carlength deck eliminated the need to "double over" the longer trains.

All eastbound and westbound trains were re-iced at Laramie. Eastbounds were serviced at the main West Laramie plant and platform. Westbound loads, which were much fewer in number, were handled by PFE lift trucks in the UP yards. Ice was secured in car load lots from the plant. Around 2000 tons annually were used to service westbound loads in this manner.

Demand for icing decreased to the point that in 1960 one mechanical icing machine was transferred to Nampa, and an artificial ice manufacturing tank and two compressors were transfered to Pocatello. In 1962 PFE transferred, sold or disposed of the balance of the ice production machinery. The plant ceased operations that year.

Cheyenne ITP. (431) Emergency icing station. Ice was purchased from the Crystal Ice Co. under yearly contract. PFE owned an ice lift truck; icing was done by UP labor, supervised by PFE agent. Re-icing done mainly on express reefers on passenger trains, or on hold cars.

UP had constructed its own ice house and platform at Cheyenne in 1902 and it was leased and used by PFE as a regular icing station until July, 1922, when Laramie became PFE's only reicing station for all through freights, eliminating Cheyenne as such. UP used the facilities for some years to re-ice express shipments and local initial loads.

An example of a PFE car service truck used to ice express reefers at passenger depots. UP Railroad Museum photo 45402, courtesy Frank Peacock.

Denver ITP. (7,755) Regular icing station. Initially natural ice was shipped from Laramie and stored for use at a UP-built facility. This and local supply proved inadequate. In 1922 PFE built an island-type platform, 15 carlengths, 1 carspot loading/unloading dock, no roof,

Denver ITP. This is the original facility that the UP built before the turn of the century. It had a 4000-ton, 24' by 480' storage house, and a 526' icing platform. UP Railroad Museum, photo 500.011.

painted gray, adjacent to IMP. Ice was secured from Denver Crystal Ice Co., which had 300 tons daily production, 5000 tons storage. PFE employees performed icing on all cars, except those cars received from the Denver & Rio Grande Western at Denver and departing eastbound from Denver in UP symbol train No. 250 or in "Omaha Specials." These trains were iced by the D&RGW at their much larger deck.

La Salle ITP. Regular icing station. PFE acquired original UP ice storage house and 18-carlength platform in 1923. The 110' by 140' storage house and 8 carlengths of the deck were retired in 1935. After that, ice was brought in by carload. Facilities closed in early 1940's due to reduction of vegetable shipments in vicinity.

Ellis ITP. (423) Regular icing station. UP owned single platform, 4 carlengths. Ice was secured from Ellis Ice Co. Icing done on shipments originating at Ellis, with labor performed by UP employees.

Salina IMP. (621) Emergency icing station. Ice secured from Western Ice Co. which owned a single platform, 7 carlengths, could manufacture 70 tons daily, store 400 tons. Ice company furnished labor.

Marysville ITP. (1,491) Regular icing station. Located in UP yards east of roundhouse. Originally a UP-built facility with a 671' platform that was leased to PFE. Facilities owned and rebuilt in 1941 by PFE, single platform, 253', 6 carlengths, no roof, painted gray, 1-carspot loading dock, 25-ton storage house. Ice secured from Marysville Ice Co. or by carload from PFE Council Bluffs plant. PFE performed icing service.

Icing done year-round for eastbound shipments routed to connections at Topeka or points short of Kansas City. Regular icing was done for westbound shipments of butter, eggs, and poultry originating west of Junction City, moving through Marysville and destined west of North Platte; and initial icing for in-transit shipments intermediate to North Platte, Kansas City or St. Joseph.

Marysville ITP. This 1925 view shows the facility built by the UP. Two PFE ice service reefers are at the unloading dock. Western History collection, Denver Public Library, courtesy Dean Dickerhoof.

North Platte IMP. Looking east from the pedestrian crossover toward the city proper. The 55-carlength platform is at left, the 17-carlength de‹ at right. In the long lines of PFE cars at left, very few "single-medallion" paint schemes survive (see Chapter 8). The UP engine terminal is in tl distance at center of photo; note the two UP 9000-class 4-12-2's drifting through the yard. Nov. 19, 1949. UP Railroad Museum photo 3091

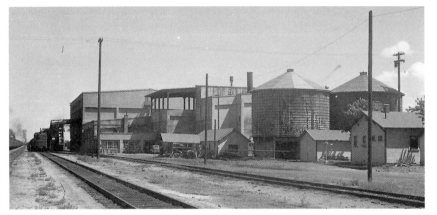

North Platte IMP. Looking east from the west end of the plant. The two water tanks supplied the boilers for hot water used in deicing westbound empties. PFE photo, CSRM.

North Platte IMP. On the south side of the plant, an icing chute was installed to ice meat loads from local packing houses. Note incline serving chute and cable between rails to move cars to machine. UP Railroad Museum photo 46832.

Kansas City ITP. (62,811) Regular icing station. Located in UP yards, 20th and Muncie, Kansas City, Kansas. PFE owned a double island platform, 4500' long, 100 carlengths, with retop icing deck for 60 carlengths, 10 carspot unloading/loading dock. The icing platform was equipped with two Preco Icing Machines, installed in June, 1954, and four Link-Belt conveyor-type top ice machines.

Ice secured from the Federal Cold Storage Co. which had one plant adjacent to the PFE deck, and delivered ice via overhead bridge with chain conveyors. F.C.S. Co. had 250 tons daily production capability, 1000 tons storage. F.C.S.Co. also had a second plant in Fairfax (north of KC) that set aside 3000 tons in storage for PFE. This ice was transported via Federal's trucks.

Initially UP and PFE ice requirements were protected with ice shipped from Laramie and stored at Armstrong, Kansas, and such ice as could be secured from local concerns. This arrangement proved unsatisfactory, and PFE built its first 970' single platform, adjacent to the privately owned IMP in 1922.

This station was PFE's last regular icing of eastbound shipments moving via UP lines or CRI&P's (Rock Island) Golden State Route. Re-icing at points east were handled by connecting carriers. Westbound shipments received by the UP were re-iced.

Gering ITP. (24) Emergency icing station. PFE-owned single platform, 176' long, 4 carlengths, 1 carspot unloading/loading dock, 14' x 44' 30-ton storage house at one end, painted gray. Ice secured from Scottsbluff Ice Co. Icing done by ice company on hold cars or shipments originating in the area.

North Platte IMP. (10,832) Regular icing station. Located in UP yards west of city. PFE owned an IMP capable of 120 tons daily, 14,200 tons storage. When this plant was built in 1920 to replace the NIP, it utilized the steam-driven ammonia compressors from Roseville as that plant was converted to electric. The steam boilers were converted at North Platte to use coal instead of oil.

There were two platforms: an island-type, double track, 55-carlength roofed deck, on the north side of the plant, and a single, 17-carlength unroofed platform on the south side. All but two carlengths of this latter platform was dismantled in 1950. When the new UP classification yard was built in the 1950's, a single 12-carlength platform was built there.

At North Platte PFE operated an unusual and perhaps unique icing practice in that on one track adjacent to the ice house the cars were brought to an icing machine rather than the machine moving to the cars. The UP would set out cars used for local packinghouse products on this track. An endless cable was used to pull the cars past the one icing spot. A string of five cars could be moved by the cable. The machine operator controlled the movement of cars. Ice came up an incline conveyor from the store room,

Grand Island ITP. The original plant shown in this 1918 view was built by the UP at the turn of the century, later leased to PFE. The 214' platform is served by a 6800-ton storage house. Observe that the telegraph poles have been used as part of the deck structure. UP Railroad Museum photo 500.005.

was crushed, and dropped into the chute for delivery to the bunkers. A gate diverted the ice into either the outboard or inboard hatch. Overhead salt storage, with a power auger, measured and spilled the correct amount of salt into each ice bunker.

Icing at North Platte was done on eastbounds except traffic originating at or west of Laramie or Denver. Westbound shipments were iced if required. This was also the main deicing station for westbound empties. Hot water was used to flush and clean ice bunkers and car interiors before cars continued west. Up to 200 cars could be deiced per day, and thousands of tons of ice were removed annually. This operation is described further in Chapter 11. Westbound empties thus could dry en route.

Grand Island ITP. (1,372) Regular icing station. Originally a UP facility, leased to PFE. PFE later built and owned a single platform, 308' long, 7 carlengths, 12' x 16' ice storage house at platform level, 20-ton capacity, 1 car unloading spot with conveyor ramp to ice house, painted gray. Ice secured by carload from Council Bluffs plant or locally under UPRR contract. PFE performed icing.

The station provided initial icing in transit or eastbound shipments originating between North Platte and Grand Island from mid-April to mid-November, except potatoes billed to points east of the Missouri River, July 15 to November 15, inclusive. Also listed as emergency icing station if specific through loads required service.

Omaha ITP. (9,932) Regular icing station. Located in UP's 8th Street yard. PFE's first facility, built in 1925, had a 20-carlength island platform, 100-ton storage house. By 1952, it was 17 carlengths, with a 25-ton storage house. Ice was secured in carload lots from the Council Bluffs plant. Icing done by PFE. This station was established as an adjunct to Council Bluffs facility to lessen switching and transfer of cars used in Omaha meat packing house loadings. Icing also done for cars delivered to or received from connecting railroads.

Council Bluffs IMP. (62,190) Regular icing station. Located on the south side of UP's main lines/transfer lines to Omaha, at west end of Council Bluffs yard. The PFE-owned plant could manufacture 280 tons of ice daily, had winter storage of 23,000 tons, daily storage 350 tons. This plant was put into operation after a very rapid four-month construction on August 1, 1921 to replace the original natural ice plant and pond that was totally outmoded.

PFE owned two platforms. No. 1 platform, island type, 3740', 80 carlengths, (originally 55 carlengths) was at the main line grade level. No. 2 platform, island type, 1012', 23 carlengths, started at the northeast corner of the winter storeroom and ran east at the level of the plant, which was considerably below the main line grade level. Ice was transferred to the No. 1 deck via an overhead bridge.

Platform 2 was known as the "meat car" deck, and serviced all cars loaded at the Omaha slaughtering yards

Omaha ITP. The perishable team tracks and ice deck are shown in this July 14, 1925, view. UP Railroad Museum photo H7-130.

Council Bluffs IMP. In this early summer, 1922, view, the new 55-carlength platform, with its timber footings, and ice crossover bridge are shown. This eastward-looking photo was taken shortly before the severe summer windstorm which destroyed much of the deck shown. The UP yards are in the distance. Sheelor Bros. photo for PFE, CSRM.

Council Bluffs IMP. These two views show the devastation caused by high winds in 1922, as related by Pete Holst in the text. Note twisted metal of conveyor bridge above, and McKeen motor car below. PFE photos, CSRM.

and meatpacker holdover cars. Located under the west end of No. 2 platform was the deck for ice loading, 3 carlengths, and unloading, 6 cars.

All eastbound trains pulled alongside No. 1 platform for re-icing prior to transfer to connecting railroads. On special occasions an 80-car train could be re-iced in as little as 25 to 30 minutes. The normal PFE standard to re-ice a car manually was 50 to 60 seconds. Icing for westbound shipments was performed by truck in the UP hump yard by City Ice Co. and their labor.

Recollections of Pete Holst:

"The new Council Bluffs plant built in 1921 was about 25 feet below the UP tracks that came across the bridge over the Missouri River. The new platform was 55 car-lengths and the incline overhead ice conveyor bridge was 10 carlengths from the west end of the deck. Due to the fact that the platform was built on new land fill, the posts under the deck were not set into the fill as would be normal, but were on heavy timbers so that leveling of the platform could be easily maintained as the fill settled.

I had just arrived in Omaha in 1922 after my marriage and was staying in a hotel when one evening we had a real big storm with heavy winds and rain. My boss, George Wall, called me and said the Council Bluffs plant had been badly damaged by the storm. When we got out there, we found all but 10 carlengths of the ice platform tossed upside down in a cornfield east of the plant. The wind had just picked it right up from the foundation timbers. We had to salvage what was left and rebuild in a hurry as the heavy season was just about to start."

In 1956, major modifications were done at the Council Bluffs facilities. The No. 1 platform was rebuilt, including removal of the roof, to accept two Preco Icing Machines and two salt machines. During the winter months the platform was heavily used for heater work as PFE heaters were removed from cars and replaced with those of connecting lines. The shorter No. 2 platform was removed, and later trailer facilities were constructed in its place. Ice was transferred from the ice manufacturing plant through a tunnel under the track instead of the old overhead bridge.

In 1969, part of the winter ice storage building was converted to a refrigerated trailer repair center, and steam

boilers and high-pressure equipment was installed to clean trailers and mechanical cars. Many westbound empties were then cleaned at Council Bluffs. An important subsidiary operation was the scouring of meat hooks to equip the vehicles. About 4000 hooks per day were processed through two machines. Council Bluffs thus became PFE's first combined ice plant and equipment service operation.

Ice usage peaked about 1952, when more than 2.5 million tons were consumed. By 1958, 1.69 million tons were used, and by 1968 it would fall to 0.58 million tons. Mechanical refrigerator car shipments started in 1953, and

Council Bluffs IMP. (Left) This eastward view in 1956 shows the new platform with icing machines and the ice transfer tunnel. UP Railroad Museum photo 7115200, courtesy Frank Peacock.

(Below) This 1969 aerial view shows the icing platform and the car and trailer repair and cleaning tracks. Across the Missouri River to the west is the Omaha skyline. UP Railroad Museum photo 57057.

by 1956 numbered 6966 carloads, all frozen food at that date. By 1960 it was evident that ice-cooled shipments were strongly declining, and were unlikely to recover (see Chapter 1). The parent railroads were questioning the expense to PFE of operating ice manufacturing plants that were showing increasing costs per ton of production and delivery, and lower use rates.

PFE considered the feasibility of going into the wholesale commercial ice business. There had been a consistent reduction in output of such ice since World War II. Household ice sales were practically non-existent by this time. Hotels, restaurants, hospitals, etc. were purchasing their own self-contained ice manufacturing machines. Clear ice was desired by most consumers rather than the opaque ice (caused by minute air bubbles trapped during rapid freezing) produced by most PFE plants. Special clear ice equipment had only been installed at Council Bluffs, Las Vegas and Pocatello.

Also hindering PFE's becoming a commercial provider was the fact that many plants were buried deep in rail yards with inadequate access to trucking, e.g., Roseville, Los Angeles, Colton. Other plants were located where there was not enough local commercial demand, e.g., Laramie, Modesto, Nampa, North Platte, Pocatello, and Sparks.

Four ice facilities had been discontinued since 1950: Carlin in 1951, Wallula in 1952, Gerber in 1954, and Visitacion in 1955. Sparks, Modesto and North Platte by 1957 were operating only on a seasonal basis, and would be

eliminated as soon as running time of through trains was reduced. By the mid-1960's, only eleven of the original nineteen ice manufacturing plants remained.

PFE began leasing portions of their storerooms and plants to commercial firms to offset expenses, and curtailed activities at other locations by shutting off portions of the facilities. Ice requirements at small locations were purchased from commercial firms, and secondary facilities were gradually phased out of service. By 1972, icing requirements were insufficient to justify continued economical operation of any icing facilities, and PFE and other refrigerator car owners petitioned the ICC for permission to discontinue ice refrigeration services (though top icing and ventilation would remain available).

Under authority of the ICC decision rendered in I&S 8720, PFE discontinued all icing services effective September 2, 1973. Since the icing and related facilities were no longer required, they were retired immediately to eliminate the costs of ownership. Nearly all owned facilities, which included ice manufacturing plants and equipment, storage houses, platforms and icing machines, and trackage were officially retired on September 24, 1973. They were then either sold to private operators or dismantled. The ledger value of the property retired was over $10 million, which was written off. The net cost to PFE for the purpose of retiring all facilities was $1.77 million.

With this single move, the 67-year ice refrigeration era for the Pacific Fruit Express Company came to an end.

ICE PLANT PRODUCTION (TONS)
Year 1956 Compared to 1949

Main Stations	1949	1954	1955	1956	% 1956 to 1949
1. Bakersfield	62692	60052	71704	70270	112.1
2. Fresno	153309	161952	166989	160947	105.0
3. Roseville	232916	190071	201597	185497	79.6
4. Sparks	41215	39485	46397	44207	107.3
5. Ogden	76546	79874	81552	77566	101.3
6. Laramie	88101	126510	125712	115193	130.8
7. Council Bluffs	53472	74023	75928	74506	139.3
8. Colton	79953	48804	56337	56776	71.0
9. Nampa	49520	48546	35721	45745	92.4
10. Pocatello	38619	37385	33350	35013	90.7
Secondary Stations					
1. Las Vegas	16749	19919	18274	17122	102.2
2. Los Angeles	59933	52397	46757	38960	65.0
3. Modesto	50633	41275	58021	45655	90.2
4. North Platte	68557	14280	15795	11840	17.3
5. Tucson	49436	41509	26546	16997	34.4
Discontinued					
1. Carlin	39467	–	–	–	0.0
2. Gerber	9492	2080	–	–	0.0
3. Visitacion	8678	7626	1551	–	0.0
4. Wallula	13312	–	–	–	0.0
Grand Total - Tons	1192600	1045788	1062231	996294	83.5

A scene repeated at thousands of packing sheds all over PFE territory. Crates of "Pebble Beach" iceberg lettuce are being loaded into an ice reefer at the Salinas Valley Vegetable Cooperative's shed in Salinas. A chain conveyor moves the containers along the loading dock, then they are diverted onto roller trays into the car, where another workman stacks and braces them. The cigar-chewing loader is recording the crate count. A normal load of iceberg lettuce was 800 of these 36 to 45-pound

14

WESTERN PERISHABLES

The Hollister local trundles through fields of iceberg lettuce with a string of loaded reefers destined for eastern markets. In this train are two MDT cars, a Santa Fe, and two URTX Milwaukee Road reefers, along with 15 or so PFE cars. SP photo, 1936.

Because of ideal climate conditions, the fertile valleys of Oregon, California, Arizona, New Mexico, Texas and western Mexico produce some form of fruit or vegetable the year round. To a lesser extent, owing to more severe winter temperatures, the western states of Washington, Idaho, Nevada, Utah and Colorado also contribute to the perennial garden basket that once required thousands of rail carload shipments to nationwide markets. Load purchase records soon established the major market as being the great population and industrial areas from Chicago and on to the east, and was generally north of the Mason-Dixon Line. New York City and the State of New York were one of the most important markets for both fresh and processed fruits and vegetables.

It is interesting to note that the western states, which contributed so much to change the dietary habits of the nation, did so with fruits and vegetables that were totally introduced to the locale. None of the major commodities grown were native to any of the states.

The early Spanish explorers found a western coastal region devoid of any fruit trees. Small bush fruits and wild berries were all that existed in what is now California. The Spanish Fathers brought Old World fruits with them from Spain and Portugal, some that had actually been introduced to them from China by early explorers: the grape, orange, pear, peach, apple, apricot and fig. By 1792, missions from San Diego to as far north as Santa Clara had flourishing orchards and cultivated gardens.

The California citrus industry, more than any other commodity, launched the Western perishable shipping business. It had its birth at the San Gabriel Mission in 1804 when the first orchard of any size was planted, but it was not until 1841 that a pioneer settler, William Wolfskill, first experimented with oranges in a commercial way. He got trees from the San Gabriel Mission, planted two acres near what is now downtown Los Angeles and sold his crops locally.

Small plantings followed in other nearby sections, but the citrus trade really became viable in the early 1870's, when 4000 acres of desert land, now the site of Riverside, were sold to settlers. It was here that Mrs. Eliza Tibbets, in 1873, planted two small Navel orange trees sent by her husband from Brazil. These two trees were the initial progenitors of all the Navel oranges since the seedless Navel

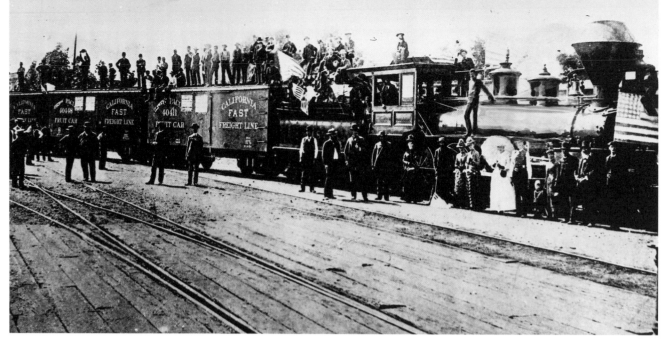

This photo has often been captioned (quite likely incorrectly: see below and Chapter 3) as the first complete fruit train to head east. The 16-car consist shown departed from Sacramento June 24, 1886. It was chartered by W.R. Strong and Co. of Sacramento and Edwin T. Earl of San Jose, wholesale fruit and produce merchants. The loads were deciduous fruits, likely pears, rather than the citrus which later dominated shipment from California. California Fast Freight Line ventilated box cars were used (described in Chap. 3). Ice blocks were piled in each end of the cars, but when this ice melted (these were not insulated cars), the shippers trusted in ventilation to get the fruit to Chicago destinations in saleable condition. R.J. Church collection.

orange is propagated from cuttings. The new fruit, larger and very sweet, quickly gained favor. Other growers soon planted more of this type tree and thus launched the beginning of a major enterprise. To Mrs. Tibbets went the distinction of being the "Mother of the California Citrus Industry." One of her original two trees was still bearing fruit in the 1950's.

The rapid settlement subsequent to the 1848 Gold Rush had led to the planting of small orchards of citrus and deciduous fruits wherever communities sprang up. Innovative fruit shippers began moving California crops via the Pacific Railroad within a few weeks of its completion. Early shipments originated from the Sacramento River Delta, and these were deciduous fruits, principally pears and plums. The first carload of deciduous fruit from this district was packed at Courtland in July, 1869, and shipped upstream by river steamer to Sacramento. There it was loaded into a ventilated boxcar and forwarded by the Central Pacific, Union Pacific and connections to Chicago under the consignment of the Porter Bros. Company.

Although acreages of deciduous and citrus trees gradually increased, the market was limited. It was not until the pioneer rail line of the Southern Pacific of California joined southern California with the remainder of the state and the transcontinental railroad at Sacramento in 1876 that the citrus industry received its first stimulus. Then, when the SP's Sunset Route was finished in 1883, the orange growers were brought even nearer to their eastern customers.

Also in the year 1883, C. P. Huntington organized the Transcontinental Cold Storage and Shipping Co. with the intention of running a line of refrigerated and ventilated cars between San Francisco and Newport News, Virginia. He had major financial interests in the Southern Pacific of California and he desired to ship southern California fruit east over the SP and connections to the Chesapeake and Ohio Railway (another road that he had ownership in and exercised control over) and use that road for eastern distribution.

In 1889 Huntington gave up or lost control of his interests in the eastern railroads, but it is interesting that he had an idea of developing a private refrigerated car line that would utilize his own railroads to forward such cars, an idea that Harriman cultivated a quarter century later.

In 1876 the first Valencia orange trees were brought from England to Southern California, and this variety would eventually become the most popular orange for juice. Vegetable production was somewhat slower in reaching shipping volume, but mixed carloads were being shipped by the 1880's, and a significant volume was moving to eastern markets by the turn of the century.

Although individual carloads of fruit had been shipped from California since at least as early as 1869, and complete trains at least since 1871, the above photo has been claimed to show the first solid train of fruit cars sent from California to eastern markets. The train may have been the first chartered by fruit merchants, and was composed of sixteen ordinary ventilated cars. In the 1886-87 season, the fledgling citrus industry shipped 2,212 carloads of citrus fruits within California and to "foreign" (out of state) markets. The next year the California Fruit Transportation Company began shipping California fruit under ice refrigeration. The perishable business had gotten its start.

By 1901 the citrus and other perishable business had expanded so rapidly that the SP and AT&SF just could not handle the volume with available car fleets. Orange and lemon shipments over the two railroads had jumped from 11,600 cars in 1899 to 22,500 in 1900, and was anticipated to be over 26,000 cars in the 1901 season. Another great railroad magnate, James J. Hill of the Great Northern Railway then stepped into the picture.

Hill attempted to encourage shipments of California citrus over his own railroad. He enticed some shippers to send their oranges by sea to Seattle, then by GN rail across his northern route to St. Paul and on to New York. Test trains with fruit shipped this way, on special schedules, took only 10 days on the railroad, versus an average of 15 to 16 days with SP or AT&SF routing.

The SP and AT&SF, though, "politely" refused to establish lower rates to haul the citrus carloads to coastal ports and divert the traffic from their own transcontinental lines. They stated such hauls could not be handled for less than $4.50 a ton, and at that rate the loss was too great for the shippers. Thus, the northern routing and competition was not established.

James Hill never made a serious attempt to fight the price resistance of the California railroads, and one wonders if he was just making a personal statement to Harriman. The two had come to head-on collisions when they both had tried to gain control of the Chicago, Burlington & Quincy Railroad, as both men desired that line as an access to Chicago. Harriman had also tried to get control of the Northern Pacific, a well-documented struggle in which Hill's defensive strategy led to the famous Northern Securities Case in the U. S. Supreme Court.

The dominance that the three western states of California, Oregon, and Arizona gained in crop production is shown in 1929 Department of Agriculture statistics. Those states grew: 90% of all the grapes in the US, 45% of the country's peaches, 60% of its cantaloupes, 50% of the pears, 70% of its lettuce, 62% of the citrus fruits, 40% of the asparagus, 30% of the celery, and 45% of the carrots consumed across the entire country. By 1936, the three states' crop production had increased so that lettuce amounted to 95% of the national total; and included 98% of the grapes, 57% of the citrus fruits, 79% of the cantaloupes and melons, 70% of fresh prunes and plums and more than half the pears and cherries grown.

At this time, about 80% of all the money the Southern Pacific took in was generated by freight hauled. In 1937, the SP's Pacific Lines received a total gross revenue for freight of $122 million, and of this, $28.5 million, or 23%, was generated by PFE fruit and vegetable business from the three states mentioned above. The importance of perishable business is readily recognized.

Early settlers in the Imperial Valley brought their melons to the Southern Pacific tracks in horse-drawn wagons, where they were loaded directly into early refrigerator cars (note the NC&StL car) and even a few box cars. Photo is undated but the SP medallion on the box car, a style adopted in 1919, means that the date cannot be earlier than 1919. Wm. A. Myers collection.

During the 1930's and into the 1940's the enormous increase in fruit and vegetable production continued. The estimated production figures by the Department of Agriculture for vegetables grown in 1928 was 12,000,000 tons. By 1948 that crop aggregate reached 18,000,000 tons and the trend was continually expanding. The combined fruit crop in 1948 was about 17,000,000 tons, a figure that did not show as great a gain.

In spite of these increases in crop production, rail movement of produce, on a national basis, started a steady decline. The eastern railroads were losing their relatively short haul loads to trucking, so that by the mid-1940's, the bulk of shipments were originating only in the far west. While total rail shipments in the United States declined from 838,600 cars in 1942 to 723,600 cars in 1951, California's share of total traffic rose from 30 percent to 38 percent. During that period, the Golden State's loadings grew from 249,400 to 273,000 cars. Shipments from other far western states also maintained their level or most often improved in this same period.

An interesting fact should be pointed out here, and that is that between the two PFE owners, the Southern Pacific lines serviced the states where the principal crop producing areas were located. The Union Pacific did reach Southern California via Las Vegas, but did not have access to the fertile farmlands as did the SP. The same situation was true in Oregon, and the UP had no rails in Arizona or Texas. Originating load records from 1908 to 1970 (see Appendix) show that the Southern Pacific averaged about 70% of the originating traffic. This very fact became a persistent point of contention between the two roads when profits of PFE were divided, as described in Chapter 1.

The total loadings from all PFE contract lines in 1946 was 380,266 cars. The national decline in rail shipments of perishables was also reflected in PFE's carload totals. They showed a slow steady decrease that averaged around 6000 loads each year, so by 1955, PFE handled system-wide a total of 326,108 carloads, a decrease of 54,158 cars from the 1946 total, or a 14.2% drop in business.

Many of these lost shipments were short haul loads that were picked up by increasing truck competition. As seen above, though, western states, especially the California, Oregon, Idaho, and Arizona districts, originated more long haul loadings for PFE in the late 1940's and early '50's.

Carloadings on PFE over its history. The great climb in loads in the 1920's, the Depression low, and post-World War II peaks are all evident, as is the steady fall in loading after 1953. A.W. Thompson graph from PFE data.

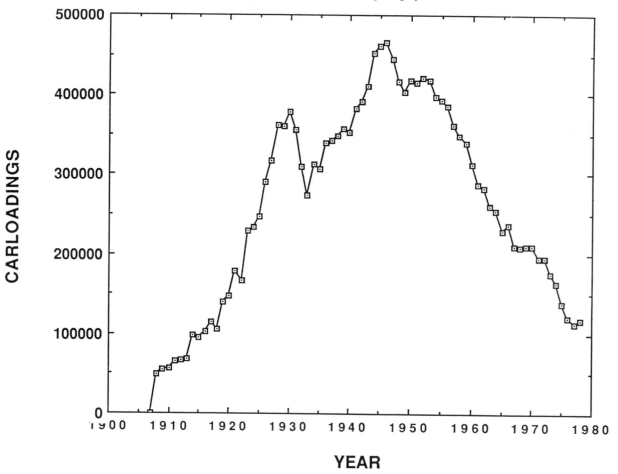

PROTECTIVE SERVICES

It was very important for the shipper and the receiver to have a working knowledge of all applicable tariff rules and protective services available. This allowed them to select the most desirable rail protective services they required, based on commodity characteristics, seasonal needs, geographic location, and cost. Table 14-1 shows the recommended shipping temperatures for a variety of fruits and vegetables. If outside air temperatures during shipment were above these suggested levels, some type of refrigeration would be specified, while if air temperatures were about the same, ventilation would suffice. If they were significantly colder, heating could be specified.

The various rail protective services and rules were described and numbered in a handbook called the *Perishable Protective Tariff*, modified and published periodically by the National Perishable Freight Committee. There was also a Protective Tariff booklet prepared by the Railway Express Agency (REA) for refrigerated express cars. The tariffs also included charges assessed for the various protective services offered, based on origin and destination of the shipment.

There were and are three general types of protective services: refrigeration, ventilation, and heating. A brief description of each, taken from *Perishable Protective Tariff No. 18* and REA *Tariff Handbook No. 27A*, follows.

Refrigeration

Refrigeration was by four general methods: bunker icing, body icing, mechanical refrigeration, and liquified gas. Sources of refrigeration to provide the necessary means for absorbing heat from the commodities to be cooled were: ice, ice and salt, solid carbon dioxide (dry ice), mechanical refrigeration, liquified gas refrigeration, evaporation, and ventilation with outside air. Definitions and standard names of refrigeration services were as follows.

Standard Refrigeration Service. Involved pre-icing or

Table 14-1
Desirable transit temperatures for certain fresh fruits and vegetables

Fruits	Desirable transit temperature	Vegetables	Desirable transit temperature
	°F.		°F.
Apples	32–40	Artichokes	32
Apricots	32	Asparagus	32–36
Avocados:		Beans (snap)	45
Most varieties	45	Beets (bunched)	32
West Indian varieties	55	Broccoli	32
Bananas (green)	56–60	Brussels sprouts	32
Cherries (sweet)	32	Cabbage	32
Cranberries	36–40	Cantaloup	35–40
Dates	40–50	Carrots	32
Figs (fresh)	32	Cauliflower	32
Grapefruit	50–60	Celery	32
Grapes (Vinifera)	32	Corn (sweet)	32
Lemons	50–55	Cucumbers	45–50
Limes	48–50	Eggplant	45–50
Oranges:		Endive and escarole	32
Ariz. and Calif.	40–44	Honeydew melon	45–50
Fla. and Tex.	32–40	Lettuce	32
Peaches and nectarines	32–45	Onions (dry)	32–40
Pears	45–55 / 32	Peas (green)	32
		Peppers (sweet)	45–50
Pineapples:		Potatoes:	
Mature green	50–55	Early crop	50–60
Ripe	45	Late crop	40–50
Plums (including fresh prunes)	32–45	For chipping:	
Strawberries	32	Early crop	65–70
Tangerines:		Late crop	50–60
Calif.	36–45	Radishes	32
Fla.	38	Spinach	32
		Sweetpotatoes	55–60
		Tomatoes:	
		Mature green	55–65
		Pink	45–50

From USDA *Agriculture Handbook 195,* 1961.

initial icing of car bunkers and re-icing to capacity at all or specified regular icing stations in transit. In an end bunker car the ice sizes included chunk ice (pieces not exceeding 100 lbs), coarse ice (pieces averaging 10 to 20 lbs), and crushed ice (pieces the size of a man's fist). Average ice consumption in transit was about 50 pounds per hour.

Preicing – bunkers of cleaned, empty refrigerator cars were iced to capacity before loading. On most PFE cars, this would amount to 10,500 lbs. of ice.

Initial icing – to ice (replenish) car bunkers for the first time after loading was completed, generally at the first icing station en route.

Re-icing – service after certain lapse of time entered on bill of lading, such as "re-ice in transit at third and fifth icing station." As train schedules grew faster, the shipper or agent would determine locations of re-icing.

Standard Service always meant the entire ice bunkers were filled to capacity each time they were serviced.

Half-stage Refrigeration Service. This meant using only the upper part of the car bunkers. In cars equipped for this service, the ice grates could be raised to a point midway between the top and bottom of the bunkers and only the top half was filled with ice. The shipper had to order a car equipped for half-stage icing and specify "Half-stage Refrigeration Service" on the bill of lading.

Salt. If additional cooling was required, certain percentages or quantities of salt were added to the ice to produce lower air and commodity temperatures in the car. The salt, NaCl, was added to the ice in an amount up to 5 percent by weight (5 lbs. per 100 lbs. of ice) for fresh produce, 12 percent for meats and the maximum, 30 percent, for frozen foods. When salt was used with chunk ice, the percentage of salt was added after the icing had been completed. When the salt was added with coarse ice, the salt and ice were added to the bunkers in alternate layers. The salt was provided at any icing as ordered by the shipper. An additional charge was made for salt added under this rule.

Top or Body Icing Service. This service, used mainly for leafy vegetables, root vegetables, melons, keg or draught beer, and Christmas trees, consisted of the placing of finely crushed ice blown into the car over the top of the load. The amount, or net quantity, was specified by the shipper. Ventilation was sometimes specified with this type transit. Re-top icing could also be specified by the shipper as required in transit.

Mechanical Protective Service. This service provides in general for the application of mechanical refrigeration or

heat, controlled thermostatically, for frozen and non-frozen commodities. Body icing could be specified also.

Liquified Gas Refrigeration Vehicles. Limited numbers of refrigerator cars and piggyback trailers used liquid nitrogen or liquid carbon dioxide for frozen foods. These units were controlled thermostatically and had various mechanical designs.

Ventilation

Three general types of ventilation service were offered: standard, special, and combination. Ventilation was the manipulation of ventilating devices (hatch covers and plugs) of car bunkers to permit or prevent passage of the outside air to the car interior. Ventilation was used extensively in the spring and fall seasons when outdoor air could be used as a cooling medium to approximate the desired in-transit commodity temperature.

These classes of ventilation services varied with the kind of commodity, the geographic location of the shipping point, and the time of year. Car vents were adjusted at regularly assigned inspection points, except when trains were delayed.

Standard Ventilation – This was the manipulation (opening or closing) of vents at certain temperatures as prescribed in the tariff rules.

Special Ventilation – This was the manipulation of vents at temperatures or stations specified by the shipper.

Combination Ventilation – A service which combined the use of both Standard and Special Ventilation, each on a part of the route. The carrier would also accept instructions to keep the vents closed throughout the entire handling of the shipment.

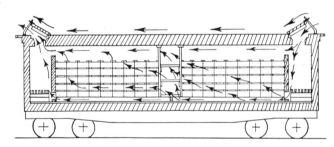

Air circulation under ventilation. SP *Bulletin*, Feb. 1928.

Heater Service

Protection against frost or freezing was provided by the use of heaters furnished, initially fueled at origin, and installed by the shipper (PFE provided this service to its customers on line). The heaters were serviced by PFE as the shipper directed.

(Above) Automatic alcohol-burning heater made by Preco. PFE photo, CSRM. (Right) Here a charcoal heater is lifted with a portable boom to the car roof. One heater was placed in each end bunker, and a plaque was attached to each door and ice hatch, bearing a skull and crossbones to warn of carbon monoxide. UP Railroad Museum, North Platte, ca. 1919.

Heater service for other than mechanical refrigerator cars and trailers was first provided by charcoal heaters, one placed in each bunker. These heaters were lighted and extinguished at temperatures shown in various perishable tables. Shippers could also specify the outside temperature at which they required the heaters to be used. When portable charcoal heaters with uncontrolled burning rate were used in nonfan cars, there was constant danger that high temperatures could build up in the top layers of the load. This would result in overripening or spoilage. Periodic inspection of the car load was a necessity.

In the 1940's the use of "LF heaters" began. These were thermostatically controlled liquid fuel (alcohol) heaters. Automatic LF heaters eliminated the need to contend with lighting and extinguishing of charcoal heaters.

Protection against freezing in most general service mechanical cars and trailers is provided thermostatically either by electric heating elements or by hot gas in the refrigerating unit under reverse-cycle operation.

SPECIAL METHODS OF
PRECOOLING COMMODITIES

Precooling is the rapid cooling of a commodity by removing field heat to attain a suitable transit or storage temperature soon after harvest, before it is moved in transit or placed in storage. The idea of "field heat" includes two different effects, the thermal heat imparted by the warm air and sunshine upon the produce, and the biological heat generated by continuing life processes within the fruit or vegetable itself, even though it has been detached from its parent plant. Removal of field heat thus means lowering the temperature of the produce to a suitable level, which

slows ripening as well as suppressing the action of decay organisms. Moisture losses must also be controlled to retard wilting and shrinkage of the produce.

It was possible, and before World War II common, simply to load and ship warm produce and rely on the ice refrigeration itself to cool the produce to shipping temperature during transit. The problem was that the desired, optimum shipping temperature would only be achieved over a period of two to four days. Precooling, on the other hand, is a controlled and faster means of reaching the desired temperature.

The types of precooling included: car precooling with ice and mechanical devices, package and top icing, hydro-cooling, vacuum cooling, and room cooling.

The practical aspects of precooling basically came down to two elements, time and economy. The shipper always wanted his cars to roll to market as soon as they were loaded, yet he desired the optimum conditions within the car for his commodity; hence, the precooling method had to remove large amounts of heat quickly. Also, most shippers operated only a few weeks a year at a given location and they did not normally invest the capital to build refrigeration precooling plants.

For these reasons and also because of its availability and freedom from trouble, the use of ice found great favor among shippers for precooling purposes. From the standpoint of numbers of cars shipped with precooling, the method in most general use up to 1946, was the practice of car precooling with ice.

Car precooling

This method, which involved rapid cooling in the car of

A portable precooling fan is mounted in this R-30-16 which is partially loaded with melons. Another fan is at the other end, and both bunkers are filled with ice. The greatly increased air movement in the car helped remove field heat from the load. *Railroad and Railfan* collection.

a warm commodity that had been loaded, was accomplished through: (1) utilizing the bunker ice by operating either car fans, portable precooling fans mounted in the car, or both; (2) using mechanical precooling units mounted along the tracks or on trucks; (3) using top ice on the load with or without package ice; and (4) circulating cold air from an ice storage plant cooling system into the car. (See Chapter 13, Roseville and Colton IMP's, for description of the intermittent vacuum car precooling system.) Top ice is beneficial to moisture retention.

In 1941 PFE began equipping their cars with built-in fans to operate from the car axles during transit and also for external operation by portable motors during precooling. A car so equipped had the advantage that when time did not permit complete precooling at the loading point, the

continuous induced circulation of air would complete precooling in transit. A precooled load would then need less ice in transit, saving icing costs to a shipper.

Most mechanical fan equipment with bunker icing could reduce commodity temperature to 40-50°F in 18 to 24 hours. Since melting ice without salt automatically maintained a temperature no lower than 32°F, there was no danger of sub-cooling of the commodity, and the melting ice maintained high humidity. Heavy tree fruits such as oranges or pears were obviously slower to cool than a carload of cherries or grapes.

Top or package ice precooling

This method was most effective in precooling leafy vegetables, cantaloupes, and similar products. The placement of crushed or snow ice in the shipping container as it was packaged, or the blowing in of a layer of snow ice over the load inside the car, or both, contributed to precooling and moisture retention. By allowing melting all the top ice before transit, the shipper was relieved from paying certain charges ordinarily assessed with cars billed as forwarded with top ice tariffs. "Package" icing meant inserting ice into or between the produce cartons or containers themselves. It was often combined with top icing.

Hydrocooling

About 1925 interest developed in the possibility of obtaining rapid and efficient cooling of packed vegetables with water or water sprays. Although efficient because of the good thermal conduction from produce to water, it was at first deemed uneconomical. Later, in 1932, the idea was reinvestigated for immersion cooling for asparagus. "Grass" was one of the most difficult commodities to cool in that

(**Left**) Top-icing at Watsonville in 1936. Slinger-blower machines for crushed ice (shown here) were first introduced to the industry at Salinas around 1930 for lettuce loads. SP photo. (**Right**) A load of bagged carrots that has just been top-iced. UP photo.

it develops great quantities of biological heat. Therefore, it must be completely cooled before shipment to prevent spoilage. As a result of this interest, the hydrocooler was developed and perfected.

These machines were portable or stationary, some 30 feet in length, and contained a tank of water over which a conveyor transported the packaged asparagus. A spray of refrigerated water, recirculated and cooled by crushed ice, was run over the goods as they moved through the machine. These machines consumed ice at a rate of only three tons per hour, thus being extremely efficient. It completely precooled asparagus in 10 to 12 minutes, as compared with about 10 hours required with car ice precooling.

Hydrocoolers were and are used commercially to precool celery, asparagus, peas, cauliflower, sprouts, artichokes, green lima beans, and carrots, and to a lesser extent for citrus and other fruits. Both spray and float (immersion) applications of cold water are used. Frozen food shippers and processors likewise realized the value of this type of precooling and use it extensively.

Vacuum precooling

This is based on the simple principle that water evaporates rapidly from a commodity under a reduced atmospheric pressure, a partial vacuum. The evaporating water absorbs its heat of evaporation (the same as the heat supplied in boiling) from its surroundings, in this case the produce on which water droplets are located. Thus the goods are cooled by this rapid evaporation. The commodity to be cooled, either before or after packaging, is usually sprayed lightly with water and placed into a steel chamber that can be tightly sealed, and a vacuum is drawn. This

Vacuum cooling chamber for boxed produce, which was then loaded into rail cars or trailers. UP photo 167-7-9, courtesy Frank Peacock.

could be done with the commodity just brought in on a field trailer, or a packing shed cart after packaging, or at some vacuum plants, an entire loaded refrigerator car or trailer could be placed into the vacuum cooler.

The rate of cooling under vacuum depends on the ratio of surface to volume so it is particularly adapted to leafy vegetables such as lettuce, celery, spinach, etc. Evacuating the chamber and cooling the product requires about 30 minutes for leafy vegetables. Dense items such as melons, with a low surface to volume ratio, require repeated water spray to cool effectively. For all produce, careful control is necessary so that only superficial water is removed, not essential moisture content from within the produce.

This process became prevalent in the late 1940's, and replaced the ice bunker precooling for the above listed commodities that were suited for this type handling. Because of the high initial and operating costs of the complex equipment, permanent vacuum installations were and are limited to large-volume business in central crop production locations. There were also some portable vacuum cooling units developed and used.

Room cooling

This is a simple process, involving only storing the commodity in a cold room until field heat is removed, and a predetermined temperature is reached. The load entering the refrigerator car is then already at its preferred shipping temperature. This method requires a significant investment by the shipper to have adequate capacity to store large amounts of harvested produce, typically for 12-24 hours or more. Given the highly seasonal nature of most produce harvests, it is understandable that only the largest shippers, or shippers' cooperatives, used this method, although it is effective. The entire quantity of produce is uniformly cooled, and the process is under the shipper's control. The biggest drawbacks are cost, and that the cooling is typically slower than other methods.

Vacuum cooling chamber at Salinas, for loaded rail cars or highway trailers. PFE photo, CSRM.

PERISHABLE LOADING

Refrigerator cars were loaded in very well-defined ways, depending on the type of perishable being shipped, the applicable tariff, the season, and to some extent on the shipper's own preferred loading arrangement.

Each perishable commodity is best shipped in a particular package, to protect it in shipment, permit efficient cooling (or heating) and humidity control, and serve as a merchandising unit upon arrival. The once-standard wooden crate began to be supplanted in the 1950's by fiberboard or corrugated cardboard cartons, by tray packages, and the use of plastic film wrapping. For each commodity and type of packaging, the industry has striven to standardize the packages to enhance shipping efficiency.

Depending on the size and shape of the carton or crate used for a particular crop, certain ways of arranging the packages would fit into the standard car most efficiently and also provide adequate air circulation. Each arrangement was devised to take advantage of the inherent strength and stacking capability of the package, to maintain adequate air channels, and to use filler or bracing material to minimize load shifting in transit (or more recently, use a car with load restraining devices).

As shown below, containers could be arranged in three basic ways in the car. The upright method, for example, was typically used with orange crates (examples are shown on pages 98 and 167). The second characteristic of a load was whether it was a "through load" or a divided load. The through load permitted more packages in the car, but was more difficult to finish loading, to unload, to inspect, and to ensure good air circulation. In either type of load, the preferred arrangement was to load "tight" in the car, with pre-cut filler or bracing material used to snugly fill the car length and width and to provide air channels. In some loads, it was even the practice to exert leverage and "squeeze"

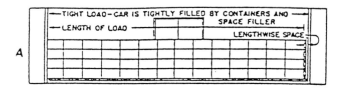

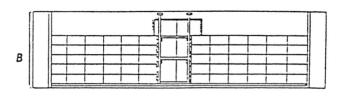

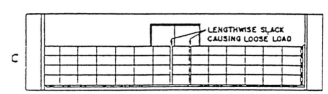

Types of load arrangement. (A) Through load, with filler at end of load to keep load "tight." (B) Divided load, with center bracing. (C) Loose load with lengthwise slack. From USDA *Agriculture Handbook 195.*

the packages, thus keeping them under pressure during shipment and lessening the chance of movement developing among the packages. Sometimes a "loose" load would be shipped, but only if the spaces remaining in the car were small enough to give no concern about shifting.

When larger cars, 50 ft. and more in length, began to be used, incentive tariffs were introduced to stimulate use of the new cars. This led to heavier car loading to obtain the lower per-package freight rates. The attraction of these rates to the shipper had to be balanced against the dangers of heavier stacking in the car. Such stacking could damage packages and reduce air circulation.

It was always essential in an ice refrigerator not to block the openings at the top of the ice bunker bulkhead, as these were essential to air movement and thus to refrigeration. Accordingly, what was considered a full load in a refrigerator car might at first glance appear to be only partially full. Thus the standard orange load in a nominal 40-ft. ice car was 462 boxes, which filled the car to about two-thirds of its inside height.

Methods of loading perishables into cars varied widely, from manual carrying, to handtrucks (less used since the 1960's), to fork lift trucks. Palletized loads were usually removed from the pallets in order to fill the car as full as practical. It was common to use chutes or roller trays at packing sheds, where two men could work at either end, one sending packages into the car and the other stacking the load. In addition to the photos on the facing page, a number of examples are presented elsewhere in this book.

Arrangement of containers in car. (A) Lengthwise. (B) Crosswise. (C) Upright. From USDA *Agriculture Handbook 195.*

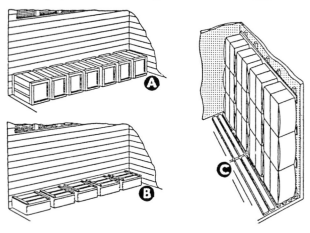

(Left) Hampers of green peas were alternately stacked to fill the car, and then were top-iced. The car is PFE 71228, an R-40-2 rebuild, about to be re-top-iced at Chicago, July 1936, *Railfan and Railroad* collection. (Above) Loading Bartlett pears from a roller tray. These are stacked lengthwise. Note chunk ice in bunker. PFE photo, CSRM.

(Left) Loading cherries in the San Joaquin Valley in 1962. The car is PFE 301063, an R-50-6. Note the bracing for this divided load, and the lift truck partly hidden behind the men at right. E.S. Peyton photo, N19325, M.D. McCarter collection. (Right). Celery loading in a two-track arrangement with cars abreast. The car is an R-30-12, PFE 17163, with a roller tray assisting in moving the packages. Crates are stacked very high and will be top-iced. California, 1928, *Railfan and Railroad* collection.

Because top icing continued to be prevalent from the World War I period until the 1970's, packaging for perishables which were so treated had to be resistant to moisture. Wood, waxed fiberboard and waxed paper liners, plastic, and plastic-impregnated cardboard cartons, have all been used. With the advent of plastic films, care had to be taken that adequate air circulation was maintained, although water resistance became less of an issue. Ingenious designs of interlayers and trays in cartons were introduced to provide air passages as the packing materials themselves became impervious to air as well as moisture.

The presence of ventilating holes in cartons is now commonplace, something not necessary in the loose-fitted wooden crate once ubiquitous for everything from oranges to deciduous fruit to vegetables.

Frozen foods, being relatively rigid and resistant to mechanical damage in shipping, require less attention to packaging, yet care must still be taken to prevent crushing of cartons, load shifting, and even air circulation to maintain the desired shipping temperature. But with the advent of load dividers, frozen or perishable loading has become rapid and dependable, and less of the art it once was.

MAJOR COMMODITIES HANDLED

To appreciate the magnitude of PFE's produce "deals," the task of supplying, moving, diverting, and servicing thousands of cars annually to haul western produce to eastern markets, it is essential to look at the major perishables shipped and how PFE handled them when the Company dominated the perishable transportation business in the "Golden Years," the period from the mid-1920's to the mid-1950's. The system map, page 432, may also help.

As agricultural areas developed along the parent roads, certain locations became the concentration points for the eastbound carloads moving over the Union Pacific and the Southern Pacific. Here the traffic was made up into fruit blocks for through movement to the eastern destinations. PFE's designated major concentration points and the territories they served were:

Reith, and after 1951, Hinkle, Oregon, on the OWR&N (UP) for the Washington and Oregon territory.

Nampa and Pocatello, Idaho, on the OSL (UP) for the Intermountain territory.

Eugene, Oregon, on the SP for the Oregon territory.

Roseville on the SP and Sacramento on the WP for the Central and Northern California territory.

Colton, California, on the LA&SL (UP) and SP for Southern California territory.

Yuma, Arizona, on the SP for the Arizona, Imperial Valley and Mexico territory.

Edinburg, Texas, on the SP for the Lower Rio Grande Valley territory.

Each fruit block was given a symbol number as it left the concentration point and this number was used to identify it through to its destination. (e.g. RV FB 132 E designated Roseville Fruit Block, the 132nd Roseville Eastbound reefer train that year.)

It is historically significant to consider each of the territories from which PFE's shipments were generated and to examine how each perishable commodity business developed. We will also gain insight as to how PFE managed the complexities of handling each "deal" year after year.

Citrus Fruit

By the mid-1930's, citrus fruits, oranges, lemons and grapefruit, ranked at the top of the list of PFE perishable fruit traffic. There were 320,000 acres of groves in California and Arizona, with additional acreage developing in southern Texas. Some orchards in California were as far north as Oroville in the Sacramento Valley, and plantings totalling 42,000 acres were in Tulare, Fresno and Kern Counties in the San Joaquin Valley. But 85% of California's oranges, 97% of the lemons, and nearly all the grapefruits were grown from Santa Barbara south to the Mexican border.

Citrus culture began in Arizona in the 1880's and flourished in the Phoenix-Salt River Valley region and around Yuma. Plantings began shortly afterward in southern California. The largest growth occurred after 1907, when the California Fruit Growers Exchange began advertising California oranges in the East. In that year, E.O. McCormick of the Southern Pacific offered to spend a dollar on citrus advertising for every dollar spent by the Exchange. The Exchange adopted specially-marked fruit boxes, and the railroad paid for billboards proclaiming "Oranges for Health – California for Wealth." It was also during this 1907 campaign that the Exchange adopted its now-familiar trademark, "Sunkist." Indeed, the Exchange's name today is "Sunkist Growers, Inc."

From the California and Arizona districts 98,680 carloads of oranges, lemons, and grapefruit were shipped to the nation's markets in a record-producing 1934-35 season. That amounted to about 60% of all the oranges, 95% of all the lemons, and 30% of all the grapefruit consumed in the U.S. and Canada. Florida, Texas and foreign countries contributed to the rest of the demand.

The seedless Navel orange ripens in the fall and winter, being picked and shipped from November to May. The Valencia thrives in cooler coastal regions and ripens during the summer months, so the two varieties provided for year-round supply and rail shipping business. Probably no crop in the world is grown with greater care and attention than these "Golden Fruits." After it has been picked, the fruit is handled all the way to market as carefully as if it were eggs.

Workers at a Sunkist packing plant sorting and hand-wrapping lemons. Keystone photo for Sunkist, 1928, *Railroad and Railfan* collection.

One of Chicago's auction show rooms. Hundreds of carloads of oranges, lemons and other fruits were displayed daily. Buyers inspected and bought the fruit, and distributed it to stores. Keystone photo for Sunkist, 1928, *Railroad and Railfan* collection.

At the packing houses the citrus fruit was washed and gently scrubbed, blown dry and rolled over brushes that coated them with a wax for polish and protection against shrinkage. They were graded as to size and then hand wrapped in tissue and packed in shipping crates. The fruit was then ready to be loaded into refrigerator cars to be sent to every state, to Canada, Mexico, or shipping ports for export. Preferred shipping temperature is 40-45° F.

Lemons are unusual in that trees blossom for extended periods while bearing fruit in various stages, so that the lemon harvest extends over much of the year. Lemons are typically picked with a thick "rind," then conditioned in packing houses at ambient temperature until the skins become thin enough for market. They are shipped with relatively high temperatures for citrus, 50-55° F., which for much of the year means ventilation or half-stage icing. Grapefruit are generally similar to lemons in shipping.

Much research was done over the years in an endeavor to improve shipping conditions for citrus. There were various classes and types of tariff services available from precooling to standard icing practices. In 1928, the Citrus Investigation Section of the U.S. Bureau of Plant Industry collaborated with the California Citrus League and Sunkist. They were assisted in these tests by the PFE Company, the SP, UP, AT&SF and other lines over which the cars were transported.

It was found that the best method to assure fruit in the finest condition was to provide prompt cooling by having the cars arrive at the packing sheds precooled. The bunkers were filled with a full 10,600 lbs. of chunk ice to precool the car. Then after loading they would be re-iced at the major assembly point prior to the transcontinental trip. One re-icing was done in transit and any supplemental icing found necessary afterwards.

Approximately 50 percent of the citrus fruit moved under some type of refrigeration, the balance being shipped under ventilation. The time consumed during rail transportation varied from two to three days for loads going to harbor for reloading onto ships, up to a maximum of 30 days to transport to the eastern states or Canada in cases where the cars were delayed by diversions, etc. The average time for transcontinental hauling of citrus was around 12 to 15 days. (See Appendix for perishable schedules.)

The main concentration point in the Southern California citrus districts was at Colton, where cars received precooling and re-icing service as instructed by the shipper. Loaded cars were assembled into solid "fruit blocks" for the eastbound movement via El Paso. Roseville was the main concentration point for shipments originating in the northern part of the state, and Yuma was where Arizona citrus loads were iced, classified and shipped on east.

Citrus fruits represented the largest individual crop transported from the Lower Rio Grande Valley. By 1940 over eight million trees were producing 30,000 carloads annually, divided 83% grapefruit and 17% oranges. Competition here for this business between various railroads and agencies of transportation was keen, particularly since the government spent several million dollars in dredging a ship

This portable, experimental precooling plant of the U.S. Dept. of Agriculture (USDA) was used to conduct early tests of precooling technique at points having rail facilities. In 1908 the USDA outfitted a car with a 12-ton ammonia compressor system with fans. Cold air blew through the 20" insulated piping fitted to the ice hatches of a refrigerator car on an adjacent track. It was used in Georgia and California for oranges in 1909, and is shown here at Lodi, Calif., in 1910, in use with table grapes. Also of interest is the SP's single-stall engine house and "gallows" turntable at far left. From USDA *Yearbook*, 1910.

channel from Brownsville to the Gulf. Even so, the railway shipments accounted for about 42% of the total business, and PFE's share would amount to around 3600 carloads annually. Edinburg was the concentration point.

Grapes

The founding of the first Mission at San Diego in 1769 also marked the birth of the grape industry in California, an industry that expanded all the way from the Mexican border to as far north as Eureka, and at one time became the state's second largest agricultural enterprise in point of acreage and was outranked only by citrus and hay in the value of its produce.

Vineyards flourished, and by 1858 more than 6,500 acres had been planted. Approximately 140,000 acres were producing in 1883, and plantings had jumped to an all-time peak of more than 680,000 acres by 1927. Following the repeal of Prohibition, the crop average dropped to 507,000 acres, of which 88,200 were table grapes, 186,600 were for wine, and 232,200 were raisin grapes. Normal production ran in excess of 2,000,000 tons annually, and amounted to 90% of all the grapes produced in the United States. Preferred shipping temperature is 32° F.

Carloads of grapes moved from California to the East as early as 1869. One carload shipped from Vacaville in 1876 was used for display at the Centennial Fair held in Philadelphia that year. The same district shipped several other cars east in 1881, some loads bringing as much as $3000 each! By 1895, grape shipments out of California ran as high as 1,000 cars annually, and by 1916, the movement was close to 10,000 cars. Until then, table grapes were almost the only variety shipped east in the fresh state. Wine and raisin varieties were processed into marketable products within the state.

The passage of the Volstead Act (Prohibition) in 1919 changed the entire picture in the grape industry. California could no longer dispose of its grapes in the wineries, except for a small amount permitted for medicinal and sacramental purposes. The answer of what to do with 90,000 acres of wine grapes came from the East and Northeast.

Some of the population there had ethnic heritage that was accustomed to the use of wine in their daily diet. The Volstead Act permitted the making of up to 250 gallons annually for home use. The West began shipping train-loads of fresh wine grapes eastward for fermentation in the basements of homes and, undoubtedly, also to illegal establishments of bootleggers. The demand so increased the interstate shipment of all varieties of fresh grapes from California, that carloads climbed from 16,358 in 1918 to 52,337 in 1923, and to the all-time high of 73,085 in 1927, with about two-thirds of the loads handled by PFE. This placed the grape at the top of all PFE load commodities handled that year.

The tremendous rise in carload shipments of grapes in addition to the expected increases in other produce caused a critical shortage in the fall of 1922 to the availability of empty cars. The problem was in the east. The fruit would move east at a rate of a thousand cars per day, while hundreds of cars remained loaded in the eastern terminals. Distributors would hold loads trying to guess the demands of the home-brewing consumers, using the car as a cold storage shed and holding them from 5 to 20 days. They would also

A two-car fumigation station. At times cars had to be fumigated, usually if insect infestation had been found in the car. In some cases fumigation was also done if a load had spoiled in transit. SP photo, courtesy Steve Peery.

peddle directly from the car. It was not slow unloading, but an absolute paralysis, no unloading at all. In late October there were nearly 1300 cars sitting loaded in the large eastern terminals, with Pittsburgh, Chicago and New York accounting for 926 of these loads. Since the cars moved under mileage rather than per diem charges, there was no expense to railroads on whose rails the cars sat, and only small demurrage charges to car receivers who retained cars.

In many small New England communities the newspapers would headline the fact that the first refrigerator cars of grapes would be due in town on a given day. The broker would actually sell the grapes directly from the car with people lined up to sample and buy. This would delay the return of the car for many days.

Western shippers were receiving less than a third of the cars they needed. The Car Service Division of the American Railway Association called upon the principal fruit and vegetable associations of the country to make an investigation and adopt a plan that would prevent the great waste of refrigerator cars due to the improper practices on the part of receivers of the perishable traffic. The Southern Pacific became so desperate that it requested the Interstate Commerce Commission to prod the eastern railroads to return the cars to California, and suggested a much higher demurrage rate, up to $25 per day, to help dynamite the aggregations of immovable cars. Of course the slow process of government hearings did not provide an immediate solution to this problem.

The PFE and shippers had to struggle through the har-

vest that year, but the ICC did eventually authorize a substantial increase in the demurrage rate. It was found, though, that consignees considered prompt release of cars of no consequence to them and that they were willing to pay whatever demurrage, track storage and refrigeration charges were assessed against them, as long as they could hold shipments in the cars until a profitable market price was obtainable. The PFE Pittsburgh District Agent was quoted in *Railway Age*, stating, "The rank and file of the produce trade consider it transportation, and the means of transportation were subjects to play with as they saw fit." The railroads and PFE continuously had to fight for and promote quick unloading and return of empties.

During this same period the Tokay grape had become a prized table grape, and nearly all of that variety grown in California, which meant the U.S., came from the Lodi-Florin districts of the Central Valley, just south of Sacramento. That area would generate around 5,000 carloads of Tokays annually.

Roseville was the concentration point for most of the grape and other perishable shipments loaded in central and northern California, On a peak day such as September 26, 1929, there were 94 freight (including reefer) trains, and 38 passenger trains handled through that yard, for an average of one train every eleven minutes.

The Depression brought a drop of grape shipments to 26,398 carloads in 1933, and following the repeal of Prohibition, the loadings leveled to around 15,000 cars annually. Most of the grapes went to local vintners. By the 1935

Southern Pacific Consolidation 2532 is seen working the lettuce sheds near Watsonville, Calif. Many such locals operated each day, switching out loads and empties during the busy harvest season. Both photos, SP, 1937, courtesy John Signor.

season, only 15,402 refrigerator cars were loaded with California grapes on SP lines. Total grape loads handled by PFE over the entire system in 1956 was 15,645 cars.

An interesting footnote to California's grape industry is that it played an important part in the great nineteenth-century phylloxera epidemic that affected European vineyards. The phylloxera root louse is native to eastern North America, where it does little damage to native grape species. Around 1870, American root stocks were taken to British and French botanical gardens, and the phylloxera went with them. Within a few years it infested the historic vineyards of France, Spain, northern Italy, Austria and southern Germany. The European grape species, *vitis vinifera*, then and now the foundation of the world's winemaking, was not resistant to this insect, and the effect was devastating. By 1879 many vineyards, and more than 75 per cent of the annual wine production of Europe, were completely destroyed.

The only way the industry could be saved was to use resistant North American root stocks, onto which the European varieties could be grafted. Some of those varieties were brought back to Europe from California, where they had been taken decades earlier to found California's own vineyards. Thus the debt of the young wine industry of California to the vineyards of Europe was partly repaid from this "reservoir" of varietal plantings. European recovery was slow, and it was not until 1899 that another great vintage appeared in France, to follow the renowned vintages of 1875 and 1877.

California, too, suffered from phylloxera when the louse was inadvertently brought from the East Coast, though the damage was much less than in Europe. California's extensive plant quarantine laws had their origin in statutes devised to limit the importation of eastern grape plants in the 1870's.

Lettuce

The movement of California and Arizona "Icebergs" provided SP and PFE an all-year "deal" and responsibility, for there was, and is, continual production of lettuce in one or more areas in the two states from January through December. The first crop of Arizona lettuce is ready to move in early December, and the "deal" is over in late January. Imperial Valley lettuce begins to move about the middle of December and continues into April. The Watsonville-Salinas district lettuce harvest starts in April and continues to early December. During the 1935 season there were 46,978 carloads of lettuce shipped from all sections of the country, and of that amount, over 93% was grown in these two states. Of that amount, 88% of the shipments were handled by PFE, as the loads were originating along SP lines.

Prior to 1915 the lettuce produced in California was of a nondescript, leafy type that was not popular in the average family's diet. In that year only 5 carloads were shipped east, all from the Imperial Valley. Seed companies had been perfecting the "Iceberg" variety (imported from France and first grown in Los Angeles in 1901), and as increased production of that variety came from the Imperial Valley, housewives welcomed it to their table.

The first Iceberg crop of 37 carloads moved from the Salinas-Watsonville district in 1921, and by 1925 shipments numbered 5,289. The Salt River Valley of Arizona shipped its first carload of lettuce in 1921 also. The Santa Maria-Guadalupe area joined the producing districts in 1922 with 203 carloads. Yuma Valley followed in 1923 with 85 cars, and in that year these five lettuce districts, including the Imperial Valley which was the original growing area, combined to ship a total of 10,319 loads. From that year on the development of the lettuce industry can only be described as phenomenal.

A string of reefers, headed by 2-10-2 3662, passes 16th Street tower in Oakland, in this photo taken from the upper (electrified) level of the Oakland depot. Cars are headed for Salinas and Watsonville. W.C. Whittaker photo, March 6, 1936.

By 1935, these major lettuce districts shipped 41,256 carloads; 23,749 cars moved from the Salinas-Watsonville-Hollister area, 6,539 from the Salt River Valley, 5,844 from the Imperial Valley, 3,529 from the Yuma Valley, and 881 from Santa Maria-Guadalupe. An additional 2,586 carloads originated on the SP from other scattered areas within these two states. These totals did not include the volume on a carload basis shipped to local markets by truck. The Los Angeles market annually consumed the equivalent of over 5,700 carloads, second only to New York City. The bulk of the lettuce going to Los Angeles was shipped by truck from the Santa Maria-Guadalupe fields.

In the early 1930's there developed quite a lettuce producing area around Nampa, Caldwell, and Payette, Idaho. A major shipper was B.F. Hurst. Annual totals of around 250 cars were shipped, but tapered off by the 1940's.

Though the Imperial Valley would eventually ship up to 12,000 carloads of lettuce annually, the SP railroad and PFE forces met their greatest test for efficiency and speed in the Salinas-Watsonville-Hollister district which comprised more than 500 square miles of lettuce plantings, amounting to 64,430 acres. Shipments from this one district ran mid-April to the end of November and would average 74% of the total United States carload movements of lettuce during that same period.

Salinas, Watsonville and Watsonville Junction yards were the railroad's focal points in the district. The 41 packing sheds at Salinas, in 1935, originated 17,215 carloads of lettuce, all but 6,534 cars of the entire district's output. Six switch engines took care of the cars in the Salinas Yard, while PFE agents at the station handled car billings and diversions. At the season peak, it was 24-hour non-stop

work. Cars loaded at Salinas, as well as Watsonville, Del Monte Junction, Cooper, Molus, Graves, Consales and Vega were moved over to the Watsonville Junction yard.

Record days at "The Junction" would see 1900 to 2000 cars handled in and out of the yard, in addition to about 200 cars on through trains. Up to fourteen switch engines, 2-6-0's and 2-8-0's, operated constantly, switching the yard and bringing in loads from sheds at the city of Watsonville. Four road engines were used in handling 99-car trains of empties and loads to and from Salinas. At Watsonville Junction all cars were classified as to destinations, assembled into trains, and moved to the concentration points of either Roseville or Colton where they started their way to eastern markets. Arrival in Chicago via Roseville and Ogden would be the morning of the 7th day, or into Kansas City the 6th morning; and via El Paso and the StLSW or Cotton Belt into St. Louis by the 7th evening.

Besides lettuce, some 35 other fruits and vegetables were shipped in straight carloads from the Salinas-Watsonville district. A total of 59,496 cars were shipped out from Watsonville in 1952 with lettuce leading the total with 38,155 cars. There were 7,304 cars of mixed vegetables, 6,444 cars of carrots, 1,962 cars of celery adding to the total. The city of Salinas originated an additional 42,806 carloads that year.

The magnitude of the impact this area had is demonstrated by the fact that by 1950 there were 16 frozen food processing plants in the Western District, and 12 of those were centered in the Watsonville and Santa Cruz areas, where 1,893 cars of frozen food originated in 1953. The Western District shipped in excess of 4,000 cars of frozen food that year, almost 50% of the annual frozen food loads moved by PFE. Strawberries were the prime fruit crop in this area, and because they were such a perishable commodity, they were one of the initial crops that entered frozen food packaging. Under ice protective service, the strawberry and berry crops were normally handled by express reefer service.

Winter vegetables grown in this district consisted mainly of artichokes, Brussels sprouts, broccoli, cauliflower, and celery. Artichokes were grown along the seacoast where they were nurtured by coastal fogs. The artichoke belt extended south from Halfmoon Bay (just south of San Francisco) to Castroville and the Carmel Valley. These areas were and are the only sections of the United States where artichokes are grown to any commercial extent.

Much advance preparation had to be done by PFE to insure that adequate cars would be available to successfully handle the projected lettuce "deals." Each year a forecast was made as to the probable crop production, the date of first shipment, the volume by weeks and months, and the probable peak shipment period. This was done by PFE agents that were well trained and qualified for this specific and vital task. Such estimations were done for all crops that PFE handled. The agents had to take into account the acres planted, the time planted, and the weather during the growing season. It was an extremely critical forecast since errors could mean unnecessary movement of cars and possible shortage or surplus of cars in a certain district.

The car movement westward was calculated so sufficient cars were always kept at loading stations to take care of one day's supply, the reserve supply for the Salinas-Watsonville-Hollister district being kept at Watsonville Junction and San Jose. The main source of daily car supply to all northern California points was Roseville. From there enough empty cars were billed each night for the following day's loadings, and also enough cars to replenish the "car reservoir" at San Jose and Watsonville Junction. The reserve was maintained to avoid a shortage of cars in case of train interruptions east or west of Roseville, and because it was impractical to maintain a full day's supply of empties on sidings at the packing sheds or nearby yards. The supply to loading stations was sometimes replenished two or three times daily. Other primary "car reservoirs" were maintained at Yuma and Pocatello.

The icing of cars of lettuce did not require as heavy a service from PFE forces as did some other crops such as cantaloupe. "Top icing" to remove field heat became prevalent by the mid-1930's and this reduced bunker icing. Cars used at Salinas were then iced only once, with pre-icing done at Watsonville Jct. In packing the crates of lettuce, a layer of lettuce was placed at the bottom of the crate, then a layer of crushed ice between each of the four layers of lettuce heads, and a final layer of ice on top. After the crates were loaded in the cars, the top-icing of the entire load was accomplished by a machine that blew chipped ice over the tops of the crates inside the car. This icing sometimes carried the load through to the destination, or if required was replenished by top-icing enroute, called "re-top icing." The

Two of the many activities that took place 24 hours a day at Salinas. (**Left**) The double-sided mechanical car icer was owned by one of the private ice companies. PFE photo, CSRM. (**Right**) Waterproof corrugated cartons of lettuce are "switched" off a conveyor belt into trailers. UP photo 167-7-10, courtesy Frank Peacock.

A third section of Imperial Valley lettuce passes eastbound through Separ, N.M., marked by the distinctive exhaust of the three-cylinder 5026, an SP class 4-10-2. Stan Kistler collection, April 9, 1941.

recommended lettuce shipping temperature was 32° F.

All ice for bunker or top-icing was furnished at Watsonville by private ice companies. The total annual volume was immense, and often the demands so heavy that the local supply had to be augmented with shipments by carload, sometimes 40 to 50 cars daily, from as far away as Stockton. Top-icing continued even with mechanical cars, and in later years many icers were converted for top-ice loads only, thus utilizing the old cars for a few more years.

The advent of "precooling" entered the process in 1932. The cooling was accomplished by means of electric fans placed at either end of the car which circulated cold air from the iced bunkers at the rate of about 6500 cubic feet per minute. This would remove field heat from the crop shipped, and greatly reduced the amount of ice needed to get the carload temperature to tariff specifications. Most of the shipments were precooled at loading stations if those facilities were available.

In 1951 PFE and local private packers introduced "vacuum cooling" to the Salinas-Watsonville area and the Imperial Valley. This was another process to take field heat out of fresh picked lettuce and other crops, and was a means of further lessening the requirements for icing. Most of these units were independent of ice plants. They operated by attaining a moderate vacuum through the use of steam Venturi jets. This partial vacuum greatly accelerated evaporation, thereby cooling the produce. The lettuce, now packed in crates at the field, was trucked directly to the vacuum plant and run into tubes 7-½ feet in diameter and approximately 50 feet in length.

The tube, with the load inside, would be sealed on both ends by heavy steel sliding doors and as the partial vacuum was established (in about 30 minutes) the temperature of the lettuce was reduced from an initial 70 degrees or higher to 33 to 34 degrees. The crates were then loaded within 15 to 20 minutes into pre-iced and pre-salted cars and billed under standard refrigeration. The shipper would sometimes top-ice this type load. Fan equipped cars were essential to the movement of vacuum cooled loads, particularly when no top-ice was used. These vacuum plants proved

Iceberg lettuce loading, Mesa, Ariz. SP photo.

very effective and helped PFE efficiently move a total of 62,939 cars of lettuce in 1955.

Cantaloupes

The Imperial Valley's annual melon "deal" created the heaviest concentrated freight traffic movement handled on the entire Southern Pacific system and by the Pacific Fruit Express Company. The harvest depended upon the weather and ripening, but generally it was from mid-April to mid-August, with the peak hitting in June. First plantings of cantaloupe were tried there in 1902, and PFE shipped 1,804 carloads in 1908. Acreage increased so that by 1927, 16,848 carloads of "Valley" melons were marketed. That year also saw the movement of the longest cantaloupe train on record, a 149-car "melon block" handled from Brawley to Yuma on the first lap of the journey east.

Imperial Valley carload shipments of cantaloupes (also including honeydews, honeyballs, casabas and watermelons) reached 21,504 cars in 1931 to gain prominence in the list of freight commodities (within a decade the annual carloads would reach 31,000). In addition to the Imperial Valley shipments, which produced 50% of the cantaloupes grown in the U. S., considerable traffic was generated from three other significant melon districts. During the 1935 season, 1239 carloads were shipped from Yuma Valley, 1005 from the Salt River Valley in Arizona, and 2000 cars from the Turlock district in the San Joaquin Valley.

Cantaloupes are very perishable and require quick loading and refrigeration. The melons had to be cooled from hot fields to the shipping temperature, 35-40° F. At the height of the season between 500 and 600 men were employed by PFE at icing facilities at Brawley, El Centro and Calexico. These three points would dispense 135,000 tons or more of ice during the cantaloupe season.

A reserve of about 5000 empties was readied at Tucson and then moved to storage tracks in the vicinity of the Valley prior to the shipping season. When the cars were ordered, they were first set at the icing decks for preicing and were then taken to the loading points. After loading, they were again returned to the icing plants for replenishment icing before being forwarded in trains. If the cars were delayed more than five hours in departing, they were again set at the ice deck for re-icing. After leaving the valley, the cars were reiced at Yuma, eastbound, and Indio, westbound. About 15% of melons moved westbound.

Rail operations in the Imperial Valley were under the SP trainmaster of the Indio-Calexico Subdivision, and he moved his headquarters to Brawley during cantaloupe movement season. He controlled all operations in the valley, and directed every movement between Calexico and Niland. An assistant trainmaster at Brawley and two assistants at El Centro aided in the supervision, these men also being appointed for the cantaloupe season only. Normally about

Brawley was the hub of the vast activities in the Imperial Valley. In this 1924 view, cars are being iced at the Imperial Ice and Development Company's deck (left) and the PFE deck (right). Southern California Edison collection, courtesy Wm. A. Myers.

One of the many daily locals working the "Valley" starts out of Calexico in the late afternoon. Here a C-9 Consolidation with its whaleback tender, inherited from a cab-forward, is passing the PFE ice deck. Stan Kistler photo, Jan. 15, 1955.

150 additional men were used in the valley by the SP during the melon season.

Besides the SP, there was also trackage and service by the San Diego & Arizona Eastern, the Inter-California, and the Holton Inter-Urban Railway (owned by SP after 1925). The SP's trackage in the cantaloupe district consisted of 33 miles of branch line from Calipatria to Calexico, and two branches that junctioned at Calipatria; one of 22 miles to Sandia, and one of 14 miles to Westmoreland. The 10-mile Holton connected with the SP at El Centro.

Unlike most loading districts, the packing sheds here were not grouped close together. This created a real operating challenge for the railroad, as the placing of empty cars and picking up of loaded cars was not a switching movement, but more like a local freight run. There were approximately 58 shippers in the Valley, and 50 packing houses operating. There were 12 loading points situated on the line between Niland and Calexico, the rest being on the Westmoreland and Sandia branches, and on the Holton Inter-Urban. Melons were brought in from the fields in the afternoon and early evening, and the empties and loads were spotted and picked up around the clock.

SP Lines in the Imperial Valley.

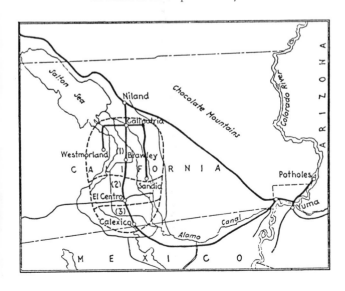

About 18 switching engines, 2-6-0, 4-6-0 and 2-8-0 types, and crews worked the Valley during the height of the season. There were five switchers at Calexico, six at El Centro and seven at Brawley. Running repairs and monthly boiler washouts were done at the Calexico enginehouse. Road engines, normally 2-10-2 types, worked in and out of pools maintained at Los Angeles.

Some packing sheds were pulled six or seven times per day! The crews were recruited from the regular road crews on the division, the runs being bulletined and bid in on the basis of seniority. Each crew was assigned to a certain territory and the runs arranged so as to give the maximum service. To appreciate the extent of the work done by the railroad and PFE it is of interest to see the daily schedule of runs on a typical day at Brawley.

The first job called at Brawley began at 7 AM, the locomotive being double-crewed with two 12-hr. shifts, to perform switching work in the vicinity of Brawley. The second run started at 8 AM and comprised a turn on the Westmoreland branch with a train of empties for spotting, working there during the day and bringing back a train of loads, before going off duty at Brawley at 8 PM. The third and fourth jobs were 12-hr shifts, one beginning at 10:30 AM, the other 12 noon, both being used in switching the loading sheds at Brawley. The fifth crew went on at 2 PM proceeding at once to the Sandia branch with a train of empties, serving the loading points on this branch and returning by midnight with a train of loads.

The sixth crew went on at 3 PM and proceeded to the Westmoreland branch to relieve the second crew. It returned with loads at 1 AM and then helped to clean up the yard work at Brawley. The seventh crew went on at 5 PM, switching at Brawley until 7 PM, then made a trip to the Westmoreland branch for loads. Upon returning, it was kept occupied until 5 AM switching Brawley. The crews at El Centro and Calexico were operated on a similar basis, so it is evident that this was a dispatching nightmare. There were so many train movements that 15 special flagmen were placed at busy grade crossings to avoid accidents.

Because of these heavy switching movements, a novel method was used to control the trains. All first-class trains operating in the area ran under train orders, but as soon as the trainmaster was established at Brawley for the cantaloupe "deal," an order was issued by the train dispatcher requiring all switching crews to call the trainmaster at Brawley for a permissive card. This card gave authority to move from one designated point to another. There was a double phone line between Niland and Calexico and on both branches, that was utilized for all these calls. The conductor of a train working a "turn" of the sheds would call Brawley when his train reached its designated point. This would release the block to the trainmaster, and he would then obtain permission to move his train from that point to the next. The trainmaster or yardmaster was thus able to move the switchers to and from outside points without the necessity of the train crew obtaining orders. The system was an absolute necessity for quick and efficient operations during this heavy season.

As stated earlier, the first carloads of cantaloupe from the Imperial Valley were shipped by mid-April and the last were usually by mid-August. It was not uncommon for brokers to request express refrigerator cars at the initial picking of a crop so they could send shipments east as fast as possible and receive highly inflated prices on the "first of the season" fruit.

Peak loading days for cantaloupes, which occurred during a four to six week period around mid-June, could see 400 to 500 cars a day. A record day, June 27, 1922, saw 647 cars moved out. In 1931 there was a two-week period in which over 500 cars moved each day. That meant initial icing of the empties, which took 10,500 pounds of ice per car; then switching the cars to the packing sheds where they were loaded with hot cantaloupes just picked from the field; and returning the loaded cars to the ice deck for re-icing, which would usually take another 7000 pounds. The amount of ice issued was phenomenal, considering an average of 8 to 9 tons per car. Vacuum cooling, introduced here in the early 1950's, greatly reduced ice consumption.

During May and June there was an average of 4 to 6 melon blocks per day leaving the Imperial Valley for Yuma. All eastbound trains, known locally as "Haulers," started from Brawley, filling out to the full normal tonnage of 124 cars at El Centro and Calexico. By arranging for each train to pick up cars at all three points, a steadier movement of loads was maintained and the yards kept free from backlogs and delays. Normally two melon trains operated westbound each day. There was also movement of other crops at the same time, notably carrots and sugar beets. Twelve to sixteen trains would be dispatched from the Valley daily.

The eastbound Haulers were handled principally by big 2-10-2 locomotives, with a few three-cylinder 4-10-2 en-gines occasionally showing up. These locomotives handled the trains to Yuma, 84 miles, in six hours, including time spent in filling out tonnage and the inspection at the Mexican border at Calexico. In the early 1950's, when steam was being withdrawn from some territories, SP cab-forward 4-8-8-2 locomotives appeared on the scene in the Valley to haul the fruit blocks, and soon thereafter diesel road units made their appearance. At least two of the daily runs made a quick turnaround and returned the same day with empties from Yuma.

From Yuma, the trains operated to El Paso, either over the SP through Phoenix, or via Tucson and the El Paso & Southwestern line of the SP. East of El Paso about half of the movements went via Tucumcari and the Rock Island. The remainder were divided about equally between the Texas & Pacific, which moved the loads via Fort Worth for delivery to the Missouri-Kansas-Texas, or to Texarkana for delivery to the Missouri Pacific; or the loads continued on the SP's T&NO lines that delivered to the St. Louis Southwestern at Corsicana, Texas, for movement to St. Louis and beyond.

Recollections of Pete Holst:

"In 1923 I went to the Imperial Valley. At first, I was more or less observing there, and traveling between Imperial Valley, Yuma, Tucson and El Paso, seeing how the Icing Department was handling the icing. The next year the whole icing thing was transferred back into the Car Service Department, and they said, 'You're it. You're going to handle the Imperial Valley.' I knew what was going on down there, they'd been having labor trouble for years, and in a hotshot melon 'deal' like that, you can't have any disruption in your labor, especially on the ice deck. If you don't ice the car, you buy the cantaloupes!

We ran three big boarding houses, at Brawley, El Centro and Calexico. We paid fifty cents an hour, board and room was a dollar a day, and we gave them transportation. So, I got busy and wrote all our agents and ice plant managers along the line, and told 'em we had these 'deals' coming up in the Imperial Valley. I lined up enough ice men that I knew I could beat any strike, and I did that every summer. The 'deals' kept building up each year. In 1928 we had about 28,000 cars out of the Imperial Valley, and in 1930 we had over 30,000. Now you're talking in a 6-week period.

You think I didn't wear out some pencils down there, figuring how much ice we're gonna use, what I've got in storage, all that! We had no ice manufacturing plants down there, it was all contracted locally. You know, thirty thousand tons of ice wouldn't go very far when you used five thousand tons a day. And you couldn't just say, 'Give me this ice tomorrow.' I had an old friend, George Corwin, Chief Clerk in the General Agent's Office in Los Angeles,

An eastbound "hauler" rumbles through Mexico on the Inter-California Railway Co. headed for the SP's Sunset Route connection at Araz Junction. The big 2-10-2, 3663, is supplemented with an extra water car in this dry country. R.P. Middlebrook photo, Arnold Menke collection.

and he knew the country and every ice plant around there. Some of the citrus houses even had their own plants, so he'd pick up ice from them. We shipped in ice from LA and Colton, and if we got to the last resort, I'd even take some from the Santa Fe.

The empties came in from Yuma. They'd store some cars in the Valley, but they stored more in Mexico on all the sidings on the Inter-Cal. You can figure what the railroad was doing when you bring in and take out 500 cars a day. We'd pre-ice the empties and we initial iced them after they were loaded, we chalk marked them on the side, the date and hour they were iced. If they were delayed in getting out for more than five hours and got 'sour' we'd have to bring 'em back and touch 'em up.

The cantaloupes practically all went east and the watermelons moved west. The eastbounds moved through Mexico, and SP at that time had to have a helper to get over the grade at Algodones coming out from below sea level. One of those old steam engines just couldn't do it. They'd give the trainmaster hell for having 100-car or bigger trains. He'd be calling brakemen every hour, five or six brakemen on the roofs. That was the damnedest railroading you ever heard of.

We had quite a business in watermelons and sometimes we got in trouble with 'em, too. The shippers would load everybody up too much with carloads of watermelons, see. They'd start the cars out, maybe billed to Fresno. By the time the cars got to Fresno, why, they were oversold there. All right, they'd move 'em to Sacramento, and there, the same fix, so they'd send them on up to Portland. I remember once they had as many as a hundred cars of watermelons scattered around, no place to go, no place to sell, the end of the line, see. And they sat there until the juice was running out the doors. You think we didn't have a time getting rid of that rotten stuff! We had a cleaning crew up there, but God, those rotten melons. They didn't even want to open the doors."

Another principal melon-producing area was the Huron-Westside District of the Central Valley of California. Several melon growers and shippers pioneered the first melon "deal" from this area in the late 1920's. The Westside melons were of excellent quality and the district was home to the famous

Mendota melons. Eastern buyers started purchasing from this district in large quantities in 1934, when the Colorado melon crop failed, and from that time crop acreage increased to where 45,000 acres were planted with different varieties of melons. The acreage has remained in that same magnitude for the past decades, and has always been an important PFE business, yielding from 9,500 to 10,000 cars (and later, trailers) annually.

Knowing the tremendous possibilities of converting desert country into rich cantaloupe-producing acreage, the Southern Pacific and county agricultural agents for the state of Nevada worked together in 1921 to develop a cantaloupe industry in that state. In that year two carloads of "Hearts of Gold" cantaloupes were shipped from the Fallon Valley. They were of such high quality and exceptional flavor, and commission merchants requested so much for the next year, that acreage was planted both around Fallon and Fernley, and the industry grew to ship 231 cars of melons in 1925. Farmers in the rich Lovelock and Mason Valleys also began planting cantaloupes so that by the mid-1920's there were estimated to be 2000 acres of the melons in these areas.

An initial advantage of the Nevada cantaloupe industry was the lateness of their season, late August to early September, which placed them on the market at a time when the California cantaloupes were gone. In 1925 a six-car ice platform was built at Hazen just for icing these shipments. However the late harvesting season came into direct competition with cantaloupe districts developing in Colorado, and in the ensuing years the Nevada growers and shippers began losing profits, until by 1932, there were only 25 carloads shipped, and by 1935 the industry had disappeared and Hazen was closed.

To a lesser but important degree, a good number of carloads of cantaloupes and watermelons were moved out of the Beeville, Texas, area during June. (See Chapter 13, Southern District, for more about this territory.)

The melon industry has continued to flourish, but the majority of shipments has gradually gone to trucking. In the 1950's though, it still remained one of PFE's top commodities handled, ranking number four in total carloads in 1955. That year saw 26,451 carloads of cantaloupes and 3,387 carloads of watermelons moved by PFE.

Imperial Valley's Cantaloupe Crop Goes to Market

HOW Imperial Valley produces the world's largest crop of cantaloupes and how Southern Pacific rushes them to eastern markets was the interesting theme of a three-page pictorial story reaching nearly 12,000,000 readers of the July 15 issue of *Life Magazine.*

Life's photographs were the work of *Life* photographer George Strock. Accompanying Strock on his job in the valley, and carrying on the photographic story over SP, T&NO and Cotton Belt lines through to St. Louis for the benefit of *Bulletin* readers, was SP staff photographer Al Rommel, results of whose work appear in this layout.

"Life's" Photographer Strock, perched atop one of the trailers which carry the melon crop to the packing sheds, shoots a crew of Mexican pickers hard at work in one of the many big fields near El Centro. Pickers work in gangs under direction of a contractor, members sharing equally the day's earnings of 14 cents per crate.

PFE "Reefer" Cars are loaded at shed. Air blown through ice bunkers pre-cools melons to 40°, halts maturing, prevents over-ripening.

Re-Icing After Pre-cooling, as well as initial icing before melons are loaded, is done at PFE decks at El Centro, Brawley, Calexico. Each car takes five to six tons initially, and three more tons after pre-cooling.

Diversion: As loaded car moves east, shipper may change its destination to any city promising best market conditions. PFE office, El Centro, keeps record of each car's location, teletypes diversion orders.

Keeping Melons Cool despite outside temperatures of 110° is 24-hour job. Shown is a Tucson PFE "iceman" refilling bunker.

Highest Point on the Imperial Valley-to-St. Louis route is Paisano, Texas, on T&NO lines. Shown is the perishable block crossing the 5047-ft. hump.

Engine Takes a Drink at Marathon, Tex., with T&NO Fireman R. A. Hurst of Valentine officiating up on top of the big tank.

Train Orders giving the perishable block the right over a westbound freight are picked up by Fireman Guy Berry at Dryden, Tex.

Oiling Up his Cotton Belt engine before pulling out of Texarkana is Eng'r Sam Brooks.

The Blue Streak, Cotton Belt's fast merchandise train, southbound, roars by the northbound perishable near Brinkley, Ark.

Crossing the Mississippi from Missouri into Thebes, Ill., the melon train moves over the Cotton Belt's beautiful steel and masonry bridge, into the last lap of its run to the East St. Louis yards.

Pickers must be highly trained to know when melons are exactly right for picking. Fruit is placed in "trap sacks" for trailers.

Govt. Test: D. A. Harrigan, agricultural com., uses a refrachrometer to see melon's sugar content is at least 10%.

Packers must be able to select by instinct various grades of melons, pack each in proper size crate. For this they earn 9 cents per crate; can make up to $35 daily.

Counting Machine operator tallies number of crates of each grade, number crates packed by each packer as day's wage basis.

Road to Market for Imperial Valley's vast melon production is Southern Pacific, and secret of the valley's fertility is an abundant water supply from the Colorado river. Here a powerful articulated cab-in-front locomotive pulls an eastbound solid train load of melons across the new All-American Canal at Araz Junction. Almost completed, the canal will add to the present water supply, increase the valley's productive area.

Office on Wheels is conductor's desk in fruit block caboose. Conductor Mark Mullins of Tucson checks over a big sheaf of waybills.

Thirty Tons of Ice crash down into car bunkers from the long deck at Hearne, Texas, to make up for loss by melting since re-icing at Del Rio. Frequent check of bunkers and re-icing guard fruit against heat throughout journey.

Fastest Interchange in the country is that from T&NO to Cotton Belt lines at Corsicana, consuming only 15 minutes in the uniformly high-speed Imperial Valley-to-St. Louis schedule. Shown backing to a coupling is Cotton Belt's No. 805, 4-8-4 type with 70-inch drivers, specially designed for fast freight service.

At St. Louis the melons move from refrigerator cars to consignees' trucks (left) thence to city's fruit stands.

Picked 6 Days Ago in California, melons are purchased in St. Louis by Mrs. Leo E. Riley and Patsy Ann.

IMPERIAL Valley's Melon Crop this year ran to about 1,700,000 crates, was valued at $3,500,000. The movement, all originated by SP, involved some 5100 PFE cars. Great majority of these moved either SP-Cotton Belt through St. Louis or SP-Rock Island through Chicago for eastern distribution.

A lone Northern Pacific stock car is the only break in a solid PFE train of Idaho spuds and onions heading east under ventilation service. The F9 rebuilds (in F3 carbodies) are near Inkom, just east of Pocatello, Idaho. UP Railroad Museum photo 68-362.

Potatoes and Onions

Handling the potato and onion crops of the Pacific Northwest and Pacific Coast did not entail any unusual operating problems. Shipments of these two vegetables moved in ventilated service, or heater protective service in colder months, and ice was normally not required. Most of the crop was placed in storage close to points of production and held for shipment as the market demanded. The West never gained the dominance in potato production that it did in most of the other crops produced for market. After the mid-1950's, though, the potato and frozen potato products eventually became PFE's number one crop handled yearly, even surpassing lettuce. These products lend themselves to large-volume shipping in refrigerator cars.

The state of Maine was initially the leading potato producer in the nation, and of a national total of 223,507 car shipments in 1934, the bulk came from Maine with 50,012 cars. At that time Idaho ranked second, and in the same 1934 period, shipped 31,677 carloads. Other states that were primary producers of this staple and their comparison carloads for that same year were: Wisconsin, 10,616 cars; Virginia, 16,092 cars; North Carolina, 10,753 cars, California, 10,595 cars; and Michigan, 7,695 cars. Because of this broad spread of growing areas, most western potato movements did not extend to the Midwestern or Atlantic states.

The exception was the Idaho potato, especially the Russet, which by 1928 made up 75 percent of that state's potato output. This potato had gained a reputation in discriminating distant markets, particularly in fine restaurants. The Idaho producers recognized this and developed strict grading and packing standards by law and custom. The Idaho "fancy bakers" were shipped in fifteen and thirty pound cartons containing from thirty to seventy individually wrapped spuds. The reputation was maintained by seeing to it that only the high quality potatoes that people had come to think of as Idaho products were sent to them.

The importance of seed selection was unmistakable in gaining this national market. The Caldwell-Wilder district developed an early variety that would go on the market in time for higher prices, while north of Pocatello, in the upper Snake River Valley, the Russet had gained such a dominance that by 1927, 23,000 carloads of potatoes were shipped out of Idaho to no less than 35 states.

Digging potatoes near Caldwell, Idaho, mid-'40's. UP photo.

Nampa, Idaho, was the major concentration point on the OSL (UP) for the Intermountain territory. Here a non-dynamic braked UP Geep switches the yard, marshalling a UP hotshot "NF" or Nampa Fruit block for eastward movement. Milton G. Sorensen photo, 1962.

Idaho was by far the leading potato producer of the west, and by the mid-1940's had gained the number one ranking in the nation, a position it continues to hold annually. Croplands paralleled the Snake River and the Union Pacific rails through southern and western Idaho, and bordering eastern Oregon. Major tonnage on many branch lines in these areas was spuds and onions, from packing sheds, to storage sheds, and then to market. The early crop was shipped at 50° F., the late crop at 40° F.

The state of Idaho generated 66,419 carloads in 1951, but that figure had dropped to 60,973 cars by 1958, as more and more of the potato crop was processed rather than shipped as whole potatoes. The potatoes were sometimes protected with ice in the spring when the last of the old potatoes were shipped and in the early fall when the new crop was coming off. The bulk of movements, though, were from storage sheds throughout the winter, and were under heater protective service.

To a lesser degree, there were potato producing districts along the UP in south-central Washington, and the Hood River Valley of north-central Oregon. Other states served by the UP, such as Utah, Nebraska, and Colorado, had smaller producing areas for potatoes and onions, but these originated relatively few loads for PFE; instead, shipments were local, by truck.

There were 21 major potato and onion growing districts along the Southern Pacific lines scattered over California, Oregon, Arizona, Nevada and New Mexico. In addition, the SP had two sweet potato districts located around Turlock and Atwater in California's Central Valley. The Lower Rio Grande Valley district between Edinburg and Brownsville also produced potatoes. These SP districts would generate for PFE about 25% of the total potato carloads hauled in the U.S. The principal potato districts on the SP and 1935 carloads were: Willamette Valley and Oregon Coast, 163 cars; Klamath Falls, 2605 cars; Stockton-Lodi (the Delta), 914 cars; Guadalupe-Santa

Maria, 572 cars; Los Angeles, 223 cars; Bakersfield, 109 cars. The AT&SF handled most of the Bakersfield potatoes, 911 cars in 1935.

Potatoes from Pacific Coast points were grown in two distinct crops, early and late. The early crop was planted in early spring and the heaviest shipments moved in July and August, many moving to the Pacific Northwest, Rocky Mountain states and the Southwest. The late California crop was planted in May, June and July. This crop was dug fully mature and stored for winter and early spring markets, competing with the Washington and Idaho crops. The California late market was mainly a local one.

The Klamath Basin area in Oregon and Siskiyou County in Northern California rapidly became producers of late potatoes, the Klamath area cultivating 90,000 acres and generating around 7,000 cars in 1936. Markets were nearby, with California and Oregon taking 90% of the crop.

The Rio Grande Valley of Texas produced potatoes from mid-March to mid-May; the crop was not a major contributor on a national basis. The market was local and hauls were to and from storage sheds to Texas consignees.

After World War II the production of processed foods grew immensely, and Idaho began producing more frozen, flaked and powdered potato products than any other state. PFE contributed heavily in the continuing growth of this industry. By the late 1940's and on into the fifties, potatoes became unquestionably the number one crop hauled by PFE. During that period, the average annual loadings were between 70,000 and 74,000 cars.

Turning to onions, the onion industry grew to where annual originating loads for PFE averaged 10,000 to 11,000, with a peak year in 1954 showing 12,244 carloads. The onion varieties grown in the West were harvested in three distinct crops: the early harvest required movement April to June, the intermediate crop moved June and July, and the late crop August and September. They are typically shipped at temperatures between 32 and 40° F.

In 1958, the Ford 861 Powermaster diesel is the latest in tractors. This scene shows harvesting potatoes in Colorado, judging by the truck license plate. UP Railroad Museum photo 42748.

Onion growing in California on a commercial basis began in 1915 for early and late crops and in 1926 for intermediate yields. Idaho and Texas production had developed by 1920 and were the other major onion growing areas on the UP-SP. Like potatoes, onions were grown all across the country, so PFE shipments tended to be only to western markets.

The bulk of Union Pacific onion shipments originated in Idaho, from areas around Nyssa, Parma, Wilder, Caldwell, Nampa and Boise, and in the south around Twin Falls. Eastern Oregon districts that bordered the Snake River and southern Washington generated 200 to 400 annual carloads, and the farming districts around Salt Lake City and Ogden also grew and shipped onions by PFE.

Southern Pacific onion loads came from four main locales: around Brooks in the Willamette Valley of Oregon, around Stockton in the San Joaquin Valley, the Imperial and Coachella Valleys of Southern California, and the Rio Grande Valley of Texas. Leading onion producers in 1934 were: Texas with 6,511 cars, Michigan with 6,148 cars, California with 2,840 cars, and Idaho with 2,345 carloads. In 1956, PFE handled 9,451 carloads of onions.

Asparagus

Practically all of the canning asparagus and about 45% of the table asparagus produced in the United States was grown in California. Contrasted with only 2400 acres in 1899, there was over 69,000 acres devoted to the asparagus industry by 1937. One of the earliest mention of asparagus growing in California is made in a 1858 California Department of Agriculture report, in which appears a statement that E.B. Crocker, later one of Central Pacific's early officers, had asparagus growing in his home garden.

By 1900, early Los Angeles shippers were sending asparagus east along with green peas and artichokes. The growth of the industry was steady, and eventually the main growing districts became the Sacramento River Delta, the Imperial Valley, and the San Fernando Valley. By 1919

this crop was originating about 250 carloads for Eastern consumers from the Walnut Grove Branch in the Delta.

California started shipping asparagus each year in mid-March. Imperial Valley shipments continued until eastern asparagus matured in quantity, usually about mid-April. About 75% of the "Delta Grass" was utilized for canning by local canneries. The long-distance shipments decreased drastically when harvesting in the Midwest and East commenced. Carloads shipped by PFE in 1936 amounted to: Sacramento River Delta, 578 cars; Imperial Valley, 76 cars; Arizona, 37 cars; for a total of 691 cars.

The Hood River Valley in Oregon would also generate between 20 and 30 carloads of asparagus annually.

Celery

Celery, as a commercial crop in California, was first grown in the early 1890's. Production areas were principally centered in Orange and Los Angeles Counties, and by 1900 approximately 1,800 carloads of this specialty vegetable were shipped to eastern markets. By 1923, shipments reached 3,500 carloads, and up to that time southern California still held the monopoly on the crop.

To the north, in the Sacramento and San Joaquin River Delta, a major reclamation of tracts and islands had been taking place between 1918 and 1925. A system of levees opened up over 55,000 acres to farming. Blight and heavy continuous croppings in the southland caused the celery acreage to shift to the virgin Delta tracts. Northern California celery shipping centers in 1921 had established themselves at Antioch, Walnut Grove, Stockton and Sacramento, with over 2,500 carloads originating from these points, while Southern California carloads dropped to about 900.

As a result of the Delta celery crop, a unique operation was established specifically for its handling. In 1927, the Western Pacific Railroad built an eight-mile extension from a new location, Terminous Junction (a half mile east of Kingdon, a siding on WP's mainline near Lodi), west to Terminous. At a cost of $500,000 the branch provided spur tracks, warehouses, fruit and vegetable packing houses, wharves and docks. The channel at Terminous was 30 feet deep at low-water periods, allowing access for a large range of river and seagoing vessels.

The Western Pacific also constructed and organized a "mosquito fleet" of small vessels to ply the waters of the various Delta channels to bring in produce from all the islands and tracts in the area. Terminous soon became the celery packing center for California.

From 1927 to 1934, the celery plantings in the Delta varied from 7,500 to 10,500 acres, which was about 90 percent of the total California crop, and it ranked sixth in monetary value for the state's vegetable crops. Almost all this celery crop passed through Terminous. The wharf warehouse, 726 feet long, had three tracks that could handle 52 cars for loading at one time. Direct telephone and telegraph facilities were provided, as well as team and platform scales, and offices for shippers. There was also a potato and onion loading platform with a track capacity of 14 cars that provided direct loading from barges.

The celery was loaded onto a conveyor belt system from the "mosquito boats" or trucks. It was washed and water cooled, then sorted before packing. Initially the packers dumped the cull stock and debris directly into Little Potato Slough. The sheer volume actually filled the slough to the point that it interfered with navigation, so around 1932, a large three-story culling chute was erected on site. Packers then passed the inferior stock along a belt system into a cull trough which floated the debris under the chute. Here a conveyor belt carried it up into the chute, where it was reloaded into trucks to be hauled away for livestock feed or fertilizer.

It was as true in 1930 as it is today, that Florida was California's chief competitor for the celery market. By 1983 the total California acreage was down to 6,000 to 8,000 annual acres, with the emphasis shifting back south, now to Ventura County. No appreciable celery is presently grown in the Delta. Florida annually has from 10,000 to 12,400 acres of celery plantings. The Delta has shifted to other products.

Also changed is Terminous. The Western Pacific discontinued service to the site in the 1964, and the rails were torn up in early 1965. The packing sheds are now a marina, and the tall culling chute, which still stands, has been placed on the National Register of Historic Places.

The 1920's saw the development of commercial celery production in the state of Utah. It was a "green" type as distinguished from the White Plume and Golden Self-blanching varieties grown in California and Florida. It was grown in Box Elder, Weber, Salt Lake and Utah counties. The rich, heavy dark soil found there was particularly suited to this Pascal type of celery brought in by the Chinese some

25 years earlier. It was known for its tenderness, crispness, sweet flavor, and absence of "strings." The periodic banking of the soil deeply against the stalk through its growing period produced a blanched celery with a very distinctive flavor. The state of New York was a major recipient of carload shipments. So popular was "Utah celery" in Albany, N.Y. that many people ordered packages directly for their Thanksgiving tables rather than chance missing it in the markets. Most of this produce, harvested in October, was sold locally, but PFE handled 25-40 carloads of the crop annually.

Other Fruits

Deciduous fruit growing took its place alongside farming and stock raising very early as a commercial enterprise. Among the first commercial orchards in the West were those along the Sierra foothills, near the "gold diggins," and the Sacramento River Delta. It was from those districts that the major share of California's deciduous fruit crop was harvested as acreages increased over the years.

In Oregon, the principal fruit shipments originated from the Rogue River Valley on the SP, where the first commercial pear orchards were planted in 1885, and from the apple and pear orchards in the Hood River Valley that the UP opened up when its rails reached there in 1882. In the 1929 season Hood River shipped 3,453 cars of commercial apples, 538 cars of canning apples, 484 cars of commercial pears and 70 cars of canning pears. Idaho originated apple, pear, and cherry shipments from the Emmett, Payette, and Wilder districts.

The Yakima Valley was a major fruit-producing district on UP's Washington lines. The states of Washington and New York vie annually for the honor of being the "apple

Here Yakima Valley Transportation Co. motor 297 moves a string of apple loads toward the UP interchange. A single Santa Fe reefer is the only break in the solid consist of PFE cars. W.C. Whittaker photo, September 1945.

capital" of the country. In Washington, the two top apple producing areas were the Wenatchee area served by the Great Northern Railway, and the Yakima Valley area served by the UP and PFE, and by the Northern Pacific.

The first apple trees in what is now the State of Washington were planted as seeds by the Hudson Bay Company at Fort Vancouver in the spring of 1827. Apples were initially planted in the Yakima Valley area in the early 1860's by a Catholic missionary. Commercial apples were first harvested in the early 1890's when irrigation ditches and canals were first constructed. By 1911 there were 762,000 apple-bearing trees in the Yakima Valley, and the acreage increased so that by 1969 there were approximately 2,500,000 trees producing.

The Union Pacific first directly served the Yakima area when they opened their branch line on March 22, 1911, although they had acquired a controlling interest in the Yakima Valley Transportation Co. electric railway in 1909. During 1911, PFE handled just under 400 carloads of perishables from this area, of which apples were the major commodity. The annual perishable shipments increased rapidly each year so that by 1925, carlot shipments reached 14,500. By 1969 the number of loads was around 18,000 annually. While the number of carloads did not increase proportionately over the later years, it must be realized that the number of boxes per carlot had increased greatly with the use of the larger mechanical cars. Where 800 boxes of apples were considered standard for the iced car, it was not unusual to stow 1200 to 1300 boxes in the larger mechanical car, and some mechanical cars were loaded with as many as 2200 boxes.

The Southern Pacific and its short-line connections originated about 85% of all fresh fruit movements from the Pacific Coast. By the mid-1930's, the industry was yearly shipping over 20,000 loads of deciduous fruit that started on SP rails. Of the fruit loads, three-quarters were to fresh fruit markets, and one-fourth was to canneries. From California, pears ranked first in 1930 fruit shipments, totalling 11,352 cars, with plums second, totalling 5,937 cars, and peaches third, with 5,753 carloads.

The Rogue River Valley, with Medford as the principal originating station, was harvesting enough pears, peaches, and apples to generate 4,838 carloads in 1930. Peaches and plum movement started in July and ran through August. Apple shipments started here in late August and ran through mid November.

Recollections of Pete Holst:

"I'd just gotten back from the Imperial Valley and got a call from Portland. They were having trouble in Medford. The shippers all started ordering salted cars, in other words, salt the pre-iced car before it went to their packing shed. Well, in a little layout like that, with 40 to 50 cars to switch a day, they just had the railroad tied up. And, they weren't all the same, one would order 2 per cent salt, and another guy would want 3 per cent. So, I got the agent and we sat down and talked to every shipper.

I said, 'Now you fellows are just spending your money and losing it. You're ordering these cars initially salted, and as soon as that salt hits the ice in there, the water starts pouring out. Then it gets to your shed and you open the doors for two hours while you load the car. You've used up

Florin, Calif., south of Sacramento, was a major strawberry-producing area in the 1920's and '30's, and was a typical small farming town with a depot and many packing sheds nearby. Here a 2-6-0 backs down the passing track to pick up a PFE reefer in front of the depot. When this photo was taken in the late 1930's, there were six packing sheds, two wineries and a basket factory within a mile of the depot. Berries were shipped in express reefers, and Shipping Inspector Bob Fletcher recalls that the trainmaster would send the engine out from Sacramento before loading was completed, so as soon as cars were loaded they could be moved for initial icing, and placed in the first eastbound passenger train. Bob Fletcher collection.

half a bunker of ice and you haven't gotten any use of it. If you'll just load in a regular iced car, and then bill for what per cent salt you want on re-icing, we'll take care of it and you'll get the full refrigeration that you're entitled to.' Well, they could see that they were just wasting their money, and we got them to settle on salting after the car got back to our ice deck."

A record peach movement that deserves comment was an outcome of the routine and efficient handling by the SP of the harvest in Sutter County, north of Sacramento. A total of 3973 cars of peaches were handled by the crews on the Knights Landing Branch in 1939. The average daily output picked up by the local trains was 117 cars, but on one day in the season, the line generated a solid 85-car train and a second 60-car train of Phillips Cling peaches, the longest such trains of one type peach recorded. The most significant part of the movements of this fruit was that the crews picked it up and delivered it to Davis in four hours. The Western Division in turn delivered the shipments to canneries at San Jose, Redwood City and other Bay Area points by 7 AM the following morning.

By the mid-1950's, PFE's systemwide fruit carloads averaged: pears, around 11,000; apples, around 6,100; peaches, around 2,900; and plums, around 2,100 cars.

Western apricot production was mainly in northern and central California, primarily in Contra Costa, Santa Clara and Yolo Counties. There were also some acreages in Oregon and Washington. The bulk of the crop was dried or sold to canneries, with the fresh fruit shipments only averaging about 400-500 cars annually.

Cherries and berries were also grown across the country, but were prized fruits early in the season. Western crops would mature earlier in the warmer climates and obtained high prices at eastern fresh fruit markets. The majority of these shipments, which could number around 800 to 1200 carloads annually, would go by express refrigerator car service, and were handled under the highest priority. The cars were either sent east in short, passenger- speed fruit blocks or attached directly to passenger trains.

A Pacific Electric banana train from the Port of San Pedro is being shoved in on the SP interchange track at Colton. Note that the freight motor is nearly at the end of the catenary. James N. Spencer photo, 1940's, Jeffrey Moreau collection.

Bananas

Although not a crop grown in the continental United States, bananas nevertheless provided PFE a significant number of annual loads. San Francisco became the banana distribution center of the West on November 7, 1927, when the S.S. *Limon*, first ship of the United Fruit Company fleet to make the run to that port, unloaded thirty thousand bunches of the popular fruit at a newly constructed terminal on the Southern Pacific wharf.

Prior to that date, Central and South American bananas destined to markets in the west were unloaded at New Orleans and shipped by rail. The new San Francisco terminal marked the establishment of another important industry on the West Coast. The San Francisco wharf had four covered platforms serving eight loading tracks with a 47-car capacity.

United Fruit Company was the largest shipping organization of its kind, operating 91 ocean steamers of its own. Each ship carried an average cargo of 30,000 bunches of

(Right) SP's new banana shed facilities at San Francisco, with four covered loading platforms, and 8 tracks with a 47-car capacity. The SP Terminal Building is in the background. (Below) United Fruit Company's 400-ft. steamer *San Mateo*, with a capacity of 30,000 bunches of bananas, docked at the SP sheds. From Dec., 1927, SP *Bulletin*.

Southern Pacific cab-forward 4188, a rear helper on an eastbound banana train, has just taken on water at Colfax, and is awaiting the signal from the road engine at the head end to start up. Note the rider coach ahead of the steel caboose. The coach was used for the "banana messenger" who accompanied the train to inspect all cars for temperature at regular intervals. Al Phelps photo, 1949.

bananas, and the company imported about fifty million bunches each year.

The banana boats would arrive each week on scheduled days, and PFE would have the cars waiting for loading. Within a few years, banana docks were also built at Los Angeles Harbor to assist in meeting the demand by westerners for this fruit. From these two facilities, PFE shipped this commodity to all the western states. The Pacific Northwest railroads, particularly Northern Pacific, competed for the northern market through a similar terminal subsequently built in Seattle. The PFE banana shipments would eventually average from 12,000 to 14,000 loads annually, including a hundred or so loads that came by rail from Mexico.

The handling of banana shipments by the large banana importers was unique in that trained perishable freight inspectors decided how much heat, refrigeration, or ventilation each carload required. These inspectors opened the car doors at certain stations and checked the temperature and conditions of the bananas every 12 to 18 hours in transit. The inspectors sometimes accompanied the shipments in transit and obtained round-trip rail transportation from the carriers at no charge. Quite often on the SP a banana train had a rider coach instead of, or in addition to the caboose for the comfort of the fruit inspectors. As a result of this close supervision of protective services, bananas showed less railroad loss and damage claims paid per car than any other perishable commodity.

An additional detail of importance is that bananas, like coconuts, were only iced in the hottest weather, as cold temperatures damaged them. Instead, ventilation was usually employed, or sometimes heater service. Because of this, PFE, like other refrigerator car operators, often assigned old cars with thinner insulation to the banana trains.

This 1928 photo of a huge produce terminal in Los Angeles shows the unusual diagonal tracks on which refrigerator cars were spotted for unloading. Note the Los Angeles Junction Railway Company's 0-6-0 No. 201. There were two large truck transfer sheds at the rear of this building. Photo from *Union Pacific Magazine*, 1929, UP Railroad Museum.

An empty mechanical refrigerator is being moved to a packing shed dock at Mesa, Ariz. by an SP Geep, preparatory to perishable loading. SP photo, neg. N7524-1.

Other Commodities

Fresh and frozen meats and other packinghouse products provided originating loads mainly in UP territory. The states that shipped much of this product were Colorado, Nebraska, Kansas, Utah and Wyoming. Plants served by PFE solely on UP rails were located at Greeley and Sterling, Colorado, and Lexington, Darr, Schuyler, North Platte and Mead, Nebraska. About 15 more packing plants were served jointly with other railroads at Denver, Colorado; Omaha, Grand Island and Fremont, Nebraska; Council Bluffs, Iowa; and Kansas City and St. Joseph, Missouri.

In the lamb industry, Ogden, Utah, had the largest lamb slaughtering plant in the United States and was served by PFE. The lamb carcasses were hung whole on meat hooks that PFE furnished and the loads were directed to the primary lamb markets of Philadelphia and New York.

The packinghouses, mainly in the Eastern District with a few that were on other districts, generated from 7,000 to 8,000 loads for PFE in the 1940's and '50's as the refrigerator car fleets of the meat packers declined in size. With the advent of mechanically refrigerated cars and trailer vans, that figure rose to between 10,000 and 11,000 shipments annually by the late 1960's.

Tomatoes and peas would account for 10,000 to 12,000 carloads each year, with the majority of these shipments being winter crops that originated from western Mexico and were shipped all over the U.S. and Canada. In 1943, 7,638 carloads of tomatoes, 727 loads of green peas, and 447 cars of green peppers passed through Nogales to go on to northern markets. During the summer months when these vegetables were harvested in the U.S., the shipments

(Left) Loading an R-30-13 with perishables (evidently pears) at Loomis, Calif., by the time-honored hand truck. This simple piece of equipment was saving backs at PFE's beginnings and still does today. SP photo, neg. N399-5. (Right) This mechanical car, PFE 456203, an R-70-18 with Landis doors, is being loaded with fresh cauliflower at the Central Cooling Co. plant in Fremont, Calif. by the modern fork lift truck in 1968. SP photo. Both photos, PFE collection, CSRM.

were normally local, more often by truck, as eastern and midwestern truck farms came into production.

Beverages and canned goods were also carried by PFE. Not only were western products moved east, but canned items, especially beer, provided ideal backhaul tonnage from eastern or midwestern breweries and canneries. These carloads would amount to between 25,000 and 30,000 shipments annually during the 1940's and 1950's. Such shipments were not usually refrigerated, merely requiring an insulated freight car to avoid temperature extremes.

There were many other fruits and vegetables, such as avocados, carrots, beans, broccoli, cauliflower, dates, and pomegranates, that moved in smaller quantities. An unusual commodity which moved during February was the common dandelion. Though most lawn owners would classify it as a weed, it was raised as a salad green in the Imperial Valley, and up to 50 carloads could be shipped annually.

Specialty loads also provided PFE with tonnage miles. Shipments of flowers were common in express refrigerators, and it is recalled by one retired PFE officer that the class R-70 "Super-Giant" wood icers were also used often in this service. From the Northwestern District there were loads of nursery stock, and ferns, huckleberry, and evergreens accounted for 732 cars in 1952.

Frozen food shipments dated all the way back to 1931 when PFE handled a meager 71 loads, which consisted mostly of peas and berries from the Northwestern District and shrimp and other seafood, mainly from Mexico. The basic problem with ice and salt alone, as described in Chapter 9, was that it was nearly impossible to maintain an entire carload at a sufficiently low temperature. There would inherently be areas of the car where the commodity would soften or even thaw, and some spoilage was normal. Still, loads slowly increased until by 1941, 678 carloads were shipped under this protective tariff.

The company built its first mechanical refrigerator cars in 1953, specifically for frozen food, and in that year handled 8,208 carloads of frozen commodities, though most of these shipments were still in ice cars. In the early 1950's processing plants for frozen packaging of vegetables and fruits were being set up in all the major growing areas by the new industry, Birdseye and Jolly Green Giant companies being at the forefront. The nation's eating habits were changing, with the quality of frozen foods gaining favor over canned goods. Also, the beginning of the "fast food era" was starting to sweep the country. With it came enthusiasm for the hamburger and french fry diet. This escalated the need for frozen potato products enormously, and Idaho became a major shipping center for these loads.

By 1955, PFE frozen food loads were up to 10,465 cars, and of these loads, 3,405 were shipped in mechanical refrigerator cars. As the frozen food industry developed, along with it came the demand for guaranteed delivery of the shipment in first-class condition without spoilage, and in ever-larger loads. PFE responded by increasing its fleet of mechanical cars, eventually increasing their size to 57 ft. in length. Perfection of this car design in the late 1950's led to modifications for produce use, as Chapter 9 explains, and this was finally to mark the end of the ice era.

The Pacific Fruit Express Company became the principal and dominant carrier of western produce by the mid-1920's, when it established itself as the world's largest refrigerator car operator. The company's ability to deliver perishables in a reliable and expedient manner to markets all across the U. S. and Canada supported and allowed for the tremendous expansion of the West's greatest industry, agriculture. No matter what the demand, PFE met the challenge. Growers, shippers, and brokers depended upon PFE's access to all markets, and were rarely disappointed. The Pacific Fruit Express Company distinguished itself by securing a notable place in the historical annals of Western railroading and Americana. It was a remarkable achievement by a remarkable company.

A clean pair of Union Pacific GP9's heading east at Hinkle, Ore., with a string of mechanical refrigerators in 1964 or 1965. UP Railroad Museum, photo 45490.

This eastbound freight, with a reefer block at the head end, has the quintessential SP motive power combination, an AC cab-forward road engine and a GS *Daylight* engine as point helper. The GS drew this freight assignment because it had just been shopped at Los Angeles. It was customary system-wide after major shopping to run in new journal brasses and shake down appliances in helper service, and even though this is GS-5 4458, with Timken roller bearings, the usual break-in run is underway. Photo

PFE IN ACTION

An eastbound perishable block, X808, hammers through Valley, Nebr., whistle screaming for the grade crossing and not a hint of speed reduction. Council Bluffs is just 26 miles away. The big 4-8-4 was pulled out of storage for the fall perishable season, its last service. Wm. W. Kratville photo, August 1958.

This chapter brings together all the information, activities and procedures described previously to present examples of PFE's operations. To begin, three reefer trips, in quite different eras, provide a perspective on the interactions among shippers, railroads, and PFE. Each trip description highlights different aspects of operations, such as icing, ventilation, train handling, and mechanical car servicing. Then a number of photographs are presented to illustrate many of the same operations.

Oregon to New York – 1925

This trip description is for a wood ice refrigerator car of PFE's most numerous class, R-30-12. Car 30814 was built in 1924, and thus is relatively new at the time of this trip in the winter of 1925.

It is February, and the Apple Growers Association in Hood River, Oregon, along the lines of UP's Oregon-Washington Railway & Navigation Co. subsidiary, has requested six cars to ship apples from storage. PFE 30814 had been cleaned and "OK'd" for loading at PFE's small cleaning and light repair yard in Nampa, Idaho. (The major PFE car shop at Nampa will not open until May, 1926.) The car is directed westward to Hood River. On Feb. 10, the car is part of a cut of six cars spotted on the Association's spur, and by 1:30 PM the next day is loaded

(**Above**) Car 30814, whose trip from Hood River, Oregon, to New York City is described in the text. PFE photo, courtesy Steve Peery. (**Right**) UP No. 2551, a 2-8-2 Mikado of USRA design, pauses at the Pocatello, Idaho, ice deck for crews to install and light alcohol heaters. Air temperatures are more than 20° below zero, and cargoes need protection. Milton G. Sorensen photo, January, 1949.

with 756 boxes of "Defiance" brand Yellow Newtown apples, giving a total lading weight of 37,422 pounds. The apples are inspected as they are loaded, and appear to be in fine condition.

The car has been consigned to Sgobel and Day, fruit brokers in New York City, and will travel over the UP as far as Council Bluffs, Iowa, thence via Illinois Central to the Chicago area, and eastward on the Erie.

At the time of loading, outside temperatures at Hood River are just above 40° F., not much above the temperature at which the apples have been stored, so no refrigeration is needed. Ice hatches are closed, and the car is picked up by UP's local freight train. The following day, the car is added into an eastbound train, which moves it to Reith, Ore. There, the ice hatches are opened to permit air circulation to ventilate the car.

The train leaving Reith is heavy, requiring one of the OWR&N's 3600-class compound Mallet 2-8-8-0 locomotives to head the train, as it moves toward the 4205-ft. summit of Oregon's Blue Mountains. Tonnage is heavy enough to require a 5000-class 2-10-2 helper on the rear end, as far as Kamela. Though air temperatures are below freezing in these mountains, the car's insulation and the thermal mass of the cargo prevent any significant change in temperature of the fruit. Huntington is reached at 7:45 PM, and here the hatches are closed again in anticipation of colder weather to the east.

At 5:20 AM on Feb. 14, the car reaches Pocatello, Idaho. Air temperatures have fallen to 22° F, and charcoal heaters are placed in the bunkers as a precaution, although since the load temperature is about 36°, the heaters are not lighted. The next day, the car continues eastward through Montpelier behind a 2-10-2 locomotive, heading for Wyoming. A 2-8-0 helper is added at Fossil to boost the train over Hodges Pass to Kemmerer, reached at 12:25 AM. The train joins the Overland Route at Granger.

Here in Wyoming, air temperatures descend below 10° and when the car stops in Green River, heaters are lighted.

Departing Laramie at 11:50 AM for the climb over Sherman Hill, another "Bull Moose" 2-8-8-0 heads the train. By late afternoon at Cheyenne, the weather has warmed to near freezing, and the heaters are extinguished again. After a change of locomotives, this time to a 2-8-2, the car departs Cheyenne at 8:10 PM on Feb. 17.

Car 30814 is inspected at dawn the next day, during a stop at North Platte, and load temperatures are found to be 34°. As temperatures above freezing are expected eastward, the hatches are opened again for ventilation. At Council Bluffs on Feb. 18, PFE's heaters are removed, and at 11:30 PM the car reaches Illinois Central (IC) rails.

At about 9 AM the next morning in Fort Dodge, Iowa, the car's hatches are closed by IC inspectors in anticipation of colder weather in Illinois. But the air remains in the midthirties across Iowa and Illinois, and is 35° at Blue Island when PFE 30814 arrives there at 12:30 AM on Feb. 21. At 8:45 AM, the car is picked up from the IC by the Indiana Harbor Belt and moved to Hammond, Ind. by 1:10 PM, where it is transferred to the Erie in mid-afternoon.

The Erie takes great pride in its fast perishable service to New York, and is already making up the "red ball" to New York, train NY-98, when car 30814 arrives. It is promptly added to 98, which leaves at 6:00 PM. Cars of southwestern perishables are added in Huntington, Ind., and by 3 PM the next afternoon, Feb. 22, NY-98 arrives in Marion, Ohio. Air temperatures have risen to 45°, and the car's hatches are opened again for ventilation. Here NY-98 is reblocked to include cars from Lima and Dayton, Ohio, and from the New York Central interchange.

Leaving Marion, one of Erie's 6-year old 2-8-2 Mikado locomotives of class N2 is attached to NY-98 to handle the hilly profiles of the Kent and Mahoning Divisions between

An example of an Erie Railroad car float crossing the Hudson River from New Jersey to Manhattan, with predominantly PFE cars on the barge. Although the date of the photos is 1956, the operation was similar at the time of the 1925 trip described in the text. (**Left, above**) Erie's tug "Rochester" nudges a float away from the Jersey dock. (**Right**) The float in mid-Hudson, with a full load of 16 40-ft. cars. (**Right, above**) Three floats docked at Piers 20 and 21 in Manhattan. Note that roofed walkways run down the center of each float, permitting sheltered unloading and buyers' inspections. Three photos, Erie Lackawanna Historical Society, D.G. Biernacki collection.

Marion and Meadville, Penna. The run continues into New York state, and at 7:45 AM on Feb. 23, car 30814 comes to rest in Hornell, N.Y. Colder air here, about 33°, leads to closing the hatches again. In Hornell, the Erie couples on a fresh Mikado and a 2-10-2 helper locomotive of class R3 to NY-98, for the train will be passing over Gulf Summit en route toward New York.

About 1 PM, car 30814 passes upgrade over famous Starrucca Viaduct as it nears Gulf Summit, and by midnight is being inspected along with the rest of NY-98 in Port Jervis, N.Y. At 2:20 PM on Feb. 25, NY-98 stops on the arrival yard tracks in Croxton, N.J., just across the Hudson River from New York. The Hood River apples are nearly to their destination.

By 4 PM, the car has been switched to the "fruit holding yard," where cars are made ready to move over the river by car float. Shortly after sundown, one of Erie's ubiquitous 0-6-0 switchers moves car 30814 onto the car float with 15

other cars. Powered by one of the railroad's own tugs, the float's destination is Pier 21 in Manhattan, one of two piers leased by the Erie from New York's Harbor Dept. to serve its Duane Street produce market

Meanwhile, a notice of arrival has been delivered to the consignee in New York, who has been receiving daily reports of car 30814's whereabouts, not only from the Erie but from the IC and UP earlier in the journey.

The apples are inspected on arrival, and only 2% show any "storage scald," decay spots or other slight blemishes. The overall report is "excellent." Throughout its trip, the load has been above freezing but below the desired maximum temperature for apples, 41°, so the handling railroads have done a good job moving the car through sub-freezing temperatures in parts of the country.

A few boxes of the apples are chosen from the car to be displayed by Sgobel and Day's agent in the produce market. Buyers arrive early and inspect the fruit, then proceed to Erie's auction room upstairs for the 8:30 AM deciduous fruit auction. Before noon all 124 cars of produce at Duane St. today will be sold to local area retail food merchants.

The PFE agent in New York is aware of the arrival and unloading of car 30814, and reminds the Erie office in New Jersey that the car is needed by PFE in the west. Two days later, car 30814 leaves Croxton Yard westbound for Chicago. There, directions are given by the local PFE office, that of the Chicago Assistant General Manager (AGM), ordering that the car be sent to Arizona. In 9 days, car 30814 will reach Yuma to be cleaned and made ready for loading again.

(Compiled by A.W. Thompson from historical material and USDA trip reports.)

Southern California to Philadelphia – 1953

The revenue trip described here is for a steel PFE ice bunker car. The time frame for this shipment is the late summer of 1953.

The car we will follow is PFE 9572, of class R-40-26, one of an order of 2000 cars of all-steel construction which were built in 1951-52. The car is equipped with Preco air-circulating fans and convertible ice tanks; that is, the ice tanks contain "stage grates" which can be swung up and locked to allow just the top half of the ice tanks to be filled. For citrus fruit, this half-stage refrigeration is all that is normally needed during much of the year, and saves the shipper money on icing charges.

The 9572 has just been released from the shop at

PFE car 9572, the focus of the accompanying trip description. March, 1952, photo by W.C. Whittaker.

Colton as "OK for loading," having been cleaned and given some light running repairs.

An order has been placed by the PFE agent at Oxnard, Calif., on the Southern Pacific's Coast line. This PFE seasonal agency serves the lemon and orange growers of the Ventura and Santa Clarita Valley areas, one of the most productive in the state.

The order is placed with the Los Angeles Car Distributor's office for 90 "dry" (non-iced) cars. This string of cars will be sent to Oxnard as soon as possible. Since this is enough for a complete train, a separate "drag" is called from Southern Pacific's Colton Yard to bring the cars into Taylor Yard at Los Angeles. If only a few reefers were needed, they would be placed on the next westbound train by Colton and then attached to the first available train up the Coast Line from Taylor to Oxnard.

Out of Los Angeles the empty reefer block is identified as an "Oxnard Turn" and a new crew takes over since the trip up the Coast is over a new subdivision. The turn arrives late in the afternoon and spots the reefers on one of the yard

Here SP Ten-wheeler 2381, working the Goleta turn in late afternoon, rolls south near Santa Barbara along Highway 101, on November 11, 1954. It is typical of the numerous locals which served packing sheds throughout the territory served by PFE. John C. Illman photo.

A typical citrus packing house on SP's Santa Paula branch, such as is described in the trip of car 9572. Don Sims photo, 1962.

tracks so the night switcher can begin making up the locals for the next day. If there is any dead freight or empties going back toward Los Angeles, the turn will take it and further earn its keep.

Since the shipper has ordered this car as a pre-iced car, the switcher takes car 9572 to the Union Ice Co. deck to be iced. Other cars are ordered "dry" and will be iced or precooled after loading. Although at main-line ice decks crews can ice cars in an average of one minute each, here at Oxnard things move a bit more slowly.

Car 9572 will go out on the Piru local along the Santa Paula branch the next afternoon to be spotted at the Piru Citrus Association (PCA) packing house for loading with lemons. Once the car is loaded, usually a day later, the traffic manager at the packing house notifies the SP agent at Fillmore that it is ready for pickup, along with additional cars. Other packing house managers have given orders for pick-ups as well. Our reefer is being sent out as a "roller" or unconsigned load, owned by the shipper. Like 85% of PFE's loads, its routing instructions will be changed one or more times before reaching its destination. The agent at Fillmore makes out waybills for each car giving shipper, consignee and route and telephones a switch list to the SP telegrapher-clerk at Oxnard.

The Piru local goes out behind a venerable 2-6-0 Mogul with the day's empty cars and picks up loads including car 9572 at the PCA shed. The PFE agent at Oxnard has been in touch with the PFE Car Distributor with his projections of car needs for many days ahead. He has also been in touch with the people at the packing houses to get projections on

how much fruit will be loaded out in the near future. This information is also forwarded to the PFE Transportation Bureau in San Francisco, responsible for the supply of empties, so system-wide car distribution patterns and needs can be calculated.

Meanwhile, the Piru local crew has received the message, "set the [initial] icers to the Oxnard deck and the precoolers to track three" from the SP night Chief Clerk. Our car goes back to the deck to have its ice bunkers topped off for the trip east.

The "precoolers" are cars which have been loaded with citrus fruit which has not had field heat removed. Many of the packing houses have cold rooms in which fruit can be precooled prior to loading. These houses usually order the pre-iced empties. Those without cold rooms make use of PFE's precooling service at Colton or at Taylor Yard. The precooler cars are held for eight hours while cold air from the ice plant is blown through canvas sleeves into the ice bunkers and out the car doors. Once cooled to around 40 to 44° F., the load is then iced and sent on its way. This is also another way for a shipper to hold a car 24 hours without charge, until market conditions improve.

Our ice car at Oxnard has received attention from the night switcher, a 2-8-0 nearing the end of its career, which has blocked all outgoing loads and placed them on a track convenient for pickup by the "SMV," Santa Maria Vegetables. This is a symbol perishable train originating at San Luis Obispo and is known as the "Smokey" by railroad employees. All perishables originating south of Santa Margarita will be gathered at concentration points and come

Until Dec. 26, 1952, when the last steam engines operated, fast merchandise and reefer blocks on the Rock Island were handled by the R67-class 4-8-4's between Tucumcari, N.M., and Kansas City, Kansas. Rock Island's fleet of 4-8-4's was 85 engines, the largest in the U.S. Here 5036 rolls reefers eastward in an Otto Perry photo, Denver Public Library.

south on the Smokey; loads originating north of Santa Margarita will be routed via Salinas, Roseville and Ogden.

The Smokey arrives at Oxnard behind a 3-unit set of F7 diesels. Until this year, this train would have been handled by one of SP's distinctive cab-forward 4-8-8-2's. The Smokey picks up the bulk of its train here. It started out with loads of lettuce which originated around Guadalupe and perhaps a car or two of strawberries.

Once the rush of getting the Smokey out of town subsides, it's time for the SP telegrapher to go to work; he's been given a consist report to send down to Los Angeles ahead of the arrival of the Smokey. This report is laid out so the output from Oxnard's teletype can be used to produce IBM punch cards at Los Angeles in the first step in making a fruit block. The operator at Oxnard has only his keyboard to work with so he sits down and hand-enters the information in an exacting format into his tape perforator. The tape is then fed into a transmitter and sent on to Taylor Yard where it is received both as hard copy and punched tape for use by clerical forces there.

The Smokey wastes no time making the 75-mile trip from Oxnard to Taylor Yard. As it nears Burbank Junction where the San Joaquin Valley line joins the Coast line, it leans into the right-hand curve at 40 miles per hour and water from the melting ice flies out of the bunker drains nearly eight feet. The operator is glad he is on the second floor of the ancient interlocking tower.

Once PFE 9572 and its block arrives at Los Angeles it is given a "Colton Perishable Block" (CPB) number. Information on each car in the block is transmitted by wire to PFE and SP agency offices and the information given to interested parties, shippers and receivers alike. Since this car carries an unsold load, the departure time of its CPB is

given the next morning to the traffic manager at the PCA office in Piru.

The original routing of car 9572 is via Southern Pacific to Tucumcari, N.M., then Rock Island to Chicago, Ill. The load is now consigned to a broker in Chicago. Information about sale of the load is given to the PFE agent, who contacts the Los Angeles Diversion Bureau. It in turn notifies Chicago about the sale.

On the second day, the Chicago broker notifies PFE he has sold the load to Bottecillo Produce in Philadelphia, Penna., and wants it diverted via St. Louis, onto the Pennsylvania Railroad to Philadelphia. The PFE passing advice service locates the car moving in its fruit block between Tucson, Ariz. and El Paso, Tex. The car has been iced at Tucson in accordance with the tariff rules for half-stage standard refrigeration; regular icing stations are placed at approximately 24-hour intervals.

Temperatures have been moderate and only a topping-off of the ice bunkers is required. Higher temperatures are expected east of El Paso, however, and PFE Ice Department and Car Service Department forces start rounding up all the ice they can find in advance of the heat wave.

PFE 9572 leaves Tucumcari behind an A-B-A trio of Rock Island FT units. A year earlier, an R67 class 4-8-4 would have done the honors. Because of the diversion, car 9572 is cut out of the fruit block at Topeka, Kansas, and will join another fruit block which has come east from Denver. Again, the Diversion Bureau is notified and the information reaches all interested parties, including the receiver in Philadelphia. By the time the car reaches St. Louis, there has been a sag in the market for lemons in Philadelphia which the receiver sees as temporary, so he asks for a 24-hour hold on the car at St. Louis.

If market conditions do not improve in Philadelphia, he will resell the load and divert it to Toledo or Cleveland. Arrangements are made to protect the shipment with an additional icing while it waits at St. Louis. Market conditions do improve in Philadelphia, however, and the load in 9572 travels Pennsylvania rails to its final destination.

The car has had its shipping instructions changed four times since it left Piru. Five or ten changes are not unusual, and instances of 20 or more changes have occurred. In busy years, PFE offices handled 300,000 to 400,000 such diversions annually, with less than 0.02% errors. Such accuracy was essential to shippers.

Car 9572 is unloaded and released back to the PRR which switches it to a concentration point for empty reefers coming out of the Philadelphia area. The PFE District Agent in Philadelphia has been in contact with the Pennsy agents and makes every effort to get the car blocked westward as fast as possible. The District Agent notifies both the Chicago General Office and the San Francisco Transportation Bureau of the empty equipment he has on hand and where it will be routed; this particular car will go via PRR to Chicago, thence via the Chicago & North Western to Council Bluffs and thence via UP to North Platte, where it will be initially cleaned and de-iced if necessary, then sent on to northern California.

Car Service Department forces foresee a need for cars in California's San Joaquin Valley, so PFE 9572 takes a direct route via UP to Ogden and then SP to PFE's Roseville shops where it pauses for running repairs. Heavy handling necessitates an adjustment to the draft gear, the brakes are due for inspection and one truck needs to be changed out due to excessive wheel wear. This is all accomplished systematically by the shop forces at Roseville and once again our reefer is made "OK for loading."

The repaired 9572 joins a train of empty reefers out of Roseville for Fresno Yard where it will be sent out to be loaded with cantaloupes at Firebaugh in the San Joaquin Valley. (Compiled by Bruce Jones from personal experience as an SP operator at Burbank Junction and Oxnard, and from historical material.)

Salinas to New York – 1968

During the 1960's, ice refrigeration was making a last stand for perishable shipping. Mechanical refrigeration was rapidly taking over, and by the latter part of the decade, the majority of PFE's loads were in mechanical cars. This section describes a turn-around of a typical PFE mechanical car. The year is 1968.

It's 12:42 AM and on this early summer morning an SP empty PFE westbound drag is edging slowly through the darkness at the eastend crossovers, entering Roseville after coming off "The Hill." The smells of dynamic brakes and retainer-controlled brakeshoes are still pungent as the 104-car train eases through the SP yard and makes its way through the entrance of the PFE light repair (LR) yard, coming to a stop on Track 3.

The road engines are cut off and SP switch crews "cut the crossings" to provide an opening at each of the five vehicle crossings in the LR yard. They then take the

(Above) PFE 452314, an R-70-15 car whose 1968 trip is described in the accompanying text. Photo by Pacific Car & Foundry for PFE, CSRM.

(Below) Loading a mechanical refrigerator car by fork lift truck in California. Note the portable steel bridge, and the Equipco load dividers being closed against the load (see Chapter 9 for more on these dividers). UP Railroad Museum, photo 470-9-6, courtesy Terry Metcalfe.

Our Southern Pacific perishable block is laboring up "The Hill," as generations of SP railroaders have called Donner Pass. It is seen here on the outside track at Cape Horn, above Colfax, Calif. Robert J. Church photos, June, 1968.

caboose back to the SP yard. The string of cars, with 452314 back 27th in line, is set for the PFE crews. The car is an R-70-15 class mechanical car, equipped with an Emerson 2-71, 2 cylinder, 35 h.p. diesel engine capable of maintaining temperatures from -10°F to +70°F.

At 6:30 AM the blue flags are in place and the early crews begin removing dunnage left from the previous load. Car Inspectors start checking any items that need repair or replacement. Engine oil is checked; 452314's is at a safe but low level, so the engine is started and left to run. Following the Inspectors is the Store Department material train, moving and issuing all needed materials. "Pak-Mor" trucks come along to pick up debris, not only from the previous load, but that thrown in by someone cleaning out their warehouse back east.

At 7:00 AM the main LR work force arrives on the scene. Carpenters are pushing their rubber-wheeled tool boxes, and the iron workers on "Kalamazoos" are equipped with tools, jacks, and torches to do any truck and under-frame work. Other employees raise the floor racks and

wash and clean the floors. Drain holes at each car end are given special attention to assure they are clear of debris. Yes, mechanicals had drains too, to accommodate body icing. The Inspector places a "bad order" tag for one floor rack slat and three brakeshoes, and notes the low oil.

The Mechanical Foreman spots the oil leak and radios to have the engine replaced. The Store Department sends a replacement engine and a change crew arrives with the mobile crane. After the change and checkout start and run, the fuel truck arrives and pumps 340 gallons of fuel into the 500-gallon tank in just a few minutes.

As quitting time approaches for the major portion of the day repair crew, the doors on car 452314 are closed, locked and sealed. The seal holds a white tag which reads "This car is clean and ready for service." It's 3:30 PM and the car is picked up by the SP switch crew to be placed into a train heading for a loading territory.

Disposition instructions are given by the Car Service Agent to the PFE Car Distributor at Sacramento for relay to the SP Yardmaster at Roseville and the Chief Dispatch-ers of the Sacramento, San Joaquin and Western Divisions. Later the same evening the empty reefer drags will begin moving to all loading points. PFE 452314 is placed in a 95-car train headed for the Salinas-Watsonville area. Arrival in Salinas will be early Monday afternoon.

Shippers have already ordered their cars for the following day's need. Our car is moved into a packing shed siding in the Watsonville District and is ready for Tuesday loading. Lettuce is picked starting early in the morning. Flatbed trucks move the palletized lettuce cartons to vacuum coolers, where field heat is removed quickly and the temperature is brought down to 34°F. Conveyors then move the packaged product into PFE 452314 where loaders, paid at piece-work rates, stack 1280 of the 45 to 50-lb. cartons into place in the car. Our car's thermostat is set at 34°F as specified by the shipper.

The railroad has established 9:00 PM as the cutoff time when cars must be ready for pick-up to be taken to Watsonville Yard for classification and sealing. By about 11:30 PM, Tuesday, the first Salinas Vegetable (SV) Block is on the move. A short stop is made at Watsonville Junction to pick up waybills from the Centralized Billing Office. Early Wednesday, at 3:00 AM, PFE 452314 clears San Jose, entrained in the 1st SV enroute to Roseville, via Oakland and Sacramento.

The train arrives at Roseville at 8:30 AM on Track 21, and is blue flagged for one hour to allow the Clerk Inspectors to make mechanical inspections and M&E CMR crews to make any repairs. Inspection reveals our car temperature inside is 34°F, and the unit is running and operating properly, with fuel at 450 gallons.

In the yard office PFE clerks copy waybills and begin preparation of a PFE Roseville Fruit Block consist by keypunching block cards with pertinent data about each shipment. Within a few minutes the railroad will assign an "R Block" number, issue a call time and furnish an outbound train list. Appropriate cards are then pulled, sorted in numerical order and fed into the card-to-tape machine (later computers were used for this). The tape is transmitted to SP Communications for dissemination to various PFE western and eastern offices. This was an important segment of PFE operations as shippers, receivers and brokers had to be able to quickly locate and divert their shipments to meet market demands. Fruit Blocks were the basis of a system which enabled PFE to provide diversion and passing service unequalled in speed and efficiency.

This is a transition period for both PFE and SP. The train is a mix of "icers," mechanicals, and trailers. The road engines are three SD45's and one venerable F7, while the mid-train helper engines consist of an SD40 and four F7's. Just before 10:00 AM Wednesday morning 21,300 horse-

power start moving PFE 452314 and 115 other perishable loads out of Roseville east towards Donner Summit. Sparks lies 8-½ grueling hours ahead, and after continuing across the Nevada and Utah deserts, the car will be in Ogden tomorrow morning.

PFE 452314 arrives Ogden on Thursday morning in Roseville Fruit Block R28, the third block of the day for Ogden to handle. The train pulls into East Yard Track 8, one of two icing platform tracks, ten minutes ahead of scheduled arrival. East Yard 9 has R27 still being worked. A partial ice deck crew commences running ice to bunker cars on R28 while the balance of the crew completes R27.

When R27 is finished, one ice inspector and icemen start at the head end of R28, working toward the middle while a similar crew starts at the middle working toward the rear. Two other Car Service inspectors start at each end working toward the center, checking trailers and mechanical cars. Four carmen check all running gear for bad order problems. They call the Yardmaster, and PFE work is interrupted as a UP switch engine cuts out two B/O (bad order) cars. This takes about fifteen minutes, and then servicing continues.

The UP caboose and road engines are coupled on R28 with PFE 452314 the 16th car from the rear end. The train is on the move just before noon. Within an hour the long string of orange cars is winding up the grade through Weber Canyon. Today's locomotives combine 12,500 horsepower, with a 2,500-hp GP35 point engine leading two DD35 5000-hp units. Brute strength moves the perishables through the Wasatch Mountain Range.

In the first few minutes of early Friday morning, R28 rolls into the receiving yard at North Platte, Nebr. on the eastern slope of the Continental Divide. The train is met by two tank trucks. All trailers are refueled to capacity and mechanical cars which have less than 150 gallons of fuel are brought up at least to that amount. Bad order cars are tagged, either for quick repair in the departure yard or switching out. PFE 452314 is right on temperature and after the ice cars are serviced, is switched to the bowl tracks with the rest of the train.

Our car is routed to New York City via Council Bluffs connection. The train is trimmed down and at 5:00 AM Central Standard Time is ready for departure. Expedited schedule calls for arrival at Council Bluffs at 1:00 PM Friday with cut-off time for delivery to the connecting railroad at 2:30 PM. Fourth morning expedited schedule (based on Chicago arrival) is being maintained and the car is ready to start the last stage of its long cross-country trip.

Around 3:30 PM the car, with 40 other perishable loads and some mixed freight is on its way via the Rock Island Railroad to Chicago. The New York receiver to whom this

Four UP GP20's, trailed by an SD24, with a block of PFE mechanical and ice refrigerator cars, here at North Platte, at about the same period as the trip described in the accompanying text. Photo 45496, UP Railroad Museum.

carload of lettuce was sold had decided to sell the lettuce in 452314 to a Chicago consignee. Instructions to divert the car to Chicago and deliver to the new consignee were filed by wire with the PFE agent before the train left Council Bluffs.

The train is scheduled to stop at Silvis, Illinois, for inspection. The carrier has relayed the diversion information to Silvis and the diversion is accomplished there by means of endorsing the waybill covering this shipment carried by the conductor. After inspection of all perishable cars and trailers, the train continues on schedule, arriving at Chicago at 1:30 AM Saturday.

The Rock Island switches the car to the Chicago Produce Terminal (CPT) concentration yards. A large percentage of perishable shipments are unloaded here, but the consignee of our car wants to hold the car until Monday. Inspection that morning reveals the lettuce is still in first class condition. Lettuce prices have been rising so the Chicago merchant decides to try and sell the carload to another New York receiver. The sale is arranged and he files diversion instructions with the PFE General Agent's office at Chicago, located at the CPT yards. The CPT forces inspect the cars ordered for outbound movement, refueling and doing any light mechanical repairs. The car is then switched to the outbound eastern railroad's receiving tracks.

PFE 452314 departs Chicago at 10:00 PM Monday night in a Penn Central eastbound. Its route carries it through Syracuse, New York, where early Wednesday morning at the former New York Central's DeWitt Yard an in-transit inspection is again made. Our car is operating perfectly. The next stop is New York City and the car is switched at 8:00 PM into the Hunts Point Market, a

modern produce market located on the rails of the NYNH&H (New Haven). The load is given another inspection which shows good temperature.

In addition, arrangements have been made to have the Railroad Perishable Inspection Agency (RPIA) inspect the commodity. Their inspection confirms the condition of the lettuce to be firm, excellent quality with only slight bud discoloration, a normal and satisfactory arrival. The RPIA is an independent inspection agency, supported by the railroads, whose function is to inspect and furnish quality and condition reports, upon request of either consignees, the railroads, or both. They operate in the eastern portion of the United States.

The receiver removes samples of the lettuce from the car and places them on display at units in the Hunts Point Market prior to 4:00 AM Thursday, which is the opening hour for sales. The entire 1280-carton load is sold by 11:00 AM to seven different buyers from retail outlets.

In an hour the car is unloaded, and the New Haven Railroad Agent is advised the car is released back to the railroad. PFE 452314 is then forwarded empty from Hunts Point Thursday evening for interchange with the Penn Central and westbound movement back through Syracuse and Buffalo to Chicago. Monday will find the empty promptly dispatched west in accordance with directives issued by the PFE Assistant General Manager in Chicago. In a few days this car will again be in a PFE shop for pretripping. Then, another carload of perishables!

(Compiled by R.J. Church from PFE *Newsletter* articles and other historical material.)

An eastbound Roseville Fruit Block is just getting underway after being iced. The mid-train helper, AC-11 4270, is easing under the PFE pedestrian overcrossing. In just a few minutes, once the train has gone through the east end crossovers onto the main, the throttles will be shoved wide open, and trackside houses will experience another of the periodic eclipsings of the sun as pillars of steam and oil smoke signify that another train is "leaving town" and attacking the long Sierra grade. Roseville, 1948. Southern Pacific photo N1539-12, courtesy Don Hofsommer.

Recollections of G.M. "Buck" Haynie, SP engineer:

"I remember one day I had come in with an eastbound freight at Roseville. I climbed off my engine and walked over to the rear helper of an eastbound fruit block that had been iced and was getting ready to leave, as I knew the crew. Trackwork along the ice deck was always sitting in mud and water from the melting ice. The ties would be half rotten, the spikes loose, and the rail joiners and bolts rusty. In those days three Mallets were used on a heavy train. (SP railroaders always seemed to refer to the AC's as Mallets even though they were not compound engines.)

They would have the rear helper two to four cars ahead of the caboose, and the mid-train helper eleven cars ahead of the rear engine. The spacing was that way because that was the distance the rear end water columns were spaced on "The Hill." So, most of the time the two rear engines could take water at the same time, without uncoupling. When stopping for water, the road engine would always spot himself, and the rear part of the train would have to uncouple from the head end and spot themselves at the two rear water columns.

When ready to start a train like this, the road engineer would signal by whistle, and also by making a fluctuation in the brake pipe pressure with the automatic brake valve. The rear helper engineers would watch the brake pressure gauge for this signal, as often the whistle signal couldn't be heard, especially in the mountains. They would ease open their throttles and the road engineer simultaneously released the air brakes. When he felt the "boot in the rear" on his tender as the slack came in, he would open his throttle, and the train would start off. If the road engine started first, there would be too much stress on the couplers, and a knuckle could break. In the level yard, starting would not be too much of a problem, but it was a real art when starting on a grade in the mountains.

Anyway, this time at the ice deck, when they got the signal to start from the head end, the mid-train engineer started first, and with too much throttle. The one Mallet was trying to move the whole train. With all that power, it just bit into the rails and spit them right out from under the engine. All the drivers ended up going on the ground and through the rotten ties, and sections of rail were back under the tender. That was quite a sight!"

A 4-unit set of Cotton Belt FT's, in their original gray bodies with yellow wings and red pinstriping, easing a reefer train through a "slow order" section of track being worked on by "gandy dancers" in Arkansas. The period is prior to 1949 when the units received the SP's "Black Widow" paint scheme. StLSW photo, courtesy Don Hofsommer.

(**Above**) A UP "veranda" gas turbine, No. 65, heads an eastbound at Peterson, Utah, on the center passing track along the Weber River. The 15 locomotives of this class were built in 1953-54, numbered 61-75. Two BAR cars are second and fourth in the train. Weber Canyon and Devil's Gate are in the background. UP photo, courtesy George Cockle.

(**Below**) Southern Pacific 4-10-2 No. 5047 starts the first section of manifest train 402 out of the siding at Shinn, just west of Niles Junction, Calif. PFE 76305, an R-30-16 with a mechanical fan shaft, is from the first group of 500 PFE cars to have such fans (see Chapter 7). John Illman photo, Oct. 5, 1952.

Western Pacific X483 East
working hard in Niles Canyo[n].
The 4-8-4 is one of six th[at]
were duplicates of SP's GS[-?]
class, delivered from Lima [in]
the summer of 1943. Shovi[ng]
near the rear end is 2-8-2 N[o.]
320, built by Alco in 192[?].
John C. Illman photo, Nov. [?]
1950.

(Right) AC-10 rear helper 3814 awaits the highball to shove a westbound out of Truckee, 15 miles from the summit at Donner Pass. PFE 6725 is a load, and meltwater streams from the ice bunker drain. Jim Orem photo, 1950.

From collections of Bill Fisher, signal maintainer:

"I surely do remember the reefer trains giving us signal maintainers a bad time. In WW II we averaged 50 trains in 24 hours, and with all the grading, the track men could hardly keep up with rail replacements, and had no time to clean ballast. Then reefer trains dripped salt water into that sand. Fall rains soaked the sand, making brine which sapped the signal track voltage. Many times I was out all night between Colfax and Emigrant Gap to boost chargers and cut out all possible resistance at each signal and still most would stay red. When it was humid at night, we'd be putting 2 amperes into the track and only get 25 milliamps at the signal. You could bump the relay with your hand and the signal would clear, but if a train went through it stayed red after he was gone. Track batteries would last about three weeks."

(Below) A UP "Big Boy" heads a long string of westbound empties over Sherman Hill, just east of Dale on the new line. Wm. W. Kratville photo, Nov. 1958.

(**Above**) Union Pacific X802 West is a Christmas rush mail train, using cleaned and dried PFE ice cars. This was done quite often at the holidays, even in diesel days. Wm. W. Kratville photo, Dec. 1955. (**Below**) A UP Challenger shoves through the crossover at Wahsatch, Utah, top of the eastbound grade out of Ogden and just a few mileposts from Wyoming. Don Sims photo, 1956.

Local X2724 at Redlands, Sept. 1954, John Edwards collection, courtesy John Signor.

"Pick 'em up,
get 'em to the ice deck,
move 'em east.
That's what we did, day after
day for PFE."

— SP dispatcher.

(**Above**) A Salinas perishable block rolls through Oakland at First and Franklin on its way to Roseville. Power is SP 2-8-0 No. 2798. Fred Mathews photo, Nov. 27, 1947. (**Below**) Moving east near Auburn, Calif. There is also a 4-unit F7 helper on the rear. Al Phelps photo, July 27, 1952.

(**Above**) Union Pacific's 3-cylinder 4-12-2's were built by Alco during 1926-30 to handle heavy trains in the Cheyenne-Ogden freight pool. Some also operated for a time between Reith and Huntington on the OWR&N. Here a "Nine," as these 9000-class engines were called, pounds upgrade with an eastbound reefer block near Rock River, Wyoming. Engine 9002 and its 72-car train, running at 35 mph, were photographed on June 9, 1935 by Otto Perry. Western History Dept., Denver Public Library, photo OP-19059.

(**Below**) In the Central Valley of California, almost any road engine could be called to haul a freight train over the relatively flat terrain. Here 4-6-2 No. 2450, normally assigned to passenger service, high-steps 74 cars westbound out of Roseville, on July 22, 1938. Otto C. Perry photo OP- 15817, Western History Dept., Denver Public Library.

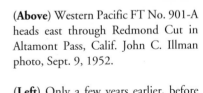

(**Above**) Western Pacific FT No. 901-A heads east through Redmond Cut in Altamont Pass, Calif. John C. Illman photo, Sept. 9, 1952.

(**Left**) Only a few years earlier, before they were displaced by FT's, the Class 257 2-8-8-2 simple articulateds were the ultimate in WP power. Here the first engine of the class heads a reefer block eastward near Portola. Otto C. Perry photo OP-20017, Western History Dept., Denver Public Library.

Pacific Electric motor 1613 is coming off the four-track main near downtown Los Angeles, and will soon reach the 8th Street Yard area where PE had a huge warehouse and industrial track complex. Don Sims photo, 1950.

This SP Baldwin switcher, equipped with trolley poles to activate track circuits while operating on the Pacific Electric, is pulling a string of reefer loads from a ship at the Wilmington docks. The train, near what is now Dolores Yard on the SP, is headed for Butte St. Yard and the SP interchange. Don Sims photo, 1950.

Sacramento Northern motor 430 hums into the yard at Marysville, Calif., to set out cars, while motor 650 is idle on the siding. John E. Shaw photo, May 27, 1956.

The Weber Canyon walls at Devil's Gate echo syncopated exhausts of UP 2-10-2's, No. 5000 on the point and road engine 5528, working a 65-car eastbound at 20 mph. Richard H. Kindig photo, Oct. 1, 1947.

(Left) A hobo escapes the chilly wind by catching a ride in a ventilated load (he's probably standing on the half-stage ice grates) on a northbound train at Grass Lake, Calif. The winter snows have not yet melted on the mountains. Richard Steinheimer photo, March, 1953, DeGolyer Library.

(Below) A westbound train, predominantly empties from the Pacific Northwest, drifts downgrade through Mount Shasta, Calif., just before it hits the steep descent into the Sacramento River canyon and on to Dunsmuir. John C. Illman photo, June 11, 1950.

(Above) Midnight at Council Bluffs. Union Pacific 4-8-4 No. 839 has just arrived with an eastbound reefer block. As it sits with turbogenerator whining and air pumps panting, a switcher pulls up to the north side of the platform with meat cars from Omaha packing plants. The main line rails glow with the lights of yet another eastbound freight. Wm. W. Kratville photo, Sept., 1956.

(Left) El Centro on a hot summer night in 1952. Pre-icing and initial icing went on around the clock during a perishable rush. Richard Steinheimer photo, DeGolyer Library.

(Below) A late-night lull at PFE's ice deck in El Centro, Calif. The background train is an SP Alco roadswitcher, SD&AE combine 173, and SP caboose 756. Don Sims photo, 1953.

(**Above**) Reefer blocks from the west were usually split up as the cars neared different eastern destinations, so it was uncommon to see complete trains of PFE cars. Here PFE and other ice cars are hustled along New York Central's famous 4-track "Raceway." Mikado 2775 has the duty. Ed Nowak photo, Jeff Moreau collection.

(**Below**) An eastbound "meat train" with reefers from the South Omaha Terminal RR heads out of Council Bluffs on the Illinois Central. The engineer of Mikado 1594 whistles for photographer Wm. W. Kratville in this July, 1952 scene.

(**Above**) UP Challenger 3814 has brought an eastbound reefer block to the Council Bluffs ice deck. Note the "blue flag" semaphores and special blades.

(**Right**) The high drivers of UP 7022, a 4-8-2, race a string of eastbound refrigerators across Nebraska corn country at milepost 79, just east of Columbus, on a cold, windy November day in 1952.

(**Below**) A string of PFE westbounds rolls on UP steel near Dodge Street (Omaha), the distinctive syncopated exhaust of a 3-cylinder "Nine" shattering the warm August, 1953 afternoon. Three photos, Wm. W. Kratville.

(**Above**) A trio of F3's labors upgrade with 86 reefers near Peterson, Utah, having left Devil's Gate and Weber Canyon a few minutes earlier. No. 3713, a 4-6-6-4, makes a pillar of smoke as it shoves mightily at the rear. Oct. 12, 1953. Both photos, Richard H. Kindig.
(**Below**) Extra 3814 East is running along the Snake River near Glenn's Ferry, Idaho. A few miles ahead at Ticeska, another 4-6-6-4, No. 3810, will be added behind the caboose, for the short, stiff climb up King Hill out of the river valley to Shoshone. Oct. 15, 1953.

In the unmistakable precincts of Sherman (above), a reefer block rolls east on UP rails behind a Big Boy. Note the apparent range of paint colors, due to weathering, of these PFE cars, all of which at some point were certainly painted Color No. 8 (p. 419). Clark Bauer collection.

Train No. 429, a westward reefer block, is crossing Altamont Pass behind a pair of Alco RS-11 road switchers in July, 1956; the second locomotive still wears the demonstrator paint scheme in which it arrived on SP property. The cars are loads in ventilator service. John Shaw photo.

Baltimore & Ohio freight No. 92 (above) is caught at Hammond, Indiana at 10:50 AM on May 30, 1953. In the lead is Alco FA locomotive No. 815. Though B&O handled fewer eastbound perishables than the Erie, it usually carried far more than rival Pennsylvania; this 79-car freight is heavy with reefers. R.R. Malinoski photo.

Perishable traffic moved rapidly along the New York-Washington axis of Pennsylvania's electric lines. In this view (below), freight motor No. 4784 has 96 cars well in hand at Iselin, New Jersey. This handsome power may look like a GG-1, but it's one of 92 engines of Class P-5a, with a 2-C-2 wheel arrangement. It's a little before noon on Sept. 8, 1955. R.R. Malinoski photo.

(**Above**) UP 2-8-8-0 No. 3536 works hard to move 61 cars of Manifest 1-260 near Campbell, Ore., at 45 mph, on Dec. 24, 1939. Behind the UP Harriman box car at the head end, it looks like all PFE reefers. Massive steam lines, cylinders, and boiler led to the nickname "Bull Moose" for this UP locomotive type.

(**Below**) Point helper 3813 and "Big Boy" 4010 pound upgrade with 108 westbound cars, many of them empty reefers, at 35 mph, as a 3900 with a downhill train drifts by near Sherman, Wyo. Aug. 3, 1949. Both photos, Richard H. Kindig.

(Above) GS-1 4407 heads a PFE block down the San Joaquin Valley near Delano, Calif. Stan Kistler caught the action in June, 1954.

(Below) Here an Alco-built Mt-1, 4-8-2 No. 4315, heads an eastbound Salinas Vegetable Block near Martinez, Calif., in this July, 1950 scene with an oil refinery in the background. Albert C. Phelps photo.

(**Above**) An AC-class 4-8-8-2 shoves hard to keep an eastbound moving through Niles Canyon and toward Altamont Pass. John E. Shaw photo, May 31, 1956.　　(**Below**) Engineer Doyle McCormack and *Daylight* engine 4449 made an elegant shakedown run with a revenue-producing reefer block of freshly painted SPFE cars, seen here just south of Brooklyn Yard (Portland), Ore., prior to the 1984 World's Fair trip. PFE used this photo on their Christmas card.

(**Above**) Extra 4015 is seen working just east of Green River, Wyo., in this Sept. 3, 1955 photo.   (**Below**) UP 3713 is the rear helper "leaving town" on gas turbine-powered X54 East out of Ogden, Utah, August 28, 1955. Both photos, John E. Shaw.

(Left) The whine of dynamic brake fans of eastbound train 8314 disturbs the high mountain serenity at Eder. The SD40T-2's and SD40's have just crested the Sierra summit within the "long bore" behind them. The original line, used for some westbound traffic, can be seen above the tunnel portal. Clint Nestell photo, Aug. 20, 1984.

(Below) Triple meet at "Sawdust" (Saugus, Calif.) as Manifest train 804, a reefer block, eases by on the main behind a 4-unit set of F7's. Waiting in the siding is the first section of its westward counterpart, 1-803; its rear helper, about to be added, is the Mt-class 4-8-2 standing alongside. The third train, not visible here, is Second 51, a steam-powered Korean War troop train, taking on water. Bercaw's Store, being restocked with Coca-Cola, was a favorite spot for crews to pick up a cold soft drink. Richard Steinheimer photo, July 17, 1950, DeGolyer Library.

(**Above**) "Bull Moose" 3555 drifts into Cheyenne with 58 eastbound refrigerator cars under ventilation service, thus probably loaded with Idaho potatoes or onions. This photo epitomizes UP railroading in Wyoming: treeless high plains with little more than rails, pole lines and wind (note the turbo exhaust). Richard H. Kindig, Oct. 29, 1938.

(**Below**) A brace of FCP (Ferrocarril del Pacifico) Alcos start south out of Nogales, Sonora, with empty PFE vans on a PFE flat car, to be loaded from the agricultural areas along the west coast of Mexico south of Empalme. In later years, surplus PFE trailers were sold to the FCP (see Chapter 10). Photo from the late 1960's, courtesy John Signor.

A train in the era of mixed ice, mechanical, and trailer equipment is caught (above) rounding a curve in the Sierra foothills. The variety of size in both cars and trailers is evident. Though the photo is undated, the white trailers mean that the time is at least as late as 1966. PFE photo, CSRM.

Train LAWJY, formerly the "West Coast Peddler," rounds Horseshoe Curve above San Luis Obispo amid the green grasses of spring on March 16, 1984 (below). After completing its climb over Cuesta Summit, the train will run downhill all the way to Watsonville Junction. Bruce Veary photo.

This interesting view (above) shows a mix of ice and mechanical cars in an eastbound perishable train circa 1965. The dirtiness of the older mechanical cars as well as the ice cars is evident in this era when washing had been discontinued for some time. Location is near Emigrant Gap in the Sierra. PFE photo, A.W. Thompson collection.

A long block of mechanical reefers crosses Gaviota Trestle on Southern Pacific's Coast Line as part of empty reefer train TUWJR, operating as X8705 west. It's 12:45 PM on November 19, 1978, and many of these cars were cleaned in Tucson and are bound for loading in the Salinas and Watsonville areas. Bruce Veary photo.

WARNING
POISONOUS FUMES

HEATED CAR

This car, initials_____ Number_____

contains heaters using_____as fu
(State kind of fuel)

and they are located in the_____
(State whether in body or bunke

When cars are equipped with heaters using either char
or charkets, ALL PERSONS ARE WARNED against
maining in such cars WITH DOORS AND HATCH
closed. Doors or hatches must be left open for a few n
utes before entering.

Must not be placed next to cars placarded
'Explosives' or 'Inflammable'

ONE OF THESE CARDS MUST BE APPLIED TO DOOR
EACH SIDE OF EVERY CAR EQUIPPED WITH HEATE
AND CARD TAKEN OFF WHEN HEATER IS REMOVI

(**Above**) Standard door placard.

(**Left**) A workman at Blue Island, Ill., lowers a hea
into a refrigerator car in wintry conditions. The sk
and crossbones placard will be tacked on the outside
the hatch; it reads "DANGER – GAS FUMES
KEEP OUT." Jack Delano photo, 1943, neg. I
USW 3-14135-D, Library of Congress.

(**Left**) A screw-operated lift platform is being used here in Milwaukee
to re-ice a PFE reefer at a location with no handy ice deck. Note pipes
and pipe caps to cover the screws, which are gear-driven from the
truck engine. White Motor Co. photo, 1924, courtesy Donald F.
Wood.

(**Below**) Initial icing of express refrigerators, likely loaded with
strawberries, at Oxnard, Calif. The Union Ice truck is an International
Model D-500 (1937-39) cab-over; a small gasoline engine powers
the conveyor. Alden Armstrong photo, about 1951.

(Left) Ice was shipped in to many points if there was no ice manufacturing plant, or if local production was insufficient. Here a workman manhandles blocks from an ice service reefer onto the loading conveyor up to the deck at Hinkle, Ore. UP Railroad Museum, photo 33326. (Above) Icing PFE cars at Dupo, Ill. on the Illinois Central in the summer of 1955. Like many ice decks in the country, this one has no roof or aprons. The man at left wears shorts lettered "Dupo Track," for the local high school. UP Railroad Museum photo.

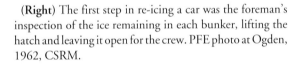

(Right) The first step in re-icing a car was the foreman's inspection of the ice remaining in each bunker, lifting the hatch and leaving it open for the crew. PFE photo at Ogden, 1962, CSRM.

(Left) The inspector is chalking the amount of ice needed for each bunker (in hundredweights). The amount is also recorded on his clipboard as a basis for charges to the shipper. PFE photo at Ogden, 1962, CSRM.

This photo (above), with men obviously posed, depicts manual icing from a deck with drop aprons, with the classic bident and pickaroon tools shown clearly. Photo KE4-16, Union Pacific Railroad Museum.

After icing, crews used rods to "settle" the ice and reduce voids in bunkers (below) before closing hatches. Note the double chain for the icing machine. PFE photo, A.W. Thompson collection.

The Ogden-Riverdale ice deck was mechanized in August, 1954. Installed to serve 110 cars on each side of an island deck, the three icing machines ran on rails atop the old deck (below). As can be seen, ice was still delivered to the icing machines using the old deck chain. Two of the Preco single-end machines are visible in the side view (above), with ice chutes rotated parallel to the deck. Salt machines are next to them. Note blue flag on the end car. A crew of workers still had to open all hatches, then close them after icing was complete; but the speed of icing an entire train was considerably faster, and more importantly, the crew size was much smaller. The machines could also be set to direct any size of ice, from chunk to crushed, into each individual car. PFE photos, CSRM.

Icing Reefers

I still remember
that icehouse summer,
blocks of ice on wooden decks
fifteen feet above the ground,
four of us learning teamwork
in relentless sunlight.

We mined the ice,
three hundred pounds a block,
at dim depths in the storage house,
let the conveyor take it out
along the deck, to wait under burlap sheets.

Hearing the distant whistle signal,
we took our places, tanned and shirtless,
waiting for the train.
Soon the locomotive panted past us,
light throttle stretching slack, slowing,
trailing wisps of steam and smoke.
A long line of orange cars trailed after,
filled with produce picked yesterday
in California valleys.

As the cars stopped, we stepped onto roofs,
flung open hatches, started moving ice.
The chopper broke the blocks, the passer
moved them toward the edge,
we two car men stuffed them in the bunkers.
Ice fragments flew, sparkling in the sun,
as big chunks boomed on the grates.
Block followed block to fill the tanks.

Slamming home the hatches,
we jumped back for the next string.
Again the train moved, again we strained muscles
wrestling ice into hatches. Finally
two short whistle blasts and the train was away,
reefers rolling eastward.
We leaned on railings, smoked 'em if we had 'em,
chewed the fat awhile, and
went back to mining ice.

Anthony Thompson

416

Appendix

MASTER LIST OF PFE CAR SPECIFICATIONS AND CLASSES

Class	Specification	Outcome	Year	Chapter
30-1	58	built	1906-07	4
30-2	58-A	built	1907	4
30-3	58-B	unbuilt	1908	4
30-4	58-C	built	1909	4
30-5	58-D	built	1909-11	4
30-6	58-E	built	1912-13	4
30-7	58-F	unbuilt	1912	4
30-8	58-G	unbuilt	1914	4
30-9	58-H	unbuilt	1914	4
30-10	58-J (I?)	unbuilt	1914	4
30-11-1/2	58-J	built	1917-18	5
30-11	58-K	built	1917-18	5
30-12	58-L	built	1920-24	5
30-13	58-M	built	1920-26	5
30-14	58-N	built	1926	5
30-15, -16	--	rebuilds	1939-55	7
30-17	--	rebuild	1940	7
30-18, -19	--	rebuilds	1942-45	7
30-21, -24	--	rebuilds	1945-48	7
30-25	--	unbuilt	1947	7
40-1	65	built	1927	6
40-2	66	built	1928	6
40-3	--	unbuilt	1928	6
50-1	67	built	1930	6
40-4	68	built	1930	6
40-6	69	built	1931	6
40-7?	70	unbuilt	1931	7
40-8	71	built	1932	6
40-9 (R-30-9)	--	rebuild	1937-40	7
70-1	72	unbuilt	1931	6
70-2	73	built	1932	6
70-3	73	built	1939	6
70-4	--	built	1940	7
40-10	74	built	1936-37	8
40-12	74-A	unbuilt	1940	8
40-14	74-B	built	1941	8
40-15	74-C	unbuilt	1942	8
40-15, -16	--	rebuilds	1939-55	7
40-18, -19	--	rebuilds	1942-45	7
40-20	74-D	built	1945	8
40-14, #45698	74-E	built	1946	8

Class	Specification	Outcome	Year	Chapter
R-40-14, #44739	74-F	built	1947	8
R-40-21	--	rebuild	1945	7
R-40-22	--	unbuilt	1945	7
R-40-23	74-G	built	1947	8
R-40-24	--	rebuild	1947-49	7
R-40-25	74-H	built	1949-50	8
R-40-26X	74-J	unbuilt	1948	8
R-40-26	74-K	built	1950-51	8
R-70-5	74-L	built	1952-54	8,9
R-70-6	--	ART cars	1950	8,9
R-70-7	--	built	1953	9
R-70-8	74-M	built	1954	9
R-70-9	74-N	built	1956	9
R-70-10	74-P	built	1956	9
R-40-27	74-Q	built	1956-57	8
R-40-28	74-R	built	1957	8
R-50-6	75	built	1957	9
R-40-30	76	built	1958	9
R-70-11	77	built	1959	9
R-70-12	78	built	1960	9
40' trailer	79	built	1961	10
85' flat	80	built	1961	10
85' flat	81	built	1962	10
R-70-13	82	built	1962	9
40' trailer	83	built	1962	10
F-70-30	84	built	1964	10
R-70-14	85	built	1965	9
Trailer, container	86,86B	built	1964	10
insul. container	87	built	1965	10
R-70-15	88	built	1966	9
89' flat	89	built	1967	10
R-70-16	90	built	1966	9
F-70-31	91	built	1966	10
40' van	92	built	1966	10
R-70-17	93	built	1967	9
R-70-18	94	built	1967	9
40' trailer	95	built	1966	10
40' trailer	96	built	1966	10
40' trailer	97	built	1967	10
R-70-19, Keystone	98	built	1968	9
R-70-19, Hydra-C.	99	built	1968	9
R-70-20 to -25	100	built	1968-71	9

PAINTING AND LETTERING

This page summarizes PFE paint schemes over the years, with dates of introduction of new paint and lettering arrangements. It is typical of most freight cars that paint schemes can remain in service for years after their owner considers them obsolete, but wood-sheathed cars in general, and refrigerator cars in particular, tend to be exceptions in that repainting was needed more often. In PFE's case, the policy was to repaint wood-sheathed cars every four to six years, and the evidence indicates that this was done. Particularly since PFE cars passed through company shops for inspection, cleaning and repair several times a year (see Chapter 11), it was practical for paint schemes to be kept up to date, if that was management's wish. Prior to about 1960, it appears that such was almost always the case.

For steel cars, repainting was needed much less often, so older schemes survived longer, perhaps as much as ten years beyond the obsolescence date. After 1960, painting was only done when necessary because of repairs, and after 1970, paint might be touched up even after a major repair, rather than repaint the entire car.

Principal paint schemes are listed below by date of introduction. Dates of changes are also listed, with text references. Drawings cited begin on page 432.

1906-1922. Yellow car sides, freight car red roofs and ends; trucks, underframe and iron hardware black; plain lettering (no emblems). Primary description, pp. 74, 75, drawing C-1483; photos, Ch. 4, 5. Express cars, olive with black roof, p. 75. Color drifts, p. 419.

> **1909.** Car number and capacity data moved from right of car side to left (p. 75).
> **1911.** "U.S. SAFETY APPLIANCE LETTERING" introduced; space under door changed from black to freight car red (p. 75, 81).
> **1920.** Black color begun for outside metal roofs (p. 99).

1922-1946. Single railroad medallion, each side. Primary description, pp. 99, 100; photos, Chaps. 4-8. Express cars, olive and black, pp. 104, 165. WP cars, p. 105.

> **1925.** ARA lettering changes, including introduction of 1-in. stripes above reporting marks and below car number, standardized lettering sizes, and data groupings, introduced (p. 99). Drawing C-4228.
> **1928.** Porcelain enamel medallions introduced (pp. 112, 113); removed in late 1930's.
> **1929.** Car side color changed from yellow to orange (p.

117). Evidence (Chapter 6) indicates that this change-over in color had been completed for the entire PFE fleet by 1934. Color drift, p. 419.

> **1932.** Solid steel roofs painted freight car red; outside metal roofs similarly changed, 1935-40 (p. 124).
> **1936.** UP shield changed to remove word "system" from upper field, p. 99.
> **1936-41.** Experimental paint schemes, pp. 137, 138.
> **1938.** Repack rectangle introduced, p. 133.
> **1942.** UP shield changed to remove diagonal "Overland" slogan, pp. 165, 174.

1946-60. Both railroad medallions on each side of car, otherwise much like 1922-46. Primary description, p. 176, drawing C-9359; see also p. 144, 173. Cars with fans, 1" or 1½" dot on end (depending on class), Chap. 8. Photos, Chaps. 7-9.

> **1949.** Most side hardware changed from black to orange, pp. 135, 179.
> **1950.** UP medallion changed from red-white-blue to black and white, p. 185.
> **1951-53.** All side hardware changed from black to orange, 1951, p. 185; stripes removed from reporting mark area, 1952, p. 185; periods in "PFE" removed, 1953, p. 186. Express cars, pp. 165, 166.
> **1953.** Frozen food car roofs changed from gray to aluminum, pp. 187, 201; mech. car ends black, p. 201.

1960-78. All lettering Gothic, large PFE name at right side of car. Primary description, p. 207; see also pp. 158, 188, 189, 215. Photos, Chap. 7-10; flat cars, pp. 236, 237.

> **1961.** SP medallion changed from "circle and bar" style to Gothic SP in center, pp. 144, 189, 190, 214.
> **1962.** Ice car roofs changed to aluminum, ends to black, pp. 159, 189. Wood interiors changed from varnish to gray, p. 189. Trailers, pp. 241, 242.
> **1965.** Black rectangle for reporting marks, pp. 190, 219, 237; roofs became white instead of aluminum, p. 215.
> **1968.** Outline initial letters "PFE" introduced, p. 224. Drawing DR-4900 is revised to this scheme.
> **1970.** 14" black reporting marks and car number, p. 224.
> **1971.** Upper field of UP shield returned to black color as in 1952-60; SPFE, UPFE marks begun; p. 224.
> **1975.** Car ends orange, "Scotchlite"™ reporting marks and numbers introduced, p. 226.

Post-1978 Schemes. See pp. 227-231, 406, 410, 425.

PFE Standard Refrigerator Orange (car sides)
CS 22 Color #8 (introduced 1929), pp. 117, 418
Panel #7, Spec. 408 (1956)

PFE Standard Freight Car Red (car roofs and ends)
CS 22 Color #11, "Metallic" (1907), see p. 418
Panel #3, Spec. 403 (1956)

PFE Standard Refrigerator Yellow (car sides)
CS 22 Color #8 (1907-1929), see p. 418
CS 22 Color #8-B after 1930, see p. 117

PFE Standard Exterior Gray (ice decks, wood structures)
Apparently no CS 22 Color number
Panel #2, Spec. S-4554 (1928 and 1956)

A rather tired R-30-24 rebuild, PFE 67364, shows its 1950's paint scheme in this 1962 photo at Dallas, Tex. (Reweigh date is 3-60.) Ends appear black in this photo. By this time, the asphalt emulsion used on car roofs and ends was black, and either the freight car red paint applied to it could weather off, or in the late 1950's, it might be left unpainted. Lettering diagrams for ice cars, however, called for red roofs and ends until 1962. Dick Kuelbs photo.

The first of its class, brand-new PFE 200126, an R-70-5 with ice bunkers, shows off its red ends and gray roof at Roseville in May of 1952 (see Chapter 8 for more on this class and its paint scheme). The white wheel rims were only for the car inspection. When such wheel paint proved slippery in car retarders, PFE removed it before the inspected cars entered service. In 1955, this class was reconfigured for mechanical refrigeration, as described in Chapters 8 and 9. PFE photo, CSRM.

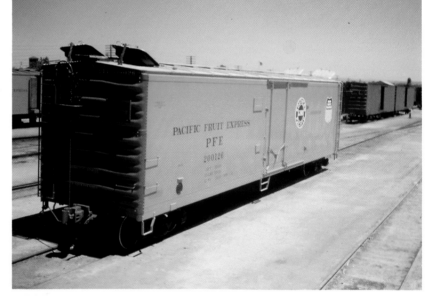

The interesting angle of this photo of PFE 454010, an R-70-16, clearly shows the ribbed roof typical of classes R-70-14 through -19. This SP-owned car has a Hydra-Cushion underframe and the full-height ladders typical of pre-1966 construction (see Chapter 9). Note that roof is white and ends are black. Dick Kuelbs photo at Fort Worth, Tex., on May 22, 1966.

This very dirty PFE car from the WP fleet, No. 55765, was captured in one of SP's Los Angeles yards in May, 1961, and reveals both the extent and color of heavy dirt on these cars in later years, when car washing had been discontinued. Morris Abowitz photo, Bill Sheehan collection.

Plywood-sided No. 67026, one of the last of the R-30-24 class, shows wear and tear in this 1961 view. As explained in Chapter 7, the application of plywood as car sheathing was disappointing in practice, and the majority of cars which were rebuilt with plywood sides ended up getting tongue-and-groove replacement siding. Rob Evans collection.

This R-30-9 (left) has been assigned to banana loading, as shown by the white placard stencil; it reads

BANANA LOADING ONLY

PE RAILS

RETURN TO

LA HARBOR WHEN EMPTY.

This view dates from July, 1961. Morris Abowitz photo, Bill Sheehan collection.

This view from the west (right) shows the automobile road across PFE's Los Angeles General Shop, with the rebuilding shed in the distance, in 1954. Foreground tracks are the light repair yard (for map, see page 266). Alden Armstrong photo.

During 1959-62, PFE experimented with conversions of ice cars to mechanical refrigeration. This car, PFE 101002 (two top photos), used an underslung Witte diesel-generator set with a side exhaust stack. Mass conversions of ice cars did not follow (see page 211). Photos taken at Taylor ice deck in September, 1961.

Underframes for the last new cars built at the Los Angeles Shop, Class R-70-12, were built at Gunderson Engineering in Portland, Oregon, and are shown here (center) on arriving flat cars in April, 1960.

Three photos above, Morris Abowitz, Bill Sheehan collection

The first PFE ice cars with sliding (plug) doors was Class R-40-26, delivered in 1951-52. Here (right) PFE 9586, still in original paint, is shown with its six-foot door open. The car has just completed a trip in vent service, and is open for inspection. This view dates from 1959 at Roseville. PFE photo, A.W. Thompson collection.

(**Top**) This view shows roof overspray (orange on the white roof) on a 40-ft. mechanical car, PFE 100302, photographed in 1962. Given the methods in use for car painting at the time (see page 269), the overspray is not surprising. Dick Kuelbs photo at Ft. Worth, Texas.

(**Center**) Photos of new cars at Pacific Car & Foundry were often posed in the plant yard, which like most yards had a dirt surface. A segment of a photo of a green lawn was then stripped into the photo to provide a more attractive foreground, as in this view of an R-70-19. This procedure is evident in several PC&F photos in Chapter 9. PC&F photo for PFE, CSRM.

(**Bottom**) Freshly rebuilt "Ice Tempco" cars are shown at SP's Taylor Yard, adjoining the PFE shop facilities. Visible here on the silver roofs are the single ice bunkers at the "B" end, the idea being that the air circulation could provide adequate cooling from a single source. Morris Abowitz photo, Bill Sheehan collection.

At times of car shortage, such as Christmas mail rushes, reefers including PFE cars, were often loaded with mail. Here (top) is an example of such car loading at the Postal Annex of Los Angeles Union Passenger Terminal, during the Christmas mail season of 1961. Morris Abowitz photo, Bill Sheehan collection.

It is common to expect cars assigned to ice service to be the older cars, with rough interiors and, often, obsolete insulation. But in the late days of the ice car fleet, this could even include the early steel cars, as shown in this June, 1961 photo (center) of a freshly-painted R-40-10 which had been assigned to ice service. Morris Abowitz photo, Bill Sheehan collection.

Alongside the Calexico ice deck (below), Consolidation No. 2799 is running as a cab hop with caboose no. 756. Reefers line the deck on January 15, 1955. This is a companion view to that on page 361. Stan Kistler photo.

Several of the early classes of PFE mechanical cars had different style stampings at each end. At the A end, which housed the mechanical equipment, an interior bulkhead permitted use of the older and less stiff style of "original Dreadnaught" end, as shown here on PFE 300983, a member of class R-50-6, pictured new at Los Angeles in 1958. Photo KE4-197, UP Railroad Museum.

(**Below**) When Southern Pacific and Union Pacific divided PFE in 1978, consideration was given at the new UPFE organization to use a green paint scheme like the one shown, on a car of Class R-70-19. Ed Chiasson, who had moved to UPFE and who termed this color "lettuce green," remarked that when a sample car in this scheme was shown to John Kenefick, UP President, he said, "I don't think so, Ed. I think you'd scare all the cows in Nebraska with that car." Instead, traditional Union Pacific yellow was used for UPFE cars, as described on pages 228-230. UP Railroad Museum photo.

(**Above**) As the split-up of PFE between SP and UP approached in 1977, several sample paint schemes were tried on the SP side. Shown is a car of Class R-70-22, with its Hydra-cushion cylinder evident below the car door. Pictured at Salinas, this scheme was not used after the 1978 split-up; instead, cars were painted white. SP photo, CSRM.

(**Below, right**) In 1975, SP had considered a color emblem to brighten up the PFE paint scheme (see page 227). Here is the original colored-pencil sketch of its proposed appearance. PFE collection, CSRM.

In this view, an SP loading operation is using a standard highway tractor to back a semi-trailer down the string of piggyback flat cars. Though the tractor is marked "Southern Pacific," its cab number betrays its ownership by SP's Pacific Motor Trucking subsidiary. Photo at Los Angeles by PFE, A.W. Thompson collection.

By the time PFE trailers were put into service, many operators of piggyback traffic had devised a variety of special equipment for the job. Here, a purpose-built UP tractor is carrying out circus loading. The nearest trailer in all-white shows the date to be about 1966 or later. Photo KE4-644, UP Railroad Museum.

These two trailers on a PFF flat car, photographed at Omaha, reveal how dirty these flat cars could get (the reporting mark area has been wiped clean). Photo KE4-447, UP Railroad Museum.

The earliest PFE trailer services were accomplished with leased SP piggyback flat cars, and this view (left) depicts one such car, PFF 513149 (which still retains its SP slogan, TRAILER-FLATCAR SERVICE). Note at left the Rock Island trailer on one of Rock Island's "war emergency" gondolas, converted for trailer service. View dates from October, 1963, at SP's Shops yard in Alhambra. Morris Abowitz photo, Bill Sheehan collection.

This posed photo (right) shows a pair of Strick-built PFE vans of the "refrigerated container" type, Class RCM-40-1, on a PFE flat car (Class F-70-30). PFE managers may have wished their trailers would ride on their own flat cars, but this was not particularly common in practice. Note the blue-gray refrigeration unit, a style which appeared in the late 1960's. PFE photo, A.W. Thompson collection.

This General American builder photo (left) shows PFF 835043, one of the first batch of new F-70-30 cars, at the East Chicago plant prior to delivery in October, 1963. The body is all orange. GATC photo for PFE, CSRM.

427

This superb view (above) of the cleaning tracks at Roseville show several aspects of car work, from the emptying bunker drain at lower left and body ice on the asphalt, to the broom clips on car doors (center), to the small equipment carts and the inspector's chalk marks on the car at left. The workmen are oiling a journal box. Date is November, 1962. PFE photo, A.W. Thompson collection.

The mobile car icing machine at Eugene was a system unique, as described on page 298. It is shown here (right) on one of those central Oregon days not shown in tourist brochures, with a steady drizzle falling from a gloomy sky in the fall of 1962. Shelter for the operator is minimal. PFE photo, A.W. Thompson collection.

When the Class R-50-5 cars were rebuilt, they retained the deep center sills of the original cars. Here (top) is a well-lit view of this feature. Rob Evans collection.

At Roseville (center), the experimental R-40-29's, 40 ft. long and mechanically refrigerated (cars 100001 and 100002) are ready for inspection. At far left Gus Torburn (Supt. of the Car Dept.) in the gray suit, and Earl Hopkins (Asst. Supt.), are examining the door closure on the cars. The date is September, 1957. PFE photo, CSRM.

After PFE moved out of SP's Taylor Yard in 1962, icing was conducted at City of Industry with equipment such as that shown here (bottom). The work of the men getting ice into bunkers from atop the cars, however, was much as it had been fifty years earlier. PFE photo, A.W. Thompson collection.

The World's Largest Fleet
—of Refrigerator Cars

Pacific Fruit Express Company has, since its inception, maintained leadership in the refrigerator car field. It is more than a car line—it is a service institution, currently operating 36,400 refrigerator cars—the largest fleet in the world. When the 5,000 new cars are added, P.F.E. will have more than 41,000 cars in service.

Six huge car shops have been built in strategic areas, to keep these cars in good repair. Many light repair stations have also been established in important producing areas.

In addition, P.F.E. owns 19 ice plants.

P.F.E.'s total ice manufacturing capacity at all 19 ice plants, located along Southern Pacific and Union Pacific lines, amounts to 5,110 tons daily, with storage facilities sufficient to accommodate 296,500 tons of ice.

P.F.E. also owns the largest number of car heaters—10,660 in all. 1,600 use alcohol as fuel, 600 being thermostatically controlled. The balance burn charcoal and are manually controlled.

P.F.E. handles icing, heater service, diversions, passing reports and many other services to the trade for Southern Pacific and Union Pacific. In addition, it handles car distribution for its owners, as well as for the Western Pacific.

The widespread facilities of the S.P. and U.P. are always at the disposal of Pacific Fruit Express, including direct wire service to Chicago, New York and many other important markets. These facilities have enabled us to render service to our patrons that is unsurpassed anywhere in the world.

PACIFIC FRUIT EXPRESS CO.

In shipping perishables, think of P. F. E.—
A FRIENDLY AND PROGRESSIVE INSTITUTION

INTRODUCING
40 Miles
of new post-war Refrigerator Cars

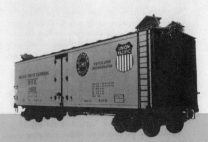

PACIFIC FRUIT EXPRESS
COMPANY

Spotlighting
P.F.E.'s LIGHTWEIGHT EXPERIMENTAL
Refrigerator Car

PACIFIC FRUIT
COMPA...

GOOD NEWS for shippers!

DOUBLE-FAST ICING AT EL PASO

PACIFIC FRUIT EXPRESS COMPANY

THE SOUTHWEST'S NEWEST AND FINEST REFRIGERATOR CAR ICING PLANT

Cars are iced here in less than a minute

"Double-fast" icing in the Southwest became a reality when Pacific Fruit Express opened its large new streamlined icing platform at El Paso, Texas, for re-icing shipments of perishables en route to eastern and southern markets. The platform is strategically located on Southern Pacific Lines and is six-tenths of a mile in length. It is double-decked and double-sided for double-fast icing. The new installation permits icing complete trains of as many as 140 cars, 70 on each side, at one time. Cars are iced in an average of *less than a minute* per car.

GREATLY IMPROVED TOP-ICING FACILITIES

The double-decked construction of the platform permits simultaneous bunker-icing and top-icing. Bunkers are iced from the top deck and top-icing handled from the lower deck. The "slingers" used for top-icing are the result of intensive research by P.F.E. engineers to develop a machine that would allow cars to be, literally, "iced on the run" and at the same time completely and perfectly refrigerated. The "slingers" are mounted on rails, thereby providing flexibility and speed in operation. Despite the 3-ton weight of a "slinger," one man

may quickly roll a machine to any point along the deck.

To further streamline the icing operations at the new El Paso dock, a public address system consisting of 18 two-way speakers, and a pneumatic tube system 2,700 feet long have been installed. Voice and paper communications between the platform, yard and other offices are greatly facilitated and speeded up.

The platform is so designed that it can be enlarged to handle 100 cars at a time on either side, which would make the facility the largest of its kind in the country.

In addition to the El Paso platform, the Pacific Fruit Express has new projects at Holtville in the Imperial Valley, Houston, Texas, and Los Angeles, California. Also enlarged and improved facilities at Yuma, Arizona, and Roseville and Bakersfield, California. No expense is being spared to provide shippers of perishables with the fastest and most modern service.

PFE

NOW LOOK INSIDE AND SEE HOW **DOUBLE-FAST ICING** WORKS!

PFE issued a great many tri-fold brochures to customers, on a wide variety of subjects. A few examples are here. CSRM collection.

NEW FEATURES

★ **CONVERTIBLE BUNKERS** provide 39-foot loading space in the car when bunkers are in retracted position. (See photograph.)

★ **HALF STAGE ICING GRATES**, hinged for easy handling, reduce capacity for ice to about 5,600 lbs.—as against full bunkers of 11,600 lbs.—thus helping the industry effect economies during cooler months.

★ **SIDE WALL FLUES**, a new feature conceived by the trade to break direct contact between the car walls and the load.

★ **IMPROVED AIR CIRCULATING FANS** step up circulation of air within the car, maintaining more uniform temperature throughout. This feature benefits both refrigeration and heater service.

★ **DIAGONAL FLOOR RACKS**, like sergeant's stripes, provide more bearing surface for all types of lading, without impairing circulation of air.

★ **EASY RIDING HIGH SPEED TRUCKS** reduce breakage and settling of loads.

★ **LIGHT WEIGHT STEEL**, used throughout, provides an estimated weight saving in excess of 4,000 lbs. per car.

★ **INCREASED INSULATION** of an additional inch all around, gives these new cars four inches in the side walls and ends, and four and one-half inches in roofs and floors.

★ **STANDARD DIMENSIONS** of 33' 2½" length, 8' 3" width and 7' 3" height above floor racks have been maintained, in conformity with Trade Committee recommendations.

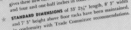

Out in front again – with 3000 more NEW REFRIGERATOR CARS

PFE

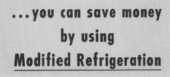

...you can save money by using Modified Refrigeration

UNDER SUITABLE CONDITIONS AND AT THE PROPER TIME OF YEAR

Since the war, refrigerator car lines of the United States have placed in service more than 25,000 new or rebuilt cars equipped with air circulating devices, thicker insulation, and half-stage ice grates.

Pacific Fruit Express Company leads the field with more than 13,000 of these new cars. For that reason we are anxious to see our patrons benefit by these improvements, which were made at a cost of millions of dollars.

FULL BUNKER ICING   HALF STAGE ICING

PFE

PACIFIC FRUIT EXPRESS COMPANY

Are you wasting money on excess refrigeration?

DURING SUMMER MONTHS...
Maximum refrigeration is essential for safe transportation of highly perishable commodities.

BUT IN FALL, WINTER AND SPRING...
Worthwhile savings often can be made through use of "modified" refrigeration service, plus good judgment on the part of the shipper.

LOOK INSIDE FOR MONEY SAVING EXAMPLES ▶

PFE

PACIFIC FRUIT EXPRESS COMPANY

...outhern Pacific and Union Pacific

With traditional faith in the future have again taken the lead in authorizing P.F.E. to purchase 3,000 new refrigerator cars (25 miles of 'em). This brings to 10,000 the number of new refrigerator cars purchased since 1941.

...RVICE has always been the constant aim of ... With these 3000 new cars greater protection is as-... for all of its patrons.

...ADERSHIP of the P.F.E. in the refriger-...car field has long been recognized, and rightfully so! ...ating approximately 40,000 cars and serving the most ...tive areas in the United States, it has established a ...ation for service and accomplishment that is unex-...anywhere in this country.

...COMPLISHMENTS—In spite ...erial shortages that began to develop as early as 1941 ...hich grew progressively worse during and after the ...E. was successful in purchasing:

1000 new cars in 1941	
1000 new cars in 1945	
5000 new cars in 1947*	
7000 Total	

...hese were delivered in 1947 but a few will carry over into the first ...f 1948.

...000 new cars now authorized will swell the total ...ses, 1941 to date, to—

10,000 new cars.

... is proud of that record!

PFE   **UNION PACIFIC**

IN ADDITION—Since 1941 P.F.E. has rebuilt at its shops over 9300 cars (these cars all have brand new superstructures) and in 1948 another 2500 cars will be rebuilt which will bring the total up to 11,800 cars for the eight year period.

This is also an outstanding accomplishment!

MORE OF EVERYTHING

Sounds like bragging! And perhaps it is! But again, P.F.E. is proud of its position in the carline field, for it has:

More refrigerator cars than any other carline agency in the world—close to 40,000 of them.

More cars equipped with air-circulating fans.

More cars equipped with convertible ice bunkers.

More cars with half-stage icing grates. An economy feature for the Trade.

More cars with sidewall flues. Valuable in breaking contact between the lading and the outer car walls.

More cars with diagonal floor racks. A good bearing surface for all types of lading.

More icing plants—19 of them.

More ice transfer platforms—20 miles of them.

More car heaters—both alcohol and charcoal—some of which are thermostatically controlled.

Do You Wonder that We Brag a Bit?

KEEP 'EM FRESH!

CALL

PACIFIC FRUIT EXPRESS

For further information on the availability and use of this versatile equipment, contact your nearest PFE, Southern Pacific or Union Pacific representative.

PFE

UNION PACIFIC–SOUTHERN PACIFIC

BIG NEWS FOR

WESTERN

GROWERS & SHIPPERS!

COMING INTO SERVICE

🤠 2,000 MORE BIG 70-TON CUSHION-UNDERFRAME MECHANICAL "REEFERS"

🤠 1000 MORE PIGGYBACK TRAILERS

FOR EASTBOUND LOADS OF FRESH OR FROZEN PERISHABLES

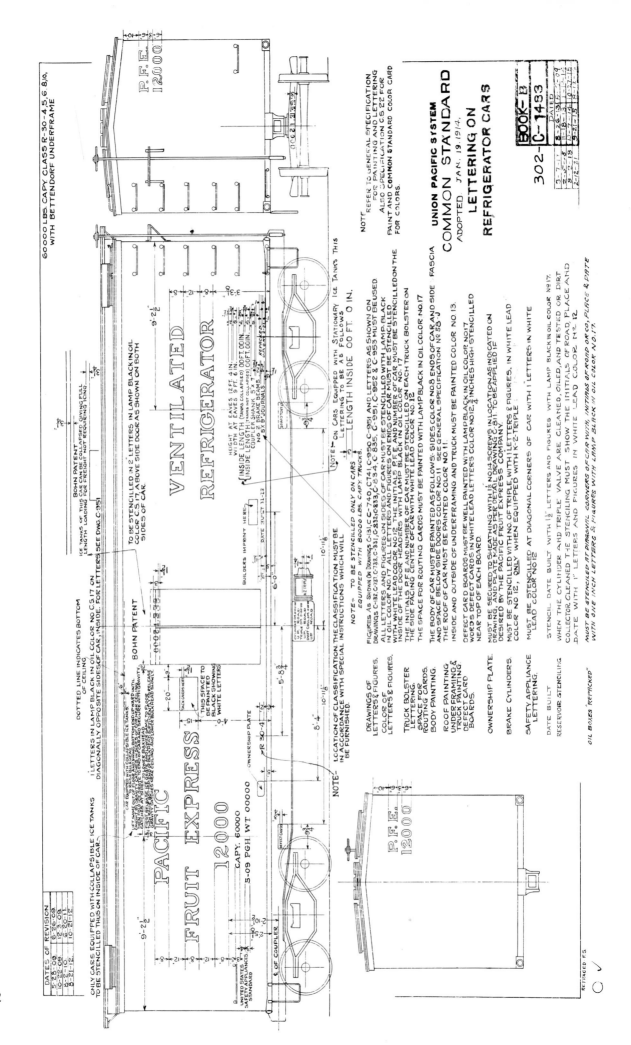

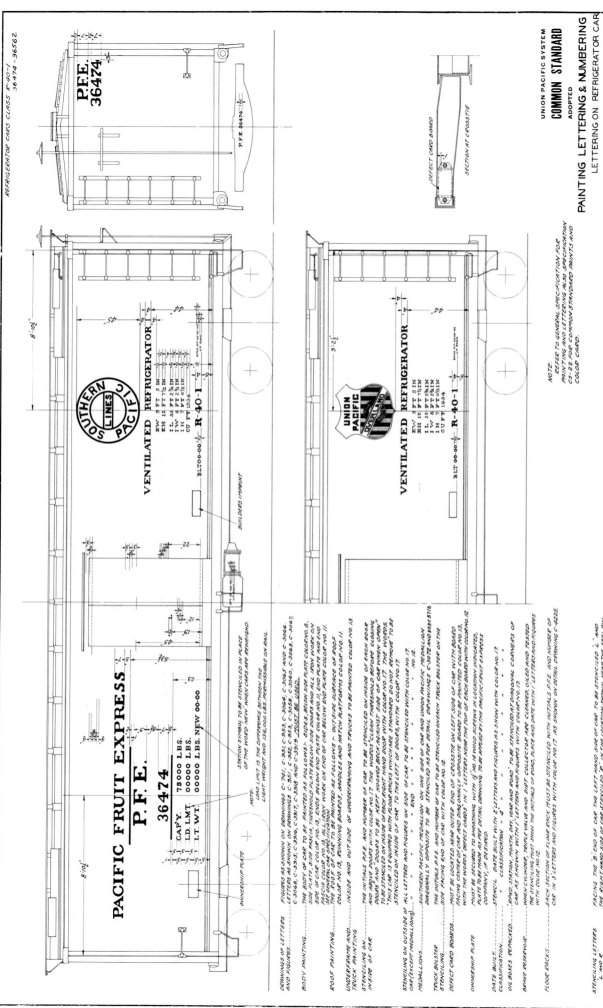

UNION PACIFIC SYSTEM
COMMON STANDARD
ADOPTED

PAINTING LETTERING & NUMBERING
LETTERING ON REFRIGERATOR CAR

303 C-4228

	DATED	
	4-2-27	
	12-6-27	
	10-20-32	
	12-12-35	

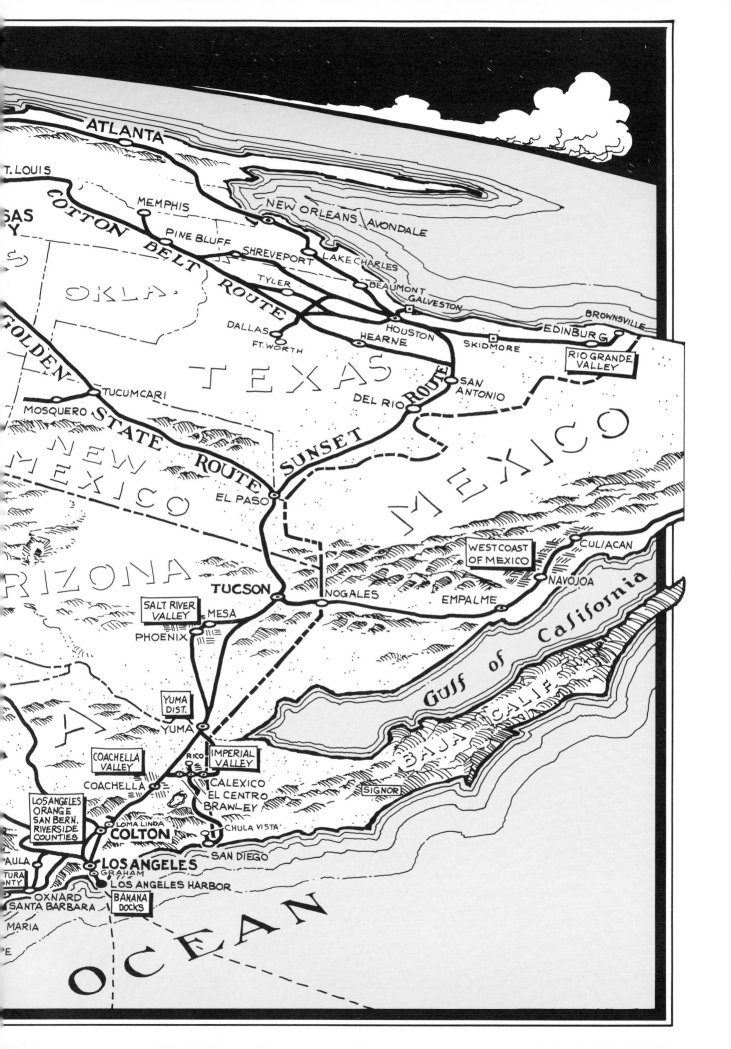

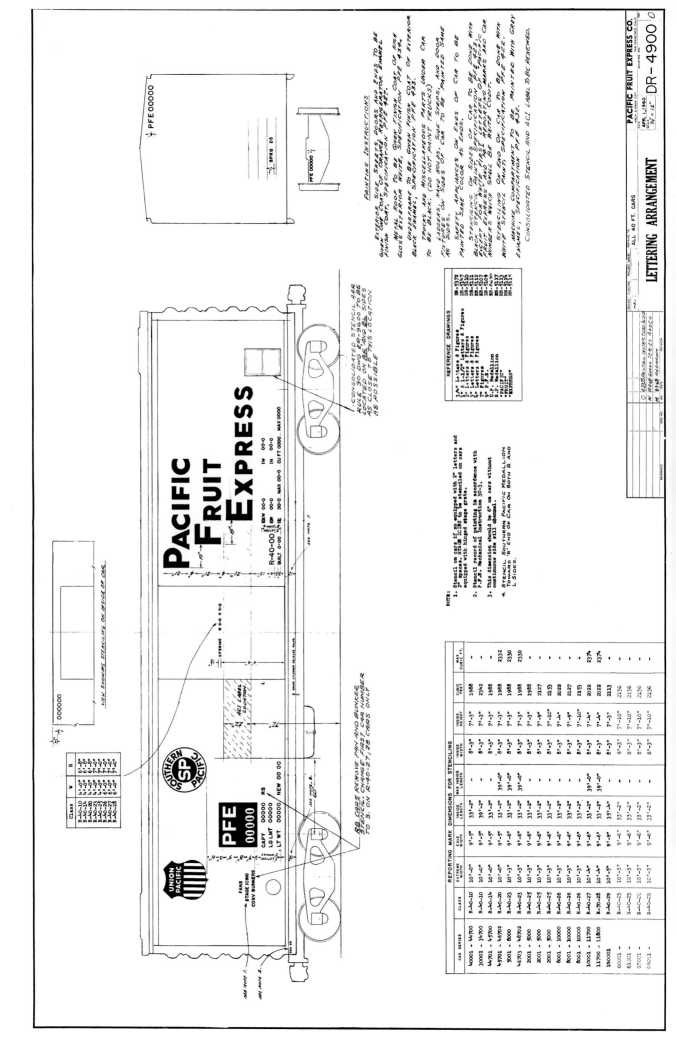

PACIFIC FRUIT EXPRESS

SHIPPING DISTRICTS AND PRINCIPAL ROUTES

⊙ PFE OWNED FACILITY
○ PFE CONTRACTED SERVICE
▣ PFE FACILITY OBSOLETE BY 1952
★ NATURAL ICE PRODUCTION

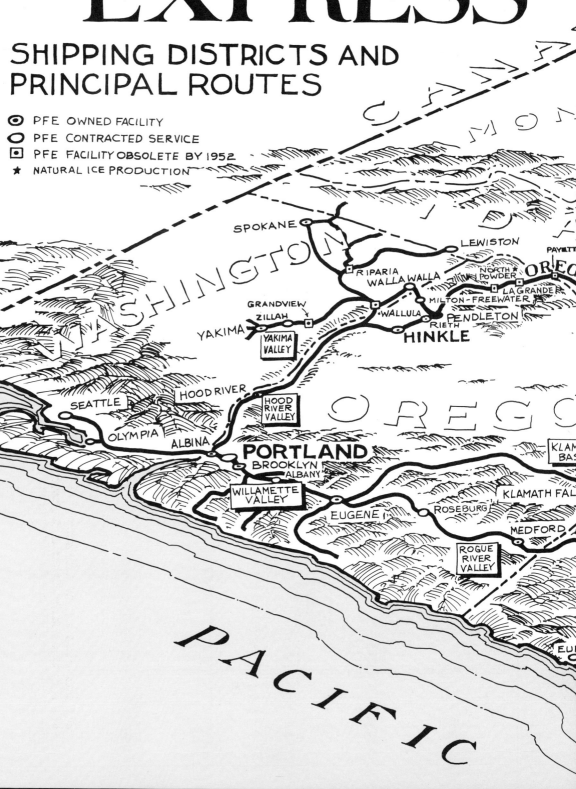

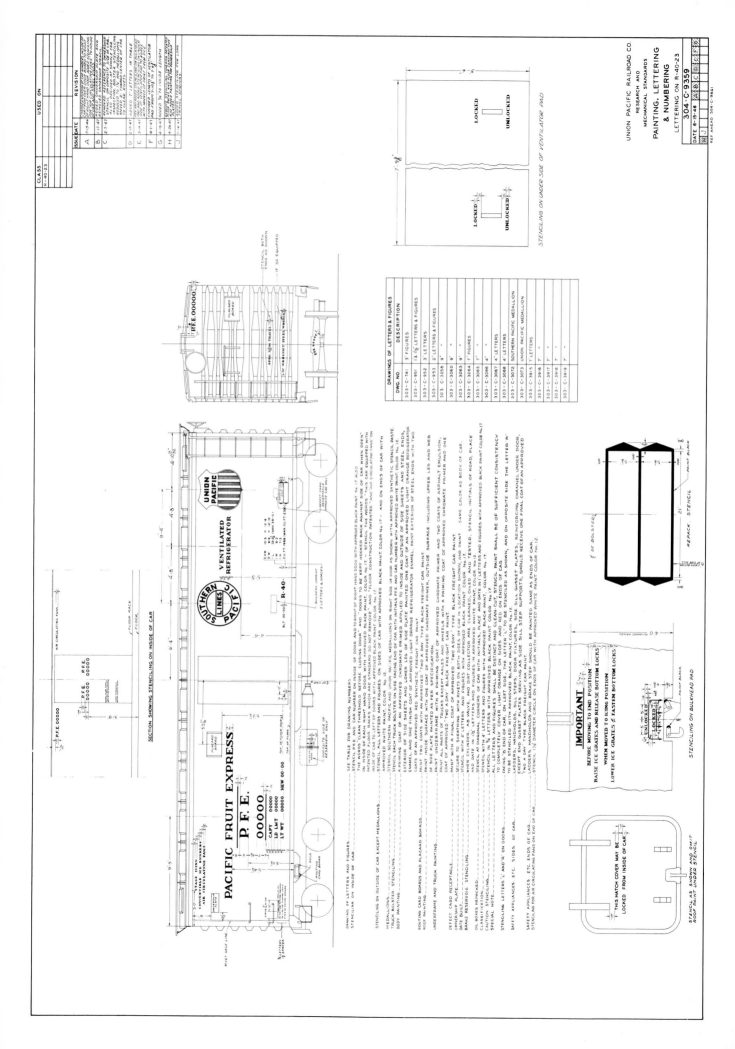

Union Pacific's largest steam power operated out of Cheyenne. In this view , Big Boy No. 4020 gets a PFE train underway in 1954. *Railroad and Railfan* collection.

Tabular Material

On this and the following pages are several perspectives on the PFE car fleet. On the following two pages (pages 434,435) are listed car specialties, taken from available PFE tabular material at CSRM. These convenient listings merely summarize the original specification packages for car orders (as listed on page 417).

The specialty listing here is not complete, as a great many additional purchased items were specified, including such items as journal bearings, brake beam supports, draft gear, ice tank screens, journal box lids, insulation, truck springs, and wheels. These were thought to be of less interest and were not tabulated here.

Nearly every purchased specialty item also specified the applicable PFE part drawing. One example is given here, for truck side frames, to help illustrate how constancy in part designs, regardless of vendor, can be traced by reference to these drawing numbers.

The period covered in this listing was that of the PFE document, namely 1920 until 1941. Similar information for cars built prior to 1920 and after 1941 can be found in the specification packages at CSRM and at the Union Pacific Railroad Museum. Rebuilt cars, which were modified in company shops, did not have specialty lists issued.

Next are examples of PFE car cards, Form 120 (pages 435, 436) and, on page 437, a typical page from the *Official Railway Equipment Register* (or ORER, as it is often called), in this case for 1929, to illustrate the way in which information was provided monthly (until 1932, and quarterly since then) about the car groups. Various car dimensions are given to the nearest sixteenth of an inch.

A more convenient summary of car dimensions for a wide range of the wood and steel ice cars is included on the following pages (pages 438 and 439), with values rounded to the nearest inch. This will provide a sufficient insight into most aspects of car size. Following those tables is a timeline for the wood cars as they were scrapped or rebuilt into other classes over time, a useful way of viewing the evolution of the wood-car fleet in a single graphic (pages 440 and 441).

The car size tables and timeline are provided courtesy of Dick Harley, whom we thank for making these tables available.

Following the car data are several pages of information about perishable crops grown in regions throughout the territories of Southern Pacific, giving the peak months (shown in black) and secondary months (shown in gray) of shipping for each crop in each district (pages 442 through 447). These were provided by Greg Henschen from an original SP document .

Also on page 447 are two examples of Southern Pacific perishable train schedules, originating on the Coast Route in California, taken from the 1963 SP book entitled *Through Manifest, Merchandise and Perishable Freight Schedules Between Principal Points*, and on page 448 are a number of PFE schedules from 1943, likewise taken from SP documents. These furnish only a snapshot of a large number of both UP and SP schedules for these essential trains over the years.

The appendix concludes with a variety of perishable loading data reproduced directly from the original typewritten PFE documents, on pages 449 and 450.

PACIFIC FRUIT EXPRESS COMPANY
CAR SPECIALTIES

Car Class	Numbers	Order No.	Roof	Underframe	Trucks, Drawing No.	Coupler Release
R-30-12	15920-18919	5591	X.L.A. Flexible, SRECo*	Bettendorf	Vulcan, C-2820	Carmer, UMPCo*
R-30-13	18920-19919	5591	X.L.A. Flexible, SRECo	R.R. design	Vulcan, C-2820	Carmer, UMPCo
R-30-12	19920-21569	P-328	Murphy Type A, SRECo	Bettendorf	Bettendorf, C-1507	Carmer, UMPCo
"	21570-22519	P-328	Murphy Type A, SRECo	Bettendorf	ASF, C-2821	Carmer, UMPCo
"	22520-23219	P-329	Murphy Type A, SRECo	Bettendorf	ASF, C-1507 & C-2821	Carmer, UMPCo
"	23220-24719	5627-9	Chicago-Cleveland*	Bettendorf	ASF, C-1507 & C-2821	UMPCo
"	24720-25719	5627-3	Interchangeable Type A, SRECo	Bettendorf	Bettendorf, C-1507, -2821	UMPCo
"	25720-26219	5627-5	Chicago-Cleveland	Bettendorf	ASF, C-1507 & C-2821	UMPCo
"	26220-26719	5627-7	SRECo	Bettendorf	ASF, C-1507 & C-2821	UMPCo
R-30-13	26720-27219	5627-7	SRECo	R.R. design	ASF, C-1507 & C-2821	UMPCo
"	27220-28249	5627-6	SRECo	R.R. design	Bettendorf, C-1507, -2821	UMPCo
R-30-12	28250-28749	P-347	Type A, SRECo	Bettendorf	Bettendorf, C-2821, -3303	Carmer, UMPCo
R-30-13	28750-29649	P-348	Interchangeable Type A, SRECo	R.R. design	Bettendorf, C-2821, -3303	Carmer, UMPCo
R-30-12	29650-30449	P-349	Interchangeable Type A, SRECo	Bettendorf	ASF, C-2821 & C-3303	Carmer, UMPCo
"	30450-31249	P-350	Interchangeable Type A, SRECo	Bettendorf	ASF, C-2821 & C-3303	Carmer, UMPCo
R-30-13	31250-31306	P-348	Interchangeable Type A, SRECo	R.R. design	Bettendorf, C-2821, -3303	Carmer, UMPCo
"	31307-31434	5669-6	Murphy Type A Flexible, SRECo	R.R. design	Bettendorf, C-2821, -3303	Carmer, UMPCo
"	31435-32434	P-358-1	Murphy Type A Flexible, SRECo	R.R. design	Bettendorf, C-2821	Carmer, UMPCo
R-30-14	32435-32934	P-359	National Flexible, Chicago-Cleve.	Bettendorf	Bettendorf, C-2821	Carmer, UMPCo
"	32935-33434	P-359	Murphy Type A Flexible, SRECo	Bettendorf	Bettendorf, C-2821	Carmer, UMPCo
R-30-13	33435-34434	P-360	National Flexible, Chicago-Cleve.	R.R. design	Columbia Steel, C-3344	Carmer, UMPCo
"	34435-35473	P-361, 361A	Murphy Type A, SRECo	R.R. design	ASF, C-3344	Carmer, UMPCo
"	35474-36473	P-362	National Flexible, Chicago-Cleve.	R.R. design	ASF, C-3344	Carmer, UMPCo

Foregoing cars all had wood ends, Miner door hardware, New York air brakes, and NM&SC* vertical-staff handbrakes; all coupler release rigging was from UMPCo (type shown where specified). (See Table 5-2, page 90, for other details.)

Car Class	Numbers	Order No.	Roof	Underframe	Trucks, Drawing No.	Hand brakes
R-E-1	500-799	5631	metal	built up	Commonwealth Steel	Miner lever
R-40-1	36474-36562	5701	Murphy Improved Pivoted, SRECo	ARA	Columbia Steel, C-4302	NM&SC vertical
R-40-2	36563-37062	P-369	National, Chicago-Cleveland	R.R. design	ASF, C-4302	NM&SC vertical
"	37063-37562	P-369	National, Chicago-Cleveland	R.R. design	Bettendorf, C-4302	NM&SC vertical
"	37563-38562	P-370	Murphy Type A, SRECo	R.R. design	Columbia Steel, C-4302	URECo*
R-40-4	38563-38812	PFE	National Flexible, Chicago-Cleve.	R.R. design	U.S. Steel Prod., C-5065	Ajax
"	38813-39062	PFE	Murphy Improved Pivoted, SRECo	R.R. design	U.S. Steel Prod., C-5065	Univ.* One-hand
R-50-1	100001-100200	5759-6	Murphy, SRECo	built up	Columbia Steel, C-4942	URECo
	100201-100400	5759-6	National, Chicago-Cleveland	built up	Columbia Steel, C-4942	URECo
R-70-2	200001-200100	PFE	Murphy Solid Steel, SRECo	R.R. design	Columbia Steel, C-5402	Univ. One-hand

Classes R-40-1, R-40-2, and R-50-1 received metal medallions from General Porcelain Enameling Co.; R-40-4 and R-70-2 from California Metal Enameling. All cars had Miner door hardware, New York air brakes, UMPCo coupler release rigging, and wood ends, except R-70-2: steel Dreadnaught ends, UMPCo. (See Table 5-2, page 90, and Table 6-1, page 111, for other details.)

*Abbreviations: ASF = American Steel Foundries; Chicago-Cleveland = Chicago-Cleveland Car Roofing Co.; NM&SC = National Malleable & Steel Castings Co.; SRECo = Standard Railway Equipment Co.; UMPCo = Union Metal Products Co.; URECo = Union Railway Equipment Co.; Univ. = Universal Draft Gear Attachment Co.

Car Class	Numbers	Order No.	Roof	Ends	Underframe	Trucks, Drawing No.	Hand brakes
R-40-10	40001-40400	P-382	Murphy Solid Steel, SRECo	UMPCo	AAR built-up	Columbia Steel, C-5885	Ajax
"	40401-40700	P-383	Murphy Solid Steel, SRECo	UMPCo	AAR built-up	Columbia Steel, C-5885	Ajax
"	40701-41200	P-378	Solid steel, Chicago-Hutchins	UMPCo	AAR built-up	Columbia Steel, C-5885	Universal
"	41201-41400	P-381	Solid steel, SRECo	UMPCo	AAR built-up	ASF Barber, C-5888	Miner
"	41401-41700	P-381	Solid steel, SRECo	UMPCo	AAR built-up	ASF, C-5885	Ajax
"	41701-41900	P-379	Solid steel, SRECo	UMPCo	AAR built-up	Type B, NM&SC, C-5890	Miner
"	41901-42200	P-379	Solid steel, SRECo	UMPCo	AAR built-up	ASF, C-5885	URECo
"	42201-42700	P-380	Solid steel, SRECo	UMPCo	AAR built-up	Bettendorf, C-5885	Equipco
"	42701-43200	NC-305	Solid steel, SRECo	UMPCo	AAR built-up	Columbia Steel, C-5885	Universal
"	43201-43400	NC-304	Solid steel, SRECo	UMPCo	AAR built-up	Type B, NM&SC, C-5890	URECo
"	43401-43700	NC-304	Solid steel, SRECo	UMPCo	AAR built-up	ASF, C-5885	URECo
"	43701-44200	NC-302	Solid steel, Chicago-Hutchins	UMPCo	AAR built-up	Bettendorf, C-5885	Equipco
"	44201-44400	NC-303	Solid steel, Chicago-Hutchins	UMPCo	AAR built-up	ASF Barber, C-5888	Miner
"	44441-44700	NC-303	Solid steel, Chicago-Hutchins	UMPCo	AAR built-up	ASF, C-5885	Miner
R-40-14	44701-45200	NC-101	Solid steel, SRECo	SRECo	AAR built-up	Col. Steel Barber, C-8176	Klasing
"	44201-45700	NC-101	Solid steel, SRECo	SRECo	AAR built-up	Col. Steel Barber, C-8176	Equipco
R-70-3, -4	200101-200125	—	Solid steel, SRECo	SRECo	PFE design	Columbia Steel, C-7026	Equipco

Foregoing cars all had Miner or Universal door hardware, New York air brakes, and geared handbrakes; all coupler release rigging was from UMPCo (all R-40-10 cars) or SRECo. (See Table 8-1, page 163, for other details.)

Car (PFE Form 120 or 78-1), recorded all significant work done in the shops on each car (see page 249). Shown here are a few examples from the collection at CSRM. First, upper left below, is 51797, a WP car "returned for disposition" in 1951, but selected for reconditioning in 1953, at which time it became PFE 55124. At upper right is the card for 38756, an R-40-4 built by PFE and illustrating a somewhat different car card format. At lower left is R-40-10 41250, while at lower right is 300401, an R-70-5. This car is interesting, because it was built as an ice

car, numbered 200189, converted to mechanical in 1956, and eventually given meat rails in 1968 and renumbered to 200401.

On the next page at full size are both sides of the card for 1918-built PFE 14762, showing not only its repair history and the mix of handwritten and stamped notations, but recording repaints in 1923 (when SP and UP medallions were added), 1927, 1929 (metal medallions), 1931 (rebuilding and orange paint), 1939, 1949, 1952, and 1957, before being destroyed in a wreck at Yuma on July 6, 1964–more than 46 years of service.

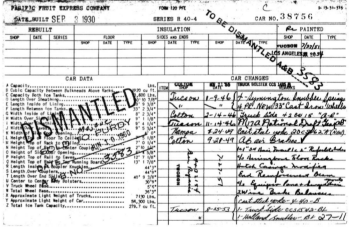

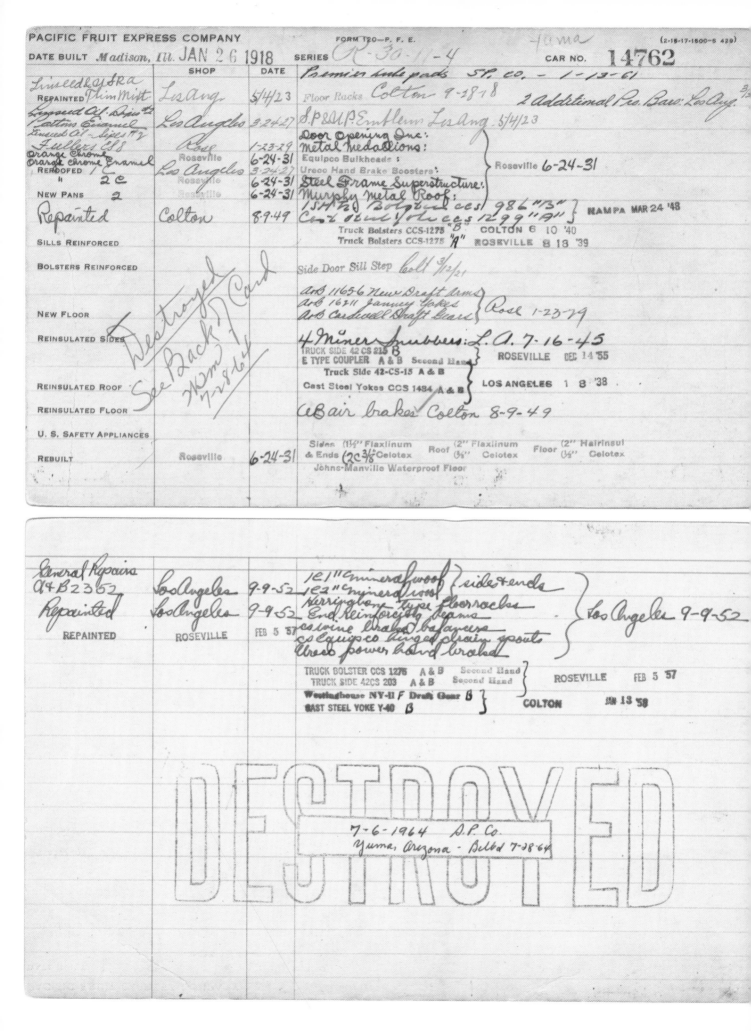

PACIFIC FRUIT EXPRESS COMPANY FORM 120—P. F. E. ~Yuma (2-15-17-1500-S 429)

DATE BUILT *Madison, Ill.* JAN 26 1918 SERIES R-30-11-4 CAR NO. 14762

	SHOP	DATE	
Linseed & SRA			*Premier lube pads SP. Co. — 1-13-61*
REPAINTED *Thin Mist*	*Los Ang*	5/4/23	Floor Racks *Colton 9-28-18* *2 Additional Pro. Bars. Los Ang.*
Linseed Oil Disc'd			
Pattons Enamel	*Los Angeles*	3-24-27	*S.P.& U.P. Emblem Los Ang. 5/4/23*
Linseed Oil — Sizes #2			Door Opening Inc':
Fullers ELS	*Rose*	1-23-29	Metal Medallions:
Orange Chrome	*Roseville*	6-24-31	Equipco Bulkheads :
Orange chrome Enamel	*Los Angeles*	3-24-27	Ureco Hand Brake Boosters': } *Roseville 6-24-31*
REROOFED 1	*Roseville*	6-24-31	Steel Frame Superstructure:
2 C			
NEW PANS 2	*Roseville*	6-24-31	Murphy Metal Roof:
			1514 #2 Bolsted ccs 986 "B" } NAMPA MAR 24 '48
Repainted	Colton	8-9-49	*Cast steel Yoke ccs 12-99 "A"*
			Truck Bolsters CCS-1275 "B" COLTON 6 10 '40
SILLS REINFORCED			Truck Bolsters CCS-1275 "A" ROSEVILLE 8 18 '39
BOLSTERS REINFORCED			Side Door Sill Step *Colt 3/12/21*
NEW FLOOR			A&B 11656 New Draft Arms
			A&B 16711 Janney Yokes } *Rose 1-23-29*
			A&B Cardwell Draft Gears
REINSULATED SIDES			4 Miner Snubbers: L.A. 7-16-45
			TRUCK SIDE 42 CS 215 "B"
			E TYPE COUPLER A & B Second Hand ROSEVILLE DEC 14 '55
			Truck Side 42-CS-15 A & B
REINSULATED ROOF			Cast Steel Yokes CCS 1484 A & B LOS ANGELES 1 8 '38
REINSULATED FLOOR			Air brakes Colton 8-9-49
U. S. SAFETY APPLIANCES			
			Sides (1½" Flaxlinum Roof (2" Flaxlinum Floor (2" Hairinsul
REBUILT	Roseville	6-24-31	& Ends (2C 3/8 Celotex (½" Celotex (½" Celotex
			Johns-Manville Waterproof Floor

Destroyed See Back of Card WM 7-28-64

	SHOP	DATE	
General Repairs A&B 2352	*Los Angeles*	9-9-52	*1C 1" Mineral wool } side + ends*
			1C 2" Mineral wool
Repainted	*Los Angeles*	9-9-52	*Herringbone type floor racks*
			End Reinforcing beams
REPAINTED	ROSEVILLE	FEB 5 '57	*C S Ajine brake balancers* } *Los Angeles 9-9-52*
			C S Equipco hinged drain spouts
			Ureco power hand brakes
			TRUCK BOLSTER CCS 1275 A & B Second Hand } ROSEVILLE FEB 5 '57
			TRUCK SIDE 42CS 203 A & B Second Hand
			Westinghouse NY-11 F Draft Gear B } COLTON JAN 13 '58
			CAST STEEL YOKE Y-40 B

DESTROYED

7-6-1964 A.P. Co.
Yuma, Arizona - Bclld 7-28-64

PACIFIC FRUIT EXPRESS COMPANY.

GENERAL OFFICES,
65 MARKET STREET, SAN FRANCISCO, CAL.
CHICAGO OFFICE, 58 E. WASHINGTON STREET.

H. GIDDINGS, Vice-President and General Manager....San Francisco, Cal.
R. G. HERDA, Assistant to Vice-President and General Manager.... "
J. B. CRAWFORD, Assistant General Manager....Chicago, Ill.
R. J. MARTIN, Assistant General Manager....San Francisco, Cal.
H. T. WHYTE, Assistant General Manager (Engineering and Refrigeration).... "
L. L. YATES, Gen. Superintendent Car Department.... "
C. H. WESTON, Auditor.... "
C. E. CARNER, Traffic Manager....Chicago, Ill.
A. J. MELLO, Purchasing Agent....San Francisco, Cal.
J. J. COWEN, Assistant Traffic Manager.... "
R. B. HOFFMAN, Superintendent Transportation....Chicago, Ill.

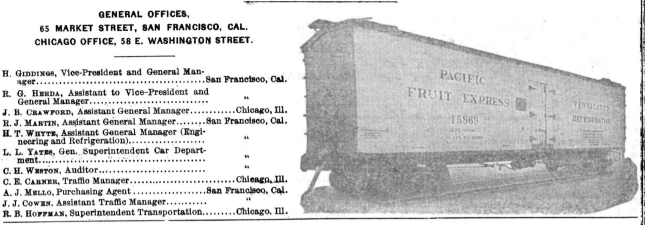

REFRIGERATOR EQUIPMENT.

The refrigerator cars of this Company are numbered and classified as follows:

M. C. B. Designation.	Markings and Kind of Cars.	Numbers.	Dimensions: Inside: Length: Between Ice Tanks—Bulkheads in Place. ft. in.	Inside: Length: Between Linings Clear (Bulkheads Collapsed). ft. in.	Inside: Width, Inside. ft. in.	Inside: Height, Inside. ft. in.	Outside: Length. ft. in.	Outside: Width at Eaves. ft. in.	Outside: Extreme Width. ft. in.	Outside: Height from Rail: To Extreme Width. ft. in.	Height from Rail: To Eaves. ft. in.	Height from Rail: To Top of Running Board. ft. in.	Height from Rail: To Extreme Height. ft. in.	Doors: Side Doors: Width. ft. in.	Side Doors: Height. ft. in.	Capacity: Capacity of Ice Tanks: Pounds: Total Capacity for Crushed Ice. lbs.	Total Capacity for Chunk Ice. lbs.	Measure of Capacity: Cubic Feet.	Measure of Capacity: Depth. ft. in.	Capacity of Car: Cubic Feet Level Full: Between Ice Boxes—Bulkheads in Place.	Clear Capacity (Bulkheads Collapsed).	Pounds.	Number of Cars.
	PASSENGER.																						
BR..	A. R. E. Refrigerator, Passenger equipped, in the service of, leased to, and controlled by American Railway Express Notes B, D, E	500 to 799	41 6½	....	8 8¼	Note AA. 7 1⅝	50 ...	10 0⅞	....	....	12 4¾	13 10	13 10	5 ...	6 0½	13080	12000	325.5	....	2586	....	63000	298
	Total Passenger Refrigerators...		....	....	....	....	....	....	....	....	....	....	....	....	....	....	....	....	....	....	....	....	298
	FREIGHT. REFRIGERATOR.																						
RS..	P. F. E. Ventilated..Notes B, E	1 to 6600	33 2¼	....	8 2¼	7 7 1/16	41 10	9 4¾	....	....	12 3⅛	12 11 13/16	13 7¼	4 ...	5 9¾	11550	10600	279.7	....	1964	....	50000	5544
RS..	" Notes B, C, E	" "	"	....	"	"	"	"	....	....	"	"	"	"	"	11990	11000	292.9	....	"	....	"	152
RB..	Beer and Ice, Notes A, B, E	" "	....	39 8¼	"	"	"	"	....	....	"	"	"	"	"	....	....	....	....	....	2478	"	27
RS..	Ventilated. Notes B, E	6601 to 7100	33 2¼	....	8 2¼	7 5 3/16	40 9⅝	9 6	....	....	12 3 11/16	13 0⅛	13 8¼	4 ...	5 9¾	11550	10600	279.7	....	1921	....	49200	474
RS..	" ..Notes B, E	7101 to 10121	33 2¼	....	8 2¼	7 5 3/16	40 9⅝	9 6	....	....	12 3 11/16	13 0⅛	13 8¼	4 ...	5 9¾	11550	10600	279.7	....	1921	2807	49500	2540
RS..	" Notes B, C②E	" "	"	39 4¼	"	"	"	"	....	....	"	"	"	"	"	11990	11000	293	....	"	"	"	295
RS..	" ..Notes B, E	10122 to 13219	33 4¼	....	8 2¼	7 5 3/16	40 9⅝	9 6	....	....	12 3 11/16	13 0½	13 8¼	4 ...	5 9¾	11550	10600	279.7	....	1928	2807	50200	2939
RS..	" Notes B, C④E	" "	"	39 4¼	"	"	"	"	....	....	"	"	"	"	"	11990	11000	296	....	"	"	"	8
RS..	" ..Notes B, E	13220 to 13279	33 2¼	....	8 2¼	7 5 5/16	40 9⅝	9 6	....	....	12 3 11/16	13 0⅛	13 10	4 ...	5 9¾	11550	10600	280.6	....	1924	....	50800	59
RS..	" ..Notes B, E	13280 to 15919	33 2¼	....	8 2¼	7 5 5/16	40 9⅝	9 6	....	....	12 3 11/16	13 0⅛	13 10	4 ...	5 9¾	11550	10600	280.6	....	1924	....	66000	2599
RS..	" ..Notes B, E	15920 to 18919	33 2¼	....	8 2¼	7 5 1/16	40 9⅝	9 4⅛	....	....	12 3⅞	13 1 13/16	13 10	4 ...	6 4½	11550	10600	279.7	....	1918	....	66000	2969
RS..	" ..Notes B, E	18920 to 19919	33 2¼	....	8 2¼	7 5 1/16	40 9⅝	9 4⅛	....	....	12 3⅞	13 1 13/16	13 10	4 ...	6 4½	11550	10600	279.7	....	1918	....	70000	988
RS..	" ..Notes B, E	19920 to 26719	33 2¼	....	8 2¼	7 5 1/16	40 9⅝	9 4⅛	....	....	12 3⅞	13 1 13/16	13 10	4 ...	6 4½	11550	10600	279.7	....	1918	....	66000	6758
RS..	" ..Notes B, E	26720 to 28249	33 2¼	....	8 2¼	7 5 1/16	40 9⅝	9 4⅛	....	....	12 3⅞	13 1 13/16	13 10	4 ...	6 4½	11550	10600	279.7	....	1918	....	70000	1523
RS..	" ..Notes B, E	28250 to 28749	33 2¼	....	8 2¼	7 5 1/16	40 9⅝	9 4⅛	....	....	12 3⅞	13 1 13/16	13 10	4 ...	6 4½	11550	10600	279.7	....	1918	....	66000	499
RS..	" ..Notes B, E	28750 to 29649	33 2¼	....	8 2¼	7 5 1/16	40 9⅝	9 4⅛	....	....	12 3⅞	13 1 13/16	13 10	4 ...	6 4½	11550	10600	279.7	....	1918	....	70000	897
RS..	" ..Notes B, E	29650 to 31249	33 2¼	....	8 2¼	7 5 1/16	40 9⅝	9 4⅛	....	....	12 3⅞	13 1 13/16	13 10	4 ...	6 4½	11550	10600	279.7	....	1918	....	66000	1592
RS..	" ..Notes B, E	31250 to 36473	33 2¼	....	8 2¼	7 5 1/16	40 9⅝	9 4⅛	....	....	12 3⅞	13 1 13/16	13 10	4 ...	6 4½	11550	10600	279.7	....	1918	....	70000	5211
RS..	" ..Notes B, E	36474 to 36562	33 2¼	....	8 2¼	7 5¾	41 1½	9 5½	....	....	12 7¼	13 4	14 1½	5 ...	6 5	11550	10600	279.7	....	1918	....	79300	89
RS..	" ..Notes B, E	36563 to 38562	33 2¼	....	8 2¼	7 5 1/16	40 9⅝	9 4⅛	....	....	12 7¼	13 1 13/16	13 10	4 ...	6 4½	11550	10600	279.7	....	1918	....	80000	1999
RS..	" ..Notes B, E	50001 to 52775	33 2¼	....	8 2¼	7 5 1/16	40 9⅝	9 4⅛	....	....	12 3⅞	13 1 13/16	13 10	4 ...	6 4⅝	11550	10600	279.6	....	1918	....	70000	2760
RS..	" ..Notes B, E	70001 to 71000	33 2¼	....	8 2¼	7 5 1/16	40 9⅝	9 4⅛	....	....	12 7¼	13 1 13/16	13 10	4 ...	6 4½	11550	10600	279.7	....	1918	....	80000	293
	Total Freight Refrigerators....		....	....	....	....	....	....	....	....	....	....	....	....	....	....	....	....	....	....	....	....	40215

Note AA—"Height inside" is figured from top of floor to bottom of ceiling line and does not take into consideration the height of the floor racks. which in both our passenger and freight refrigerator cars is 4⅞ inches.

▲ Denotes additions. ◆ Denotes increase. ⬇ Denotes reduction. (See Page xviii.)

PACIFIC FRUIT EXPRESS
Selected O.R.E.R. Dimensions
Ventilated Reefer Database
40 ft. Wood Cars (1936-1970)

PFE Class	Period	No. Built	Numbers	In Length	In Width	In Height	Out Length	Eave Width	Extr Width	Hgt to EW	Hgt Eave	Hgt Top RB	Door Width	Door Heigh	Capy CuFt	Capy Lb	Dimen Date
R-30-2-13	1925-1941	(~200)	1 - 499	33 - 3 -	8 - 3 -	7 - 2	41 - 10	9 - 5	9 - 11-	3 - 5	12 - 3+	13 - 0-	4 - 0	5 - 10-	1,964	50,000	1942
R-30-2-13	1925-1941	(~2,300)	800 - 6900	33 - 3 -	8 - 3 -	7 - 2	41 - 10	9 - 5	9 - 11-	3 - 5	12 - 3+	13 - 0-	4 - 0	5 - 10-	1,964	50,000	1942
R-30-4	1909-1938	500	6601 - 7100	33 - 3 -	8 - 3 -	7 - 0	42 - 2	9 - 6	9 - 11+	3 - 5-	12 - 4	13 - 0+	4 - 0	5 - 10-	1,921	50,000	1940
R-30-5	1909-1938	3,021	7101 - 10121	33 - 3 -	8 - 3 -	7 - 0	42 - 2	9 - 6	9 - 11+	3 - 7	12 - 4	13 - 0+	4 - 0	5 - 10-	1,921	50,000	1942
R-30-5	1929-1938	(100)	80001 - 80100	33 - 3 / 39 - 5-	8 - 3 -	7 - 0	42 - 2	9 - 6	9 - 11+	3 - 7	12 - 4	13 - 0+	4 - 0	5 - 10-	1,921 / 2,307	66,000	1942
R-30-6	1912-1938	3,098	10122 - 13219	33 - 3 -	8 - 3 -	7 - 0	42 - 2	9 - 6	9 - 11+	3 - 7	12 - 4	13 - 0+	4 - 0	5 - 10-	1,928	50,300	1942
R-30-11.5(-4)	1917-1958	60	13220 - 13279	33 - 3 -	8 - 3 -	7 - 0	42 - 2	9 - 6	9 - 11+	3 - 5	12 - 4-	13 - 0+	4 - 0	5 - 10-	1,924	66,000	1942
R-30-11(-4)	1917-1958	2,640	13280 - 15919	33 - 3 -	8 - 3 -	7 - 0	42 - 2	9 - 6	9 - 11+	3 - 7	12 - 4-	13 - 0+	4 - 0	5 - 10-	1,924	66,000	1942
R-30-12	1920-1950	3,000	15920 - 18919	33 - 3 -	8 - 3 -	7 - 0	41 - 8+	9 - 4+	9 - 11-	3 - 5	12 - 4	13 - 2-	4 - 0	6 - 4+	1,918	66,000	1942
R-30-12	1922-1950	6,800	19920 - 26719	33 - 3 -	8 - 3 -	7 - 0	41 - 8+	9 - 4+	9 - 11-	3 - 5	12 - 4	13 - 2-	4 - 0	6 - 4+	1,918	66,000	1942
R-30-12	1924-1950	500	28250 - 28749	33 - 3 -	8 - 3 -	7 - 0	41 - 8+	9 - 4+	9 - 11-	3 - 5	12 - 4	13 - 2-	4 - 0	6 - 4+	1,918	66,000	1942
R-30-12	1924-1950	1,600	29650 - 31249	33 - 3 -	8 - 3 -	7 - 0	41 - 8+	9 - 4+	9 - 11-	3 - 5	12 - 4	13 - 2-	4 - 0	6 - 4+	1,918	66,000	1942
R-30-13	1920-1949	1,000	18920 - 19919	33 - 3 -	8 - 3 -	7 - 0	41 - 8+	9 - 4+	9 - 11-	3 - 5	12 - 4	13 - 2-	4 - 0	6 - 4+	1,918	70,000	1942
R-30-13	1923-1949	1,530	26720 - 28249	33 - 3 -	8 - 3 -	7 - 0	41 - 8+	9 - 4+	9 - 11-	3 - 5	12 - 4	13 - 2-	4 - 0	6 - 4+	1,918	70,000	1942
R-30-13	1924-1949	900	28750 - 29649	33 - 3 -	8 - 3 -	7 - 0	41 - 8+	9 - 4+	9 - 11-	3 - 5	12 - 4	13 - 2-	4 - 0	6 - 4+	1,918	70,000	1942
R-30-13&14	1924-1950	5,224	31250 - 36473	33 - 3 -	8 - 3 -	7 - 0	41 - 9+	9 - 4+	9 - 11-	3 - 5	12 - 4	13 - 2-	4 - 0	6 - 4+	1,918	70,000	1942
W.P. (R-30-13)	1923-1941	2,775	50001 - 52775	33 - 3 -	8 - 3 -	7 - 0	41 - 9+	9 - 4+	9 - 11-	3 - 5	12 - 4	13 - 2-	4 - 0	6 - 5-	1,918	70,000	1940
R-40-1	1927-1955	89	36474 - 36562	33 - 3 -	8 - 3 -	7 - 0	42 - 3	9 - 5+	10 - 1+	3 - 4	12 - 7+	13 - 4	5 - 0	6 - 5	1,918	78,200	1942
R-40-2	1928-1949	2,000	36563 - 38562	33 - 3 -	8 - 3 -	7 - 0	41 - 9+	9 - 4+	9 - 11+	3 - 5+	12 - 7+	13 - 2-	4 - 0	6 - 4+	1,918	80,000	1942
R-40-2	1928-1949	(1,443)	70001 - 71585	33 - 3 -	8 - 3 -	7 - 0	41 - 9+	9 - 4+	9 - 11+	3 - 5+	12 - 7+	13 - 2-	4 - 0	6 - 4+	1,918	80,000	1942
R-40-4	1930-1962	500	38563 - 39062	33 - 3 -	8 - 3 -	7 - 0	41 - 9	9 - 6	9 - 11+	3 - 7	12 - 7+	13 - 2-	4 - 0	6 - 4-	1,918	78,500	1942
R-40-4	1929-1962	(510)	71273 - 71953	33 - 3 -	8 - 3 -	7 - 0	41 - 9+	9 - 4+	9 - 11+	3 - 7	12 - 7+	13 - 2-	4 - 0	6 - 4+	1,918	77,800	1942
R-40-6	1935-1960	(50)	80101 - 80150	33 - 4	8 - 3+	7 - 1	41 - 8+	9 - 10-	10 - 3+	3 - 7	12 - 8+	13 - 4+	4 - 0	6 - 3-	1,948	75,200	1942
R-40-8	1935-1961	(400)	90001 - 91021	33 - 3 -	8 - 3 -	7 - 2	41 - 9	9 - 6	9 - 11+	3 - 7	12 - 9+	13 - 4+	4 - 0	6 - 3-	1,974	77,800	1942
R-30-11-8	1935-1960	(521)	90001 - 91021	33 - 3 -	8 - 3 -	7 - 2	41 - 9	9 - 6	9 - 11+	3 - 7	12 - 9+	13 - 4+	4 - 0	6 - 3-	1,974	66,000	1942
R-30/40-9	1938-1960	(5,502)	91022 - 96523	33 - 3 -	8 - 3 -	7 - 3	41 - 8+	9 - 6	9 - 10+	3 - 7-	12 - 9-	13 - 8	4 - 0	6 - 10+	1,988	70,000	1942
R-30/40-9	1940-1960	(2,195)	96524 - 98718	33 - 3 -	8 - 3 -	7 - 3	41 - 8+	9 - 6	9 - 10+	3 - 7-	12 - 9-	13 - 8	4 - 0	6 - 10+	1,988	70,000	1942
R-30/40-9	1942	(5)	95737 - 95741	39 - 0	8 - 3 -	7 - 3	41 - 8+	9 - 6	9 - 10+	3 - 7-	12 - 9-	13 - 8	4 - 0	6 - 10+	2,333	70,000	1942
R-30-9_16	1937-1958	(275)	85001 - 85275	33 - 3 -	8 - 3 -	7 - 3	41 - 8+	9 - 6	9 - 10+	3 - 7-	12 - 9-	13 - 8	4 - 0	6 - 10+	1,988	70,000	1950
R-30-9	1950-1954	(10)	85276 - 85285	33 - 3 -	8 - 3 -	7 - 3	41 - 8+	9 - 6	9 - 10+	3 - 7-	12 - 9-	13 - 8	4 - 0	6 - 10+	1,988	70,000	1950
W.P. (R-30-9)	1938-1952	(~2,660)	50001 - 52775	33 - 3 -	8 - 3 -	7 - 3	41 - 8+	9 - 6	9 - 10+	3 - 7-	12 - 9-	13 - 8	4 - 0	6 - 10+	1,988	70,000	1942
W.P. (R-30-9)	1952-1963	(899)	55001 - 55899	33 - 3 -	8 - 3	7 - 3	41 - 9	9 - 6	9 - 10+	3 - 7	12 - 9	13 - 8	4 - 0	6 - 10+	1,988	70,000	1954
R-30/40-15	1939-1963	(52)	99001 - 99052	37 - 10+	6 - 2-	6 - 6-	41 - 9+	9 - 10-	10 - 3+	3 - 4+	13 - 3-	13 - 8	2 - 8	5 - 3	1,500	70,000	1944 & '54
R-30-12-17	1940-1950	(5)	79995 - 79999	39 - 6+	8 - 3	6 - 4+	41 - 8+	9 - 10-	10 - 2-	3 - 4+	13 - 3-	14 - 0+	4 - 0	6 - 9+	2,132	70,000	1942
R-30/40-16	1940-1964	(3,554)	73001 - 76554	33 - 3 -	8 - 3	7 - 3	41 - 8+	9 - 6	9 - 10+	3 - 7-	12 - 9	13 - 6	4 - 0	6 - 10+	1,988	70,000	1942
R-30/40-18	1942-1951	(2,500)	60001 - 62500	33 - 3 -	8 - 3	7 - 3	41 - 8+	9 - 7+	10 - 0-	3 - 7-	12 - 9-	13 - 8	4 - 0	6 - 10+	1,988	70,000	1942
R-30/40-18	1951-1962	(~2,450)	60001 - 62500	33 - 3 / 39 - 0	8 - 3	7 - 3	41 - 8+	9 - 7+	10 - 0-	3 - 7-	12 - 9-	13 - 8	4 - 0	6 - 10+	1,988 / 2,332	70,000	1952
R-30-19, 21, 24	1944-1955	(6,030)	62501 - 68532	33 - 3 / 39 - 0	8 - 3	7 - 3	41 - 8+	9 - 7+	10 - 0-	3 - 7-	12 - 10-	13 - 9+	7 - 0-	6 - 10+	1,988 / 2,332	70,000	1945
R-30/40-19	1955-1965	(~970)	62501 - 63500	33 - 3.	8 - 3	7 - 3	41 - 8+	9 - 7+	10 - 0-	3 - 7	12 - 10-	13 - 9+	4 - 0	7 - 0-	1,988	70,000	1956
R-30/40-21&24	1955-1965	(~4,880)	63501 - 68532	33 - 3 / 39 - 0	8 - 3	7 - 3	41 - 8+	9 - 7+	10 - 0-	3 - 7	12 - 10+	13 - 9+	4 - 0	7 - 0-	1,988 / 2,332	70,000	1956

June 16, 1998

PACIFIC FRUIT EXPRESS — Selected O.R.E.R. Dimensions

Ventilated Reefer / Steel Cars (1936-1978) — Database

PFE Class	Period	No. Built	Numbers	In Length	In Width	In Height	Out Length	Eave Width	Extr Width	Hgt to EW	Hgt Eave	Hgt Top RB	Door Width	Door Heigh	Capy CuFt	Capy Lb	Dimen Date
R-40-10	1936-1969	4,700	40001 - 44700	33 - 3	8 - 3	7 - 3	41 - 8+	9 - 5	10 - 0+	3 - 7+	12 - 7-	13 - 5-	4 - 0	7 - 1-	1,988	82,000	1944
BR-40-10	1953-1961	(50)	901 - 950	33 - 3	8 - 3	7 - 3	41 - 8+	9 - 5	10 - 0+	3 - 7+	12 - 7-	13 - 5-	4 - 0	7 - 1-	1,988	82,000	1954
R-40-10	1963-1967+	(~400)	30001 - 34700	39 - 2	8 - 3	7 - 3	41 - 8+	9 - 5	10 - 0+	3 - 7+	12 - 7-	13 - 5-	4 - 0	7 - 1-	2,342	82,000	1963
R-40-14	1941-1967+	1,000	44701 - 45700	33 - 3	8 - 3	7 - 3	41 - 11	9 - 4+	10 - 0+	3 - 7	12 - 7+	13 - 4+	4 - 0	7 - 1-	1,988	80,000	1942
R-40-14	1947-1966	1	44739	33 - 3 - / 39 - 0	8 - 3	7 - 3	41 - 11	9 - 4+	10 - 0+	3 - 7	12 - 7+	13 - 4+	4 - 0	7 - 1-	1,988 / 2,330	80,000	
R-40-14	1946-1952	1	45698	33 - 3 - / 39 - 0	8 - 3	7 - 3	41 - 11	9 - 4+	10 - 0+	3 - 7	12 - 7+	13 - 4+	4 - 0	7 - 1-	1,988 / 2,330	80,000	
R-40-20	1945-1967+	1,002	45701 - 46702	33 - 3 - / 39 - 0	8 - 3	7 - 3	41 - 11	9 - 5	10 - 0+	3 - 7	12 - 9-	13 - 6	4 - 0	7 - 2-	1,988 / 2,330	78,000	1945
R-40-23	1947-1972	3,000	5001 - 8000	33 - 3	8 - 3	7 - 3	41 - 9-	9 - 6	10 - 3+	3 - 7	12 - 9+	13 - 7+	4 - 0	7 - 6-	1,988 / 2,330	80,000	1950
R-40-23	1947-1972	2,000	46703 - 48702	33 - 3 - / 39 - 0	8 - 3	7 - 3	41 - 9-	9 - 6	10 - 3+	3 - 7	12 - 9+	13 - 7+	4 - 0	7 - 6-	1,988 / 2,330	80,000	1950
R-40-23	1960-1971+	(1,000)	20002 - 21001	36 - 6	8 - 3	7 - 6	41 - 9-	9 - 6	10 - 3+	3 - 10	12 - 9+	13 - 7+	4 - 0	7 - 6+	2,248	80,000	1962
R-40-23	1962-1967+	(1)	25001	36 - 6	8 - 2	6 - 8	41 - 9	9 - 6	10 - 4	3 - 10	12 - 10	13 - 8	4 - 0	7 - 7	2,005	60,000	1962
R-40-23	1965-1971+	(~300)	35001 - 36000	33 - 2	8 - 3	7 - 5	44 - 9	9 - 6	10 - 4	3 - 10	12 - 10	?	4 - 0	7 - 7	2,048	80,000	1967
R-40-23	1967-1970	(239)	36001 - 36500	39 - 0	8 - 3	7 - 3	44 - 9	9 - 6	10 - 4	3 - 10	12 - 10	?	4 - 0	7 - 6	2,330	86,000	1967
R-40-23	1965-1968	(15)	1001 - 1015	34 - 0	8 - 8	8 - 0	44 - 9	9 - 6	10 - 4	3 - 7	12 - 10	13 - 8	6 - 0	7 - 5	2,357	80,000	1967
R-40-23	1968-1975+	(15)	36501 - 36515	39 - 2	8 - 8	8 - 0	44 - 9	9 - 6	10 - 4	3 - 7	12 - 10	13 - 8	6 - 0	7 - 5	2,716	80,000	1970
R-40-25	1949-1971+	3,000	2001 - 5000	33 - 3	8 - 3	7 - 3	41 - 9-	9 - 6	10 - 3+	3 - 7-	12 - 9+	13 - 7+	4 - 0	7 - 6-	1,988	80,000	1950
R-40-25	1963-1970	(85)	82001 - 85000	33 - 3	8 - 3	6 - 8+	41 - 9-	9 - 6	10 - 3+	3 - 7-	12 - 9+	13 - 7+	4 - 0	7 - 6+	1,836	60,000	1965
R-40-25	1965-1975	(~525)	12001 - 15000	33 - 2	8 - 3	7 - 10	41 - 9-	9 - 6	10 - 3+	3 - 7-	12 - 9+	13 - 7+	4 - 0	7 - 6+	2,153	86,000	1965
R-40-25	1965-1975	(~100)	12001 - 15000	33 - 2	8 - 3	7 - 9	41 - 9-	9 - 6	10 - 3+	3 - 7-	12 - 9+	13 - 7+	4 - 0	7 - 6+	2,127	86,000	1965
R-40-25	1970-1975+	(90)	60000 - 60999	33 - 2	8 - 3	7 - 10	44 - 9	9 - 6	10 - 4	3 - 7	12 - 10	13 - 8	4 - 0	7 - 7	1,988	86,000	1971
R-40-25	1970-1975+	(90)	65000 - 65999	33 - 2	8 - 3	7 - 10	44 - 9	9 - 6	10 - 4	3 - 7	12 - 10	?	4 - 0	7 - 7	1,988	86,000	1971
R-40-26	1951-1974	2,000	8001 - 10000	33 - 3-	8 - 3	7 - 4+	41 - 9-	9 - 6	10 - 3+	3 - 7-	12 - 9+	13 - 7+	6 - 0	7 - 5-	2,011	80,000	1952
R-40-26	1960-1971	(1)	20001	36 - 6	8 - 3	7 - 4	41 - 9-	9 - 6	10 - 4	3 - 7	12 - 10	13 - 8	6 - 0	7 - 5	2,208	60,000	1962
R-40-26	1960-1970	(1)	21002	36 - 6	8 - 3	7 - 4	41 - 9-	9 - 6	10 - 4	3 - 7	12 - 10	13 - 8	6 - 0	7 - 5	2,223	80,000	1962
R-40-26	1965-1975+	(275)	18001 - 19999	33 - 2	8 - 3	7 - 10	41 - 9-	9 - 6	10 - 3+	3 - 7-	12 - 9+	13 - 7+	6 - 0	7 - 5-	2,153	86,000	1965
R-40-26	1965-1975	(109)	18001 - 19999	33 - 2	8 - 3	7 - 9	41 - 9-	9 - 6	10 - 3+	3 - 7-	12 - 10	13 - 7+	6 - 0	7 - 5-	2,127	86,000	1971
R-40-26	1970-1975+	(109)	61000 - 61999	33 - 2	8 - 3	7 - 10	44 - 9	9 - 6	10 - 4	3 - 7	12 - 10	?	6 - 0	7 - 6	2,011	86,000	1971
R-40-26	1970-1975+	(110)	66000 - 66999	33 - 2	8 - 3	7 - 10	44 - 9	9 - 6	10 - 4	3 - 7	12 - 10	?	6 - 0	7 - 6	2,011	86,000	1971
R-40-27	1957-1975+	1,700	10001 - 11700	33 - 3 - / 39 - 0+	8 - 3	7 - 4+	42 - 9-	9 - 6	10 - 3+	3 - 7-	12 - 9+	13 - 7+	6 - 0	7 - 5-	2,022 / 2,374	80,000	1958
R-40-27	1968-1975+	(5)	34701 - 34705	39 - 2	8 - 3	7 - 4	45 - 3	9 - 9	10 - 5	5 - 7	13 - 5	?	6 - 0	7 - 5	2,368	73,000	1970
R-40-27	1971-1975+	(98)	30001 - 31700	39 - 0	8 - 3	7 - 4	45 - 3	9 - 6	10 - 4	8 - 7	12 - 10	?	8 - 0	7 - 5	2,374	80,000	1975
R-40-27	1972-1975+	(414)	190003-190502	35 - 4	8 - 3	8 - 2	45 - 5	9 - 6	10 - 4	3 - 10	14 - 0	?	6 - 0	8 - 2	2,380	80,000	1975
R-40-27	1972-1975+	(50)	190029-190318	35 - 4	8 - 3	8 - 2	45 - 5	9 - 6	10 - 4	3 - 10	14 - 0	?	6 - 0	8 - 2	2,380	90,000	1975
R-40-28	1957-1975+	100	11701 - 11800	33 - 3 - / 39 - 0+	8 - 3	7 - 4+	42 - 9-	9 - 6	10 - 3+	3 - 7-	12 - 9+	13 - 7+	8 - 0	7 - 5+	2,022 / 2,374	80,000	1958
R-40-28	1971-1975+	(2)	31701 - 31800	39 - 0	8 - 3	7 - 4	45 - 3	9 - 6	10 - 4	8 - 7	12 - 10	?	8 - 0	7 - 5	2,374	80,000	1975
R-70-5	1952-1955	75	200126 - 200200	43 - 6	8 - 6	8 - 0	52 - 9-	9 - 10-	10 - 7+	3 - 5+	13 - 8-	14 - 8-	6 - 0	8 - 3-	2,958	130,000	1954
R-70-5	1954-1955	100	200601 - 200700	43 - 6	8 - 6	8 - 0	52 - 9-	9 - 10-	10 - 7+	3 - 5+	14 - 0-	14 - 6-	6 - 0	8 - 3-	2,958	135,000	1954
R-70-6	1950-1954	12	200226 - 200237	50 - 0	8 - 3	7 - 2+	52 - 9	10 - 0-	10 - 7+	3 - 7+	13 - 11-	14 - 8+	5 - 0	6 - 8-	2,865	120,000	1952

June 17, 1998

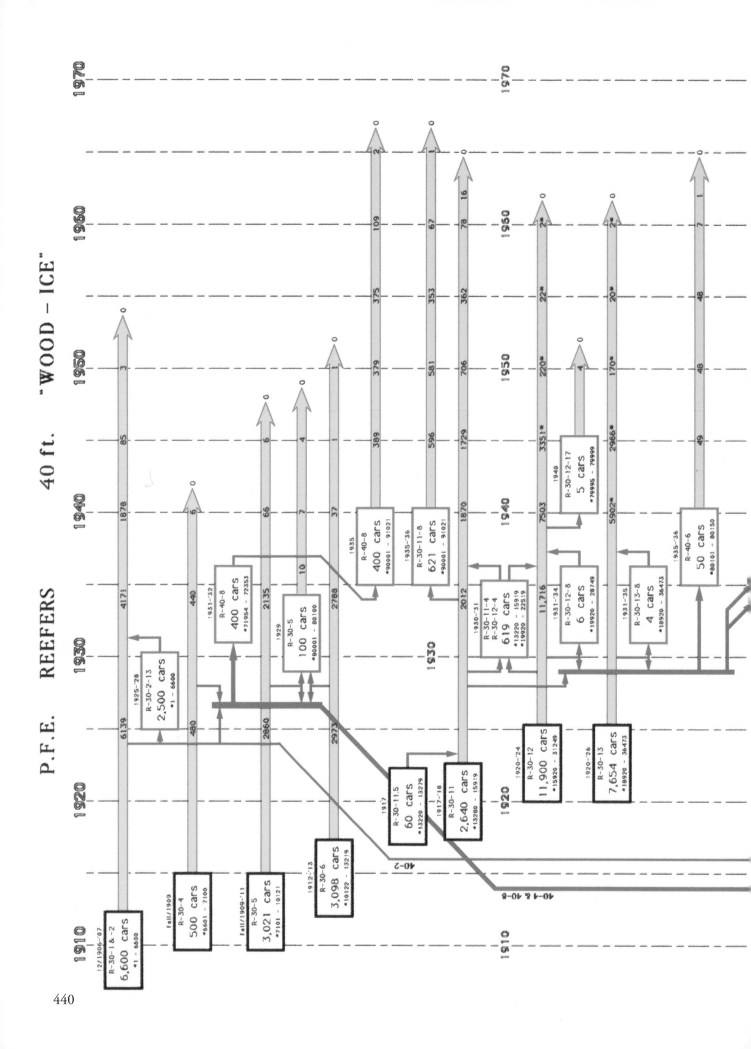

P.F.E.   REEFERS   40 ft.   "WOOD – ICE"

440

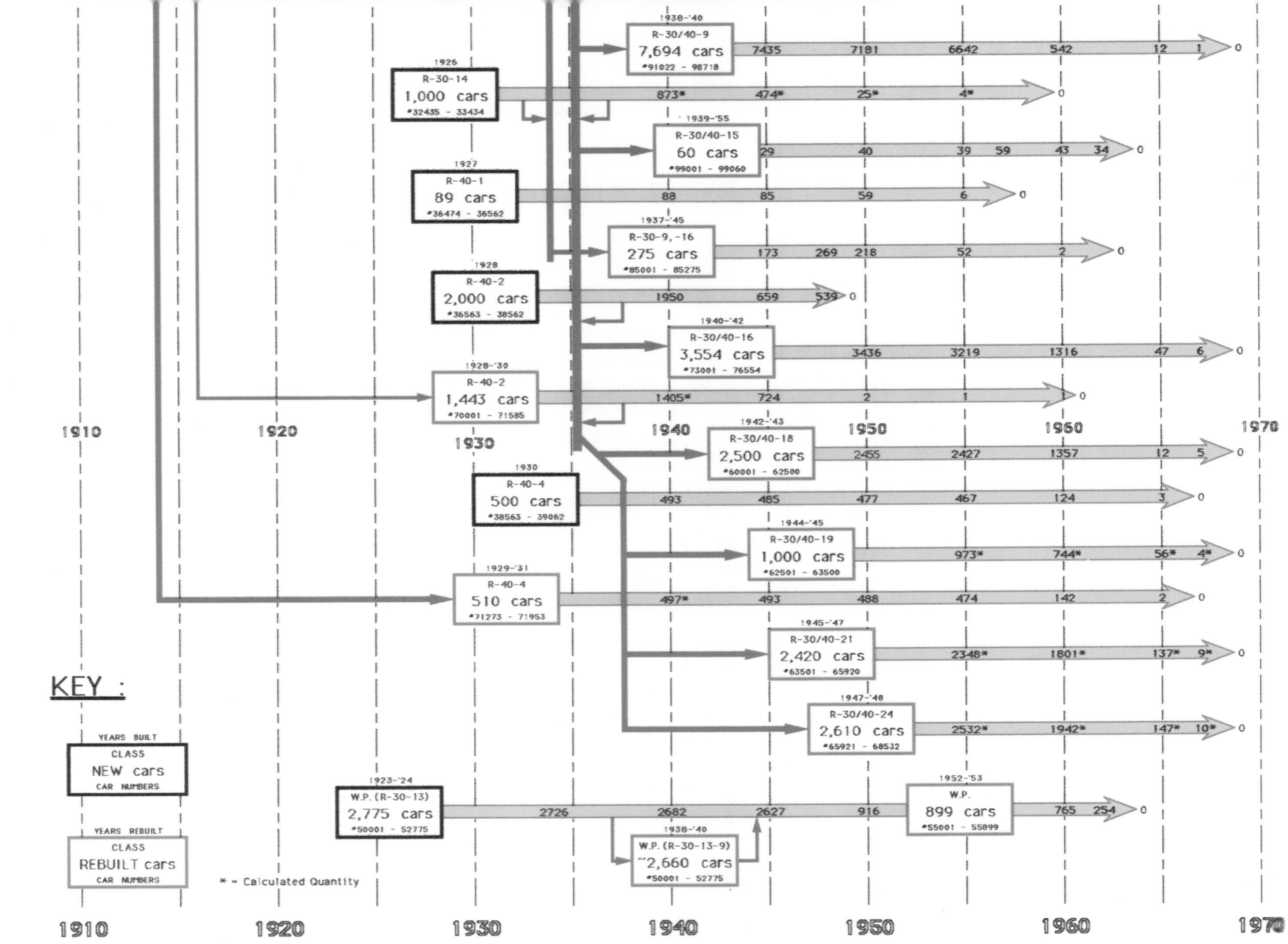

© 1994, 1998 R.D. HARLEY

October 20, 1999

1910   1920   1930   1940   1950   1960   1970

* = Calculated Quantity

1926
R-30-14
1,000 cars
#32435 - 33434

1938-'40
R-30/40-9
7,694 cars
#91022 - 98718

1939-'55
R-30/40-15
60 cars
#99001 - 99060

1927
R-40-1
89 cars
#36474 - 36562

1937-'45
R-30-9,-16
275 cars
#85001 - 85275

1928
R-40-2
2,000 cars
#36563 - 38562

1940-'42
R-30/40-16
3,554 cars
#73001 - 76554

1928-'30
R-40-2
1,443 cars
#70001 - 71685

1942-'43
R-30/40-18
2,500 cars
#60001 - 62500

1930
R-40-4
500 cars
#38563 - 39062

1944-'45
R-30/40-19
1,000 cars
#62501 - 63500

1929-'31
R-40-4
510 cars
#71273 - 71953

1945-'47
R-30/40-21
2,420 cars
#63501 - 65920

1947-'48
R-30/40-24
2,610 cars
#65921 - 68532

1952-'53
W.P.
899 cars
#55001 - 55899

1938-'40
W.P. (R-30-13-9)
~2,660 cars
#50001 - 52775

1923-'24
W.P. (R-30-13)
2,775 cars
#50001 - 52775

KEY:

YEARS BUILT
CLASS
NEW cars
CAR NUMBERS

YEARS REBUILT
CLASS
REBUILT cars
CAR NUMBERS

Normal Growing and Shipping Seasons on Southern Pacific Lines

Commodity	Producing District	Producing State	Jan	Feb	Mar	Apr	May	Jun	Jul	Aug	Sep	Oct	Nov	De
Anise	Castroville	CA												
	Guadalupe-Santa Maria	CA												
	Monterey-Salinas	CA												
	San Jose District	CA												
Apples	Medford	OR												
	Rogue River Valley	OR												
	Sonoma County	CA												
	Watsonville	CA												
Apricots	Central Valley	CA												
Artichokes	Castroville	CA												
	Davenport-Santa Cruz	CA												
	Santa Maria-Guadalupe District	CA												
	Half Moon Bay District	CA												
Asparagus	Imperial Valley	CA												
	Los Angeles District	CA												
	Sacramento Delta	CA												
Avocados	Los Angeles-Santa Barbara	CA												
	San Diego County	CA												
Beans(Snap and Lima-Green)														
	Central Valley	CA												
	Louisiana Lines	LA												
	West Coast of Mexico	MEX												
Beets	Corpus Christi District	TX												
	Laredo District	TX												
	Lousiana Lines	LA												
	Maricopa County	AZ												
	Rio Grande Valley	TX												
Broccoli	Guadalupe-Santa Maria	CA												
	Laredo District	TX												
	Maricopa County	AZ												
	Rio Grande Valley	TX												
	San Jose District	CA												
	Salinas-Watsonville District	CA												
Brussels Sprouts														
	Half Moon Bay District	CA												
	San Jose District	CA												
	Santa Cruz-Davenport District	CA												
	Salinas-Watsonville District	CA												
Cabbage	Central Valley	CA												
	Corpus Christi District	TX												
	Guadalupe-Santa Maria	CA												
	Imperial Valley	CA												
	Los Angeles District	CA												
	Louisiana Lines	LA												
	Maricopa County	AZ												
	Oxnard District	CA												
	Rio Grande Valley	TX												
	San Antonio District	TX												
	Salinas-Watsonville District	CA												
	Yuma County	AZ												
Cantaloupes	Bakersfield District	CA												

442

Commodity	Producing District	Producing State	Jan	Feb	Mar	Apr	May	Jun	Jul	Aug	Sep	Oct	Nov	Dec
	El Paso Valley	TX												
	Imperial Valley	CA												
	Kings County	CA												
	Laredo District	TX												
	Laredo ex Mexico	TX												
Cantaloupes	Maricopa County	AZ												
	Pinal County	AZ												
	Rio Grande Valley	TX												
	San Antonio District	TX												
	Turlock-Modesto District	CA												
	West Coast of Mexico	MEX												
	West Side of San Joaquin Valley	CA												
	Yuma County	AZ												
Carrots	Central and Southern California	CA												
	Corpus Christi District	TX												
	Imperial and Coachella Valleys	CA												
	Laredo District	TX												
	Louisiana Lines	LA												
	Maricopa County	AZ												
	Pinal County	AZ												
	Rio Grande Valley	TX												
	Yuma County	AZ												
Cauliflower	Brentwood District	CA												
	Central California	CA												
	Maricopa County	AZ												
	Oxnard District	CA												
	San Antonio	TX												
	San Jose District	CA												
	Santa Maria-Guadalupe District	CA												
	Southern California	CA												
	Salinas-Watsonville District	CA												
Celery	Bakersfield District	CA												
	Brooks District	OR												
	Santa Maria-Guadalupe District	CA												
	Long Beach District	CA												
Celery	Los Angeles District	CA												
	Maricopa County	AZ												
	Oxnard District	CA												
	Sacremento Delta-Stockton	CA												
	San Diego District	CA												
	San Jose District	CA												
	Salinas-Watsonville District	CA												
	Wilmington District	CA												
Cherries	Northern and Central California	CA												
Chicory	Guadalupe and Vicinity	CA												
	San Jose District	CA												
	Salinas-Watsonville District	CA												
Corn-Green	Bakersfield District	CA												
	Brentwood District	CA												
	Coachella Valley	CA												
	Hollister District	CA												
	Louisiana	LA												

Normal Growing and Shipping Seasons on Southern Pacific Lines

Commodity	Producing District	Producing State	Jan	Feb	Mar	Apr	May	Jun	Jul	Aug	Sep	Oct	Nov	De
	Maricopa County	AZ					█							
	Rio Grange Valley	TX					▒							
	Salida-Tracy District	CA									█	█		
Cucumbers	Corpus Christi District	TX				▒	█							
Endive	Rio Grande Valley	TX	▒	▒	▒									
Garlic	Maricopa County	CA					█	█						
	Northern and Central California	CA	█	█				█	█	█	█	█	█	█
Grapefruit	Coachella Valley	CA	█	█	█	█	█							
	Maricopa County	AZ	█	█	█	█	█	█	█	█			█	█
	Rio Grande Valley	TX	█	█	█	█	▒	▒						
	Riverside County	CA	█	█	█	█								
	San Bernardino District	CA						█	█	█	█	█		
Grapefruit	Tulare County	CA		█	█									
	Yuma County	AZ	█	█	█	█	▒	▒					█	█
Grapes	Bakersfield District	CA	▒	▒	▒	▒	▒			█	█	█	█	▒
	Central California	CA							█	█	█	█	█	
	Imperial and Coachella Valleys	CA						█	█					
	Maricopa County	AZ						█	█					
	Northern Cal.-Lodi-Modesto	CA									█	█		
	Sacramento District	CA									█	█		
	San Joaquin Valley	CA							█	█	█	█		
	Yuma County	AZ						▒	█					
Lemons	Maricopa County	AZ	█	█	█	█	▒	▒			█	█	█	█
	Northern California	CA	▒	▒	▒	▒	▒	▒	▒	▒	█	█		
	Santa Barbera-Oxnard District	CA	▒	▒	▒	▒	█	█	█	█	█	█	█	█
	Southern California	CA	█	█	█	█	█	█	█	█	█	█	█	█
	Yuma County	AZ	█	█	█	█	▒					█	█	█
Lettuce	Bakersfield District	CA										▒	█	
	Brentwood District	CA						█						
	Central California (Fresno—Sout	CA	▒	▒		█	▒	▒					▒	▒
	Cochise County	AZ				▒	█					█	█	
	Guadalupe-Santa Maria	CA				█	█	█	█	█	█	█		
	Imperial Valley	CA	█	█									▒	▒
	Irvington-Centerville-SnoBoy Di	CA							█	█	█	▒		
	Maricopa County	AZ	▒	▒								█	█	█
	Oxnard District	CA				▒	█	█	█	█	█	▒		
	Patterson District	CA					█	█						
	Modesto-Oakdale District	CA					█	█	█					
	Watsonville-Salinas	CA					█	█	█	█	█	█		
	San Jose District	CA							█	█	█	█		
	San Antonio	TX	█	▒	█	█	█							
	Santa Ana District	CA										▒	▒	▒
	Yuma County	AZ	█	█	█								█	█
Melons-White	Bakersfield District	CA							█	█				
	Brentwood District	CA							█	█				
	Maricopa County	AZ							█	█				
	Modesto-Turlock District	CA								█	█			
	Northern California	CA								█	█	█		
Mustard Greens	Maricopa County	AZ	▒	█										
	Pinal County	AZ	▒	█										
Nectarines	Brentwood District	CA							█	█				

444

Commodity	Producing District	Producing State	Jan	Feb	Mar	Apr	May	Jun	Jul	Aug	Sep	Oct	Nov	Dec
Mustard Greens	Maricopa County	AZ	▒	█	█									
	Pinal County	AZ	▒	█	█									
Nectarines	Brentwood District	CA							▒	▒				
Onions	Bakersfield District	CA	▒					█		▒				
	Brooks and Gaston	OR	█	█	▒	▒	▒				█	█		
	Chualar-Gonzales District	CA									█	█		
	Coachella Valley	CA					█	█						
	Corpus Christi District	TX				▒	█	█						
	Eagle Pass District	TX					█	█						
	Imperial Valley	CA				▒	▒							
	Laredo - T.M. Ry.	TX				█	█							
	Los Angeles District	CA							▒	█				
	Maricopa County	AZ				█	█	█						
	Nevada	NV	▒	▒	▒									
	North Texas	TX					▒	▒						
	Pima County	AZ						█						
	Pinal County	AZ				█	█	█						
	Stockton District	CA	▒						█	█	█	▒		
	Wharton-Yoakum District	TX			▒	█	▒							
	Yuma County	AZ				█	█							
Oranges	Bakersfield District	CA	█	█	▒							▒	█	█
	Fresno County	CA	█	█	█	█	█	█	▒				█	█
	Maricopa County	AZ	█	█	█	█	█						█	█
	Northern California	CA	▒	█	█	█	█	█					█	█
	Oxnard District	CA	▒	▒	▒	▒	▒	▒	█	█			█	█
	Rio Grande Valley	TX	▒	▒	▒								█	█
	Santa Ana District	CA	█	█	█	█	▒	█	█	█	█	█	█	█
	Southern California	CA	█	█	█	█	█	█	█	█	█	▒	█	█
	Tulare County	CA	█	█	█	█	█	█	▒	█		█	█	█
	Yuma County	CA	▒	█	█	█	█					▒	█	█
Parsley	Rio Grande Valley	TX	▒	▒	▒									
Peaches	Bakersfield District	CA					█	█						
	Brentwood District	CA							█	█				
	Merced District	CA							█	█				
	Modesto District	CA							█	█				
	Newcastle District	CA						█	█	█				
	Red Bluff District	CA							▒	▒				
	Reedley District	CA							█	█				
	Yuba City-Marysville District	CA							█	█				
Pears	Contra Costa County	CA							▒	▒				
	El Paso Valley	TX							█	▒				
	Lake and Mendocino Counties	CA								█	█			
	Locke-Walnut Grove District	CA							█	█				
	Marysville District	CA							█	█	▒			
	Medford District	OR	█	█	█	█				█	█	█	█	█
	Newcastle District	CA	▒						█	█				
	Placerville District	CA							█	█	█	█		▒
	Rogue River Valley	OR	█	█	█	█								
	San Jose District	CA	▒						█	█	█	█	█	█
Peas-Green	Bakersfield District	CA				▒	█	▒						
	Fresno–South	CA	█	█	█	█							█	█
	Guadalupe-Santa Maria District	CA				█	█	█						

445

Commodity	Producing District	Producing State	Jan	Feb	Mar	Apr	May	Jun	Jul	Aug	Sep	Oct	Nov	De
	Hayward District	CA				■	■	▒						
	Northern California	CA				■	■	■						
	Pinal Coounty	AZ				■	■	■						
	Porterville Branch	CA	▒									■	■	
	Sacramento District	CA					■	■						
	Salinas-Watsonville District	CA									■	■		
	San Jose-Gilroy-Hollister District	CA				▒	▒	■	▒	▒	■			
	San Luis Obispo District	CA			▒	▒	■	■	▒	■				
	West Coast of Mexico	MEX	■	■	■	■	■	■	■	■	■	■	■	■
Persimmons	Cottonwood District	CA										▒	▒	
Plums	Bakersfield District	CA						■	■					
	Exeter District	CA						■	▒					
	Fresno District	CA					▒	■	■					
	Lodi District	CA						▒	■					
	Newcastle District	CA						▒	■					
	Northern California	CA						■	■	■				
	Suisan-Fairfield District	CA						■	■					
Potatoes-Irish (White)														
	Bakersfield Dist.-Edison-Algosa-Arvin-Famosa-Lerdo-Saco-Maricopa	CA	▒	▒	■	■	■	▒	■	■				
	Chino District	CA						■	■					
	Fresno District incl. Madera	CA					■	■						
	Guadalupe-Santa Maria District	CA						▒	■	▒				
	Klamath Falls District	OR-CA							▒	■	■			
	Louisiana	LA				▒	▒	▒	▒					
	Maricopa County	CA					■	■						
	Nevada	NV								▒	▒			
	Owens Valley	CA								▒	▒	▒		
	Pinal County	AZ					■	■						
	Rio Grande Valley	TX	▒	▒	▒	■								
	Southern California	CA				▒	▒	▒	■					
	Stockton District	CA	■	■	■	■	■	■	■	■	■	■		
	Tehachapi District	CA									■	■		
	Salinas-Watsonville District	CA									■	■		
	Wharton-Yoakum District	TX				▒	■	▒						
	Yuma County	AZ				■	■							
Potatoes-Sweet	Atwater District	CA	■	▒	▒									
	Louisiana (Yams)	LA	▒	▒	▒	▒	▒	■	■					
	Maricopa County	AZ	▒								▒	▒	■	
	Stanislaus County	CA	▒							■	■	■		
Shallots	Maricopa County	AZ	■	■	■	▒							■	■
	Louisiana	LA		■	■	■								
Spinach	Corpus Christi District	TX	■	■	■	▒								
	Eagle Pass-Uvalde District	TX	■	■	■	▒								
	Laredo–T.M. Ry.	TX	▒	■	■									
	Rio Grande Valley	TX	▒	■	■									
	Wharton-Yoakum District	TX			▒	▒								
Tomatoes	Alameda and Contra Costa Coun	CA									■	■	▒	
	Bakersfield District	CA							■	■	■	■	■	
	Brentwood District	CA							■	■	■			
	Corpus Christi District	TX				▒	■	▒						
	Eagle Pass District	TX										■	■	
	East Texas	TX				▒	■	▒						

Commodity	Producing District	Producing State	Jan	Feb	Mar	Apr	May	Jun	Jul	Aug	Sep	Oct	Nov	Dec
	Fresno District	CA												
	Imperial Valley	CA												
	Laredo–T.M. Ry.	TX												
	Los Angeles District	CA												
	Merced District	CA												
	Oxnard District	CA												
	Rio Grande Valley	TX												
	Salinas-Watsonville District	CA												
	San Luis Obispo District	CA												
	Santa Maria-Guadalupe	CA												
	Tracy-Patterson District	CA												
	West Coast of Mexico	MEX												
Watermelons	Bakersfield District	CA												
	Imperial Valley	CA												
	Kings County	CA												
	Maricopa County	AZ												
	North Texas	TX												
	Pinal County	AZ												
	Turlock District	CA												
	West Coast of Mexico	MEX												
	Wharton-Yoakum District	TX												
	Yuma County	AZ												

Examples of Perishable Train Schedules (1964)

Coast - Overland Routes

Train - SV (Salinas Vegetable Block)

Watsonville Jct. to Roseville
(Daily)

Station		Time	Day
Watsonville Jct.	Lv	200AM	1
San Jose	Ar	415AM	1
San Jose	Lv	600AM	1
Oakland	Lv	800AM	1
Roseville	Ar	1245PM	1

SV (Salinas Vegetable Block) operates through to Roseville for connection with Roseville Perishable Blocks from Roseville first day and NCP from Roseville second day after billing date.

For schedule beyond Roseville on traffic for eastern destinations see Train-R (Roseville Perishable Blocks-Overland Route).

For schedule beyond Roseville on traffic for Pacific Northwest see Train NCP (North Coast Perishable-Shasta Route).

Coast Route

Train - SMV (Santa Maria Vegetable Block)

Guadalupe to Los Angeles
(Seasonal)

Station		Time	Day
Guadalupe	Lv	930PM PT	0
Santa Barbara	Ar	130AM PT	1
Santa Barbara	Lv	200AM PT	1
Los Angeles	Ar	530AM PT	1
Colton	Lv	1000PM PT	1
El Paso	Ar	845PM MT	2
New Orleans	Ar (T&L)	100PM CT	4
St. Louis	Ar (SSW)	800PM CT	4
Memphis	Ar (SSW)	530PM CT	4
Chicago	Ar (CRIP)	1230AM CT	5

SMV (Santa Maria Vegetable Block) originates at Guadalupe and operates through to Los Angeles for connection with Colton Perishable Block traffic from Los Angeles same day.

Perishable from Santa Maria Valley Railroad to be interchanged Guadalupe not later than 8:45 p.m., P.T.

For further detail of perishable schedule beyond Colton, see Colton Perishable Block schedule - Golden State-Sunset Routes.

PERISHABLE FREIGHT SCHEDULES

Issued 7-20-43.

ROSEVILLE TO CHICAGO

Via SP-UP and following Iowa Lines
C&NW—CGW—CMStP&P—IC—CB&Q—CRI&P

PREFERRED ROUTE

Lv Roseville, Cal.	SP	PT	11:59 A.M.	Tue 1st day
Ar Ogden, Utah	SP	PT	1:30 A.M.	Fri 4th day
Ar Council Bluffs, Ia.	UP		7:30 P.M.	Sun 6th day
#Ar Chicago, Ill.	Ia. Lines	CT	12:30 A.M.	Tue 8th day
Ar Peoria, Ill.	CB&Q	CT	11:59 P.M.	Mon 7th day
Ar Peoria, Ill.	C&NW	CT	11:59 P.M.	Mon 7th day

#Cars for Auction contemplate delivery to Chicago Produce Terminal Railway by 3:00 A.M. Central Standard Time, 8th day.

LOS ANGELES-ROSEVILLE-PORTLAND

Via San Joaquin Valley

Lv Los Angeles, Cal.	SP	PT	1:30 A.M.	Tue 1st day
Lv Bakersfield, Cal.	SP	PT	12:30 P.M.	Tue 1st day
Lv Fresno, Cal.	SP	PT	8:00 P.M.	Tue 1st day
Lv Stockton, Cal.	SP	PT	2:00 A.M.	Wed 2nd day
Ar Roseville, Cal.	SP	PT	6:00 A.M.	Wed 2nd day
Lv Roseville, Cal.	SP	PT	11:30 A.M.	Wed 2nd day
†Ar Portland, Ore.	SP	PT	3:00 P.M.	Fri 4th day

†Contemplates connections with Union Pacific and Northern Pacific night trains.

LOS ANGELES-SAN FRANCISCO-OAKLAND

Via Coast Line

Lv Los Angeles, Cal.	SP	PT	12:45 A.M.	Tue 1st day
Lv Santa Barbara, Cal.	SP	PT	5:45 A.M.	Tue 1st day
Lv Watsonville Jct.	SP	PT	8:30 P.M.	Tue 1st day
Ar San Francisco (Bayshore)	SP	PT	3:30 A.M.	Wed 2nd day
Ar Oakland, Cal.	SP	PT	5:00 A.M.	Wed 2nd day

SANTA ROSA - P&SR - NWP POINTS
— TO —
CHICAGO AND KANSAS CITY

Via SP-UP and following Iowa Lines
C&NW—CGW—CMStP&P—IC—CB&Q—CRI&P

PREFERRED ROUTE

Lv Schellville Jct., Cal.	SP	PT	2:00 A.M.	Tue 1st day
Lv Roseville, Cal.	SP	PT	11:59 A.M.	Tue 1st day
Ar Ogden, Utah	SP	PT	1:30 A.M.	Fri 4th day
Ar Council Bluffs, Iowa	UP	CT	7:30 P.M.	Sun 6th day
Ar Chicago, Ill. via	Iowa Lines	CT	12:30 A.M.	Tue 8th day
Lv North Platte, Neb.	UP	CT	9:00 P.M.	Sat 5th day
Ar Kansas City, Mo.	UP	CT	9:00 P.M.	Sun 6th day

IMPERIAL VALLEY PERISHABLES
Via SP-CRI&P
PREFERRED ROUTE

Lv Yuma, Ariz.	SP	MT	10:00 A.M.	Tue 1st day
Ar El Paso, Tex.	SP	MT	7:00 A.M.	Thu 3rd day
Ar Tucumcari, N.M.	SP	MT	10:00 A.M.	Fri 4th day
Ar Dalhart, Tex.	CRIP	CT	5:00 P.M.	Fri 4th day
#Ar Denver, Colo.	C&S	CT	7:30 P.M.	Sat 5th day
†Ar Kansas City, Mo.	CRIP	CT	9:00 P.M.	Sat 5th day
‡Ar St. Louis, Mo.	CRIP	CT	8:00 P.M.	Sun 6th day
‡Ar Burr Oak (Chicago), Ill.	CRIP	CT	12:30 A.M.	Mon 7th day
*Ar Inver Grove, Minn.	CRIP	CT	1:30 A.M.	Mon 7th day

#Via SP, CRI&P, FW&DC, C&S.
‡Contemplates connection with Eastern Lines' trains from E. St. Louis 2:00 A.M. and Chicago 7:00 A.M. Contemplates delivery on regularly assigned team tracks in St. Louis 5:00 A.M. 7th day, Chicago 7:00 A.M. 7th day.
*Cars handled in switch service to Minneapolis and St. Paul, Minn.
†Contemplates connections with trains leaving Kansas City 5:00 A.M. and later. Contemplates connection with TP&W train No. 122 leaving Keokuk 6:30 P.M., 6th day.
Note: Special Imperial Valley expedited service shown provided for lettuce and Spring cantaloupes, service being inaugurated when tonnage of these commodities reaches 10 cars per day eastbound. When shipments eastbound fall below 10 cars per day of these commodities special service discontinued and cars move on Colton Fruit Block from Yuma, Schedule No. 16 being applicable.

COLTON FRUIT BLOCK

PREFERRED ROUTE

SP or SP—CRI&P

Lv Colton, Cal.	SP	PT	11:59 A.M.	Tue 1st day
Ar El Paso, Tex.	SP	MT	7:00 A.M.	Fri 4th day
Ar Tucumcari, N. Mex.	SP	MT	10:00 A.M.	Sat 5th day
#Ar Denver, Colo.	C&S	CT	7:30 P.M.	Sun 6th day
Ar Oklahoma City, Okla.	CRI&P	CT	7:30 P.M.	Sun 6th day
Ar Kansas City, Mo.	CRI&P	CT	9:00 P.M.	Sun 6th day
Ar Des Moines, Ia.	CRI&P	CT	7:00 A.M.	Mon 7th day
Ar Inver Grove, Minn.	CRI&P	CT	1:30 A.M.	Tue 8th day
Ar St. Louis, Mo.	CRI&P	CT	8:00 P.M.	Mon 7th day
†Ar Burr Oak (Chicago), Ill.	CRI&P	CT	12:30 A.M.	Tue 8th day

#Via SP—CRI&P—FW&DC—C&S.

SALINAS-WATSONVILLE DISTRICT
— TO —
ST. LOUIS AND MEMPHIS
SP—StL&SW

Lv Watsonville Jct., Cal.	SP	PT	6:45 A.M.	Tue 1st day
Lv Colton, Cal.	SP	PT	11:59 A.M.	Wed 2nd day
Ar Memphis, Tenn.	StLSW	CT	7:00 A.M.	Tue 8th day
#Ar E. St. Louis, Ill.	StLSW	CT	8:00 P.M.	Tue 8th day

Note: For other destinations shown in Schedule No. 15, add one day to time shown therein.

*On Sundays and holidays: Lv Watsonville Jct. 6:45 A.M. (1st day)
Ar Los Angeles 11:00 A.M. (2nd day)

#Contemplates team track delivery St. Louis, Mo., 5:00 A.M., Wed. 9th day. Contemplates connection with Eastern Lines trains from E. St. Louis, 2:00 A.M.

SACRAMENTO AND SAN JOAQUIN VALLEY POINTS
— TO —
MEMPHIS, ST. LOUIS, KANSAS CITY AND CHICAGO
SP—StLSW—SP—CRI&P

Sunset Manifest—Colton Fruit Block

Lv Roseville, Cal.	SP	PT	10:30 P.M.	Monday
Lv Stockton, Cal.	SP	PT	12:05 A.M.	Tue 1st day
Lv Fresno, Cal.	SP	PT	9:00 A.M.	Tue 1st day
Lv Bakersfield, Cal.	SP	PT	2:00 P.M.	Tue 1st day
Ar Los Angeles, Cal.	SP	PT	1:30 A.M.	Wed 2nd day
Lv Colton, Cal.	SP	PT	11:59 A.M.	Wed 2nd day
Ar Memphis, Tenn.	StLSW	CT	7:00 A.M.	Tue 8th day
Ar East St. Louis, Ill.	StLSW	CT	8:00 P.M.	Tue 8th day
Ar Kansas City, Mo.	CRI&P	CT	9:00 P.M.	Mon 7th day
Ar St. Louis, Mo.	CRI&P	CT	8:00 P.M.	Tue 8th day
Ar Chicago, Ill.	CRI&P	CT	12:30 A.M.	Wed 9th day

Note: For schedules to other destinations shown in Schedule No. 15 via StL&SW or Schedule No. 16 via CRI&P, add one day to times shown therein.

Note: For Chicago Auction and Team Track Delivery at St. Louis and Chicago see Schedule No. 16.

SANTA MARIA-GUADALUPE DISTRICT
— TO —
CHICAGO AND KANSAS CITY

Via SP-UP and following Iowa Lines
C&NW—CGW—CMStP&P—IC—CB&Q—CRI&P

Lv Guadalupe, Cal.	SP	PT	1:45 A.M.	Tue 1st day
Lv Roseville, Cal.	SP	PT	11:59 A.M.	Wed 2nd day
Ar Ogden, Utah	SP	PT	1:30 A.M.	Sat 5th day
Ar Council Bluffs, Iowa	UP	CT	7:30 P.M.	Mon 7th day
Ar Chicago, Ill. via	Iowa Lines	CT	12:30 A.M.	Wed 9th day
Lv North Platte, Neb.	UP	CT	9:00 P.M.	Sun 6th day
Ar Kansas City, Mo.	UP	CT	9:00 P.M.	Mon 7th day

Note: For Chicago Auction and Team Track Delivery and Chicago, Kansas City, St. Louis and Peoria connections Eastern Lines see Schedules Nos. 1 and 2.

THE TOTAL PERISHABLE LOADING BY LINES IN SOME OF THE PRINCIPAL TERRITORIES (*)

DURING THE ENTIRE YEAR 1958

COMPARED WITH THE ENTIRE YEARS OF 1957, 1956, 1955, 1954, 1953, 1952 and 1951

REFRIGERATOR CARLOADS, ENTIRE YEAR, JANUARY TO DECEMBER INCLUSIVE

Territory or Railroad	Line	1958 Carloads	1957 Carloads	1956 Carloads	1955 Carloads	1954 Carloads	1953 Carloads	1952 Carloads	1951 Carloads
Maine - BAR	MDT	30,035	33,383	37,248	32,569	32,841	35,091	36,260	25,888
NJ-Pa-Del-Md-E.Va.	FGE	49,432	52,737	56,323	54,938	59,888	61,624	59,479	37,723
W.Va.-Va-NC-SC-Ga.	FGE	26,076	27,457	29,752	29,351	31,790	30,698	28,207	30,653
Florida	FGE	56,884	78,327	95,611	107,123	103,706	103,997	115,607	100,610
Ky-Tenn-Ala-Miss-La.	FGE	5,896	8,587	9,679	7,649	11,424	12,756	13,198	14,776
IC System	IC	24,264	28,838	28,409	29,678	33,327	31,924	32,153	36,298
GMO RR	NRL	11,182	13,361	13,244	12,714	14,077	13,654	12,842	16,654
Texas and La. (TNO)	PFE	15,776	15,355	18,971	17,132	18,826	19,531	19,134	15,049
Mo. Pac. Gulf Dist.	ART	19,032	15,358	23,154	23,291	24,039	22,482	19,232	13,753
Colo. (DRGW)	ART	8,126	7,879	7,997	10,824	12,159	12,525	16,487	13,008
Colo. & Oth.Sts. (QW)	BRE	20,164	20,903	23,658	24,124	20,728	21,606	19,211	24,200
Colo. & Oth.Sts.(UP-E)	PFE	9,038	8,916	11,153	12,562	10,851	13,191	14,788	18,624
Idaho (UP)	PFE	60,973	52,990	55,152	52,380	58,106	56,708	60,323	66,419
C&NW Ry.		35,292	33,263	36,707	35,671	34,813	35,788	34,221	38,581
CMSTP&P		93,147	102,205	110,151	85,980	87,949	91,243	111,666	100,383
Minn-ND (GN East)	WFE	20,869	25,880	27,737	35,739	32,165	31,765	31,189	27,446
Minn-ND (NP East)	NP	10,040	12,115	13,067	14,677	15,984	15,558	15,231	14,207
Pac. NW (GN West)	WFE	21,867	19,904	21,289	24,584	22,445	24,062	22,440	25,057
Pac. NW (NP West)	NP	21,160	21,872	23,954	26,388	27,640	28,161	27,057	27,465
Pac. NW (SP-UP)	PFE	22,027	23,855	25,558	28,236	25,830	30,705	28,811	29,681
Nor. California	PFE	128,278	147,967	160,271	146,395	164,774	168,901	173,347	155,764
Nor. California	ATSF	31,646	40,407	37,644	39,685	35,691	40,838	37,983	36,813
So. Calif. & Ariz.	PFE	99,385	102,078	101,034	105,643	106,803	124,180	120,395	124,396
So. Calif. & Ariz.	ATSF	41,590	43,298	44,393	48,392	44,096	54,566	47,583	55,416
TOTAL		861,179	936,935	1,012,156	1,005,725	1,029,952	1,081,554	1,096,844	1,048,864
% TOTAL PERSH. LDG. IN U.S.		78.8	80.4	79.7	78.1	79.9	80.2	80.4	77.5
TOTAL PERSH. LDG. IN U.S.		1,093,028	1,165,475	1,265,834	1,287,699	1,288,385	1,349,214	1,364,845	1,353,963
AVERAGE PER WEEK		21,020	22,413	24,342	24,735	24,748	25,875	26,103	25,966

(*)--PERISHABLE LOADING AS TAKEN FROM THE WEEKLY LETTER

PACIFIC FRUIT EXPRESS COMPANY

COMPARATIVE FIGURES FOR LOADING OF PERISHABLES

	1953	1954	1955	1956
Apples	5,967	5,993	6,834	5,738
Bananas	15,877	13,945	13,407	13,938
Cantaloupes	26,836	29,350	26,451	25,339
Carrots	16,591	13,328	12,546	12,703
Cauliflower	5,394	6,573	5,513	4,973
Celery	14,464	14,665	15,315	16,980
Citrus	34,622	28,928	29,138	31,871
Tree Fruit	3,362	2,847	4,352	3,669
Grapes	14,159	15,468	16,997	15,645
Lettuce	66,819	63,641	62,936	58,258
Onions	12,323	12,244	11,288	9,451
Peaches	2,655	2,595	3,937	2,282
Pears	10,202	11,126	10,046	12,380
Green Peas	980	923	789	753
Plums	2,665	2,094	2,727	3,271
Potatoes	85,084	74,755	73,895	72,114
Other vegetables	16,751	17,857	15,692	16,243
Tomatoes	15,979	15,087	10,858	9,612
Frozen foods	10,769	9,162	10,871	13,603
Beverages	3,278	3,085	3,471	2,877
Canned goods	25,014	23,323	24,050	26,449
Watermelons	3,078	3,761	3,387	3,118
Meat and P.H.P.	7,281	7,816	8,339	7,631
Other miscellaneous	18,556	18,900	20,127	16,591
Total	418,706	397,466	392,966	385,489

TOTAL PERISHABLE AND SEMI-PERISHABLE FREIGHT SHIPMENTS ORIGINATING ON S.P., U.P., W.P. AND THEIR SHORT LINE
CONNECTIONS, SEGREGATED BY P.F.E. AND FOREIGN CARS, ALSO SHOWING PERCENT OF GRAND TOTAL LOADED ON EACH LINE.

	SOUTHERN PACIFIC				UNION PACIFIC				WESTERN PACIFIC				TOTAL		
	PFE	FORN	TOTAL	% OF TOTAL	PFE	FORN	TOTAL	% OF TOTAL	PFE	FORN	TOTAL	% OF TOTAL	PFE	FORN	TOTAL
Season															
1907-08			36730	75.1			12172	24.9			—				48902
1908-09			40174	73.1			14750	26.9			—				54924
1909-10			43443	76.9			12953	22.9			139	0.2			56535
1910-11			49867	76.1			14451	22.1			1202	1.8			65520
1911-12			47774	71.5			17666	26.4			1394	2.1			66834
1912-13			43282	63.0			23798	34.7			1559	2.3			68639
1913-14			64000	65.6			32420	33.2			1203	1.2			97623
1914-15			67834	71.2			25974	27.3			1453	1.5			95261
1915-16			76070	74.3			23653	23.1			2806	2.6			102329
1916-17			82871	72.8			28238	24.8			2795	2.4			113904
Year															
1918			73056	68.8			32517	30.6			636	0.6			106209
1919			97369	69.9			38612	27.7			3345	2.4			139326
1920	77200	27197	104397	71.1	27171	10764	37935	25.9	3218	1218	4436	3.0	107589	39179	146768
1921	106220	15946	122166	68.5	41030	9721	50751	28.5	4547	727	5274	3.0	151797	26394	178191
1922	100754	13303	114057	68.6	43881	4148	48029	28.9	3806	337	4143	2.5	148441	17788	166229
1923	136420	17376	153796	67.3	60916	5739	66655	29.2	6833	1150	7983	3.5	204169	24265	228434
1924	150261	15166	165427	71.0	52535	6481	59016	25.3	7095	1579	8674	3.7	209891	23226	233117
1925	157917	16546	174463	70.4	51883	10508	62391	25.2	8853	2001	10854	4.4	218653	29055	247708
1926	190680	12507	203187	70.0	62916	11882	74798	25.8	11009	1135	12144	4.2	264605	25524	290129
1927	209120	22784	231904	73.3	56082	14094	70176	22.2	12152	2112	14264	4.5	277354	38990	316344
1928	236743	22075	258818	71.7	73094	11543	84637	23.4	13994	3671	17665	4.9	323831	37289	361120
1929	244952	19521	264473	73.3	68264	12691	80955	22.5	13205	1999	15204	4.2	326421	34211	360632
1930	256666	18230	274896	72.7	72551	11921	84472	22.3	16644	2410	19054	5.0	345861	32561	378422
1931	244682	7525	252207	71.0	79772	7865	87637	24.7	14774	672	15446	4.3	339228	16062	355290
1932	220477	3892	224369	72.4	66151	6415	72566	23.4	12727	267	12994	4.2	299355	10574	309929
1933	185555	2537	188092	68.8	64956	6647	71603	26.2	13400	250	13650	5.0	263911	9434	273345
1934	209842	3388	213230	68.2	75315	6925	82240	26.3	16900	176	17076	5.5	302057	10489	312546
1935	214595	5596	220191	71.8	63009	7638	70647	23.0	14633	1159	15792	5.2	292237	14393	306630
1936	228202	15277	243479	71.7	71262	9111	80373	23.7	14331	1153	15484	4.6	313795	25541	339336
1937	240108	9032	249140	72.8	67813	8580	76393	22.3	15420	1194	16614	4.9	323341	18806	342147
1938	243236	8405	251641	72.2	74572	7356	81928	23.5	14150	656	14806	4.3	331958	16417	348375
1939	246371	9777	256148	71.8	75896	8904	84800	23.7	14962	1082	16044	4.5	337229	19763	356992
1940	238462	11945	250407	71.0	75502	9304	84806	24.0	15882	1665	17547	5.0	329846	22914	352760
1941	251838	19611	271449	71.0	80000	12327	92327	24.2	18397	2040	16357	4.8	348195	33978	382173
1942	251477	33268	284745	72.7	72110	19052	91162	23.2	12273	3864	16137	4.1	335860	56184	392044
1943	218560	75194	293754	71.4	71497	31467	102964	25.0	10377	4273	14650	3.6	300434	110934	411368
1944	209128	108687	317815	70.4	82307	36661	118968	26.3	8284	6818	15102	3.3	299719	152166	451885
1945	194159	133367	327526	71.0	81347	38081	119428	25.9	8072	6413	14485	3.1	283578	177861	461439
1946	216846	115330	332176	71.4	82034	34851	116885	25.1	9854	6565	16419	3.5	308734	156746	465480
1947	212603	109189	321792	72.4	73796	34840	108636	24.4	8514	5799	14313	3.2	294913	149828	444471
1948	233488	68731	302219	72.6	75141	24276	99417	23.9	9214	5269	14483	3.5	317843	98276	416119
1949	242433	42441	284874	70.7	86162	16655	102817	25.5	11631	3742	15373	3.8	340226	62838	403064
1950	257457	48040	305497	73.1	80186	16184	96370	23.1	12212	3590	15802	3.8	349855	67814	417669
1951	250243	41056	291299	70.2	92508	15633	108141	26.0	12517	3265	15782	3.8	355268	59954	415222
1952	273214	34072	307286	73.1	83570	12653	96223	22.9	12728	4155	16883	4.0	369512	50880	420392
1953	274908	33074	307982	73.6	81783	12626	94409	22.5	13899	2416	16315	3.9	370590	48116	418706
1954	264177	24268	288445	72.6	82077	10693	92770	23.3	13895	2356	16251	4.1	360149	37317	397466
1955	258287	25089	283376	72.1	80798	12330	93128	23.7	14633	1829	16462	4.2	353718	39248	392966
1956	252542	24250	276792	71.8	81950	10225	92175	23.9	14394	2128	16522	4.3	348886	36603	385489
1957	242916	16749	259665	71.9	77862	8327	86189	23.9	13763	1597	15360	4.2	334541	26673	361214
1958	223968	19020	242988	69.8	82751	8820	91571	26.3	11744	2031	13775	3.9	318463	29871	348334
1959	217234	24410	241644	71.2	76311	9028	85339	25.1	11011	1654	12665	3.7	304556	35092	339648
1960	212052	19031	231083	74.0	62054	7472	69526	22.3	10065	1509	11574	3.7	284171	28012	312183
1961	191409	20366	211775	73.6	61099	6609	67708	23.5	7463	971	8434	2.9	259971	27946	287917
1962	174834	26302	201136	71.0	63561	10477	74038	26.1	6592	1501	8093	2.9	244987	38280	283267
1963	163959	18643	182602	70.0	59938	10177	70115	26.9	6685	1503	8188	3.1	230582	30323	260905
1964	153998	25189	179187	70.3	60132	9398	69530	27.3	5515	786	6301	2.4	219645	35373	255018
1965	144783	17340	162123	70.6	53686	7051	60737	26.5	4920	862	5782	2.5	203389	25253	228642
1966	146940	18141	165081	69.6	61304	6326	67630	28.5	3742	673	4415	1.9	211986	25140	237126
1967	132835	13032	145867	69.4	59140	4284	63424	30.2	682	215	897	.4	192657	17531	210188
1968	131961	16390	148351	71.1	55865	4399	60264	28.9					187826	20789	208615
1969	133435	19686	153121	72.8	49137	8093	57230	27.2					182572	27779	210351
1970	132761	17892	150653	71.9	48015	10907	58922	28.1					180776	28799	209575
1971	118590	13969	132559	67.9	46850	15845	62695	32.1					165440	29814	195254
1972	124448	10688	135136	69.4	47075	12450	59525	30.6					171523	23138	194661
1973	116561	2480	119041	67.5	53512	3776	57288	32.5					170073	6256	176329

	SOUTHERN PACIFIC				UNION PACIFIC				TOTAL		
	PFE	FORN	TOTAL	% OF TOTAL	PFE	FORN	TOTAL	% OF TOTAL	PFE	FORN	TOTAL
Year											
1974	112423	2040	114463	70.0	48290	838	49128	30.0	160713	2878	163591
1975	89951	2115	92066	66.7	45863	136	45999	33.3	135814	2251	138065
1976	68677	1496	70173	58.0	50538	209	50747	42.0	119215	1705	120920
1977	60667	1405	62072	54.6	51498	121	51619	45.4	112165	1526	113691
JAN-MAR 1978	9237	218	9455	39.8	14238	28	14311	60.2	23520	246	23766

Bibliography

NOTES ON SOURCES

The sources we have used are listed below, as they relate to individual chapters, or as a general bibliography. The most important source has been the records preserved by Pacific Fruit Express itself, although the company's numerous moves of headquarters over the years, the split into Union Pacific and Southern Pacific parts in 1978, and final absorption into the Southern Pacific in 1985 have greatly reduced the completeness and degree of organization of these records. Part of this material is now part of the Library collection at the California State Railroad Museum in Sacramento. A second, quite extensive record is the collected PFE material held by the Union Pacific at its headquarters in Omaha. Much in the way of correspondence, drawings, financial and legal records, photographs and memoranda relating to PFE is included, particularly in the President's Office correspondence (microfilmed) and former New York office records housed in the Union Pacific Museum, and in UP Mechanical Department records.

As mentioned in the Introduction, it is clear that most railroad historians have regarded Pacific Fruit Express as a footnote to their topic, and in a number of cases have merely rephrased the conclusions of earlier work without adding new information. Accordingly, many such comments should be read with caution. Similar remarks apply to "summaries" of the early history of refrigerator cars. A great many inaccuracies, misunderstood facts, and garbled events have been repeated verbatim in succeeding generations of histories. John White's *The Great Yellow Fleet* has corrected the great majority of the nineteenth century record on this topic, although it is less reliable after 1920. The railroad trade press, and the professional journals for both railroad and refrigeration engineering subjects, have been of considerable help in supplementing the PFE and UP records in assembling this history.

Interviews with various former PFE employees have been of great benefit. These are listed separately under the General Bibliography. Transcribed texts of these interviews are deposited with the Library of the California State Railroad Museum, with the Union Pacific Railroad Museum in Omaha, and with the A.C. Kalmbach Library of the National Model Railroad Association in Chattanooga.

This bibliography is organized into two parts, first a general section listing the publications used as background for two or more chapters in the book, then a section listing references for individual chapters. Within the general section, publications are separately listed by type.

GENERAL BIBLIOGRAPHY

Books

Armstrong, John H., *The Railroad – What It Is, What It Does*, Simmons-Boardman, Omaha, Nebr., 1977.

Athearn, Robert G., *Rebel of the Rockies: A History of the Denver and Rio Grande Western Railroad*, Yale Univ. Press, New Haven, Conn., 1967. [includes Western Pacific history]

Austin, Ed, and Tom Dill, *The Southern Pacific in Oregon*, Pacific Fast Mail, Edmonds, Wash., 1987.

Beebe, Lucius, *The Central Pacific and Southern Pacific Railroads*, Howell-North, Berkeley, 1963.

Church, Robert J., *Cab-Forward* (Revised Edition), Central Valley Railroad Publications, Wilton, Calif.,1982.

Church, Robert J., *The 4300 4-8-2's* (Revised Edition), Signature Press, Wilton, Calif., 1996.

Crump, Spencer, *Ride the Big Red Cars* [Pacific Electric], Trans-Anglo Books, Los Angeles, 1962.

DaCosta, P., *Pacific Fruit Express, Ice Refrigerator Cars, 1906-1932*, Apache Press, Eugene, Ore., 1978. [drawings only, no text]

Droege, John A., *Freight Terminals and Trains* (2nd Ed.), McGraw-Hill, New York, 1925.

Dunscomb, Guy L., *A Century of Southern Pacific Steam Locomotives*, Train Shop, Modesto, 1963.

Dunscomb, Guy L., and Fred A. Stindt, *Western Pacific Steam Locomotives, Passenger Trains and Cars*, Dunscomb-Stindt, Modesto, Calif., 1980.

Farrington, S. Kip, *Railroading from the Rear End*, Coward-McCann, New York, 1946.

——, *Railroading the Modern Way*, Coward-McCann, New York, 1951.

Hamman, Rick, *California Central Coast Railways*, Pruett, Boulder, Colo., 1980.

Healy, Kent T., *Performance of the U.S. Railroads since World War II*, Vantage Press, New York, 1985.

Henry, Robert S., *This Fascinating Railroad Business*, Bobbs-Merrill, New York, 1946.

Hofsommer, Don L., *The Southern Pacific, 1901-1985*, Texas A&M Univ. Press, College Station, Tex., 1986.

Hungerford, Edward, *The Modern Railroad*, A.C. McClurg, Chicago, 1912.

Kaminski, Edward S., *American Car & Foundry Company, 1899-1999*, Signature Press, Wilton, Calif., 1999.

King, Ernest L., and Robert E. Mahaffay, *Main Line* [SP history], Doubleday, Garden City, NY, 1948.

Klein, Maury, *Union Pacific* (2 Vols.), Doubleday, New York, 1987 and 1990.

Kratville, Wm. W., *Golden Rails*, Kratville Publications, Omaha, Nebr., 1965.

Kratville, Wm. W., and Harold E. Ranks, *Motive Power of the Union Pacific*, Barnhart Press, Omaha, Nebr., 1958.

LeMassena, Robert A., *Rio Grande...to the Pacific!*, Sundance, Denver, 1974. [includes Western Pacific history]

Loree, L.F., *Railroad Freight Transportation*, Appleton, New York, 1922.

Lucas, Walter A., *100 Years of Railroad Cars*, Simmons-Boardman, New York, 1958.

Morison, Samuel Eliot, *The Oxford History of the American People*, Vol. 3, Oxford University Press, London, 1965.

Overton, Richard C., *Burlington Route: A History of the Burlington Lines*, Knopf, New York, 1965.

Rose, Joseph R., *American Wartime Transportation*, Crowell, New York, 1953.

Sagle, Lawrence W., *Freight Cars Rolling*, Simmons-Boardman, New York, 1960.

Signor, John R., *Tehachapi*, Golden West Books, San Marino, Calif., 1983.

——, *Donner Pass*, Golden West Books, San Marino, Calif., 1985.

——, *The Los Angeles and Salt Lake Railroad Company*, Golden West Books, San Marino, Calif., 1988.

——, *Southern Pacific's Coast Line*, Signature Press, Wilton, Cal., 1995.

Signor, John R., and John A. Kirchner, *The Southern Pacific of Mexico*, Golden West Books, San Marino, Calif., 1987.

Starr, Kevin, *Americans and the California Dream, 1850-1915*, Oxford Univ. Press, New York, 1973.

——, *Inventing the Dream: California Through the Progressive Era*, Oxford Univ. Press, New York, 1985.

——, *Material Dreams: Southern California Through the 1920's*, Oxford Univ. Press, New York, 1990.

Stover, John F., *The Life and Decline of the American Railroad*, Oxford Univ. Press, New York, 1970.

Waters, L.L., *Steel Trails to Santa Fe*, Univ. Kansas Press, Lawrence, Kans., 1950.

White, John H., *The Great Yellow Fleet*, Golden West Books, San Marino, Calif., 1986. [For corrections to the PFE and SFRD chapter written by Donald Duke, see Richard H. Hendrickson, *Santa Fe Modeler* (Official Publication of the Santa Fe Modelers Organization), Vol. 10, No. 2, Spring, 1987, pp. 24-26; and Anthony W. Thompson, *The Streamliner* (Official Publication of the Union Pacific Historical Society), Vol. 2, No. 4, Oct. 1986, pp. 36, 37.]

——, *The American Railroad Freight Car*, Johns Hopkins University Press, Baltimore, 1993.

Wilson, Neill C., and Frank J. Taylor, *Southern Pacific: The Roaring Story of a Fighting Railroad*, McGraw-Hill, New York, 1952.

Articles

"A Cool, Fresh Start for Perishables," *Southern Pacific Bulletin*, Vol. 65, No. 5, May 1981, pp. 3-6.

Anderson, Oscar E., "Refrigerated Transportation," Chapter VIII, *Refrigeration in America*, Princeton Univ. Press, Princeton, 1953.

Bogart, Stephen, "Perishable – Rush!", *Trains*, Vol. 9, No. 4, Feb. 1949, pp. 26, 27.

"Chiasson leaves 42-year job with UP," *The Packer*, Sat., July 30, 1983, p. 14A.

Cockle, George R. (Editor), "Refrigerator Cars," *Railroad Car Journal*, Number 2, Kratville Publications, Omaha, Nov. 1971.

Colbert, J.W., C.P. Lentz and E.A. Rooke, "Effect of Bunker Ice Salt Concentration on Temperature," *Refrigerating Engineering*, Vol. 61, No. 10, Oct. 1951, pp. 960-962.

Dellinger, E.S., "Rolling the Citrus Gold," *Railroad Magazine*, Dec. 1948, pp. 18-45.

Dietrichson, W.F., "Developments in Refrigerated Transport," *Refrigerating Engineering*, Vol. 26, No. 1, July 1933, pp. 9-11.

Etzel, Leroy, "Refrigeration on the Rails," *Ice and Refrigeration*, Vol. 125, Aug. 1953, pp. 33-36.

Hendrickson, Richard H., "Freight Car Trucks, 1850-1950," in *Symposium on Railroad History*, A.W. Thompson, ed., Kalmbach Memorial Library, NMRA, Chattanooga, 1990, pp. 9-26.

Hukill, W.J., "Refrigerator Car Surface Temperatures," *Refrigerating Engineering*, Vol. 23, No. 4, April 1932, pp. 225-259.

Hukill, William V., and D.F. Fisher, "Present Practice with Refrigerator Cars," *Refrigerating Engineering*, Vol. 30, No. 2, Aug. 1935, pp. 75-79.

Hulse, George E., "Progress in Ice and Mechanical Refrigerator Cars," *Refrigerating Engineering*, Vol. 34, No. 1, July 1937, pp. 9-15.

Krieg, Al, "Pacific Fruit Express, Old Hand at Keeping Its Cool," *PFE Newsletter*, July, 1970, pp. 4-6 (reprinted from *Western Fruit Grower*).

Leeds, J.S., "Organization for Handling Refrigeration Transportation," *Railway Age Gazette*, Vol. 55, Sept. 26, 1913, pp. 569-71.

Lorion, A.J., "Loading the Refrigerator Car – Design as Related to Loading Methods," *Refrigerating Engineering*, Vol. 20, No. 3, Sept. 1930, pp. 151-158.

Manos, W.P., "The Evolution of Rail Freight Vehicles in the United States," Ch. 8 in *Railway Mechanical Engineering – A Century of Progress*, American Society of Mechanical Engineers, New York, 1979, pp. 185-215.

McPike, E.F., "Current Practice of Transit Refrigeration," *Refrigerating Engineering*, Vol. 18, No. 1, July 1929, pp. 1-4.

Mohowski, Robert, "End of the Ice Age," *Railroad Model Craftsman*, Vol. 51, No. 10, March, 1981, pp. 71-76.

Plummer, K.V., "Views on the Transportation of Frozen Food," address to the Eastern Frosted Foods Association in New York on May 22, 1947, manuscript, PFE collection, CSRM.

Sims, Don, "Yuma Division," *Trains*, Vol. 17, No. 4, Feb. 1957, pp. 38-51.

Smith, Don, "PFE Painting and Lettering," *The Streamliner* (Official Publication of the Union Pacific Historical Society), Vol. 1, No. 4, Oct. 1985, pp. 24-40. For additions and corrections, see *The Streamliner*, Vol. 2, No. 2, April 1986, pp. 36-38.

Sweeley, E.A., "Practice in Refrigerator Car Design," *Refrigerating Engineering*, Vol. 18, No. 3, Sept. 1929, pp. 67-70. See also *Railway Age*, Vol. 87, Jul. 20, 1929, pp. 193-195.

Thompson, Anthony, "PFE's Ice Reefers: Wood Cars," *Railroad Model Craftsman*, Vol. 55, No. 8, Jan. 1987, pp. 61-69.

Thompson, Anthony, "PFE's Ice Reefers: Rebuilt Cars," *Railroad Model Craftsman*, Vol. 55, No. 10, March 1987, pp. 81-90.

Thompson, Anthony, "PFE's Ice Reefers: Operations and Express Cars," *Railroad Model Craftsman*, Vol. 55, No. 11, April 1987, pp. 59-67.

Thompson, Anthony, "Corrections and Additions to PFE Ice Reefer Series," *Railroad Model Craftsman*, Vol. 56, No. 2, July, 1987, pp. 7, 10, 11.

White, John H., "The Beginnings of Steel Freight Cars," in *History of Technology* (11th Ann. Vol.), N. Smith, ed., Mansell Publ. Ltd., London, 1986, p. 181-207.

Periodical, Annual or Occasional Publications

ASHRAE Guide and Data Book, American Society of Heating, Refrigerating and Air-conditioning Engineers, New York.

Car and Locomotive Cyclopedia, Simmons-Boardman, Omaha. (since 1966)

Car Builders' Cyclopedia, Simmons-Boardman, New York. (since 1922)

Car Builders' Dictionary, Simmons-Boardman, New York. (prior to 1922)

Manual of Standard and Recommended Practice, Mechanical Division, Association of American Railroads, Washington, DC.

Official Railway Equipment Register, The Railway Equipment and Publications Co., New York.

Southern Pacific Bulletin, Southern Pacific Company, San Francisco.

Union Pacific Magazine, Union Pacific Railroad, Omaha.

Documents of Pacific Fruit Express Company

"Authorities for Expenditure or AFE (Form 12)," Union Pacific records, Boxes 00088, 00437, 00438, etc., UP Railroad Museum; AFE's prior to 1911, CSRM.

Bulletin (predecessor of *Newsletter*), Issues 1-5, 1949.

"Car Record (Form 120 until 1930, Form 78-1 thereafter)," 5"x 8" cards for each car, CSRM.

Equipment Diagrams (all car, trailer and container classes), 1906-1970, CSRM and UP Railroad Museum.

"Freight Refrigerator Cars" (rosters), annual since 1922.

History and Function of the Pacific Fruit Express Company, San Francisco, 1942, 1945, 1963, 1967. (contains some historical errors)

Newsletter, all issues, San Francisco and Brisbane, Nov. 1959-May 1978.

"Progressive Development of Pacific Fruit Express Co. and Their Refrigerator Cars" (part of anti-trust lawsuit response), San Francisco, 1941, CSRM.

Refrigerator Car Specialties Applied to All Cars Built Since 1920, 1940, CSRM.

"Summary of Car Shop Operation (Form 865)," Monthly Memoranda, 1920-1958, CSRM.

Other Documents

A.A.R. Refrigerator Car Research Reports, Mechanical Division, Association of American Railroads, Washington, DC, 1946-61.

Code of Rules for Handling Perishable Freight, Circular 20-F, National Perishable Freight Committee, Oct. 21, 1965 (earlier Circulars also consulted, incl. No. 20-A, Dec. 1933).

Investigation of the Body Icing of Vegetables, U. S. Dept. of Agriculture Report, Washington, DC, Dec. 19, 1927.

Jamison, W. T., *Perishable Protective Tariff No. 17*, National Perishable Freight Committee, Feb. 21, 1957. (some previous tariffs also consulted)

President's Office correspondence (microfilm), esp. File 191, 1920-1970, includes Union Pacific, Southern Pacific and Pacific Fruit Express items, UP Railroad Museum.

Redit, W. H., and A. A. Hamer, *Protection of Rail Shipments of Fruits and Vegetables*, Agriculture Handbook No. 195, U.S. Dept. of Agriculture, Washington, DC, July, 1961; revision (credited to Redit only), July 1969.

Richardson, C. A., *Railway Transportation of Perishable Freight: History – Development – Research*, Association of American Railroads, Mechanical Division Report, Nov. 1946.

Transcribed Interviews

Earl R. Hopkins, General Mechanical & Engineering Officer, PFE, 1962-74; retired 1974. At Auburn, Calif., on 27 October, 1985, by Thompson; on 10 January 1987, by Thompson and Church.

A.L. "Pete" Holst, Assistant General Manager, PFE; retired 1963, deceased Jan. 1992. At San Mateo, Calif., on 10 January 1986, by Thompson; on 1 March 1987, by Thompson and Church.

Marvin R. Dike, Plant Manager and Trailer Service Manager, PFE; retired. At Omaha, 8 April 1988, by Thompson.

Armand E. "Ed" Chiasson, Vice President and General Manager, PFE, 1973-78; retired from Union Pacific, 1983. At Omaha, 9 April 1988, by Thompson.

A.L. Holst; T.D. Walsh, Manager – Industrial Relations, PFE, retired; and D. Schumacher, Auditor, PFE, retired. At Millbrae, Calif., on 29 April 1987, by Jones.

A.L. Holst, E.R. Hopkins, D. Schumacher. At Millbrae, Calif., on 28 July 1987, by Jones.

Robert W. Torassa, formerly District Superintendent – Car Service for PFE; now with SPT Co. At Los Angeles, on 12 February 1988, by Jones.

INDIVIDUAL CHAPTER BIBLIOGRAPHIES

The following reference items, appropriate to individual chapters, were consulted in addition to the items listed above in the General Bibliography.

Chapter 1

Athearn, Robert G., *Union Pacific Country*, Rand McNally, Chicago, 1971.

Bean, Walton, *California: An Interpretive History* (2nd Ed.), McGraw-Hill, New York, 1973.

California Fruit Case: *The Railway Age (Chicago)*, Vol. 31, Feb. 16, 1900; *ibid.*, Apr. 13, 1900, p. 389; *ibid.*, Vol. 33, Apr. 25, 1902, p. 688; *ibid.*, May 16, 1902, p. 782; *ibid.*, June 6, 1902, pp. 857-859; *ibid.*, Vol. 35, Apr. 17, 1903, p. 729; *ibid.*, Vol. 38, Sept. 16, 1904, pp. 370, 395; *ibid.*, Vol. 39, March 3, 1905, pp. 288, 289; *Annual Reports of the Interstate Commerce Commission*, 19th Report, 1905, p. 31, 32; *ibid.*, 20th Report, 1906, p. 44.

Car Hire Contract,UP-SP: "UP Plan for Revision," Dec. 4, 1959; R. Sutton, memoranda, Apr. 10, 1959, May 3, 1960; Walker to Sutton, letter, Nov. 25, 1959. President's Office correspondence, File 191, UP Railroad Museum.

Car pool with AT&SF: Secrist to Adams, memo, Dec. 8, 1919; Adams to Lovett, letter, Dec. 15, 1919. File UA-22-A, UP Railroad Museum.

Chiasson, A.E., and A. Amato, "U.P.F.E. – A New, Fortified Brand of Service," *Fast Track* (UP Personnel Dept.), August, 1978.

Chiasson, A.E., quotations, from interviews and personal correspondence, A.W. Thompson.

Cranmer, W.G., "PFE – Today and Tomorrow," PFE *Newsletter*, May, 1978, pp. 2,3.

Cranmer, W.G., "PFE Five-year Plan," presentation to SPT Co. Operating Dept. meeting, Sept. 2-4, 1980, text, PFE collection, CSRM.

Daggett, Stuart, *Chapters on the History of the Southern Pacific*, Ronald Press, New York, 1922.

Denver & Salt Lake contracts: Gray to Charske, letter, May 30, 1926; Gray to Lovett, telegram, Mar. 18, 1930; McCarthy (D&RGW) to Plummer, letter, Jan. 5, 1953; copies, 1926 and 1930 contracts. President's Office correspondence, File 191, UP Railroad Museum.

Ellen, Thomas D., "The Future of the Perishable Business and PFE," memo to D.K. McNear and D.M. Mohan, June 7, 1985, CSRM.

"Equipment Orders" [Western Pacific], *Railway Age*, Vol. 72, June 19, 1922, p. 1552.

Executive Committee Minutes, UP, Dec. 13, 1906, from Vol. I, pp. 75, 76, printed record of Pacific Railroad Case. UP Railroad Museum.

Financial matters: *Poor's Railroad Manual*, various years, Poor's, New York; *Moody's Investor's Manual – Railroads*, Moody's, New York; "Value of Pacific Fruit Express to SP Co.," VP & GM Office, memo, Feb. 20, 1957, CSRM; balance sheets, File UA-22-A, UP Railroad Museum.

Hidy, Ralph W., Muriel E. Hidy, Roy V. Scott and Don L. Hofsommer, *The Great Northern Railway*, esp. Ch. 23, Harvard Business School Press, Boston, 1988.

"Historic PFE Company Ends," *Western Grower and Shipper*, Nov. 1978, pp. 69, 72, 125, 137.

Hutchinson, W.H., "Southern Pacific: Myth and Reality," *Calif. Historical Quart.*, Vol. 48, Dec. 1969, pp. 325-334.

"Investigation of the Harriman Roads," *The Railroad Gazette*, Vol. 42, No. 2, Jan. 11, 1907, pp. 52-54.

Kennan, George, *E.H. Harriman – A Biography*, 2 Vols., Houghton-Mifflin, Boston, 1922.

Kolko, Gabriel, *Railroads and Regulation, 1877-1916*, Princeton Univ. Press, Princeton, 1965.

Kriebel, F.E., "Transporting Perishables – A Perspective of the Past With an Eye to the Future," address to United Fresh Fruit and Vegetable Association, PFE *Newsletter*, May 1971, pp. 5-7.

Lavender, David, *The Great Persuader* [C.P. Huntington], Doubleday, New York, 1970.

Lease of PFE cars: 1933 proposal, President's Office correspondence, File 191, UP Railroad Museum; 1960's leases, Russell to Stoddard, letter, Jan. 24, 1963; Waterman (SP) to Bongardt (UP), letter, July 22, 1965; ice car leases, File UA-22-AF; UP Railroad Museum.

McAfee, Ward, *California's Railroad Era, 1850-1911*, Golden West Books, San Marino, Calif., 1973.

Mechanical refrigeration: Plummer to Russell and Stoddard, letter, March 1, 1957, File UA-22-A, Part #12, Section #1, UP Railroad Museum.

Mercer, Lloyd J., *E.H. Harriman: Master Railroader*, Twayne, Boston, 1985.

Mileage rates, 1919-1970: File UA-22-A1, UP Railroad Museum.

Mowry, George E., *The California Progressives*, Univ. Calif. Press, Berkeley and Los Angeles, 1951.

Olin, Spencer, *California's Prodigal Sons*, Univ. Calif. Press, Berkeley and Los Angeles, 1968.

Orsi, Richard, "The Octopus Reconsidered: The Southern Pacific and Agricultural Modernization in California, 1865-1915," *Calif. Historical Quart.*, Vol. 54, Fall 1975, pp. 197-220.

PFE split-up and perishable transportation: Cranmer to Loveland (SP), memo, Oct. 23, 1978, PFE collection, CSRM.

Plummer, K.V., "Mechanical Refrigeration Versus Ice for Railroad Shipments," *Refrigerating Engineering*, Vol. 62, No. 7, July 1954, pp. 49, 50 .

Purchase of other lines: numerous letters among PFE, SP, UP during 1952-57, President's Office correspondence, File 191, UP Railroad Museum.

"Refrigeration Charges," in *Nineteenth Annual Report of the Interstate Commerce Commision*, Govt. Printing Office, Washington, 1905, pp. 6, 7.

"Refrigerator Service on Harriman Lines," *The Railway and Engineering Review*, Vol. 46, Dec. 22, 1906, p. 989.

Reigel, Robert E., *The Story of the Western Railroads*, esp. pp. 296-304, Macmillan, New York, 1926.

Ripley, William Z., *Railroads, Finance and Organization*, Appleton, New York, 1920.

Rotating PFE Presidency: PFE files UA-22-A3 and President's Office correspondence, File 191, UP Railroad Museum.

Seely, Bruce E., *Building the American Highway System*, Temple Univ. Press, Philadelphia, 1987.

Signatures of VP & GM's, from correspondence, Files 191, AFE and UA-22, UP Railroad Museum.

"Southern Pacific Company, Pioneers of Western Progress," report, Strassburger & Co., stockbrokers, New York, Aug. 1929, CSRM.

SP Equipment Co. construction: numerous letters in 1920's, President's Office correspondence, File 191; Stoddard to Lovett, letter, Aug. 5, 1957, File UA-22A, Part #12, Section #1. UP Railroad Museum.

Spearman, Frank H., *The Strategy of Great Railroads*, Scribner's, New York, 1904.

St. Clair, David J., *The Motorization of American Cities*, Praeger, New York, 1986.

Trottman, Nelson, *History of the Union Pacific: A Financial and Economic Survey*, Ronald Press, New York, 1923.

Walsh, T.D., "Railway Transportation of Perishable Freight – How It Was – What Happened – How It Is," monograph, March, 1977.

Western Pacific car contract: Shoup to Sproule, telegram, Mar. 9, 1923; Shoup to Secrist, telegram, same date; Secrist to Shoup, telegram, Mar. 26, 1923; Secrist to Shoup, telegrams, April 3 and April 17 1923; Giddings to Gray, telegram, Dec. 3, 1936; copies of WP contracts, dated 5-23, 5-38, 5-42, 11-51; Plummer to Mercier and Stoddard, letters, May 11, Oct. 17, Oct. 24, 1951. President's Office correspondence, File 191, UP Railroad Museum.

"Western Refrigerator Line Commences Business with 2,000 Cars," *Railway Review*, Vol. 72, Jan. 13, 1923, p. 127.

Chapter 3

"Armour Car Lines," *The Railway Age* (Chicago), Vol. 41, March 9, 1906, p. 362.

Armour, J. Ogden, *The Packers, the Private Car Lines, and the People*, Henry Altemus Co., Philadelphia, 1906.

Baker, R.S., "Private Cars and the Fruit Industry," *The Railroad Gazette*, Vol. 40, Feb. 23, 1906, pp. 186, 187.

California Fast Freight Line: Rigdon File, p. 33, UP Railroad Museum.

"Cars at the 1883 Exposition in Chicago" [fruit cars], *The Railroad Gazette*, Vol. 17, June 15, 1883, p. 379.

Central Pacific refrigerator car: *National Car-Builder*, Sept. 1870, p. 3.

Clemen, Rudolf, *The American Livestock and Meat Industry*, Ronald Press, New York, 1923.

Davis, Burke, *The Southern Railway*, Univ. North Carolina Press, Chapel Hill, N.C., 1985.

Division of citrus traffic, SP and ATSF: *The Railroad Gazette*, Vol. 42, Feb. 8, 1907, p. 189.

Early fruit shipments: *Transactions California State Agricultural Society, 1868* (1869), p. 22; *Transactions Calif. State Agric. Soc., 1870* (1871), pp. 51, 449, 454; *The Overland Monthly*, Vol. 12, Mar. 1874, pp. 235-244; *ibid.*, June, 1874, pp. 560-562; *6th Annual Report*, Railroad Commissioners of California, 1885, pp. 45-49; *Railway Age (Chicago)*, Vol. 10, Dec. 31, 1885, p. 820; *Pacific Rural Press*, Vol. 33, Mar. 12, 1887, p. 1; *Annual Report*, Calif. State Board of Horticulture, 1891, pp. 56-66; *Californian Illustrated Magazine*, Vol. 2, Oct. 1892, pp. 703-708.

"New Types of Refrigerator Cars," *Ice and Refrigeration*, Vol. 27, No. 6, Dec. 1904, pp. 205-209.

Nix, John W., "The Fruit Trade," in *One Hundred Years of American Commerce*, 2 Vols., C.M. Depew, Editor, D.O. Haynes and Co., New York, 1895, pp. 602-606.

Midgley, J.W., "Private Cars. An Inquiry into Their Growth, Development and Operations," 18-part series, *Railway Age*, between Oct. 10, 1902 and April 21, 1905.

Neyhart, Louis A., *Giant of the Yards*, Houghton-Mifflin, Boston, 1952.

"Private Cars in Freight Traffic," in *Eighteenth Annual Report of the Interstate Commerce Commission*, Govt. Printing Office, Washington, 1904, pp. 10-19, 47-49.

Simmons, A.M., "An Apology for the Private Car," *The Railway and Engineering Review*, Vol. 45, July 29, 1905, p. 559.

"Standard Fruit Car - Central Pacific Railroad," *The National Car-Builder*, June, 1884, pp. 68-70.

Voss, William, *Railway Car Construction*, Van Arsdale, New York, 1892.

Weld, L.D.H., *Private Freight Cars and American Railways*, Columbia Univ. Press, New York, 1908.

Yeager, Mary, *Competition and Regulation: The Development of Oligopoly in the Meat Packing Industry*, JAI Press, Greenwich, Conn., 1981.

Chapter 4

"Abolishing Transcontinental Private Car Lines," *The Railway and Engineering Review*, Vol. 47, Aug. 10, 1907, p. 695.

"Amendment to the Safety Appliance Act," *Railway Age Gazette*, Vol. 58, 1910, pp. 982, 983.

Bettendorf underframe: informative ads in *Car Builders' Dictionary*, e.g. 1912, Advertising Section, p. 25.

"Cars Sold to California Dispatch Line," memo, PFE, San Francisco, Jul. 30, 1936, PFE collection, CSRM.

Hart, Joseph H., "Railroad Refrigeration," *The Railroad Gazette*, Vol. 42, No. 3, Jan. 18, 1907, pp. 74, 75.

Hart, Joseph H., "Improvements in Refrigerator Cars," *Railway Age Gazette*, Vol. 47, Aug. 6, 1909, pp. 237-239.

"Important Features in Refrigerator Car Design," *Railway Age Gazette*, Vol. 56, Jan. 30, 1914, pp. 215-221.

"Railroad Ownership of Refrigerator Cars" [Harriman Lines], *Railway Age (Chicago)*, Vol. 42, No. 9, Aug. 31, 1906, p. 249.

"Refrigerator Cars for the Harriman Lines," *The Railroad Gazette*, Vol. 41, Sept. 21, 1906, p. 231.

"Refrigerator Cars for the Union Pacific," *American Engineer*, Vol. 87, No. 5, May 1913, pp. 263-265.

"The Harriman Refrigerator Cars," *The Railroad Gazette*, Vol. 43, No. 14, Oct. 4, 1907, pp. 374, 375.

"The 'Siphon' System of Refrigeration" [Bohn Patent], *The Railway Age (Chicago)*, Vol. 33, Jan. 10, 1902, pp. 52, 53.

Chapter 5

"Best Representative Examples of Refrigerator Cars Built in 1922," *Railway Review*, Vol. 72, Jan. 6, 1923, pp. 44, 45.

Bettendorf frame supply problems: Kruttschnitt to Lovett, letter, Feb. 17, 1920; Englebright to Lovett, memorandum, July 7, 1920. PFE AFE correspondence, box 00437, UP Railroad Museum.

"Bulkhead and Ice Grate of All-Metal Construction" [Equipco], *Railway Age*, Vol. 78, Mar. 14, 1925, p. 746.

Cost overruns: PFE AFE correspondence during 1922-26, Union Pacific File UA-22A, box 00437, and President's Office correspondence, File 191, UP Railroad Museum.

"Comparative Tests of Refrigerator Cars," *Railway Mechanical Engineer*, Vol. 94, Jan. 1920, pp. 28-32. See also editorial comment, *ibid.*, p. 2.

"Equipco All-Metal Bulkheads," *Car Builders' Cyclopedia*, Simmons-Boardman, New York, 1925, p. 152, 153.

"Insulating Lumber for Refrigerator Cars" [Celotex], *Railway Age*, Vol. 77, Nov. 1, 1924, pp. 806, 807.

Lane, James E., "USRA Freight Cars: An Experiment in Standardization," *Railroad History* (R&LHS), No. 128, 1973, pp. 5-33.

"Pacific Fruit Express Refrigerator Cars," *Railway Age*, Vol. 69, Dec. 31, 1920, pp. 1145-1148.

Paint scheme of 1922: Gray to Lovett, telegram, 25 Feb. 1922; McDonald to Mahl, letter, March 1, 1922. Union Pacific File UA-22A, box 00088, UP Railroad Museum.

Pennington, Mary E., "Development of a Standard Refrigerator Car," *Refrigerating Engineering*, Vol. 6, No. 1, July 1919, pp. 1-24.

Pennington, M.E., "Low Temperatures in Refrigerator Cars," *Railway Age*, Vol. 77, Nov. 22, 1924, pp. 947-950.

"Refrigerator Cars for the Pacific Fruit Express Co.," *Railway Review*, Vol. 60, May 26, 1917, p. 721-723.

"Standard U.S.R.A. Refrigerator," *Railway Mechanical Engineer*, Vol. 92, Dec. 1919, pp. 663-668.

Thompson, Anthony, "PFE Express Refrigerator Cars," *Railroad Model Craftsman*, Vol. 56, No. 11, April 1988, pp. 62, 63.

Winterrowd, W.H., "Some Notes on Railway Refrigerator Cars," *Railway Age*, Vol. 73, May 20, 1922, pp. 1173-1175; *ibid.*, May 27, 1922, pp. 1229-1232.

Chapter 6

"Balsam-Wool Insulation Tests," *Railway Age*, Vol. 78, Apr. 25, 1925, pp. 1041, 1042.

Barr, W.M., and D. Wood, "Report of Committee on Investigation of Insulating Materials in P.F.E. Refrigerator Cars," Memo to L.E. Cartmill, PFE, San Francisco, 1938, PFE collection, CSRM.

Barrows, Donald S., "Synchronous Truck Spring Movement Produces Destructive Forces," *Railway Age*, Vol. 92, Feb. 27, 1932, pp. 357-362.

Birdseye, Clarence, "Preparation and Distribution of Frozen Perishable Products," *Refrigerating Engineering*, Vol. 19, No. 6, June 1930, pp. 173, 180.

Birdseye, Clarence, "Transportation of Frozen Foods," *Railway Mechanical Engineer*, Vol. 106, No. 3, March 1932, p. 126.

Car shortages: Gray to Charske, letter, Dec. 2, 1927 (see also Gray to Charske, letter, Nov. 17, 1921; Lovett to Kruttschnitt, letter, Nov. 23, 1921; Gray to Lovett, telegram, Nov. 17, 1922; Gray to Charske, letter, Nov. 13, 1925). PFE AFE correspondence, boxes 00437 and 00438, UP Railroad Museum.

Experimental design, R-40-1: Giddings to Clark, letter, Jan. 22, 1927; Gray to Charske, letter, Jan. 25, 1927. Union Pacific File UA-22-A, box 00088, UP Railroad Museum.

Exterior car washing suspended: L.E. Cartmill, telegram C-164, Aug. 11, 1931, PFE materials, CSRM.

"Freight Car Orders in 1928," *Railway Age*, Vol. 86, Jan. 5, 1929, pp. 80-86. [builder's photo of R-40-2 car 37470, p. 83]

"Glass Wool for Railroad Use," *Railway Age*, Vol. 106, June 24, 1939, pp.

Goodwin, E.G., "Steel Frame Refrigerator Cars," *Railway Mechanical Engineer*, Vol. 92, July 1918, pp. 401-405.

"Insulation for Refrigerator Cars" [Dry-Zero], *Railway Age*, Vol. 78, June 13, 1925, p. 1477.

Jones, Bruce, "PFE R-40-2," *Mainline Modeler*, Vol. 7, No. 5, May 1986, pp. 41-45.

Large-size refrigerator cars: R-50-1, memo of C. Gray, June 8, 1929, and AFE 44-A (1929); R-70-2, Giddings to Clark, letter, Mar. 26, 1931; Giddings to Wise, letter, Oct. 29, 1931; memo of C. Gray, Feb. 6, 1932. Union Pacific File UA-22-A, box 00088, and PFE AFE file, box 00438, UP Railroad Museum.

"Panel Insulation for Refrigerator Cars" [Alfol], *Railway Age*, Vol. 100, June 27, 1936, p. 1062.

"Present Extent of the Frozen Foods Business," *Refrigerating Engineer-*

ing, Vol. 22, No. 3, Sept. 1931, pp. 170-172.

Rebuilding after 1957: Plummer to Russell and Stoddard, letter, Apr. 23 and Oct. 30, 1957, President's Office correspondence, File 191, UP Railroad Museum.

"Report of Inspection of PFE Cars Insulated with Fiberglas, Los Angeles, Oct. 30, 1941," memo, issued by L.E. Cartmill, Nov. 3, 1941; PFE collection, CSRM.

Retention of T and L section trucks in service: Torburn to Gogerty (UP) and Brown (SP), letter, Aug. 8, 1945, *et seq.*, PFE materials, CSRM.

Rice, P.X., "Tests on a Refrigerator Car Model," *Railway Mechanical Engineer*, Vol. 97, June 1923, pp. 351-355.

Size of car orders: Giddings to Neill, letter, Jan. 24, 1930 (see also Kruttschnitt to Lovett, letter, Nov. 10, 1921, and Gray to Lovett, letter, Nov. 17, 1921, regarding 1922 orders for R-30-12). PFE AFE correspondence, boxes 00437 and 00438, UP Railroad Museum.

Spieth, W.S., "Truck-Spring Snubbers," *Railway Mechanical Engineer*, Vol. 114, No. 5, May 1940, pp. 175-179, 189.

Thompson, Anthony, "PFE R-40-2 and R-40-4 Reefers," *Railroad Model Craftsman*, Vol. 56, No. 6, Nov. 1987, pp. 106-113.

Thompson, Anthony, "PFE R-70-2 Reefer," *Railroad Model Craftsman*, Vol. 56, No. 2, July 1987, pp. 56-58.

Tracy, H.E., "P.F.E. Builds Seventy-ton Refrigerator Cars," *Railway Mechanical Engineer*, Vol. 106, No. 9, Sept. 1932, pp. 349-352.

"Unit Insulation for Refrigerator Cars" [Alfol], *Railway Age*, Vol. 106, June 24, 1939, p. 1086.

Chapter 7

"Burlington to Test Refrigerator Cars," *Railway Age*, Vol. 120, Mar. 2, 1946, pp. 459, 460.

Campbell, A.N., "Reefers with Overhead Bunkers," *Railway Mechanical and Electrical Engineer*, Vol. 124, No. 6, July 1950, pp. 374-378.

"Deterioration Threatens Car Supply," *Railway Age*, Vol. 118, May 19, 1945, pp. 890-893.

"Economic Aspects of the Freight Car Situation," *Railway Age*, Vol. 100, May 23, 1936, pp. 826-828.

Gorman, E.A., "Fan Circulation Improves Effectiveness of Refrigerator Cars," *Railway Age*, Vol. 98, Mar. 30, 1935, pp. 493-495.

Horizontally-grooved plywood: Torburn to Plummer, memo, Aug. 14, 1950, PFE collection, CSRM.

Lentz, C.P., and W.H. Cook, "Transport and Storage of Perishables in Canada," *Refrigerating Engineering*, Vol. 61, No. 2, Feb. 1953, pp. 160-163, 202.

Lindsay, Harvey B., "Improved Refrigerator Car Design Long Overdue," *Railway Age*, Vol. 98, May 18, 1935, pp. 769-771.

"New Refrigerator Car Arouses Interest on West Coast [R-50-1-2], *Distribution and Warehousing Magazine*, Sept. 1941.

"New Refrigerator Cars Specially Designed for Frozen Foods Now on Test," *Ice and Refrigeration*, Vol. 111, No. 5, Nov. 1946, pp. 21, 22.

"Overhead Icing in C.N. Refrigerator Cars," *Railway Mechanical Engineer*, Vol. 114, June 1940, pp. 211-215, 218.

"Pacific Fruit Express to Spend $15,500,000," *Railway Age*, Vol. 110, Jan. 18, 1941, p. 197.

"Preco Air-Circulating Fans," *Railway Age*, Vol. 110, Apr. 12, 1941, pp. 648-650.

Principles of PFE rebuilding: "Car Improvements," PFE memo, San Francisco, June 25, 1946; Torburn to Plummer, memo, Oct. 4, 1949. PFE collection, CSRM.

Reconditioning of R-30-9 cars: Giddings to Gray and McDonald, telegram, Oct. 29, 1935; Gray to Charske, telegram, Dec. 10, 1935; Jeffers to Gray, telegram, July 6, 1936; Gray to McDonald, telegram, July 9, 1936. President's Office correspondence, File 191, UP Railroad Museum.

"Report on Forced Air Circulation Investigations to Date," Refrigeration Dept. Memo, PFE, San Francisco, Mar. 19, 1942, PFE collection, CSRM.

Russell, D.J., quotation, from interviews with E.V. Hopkins.

Townshend, J.L., "Refrigerator Cars with Ice Overhead," *Refrigerating Engineering*, Vol. 45, No. 4, April, 1943, pp. 243-245.

War-time suspension of car dismantling: Jabelmann (UP), Schuster (SP) and Cartmill (PFE) to Jeffers, Mercier and Giddings, memo, May 20, 1942. President's Office correspondence, File 191, UP Railroad Museum.

Western Pacific rebuilding: Plummer to Russell and Stoddard, letter, Sept. 25, 1952; Plummer to Russell, letter, Sept. 30, 1953. President's Office correspondence, File 191, UP Railroad Museum.

Chapter 8

"All-steel Box-car Design [ARA] Presented to Mechanical Division," *Railway Mechanical Engineer*, Vol. 106, No. 8, August 1932, pp. 317-323.

Aluminum car (45698): Cartmill to R.D. Bryan (ATSF), letter C-7-74, Jan. 8, 1947, PFE collection, CSRM.

"Aluminum PFE Reefer," *Railway Age*, Vol. 121, Oct. 5, 1946, p. 570.

"Aluminum Reefer Stands Test of Time," *Railway Age*, Vol. 134, Feb. 23, 1953, pp. 57, 58.

"Box-Car Ends" [Improved Dreadnaught], *Railway Mechanical Engineer*, Vol. 119, No. 11, Nov. 1945, p. 557.

First PFE steel cars (R-40-10): Fetters to Jeffers, memo, Dec. 29, 1935; Fetters, Dailey, and Cartmill, memo to file, Jan. 4, 1936; Gray to Charske, letter, Jan. 10, 1936. President's Office correspondence, File 191, UP Railroad Museum.

"Freight Car Program Gets Slow Start" [steel allocations], *Railway Age*, Vol. 122, May 17, 1947, pp. 1024-1028, 1033.

Gorman, E.A., "Produce Protection in Rail Transit," *Refrigerating Engineering*, Vol. 58, No. 7, July 1950, pp. 668-672.

"Growers and Shippers Study Refrigerator Car Design," *Railway Mechanical Engineer*, Vol. 118, No. 10, Oct. 1944, pp. 444, 445.

Hallmark, H.C., "Time to Reduce Refrigerator Car Weight," *Railway Age*, Vol. 118, Mar. 17, 1945, p. 488.

Herringbone floor racks: Webster (PFE) to McCauley (Northern Pacific), letter, Aug. 17, 1942, UP President's Office correspondence, File 191, UP Railroad Museum.

Hauser, Gilbert B., "Aluminum for Freight-car Construction," *Railway Mechanical Engineer*, Vol. 122, No. 5, May 1948, pp. 237, 238, 241.

"How Users View Refrigerator Car Trends," *Railway Age*, Vol. 132, Feb. 18, 1952, pp. 41-43.

Kelley, John N., "Perishable Transport of the Future," *Railway Age*, Vol. 118, Feb. 10, 1945, pp. 304, 305, 307.

Kelley, John N., "Postwar Redesign of the Refrigerator Car," *Refrigerating Engineering*, Vol. 53, No. 2, Feb. 1947, pp. 112-116.

Kelley, John N., "Refrigerator Cars – A Progress Report," *Railway Age*, Vol. 130, Mar. 26, 1951, pp. 37-39.

Kelley, John N., and R. B. Tewksbury, "1952 Picture for Railroad Refrigerator Cars," *Refrigerating Engineering*, Vol. 60, No. 3, March 1952, pp. 268, 296, 298.

Kraeger, Frank W., "Freight Cars Ordered in 1936," *Railway Age*, Vol. 102, Jan. 2, 1937, pp. 73-78.

McGinnis, Arthur J., "Freight Car Orders Were Curtailed by Deliveries in 1942," *Railway Age*, Vol. 114, Jan. 2, 1943, pp. 111-116.

McGinnis, Arthur J., "Orders for Freight Cars in 1943," *Railway Age*, Vol. 116, Jan. 1, 1944, pp. 94-98.

Metcalfe, Terry, *Union Pacific Freight Cars, 1936-1951*, Metcalfe Publ., Englewood, Colo., 1989. [contains Peacock car nomenclature]

"New Cars" [R-40-10], *Southern Pacific Bulletin*, Feb. 1936, p. 6; *ibid.*, Dec. 1936, p. 3.

"Pacific Fruit Express Builds 2000 Refrigerator Cars," *Railway Age*, Vol. 132, Jan. 28, 1952, pp. 29-31.

"PFE Builds 40-ton Refrigerator Cars," *Railway Mechanical and Electrical Engineer*, Vol. 126, No. 3, March 1952, pp. 66-69.

"PFE Cars Cut Shipping Costs" [Ice Tempco], *Railway Age*, Vol. 150, Jan. 30, 1961, pp. 35, 37.

"PFE Receives Refrigerator Cars," *Railway Age*, Vol. 122, No. 24, June 14, 1947, p. 1208, 1209.

"Produce Shippers Want More Refrigerator Cars," *Ice and Refrigeration*, Vol. 110, No. 3, March 1946, pp. 21, 22.

"Railway Refrigerator Cars," Chapter 56, *ASHRAE Guide and Data Book*, American Society of Heating, Refrigerating and Air-conditioning Engineers, New York, 1962.

"Refrigerator Car Design Proposals," *Railway Age*, Vol. 117, Oct. 28, 1944, pp. 654, 655.

"Refrigerator Car Discussed before Shippers' Council," *Railway Mechanical and Electrical Engineer*, Vol. 124, No. 3, March 1950, pp. 170, 171.

"Refrigerator Car Research Progress," *Railway Age*, Vol. 126, June 25, 1948, pp. 1239-1241.

"Refrigerator Cars in Transition," *Modern Railroads*, Vol. 3, No. 2, Feb. 1948, pp. 33-38.

"Report on Car Construction, Standard Steel-sheathed Box Car, Corner Construction" [W-corner post], *Railway Mechanical Engineer*, Vol. 114, July, 1940, p. 280.

Reynolds, Michael E., "The History of PFE Class R-70-5 Cars," *Prototype Modeler*, Vol. 1, No. 4, Feb. 1978, pp. 51-55.

"Six Years' Experience with an Aluminum Reefer," *Railway Locomotives and Cars*, Vol. 127, Mar. 1953, pp. 72-75.

"The Post-War Refrigerator Car," *Railway Age*, Vol. 126, No. 5, Jan. 29, 1949, p. 259, 260.

Thompson, Anthony, and Richard Hendrickson, "PFE's Ice Reefers:

Steel Cars," *Railroad Model Craftsman*, Vol. 55, No. 9, Feb. 1987, pp. 86-95.

Torburn, G.P., remarks before the American Society of Refrigerating Engineers, Jan. 17, 1947, PFE text report, San Francisco, 1947, PFE materials, CSRM.

"Ultralite Fiberglas Insulation," *Railway Mechanical Engineer*, Vol. 120, Aug. 1946, pp. 430, 431.

"Use of Aluminum a Matter of Economics," *Railway Age*, Vol. 118, Mar. 10, 1945, pp. 460, 461. (See also reply by F.D. Foote, *ibid.*, Vol. 119, Oct. 6, 1945, pp. 565, 566.)

Chapter 9

"A Pioneer in Mechanical Cooling" [FGE], *Railway Age*, Vol. 137, Oct. 18, 1954, pp. 62-64.

Birdseye, Clarence, "Looking Backward at Frozen Foods," *Refrigerating Engineering*, Vol. 61, No. 11, Nov. 1953, pp. 1182-84.

"C&O Chairman Challenges Use of Ice in Refrigerator Cars – Here are the Facts," *Ice and Refrigeration*, Vol. 110, No. 4, April 1946, pp. 34, 64.

Daly, J.F., "Cooling of Refrigerator Cars," *Ice and Refrigeration*, Vol. 121, Sept. 1951, pp. 13-15.

Elfving, Thore M., "Moisture Problems in Low Temperature Railroad Transportation," *Refrigerating Engineering*, Vol. 63, No. 6, June 1955, pp. 48-57.

Foam insulation: Schley to Walker, memo, Aug. 6, 1963, PFE collection, CSRM.

"Fresh-produce Mechanical Reefers," *Railway Locomotives and Cars*, Vol. 135, No. 4, April 1961, pp. 25, 28.

"Frozen Food from the West," *Western Canner/Packer*, Aug. 1954, p. 33.

Harwood, William, "Refrigerator Car Design," *Model Railroader*, Vol. 34, No. 4, April 1967, pp. 35-37.

Henney, C.F., and D.C. McCoy, "Mechanical Refrigeration for Railroad Refrigerator Cars," *Refrigerating Engineering*, Vol. 62, No. 10, Oct. 1954, pp. 41-48.

"Low Temperature Railroad Reefers," *Industrial Refrigeration*, Vol. 125, Oct. 1953, pp. 32-36.

McKee, R.F., "Refrigerator Car Improvements," *Proc. 15th National Conference on Handling Perishable Agricultural Commodities*, Purdue Univ. Press, Lafayette, 1959, p. 30-36. See also Proc. 19th Conf., 1965.

"Mechanically Cooled Refrigerator Cars," *Railway Age*, Vol. 131, Oct. 29, 1951, pp. 35-37.

"Mechanical Reefers. . .Car of the Future?", *Modern Railroads*, Vol. 8, No. 9, Sept. 1953, pp. 69-80.

"Mechanical Reefers Get Traffic," *Railway Age*, Vol. 148, Feb. 8, 1960, pp. 14-26.

"Mechanical Refrigeration and Heating for Reefers" [ice car conversion], *Railway Locomotives and Cars*, Vol. 129, April, 1955, pp. 60, 61.

"Mechanical Refrigeration of Cars," *Railway Age*, Vol. 129, Dec. 23, 1950, pp. 26-28.

"Mechanical Refrigeration, Part I: What's in Today's Mechanical Reefer?", *Railway Locomotives and Cars*, Vol. 130, Sept. 1956, pp.

55-59.

"Mechanical Refrigeration, Part II: To Keep 'Em Freezing," *Railway Locomotives and Cars*, Vol. 130, Oct. 1956, pp. 63-69.

"Mechanical Refrigeration, Part III: Mechanical Refrigeration is Here to Stay," *Railway Locomotives and Cars*, Vol. 130, Nov. 1956, pp. 60-63.

"New Low Temperature Refrigerator Cars," *Ice and Refrigeration*, Vol. 121, No. 11, Nov. 1951, pp. 21, 22.

"Oversize Cars Not Adaptable," *Ice and Refrigeration*, Vol. 121, No. 7, July 1951, pp. 18, 54.

"PFE Adds 400 New Reefers," *Railway Age*, Vol. 165, Aug. 26, 1968, p. 38.

"PFE Builds New-type Reefer," *Railway Age*, Vol. 150, No. 13, Mar. 27, 1961, p. 41.

"PFE Expands Mechanical Reefer Fleet," *Railway Locomotives and Cars*, Vol. 132, June, 1958, pp. 27, 28, 46.

"PFE Gets Large Cushioned Reefers," *Railway Age*, Vol. 154, April 15, 1963, p. 12.

"PFE Mechanical Reefer Fleet Grows," *Railway Locomotives and Cars*, Vol. 134, No. 8, August 1960, pp. 29-31.

Plummer, K.V., "Mechanical Refrigeration Versus Ice for Railroad Shipments," *Refrigerating Engineering*, Vol. 62, No. 7, July 1954, pp. 49, 50 .

Ransom, Ralph W., "Does the Mechanically Refrigerated Freight Car Do Its Job?", *Refrigerating Engineering*, Vol. 62, No. 7, July 1954, pp. 51-54.

Rector, Thomas A., "Frozen Concentrated Orange Juice – Its Research Background," *Refrigerating Engineering*, Vol. 58, No. 4, April 1950, pp. 349-353.

Redit, W.H., *Transportation of Frozen Citrus Concentrate by Railroad and Motortruck from Florida to Northern Markets*, USDA Agricultural Information Bulletin 62, U.S. Dept. of Agriculture, Washington, 1951.

"Refrigerated Freight," *Central of Georgia Magazine*, Feb. 1957, pp. 8, 9.

Rill, J. C., "Transporting Frozen Foods by Rail," *Refrigerating Engineering*, Vol. 64, No. 11, Nov. 1956, pp. 46, 98, 99.

Removal of running boards: numerous letters, latest being Dahahy (AAR) to Hopkins [4-yr. extension], Oct. 6, 1972, PFE collection, CSRM.

Scotchlite medallions: Schley to Russell and Stoddard, letter, Sept. 21, 1963; Schley to Hopkins, memo, Oct. 15, 1964. PFE collection, CSRM.

Tewksbury, R.B., "Rail Transportation of Perishable Foodstuffs," *Refrigerating Engineering*, Vol. 61, No. 1, Jan. 1953, pp. 52-55.

"Temperatures Stay Below Zero," *Railway Age*, Vol. 135, Sept. 7, 1953, pp. 93-96.

Thompson, Anthony, "PFE's Mechanical Reefers," *Railroad Model Craftsman*, Vol. 56, No. 8, Jan. 1988, pp. 76-85. For corrections and additions, see also *Railroad Model Craftsman*, Vol. 57, No. 3, Aug. 1988, pp. 8, 10.

"What Makes a Mechanical Reefer Tick?", *Railway Age*, Vol. 148, Feb. 22, 1960, pp. 12-16.

Wood, E.C., "Mechanical Systems Applied to Freight Cars," *Refriger-*

ating Engineering, Vol. 26, No. 1, July 1933, pp. 11-13.

"Would Mechanical Refrigeration Hold Traffic?", *Railway Age*, Vol. 108, Jan. 27, 1940, p. 696. (See reply, *ibid.*, Apr. 20, 1940, pp. 709, 710, and response, p. 696.)

Chapter 10

"Atmosphere Control," PFE *Newsletter*, Jan. 1966, p. 7.

Chatfield, D. Scott, "Trailer Train's Traditional Cars," in *Learning from the Prototype*, A.W. Thompson, ed., The Pittsburgh Limited, Pittsburgh, 1990, pp. 53-62.

"Competitive Transportation of Perishables by Trailer-Flatcar Service," memo, PFE, San Francisco, January, 1960, PFE collection, CSRM.

Hediger, Jim, "New York Central's Flexi-Van Flatcar," *Model Railroader*, Vol. 59, No. 2, Feb. 1992, pp. 96-101.

"Matson Containers," PFE *Newsletter*, Jan. 1966, p. 2.

McKenzie, David R., Mark C. North, and Daniel S. Smith, *Intermodal Transportation – The Whole Story*, Simmons-Boardman, Omaha, 1989.

Morgan, David P., "The Paraphernalia of Piggyback," *Trains*, Vol. 20, June, 1960, pp. 37-45.

"Newest TOFC Car Can Load at Sides, Ends," *Railway Age*, Vol. 152, Apr. 2, 1962, pp. 20, 21.

"NYC Begins Flexi-Van Operations," *Railway Locomotives and Cars*, Vol. 132, May, 1958, p. 39.

Panza, Jim, "Thirty-five Years of Trailer Train," *Railroad Model Craftsman*, Vol. 59, July, 1990, pp. 72-79.

Perishables Transportation: A Fresh Look at TOFC / COFC, Report to National Commission on Productivity, Peat, Marwick, Mitchell and Co., Oct. 1975.

Chapter 11

Brown, Gordon R., "PFE's Repair Shops," *Railroad Modeler*, Vol. 5, No. 8, Aug. 1975, pp. 49-55, 70, 71.

"Car Conditioning Vital Factor in Melon Handling" [Southern California PFE shops], *Railway Age*, Vol. 86, June 22, 1929, pp. 1405-1410.

Friedman, John W., "Visit to the PFE Facilities, Roseville and Nampa, Findings and Suggestions," Pacific Car & Foundry Co. report to PFE, Reports No. 1 and 2, July, Aug. 1974, PFE collection, CSRM.

"History of Tucson Shop," draft text (unpublished) in PFE *Newsletter* file, Sept. 9, 1969, CSRM.

"Hot Water Speeds De-Icing of Reefers," *Railway Age*, Vol. 128, Feb. 4, 1950, p. 48.

"Locomotives for PFE," PFE *Newsletter*, Feb. 1969, pp. 2,3.

"Modern Refrigerator Repair Shop," *Railway Mechanical Engineer*, Vol. 104, No. 2, Feb. 1930, pp. 57-61, 68.

"PFE an Important Contributor to Nampa," *Nampa – 100 Years*, Centennial Magazine, *Idaho Press-Tribune*, Nampa, June, 1986.

"PFE Expands Mechanical Reefer Shop," *Railway Locomotives and Cars*, Vol. 134, No. 11, Nov. 1960, pp. 30, 35.

PFE shop facilities records: "AFE Files," Forms 12, with maps and legends of facilites; "Contract Agreements," Auditor's Office files; "Laramie," Amato to Peterson, memo, May 21, 1975, File C-3-11; UP Railroad Museum.

"Roseville Yard of the Southern Pacific," *The Railroad Gazette*, Vol. 43, Dec. 21, 1907, p. 783.

Strapac, Joseph A., *Southern Pacific Motive Power Annual*, Pacific Coast Chapter, R&LHS, San Francisco, 1981, 1982.

"Survey of Car and Stores Departments," Report to PFE, Emerson Consultants, Inc., April 1960, PFE collection, CSRM.

Chapter 12

Cummings, Richard O., "The American Ice Harvests," *Refrigerating Engineering*, Vol. 58, No. 4, April 1950, pp. 358-362 (abstracted from Chapters 6 and 7 of Cummings' *The American Ice Harvests*, Univ. of California Press, 1949).

Hanson, Richard, "Truckee Basin's Ice Age," *Sierra Heritage*, Vol. 7, Dec. 1987.

Hiles, Theron L., *The Ice Crop*, Orange Judd Co., New York, 1893.

Holliday, Mary, "Ice for the Comstock," PFE *Newsletter*, Jan. 1969, pp. 3,4 (reprinted from *The Nevadan*).

Lynch, W.F., "History of Donner Creek," letter, May, 1954, PFE misc. correspondence file, CSRM.

Wood, Harold B., "Handling Ice for Car Icing" [Union Pacific], *Ice and Refrigeration*, Vol. 41, July, 1911, pp. 15-17.

Wheeler, Denise, "When Wyoming Iced the UP 'Reefers,' " *In Wyoming*, 1978, pp. 28-34.

Whyte, R.T., "The Story of a Half-Million Cakes of Ice," *Southern Pacific Bulletin*, Feb. 1927.

Chapter 13

Baker, C.T., "Railway Car Icing Stations," *Refrigerating Engineering*, Vol. 19, No. 4, April 1930, pp. 106-112.

Decline in PFE ice usage: Russell to Plummer, , letter, April 30, 1957; Plummer to Russell, letter, May 20, 1957; Plummer to Russell and Stoddard, letter, June 18, 1957; Ahern to Russell and Stoddard, letter, Oct. 6, 1958. President's Office correspondence, File 191, UP Railroad Museum.

"Fast Service for Southeast Texas," *Railway Age*, Vol. 108, March 9, 1940, pp. 449, 450, 452.

"How PFE Ices Cars in a Hurry," *Railway Age*, Vol. 145, Aug. 11, 1958, p. 25.

"How to Ice a Reefer in 45 Seconds," *Trains*, Vol. 16, No. 2, Dec. 1955, pp. 24, 25.

"Lith Board," *Railway Age Gazette*, Vol. 48, 15 March 1910, p. 585.

"Million Dollar Ice Plant Started," *Ice and Refrigeration*, Vol. 120, April 1951, pp. 17, 18.

Myers, William A., *Iron Men and Copper Wires*, Trans-Anglo Books, Glendale, Calif., 1983.

"New Million Dollar Ice Plant," *Ice and Refrigeration*, Vol. 124, Feb. 1953, pp. 13-16.

"PFE Erects New Icing Plant at Bakersfield," *Southern Pacific Bulletin*, May 1922.

PFE ice facilities records: "Description of Facilities," Forms 897, CSRM. "Work Order Authority," Forms 10; "Distribution Detail of Work Order," Forms 30; "Summary of Facilities," Forms 916, UP Railroad Museum; "Joint Committee Survey of PFE Icing Facilities and Related Operations," Report of PFE Co. and SP Co., Sept.-Oct.

1950, UP Railroad Museum.

"PFE Ice Plant," *Colton Courier*, Colton, Calif., Nov. 21, 1958.

Phillips, W.C., "Establishing Icing Facilities on a Large Scale," *Railway Age*, Vol. 72, March 4, 1922, pp. 533, 534.

"Pre-cooling Plant of the Southern Pacific at Roseville, Cal.," *Railway Age Gazette*, Vol. 48, 18 Mar. 1910, pp. 725-727.

Review of PFE construction practices and costs: Mercier to Ashby, letter, Oct. 8, 1946; Plummer to Mercier, letter, Oct. 11, 1946; Plummer to Ashby and Mercier, letter and meeting minutes, Nov. 22, 1946; Prater to Lynch, memo, Nov. 22, 1946; UP President's Office correspondence, File 191, UP Railroad Museum.

Secrist, C.M., "Facilities for Replenishing Ice for Refrigeration in Transit," *Railway Age Gazette*, Vol. 55, Sept. 26, 1913, p. 568.

Sims, Don, "A Look at Ice Houses," *Railroad Modeler*, Vol. 8, No. 3, March 1978, pp. 44-49, 72, 73.

Chapter 14

Amerine, M.A., and V.L. Singleton, *Wine*, Univ. of Calif. Press, Berkeley, 1965.

California grape car plan: *Railway Age*, Vol. 81, July 31, 1926, pp. 183,184; *ibid.*, Aug. 28, pp. 359, 360; *ibid.*, Oct. 30 editorial; *ibid.*, Nov. 13, pp. 933-36.

Car shortages and grape shipments: *Railway Age*, Vol. 73, Oct. 7, 1922, p. 669; *ibid.*, Vol. 75, Oct. 20, 1923, pp. 699, 718, 719; *ibid.*, Vol. 80, June 19, 1926, pp. 1924, 1925.

Clarke, E.P., "California's Fruit Industry," *Sunset*, Vol. 13, July 1904, pp. 239-242.

Corbett, J.W. (SP), H.C. Munson (WP), A.D. Hanson (UP), C.R. Tucker (ATSF) and C.A. Mulvihill (SFRD), "Modern Railroad Operations and Transit Refrigeration," *Proc. 10th Conf. on Transportation of Perishables*, Univ. Calif., Davis, Calif., 1954, pp. 108-121, 157-159.

Craemer, Justus F. "Transportation and the Fresh Fruit and Vegetable Industry," Calif. Public Utilities Commission Report, 1952, PFE collection, CSRM.

Dennis, S.J., "Recent Investigations in the Handling of Perishable Products for Transportation," *Ice and Refrigeration*, Vol. 33, No. 6, Dec. 1907, pp. 272-274.

Donaldson, Stephen E., and William A. Myers, *Rails Through the Orange Groves* (2 Vols.), Trans-Anglo Books, Glendale, Calif., 1989 and 1990.

Dorwart, William G., "Pittsburgh Produce Terminal," *The Keystone* (Pennsylvania Railroad Historical & Technical Society), Vol. 23, No. 1, Spring, 1990, pp. 33-38.

Fogelberg, Nephtune, and A.W. McKay, *The Citrus Industry and the California Fruit Growers Exchange System*, Circular C-121, Farm Credit Administration, U.S.D.A., Washington, DC, June, 1940.

Greeves-Carpenter, C.F., "Refrigeration in the Citrus Industry - A Story of the California Fruit Growers Exchange and Refrigerated Transport," *Refrigerating Engineering*, Vol. 28, No. 2, Aug. 1934, pp. 66-73.

"Handling 11,000 Trains on Time," *Railway Age*, Vol. 87, July 13, 1929, pp. 143, 144.

Hart, Joseph H., "Refrigeration in the Transportation of Fruit," *The Railroad Gazette*, Vol. 44, May 8, 1908, p. 629.

Ice consumption: summary of 1919 ARA tests, refrigerator car section, p. 168, *Car Builder's Cyclopedia*, Simmons-Boardman, 1940.

Levy, E.D., "Transportation of Fruits and Vegetables," *Railway Age Gazette*, Vol. 54, Feb. 7, 1913, pp. 239-242.

MacCurdy, Rahno Mabel, *The History of the California Fruit Growers Exchange* [Sunkist], Los Angeles, 1925.

Mann, C.W., E.A. Gorman and W.V. Hukill, *Stage Icing in the Refrigeration of Oranges in Transit from California*, Tech. Bulletin No. 857, U.S. Dept. of Agriculture, Washington, DC, Sept. 1943.

Marshall, David, "135,000 Reefers," *Railroad*, Vol. 71, No. 2, Feb. 1960, pp. 22-27.

Nelson, G.H., and J.W. Inghram, "The Transportation of Perishable Freight," *Railway Age*, Vol. 75, Dec. 29, 1923, pp. 1213-1215.

"Pacific Coast's Greatest Freight Traffic Clearing House Located at Roseville," *Southern Pacific Bulletin*, Dec. 1922.

"Perishable Freight Schedules," Southern Pacific Freight Dept., File 572, July, 1943, CSRM.

"Perishables Require Specialized Operations" [Imperial Valley], *Railway Age*, Vol. 87, Nov. 30, 1929, pp. 1270-1272.

Rear, J.C., "Precooling Practices in California," *Refrigerating Engineering*, Vol. 53, No. 6, June 1947, pp. 503-506.

Redfearn, B.W., "Methods of Pre-Cooling Perishable Goods at Loading Stations," *Railway Age Gazette*, Vol. 55, Sept. 26, 1913, pp. 568-69.

"Shipping and Storing Oranges," *Ice and Refrigeration*, Vol. 33, No. 1, July, 1907, pp. 11, 12.

Steinheimer, Richard, "Imperial Valley," *Railroad*, Vol. 62, No. 3, Dec. 1953, pp. 36-57.

Steele, Rufus, "What Pre-cooling Means," *Sunset*, Vol. 24, March 1910, pp. 339-343.

Tassell, W.W., "The Nation's Gardens at Your Door," *Union Pacific Magazine*, May, 1929, pp. 8, 9, 23.

"Vacuum Cooling Process for Lettuce Provides Better and Faster Service," *Ice and Refrigeration*, Vol. 125, Aug. 1953, p. 27.

Wagner, P.M., *American Wine and Wine-making*, Knopf, New York, 1972.

Williams, T.H., "A Railroad Within a Railroad – Los Angeles Yard," *Southern Pacific Bulletin*, Nov. 1929.

Chapter 15

"Cold and Fresh," *Southern Pacific Bulletin*, Sept. 1957, pp. 7-12.

"Truck Elevator Unit Provides Modern Method of Track-side Car Icing," *Ice and Refrigeration*, Vol. 111, July 1946, p. 30.

Wood, Donald F., "Trucks at Work: Icing Railroad Cars," *Wheels of Time* (Amer. Truck Hist. Soc.), Vol. 2, No. 5, Oct. 1981, pp. 20-22.

Index

This book was composed in Adobe Garamond. The many versions of Garamond used since the 16th century design of Claude Garamond were joined in 1988 by this digital version, prepared by Robert Slimbach for Adobe Systems. Book design and typography by Anthony W. Thompson.